STRAND PRICE
$5.00

D1161816

Contents

Without prejudice

I started my career as a daily sports writer for *The Providence Journal*. It is a well-regarded newspaper in Rhode Island, and I loved the job. It was hard work and immensely stressful hitting deadlines night after night after night, but I loved it.

Fresh out of college, I was low man on the totem pole. Quickly I saw in my older and more experienced colleagues that the job could take its toll. Stressed-out and often chain smoking with bags under their eyes, these people were putting everything they had into every story they wrote. I so admired this quality. Nobody is more passionate about their job than a great journalist. And nobody is more respected than an honest one.

The reasons are simple: a great journalist is unbiased, and a great journalist cares deeply. What better group of people to judge an advertising show?

In an industry that is too often self-congratulatory, and too often has the same agency people judging the shows and deciding what work (often their own) is award-worthy, it is refreshing to have a steroidal injection of "journalistic integrity." The judges at Epica do not care what wins, as they have no horse in the race and no axe to grind. They do, however, care that the winners they pick represent the best of what they saw. In fact they care very much. Unbiased people who truly give a shit, a hallmark of the journalism profession.

There are shows that carry more weight. There are shows in more exotic locations. There are shows that mean more to your clients. But there is no show that your work will be more thoroughly investigated by a more unbiased and more influential audience. And there is no show that the judges themselves are the exact people who can put your work out onto the international, mass media stage with one, simple press clip.

Let's give them something to write about.

Tor Myhren is Worldwide Chief Creative Officer of Grey and President of Grey New York

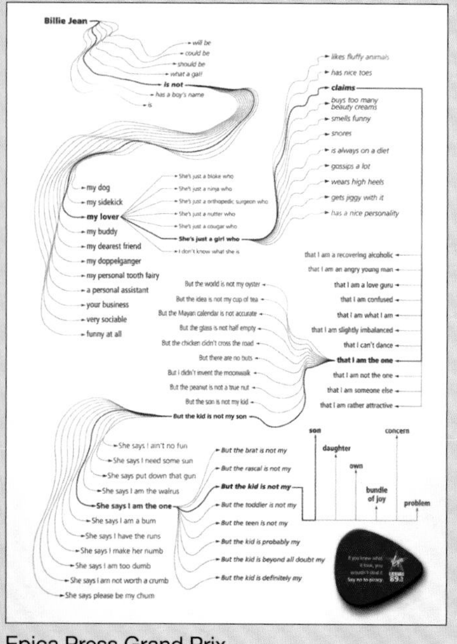

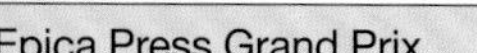
Epica Press Grand Prix

Epica Film Grand Prix

Epica Digital Grand Prix

	Country	Agency	Client
Epica Film Grand Prix	UNITED STATES	BBDO New York	GE, "The Boy Who Beeps"
Epica Press Grand Prix	LEBANON	Leo Burnett Beirut	Virgin Radio, "Making Music"
Epica Outdoor Grand Prix	FRANCE	Publicis Conseil	National Museum of Natural History, "Paris Zoo"
Epica Digital Grand Prix	NETHERLANDS	72andSunny	Google, "Night Walk in Marseille"
Epica Digital Grand Prix	CANADA	Leo Burnett Toronto	Procter & Gamble, Always, "#LikeAGirl"

FILM

Cat.	Category	Country	Agency	Client
Cat. 1	Food	SWEDEN	King	ICA, "ICA Glasses"
Cat. 2	Confectionery & Snacks	UNITED STATES	BBDO New York	Mars, Twix, "#TBT"
Cat. 3	Drinks	NETHERLANDS	Wieden+Kennedy Amsterdam	Heineken, "The Odyssey"
Cat. 4	Communication Services	SWEDEN	Forsman & Bodenfors	Postnord Logistics, "Investigating PostNord Logistics"
Cat. 5	Transport & Tourism	UNITED KINGDOM	Ogilvy & Mather London	Expedia, "Horse Whisperer"
Cat. 6	Retail Services	UNITED KINGDOM	adam&eveDDB	Harvey Nichols, "Sorry I Spent It On Myself"
Cat. 7	Financial Services	AUSTRALIA	JOY	H&R Block, "We Don't Miss A Thing"
Cat. 9	Household Maintenance	FRANCE	Leo Burnett France	Delipapier, Sopalin, "Oh My Lord"
Cat. 10	Public Interest	SWEDEN	Forsman & Bodenfors	UNICEF Sweden, "The Good Guys Christmas"
Cat. 11	Health & Beauty	UNITED STATES	Publicis Kaplan Thaler	Procter & Gamble, Crest & Oral-B "Halloween Treats Gone Wrong"
Cat. 12	Fashion, Footwear & Personal Accessories	UNITED KINGDOM	adam&eveDDB	Harvey Nichols, "Sorry I Spent It On Myself"
Cat. 13	Automobiles	UNITED KINGDOM	adam&eveDDB	Volkswagen, "Made for Real Life"
Cat. 14	Automotive & Accessories	SWEDEN	Forsman & Bodenfors	Volvo Trucks, "Casino"
Cat. 15	Media	FRANCE	BETC	Canal+, "Cameramen"
Cat. 16	Recreation & Leisure	NORWAY	TRY/Apt/POL	Norsk Tipping - Oddsen, "The Wedding Speech"
Cat. 17	Luxury & Premium Brands	UNITED KINGDOM	adam&eveDDB	Harvey Nichols, "Sorry I Spent It On Myself"
Cat. 18	Professional Products & Services	FRANCE	Buzzman	Double A, "The Double Quality Paper"
Cat. 20	Corporate Image	UNITED STATES	BBDO New York	GE, "The Boy Who Beeps"

PRINT

Cat.	Category	Country	Agency	Client
Cat. 1	Food	UNITED ARAB EMIRATES	Impact BBDO Dubai	Saudia Milk, "Broken Dreams"
Cat. 2	Confectionery & Snacks	UNITED KINGDOM	adamandeveDDB	Unilever, Marmite, "Neglect"
Cat. 3	Drinks	SWITZERLAND	Ruf Lanz	Swiss Milk Producers, "Swissmilk Cable Car Stations"
Cat. 4	Communication Services	URUGUAY	Havas Worldwide Gurisa	El Observador, "Balance"
Cat. 5	Transport & Tourism	NORWAY	Kitchen Leo Burnett	Norwegian Airlines, "The Pale Complexion Examination"
Cat. 6	Retail Services	FRANCE	Marcel	Intermarché, "Inglorious Fruits and Vegetables"
Cat. 7	Financial Services	TURKEY	Tribal Worldwide Istanbul	Sigortam.net, "Hiding Money"
Cat. 8	Homes, Furnishings & Appliances	FRANCE	Herezie	Zwilling J. A. Henckels, "The Beauty of Sharpness"
Cat. 9	Household Maintenance	GERMANY	Leo Burnett Frankfurt	Samsung Electronics, "Just 80mm Flat"
Cat. 10	Public Interest	BRAZIL	Leo Burnett Tailor Made	Fiat, "Don't make-up and drive"
Cat. 11	Health & Beauty	UKRAINE	Geometry Global	Sport Life, "One-Two-Three"
Cat. 12	Fashion, Footwear & Personal Accessories	CZECH REPUBLIC	Havas Worldwide Prague	Styx, "A Truly Masculine Living Room"
Cat. 13	Automobiles	FRANCE	Fred & Farid Paris	Porsche, "911 Rear Horsepower "
Cat. 14	Automotive & Accessories	MEXICO	Grupo Vale Havas	Continental Tires, "Grip"
Cat. 15	Media	LEBANON	Leo Burnett Beirut	Virgin Radio, "Making Music"
Cat. 16	Recreation & Leisure	FRANCE	Publicis Conseil	National Museum of Natural History, "Paris Zoo"
Cat. 17	Luxury & Premium Brands	UNITED KINGDOM	adam&eveDDB	Harvey Nichols, "Sorry I Spent It On Myself"
Cat. 18	Professional Products & Services	RUSSIAN FEDERATION	Vozduh	School of English Five O'clock, "Flags"
Cat. 20	Corporate Image	TURKEY	Leo Burnett Istanbul	Tofaş - Jeep, "Keep (Beep, Keep, Deep)"

RADIO

Cat.	Category	Country	Agency	Client
Cat. 21	Radio Advertising	UNITED STATES	Publicis Kaplan Thaler	Procter & Gamble, ZzzQuil, "Sleepline 2.0"

DIRECT MARKETING

Cat.	Category	Country	Agency	Client
Cat. 22	Consumer Direct	SWITZERLAND	Leo Burnett Schweiz	Bio Suisse, "Cow Marathon"
Cat. 23	Business to Business Direct	BELGIUM	BBDO Belgium	JCDecaux, "Street View Unpaid Bills"

MEDIA USAGE

Cat.	Category	Country	Agency	Client
Cat. 24	Media Innovation - Traditional Media	CHINA	OgilvyOne Beijing	Volkswagen, "Eyes On The Road"
Cat. 25	Media Innovation - Alternative Media	UNITED STATES	Leo Burnett Chicago	McDonald's, "Literacy Store"
Cat. 26	Creative Technology	UNITED KINGDOM	Tribal Worldwide London	Volkswagen, "Play The Road - Reinventing Driving Music"

Winners

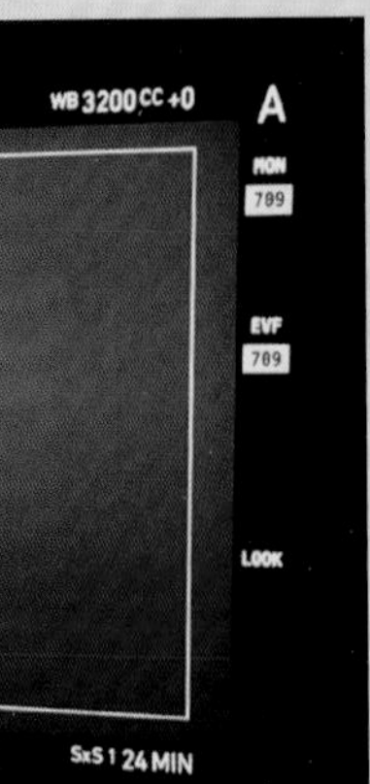

Epica Outdoor Grand Prix

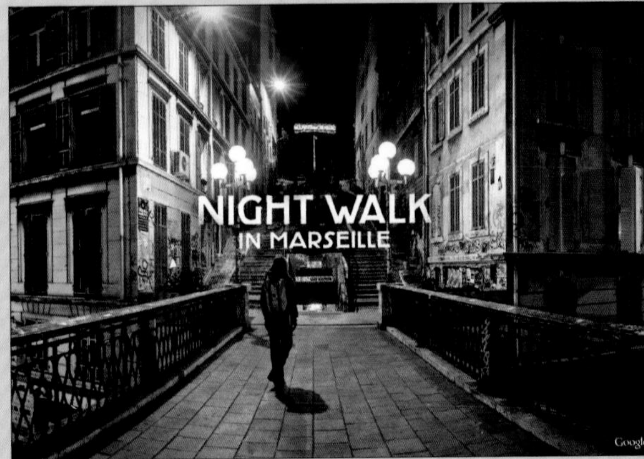

Epica Digital Grand Prix

Category		Country	Agency	Client / Title
BRANDED ENTERTAINMENT				
Cat. 27	Branded Content & Entertainment	UNITED KINGDOM	Abbott Mead Vickers BBDO	Guinness, Diageo, "Sapeurs Doc"
Cat. 28	Public Relations	BRAZIL	Leo Burnett Tailor Made	ABTO (Brazilian Association of Organ Transplantation), "Bentley Burial"
Cat. 29	Promotions & Incentives	DENMARK	Robert/Boisen & Like-minded	Spies Travels, "Do It For Denmark"
Cat. 30	Experiential & Shopper Marketing	FRANCE	Marcel	Intermarché, "Inglorious Fruits and Vegetables"
CRAFT & IMAGERY				
Cat. 31	Copywriting & Storytelling	LEBANON	Leo Burnett Beirut	Virgin Radio, "Making Music"
Cat. 32	Animation	UNITED STATES	Creative Artists Agency	Dolby, "Silent"
Cat. 33	Direction & Cinematography	AUSTRALIA	Finch	New Zealand Transport Agency , "Mistakes"
Cat. 34	Editing & Special Effects	FRANCE	Gang Films	Evian, Volvic, "Volvic The Giant"
Cat. 35	Best Use of Music	UNITED KINGDOM	Abbott Mead Vickers BBDO	Guinness, "Made of Black"
Cat. 36	Title & Credit Sequences	UNITED KINGDOM	th1ng	Fox Entertainment, "Chomet Couch Gag"
Cat. 37	Print Craft	FRANCE	Publicis Conseil	National Museum of Natural History, "Paris Zoo"
Cat. 38	Advertising Photography	FRANCE	Fred & Farid Paris	Porsche, "911 Rear Horsepower"
Cat. 39	Illustration	ITALY	TBWA\Italia	Humanitas Hospital and Cancer Center, "Smok-ink"
DESIGN				
Cat. 40	Graphic Design	SWEDEN	Lowe Brindfors	Friends, "Anti-Bullying Typeface"
Cat. 41	Publication Design	JAPAN	Dentsu	Kishokai Medical Corporation, "Mother Book"
Cat. 42	Packaging Design	SWITZERLAND	Leo Burnett Schweiz	Mario Haller, "Lightning"
DIGITAL				
Cat. 43	Online Campaigns - Food & Drink	GERMANY	Serviceplan	Deli Star Bagel & Coffee, "Audio Coffee"
Cat. 44	Online Campaigns - Consumer Services & Household	DENMARK	Robert/Boisen & Like-minded	Spies Travels, "Do It For Denmark"
Cat. 44	Online Campaigns - Consumer Services & Household	NETHERLANDS	72andSunny	Google, "Night Walk in Marseille"
Cat. 45	Online Campaigns - Public Interest	AUSTRIA	Demner, Merlicek & Bergmann	Red Noses Clowndoctors, "Red Noses. Red Button."
Cat. 46	Online Campaigns - Health, Beauty & Fashion	UNITED KINGDOM	adam&eveDDB	Harvey Nichols, "Sorry I Spent It On Myself"
Cat. 47	Online Campaigns - Automotive	SWEDEN	King	Taxi Stockholm, "Taxi Trails"
Cat. 48	Online Campaigns - Media & Entertainment	FRANCE	Grey Paris	Ubisoft, "What Are You Made Of ?"
Cat. 49	Online Campaigns - Luxury	UNITED KINGDOM	adam&eveDDB	Harvey Nichols, "Sorry I Spent It On Myself"
Cat. 50	Online Campaigns - Business to Business & Corporate	GERMANY	Serviceplan	Bytro Labs, "The Game Report"
Cat. 51	Websites	FRANCE	Grey Paris	Ubisoft, "What Are You Made Of ?"
Cat. 52	Online Ads	RUSSIAN FEDERATION	Grey Moscow	GM Russia CIS, "Skiptest"
Cat. 53	Online & Viral Films	CANADA	Leo Burnett Toronto	Procter & Gamble, Always, "#LikeAGirl"
Cat. 53	Online & Viral Films	NEW ZEALAND	Clemenger BBDO	New Zealand Transport Agency, "Mistakes"
Cat. 54	Social Networks	BRAZIL	Leo Burnett Tailor Made	ABTO (Brazilian Association of Organ Transplantation), "Bentley Burial"
Cat. 55	Branded Games	FRANCE	Wanda Productions	Guy Cotten, "Trip Out To Sea"
MOBILE				
Cat. 56	Apps	DENMARK	McCann Copenhagen	IKEA, "Showroom at Home"
Cat. 57	Mobile Sites	NETHERLANDS	72andSunny	Google, "Night Walk in Marseille"
Cat. 58	Mobile Games	SWEDEN	Shout Advertising	Liseberg, "The Fun Queue"
Cat. 59	Mobile Campaigns	THAILAND	CJ WORX	Seub Nakhasathien Foundation, "The Virtual Fence Project"
Cat. 60	Mobile Social Networks	AUSTRALIA	Leo Burnett Melbourne	SPC Ardmona, "#SPCSunday"
INTEGRATED				
Cat. 61	Integrated Campaigns	UNITED KINGDOM	adam&eveDDB	Harvey Nichols, "Sorry I Spent It On Myself"
SPECIAL				
Cat. 62	World Cup Advertising	GERMANY	Razorfish	Audi, "Audi LED Scoreboard"

adobo
WOMEN OF INFLUENCE 2015

Anuncios
'LOS ANUNCIOS DEL AÑO 2014' VIVIERON UNA NOCHE DE CINE
#initiative

ArabAd
Saudi Eyes the Future

BRIEFING
GIRLS POWER
ESTE NÚMERO É SEXISTA

Campaign Brief
The Empire Strikes Back

extradiens

ARCHIVE

Kampanje
50 ÅR
MED MEDIEHISTORIE

M&M
LUOVA KAPTEENI

MM
403 404
TIMOTEJ GALA, HTTPOOL
S TWITTERJEM V 15 DRŽAV

MARKETING
the client is not
GOD!
MARKETERS ARE
MERE MORTALS:
HOW AD AGENCIES
CAN HELP THEM WIN!

Marketing Türkiye
ÜNIVERSITELI
gençliğin

AD ASIA

GR
design δράσεις

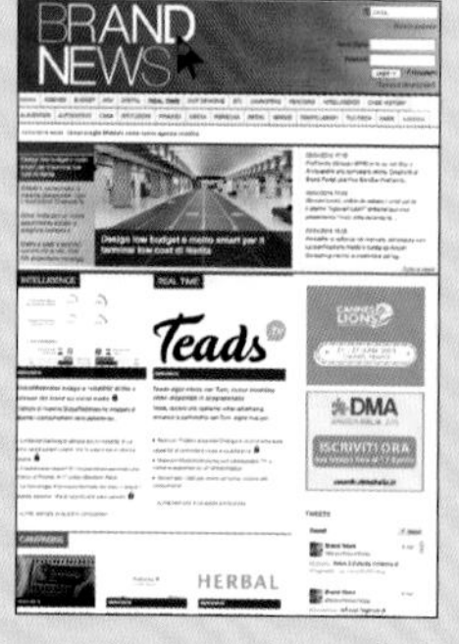
BRAND NEWS
Teads
DMA
HERBAL

Press
RAFAŁ BETLEJEWSKI: PATRZONY

Je moet in the moment zijn

STRATÉGIE
SLOBODA TLAČE S NÁSLEDKAMI
SLOVENSKÁ REKLAMA NA FACEBOOKU
TRENDY 2015
JEDNOTKA.

STRATÉGIES
LES ANIMATEURS PRÉFÉRÉS DES FRANÇAIS

strategy
CHARTING MOLSON'S COURSE
CASSIES & CREATIVE REPORT CARD
SCHOOLED: A DEEP DIVE INTO NEW LEARNING

Sostav.ru
КАРТА БРЕНДИНГОВЫХ АГЕНТСТВ

MARKETING & CREATIVITY
宣伝会議
5
TOKYO
54%
53%
49%
44%
35%
20%

THE DRUM
READY TO LOSE CONTROL?
THE DRIVERLESS CAR ISSUE

THE BEST OF GLOBAL DIGITAL MARKETING
Upcoming Events

MARKETING TRIBUNE
Homo digitalis: altijd verbonden

signcafe

persönlich
Unbequem
Harald Schmidts Bekenntnisse

CreativeReview
CREATIVITY IN HEALTH

Resumé
"DE ÄR RENT KRIMINELLA"
Bonnier-familjen delar på 150 Mkr
IQ
Innovation & Kommunikation

The jury

The Epica Jury is made up of journalists from leading advertising, design, marketing and communications magazines and websites worldwide. A total of 42 publications from 36 countries were represented on the jury in 2014. The jury president was Teressa Iezzi, editor of Fast Company's creative channel, Co.Create.

ARGENTINA	Reporte Publicidad
AUSTRALIA	Campaign Brief
AUSTRIA	Extradienst
	Lürzer's International Archive
BELGIUM	Pub
BULGARIA	Sign Café
CANADA	Strategy
CHINA	Modern Advertising
CZECH REPUBLIC	Strategie
DENMARK	Markedsføring
ESTONIA	Best-Marketing
FINLAND	Markkinointi & Mainonta
FRANCE	Stratégies
GERMANY	Werben & Verkaufen
GREECE	+Design
	Marketing Week
HUNGARY	Kreativ
INDIA	exchange4media
IRELAND	IMJ
ITALY	NC Nuova Communicazione
	Brand News
	Pubblicita'Italia
JAPAN	Sendenkaigi
LEBANON	ArabAd
MALAYSIA	Marketing Magazine
NETHERLANDS	Marketing Tribune
NORWAY	Kampanje
PHILIPPINES	Adobo Magazine
POLAND	Press
PORTUGAL	Briefing
RUSSIA	Sostav.ru
SERBIA	New Moment
SINGAPORE	AdAsia
SLOVAKIA	Stratégie
SLOVENIA	Marketing Magazin
SPAIN	Anuncios
SWEDEN	Resumé
SWITZERLAND	Persönlich
	Werbewoche
TURKEY	Marketing Türkiye
UNITED KINGDOM	Creative Review
	The Drum

EPICA AWARDS
A DIFFERENT ANGLE ON CREATIVITY
2014
euronews
MONT BLANC
MARKETING TRIBUNE
Meer over marketing
Amsterdam 2014

Welcome to Amsterdam

The Epica Awards ceremony and International Creative Circle took place in Amsterdam at the Koepelkerk on Thursday, November 20th, 2014. In the afternoon leading up to the ceremony, Epica and Marketing Tribune hosted the Creative Circle, a conference highlighting international creative work. It included speeches from Petter Gulli, Executive Creative Director at DDB Oslo; François Grouiller, Group Strategy Director, Europe at Fred & Farid Group in Paris; Darren Richardson, CCO & Managing Director at BBDO and Proximity Worldwide Düsseldorf; Clay Mills, Managing Director at Wieden+Kennedy Amsterdam; and Jonay Sosa, traveller and copywriter at ideasforfuel.com.

Humanity always wins
by Mark Tungate

Leo Burnett was not a Mad Man. Not in what has become the archetypal sense of the term. He was a short, paunchy guy who looked more like Alfred Hitchcock than Don Draper. However, Don Draper was partly modelled on a Burnett employee: a guy called Draper Daniels, who was Leo's head of creative and worked on the Marlboro account.

Looks aside, there's no doubt that as a personality and an agency, Leo Burnett helped to shape the advertising business. "He was one of the godfathers of the industry," says worldwide chief creative officer Mark Tutssel (*left*). "Here was a guy who believed in creativity, and who set out to use it in a way that changed the fortunes of many iconic brands. One need look no further than the Marlboro cowboy."

Today, the 80-year-old network honours its founder's legacy in many ways. "At the heart of everything we do is a belief in the power and potency of creativity," Mark elaborates. "Leo always said that he wanted his agency to be the best in the world – bar none. Second place simply didn't exist. He had an obsession with perfection. And we're still driven by that passion to be the best."

Hence the network's Global Product Committee, a quarterly meeting during which its creative chiefs from across the globe critique and rate their own work. Hence, also, Mark's conviction that awards are important.

"Awards are a vital barometer of your creative health." He points out that 17 different Leo Burnett agencies won Epica awards this year, implying that standards of creativity are high across the board. "We truly work as a network. By that I mean we work as one – with one goal and one vision."

As an aside, he adds that the "does creativity sell?" argument is well and truly over. "Donald Gunn (Leo Burnett's former director of creative resources, and founder of the eponymous report) conducted a persuasive study long ago; more recently the IPA (Institute of Practitioners in Advertising) proved categorically that there is a direct correlation between high creativity and marketplace success."

The drive to be the best might sound a little aggressive on paper, but Mark insists that the human element – the consumer, in other words – is never forgotten. "Leo himself left us with the attitude that became our philosophy: HumanKind. He had this amazing ability to touch people, to make that dovetail connection between brands and consumers."

The network, he says, should strive to ensure that everything it does "is designed to add value to human lives". There are a number of examples in this book, from a billionaire who threatens to bury his Bentley to raise awareness for organ donation, to a citronella-treated newspaper that warded off mosquitos during National Dengue Week in Sri Lanka.

Mark also points to Samsung's "Maestros Academy": "The first digital platform that brought great Italian craftsmen and the next generation of artisans together, through the power of technology. That's the kind of new world thinking we prize."

Is it difficult to shape that thinking within a network that has a heritage dating back to the 1930s? "Of course not, because we've all evolved over time. There's been a change of mentality. Obviously the biggest shift in communication has been from one-way to two-way. Before, we advertised AT people. Now we definitely communicate WITH them. Our ultimate goal is to create lifelong emotional relationships between brands and people."

So what about the industry's growing obsession with data, which often feels like the opposite of creativity? "Data needs to be used in the service of creativity. If I started a research agency, it would be called Read Between The Lines, because that's exactly what you have to do: use the data to uncover deeper insights and improve relevance. It's a springboard that can help you find better ideas."

The digital world is also a new source of stories, some of them a lot of fun. Mark cites Leo Burnett's campaign for insurer Allstate, which starred its character Mayhem as a social-savvy burglar. People can't resist posting pictures of their latest trip on social media; so Mayhem keeps an eye on their feeds and then breaks into their houses while they're busy filling Instagram with selfies. As they enjoy college football's Sugar Bowl, he's selling their belongings on the internet while millions watch.

"I think people are slightly alarmed by the word 'data'. But you need to convert 'data' into 'idea'. The same is true of technology. It's hugely important in terms of the way we reach people, but ultimately it's up to us to find an idea that will move them."

Take the digital Grand Prix winner, "Like A Girl", for Always. A viral video, certainly: but also a compelling piece of film with a mission to empower young women. It seems that however much the industry changes, you can't beat the human touch.

The crowd pleasers
by Mark Tungate

Adam&eveDDB owns Christmas. At least in the UK, where the agency's annual effort for the department store John Lewis is always hotly anticipated. Although the spots are very different, they have ingredients in common: a certain heartstring-tugging sensibility, along with a well-known pop song covered by an unexpected artist. (My own favourite, "The Long Wait", an Epica winner in 2012, features The Smiths' "Please, Please, Please Let Me Get What I Want" sung by Slow Moving Millie, AKA the actress Amelia Warner).

It turns out that the spot also contains something co-founder and executive creative director Ben Priest holds dear: a twist at the end. "People love a misdirect," as he puts it. "When they get the joke, there's a little sting of recognition. It makes them feel smarter."

A case in point is the award-winning commercial for Volkswagen, which was shown in cinemas and looks exactly like a movie trailer. The good guys in their VW are closing in on a bus that's been hijacked by escaped convicts. One of our heroes climbs onto the bonnet of the car and tries to board the bus – but he can't, because VW's safe distance technology slows the car.

The ad is grandiose, action-packed and satisfying. Ben confirms that the agency strives first and foremost to please the audience. "Right from the start, we said, 'Let's exist in the spotlight and do work that millions of people will see – and lots of people will love'. We want to do big, big, mainstream stuff."

Ben's advertising heroes include John Webster, the legendary BMP creative who in the 1970s wrote the slogans my generation

chanted in the playground, and David Abbott, the consummate copywriter behind Sainsbury's, The Economist, and many others.

Adam & Eve was founded in 2008 when Ben left Rainey Kelly Campbell Roalfe/Y&R with James Murphy and David Golding. "It was at the deepest darkest point of the recession, which oddly enough is a good time to start an agency. Start-ups are extremely important to the vitality of the economy."

They merged with DDB in 2012, transforming immediately from an agency of 75 to one of 400. Although DDB has an immense creative heritage, Ben says the merged entity does not have a particular philosophy (along the lines of TBWA's "Disruption" or BBDO's "the work, the work, the work"). "Nothing we've written down, anyway. In pitches, we just show what we've done. Having said that, we have a certain approach. Everyone sits open plan: we don't have a creative area or a TV area. When we merged with DDB we knocked down walls and moved people from five floors onto just two."

They also work fast. "We've never liked that ploddy, process-driven way of working that some big agencies have. Obviously that puts pressure on people, but we never leave anyone out on their own. We always say that this is rugby, not relay."

Talking of pressure, I wonder aloud if the agency ever worries that it won't be able to top the previous year's Christmas spot for John Lewis. "Well, it's a high-class problem to have," observes Ben. "I remember our client standing up in a meeting once and saying that working on the Christmas campaign is not a pressure, it's a privilege."

It's also highly collaborative. "There's no wall between agency and client. We agree and disagree passionately. And the whole thing works on gut instinct – there's no research." Is the agency a fan of research, in general? "It sort of depends on the client. I like the fact that research can inspire a good idea. But I wouldn't advocate clinging to it at every stage of the process."

So now we come to the elephant in the room: the multi-award-winning Christmas campaign for Harvey Nichols, arguably London's most upmarket department store. You know the pitch by now. The store launched a range of well-packaged but ultra cheap goodies, from elastic bands to paper clips, and called it the "Sorry, I Spent It On Myself" collection. Buy cheapskate gifts from Harvey Nicks for your loved ones, and spend the savings on a more luxurious item for your most loved one.

"The film was really a complement to the main idea," says Ben. "Harvey Nichols said they would only do it if they could actually make these products, get them into the store and sell them."

In fact the products sold out, and soon began appearing on eBay. Once again, the campaign gave consumers the impression they were in on the joke – that the brand understood them. But what's with the same agency working for two major department stores? Isn't there a conflict here?

"When we merged, both clients decided that they were happy to work with us, and they wanted to continue. As a result, you have Richard Brim and Daniel Fisher, who worked on Harvey Nichols, creating the latest John Lewis campaign."

As much as the agency excels at film, it revels in the ability to expand an idea across multiple platforms. The latest John Lewis character, Monty the Penguin, also became a cuddly toy, pyjamas, books, an app and an animal adoption scheme. However, Ben accepts that the internet has reinforced the appeal of film. "Let's just say that film has had its USP confirmed." And film remains, of course, one of the ultimate crowd pleasers.

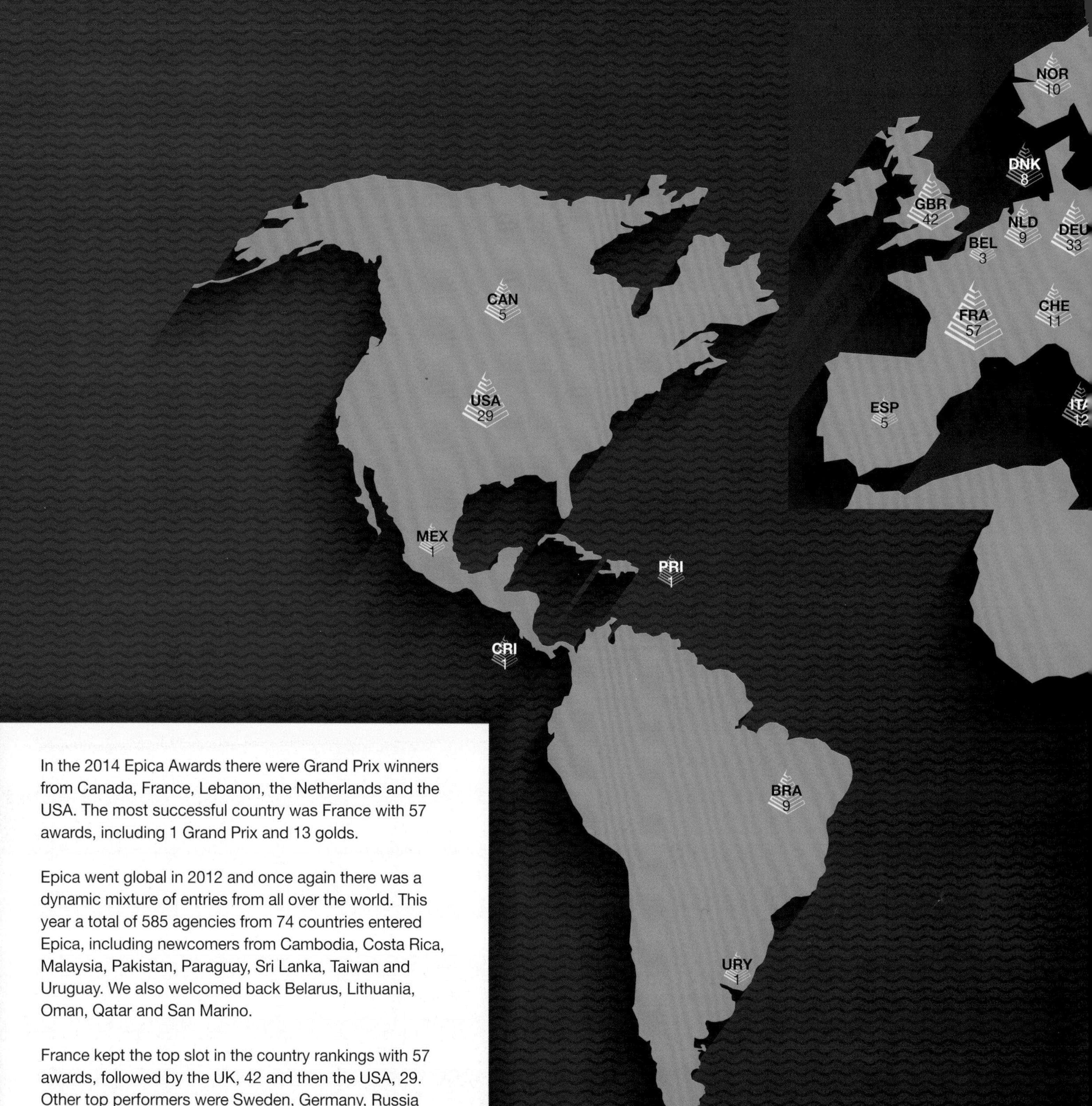

In the 2014 Epica Awards there were Grand Prix winners from Canada, France, Lebanon, the Netherlands and the USA. The most successful country was France with 57 awards, including 1 Grand Prix and 13 golds.

Epica went global in 2012 and once again there was a dynamic mixture of entries from all over the world. This year a total of 585 agencies from 74 countries entered Epica, including newcomers from Cambodia, Costa Rica, Malaysia, Pakistan, Paraguay, Sri Lanka, Taiwan and Uruguay. We also welcomed back Belarus, Lithuania, Oman, Qatar and San Marino.

France kept the top slot in the country rankings with 57 awards, followed by the UK, 42 and then the USA, 29. Other top performers were Sweden, Germany, Russia and the Netherlands.

Adam&eveDDB from London was the Agency of the Year with 14 awards including 9 golds, followed by BBDO New York with 14 awards too, including 1 Grand Prix and 1 gold. Meanwhile, Leo Burnett Tailor Made (Brazil) won 8 awards including 3 golds, while the UK's Abbott Mead Vickers BBDO scored 7 awards, including 2 golds.

With its Grand Prix, 14 golds and 47 awards in total, Leo Burnett is Epica's best-performing Network of the Year. It was followed by BBDO with 35 awards including a Grand Prix and 7 golds. DDB also performed well with 27 awards, 11 of which were golds, plus another Grand Prix. Publicis and Havas Worldwide complete the top five.

All the Grand Prix, gold, silver and bronze winners feature in this 28th edition of the Epica Book, together with a selection of other high-scoring entries.

	GP	Gold	Sil	Brz	TOT
FRANCE FRA	1	14	22	20	57
UNITED KINGDOM GBR	0	14	12	16	42
UNITED STATES USA	1	6	13	9	29
SWEDEN SWE	0	7	9	3	19
GERMANY DEU	0	4	7	7	18
RUSSIAN FEDERATION RUS	0	2	4	6	12
TURKEY TUR	1	3	1	4	12
ITALY ITA	0	2	3	7	12
AUSTRALIA AUS	0	3	2	6	11
SWITZERLAND CHE	0	3	2	6	11
NORWAY NOR	0	1	3	8	10

NETHERLAND
BRAZIL BRA
DENMARK DN
CANADA CAN
U. ARAB EMIR
SPAIN ESP
LEBANON LB
UKRAINE UK
BELGIUM BEL
CHINA CHN
JAPAN JPN

	GP	Gold	Sil	Brz	TOT
	0	3	3	2	9
	0	3	1	5	9
	0	2	1	7	8
	1	1	2	1	5
RE	1	2	0	0	5
	0	1	1	3	5
	0	0	2	3	3
	0	1	2	0	3
	0	1	1	1	3
	0	1	1	1	3
	0	1	0	2	3

	Gold	Sil	Brz	TOT
NEW ZEALAND NZL	1	1	0	2
CZECH REPUBLIC CZE	1	0	1	2
SRI LANKA LKA	1	0	1	2
THAILAND THA	1	0	1	2
FINLAND FIN	0	1	1	2
POLAND POL	0	1	1	2
HUNGARY HUN	1	0	0	2
AUSTRIA AUT	1	0	0	1
MEXICO MEX	1	0	0	1
URUGUAY URI	0	0	2	1
BULGARIA BGR	0	1	0	1

	Gold	Sil	Brz	TOT
COSTA RICA CRI	0	1	0	1
GREECE GRC	0	1	0	1
QATAR QAT	0	1	0	1
CAMBODIA KHM	0	0	1	1
INDIA IND	0	0	1	1
KUWAIT KWT	0	0	1	1
LITHUANIA LTU	0	0	1	1
PUERTO RICO PRI	0	0	1	1
ROMANIA ROU	0	0	1	1
SOUTH AFRICA ZAF	0	0	1	1
VIETNAM VNM	0	0	1	1

NEWS
The Boy Who Beeps
He speaks the language of industry
He's fluent in machine
Companies are thinking if you can talk to machines, you can do great things

A beep from the heart

by Mark Tungate

Who would have thought that a story about the internet of machines could bring a tear to your eye? But more than one Epica juror had to blink rapidly after watching "The Boy Who Beeps", the cinematic spot for GE from BBDO New York. Finally, they were moved to award it the Film Grand Prix.

The film introduces us to a little boy who, from the day of his birth, emits electronic beeps instead of talking. It soon becomes apparent that he has a kind of superpower: he's able to communicate with machines. His beeps can switch on a TV, get a vending machine to flip out a can of soda – and even fix a power outage. But only in the final frame does he utter his first real words.

Explaining the background, BBDO New York creative director and copywriter Tim Roan says: "GE makes the industrial machines that keep the world working. Their idea was to design software that would basically allow these machines to talk to one another, generating data that could be used to make them more efficient. That's the Industrial Internet."

According to GE's website, the Industrial Internet will soon link "billions of machines and devices, ranging from smartphones and thermostats to jet engines and medical scanners". The challenge for BBDO was to celebrate this development and make it relevant to the wider public, as well as GE clients.

Ironically, a TV commercial was not viewed as the primary solution. "The door was open for us to try something different in terms of length and story structure," Tim recalls. "GE wanted to approach this in a different way – maybe as a serial."

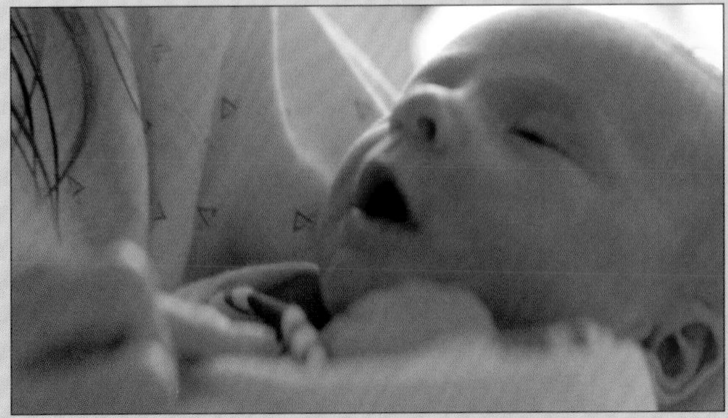

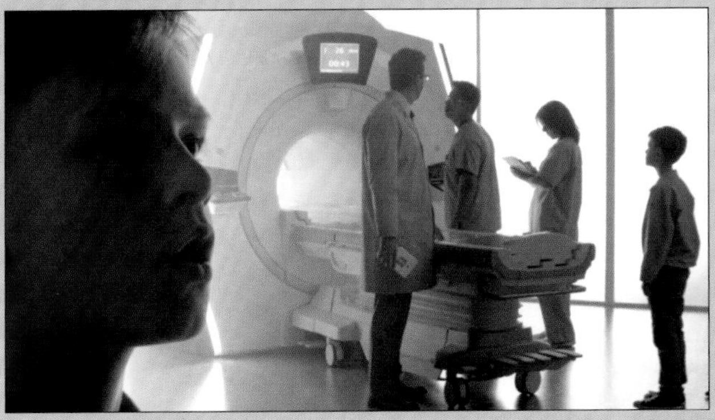

First of all, Tim and associate creative director/art director Lance Vining needed to get to the heart of the concept. Lance says: "Machines that can talk is pretty good. But what if we could talk to machines? So we thought about that for a couple of weeks."

The pair were on a shoot in Brazil when the eureka moment came. Tim says: "We were bouncing around in the back of van through rainy Sao Paulo when it hit us. What if only one person could talk to machines? What could he do with this talent? Lance had a pregnant wife, and I have kids, so this storybook feeling kept coming through. And that became 'The Boy Who Beeps'."

While talking to the director – another Lance, this time Lance Acord – a secondary love story emerged, between the boy and a girl at school, which eventually gave the film its emotional punch and eye-blurring ending.

Tim says: "There's definitely an arc the boy goes through. He experiences hardship: his parents worry about him, kids at school laugh at him. But he becomes a kind of hero. We wanted to explore what the world's attitude to him would be."

Although the boy is well aware that he's different, he is able to shrug off the sniggers of his fellow pupils, as if he's quietly aware that everything will work out in the end. To stretch a point, the girl who befriends him is almost a stand-in for GE itself, which embraces unexpected solutions. Yet both characters remain entirely human and relateable. The audience cheers on their relationship just as it feels a rush of gratification when the hero's talents are recognised.

The director was due to take his annual vacation during the period scheduled for shooting, but he signed on to the project because he didn't want anyone else to do it. Lance Vining says: "I've never had an experience like that with a director in my life. He was totally into it from beginning to end."

At one point it was thought that the film would run for five minutes, but the final cut is a perfect two. Finally, a complex industrial innovation had inspired a concise yet heartfelt TV spot; with a soundtrack by Beck to top it all off.

"It's actually two Beck tracks, which is incredible," says Lance. "The potential issues around using music by a still-famous, culturally relevant independent artist are huge."

But luck was smiling on the project, as it turned out that the film's director and editor both had connections with the musician. Once Beck saw the work, the deal was as good as done.

That the client was delighted with the result rapidly became obvious. The film was unveiled during the first game of the NFL (National Football League) season, one of the biggest televisual events of the year. Other high-profile media slots followed.

"We've had nothing but great responses," says Lance. "We got a lot of tweets suggesting we should turn it into a full-length movie." One thing the team didn't do was surround the film with digital spin-offs, stunts and clutter. "We talked about a few things, but in the end they seemed too trivial and we felt that they might blunt the impact of the film."

"The Boy Who Beeps" did get shown, however, in one of its most natural environments – the cinema. Tim Roan actually saw it when he went to the movies with his kids. Their response at the end was equally heart-warming. "Good job, dad."

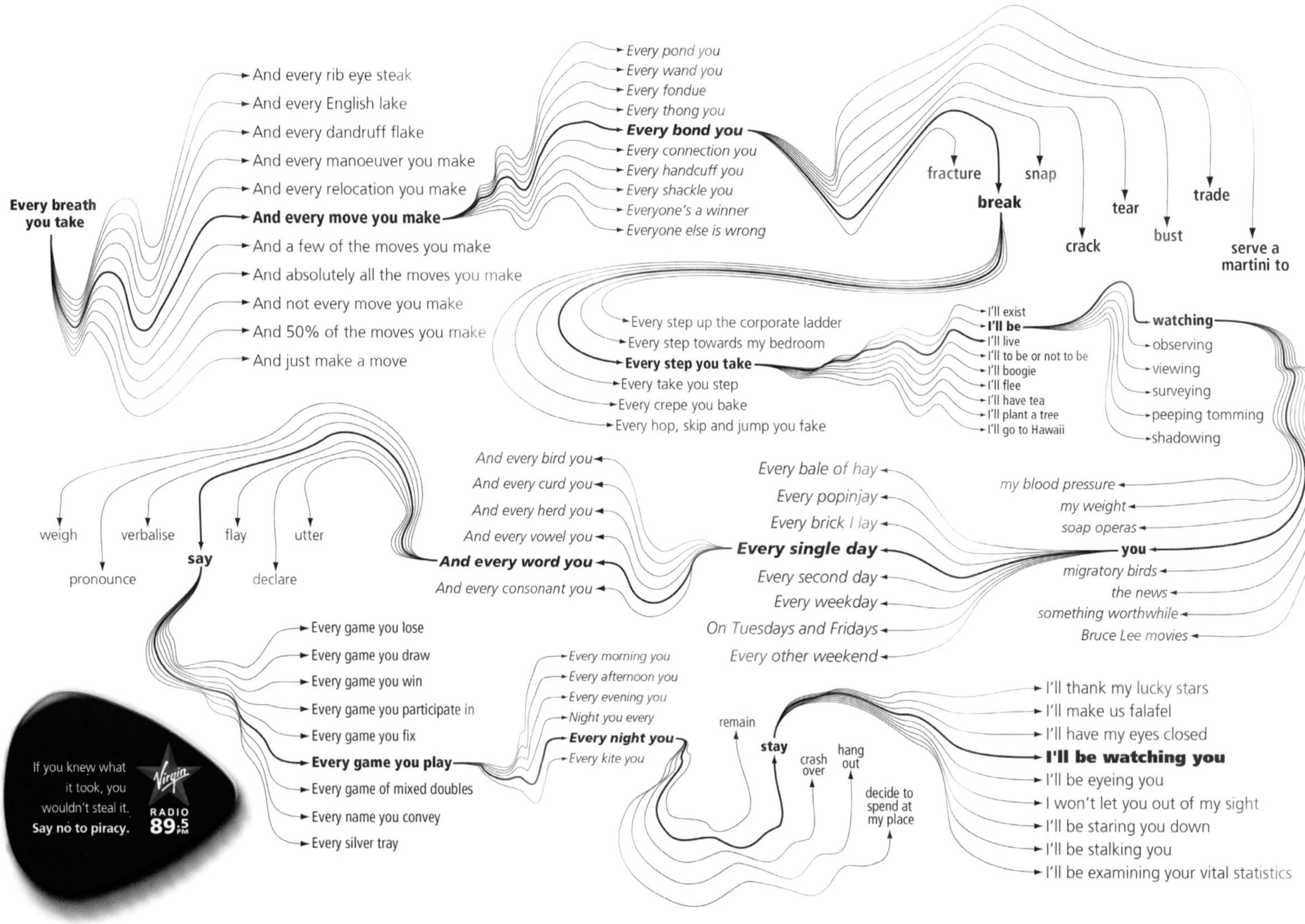

Every breath you take

And every rib eye steak
And every English lake
And every dandruff flake
And every manoeuver you make
And every relocation you make
And every move you make
And a few of the moves you make
And absolutely all the moves you make
And not every move you make
And 50% of the moves you make
And just make a move

Every pond you
Every wand you
Every fondue
Every thong you
Every bond you
Every connection you
Every handcuff you
Every shackle you
Everyone's a winner
Everyone else is wrong

fracture
break
snap
crack
tear
bust
trade
serve a martini to

Every step up the corporate ladder
Every step towards my bedroom
Every step you take
Every take you step
Every crepe you bake
Every hop, skip and jump you fake

I'll exist
I'll be
I'll live
I'll to be or not to be
I'll boogie
I'll flee
I'll have tea
I'll plant a tree
I'll go to Hawaii

watching
observing
viewing
surveying
peeping tomming
shadowing

my blood pressure
my weight
soap operas
you
migratory birds
the news
something worthwhile
Bruce Lee movies

Every bale of hay
Every popinjay
Every brick I lay
Every single day
Every second day
Every weekday
On Tuesdays and Fridays
Every other weekend

And every bird you
And every curd you
And every herd you
And every vowel you
And every word you
And every consonant you

weigh
pronounce
verbalise
say
flay
declare
utter

Every game you lose
Every game you draw
Every game you win
Every game you participate in
Every game you fix
Every game you play
Every game of mixed doubles
Every name you convey
Every silver tray

Every morning you
Every afternoon you
Every evening you
Night you every
Every night you
Every kite you

remain
stay
crash over
hang out
decide to spend at my place

I'll thank my lucky stars
I'll make us falafel
I'll have my eyes closed
I'll be watching you
I'll be eyeing you
I won't let you out of my sight
I'll be staring you down
I'll be stalking you
I'll be examining your vital statistics

If you knew what it took, you wouldn't steal it. **Say no to piracy.**
Virgin RADIO 89.5 FM

© ramzi hachicho - Fotolia

Words to save music
by Theda Braddock

How do you tackle an issue that has not only been creating obstacles for your client, but plaguing a community? That's exactly what Leo Burnett was able to do with its campaign for Virgin Radio, the winner of this year's press Grand Prix.

The brief was straightforward but challenging. In Lebanon, 95% of music is pirated and Virgin Radio, like others in the music industry, has suffered losses for years as a result. Through a collaborative effort by Leo Burnett offices in Beirut and Dubai, led by regional creative director Bechara Mouzannar (*left*), the print campaign "Making Music" was developed.

The visuals capture the thought processes behind the creation of hit music. Featuring three iconic songs (Michael Jackson's "Billie Jean", Nirvana's "Come As You Are" and The Police's "Roxanne") the posters detail all the potential lyrics the songwriters might have considered, many of them highly amusing, with the final choices in bold. The visuals aim to illustrate the complex art of composition and suggest that musicians should be rewarded, not punished with music piracy.

As a background, Bechara explains the history of radio and music piracy in Lebanon, pointing out the difficulty of tackling the problem while addressing an audience that is unwilling to change. Radio has always played an important role in the region due to its

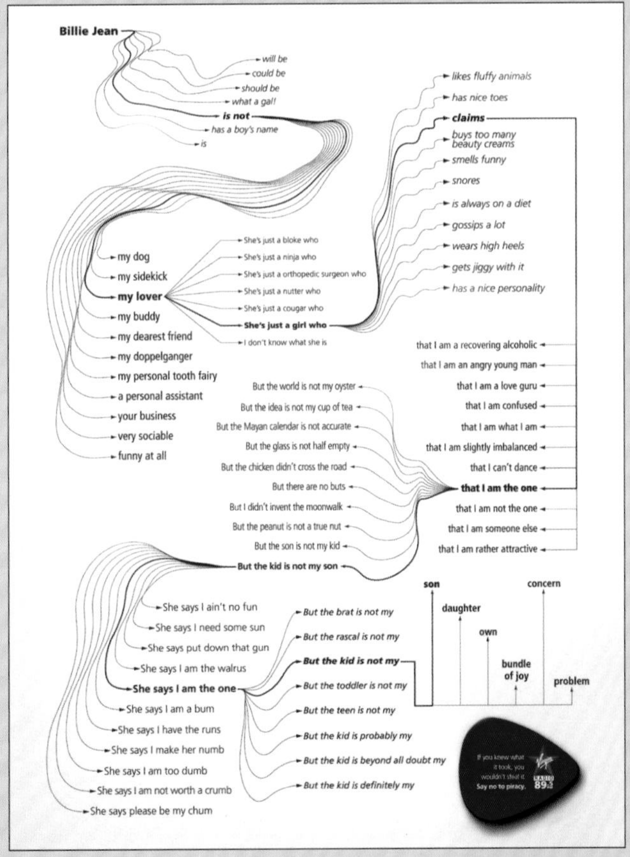

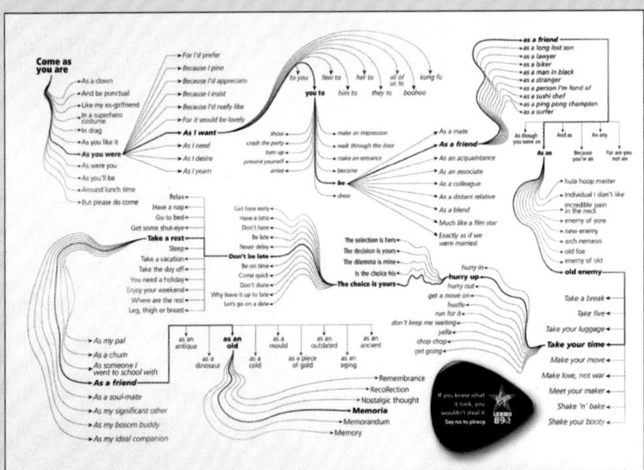

© diak - Fotolia

many conflicts, including Lebanon's own civil war, the resulting political turmoil and the most recent conflict in 2006. "Radio has been a kind of companion for people, even if they have TV. It has reported killings, massacres and crises over 30 years of trouble. Even today, there are electricity cuts for four to five hours a day."

With their easy portability, radios play a vitally informative role in people's daily lives. Music is also an important factor, offering comfort and escape, and FM stations have neglected to pay broadcasting rights.

But piracy is also pervasive among ordinary citizens, beginning with the counterfeit products that were smuggled in during the wars. "People considered it a minor sin, if anything, to purchase these products because the local music industry was so unsuccessful," says Bechara. "When the internet arrived and sharing became possible, online piracy became an even bigger problem and music brands were hesitant to set up shop. iTunes changed things as it was a solid platform for downloading music at affordable prices. At the same time, the Lebanese started to understand the importance of purchasing real DVDs and CDs, rather than pirated items."

Brands began to return to the country, with Virgin leading the way with flagship stores and events. "Richard Branson even came to visit. Virgin wanted to celebrate music for those who had suffered, in a certain sense. They became the first international brand with a major radio station, reassuring other brands who have to pay a lot for broadcast rights and position themselves in a market with hundreds of stations."

Despite these improvements, however, the problem persists, hence the awareness-raising campaign.

Bechara believes "Making Music" was chosen by the jury of journalists because "they understand the exercise of styles and the consideration of language that goes into the expression of an idea". He suggests that they may have been instinctively drawn to a campaign that "pays tribute to the complexity of words, to what you can come up with using mind and pen".

But the awards circuit is one thing. The visuals were also effective on the ground, partly because they reached a wide audience through newspapers, another vital media for the Lebanese, and because so much of the population reads English. Bechara is especially pleased that the campaign has had a positive impact on youth, citing his own son as an example. "When he saw them he told me I'd finally made a good ad!"

While he is flattered that the campaign has won so many plaudits, Bechara stresses that the greatest reward for any advertisement is when you can see that it has genuinely resonated with the audience, whether people are laughing more or talking more – or in this case, both. He believes the power to move people is the added value that agencies continue to bring to brands.

"We're able to create a bond between brands and society. Agencies do insightful things and, especially in the Middle East, a region that has suffered so much, it's up to agencies to be as truthful as possible. We're salesmen but we can also be poets, creating brands that are dearly loved."

He adds that the "Making Music" campaign "offered a double reward, first winning the heart of the customer, and then awards in major festivals". But there's no room for complacency. By the time you read this, the team will have developed a second campaign for Virgin Radio, with a completely fresh approach.

© MNHN - François Grandin

LES ANIMAUX SAUVAGES SONT À PARIS

© MNHN - François Grandin

Wild about Paris

by Theda Braddock

In the east of Paris lies a world of wildlife – from the savannah to the jungles of the Amazon. Or at least a taste of these, and three other bio-zones, at the recently re-opened Paris Zoo, formerly the Zoo of Vincennes. After a six-year reconstruction period, the zoo (a division of the National Museum of Natural History) has opened its gates as a wildlife preserve with a focus on conservation and animal welfare, by creating an environment that allows animals to live in their natural habitats.

So how to announce the grand re-opening and promote this cage-free attraction to Parisians? Cue the agency Publicis Conseil Paris, which set out to merge wildlife with the urban environment.

The stately black and white print campaign features "wild" animals on the prowl in some of the most recognisable sites in Paris. Thanks to masterful re-touching, the viewer has the impression that baboons and lionesses are perfectly at home at Notre Dame or near the Louvre. A jaguar stalks the statue of a deer in the Luxembourg gardens, while vultures wait patiently beside the statue of a lion attacking its prey in the Tuileries.

The tagline "Wildlife is back in town" informs us of the zoo's re-opening, while underlining that these beautiful animals are only steps away.

Art director Benoît Blumberger and copywriter Bangaly Fofana wanted to capture the essence of the revamped attraction. Under the supervision of creative directors Frédéric Royer and

© A. Fevrier

Olivier Altmann (who has since left to co-found agency Altmann + Pacreau), they started by focusing on the zoo's mission: protecting and saving endangered species. But eventually they came down to a single strong message – after years of silence, wildlife was back in town.

After that, the objective became clear: bringing the animals to Paris. "We had to match the calling of the zoo. We didn't want it to look like another amusement park. So the idea was: if we have to showcase animals, we have to respect their natural behaviour, and magnify it."

The team was inspired by the work of wildlife photographer Nick Brandt, known for his daring, close-up animal shots. "He brings a totally different perspective that makes the animals look majestic and graceful, which we felt would be a good way for us to stand out from all the animal advertising campaigns we've seen before."

So with photographer Ronan Merot and the retouching magic of Adrien Bénard, the team set out to create portraits of animals "behaving as though they were in their natural environment in the middle of Paris".

Bearing in mind the colourful subject matter, why choose black and white? "When you have to mix premium-ness, Paris, and photography, black and white makes sense. We also felt it would be relevant to show the timeless postcard aspect of Paris and its environment."

The campaign presented no shortage of challenges and hours of painstaking work. For a start, shooting in February in Paris is always hampered by the climate and necessitates a great deal of patience.

Photographer Ronan Merot recalls praying for good weather as he set out for weeks of shooting across the city, returning to the same places as much as half a dozen times to ensure that he had a variety of angles. Then he and the editors at the agency spent hours combining the results with stock photos of animals. Extensive retouching was supported by frequent follow-up shoots to ensure the seamless integration of the animals with their new environment.

Having worked closely with the team over a period of several months, Ronan recognises that they were given what many creatives will agree is one of the greatest and rarest of luxuries – time. He attributes a huge part of the campaign's success to the breathing room the team was given in terms of finding solutions. In fact he wishes more clients were as understanding – not just of the creative process, but of the craft that is required to turn a good idea into award-winning work.

Another important element, he adds, was the way the team worked together, with egos set aside. "The mentality really was, 'let's take the best idea, it doesn't matter if it's from you or me'," he says.

The final result was an elegant yet eye-catching outdoor campaign that stopped passers-by in their tracks.

At the time of writing, Publicis Conseil team was planning to follow up on its success with a new "season" of the campaign, this time featuring an anaconda, a crocodile and a white rhino. One can only imagine where they'll end up. If you happen to be in Paris, it's probably best to take a careful look around before you step on the metro.

Google's French connection

by Mark Tungate

Marseille is one of those towns – like Tangier or Naples – that has a reputation for being edgy; take the wrong turn and you might stray into something resembling danger. In reality it's a buoyant Mediterranean city with a thriving cultural and artistic scene.

The Night Walk in Marseille explores both dimensions. The virtual tour takes us to places we might baulk at visiting alone after dark, and strips away our preconceptions to reveal the true soul of the city. Which is not surprising, as it's based on a series of sound walks created by somebody who lives there, Julie de Muer.

The quest that bought Julie, Google, the Amsterdam agency 72andSunny, and the production company MediaMonks together is almost as labyrinthine as the backstreets of Marseille. The original brief was to create a series of films that would dramatize the Google tools that help us in our daily lives.

In 2013 72andSunny was briefed to extend the Google Stories campaign, which had originated at Google's Creative Lab in the US, to Europe. The search was on to find "ordinary people using Google's search and maps in extraordinary ways".

"Getting the casting right was the hardest part," says Graham Bednash, director of consumer marketing at Google EMEA. "I don't know how many people we rejected, but I can tell you we looked at hundreds of stories. Some were too predictable, too fanciful…we wanted something authentic."

The first story the team made for France was a film about Laurent Aigon, an amateur aviation enthusiast who uses Google to find the parts for a flight simulator, which he builds in his kids' bedroom. Agency creative director Gregg Clampffer says: "That was very much about an individual, so Google asked us if we could find something more social, something that went out into the city and involved people."

Easier said than done. The next round of research uncovered characters ranging from urban bee-keepers to Jacques Cousteau's granddaughters. "The problem is, once you get to these stories, how do you move them forward?" says Gregg. "In a presentation to Google called Storytelling 2.0 we said we wanted to create an interactive experience, one that would let people use Google's products and deepen their relationship with the brand."

One of the crazier suggestions was a combination of a night-time Street View and the TV show The Walking Dead: in other words, a night walk with zombies. "It was one of a pile of ideas we were kicking around. But basically our criteria had changed: we needed to find somebody using Google products in an interactive way.

That was when the team stumbled across Julie's sound walks, which used Google Maps to guide participants. "She lectures at the university and is an artist, so some of the tours were quite esoteric. She was exploring layers of history and the story of manufacturing in Marseille. But in interviewing her, we saw that what she really wanted to do was show another side of the city."

The focal point would be a 90-second film about Julie's walks, but the team rapidly began wondering how they could optimise the experience. "We were inspired by the way people, especially artists, hack Google Street View to create interesting anomalies – people holding signs, and so on. That led to the thought of bringing Julie's walks into Street View, to push the boundaries of a map as a utility and to make a rich experience."

Graham adds: "We were looking for ways of creating a television experience that was more native to digital. So the question was: can we make something on television much more digitally interactive? Not least because these days most people have a phone or tablet with them while they're watching TV."

The project would also give people around the world the opportunity to experience Marseille. Listening to one of Julie's sound walks, a nocturnal street art safari, the idea of the first night-time Street View resurfaced, sans zombies. Gregg says: "We wanted to recreate the actual tour part of it, which is the guy talking about street art, but also to integrate other Google products to show the history of the town."

At one point, for example, the tour zooms in on the ghostly figure of the late Jean-Claude Izzo, who wrote crime novels that are essentially a long love letter to the city.

The traditional film shoot with Julie took four days, while the night shoot using Google's Photo Sphere – a feature than enables you to take immersive 360° panoramic photos with your phone, then share them online – took another five nights. In all more than 200 spheres were shot in the Cours Julien and surrounding areas. "The trick of it was using programming languages to string all those images together and create a Google Maps experience, using an entirely different product."

The whole thing took two months, from idea to completion. And what started out as an episode in a series of films has now become a widely admired digital experience. Gregg agrees there's a certain irony to that. "When the digital part really took off, it became the element that led people to the film, rather than the other way around."

An empowering cliché

by Lisa Marks

"We knew that when we hit on 'Like A Girl', we had hit on a truth. Something truly magical happened," says Judy John, the CEO and creative director of Leo Burnett Toronto. "Our job was to look at feminine hygiene in a different way and by doing that we started a conversation."

It is a conversation that has been more far reaching than anyone expected – and if anything it's getting louder.

The brief from Always, a Procter & Gamble brand, was to move away from function and zero in on emotional confidence. The unusual result is a documentary-style commercial that asks real people to run, throw or indeed do anything "Like a Girl" – a description seen by many as derogatory – and then challenge their negative perceptions.

The idea began with the finding that that almost twice as many girls as boys lose confidence during puberty, and never fully regain it. The creative team at Leo Burnett includes a healthy mix of men and women – but naturally the statistic resonated most strongly with the women.

"It became real in the room. We talked about how we could get this message out so that people would understand how important it is to change," says Judy. "The other shift we had to make was being less TV-centric and more social."

By doing that, the Like A Girl campaign hit the zeitgeist on the nose. In a year that saw 17-year-old education activist Malala Yousafzai win a Nobel Peace Prize, and other high-profile

calls to action such as Amy Poehler's #askhermore red carpet campaign, Like A Girl quickly gained traction, becoming the engine that not only drove sales, but also ignited an important debate on gender politics.

While both men and women directors were considered, Leo Burnett brought in Lauren Greenfield to lift the idea off the page. As the award-winning director of the 2012 documentary The Queen of Versailles, her realistic yet empathetic eye was a neat fit. Again, the stars aligned.

"Our creative director in Chicago sent me Lauren's coffee table book, 'Girl Culture' and said, 'This is who we would love to shoot with'. I flipped through the book, looked at the photography and thought, 'I'm not sure we can shoot with anybody else'. Lauren's sensibility and the way she captures the honesty and realism of girls was perfect."

Real people were cast for the commercial, which took a day to shoot. There was a base script which allowed plenty of room to explore and improvise.

"You never know what you're going to get when you do one of these documentary-style experiments, because you can't script the responses; but they were honest, authentic and emotional," says Judy, who joined Leo Burnett Toronto in 1999 as chief creative officer and was promoted to CEO in 2011.

As the magic unfolded both Lauren and Judy knew they were witnessing something special.

"Here we are, on camera, with people who had never really thought deeply about what it means to do something 'Like A Girl'. Watching their reactions, you could see that even the women and girls who responded were thinking, 'Oh, I've just insulted myself'," reveals Judy.

Lauren agrees. "That moment of realization, when the women and men in our film suddenly understood that they had been sucked into this cultural cliché, is magical to witness, because the viewer also gets to experience it at the same time," says the Boston native. "When these moments of realization occurred in real time, we knew something profound was happening in front of the cameras. Both I and some of the women on set were moved to tears."

While it makes absolutely no mention of feminine hygiene products, the ad lands exactly where it should. "Women and girls feel more better about the brand in that it shares similar values to what they do," says Judy. "As a result, the brand is doing really well."

With 56 million views and rising at the time of writing, Like A Girl might be the viral hit of the year – but it also made TV history.

In a groundbreaking move, a 60-second cut of the commercial was shown during this year's Super Bowl – the first feminine hygiene product to be advertised during the NFL's season highlight. Adobe ranked it the top digital campaign of the Super Bowl, based on an analysis of mentions on a variety of social networks and Internet platforms.

"It was perfect timing," says Judy (who as a Patriots fan was doubly thrilled). "And what was interesting is that is also prompted conversation with men."

Leo Burnett and Lauren Greenfield are now working on further content for Always. "It's been such a crazy ride watching how popular this video has become," says Judy. "It's what you dream of in this business; to be part of something that is not just successful but also meaningful."

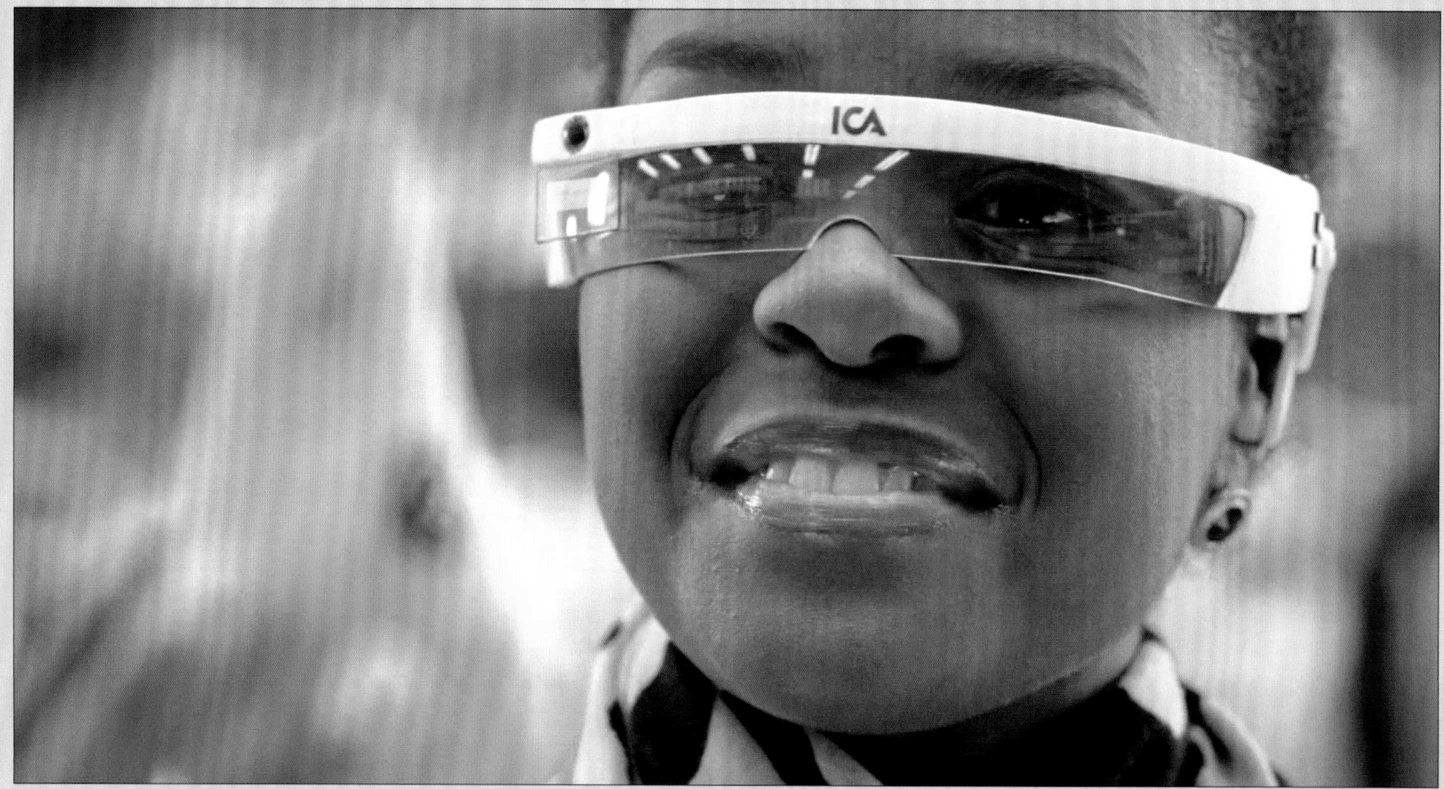

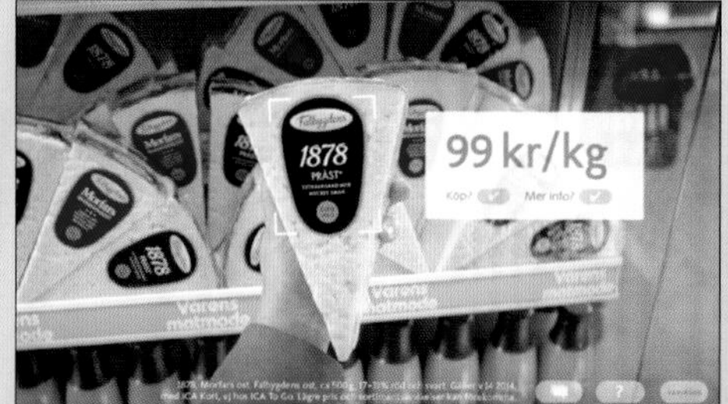

CORN FLAKES
Suddenly I have cravings for these affordable cereals!

This week! Soda, only 7 kronor!

7 kr
This week! Soda, only 7 kronor!

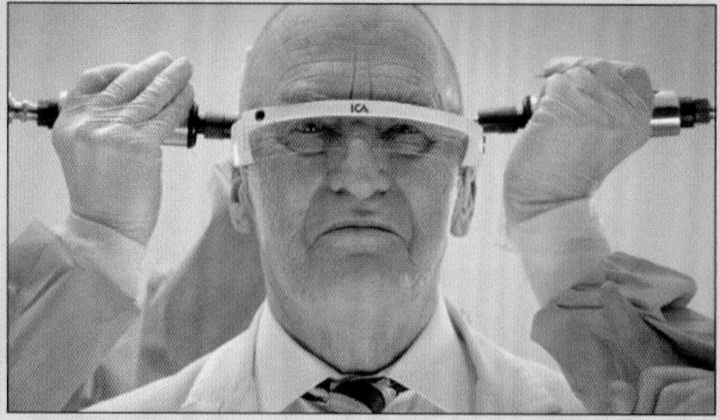

ICA glasses

Food 

Agency King, Stockholm
Creative Director Frank Hollingworth
Copywriters Pontus Thoren, Martin Sööder
Art Directors Nima Stillerud, Adam Gäfvert, Jesper Stein
Production Esteban, Stockholm
Film Directors Markus Ernerot, Alexander Brügge
Producer Olof Barr
Post Production Gangsters Post
Advertiser ICA, "ICA Glasses"

The madcap staff of the CA supermarket have been a fixture of Swedish advertising for years. But it seems they've remained bang up to date. Their new ICA glasses allow shoppers to scan bar codes, choose ingredients, summon help and add items to their shopping list – even when they're at home. And as the glasses are wired directly to the brain, they can give you a nasty shock if you neglect your diet. Not to mention a sudden craving for that week's special offer. The ad was screened on April Fool's Day.

Agency	Impact BBDO, Dubai
Creative Director	Fadi Yaish
Copywriter	Tomas Almuna
Art Directors	Gonzalo Palavecino Sergio Araya
Production	Estilo3D, Buenos Aires
Agency Producer	Clarisse Mar Wai May
Advertiser	Saudia Milk, "Broken Dreams"

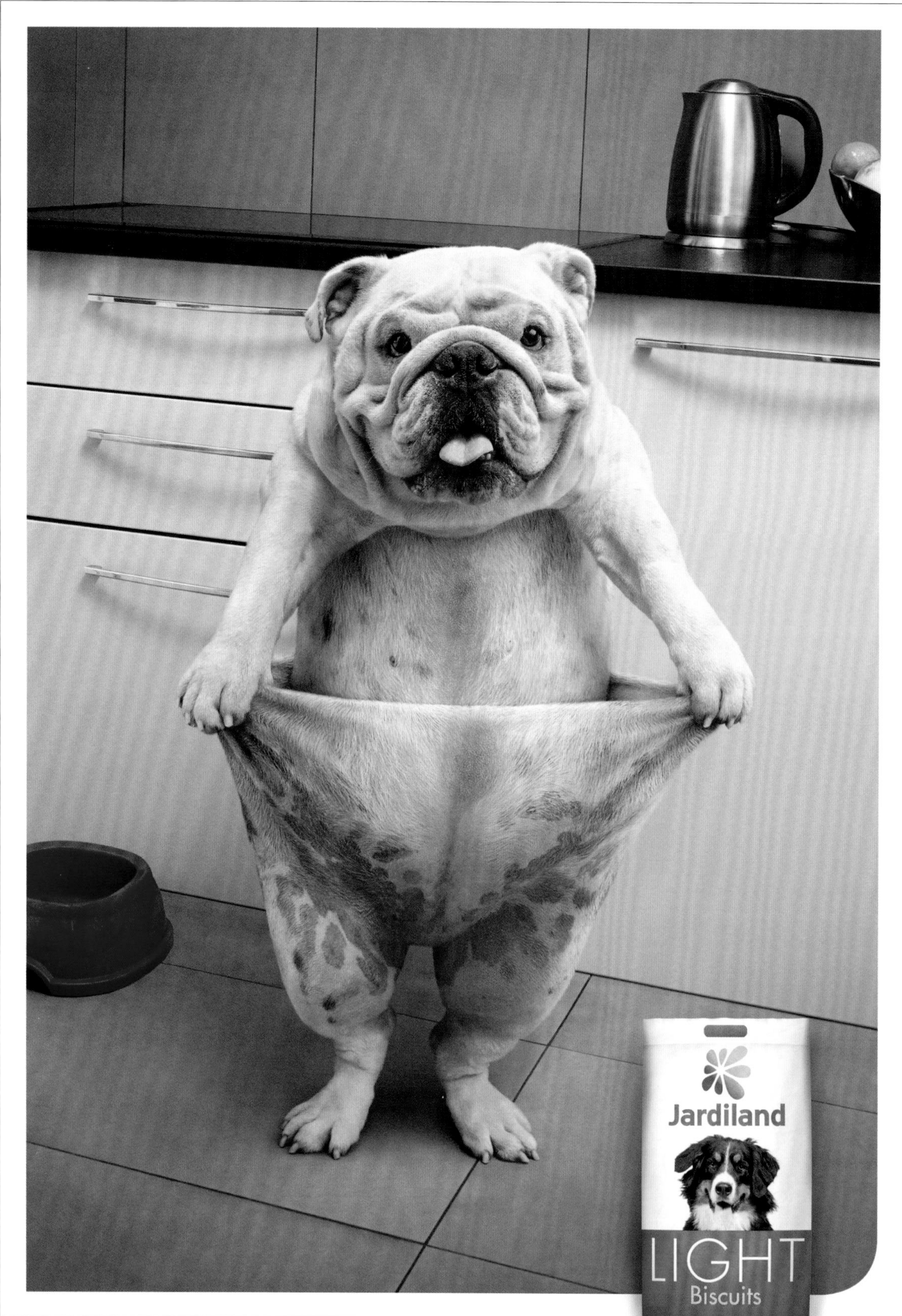

 Food

Agency	Rosapark, Paris
Creative Directors	Mark Forgan Jamie Standen
Copywriter	Jamie Standen
Art Director	Mark Forgan
Photographer	Achim Lippoth
Production	ZenithOptimedia, Paris
Agency Producer	Chloé Bartoletti
Illustrator	Christophe Huet, Asile, Paris
Advertiser	Jardiland, "Dog Fat Pants"

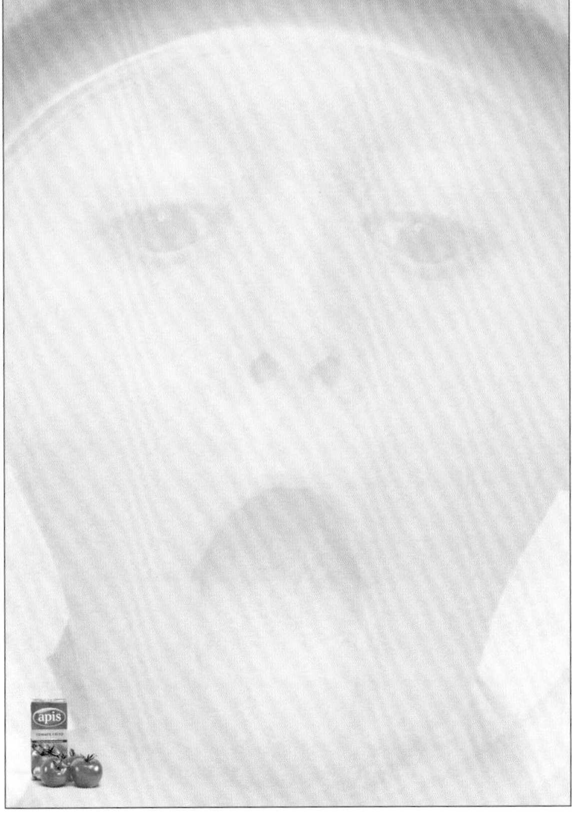

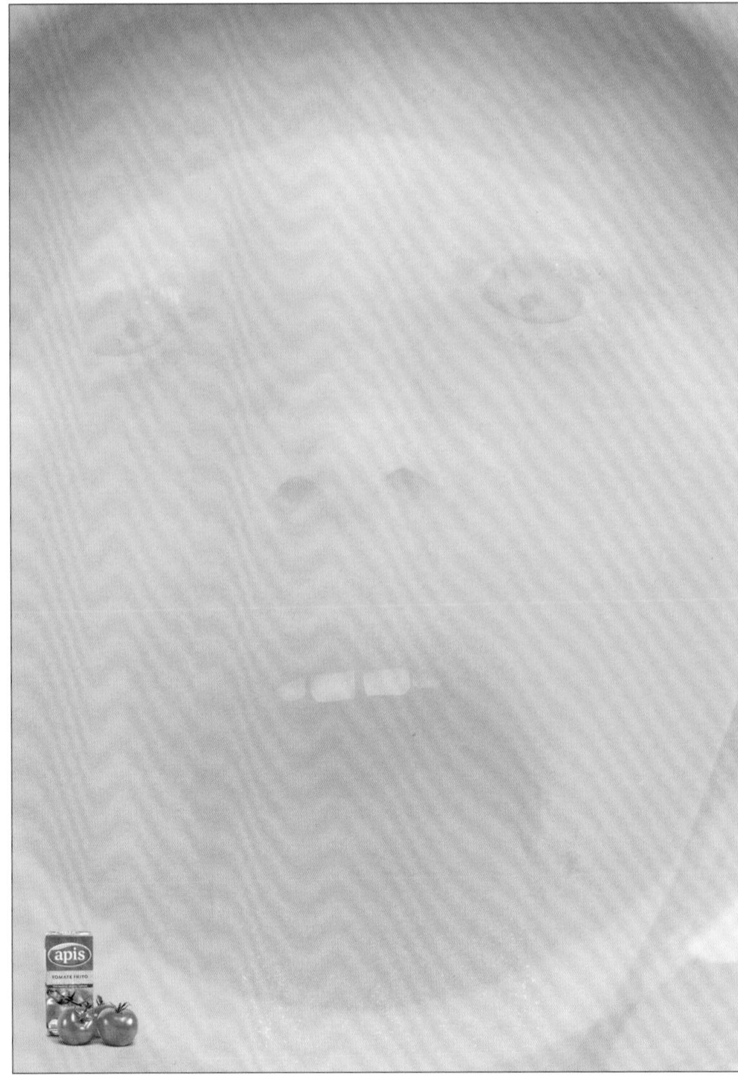

Agency	TBWA\España, Madrid	**Agency Producer**	Mariluz Chamizo
Creative Directors	Juan Sańchez	**Digital Creative Dir.**	Noelia Meltzer
	Cristina Davila	**Digit. Prod. Manager**	Javier Burgueño
	Guillermo Ginés	**Creative Programer**	Enrique Marín
Copywriter	Inés Méndez	**Advertiser**	Apis Fried Tomato Sauce, "Dazzling, Gleaming, Shiny"
Art Director	Urtzi Iñurrita		
Production	Taco De Perro, Madrid		
Film Director	Victor Manuel Gulia		

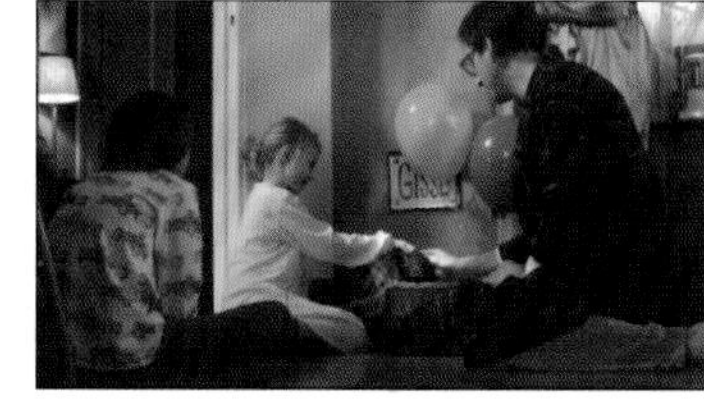

Agency McCann Oslo
Creative Directors Stein Simonsen, Torstein Greni
Copywriters Jan Petter Ågren, Stian Birkelid
Art Directors Stian Birkelid, Jan Petter Ågren
Photographer Jakob Ihre
Production Social Club, Stockholm
Film Director Jesper Ericstam
Producer Magnus Theorin
Agency Producer Beril Holte Rasmussen
Advertiser Grilstad, "The Lucky Pig"

Somewhat bizarrely, a little girl is given a piglet for her birthday. She names it Gisse. We follow the pig as it grows up, with all the complications – and smelly deposits – that process involves. The father, particularly, seems exasperated by the animal. One morning we find him in the kitchen, frying bacon. Surely he didn't…? No, of course not. He buys his bacon from Grilstad: 100% bacon, smoked with woodchips, no added water. Gisse is alive and well.

Agency TRY/Apt/POL, Oslo
Copywriter Jørgen Bøhle Bakke
Art Director Ester Hjellum
Production Bacon, Copenhagen
Film Director Kasper Wedendahl
Executive Prod. Mangne Lyngner
Producer Mari Grundnes Paus
Advertiser Tine, "Hunger"

We've all come across this guy. He's your hunger. A malicious bald bloke clad in purple, he's the one who makes you blame your boyfriend when you bump your head, snap at your family when you're doing the dishes – again! – shun your mother's clothing choices, and generally get in a tizzy when your life gets in a tangle. The only way to get rid of him? A Go' Morgen snack from Tine. Break the hunger.

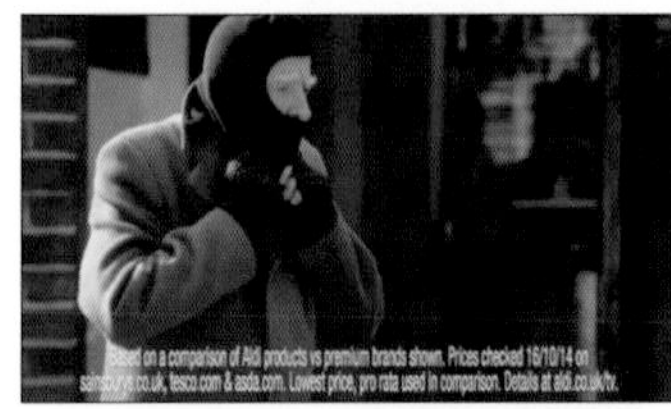

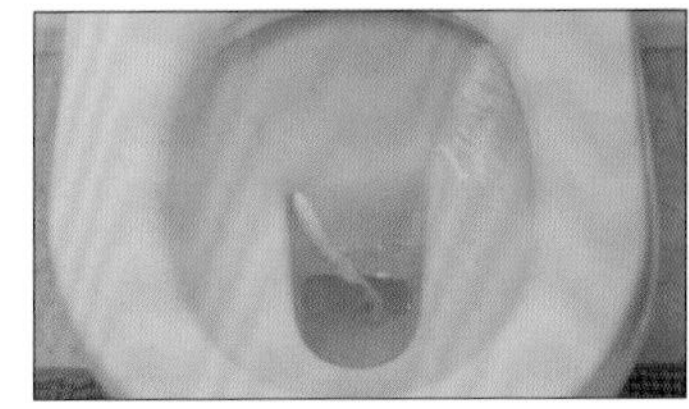

Agency	McCann Manchester
Executive CD	Dave Price
Creative Director	Neil Lancaster
Copywriter	Neil Lancaster
Art Director	Dave Price
Production	Big Buoy, London
Advertiser	Aldi Stores, "Swap and Save"

An old lady is sitting on a park bench next to her husband. Then she shuffles along and sits next to another old man, who looks mildly surprised. She holds his hand. Sometimes it's nice to swap. If you swap from your old supermarket to Aldi, you could save up to 50%.

In a second variation on the theme, a young man carrying a heavy bag offers to swap his balaclava for the cap of an old man waiting at the bus stop. The senior citizen gratefully agrees. The young man jumps into a car and it screeches away. A couple of policeman show up and grab the old man.

In the third spot, when a man drops his toothbrush down the toilet, he exchanges it for his partner's. Sometimes it's good to swap.

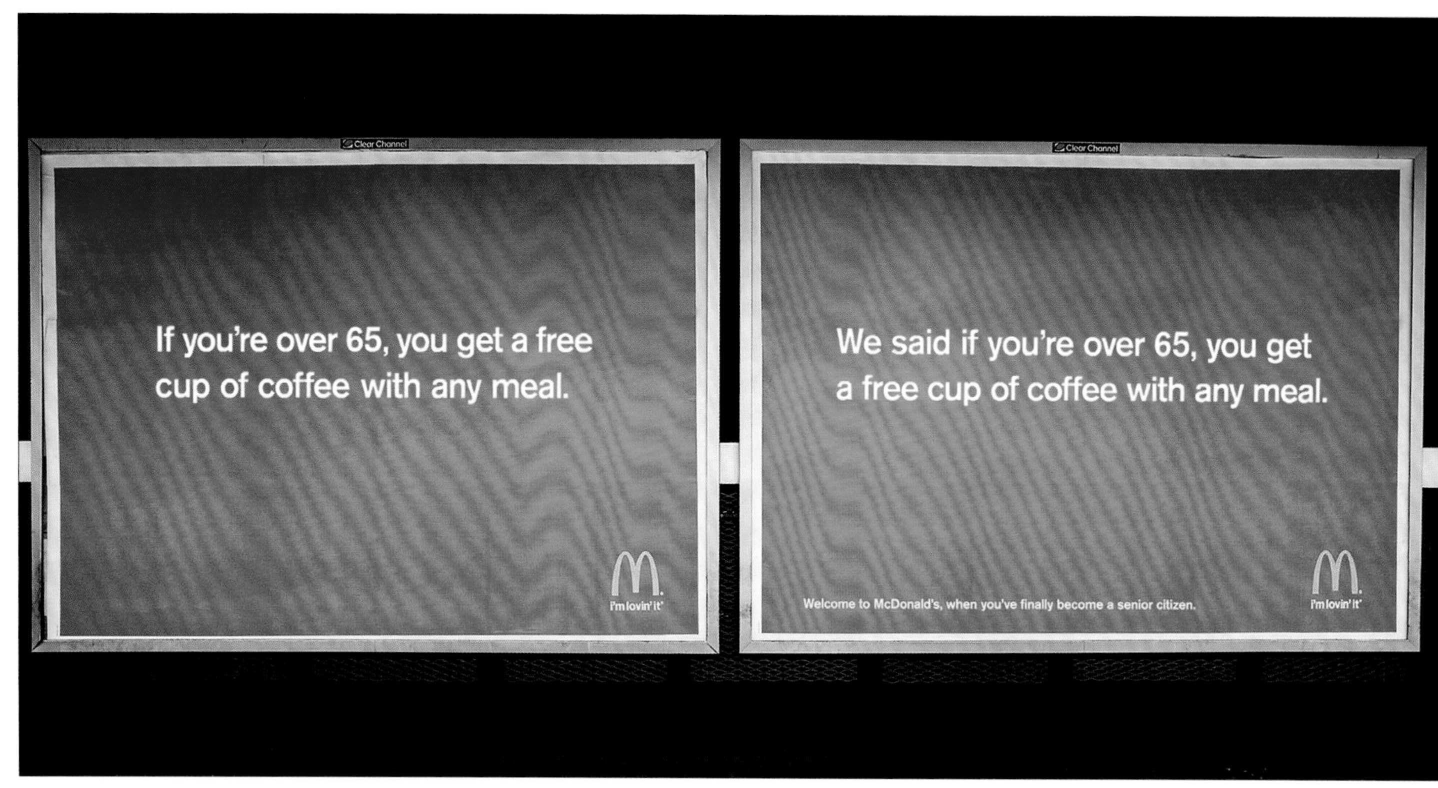

If you're over 65, you get a free cup of coffee with any meal.
i'm lovin' it
We said if you're over 65, you get a free cup of coffee with any meal.
Welcome to McDonald's, when you've finally become a senior citizen.
i'm lovin' it

Agency	DDB Stockholm
Creative Directors	Jerker Fagerström Magnus Jakobsson Fredrik Simonsson
Copywriter	David Alledal
Art Director	Gustav Holm
Graphic Designers	Pärmartin Jonsson Johanna Lundblad
Retouch	Christian Björnerhag
Advertiser	McDonald's, "McSenior"

Agency	Leo Burnett, London
Creative Directors	Matt Lee Pete Heyes
Copywriters	Laurie Smith Steve Robertson
Art Directors	Laurie Smith Steve Robertson
Production	Outsider, London
Film Director	James Rouse
Advertiser	McDonald's, "Hunter Gatherer"

A heavily pregnant woman is banging cupboard doors in the kitchen, clearly looking for something. Her husband, half-watching TV, notices her frustration. He leaves the house and takes up the search, calling at convenience stores and petrol stations. All he gets are apologetic shakes of the head. Finally he spots a McDonald's, where he is greeted warmly. Back home, he's able to satisfy his wife's craving: with a little bag of gherkins.

Agency TBWA\Paris
Creative Director Jean-François Goize
Copywriter Frank Marinus
Art Director Michael Mikiels
Illustrator Michael Mikiels
Advertiser McDonald's, "Pictograms"

McDonald's products are so iconic that they can be recognised on sight, without the aid of a name – or even a photo.

Agency	BBDO Moscow
Creative Director	Luis Tauffer
Copywriter	Evgeny Tsiklauri
Art Directors	Luis Tauffer Roman Lych
Production	Carioca, Bucharest
Advertiser	Mars, Pedigree, "Through Dog's Eyes"

Agency	McCann Tel Aviv
Copywriter	Lior Soham
Art Director	Moran Kal
Photographer	Hezi Josef
Production	Drawetc, Prague
Advertiser	Proplan Pet Food, "Dig to China"

Agency	Zulu Alpha Kilo, Toronto
CCO	Zak Mroueh
Creative Directors	Shane Ogilvie Ron Smrczek
Copywriter	Jon Taylor
Art Director	Andrea Romanelli
Photographer	Jamie Morren
Agency Producer	Kate Spencer
Manufacturing	Media Resources
Advertiser	Jack Astor's Bar, "#sharkbait"

Jack Astor's is a bar and restaurant with an irreverent sense of humour. So when Canada's largest aquarium opened just across the street, the restaurant obliged with a promotion that displayed biting wit.

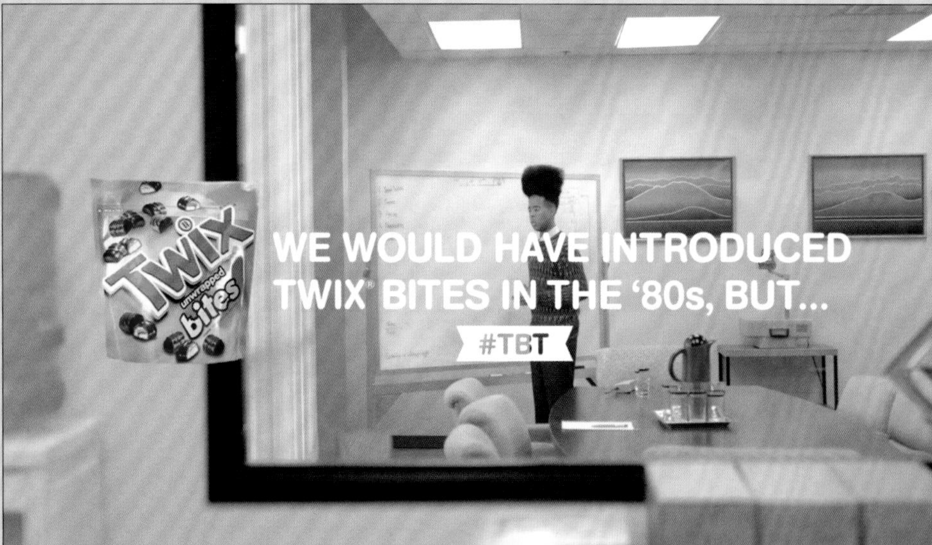

Agency	BBDO New York
Chief Creative Officers	David Lubars Greg Hahn
Executive CDs	Peter Kain Gianfranco Arena
Copywriter	Matt Herr
Art Director	Justin Bilicki
Executive Producers	Amy Wertheimer Alex Gianni
Agency Producer	Patrick Smith
Production	Smuggler, New York
Film Director	Jun Diaz
DOP	John Barr
Producers	Lisa Rich Alex Waite
Editor	Robert Ryang
Editorial Producer	Zarina Mak
Sound Engineer	Evan Mangiamele
VFX Company	Eight VFX
Advertiser	Mars, Twix Bites, "#TBT Campaign"

These spots ponder why Twix Bites weren't introduced before now. Flashing back to the 1990s, we see two guys in an office. "I'm downloading plans for some kinda bite-sized Twix," says one of them. We hear the primitive buzz and whine of a modem. "It's connecting." As the evening draws on, the second guy grows frustrated. He leans forward. "I gotta call my wife." "NO!" But it's too late – he's picked up the phone and severed the connection.

Another spot takes us back to the 80s, where a trendy dude jots an idea for bite-sized Twix on a whiteboard. "Tight," he says. Then he bends down to pump up the soles of his fashionable sneakers. As he does so, his big hair wipes the idea clean off the board. Another reason why Twix Bites have only just arrived.

Agency adam&eveDDB, London
Executive CDs Ben Priest, Ben Tollett, Emer Stamp
Creative Directors Mike Crowe, Rob Messeter
Creatives Nick Sheppard, Tom Webber
Creative Producer Craig Neilson
Photographer David Sykes
Advertiser Unilever, Marmite, “Neglect”

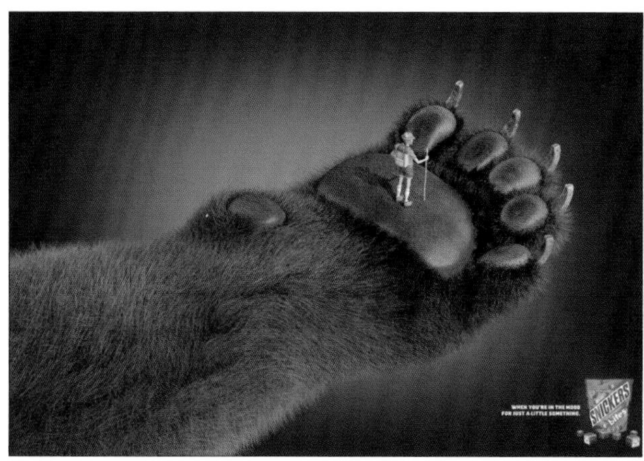

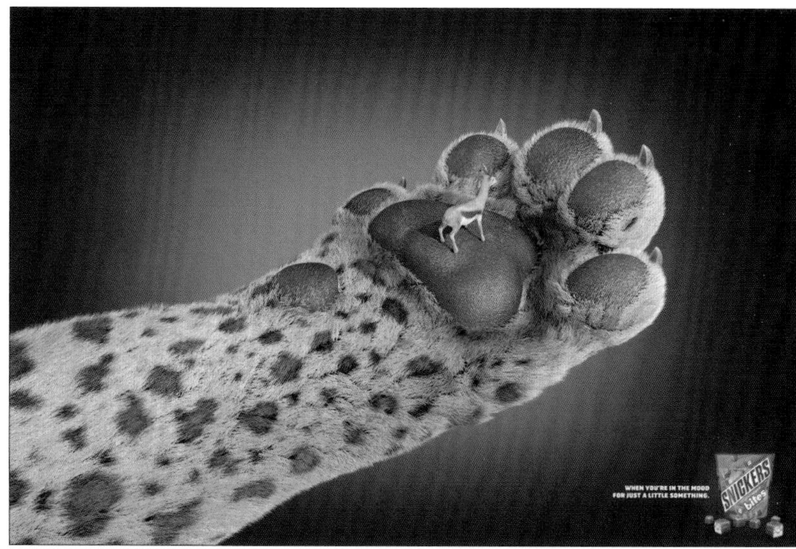

 Confectionery & Snacks

Agency	BBDO New York
Chief Creative Officers	David Lubars Greg Hahn
Executive CDs	Peter Kain Gianfranco Arena
Senior CDs	Danilo Boer Grant Smith
Copywriter	Grant Smith
Art Director	Danilo Boer
Illustrator	Un Mariachi
Advertiser	Mars, Snickers, “Snickers Bites”

Agency	Impact BBDO, Dubai
Creative Director	Fadi Yaish
Copywriter	Aunindo Sen
Art Director	Gautam Wadher
Production	Carioca, Bucharest
Agency Producer	Clarisse Mar Wai May
Advertiser	Mars, Snickers, "Unhungry"

Agency BBDO New York
CCOs David Lubars, Greg Hahn
Senior CDs Peter Kain, Gianfranco Arena
Copywriter Matt Herr
Art Director Justin Bilicki
Production O Positive, New York
Film Director Jim Jenkins
DOP Robert Gantz
Advertiser Mars, Snickers, "Snickers Bites"

Unveiling Snickers Bites, a modern-day marketing type asks: "Why didn't we think of this years ago?" Flash back to the 1950s, where an ageing executive snaps on his intercom. "Tammy – please remind me to make Snickers in a bite size. You know my memory!" But his secretary hears only static and inaudible mumbling through the faulty intercom. She tries to tell him: "There's a lot of interference, sir, it's maybe the Soviets." But he's already signed off. Snickers Bites. Finally here.

Agency The Martin Agency, Richmond
CCO Joe Alexander
Group CD Jorge Callega
CDs David Muhlenfeld, Magnus Hierta
Associate CD Bryan Lee
Sr. Art Director Brig White
Production The Martin Agency, Richmond
Illustrator Maria Raymondsdotter
Advertiser Mondelez, Oreo, "Oreo Daydream"

A catchy song and poetic animation capture a young woman's daydream. If she'd once given an Oreo to a cute guy she used to know, would he have dumped his girlfriend and ended up with her? Would they now have kids? When she tastes an Oreo, she still thinks anything is possible – because life is "wonderfilled".

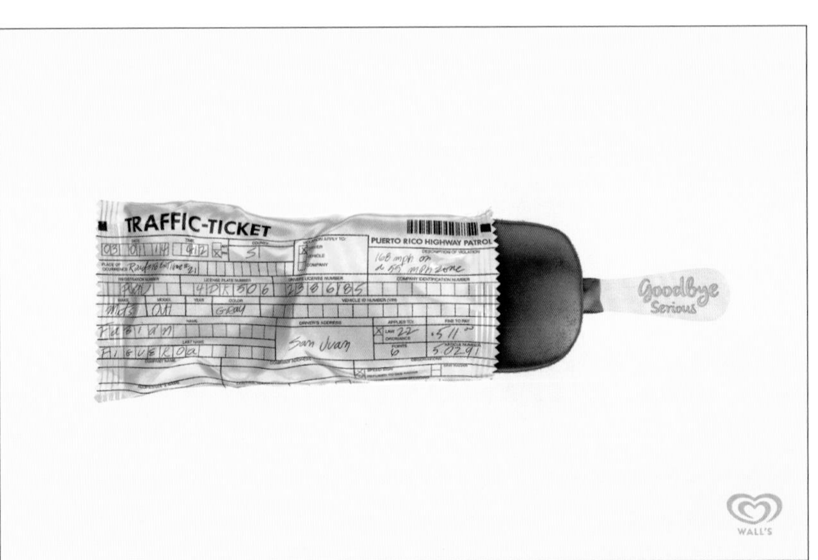

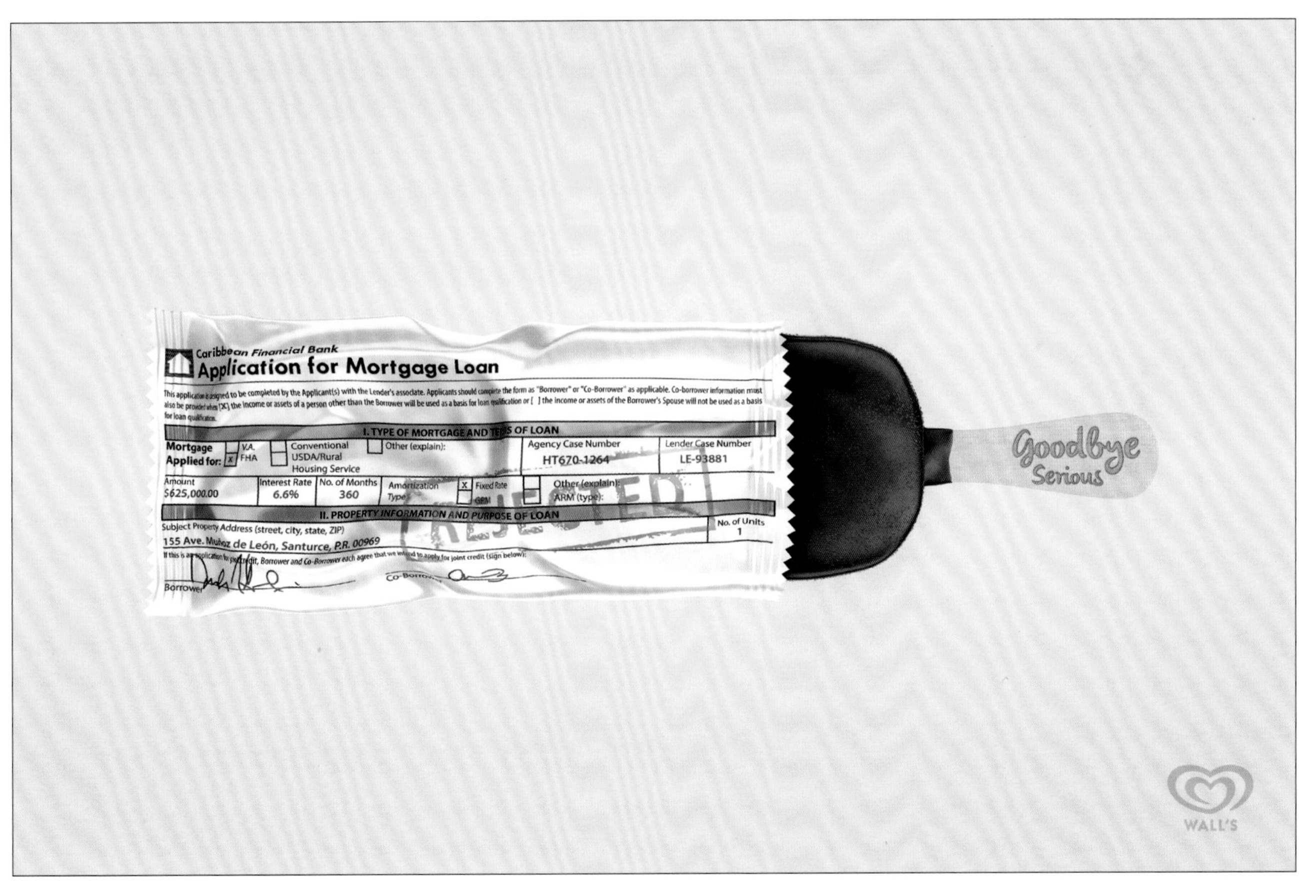

Agency	DDB Latina Puerto Rico, San José
Creative Directors	Enrique Renta Santiago Cuesta
Copywriters	Santiago Cuesta Juan Dávila Morris
Art Directors	Juan Carlos López Luis Figueroa
Illustrators	Masivo Carlos Nova
Advertiser	Unilever, Wall's, "Jury"

meow.

Και frozen και yogurt
και σε ξυλάκι

Από ελληνικό γιαούρτι,
μόνο με 114 θερμίδες

Agency	attp, Athens
Creative Director	Nikos Palaiologos
Copywriter	Nikos Hatzidakis
Art Director	Thomas Damtsios
Illustrator	Thomas Damtsios
Advertiser	KRI Frozen Yogurt, "Frozen Yogurt Meow"

Agency	Energy BBDO, Chicago
Creative Directors	Rick Hamann Andrés Ordoñez Pedro Perez
Copywriter	Nikki Patel
Art Director	Ramiro Silva
Photographer	Ken Anderson
Agency Art Producers	Liz Miller-Gershfeld Jackie Lapides
Retoucher	Salamágica
Advertiser	Wrigley, "Altoids Arctic"

Drinks

Agency Wieden+Kennedy, Amsterdam
Executive CDs Mark Bernath, Eric Quennoy
Creative Directors Thierry Albert, Faustin Claverie
Copywriter Toby Moore
Art Director Henrik Edelbring
Production MJZ, London
Film Director Tom Kuntz
DOP Tim Maurice Jones, Florian Hoffmeister
Executive Producer Debbie Turner
Producer Suza Horvat
Editor Russell Icke, Whitehouse Post, London
Sound Designer Raja Sehgal, GCRS, London
Post Production Jay Bandish, Dave Fleet, Rachel Stones, The Mill, London
Advertiser Heineken, "The Odyssey"

Heineken regularly introduces us to legendary men with impressive skills. We meet the latest candidate on a cruise ship, where he first appears as a bearded stowaway. But he has chameleon-like skills of adaptation, making friends with seagulls, changing smoothly into a suit, pulling off an uncanny curling trick and some stunning dance moves. His appearance subtly changes each time. "Who is that man?" asks a smitten passenger. "That can't be just one man," replies the captain. And indeed not – in the last shot, the stowaway is revealed as an entire cast. Everyone is legendary at something.

Agency	Ruf Lanz, Zurich	Thanks to the clever placement of these posters at ski resorts, a single cow appears to be pulling cable cars and chairlifts. Only Swiss Milk delivers such strength. The campaign itself gained strength from being shared thousands of times via social media, delivering huge exposure for a modest budget.
Creative Directors	Markus Ruf Danielle Lanz	
Copywriter	Torsten Maas	
Art Directors	Mario Moosbrugger Marcel Schläfle	
Advertiser	Swiss Milk Producers, "Cable Car Stations"	

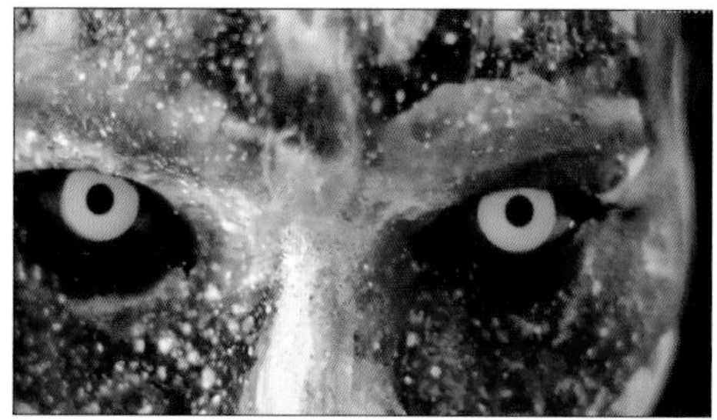

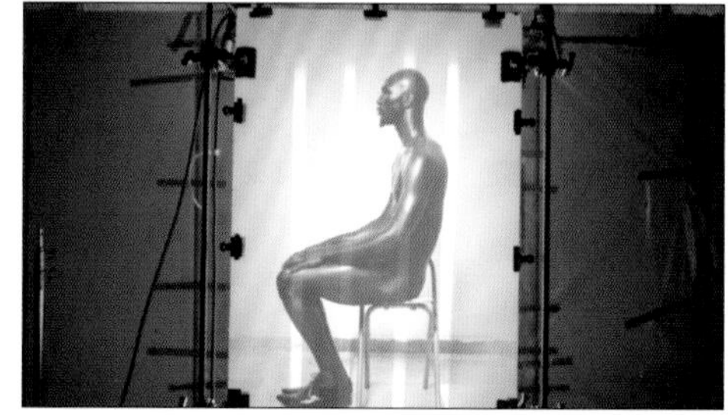

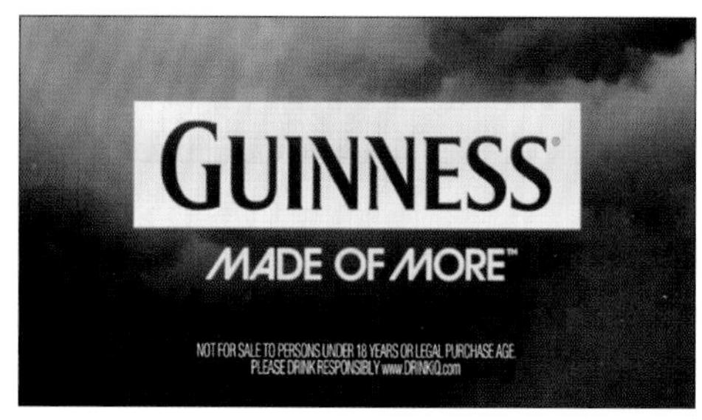

Agencies	BBDO Africa, AMV BBDO, London	Producers	James Howland
Creative Director	Mike Schalit	Post Production	The Mill, London
Creatives	Ant Nelson Mike Sutherland	Editing House	Final Cut, London
Production	Rogue Films, London	Editor	Amanda James
Producer	Nick Godden	Sound Design	Aaron Reynolds, Wave Studios, London
Film Director	Sam	Advertiser	Diageo, Guinness, "Made Of Black"

More of a rock video than a conventional spot, this film asks us "What is black?" It's not a colour, the images suggest, but more of an attitude. Radical. Artistic. Avant-garde. Subversive. Black writes its own rules. And what drink is made of black? Guinness, of course. Made of more.

Agencies	BBDO Africa, AMV BBDO, London
Creative Director	Mike Schalit
Creatives	Ant Nelson Mike Sutherland
Producer	Hannah Jones
Painter	Steve Caldwell
Pattern Designer	Dan Funderburgh, Debut Art
Client	Diageo, Guinness, "Made Of Black - Attitude, Swag & Beat"

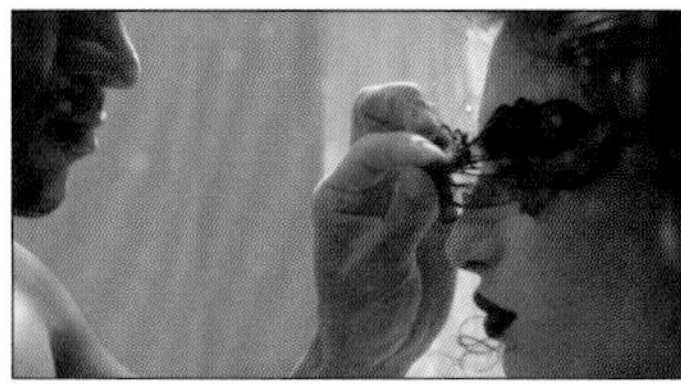

Agency Quai Des Orfèvres, Paris
Creative Director Richard Cohen
Copywriter Rudy Bamberg
Art Director Richard Cohen
Agency Producer Pauline Walhain
Production Starloo, Paris
Film Director Jeremy Charbit
Producer Stéphane Martin
Advertiser Kusmi Tea, "The Beauty of Blends"

This sensual and elegant underwater ballet is a metaphor for a new range of Kusmi teas that blend different flavours. As the dancers twist and twirl around one another, we see how beautiful a blend can be.

Agency DLVBBDO, Milan
Executive CD Stefania Siani, Federico Pepe
Creative Directors Emanuele Viora, Andrea Jaccarino
Copywriter Emanuele Viora
Art Directors Federico Pepe, Andrea Jaccarino
Photographer LSD
Advertiser Sogni d'oro, "Instant Relax"

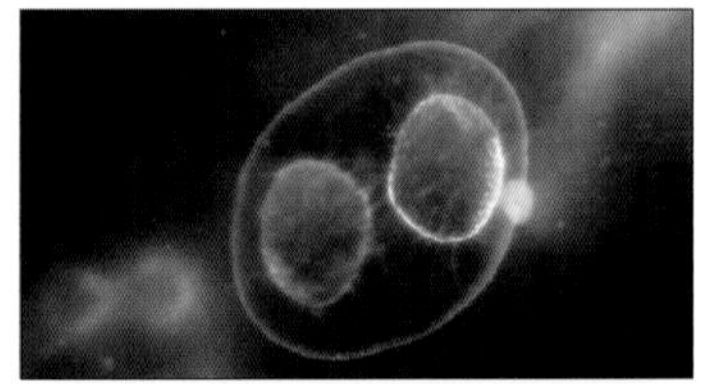

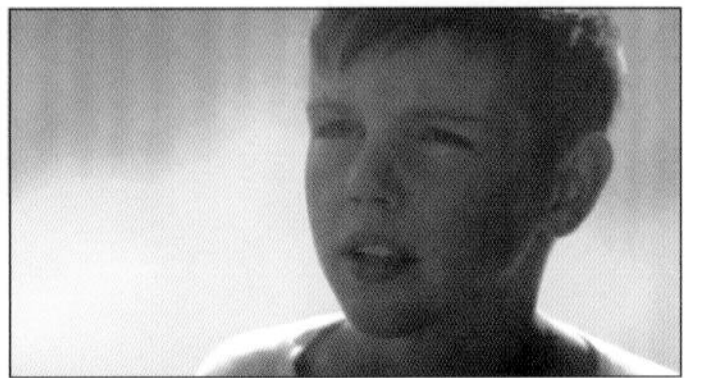

Agency Y&R, Paris
Creative Director Pierrette Diaz
Production Gang Films, Paris
Producers Jean Villiers, Nathalie Lecaer
Agency Producers Valérie Montiel, Estelle Diot
DOP Joost Van Gelder
Editors Walter Mauriot, Fred Baudet
Post Production Digital District
Advertiser Danone, Volvic, "Volvic The Giant"

This spectacular effects-driven spot explores the geological forces behind mineral water. At first it looks as though a sentient being is about to emerge from the earth's crust. "I am a giant," says the narrator. "Born from the deepest entrails of the earth. I have seen life…and made life." Historical events unfold, but have little impact on the landscape. "I am strong, unpredictable. Stronger than man – stronger than time… I am immortal." The water itself is speaking to us. Volvic. Made by time.

Agency BBDO New York
Creative Directors Rick Williams, Marcel Yunes
Copywriters Rick Williams, Marcel Yunes, Jessica Coulter, Matt Sorrell
Art Directors Marcel Yunes, Rick Williams
Production HēLō, Los Angeles
Advertiser Budweiser, "Bud Light - Ian Up for Whatever Film"

A guy called Ian is offered a Bud Light by a girl in a bar. "If I give this to you, are you up for whatever happens?" Ian agrees. In a perfectly choreographed stunt, Ian is whisked off in a limo – with Reggie Watts DJ-ing – given a posh new jacket and led into an elevator, where he meets Don Cheadle with a llama, along with the twin of the girl he just met. Next up is a sudden death ping pong match with Arnold Schwarzenegger, which puts Ian on stage with Onerepublic. Bud Light is the perfect beer for whatever happens.

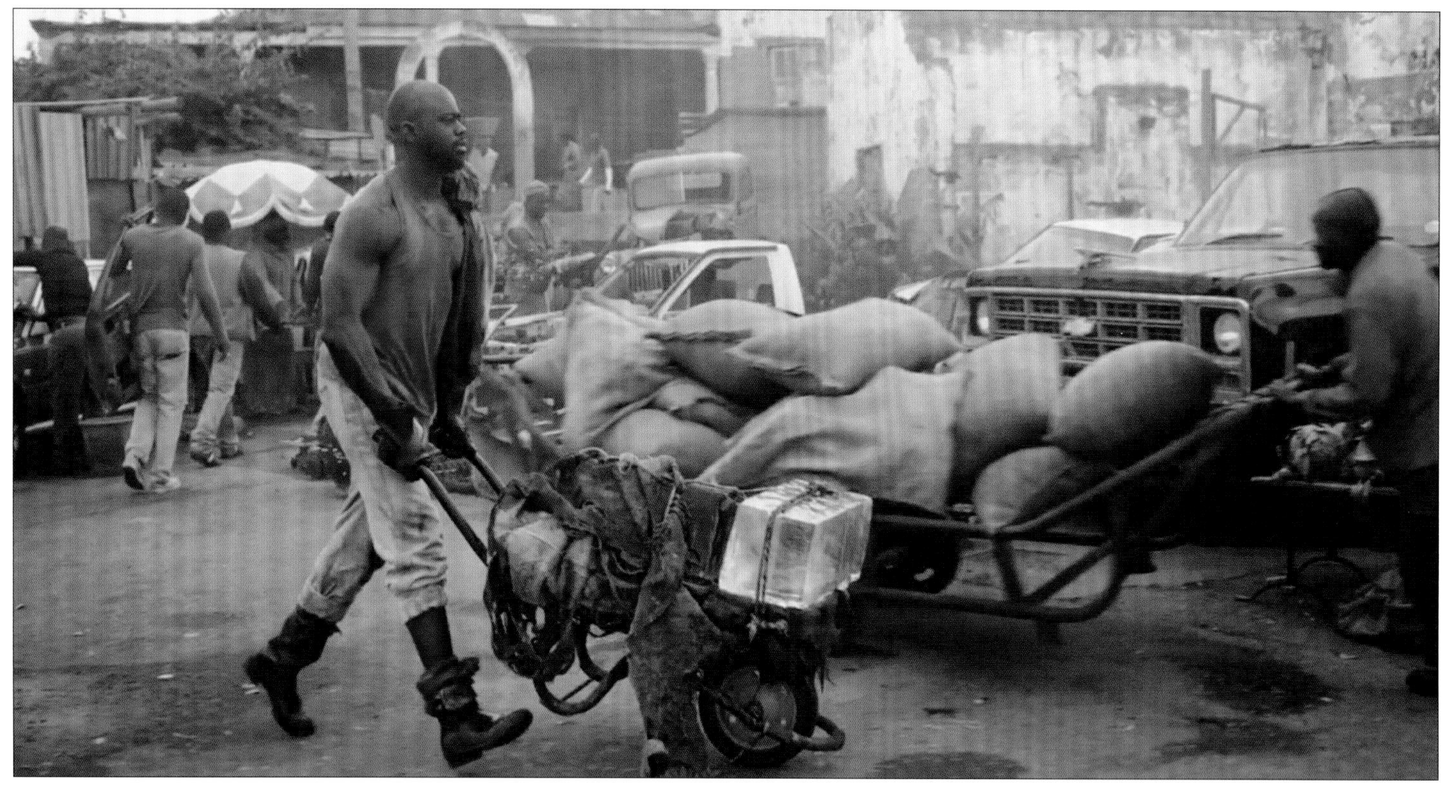

Agency	AMV BBDO, London	**Producer**	Suza Horvat
ECD	Paul Brazier	**Post Production**	The Mill, London
Creative Director	Dave Buchanan	**Editing House**	Final Cut, London
Creatives	Nadja Lossgott Nicholas Hulley	**Editor**	Rick Russell
Production	MJZ, London	**Sound Design**	Wave Studios, London
Producer	Sara Flood	**Advertiser**	Guinness, "Sapeurs"
Film Director	Nicolai Fuglsig		
Executive Producer	Debbie Turner		

Meet the Sapeurs – the society of elegant persons of the Congo. "In life, you cannot always choose what you do," says one of them, who clearly has a harsh factory job. "But you can always choose who you are." Off duty, he and his friends transform themselves into the ultimate dandies, with flamboyant suits and stylish accessories. Revered by their community, they engage in debonair dance-offs at their local bar. "With every brace and cuff-link, we say: I am the master of my fate; I am the captain of my soul." Just like the individualists who drink Guinness.

Agency	Havas Worldwide, Zurich
Creative Directors	Frank Bodin Michael Kathe
Copywriter	Jan Hertel
Art Directors	Andrea Huber Claude Eberhard
Photographer	Fabian Scheffold
Graphic Design	Jotta Ziogas
Post Production	Fred Bastide, Fluxif, Zurich
Advertiser	Bio-Strath Vegetable Elixir, "Strong Children"

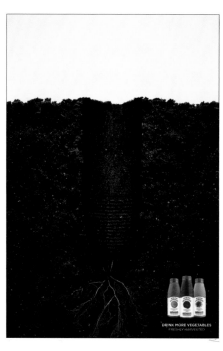

Agency	Armando Testa, Turin
Creative Directors	Dario Anania Vincenzo Pastore
Art Directors	Dario D'Angelo Dario Anania
Advertiser	Heineken, Birra Moretti, "Rio 2014"

Agency	Bulldozer, Karlstad
Copywriter	Jenny Eklund
Art Director	Andreas Österlund
Photographer	Anders Lipkin
Graphic Design	Anette Åhlén
Advertiser	Brämhults Juice, "Drink more vegetables"

Agency	Zulu Alpha Kilo, Toronto
Creative Directors	Zak Mroueh Shane Ogilvie
Art Director	Jenny Luong
Design Director	Mooren Bofill
Illustrator	Jenny Luong
Studio Artist	Brandon Dyson
Agency Producer	Kate Spencer
Advertiser	Corona, "Day of the Dead"

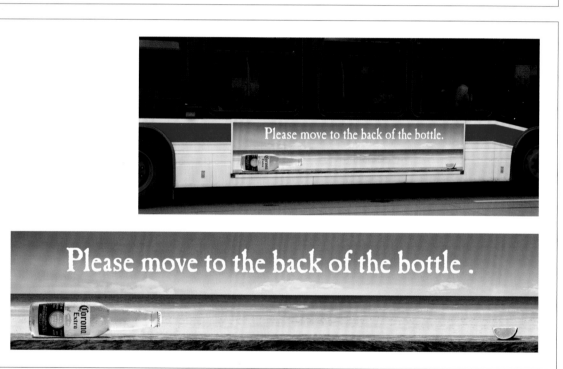

Agency	Zulu Alpha Kilo, Toronto
Creative Directors	Zak Mroueh Shane Ogilvie
Copywriter	George Ault
Art Director	Grant Cleland
Photographer	Jamie Morren
Agency Producers	Kari Macknight Dearborn Kate Spencer
Advertiser	Corona, "Corona Summer Program 2014"

LATE NIGHT CINEMA.
IT'S A LITHUANIAN ART FILM.
A ONE-MAN SHOW.
Magnesium helps your nervous system.
hohesC PLUS
Rich in magnesium.

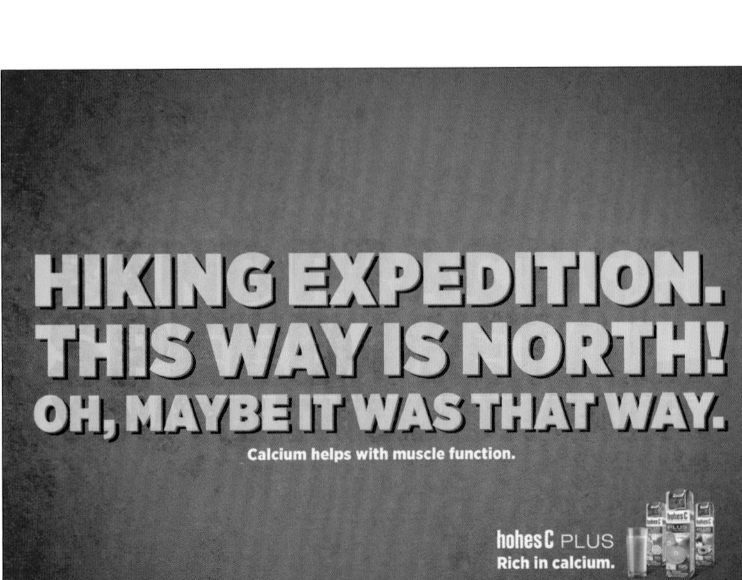

HIKING EXPEDITION.
THIS WAY IS NORTH!
OH, MAYBE IT WAS THAT WAY.
Calcium helps with muscle function.
hohesC PLUS
Rich in calcium.

LUNCH BREAK.
YOU'VE GOT 10 MINUTES.
7 HAVE ALREADY PASSED.
Dietary fibre helps satisfy the stomach, reducing hunger.
hohesC PLUS
Rich in dietary fibre.

Agency	Cluso, Budapest
Creative Directors	Lajos Horváth Gergely Fodor
Copywriter	Ambrus Horváth
Art Director	Gergely Fodor
Photographer	Szilárd Nagyillés
Advertiser	Hohes C, "Hohes C Plus"

Communication Services

Introducing a logistics company
that covers the Nordic region.
postnord

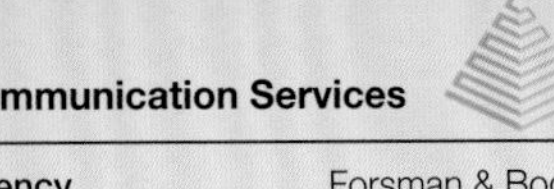

Agency	Forsman & Bodenfors, Gothenburg
Copywriter	Jacob Nelson
Art Director	Ted Mellström
Agency Producer	Magnus Kennhed
Designer	Viktor Brittsjö
Production	StandArt, Stockholm
Film Director	Peter Harton
DOP	Martin Munch
Producers	Kalle Schröder
	Josefin Kollberg
Advertiser	PostNord Logistics, "Investigating PostNord Logistics"

A smug investigative reporter stands in a remote field. "I'm here to prove that PostNord Logistics does not cover the Nordics…" But he is cut off as a PostNord truck whizzes past. He tries a remoter field. "I'm here to prove that – " but this time a train with the PostNord logo on it whooshes behind him. His next attempt is foiled by a passing boat. Finally he ends up deep in the woods, where he complains: "I think I just stepped in moose shit." He is still complaining when a PostNord delivery man strides into view. The company does indeed cover the entire Nordic region.

Agency	Havas Worldwide Gurisa, Montevideo
Creative Directors	Claudio Invernizzi Marco Caltieri
Copywriters	Juan Pablo Granito Marco Caltieri
Art Director	Marco Caltieri
Photographers	Mauro Ferraro Marco Caltieri
Production	Prospiti, Montevideo
Digital Artwork	Setharaman Nerayanan
Advertiser	El Observador, "Balance"

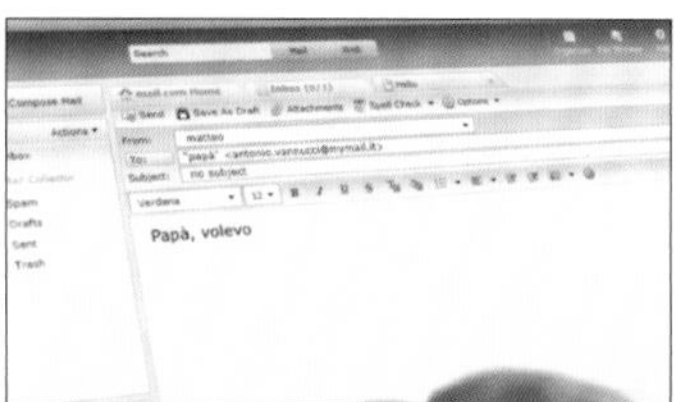

 Communication Services

Agency TRY/Apt/POL, Oslo
Copywriters Lars Joachim Grimstad, Caroline Ekrem
Art Directors Egil Pay, Sara Hødnebø
Production Bacon OSL, Oslo
Film Director Bart Timmer
Producers Magne Lyngner, Mari Grundnes Paus
Advertiser Canal Digital, "The Silver Hand"

At the canteen, a man's colleagues are laughing about "the silver hand". "Did you see the episode last night?" one of them asks. He did not. In the office loos, a co-worker shouts: "Beware of the silver hand!" On the news that night: "A classic silver hand effect on the markets." All the man's life, the silver hand haunts him. As a shark is about to attack, he's told: "Do the silver hand thing!" But what is it? Years later, old folk are still talking about it. Finally, at his funeral, the priest evokes "the silver hand". Don't miss great TV, with Canal Digital.

Agency Ogilvy & Mather, Milan
CCOs Giuseppe Mastromatteo, Paolo Labichino
Creative Directors Marco Geranzani, Giordano Curreri
Copywriter Marco Geranzani
Art Director Giordano Curreri
Agency Producer Francesca D'Agostino
Production Mercurio Cinematografica, Milan
Advertiser Wind Telecommunications, "Dad"

Through a series of flashbacks, we learn of a man's conflicted relationship with his father. They were close when he was young, but fell out in his teens. Now he lives in England, far from his native Italy, and he wants to put things right. He thinks about texting his dad, or emailing, but stops short every time. Finally, he heads for the airport. On the plane, he swipes through nostalgic photos on his tablet. At last the pair are reunited, face to face, in the bay where they used to swim together. Sometimes, technology isn't everything.

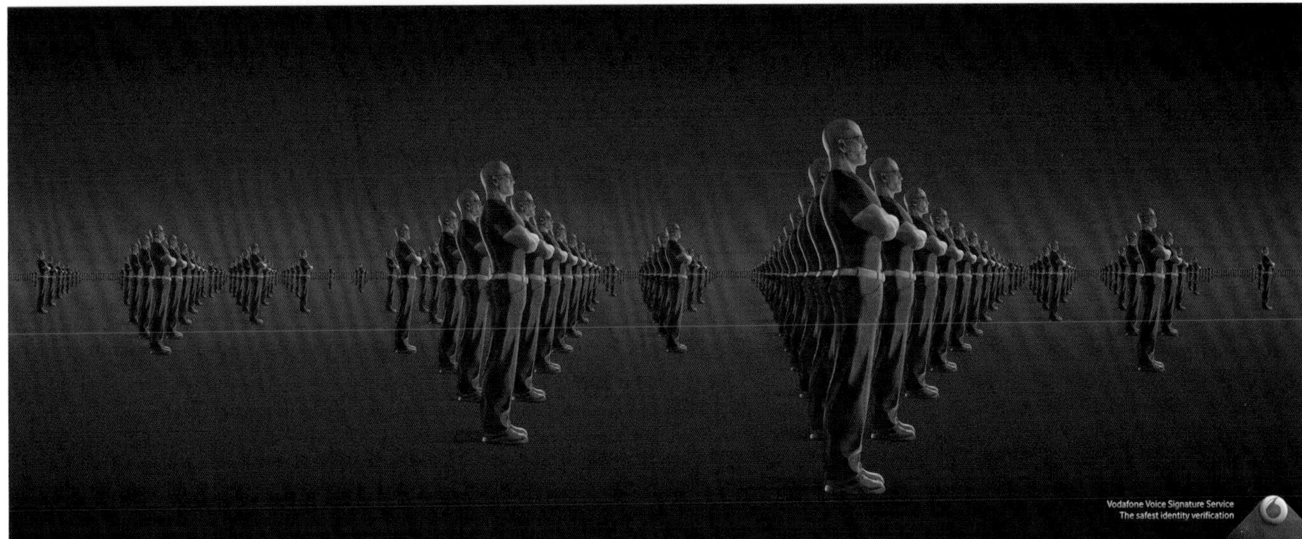

Agency	Y&R Team Red, Istanbul
Creative Director	Ayse Aydin
Copywriters	Can Arabacilar Ilker Dagli
Art Directors	Erkan Kaya Ugur Say
Production	Zoo, Istanbul
Agency Producers	Deniz Kunkut Gamze Bayindir
Graphic Design	Burak Kirpi
Advertiser	Vodafone, "Voice Signature - Swat"

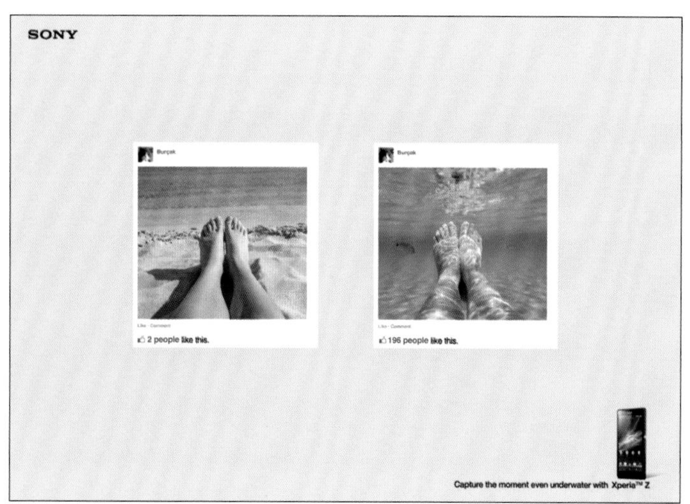

Communication Services

Agency	Rafineri, Istanbul
Creative Directors	Ayşe Bali Emre Kaplan
Copywriter	Gökhan Özdemir
Art Director	Faruk Terzi
Photographer	Nejat Talas
Advertiser	Sony Xperia, “Social Media”

Agency	Rafineri, Istanbul
Creative Directors	Ayşe Bali
Copywriter	Gökhan Özdemir
Art Director	Faruk Terzi
Illustrator	Tansu Özel
Advertiser	Sony Xperia, "The Hunters"

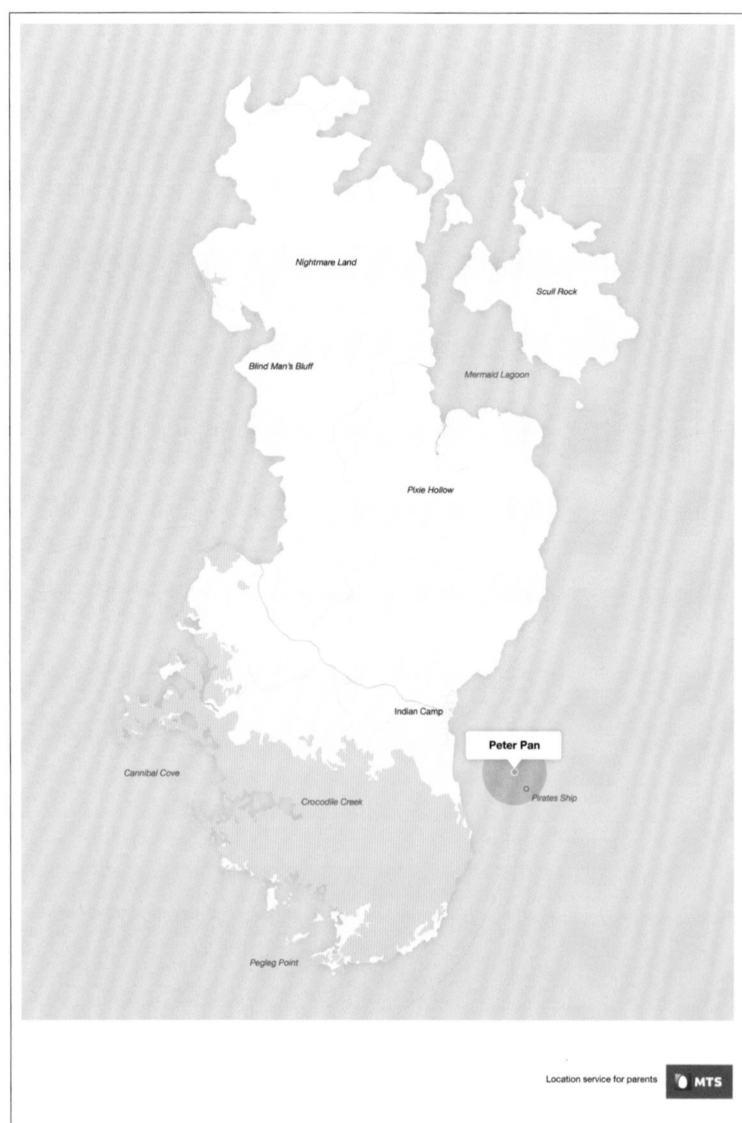

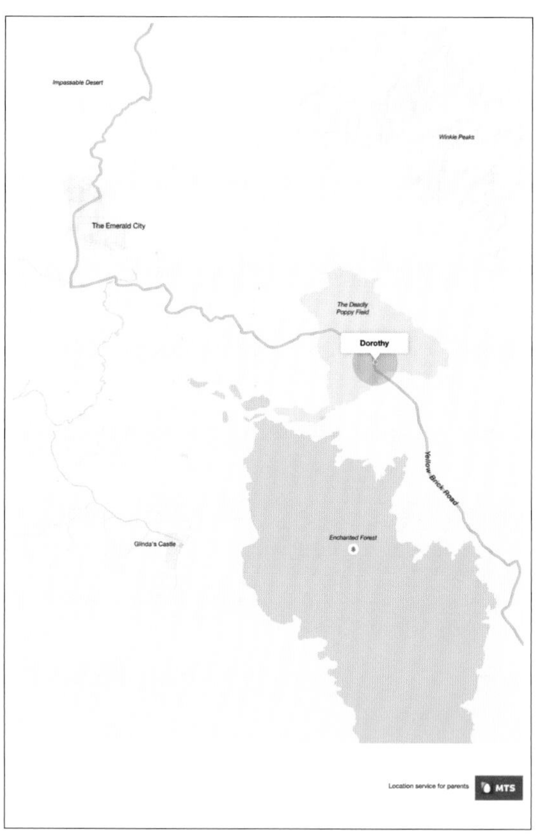

64 Communication Services

Agency	BBDO Moscow
Creative Director	Nikolay Megvelidze
Copywriter	Ekaterina Kulyukhina
Art Director	Andrey Kuznetsov
Design Production	Ignatiev Mark Usatov Konstantin Titinkov Aleksey
Advertiser	MTS Location Service for Parents, "Children's Books"

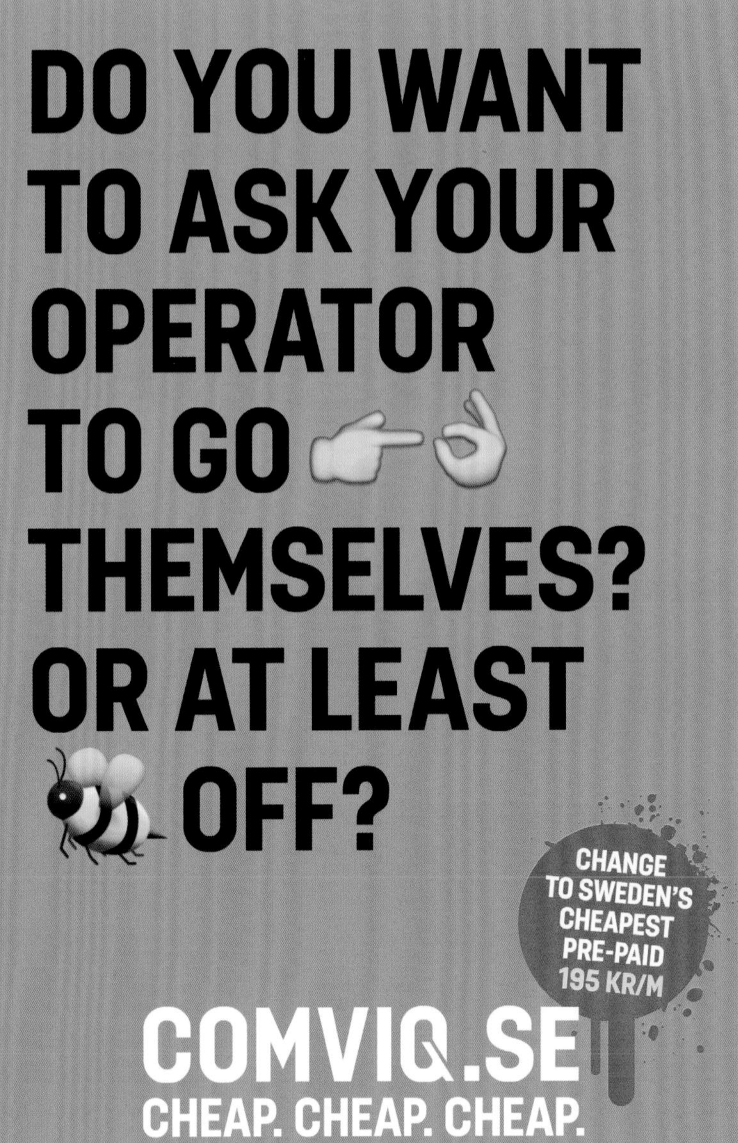

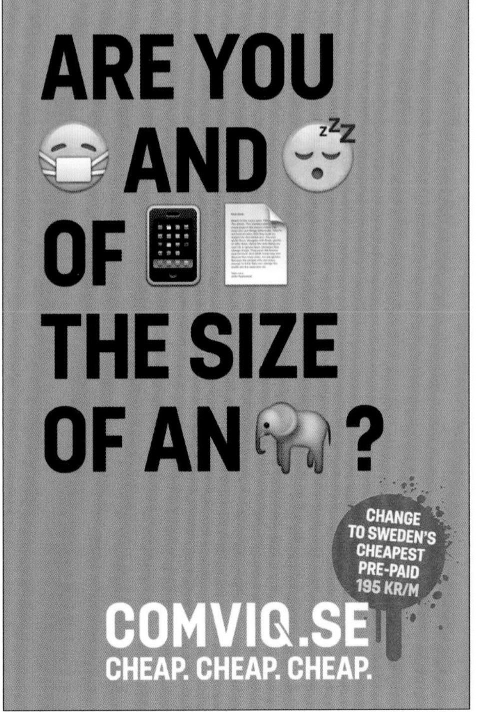

Agency	Forsman & Bodenfors, Gothenburg
Copywriter	Anna Qvennerstedt
Art Director	Silla Levin
Designer	Axel Söderlund
Advertiser	Comviq, "Emoji"

Transport & Tourism

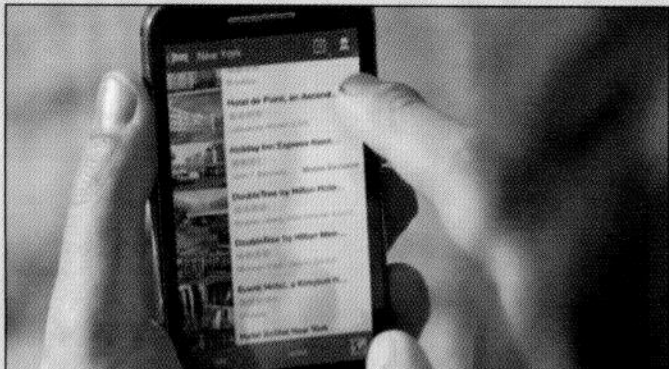

Agency	Ogilvy & Mather, London
CCO/Executive CD	Gerry Human
Copywriter	Simon Lotze
Art Director	Miguel Nunes
Production	Moxie Pictures
Film Director	Frank Todaro
Producer	Alicia Farren
Agency Producer	Henry Huang
DOP	Richard Mott
Advertiser	Expedia, "Travel Yourself Interesting"

This campaign relates what happens when you take a vacation with the help of Expedia. Take Esteban, for example. Normally, this consummate horseman rules the hacienda. But not today. No, today his limelight has been hogged by Pedro, who got a great deal on a New York hotel thanks to Expedia's mobile app. And now everyone wants to hear his tales of the Big Apple. Despite Esteban's best efforts to distract them.

Meanwhile, Hugo the magician literally cuts himself in half to attract attention. But it's no good – he's been upstaged by Brian, the sound guy, who got a cut-price holiday in Hawaii by booking his flight and hotel on Expedia's website. Hugo disappears in puff of smoke. Rather like Brad the stuntman, who loses the spotlight to Janice, the taco lady, and her awesome view of the Eiffel Tower. Expedia – travel yourself interesting.

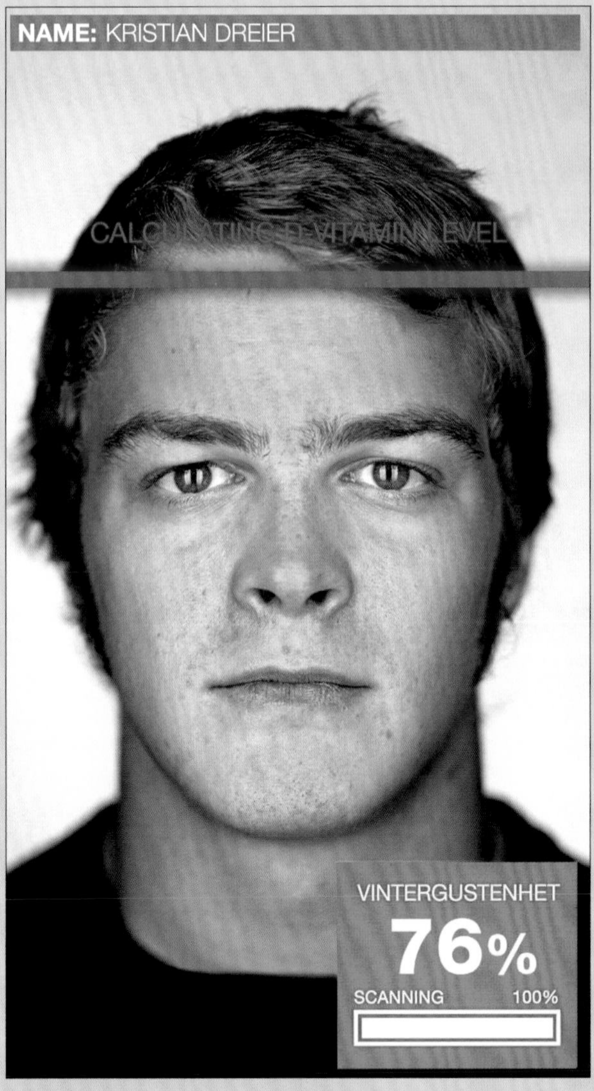

Agency Kitchen Leo Burnett, Oslo
Creative Directors Per Erik Jarl, Christian Hygen
Copywriters Christian Hygen, Thomas Askim
Art Directors Per Erik Jarl, Eirik Stensrud
Creative Producer Aram Zarkoob
Graphic Designer Pia Lystad
Advertiser Norwegian Airlines, "Pale Complexion Examination"

Norwegian Airlines bought up all the digital screens at Oslo's busy central station and put them to work. People passing through the station were stopped and tested for the paleness of their complexions. The results were shown on the screens along with the ideal remedy – tickets to somewhere sunny from Norwegian Airlines. With a new person tested every two minutes, the event was an entertaining way of contrasting Norway's grim winter with the warmer destinations offered by its airline.

Don't miss Rome on the way to Athens
Don't miss Paris on the way to Nice
With an InterRail Card you can hop on and off wherever you'd like, all over Europe.
SJ
SWEDISH RAILWAYS

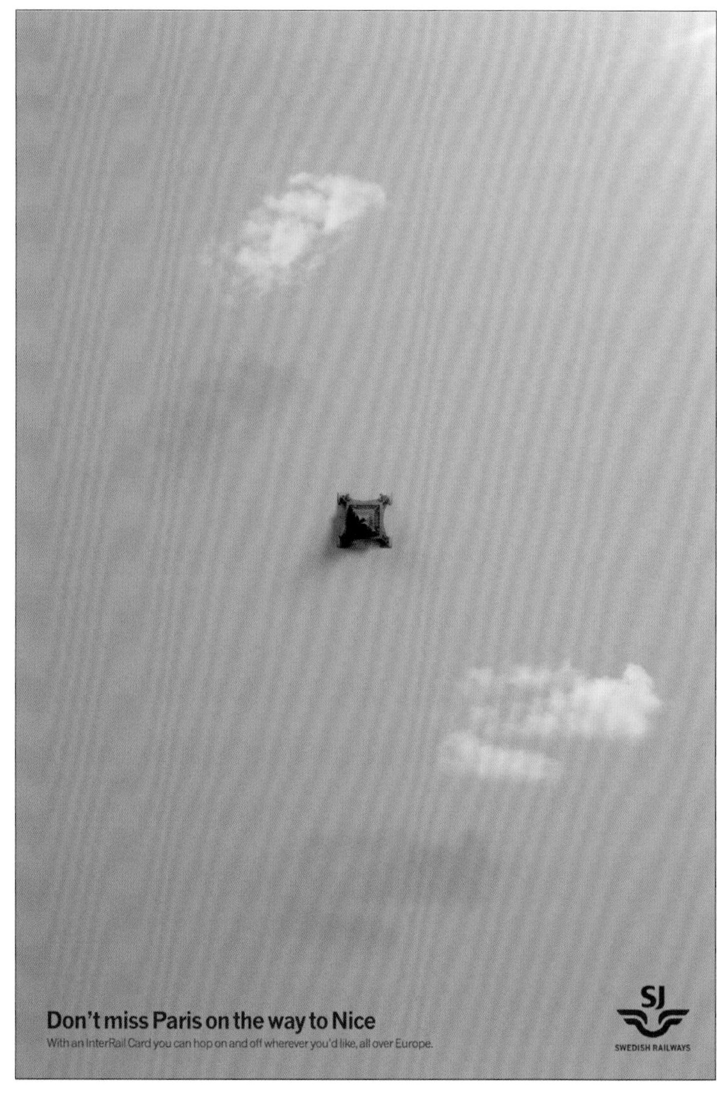

Agency	TBWA\Stockholm
Creative Director	Kalle Widgren
Copywriters	Martin Baude Andre Persson
Art Directors	Martin Baude Andre Persson
Production Company	Rithuset, Stockholm
Graphic Design	Christian Styffe
Advertiser	Swedish Railways, "Don't Miss Europe"

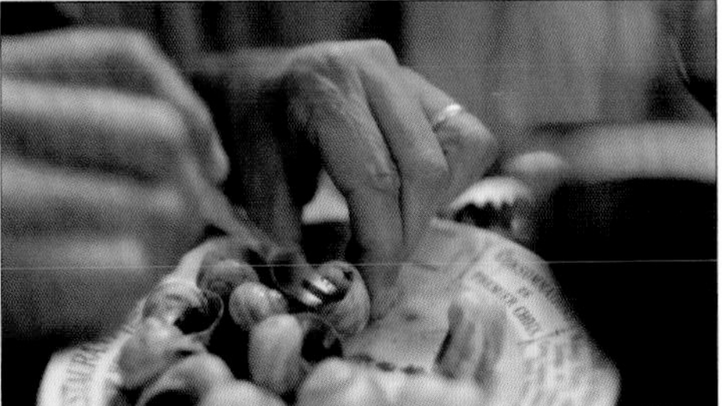

Agency	AMV BBDO, London
ECD	Paul Brazier
Creative Director	Mark Fairbanks Thiago de Moraes
Creatives	Adrian Rossi Alex Grieve
Agency Producer	Anita Sasdy
Production	HLA, London
Producer	Mike Wells
Film Director	Simon Ratigan
DOP	Martin Hill
Post Production	The Mill, London
Editing House	The Play Room, London
Editor	Adam Spivey
Sound	Parv Thind, Wave Studios, London
Stills Photographers	Simon Ratigan Matt Stuart
Grade	Seamus O'Kane, The Mill, London
Advertiser	Eurostar, "Stories Are Waiting"

A montage of short clips and images show us some unexpected sides of Paris. "Maybe," says the narrator, "you'll go left. Maybe you'll go right." Or up to Montmartre. Or down to the metro. Maybe you'll meet strange characters, see odd sites, eat weird food. Maybe you'll get spooked by the Catacombs. Or by a gargoyle. Maybe you'll fall in love. With the wine. With a person. Or with a stuffed penguin. Whatever happens, stories are waiting. Just take the Eurostar.

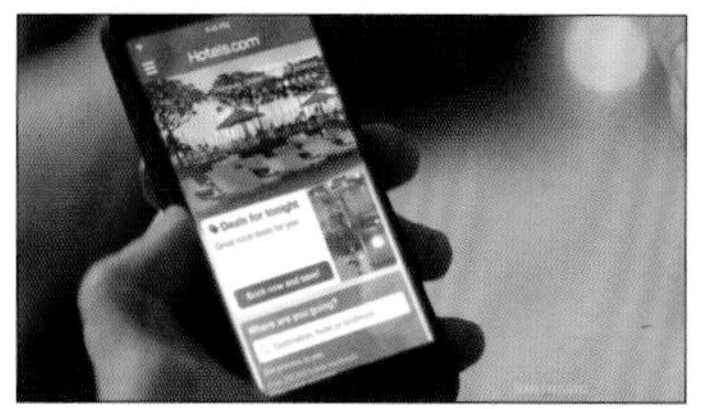

Agency CP+B, Boulder
VP, ECD Dan Donovan
VP, Exec. Dir. of Art Direction & Design Dave Swartz
Creative Directors Andrew Lincoln, Matt Talbot
Copywriter Ross Saunders
Art Director Marc Wilson
Production Imperial Woodpecker, New york
Advertiser Hotels.com, "Obvious Eye Contact"

The suave Captain Obvious thinks he's scored with a girl in a bar. He addresses the camera. "I've always found you don't know you need a hotel room, until you're sure you do." Fortunately, using the hotels.com app, he can book a room instantly. This done, he gets up to sweep the girl off her feet. But she walks right past him – to greet her boyfriend. "Or I could not book a hotel room and put my cell phone back in my pocket as if nothing happened," he adds. "Hotels. com. I don't need it right now."

Agency Lowe, Istanbul
Creative Group Head Erdem Suyolcu
Creative Director Can Faga
Copywriters Zeynep Gunes, Emine Aydin
Art Directors Ali Yigit Gumus, Okan Saykun
Agency Producers Tugrul Karadeniz, Ahmet Uygun
Production Filmpark, Istanbul
Producers Alper Evirgen, Mete Ozok
Advertiser Turkish Airlines, "Dreams"

A quartet of cute kids are watching a plane soar high above the countryside where they live. "D'you think it's going to Istanbul?" asks one. "It's not like it's going to come here," says another. Suddenly inspired, they decide to build an airfield. They work hard, even installing runway lights, but the plane doesn't land. Until one day, it does – not exactly in their field, but at a new airport just over the ridge. Turkish Airlines serves everywhere in Turkey.

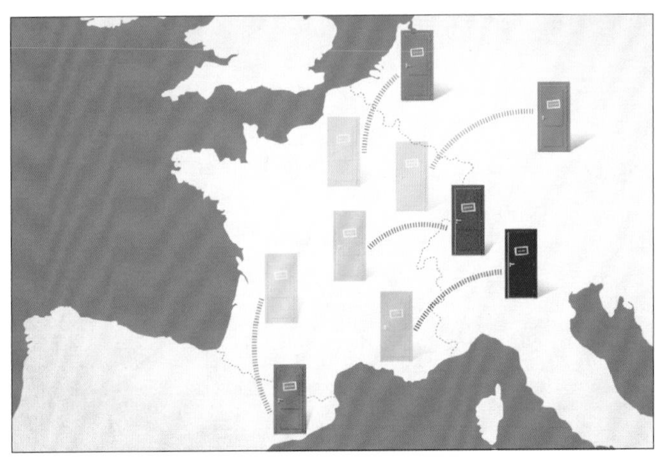

Agency TBWA\Paris
Creative Director Philippe Simonet
Copywriter Josselin Pacreau
Art Director Sébastien Guinet
Photographer Pierre Edelman
Production Stink, Paris
Film Director Nathan Besse
Producer Sylvaine Mella
Head of TV Maxime Boiron
Agency Producers Virginie Chalard, Blaise Izard
Post Producer Elise Gamboa
Music Florent Brown
Sound Designers Anaïs Khout, David Amsalem
Color Grading Anne Szymkowiak
Film Editors Hugo Lemant, Nicolas Gérard
Advertiser SNCF, French Railways, “Europe Is Just Next Door”

In France, many people think that the TGV high speed train only goes to French cities. In fact it serves major cities across Europe. To dramatize this, doors were erected that provided a virtual link to Barcelona, Milan, Geneva, Stuttgart and Brussels. Each time a passer-by opened a door, a distinctive scene was played out, giving the impression that they could almost step into the other city. The experiences were filmed and became a video and cinema ad, showing that Europe is just next door.

508 BELLS.
80 RINGS.

351 ROCKS.
270 STONES.

107 BRIDES.
13 GROOMS.

ONE MILLION DUBLINERS. ONE LUKE KELLY.

21 MONEYPENNYS.
119 BONDS.

1733 KINGS.
115 LORDS.

111 SPRINGS.
113 SUMMERS.

707 MONKS.
5 SAINTS.
68 POPES.

29
SHAKESPEARES.
ONE
BRENDAN BEHAN.

44 AYRES.
506 GRACES.

26
BREWERS.
7
BEERS.
1
BARMAN.

GLASNEVIN.
ALL HUMAN LIFE IS HERE.
GATHERING SINCE 1828
VISIT NOW
GLASNEVINCEMETERY.IE
GLASNEVIN CEMETERY MUSEUM,
FINGLAS ROAD, DUBLIN 11.

NORTH 95.
SOUTH 6.
EAST 4.
WEST 193.

Since 1828, more than one and a half million people have been buried in Glasnevin Cemetery. With more people below ground than above ground in Dublin, is your family here?

23 Kettles.
889 Boyles.

20 CUMMINGS.
10 GOINGS.

18 FRIENDS.
1 FOE.

Agency	Brand Artillery, Dublin
Creative Director	Eoghan Nolan
Copywriter	Eoghan Nolan
Art Director	Tony Purcell
Typographer	Tony Purcell
Advertiser	Glasnevin Cemetery & Museum, "Surnames"

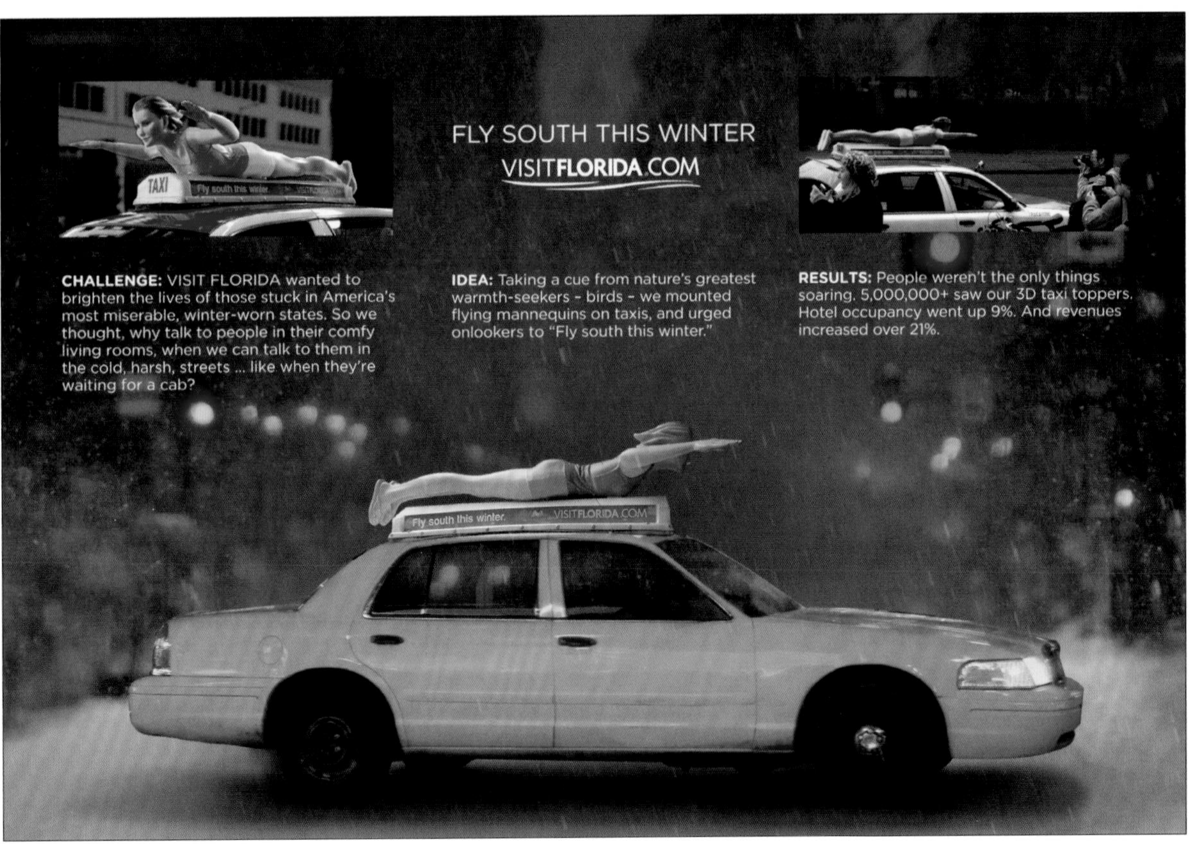

FLY SOUTH THIS WINTER
VISITFLORIDA.COM
CHALLENGE: VISIT FLORIDA wanted to brighten the lives of those stuck in America's most miserable, winter-worn states. So we thought, why talk to people in their comfy living rooms, when we can talk to them in the cold, harsh, streets ... like when they're waiting for a cab?
IDEA: Taking a cue from nature's greatest warmth-seekers - birds - we mounted flying mannequins on taxis, and urged onlookers to "Fly south this winter."
RESULTS: People weren't the only things soaring. 5,000,000+ saw our 3D taxi toppers. Hotel occupancy went up 9%. And revenues increased over 21%.
Fly south this winter.
VISITFLORIDA.COM

Agency	SapientNitro, Miami
Worldwide CCO	Gaston Legorburu
North American CCO	Gary Koepke
Creative Directors	Ronn Pearson Jordan Lipton
Associate CDs	Carol Montoto Brian Jones
Copywriter	Casey Woods
Art Director	Danielle Fay
Designers	Svetoslav Kraev Carolina Espinales
Advertiser	Visit Florida.com, "Fly South This Winter - Taxi Topper"

Agency	JWT SPOT, Athens
Vice President CCO	Takis Liarmakopoulos
Creative Director	Lazaros Evmorfias
Copywriters	Lazaros Evmorfias Dimitris Dousis
Photographer	Vasileios Michael
Illustrator	Tereza Ferentinou
Advertiser	Airfasttickets Online Travel Agency, "Tunnel"

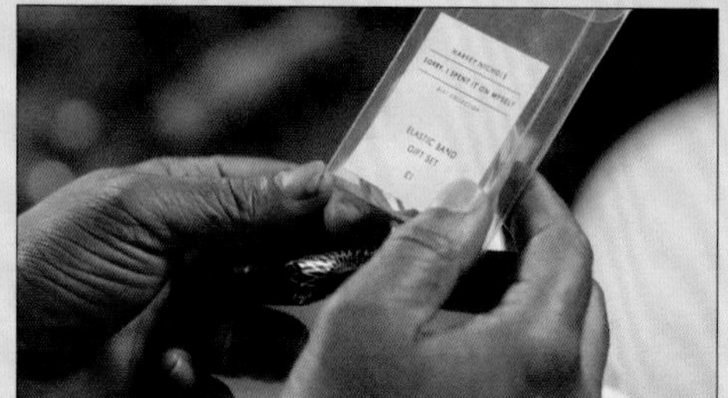

74 Retail Services

Agency adam&eveDDB, London
Executive CDs Ben Priest, Ben Tollett, Emer Stamp
Creatives Richard Brim, Daniel Fisher
Producer Daniel Moorey
Agency Producer Victoria Keenan
Production Outsider, London
Film Director James Rouse
Producer Benji Howell
Cameraman Alex Melman
Editor Bill Smedley, Work Post, London
Post Producer Josh King, MPC, London
Sound Factory Studio, London
Director James Day
Advertiser Harvey Nichols, "Sorry, I Spent It On Myself"

One of many prizes won by the Harvey Nichols campaign in this year's Epica competition. This film for the upmarket UK retailer shows people who purchased cut-price Christmas gifts for their loved ones in order to spend more on themselves. "Elastic bands?" the first victim asks, incredulously. "Elastic bands from Harvey Nichols," his daughter corrects him. She has lovely shoes, we notice. Paper clips, a sink plug and toothpicks ("You love toothpicks!") are all dispensed to disappointed relatives. Presenting the Harvey Nichols "Sorry, I Spent It On Myself" Gift Collection.

A GROTESQUE APPLE

A DAY KEEPS THE DOCTOR AWAY AS WELL.

INGLORIOUS fruits&vegetables

by Intermarché

THE FAILED LEMON
FROM THE CREATOR OF THE LEMON.

THE UGLY CARROT
IN A SOUP WHO CARES?

THE RIDICULOUS POTATO

ELECTED MISS MASHED POTATO 2014.

INGLORIOUS fruits&vegetables

by Intermarché

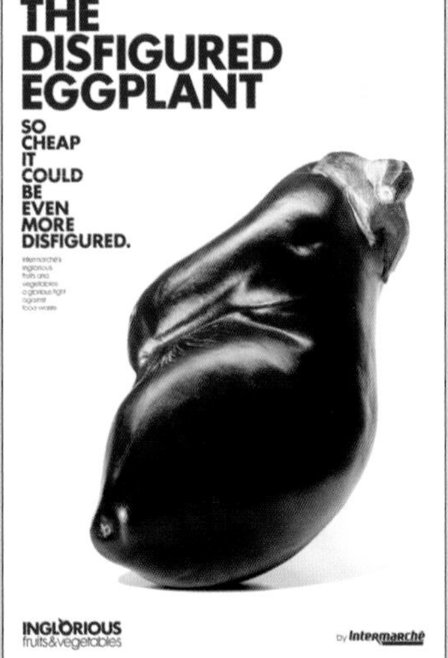

THE DISFIGURED EGGPLANT
SO CHEAP IT COULD BE EVEN MORE DISFIGURED.
INGLORIOUS fruits&vegetables
by Intermarché

Agency	Marcel, Paris
Publicis Worldwide CCO	Erik Vervroegen
Chief Creative Officer	Anne de Maupeou
Executive CD	Dimitri Guerassimov
Creative Director	Julien Benmoussa
Copywriters	Julien Benmoussa Gaëtan du Peloux Youri Guerassimov
Art Directors	Youri Guerassimov Gaëtan du Peloux Anaïs Boileau
Production	Prodigious, Paris
Global Print Manager	Jean-Luc Chirio, Publicis
Art Buyer	Soone Riboud, Publicis
Producer	Justine Beaussart, Prodigious
Photographer	Patrice de Villiers
Retouching	L'Asile, Paris
Advertiser	Intermarché, "Inglorious Fruits and Vegetables"

Supermarket Intermarché went to war against food waste by selling "deformed" fruits and vegetables that would usually get thrown out for not adhering to the norm. The operation was backed up by a print campaign that made stars of the imperfect foods, which of course tasted just as good as their flawless counterparts.

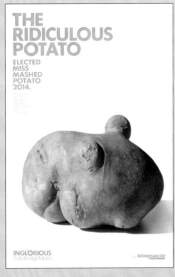

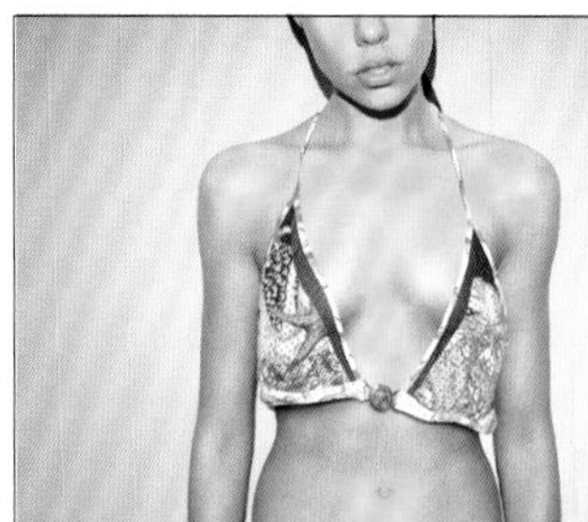

Agency	adam&eveDDB, London	**Designer**	Rob Hare Stanley's King Henry, London
Executive CDs	Ben Priest Ben Tollett Emer Stamp	**Retouching**	Gareth Ling Sophie Lawes Stanley's King Henry, London
Creatives	Richard Brim Daniel Fisher		
Agency Producer	Kirsty Petrie	**Advertiser**	Harvey Nichols, "Bad Fit"
Head of Print	Daniel Moorey		
Photographer	Matt Irwin		

Agency	adam&eveDDB, London
Executive CDs	Ben Priest Ben Tollett Emer Stamp
Creatives	Richard Brim Daniel Fisher
Creative Producer	Kirsty Harris
Head of Print	Daniel Moorey
Designer/Typographer	Alex Fairman, Stanley's King Henry, London
Photographer	James Day
Advertiser	Harvey Nichols, "Sorry, I Spent It On Myself"

Taking the idea to its logical conclusion, Harvey Nichols actually launched the "Sorry, I Spent It On Myself" gift collection. Here are the items that shoppers could purchase in store. Maybe somebody appreciated the Harvey Nichols paper clips. We're less sure about the gravel, though.

Retail Services

Agency	Heimat, Berlin
Chief Creative Officer	Guido Heffels
Creative Directors	Guido Heffels Ramin Schmiedekampf Frank Hose
Photographer	Paco Femenia
Production	Trigger Happy Production, Berlin
Film Director	Pep Bosch
Advertiser	Hornbach, "Gothic Girl"

A father drops his daughter off at school. In their perfect little town, where everything is white, beige or pastel, the teenage Goth girl pays the price for her rebellion by being teased in class and shunned by the community. She looks resigned to all this meanness – until she arrives home, to find that her father is painting the house and driveway entirely black in her honour. Hornbach home improvements – say it with your project.

Agency	Åkestam Holst, Stockholm
Creative Director	Andreas Ullenius
Copywriter	Hanna Björk
Art Director	Lars Holthe
Production	Callboy, Stockholm
Director	Max Vitali
Producer	Nils Ljunggren
Agency Producer	Camilla Geijer, Another Production
Advertiser	IKEA, "Undercover"

An elderly bearded guy in a baseball cap arrives at an IKEA store. He looks carefully at everything, opening drawers and examining items, observed in his turn by a sharp-eyed little boy. As he loads up on gifts, other children notice him too. They begin pointing and tugging parental sleeves, but the grown-ups aren't convinced. Finally the old guy climbs into a battered Volvo, which has a revealing number plate. "Did anyone recognise you?" asks an elf. "I don't think so," he replies, and drives off with a "ho ho ho".

WEST

STER

Now delivering to Central London from just £1.

TOTTEN

WHITECH

Now delivering to East London from just £1.

Agency DLKWLOWE, London
Executive CDs Richard Denney, Dave Henderson
Creative Directors Richard Denney, Dave Henderson, Tom Hudson
Copywriters Richard Denney, Ben McCarthy, Seb Housden
Art Directors Richard Denney, Ben McCarthy, Seb Housden
Photographer Patrice de Villiers
Production Trayler & Trayler, London
Agency Producer Gary Wallis
Graphic Design Ryan Self
Advertiser Morrisonsfood.com, "Up Your Street"

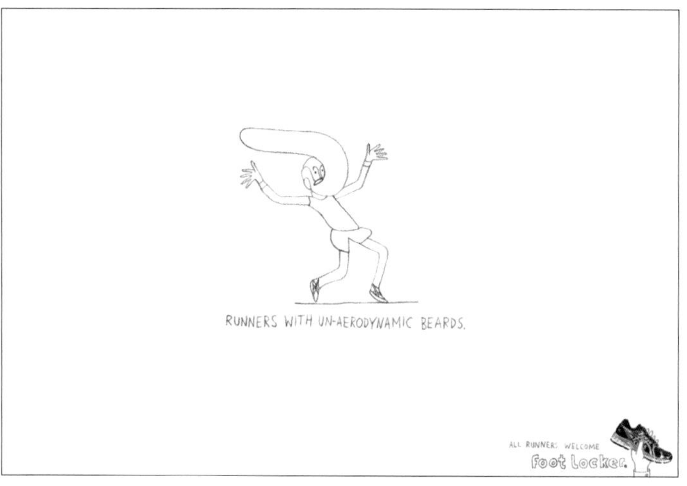

 Retail Services

Agency	BBDO New York
Chief Creative Officers	David Lubars Greg Hahn
Executive CDs	Chris Beresford-Hill Dan Lucey
Senior CDs	Grant Smith Danilo Boer
Executive Producer	Tricia Lentini
Digital Strategist	Rhys Hillman
Advertiser	Foot Locker, "All Runners Welcome"

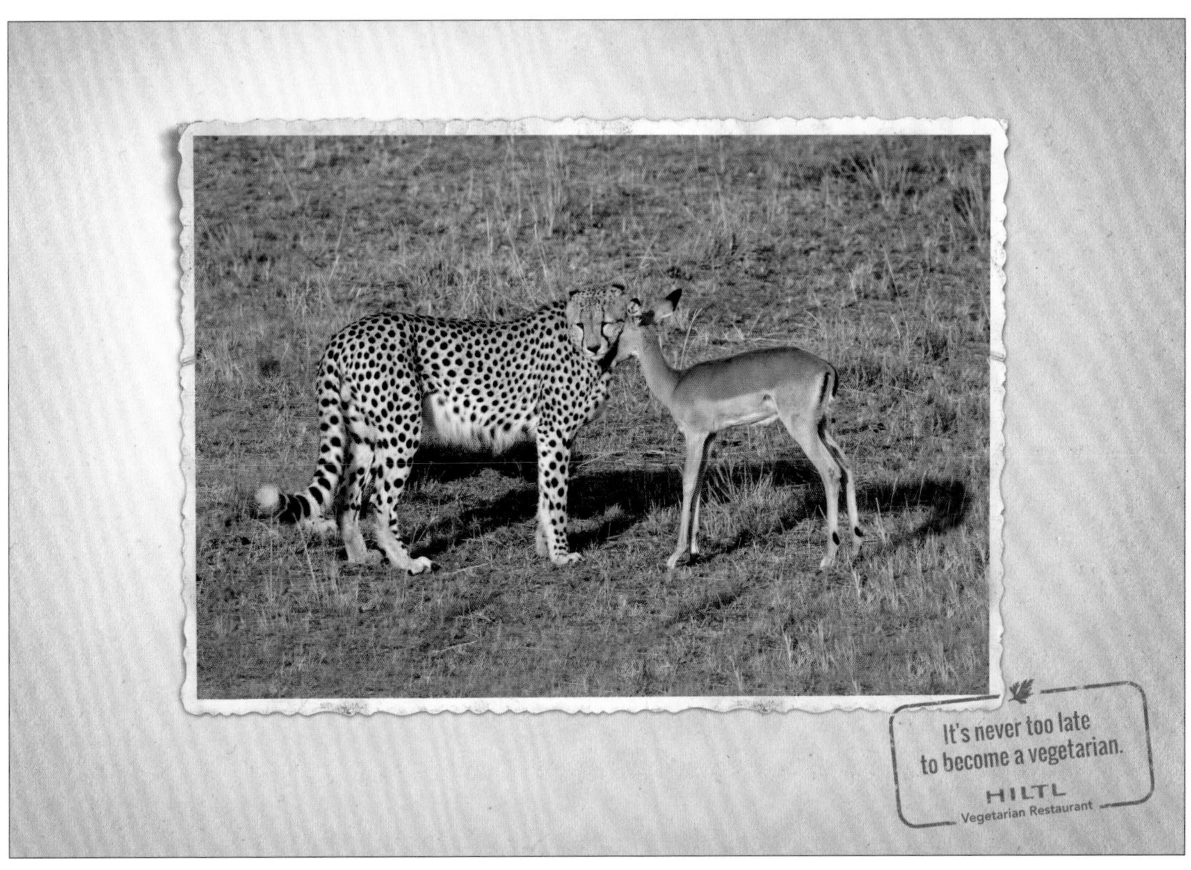

Agency	Ruf Lanz, Zurich
Creative Directors	Markus Ruf Danielle Lanz
Copywriter	Florian Birkner
Art Director	Marcel Schläfle
Graphic Design	Laura Hofer
Advertiser	Hiltl Vegetarian Restaurant, "Hiltl Animal Friendship"

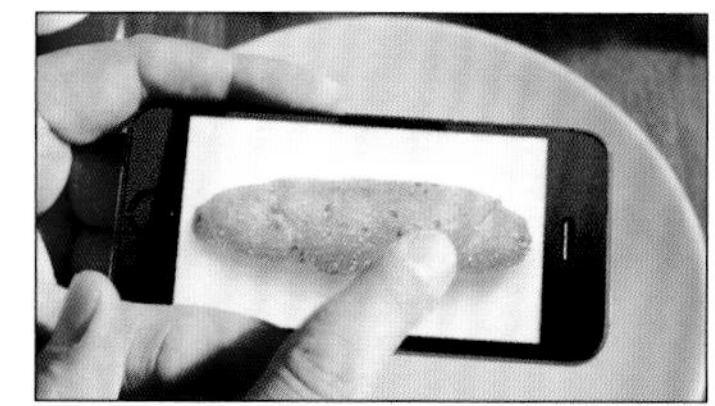

Agency Isobar, Budapest
Creative Director Marton Jedlicska
Copywriter Peter Zsembery
Art Director Daniel Deme
Film Director Péter Rudolf Kiss
Production Zoltán Mártonffy
Agency Producer Éva Bayer-Baróti
Advertiser Tesco, "Tesco In Your Hands"

A man takes his smartphone out of the fridge. It seems to have amazing qualities: first he pours milk out of it; then it puts bread on his plate. The phone also contains butter, jam and eggs – and it can slice and dice fruit and vegetables. Tesco supermarket is now in your hands, thanks to the new shopping app.

Agency Lopez Negrete, Houston
Creative Directors Fernando Osuna, Mariano German, Vicent Llopis, David Padierna
Copywriters Francisco Agüera, Ameth Barrera
Art Director Luigui Rodríguez
Advertiser BuzzMill Organic Coffee Store, "Travel"

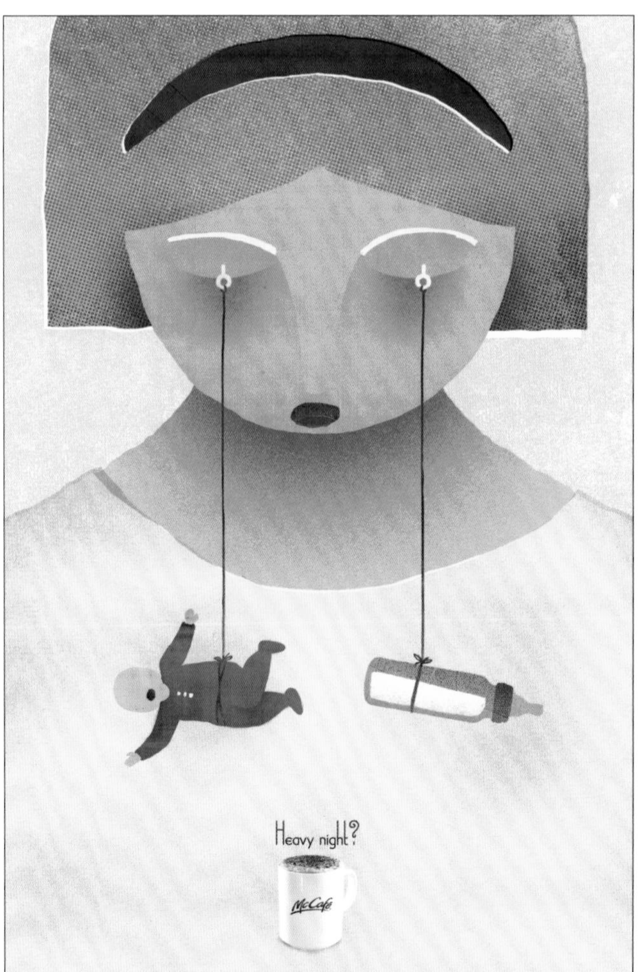

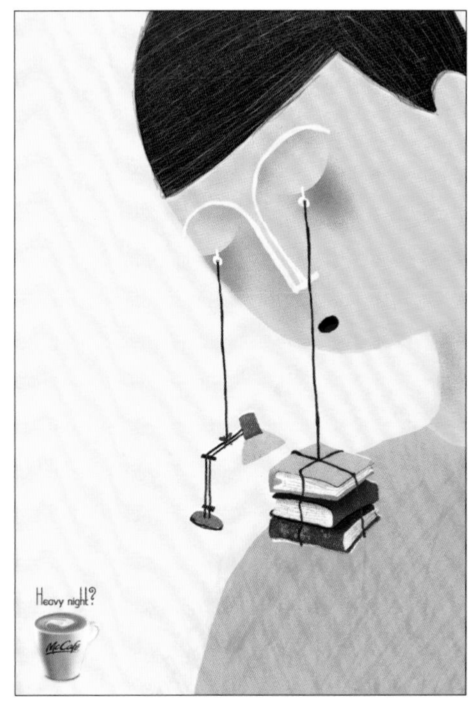

Agency	Leo Burnett, Sydney
Chief Creative Officer	Andy DiLallo
Copywriter	Grant McAloon
Art Director	Bruno Nakano
Agency Producer	Jeremy Devilliers
Illustrator	Bruno Nakano
Advertiser	McDonald's, "Heavy Nights"

Recipe

Attempt

Recipe

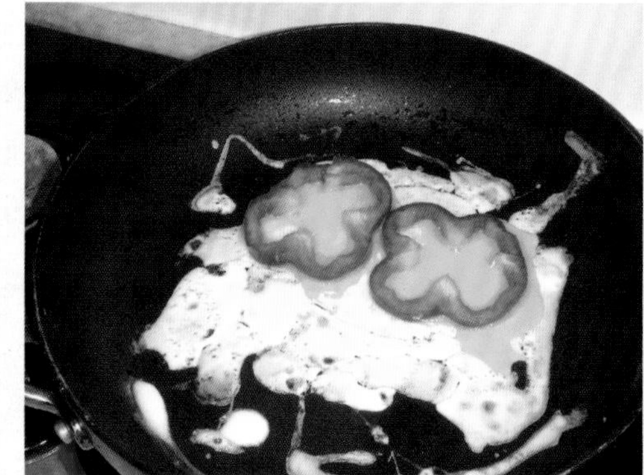

Attempt

Agency	Artplan, Rio de Janeiro
Chief Creative Officer	Roberto Vilhena
Creative Directors	Alessandra Sadock Gustavo Tirre
Copywriters	Henrique Louzada Pedro Rosas Augusto Correia
Art Director	Augusto Correia
Creative Technologist	Leonardo Marçal
Photographer	Rudy Hühold
Advertiser	Domino's Pizza, "Cooking Fails"

Agency	Australie, Paris
Creative Directors	Claire Ravut Stéphane Renaudat
Copywriters	Arnaud Lesueur Francois-Xavier Evrard
Art Directors	Frédéric Duverge Sylvain Michel
Advertiser	E.Leclerc, "Culture In Everyday Life"

Agency JOY, Sydney
Creative Director Christy Peacock
Copywriter Lauren MacDonald
Art Director Vanessa Robinson
Production Revolver, Sydney
Film Director Matt Devine
Producer Michael Ritchie
Post Production Heckler, Sydney
Sound Design Sonar Music, Sydney
Audio Engineer Stuart Welch
Advertiser H&R Block, "We Don't Miss A Thing"

A fairly innocuous-looking wall. A man walks into frame. The narrator says: "With over 40 years' experience as Australia's leading tax specialist, what's hard to spot for some is blindingly obvious to us." The man points: "There!" A brick-patterned figure emerges from the wall. "There!" A white-clad Ninja springs from the crossing. "And there!" A disguised elephant magically appears. The narrator concludes: "Which can make a big difference to your tax refund." Call H&R Block, tax accountants.

sigortam.net
Online Home Insurance
Get insurance before your own measures.

Agency	Tribal Worldwide, Istanbul
Creative Group Head	Baris Sarhan
Creative Directors	Arda Erdik Basar Bellisan
Copywriter	Cagri Erdemir
Art Director	Zeynep Ordu
Photographer	Emre Gologlu
Advertiser	Sigortam.net Online Insurance Platform, “Hiding Money”

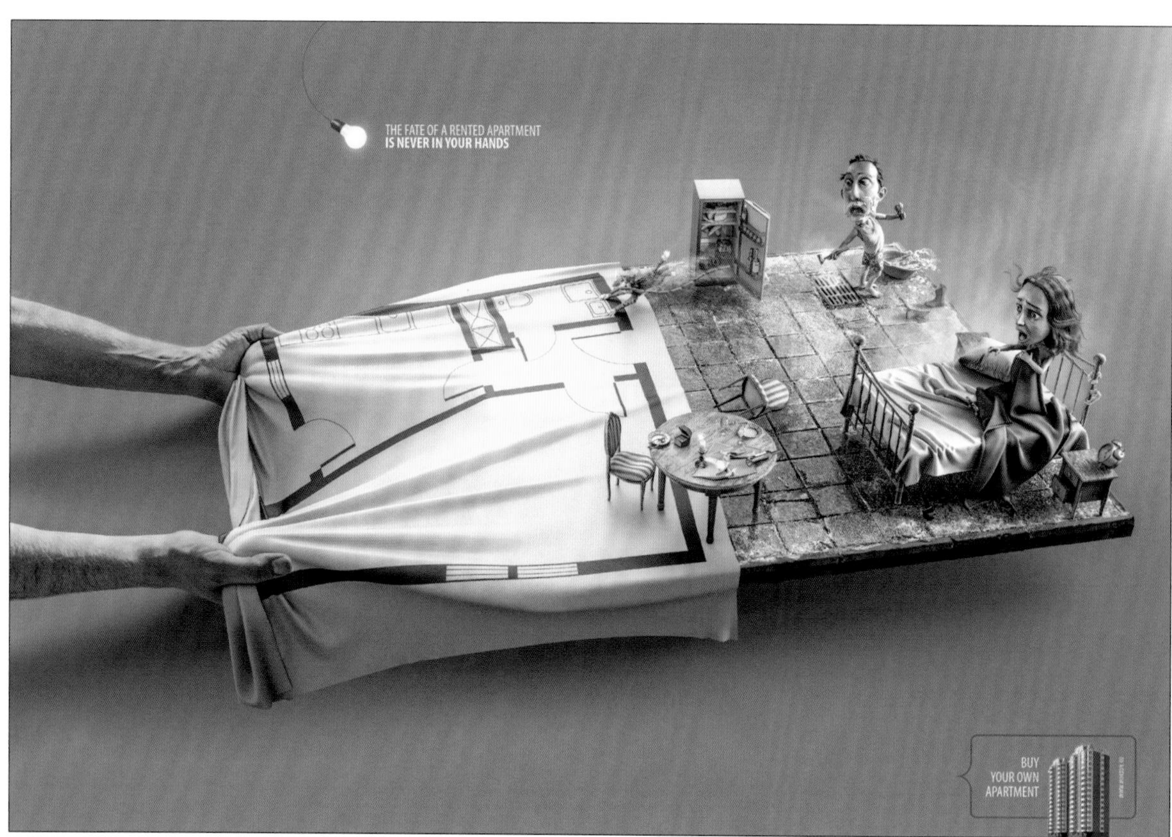

Agency	TRY/Apt/POL, Oslo
Creative Director	Lars Joachim Grimstad
Copywriters	Lars Joachim Grimstad Jonas Grønnern Camilla Bjørnhaug
Art Directors	Egil Pay Lars-Kristian Harveg Preben Moan
Production	Tangrystan, Oslo
Film Director	Andrea Eckerbom
Producer	Beate Tangre
Advertiser	DNB Bank, "The 24 Hour Ad Break"

People worry most about their finances at night – when they think nothing can alleviate their anxiety. But Norwegian bank DNB offers 24-hour customer service. In order to remind people about this, the bank bought every ad break on Norway's leading channel over 24 hours. Then it invited the public to give advice – about all sorts of things. For instance, don't watch Netflix until 6am if you have to get up at 8. Over 1000 films were shown, all providing DNB's 24-hour helpline at the end. Social media praise was widespread, and awareness of the service more than doubled overnight.

Agency	Media-Storm Advertising, Moscow
Creative Director	Evgeny Turkin
Copywriter	Evgeny Turkin
Art Director	Evgeny Turkin
Illustrator	Alexey Kraminov
Advertiser	Morton Invest, Real Estate, "The Tablecloth Campaign"

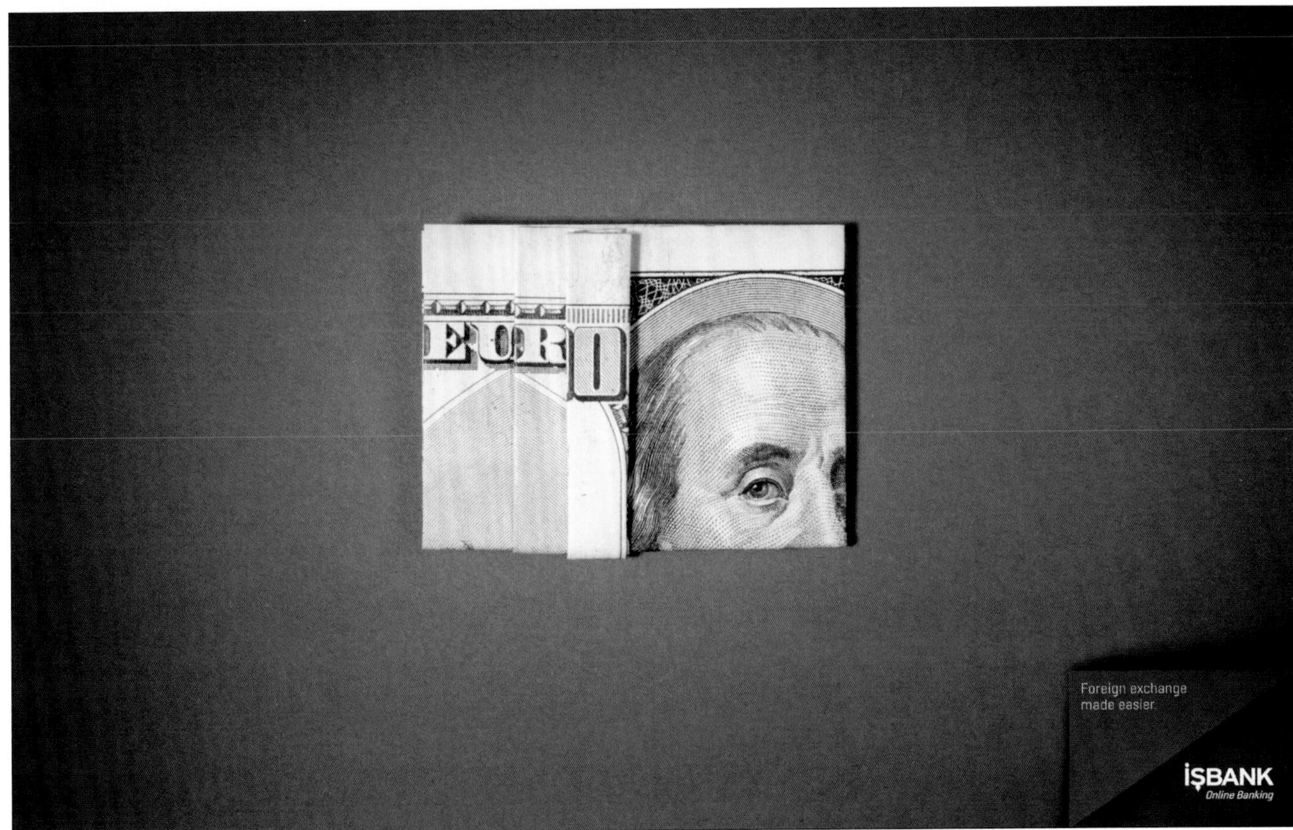

Agency	Tribal Worldwide, Istanbul
Creative Group Head	Baris Sarhan
Creative Directors	Arda Erdik Basar Bellisan
Copywriter	Tolga Mutlu
Art Director	Meric Karabulut
Photographer	Emre Göloglu
Advertiser	Isbank, "Foreign Exchange"

Agency	Honesty, Stockholm
Creative Directors	Martin Marklund Petrus Kukulski
Copywriters	Martin Marklund Petrus Kukulski
Art Director	Emil Jonsson
Finished Art	Sara Adrian
Advertiser	Riksgälden Premium Bonds, "The Ghost"

Agency	Rocky Advertising, Helsinki
Copywriter	Teijo Hintikka
Art Director	Jarkko Toijonen
Photographer	iStockphoto
Agency Producer	Mikko Toivanen
Graphic Design	If Inhouse Studio
Photo Retouching	Jyrki Loukkaanhuhta
Advertiser	If Life Insurance, "Balloon"

My finances are perfectly fine me how much?

For all life's twists and turns: Flexible financial plans.

We're a couple of things ended our relationship.

For all life's twists and turns: Flexible financial plans.

Everything is well I didn't see that coming.

For all life's twists and turns: Flexible financial plans.

We lack nothing is left.

For all life's twists and turns: Flexible financial plans.

I only have a few dollars in my hand me the caviar please.

For all life's twists and turns: Flexible financial plans.

As a boss I earn more time for the family would be nice.

For all life's twists and turns: Flexible financial plans.

Agency	Leo Burnett, Zurich
Creative Directors	Peter Brönnimann Axel Eckstein
Copywriters	Thomas Schöb Simon Smit
Art Director	Reto Clement
Advertiser	Swiss Life Insurance, "Life's Turn in a Sentence"

STABILT SEDAN 1915
www.beijerbygg.se
BEIJER
BYGGMATERIAL

– It´s my turn to lie in the upper bed.
– Don´t sound so disadvantged.

Agency	Honesty, Stockholm
Creative Directors	Martin Marklund Petrus Kukulski
Copywriters	Martin Marklund Petrus Kukulski
Photographer	Kenneth Svedlund Ishii
Film Directors	Martin Marklund Petrus Kukulski
Producer	Anders Olsson
Graphic Design	Anna Lindelöw
Music	Petrus Kukulski
Advertiser	Beijer Building Supplies, "Stable Since 1915"

A summer barbecue begins. A young lad arrives with his three new friends: sumo wrestlers. "Exchange students," his mother explains to another guest. "From Osaka." The big guys get stuck into the hot dogs. "Gotta rest my butt," says one, and drapes his bulk on the spindly wooden railing around the terrace. The others join him, but the railing doesn't budge.

In the next spot, during a badminton game, the shuttlecock ends up on the roof. A sumo goes to look for it. And because he's "visually impaired", the others join him. But the roof looks as solid as ever. Finally, in the third spot, the three sumo wrestlers share the top bunk at nap time. The boy looks perfectly relaxed reading below them. Beijer Building Materials: stable since 1915.

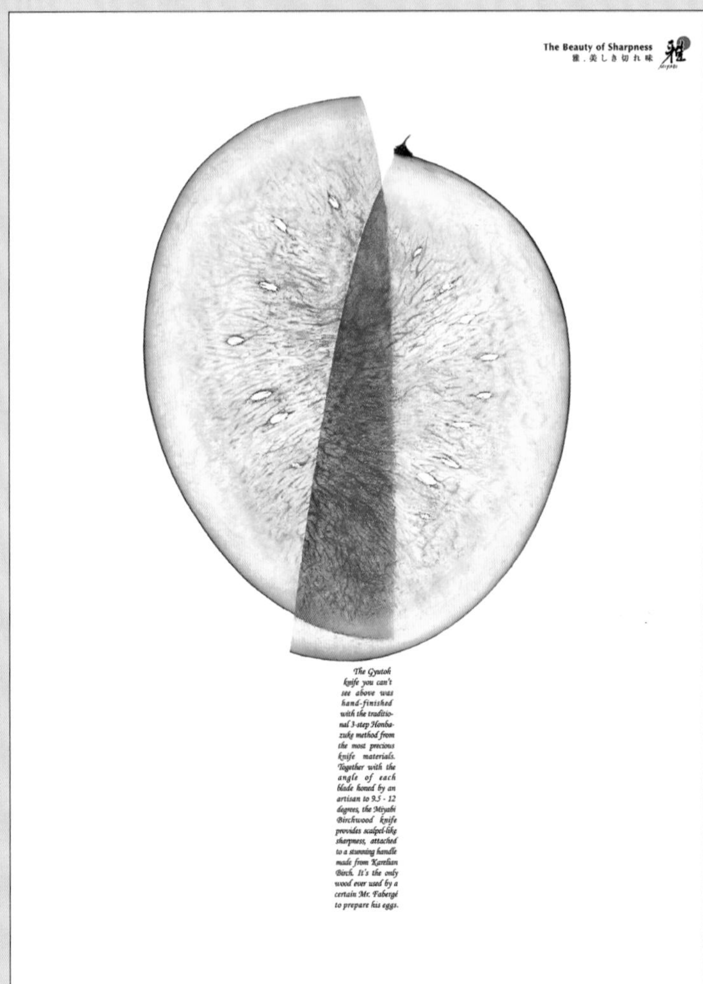

The Beauty of Sharpness
雅．美しき切れ味
The Gyutoh knife you can't see above was hand-finished with the traditional 3-step Honbazuke method from the most precious knife materials. Together with the angle of each blade honed by an artisan to 9.5 - 12 degrees, the Miyabi Birchwood knife provides scalpel-like sharpness, attached to a stunning handle made from Karelian Birch. It's the only wood ever used by a certain Mr. Fabergé to prepare his eggs.

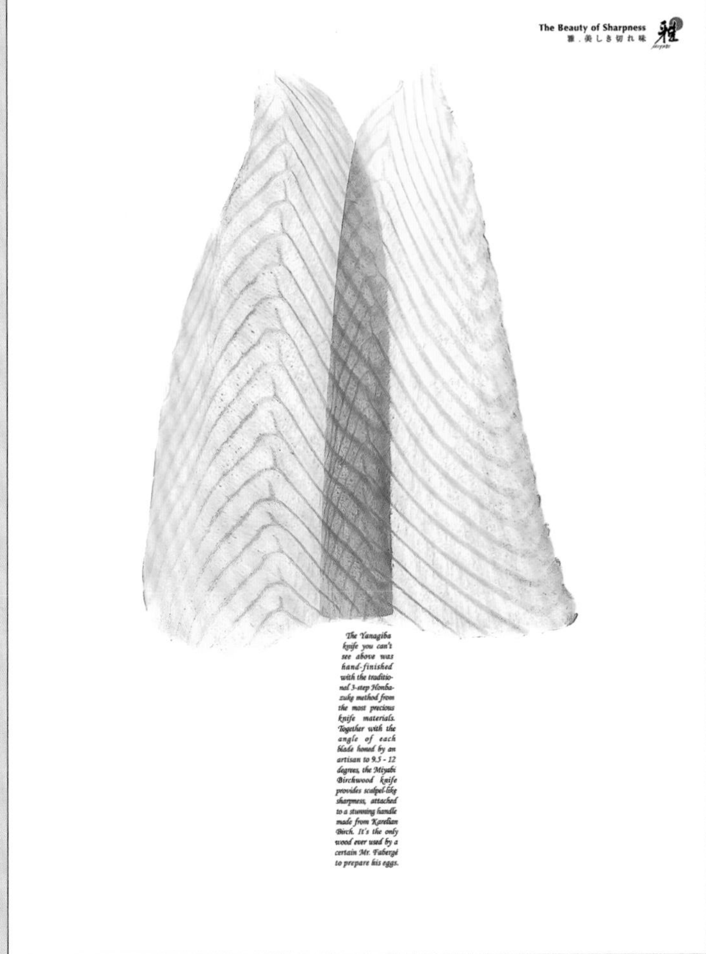

The Beauty of Sharpness
雅．美しき切れ味
The Yanagiba knife you can't see above was hand-finished with the traditional 3-step Honbazuke method from the most precious knife materials. Together with the angle of each blade honed by an artisan to 9.5 - 12 degrees, the Miyabi Birchwood knife provides scalpel-like sharpness, attached to a stunning handle made from Karelian Birch. It's the only wood ever used by a certain Mr. Fabergé to prepare his eggs.

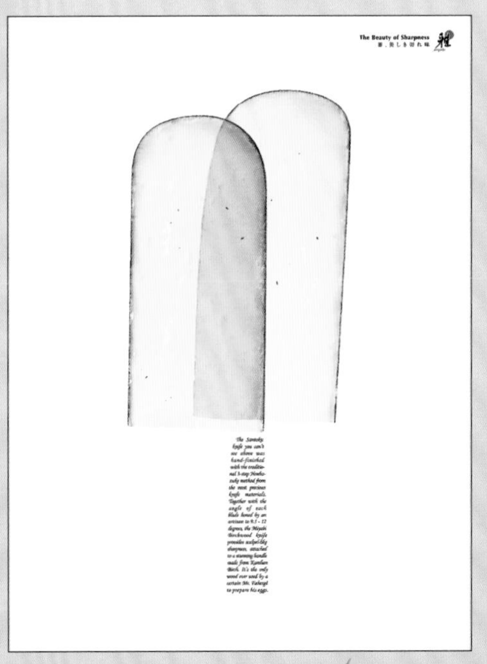

Agency	Herezie, Paris
Executive CD	Andrea Stillacci
Copywriters	Nicolas Duménil Jacques Denain Alexander Van Walsum
Art Directors	Nicolas Duménil Jacques Denain
Production	Capucine Lhermitte
Photographer	Pierre Baelen
Retoucher	La Souris Sur Le Gâteau
Producer	Thibault Zellner
Advertiser	Zwillin Kitchen Knives, "The Beauty of Sharpness"

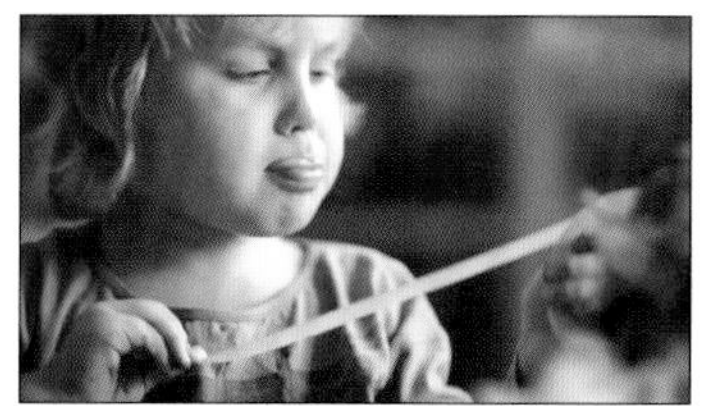

Agency TBWA\Stockholm
Creative Director Kalle Widgren
Copywriter Frida Siversen Ljung
Art Director Sanna Lengholm
Production Callboy, Stockholm
Film Director Max Vitali
Producers Sofia Bjorkman, Nils Ljunggren
Graphic Design Charlotte Habing
Advertiser Swedish District Heating, "The Unwanted Gifts"

"I love to craft," says a little boy. But what's he making? "This is a trumpet-helicopter-bunny," he says of the extraordinary but frankly hideous object. "I'm gonna give it to mommy so she can bring it to work." A title reads: "We heat homes with the things you throw away." Swedish Heating.

Agency CHI & Partners, London
Executive CD Jonathan Burley
Copywriter Micky Tudor
Art Director Monty Verdi
Production Park Pictures, London
Film Director Nathan Price
Producers Stephen Brierley, Claris Harvey
DOP Ginny Loane
Advertiser Samsung, "Coliseum"

A massive gladiatorial arena. The crowd is baying for blood. The emperor looks bored. In the midst of this scene appear…a man in a bathrobe and a young boy in pyjamas. The man has a cup of tea and a biscuit. The gladiators wait, swords brandished. The emperor gives the thumb down. The man's biscuit plops into his tea. But as the gladiators close in for the kill, we see that he and his son are watching a movie on Samsung's new curved TV, which surrounds them with the action.

BOSCHHHH®

Agency	Leo Burnett, Istanbul
Creative Group Heads	Ersin Pekin Koray Šahan
Creative Directors	Oktar Akın Emrah Akay
Photographer	Bora Sübakan
Production	PPR, Istanbul
Advertiser	Samsung, "Samsung NX Cameras"

Agency	BBDO Brussels
Creative Directors	Sebastien De Valck Arnaud Pitz
Copywriter	Sarah Huysmans
Art Director	Jasper Verleije
Head of Design	Eric Leurquin
Advertiser	Bosch, "Boschhhh"

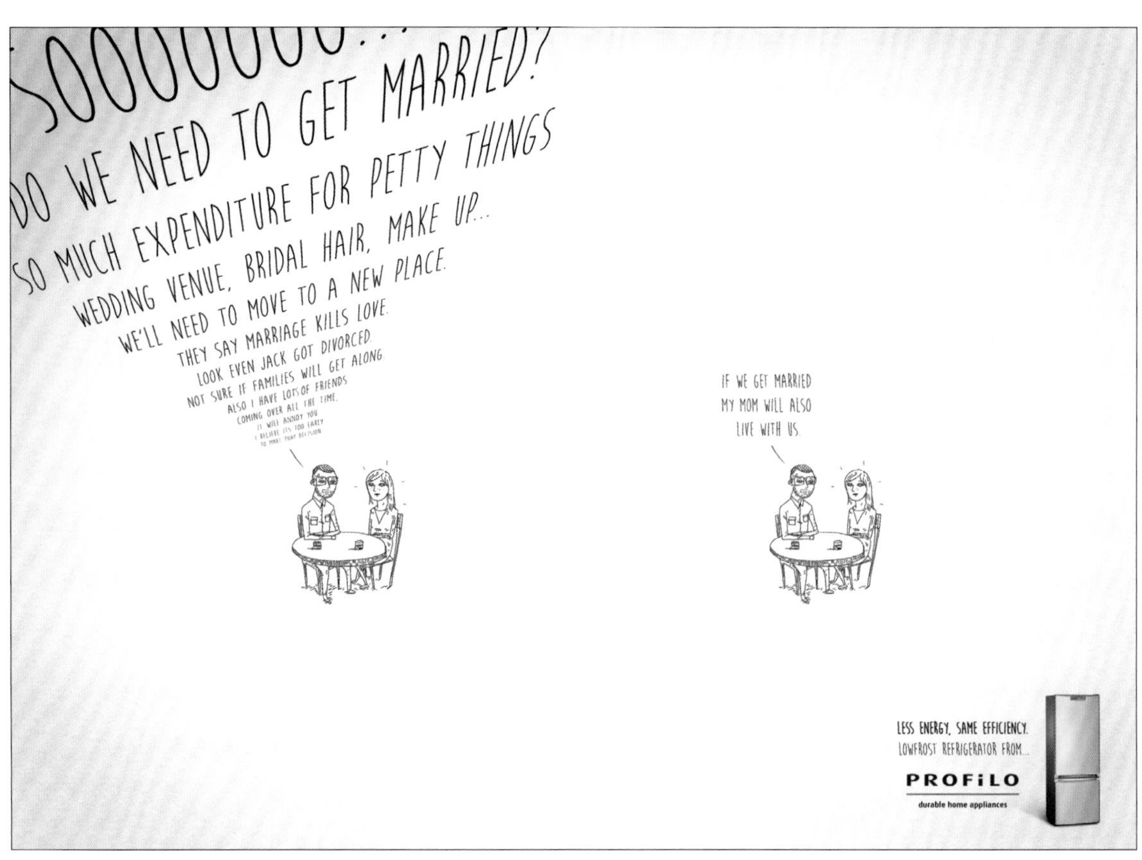

 Homes, Furnishings & Appliances

Agency	Rafineri, Istanbul
Creative Director	Ayşe Bali
Copywriters	Halil Fırat Eren Özge Yalçın
Art Director	Saydan Çelik
Illustrator	Saydan Çelik
Advertiser	Profilo, "Profilo/Lowfrost Refrigerator"

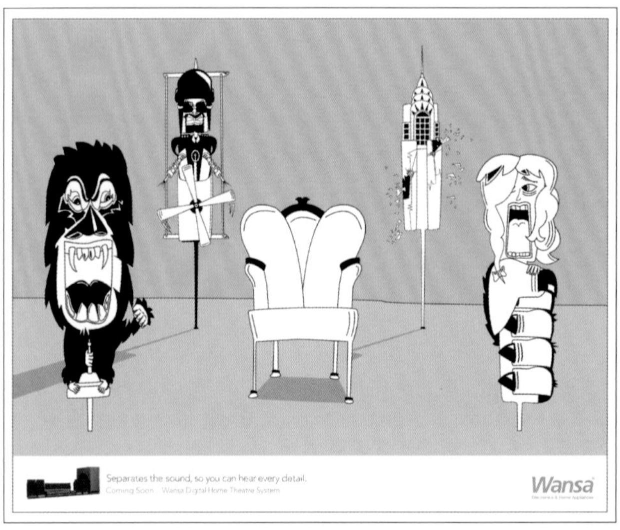

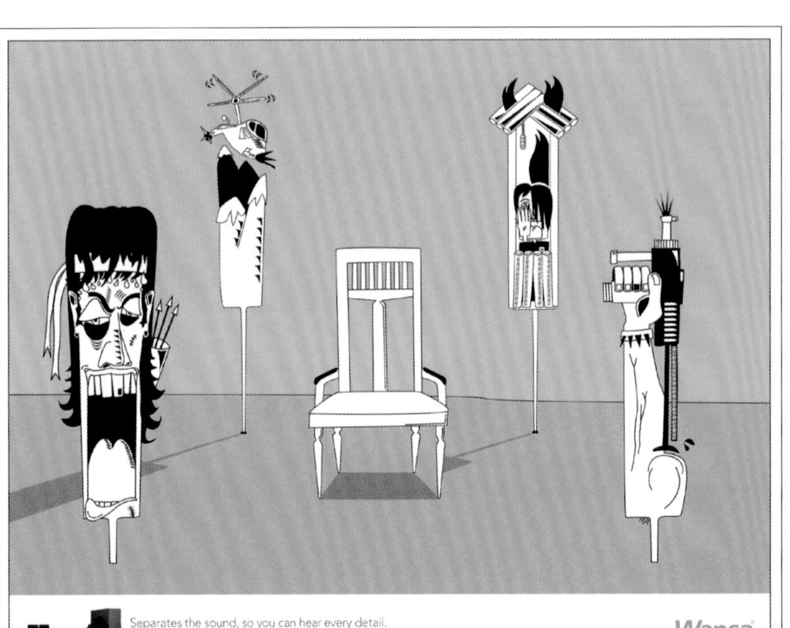

Agency	Impact & Echo BBDO, Kuwait
Creative Directors	Cesar Jachan Lokesh Achaiah Ramy Aziz Labib Hanna
Copywriter	Lokesh Achaiah
Art Director	Ramy Aziz Labib Hanna
Illustrator	Ramy Aziz Labib Hanna
Advertiser	Wansa Home Theatre, "Lifelike Sound"

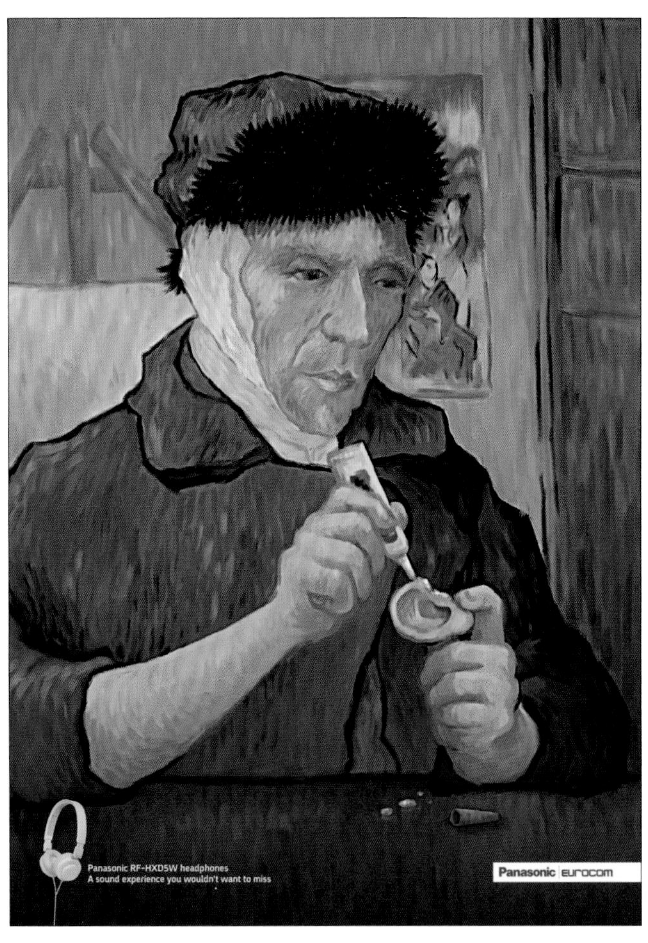

 Homes, Furnishings & Appliances

Agency	McCann Tel Aviv
VP Creative	Itay Galon
Copywriter	David Cohen
Art Director	Netanel Hagag
Advertiser	Eurocom, "Van Gogh Headphones"

Agency	Alice BBDO, Istanbul
Copywriters	Derya Banista Cagri Oral
Art Directors	Kerem Altuntas Arda Albayraktar
Photographer	Fethi Izan
Production	PBlok, Istanbul
Graphic Design	Serkan Ayrac
Advertiser	Arzum, "Even Sucks Up The Past"

Agency	McCann Athens
Creative Directors	Eleni Zisimopoulou Eleftheria Petropoulou
Copywriter	Eleftheria Petropoulou
Art Director	Popi Dimakou
Illustrator	Ampoo
Advertiser	Coral, "Mourning"

Household Maintenance

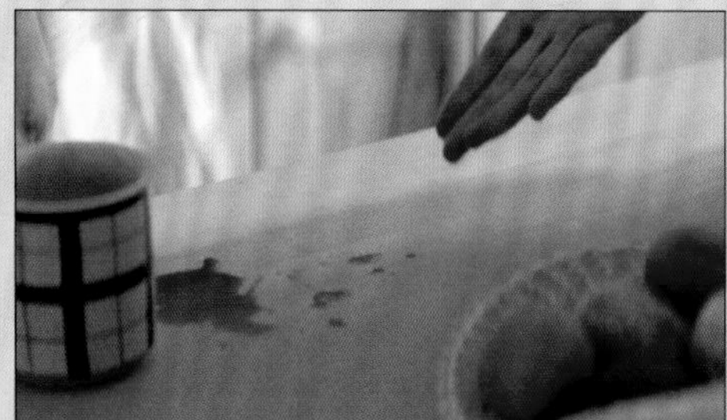

Sopalin
THE POWER
IS IN YOUR HANDS

Household Maintenance

Agency	Leo Burnett, Paris
Executive CD	Xavier Beauregard
Copywriter	Hadi Hassan-Helou
Art Director	Jérôme Gonfond
Production	Les Télécréateurs, Paris
Film Director	Vincent Lobelle
Producers	Mounia Mebarki Marie Mezerav
Agency Producer	Antoine Grujard
Advertiser	Sopalin, "Oh My Lord"

At breakfast time, a man slops coffee onto the countertop and doesn't bother mopping it up. His wife appears. She reaches for the kitchen roll, but it appears to be stuck. She struggles and heaves, going red in the face. The guy decides to show off. "This is your chance to take your crown back," intones a narrator, Excalibur-style. "Do it for your kingdom. Do it for your beloved. Do it for your people!" The man easily picks up the roll. His wife has been teasing him. She indicates the puddle of coffee. Sopalin – the power is in your hands.

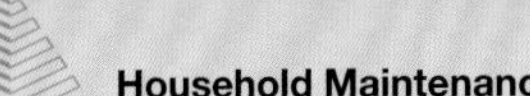

Agency	Leo Burnett, Frankfurt
Creative Directors	Andreas Pauli Irina Schestakoff Alexander Haase
Copywriter	Florian Fehre
Art Directors	Till Rothweiler Lisa Wiedemann
Photographer	Marc Wuchner
Advertiser	Samsung, "Just 80mm Flat"

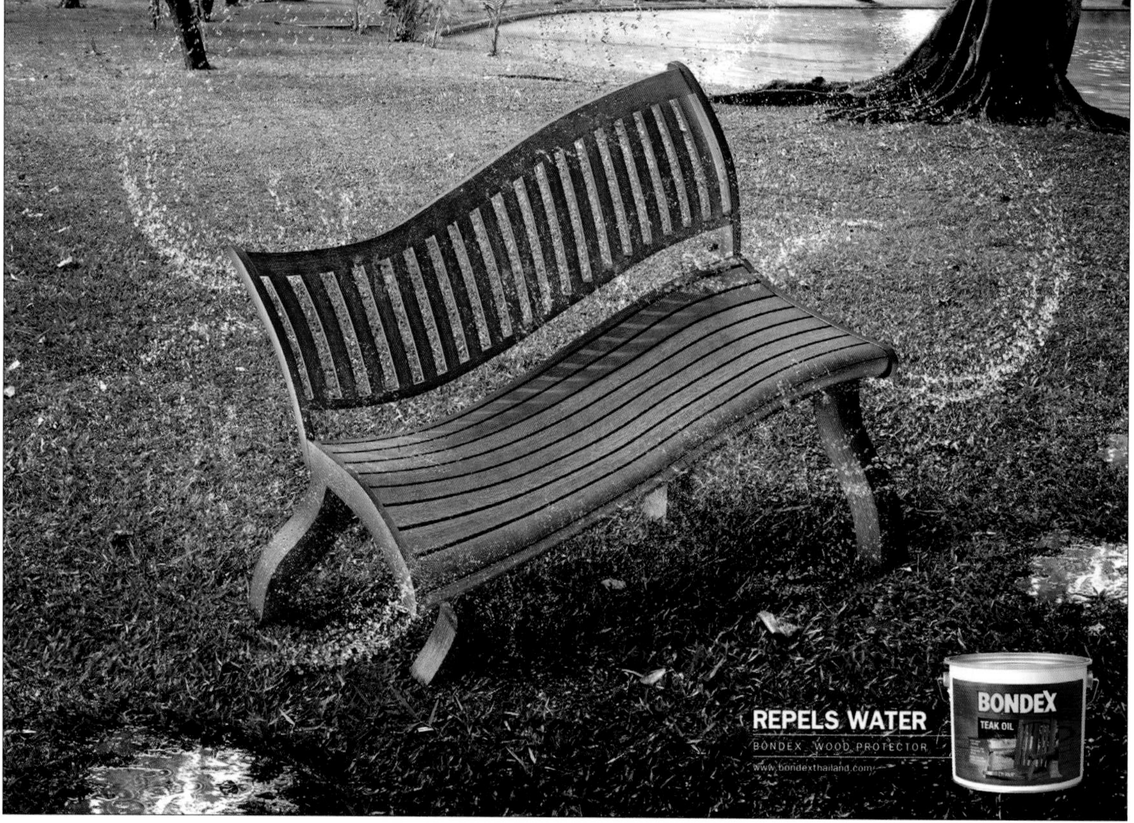

Agency TBWA\Bangkok
Creative Directors Veradis Vinyaratn
Prakit Kobkijwattana
Copywriter Susita Lueksuengsukoom
Art Directors Ditdanai Nopparat
Wasawad Panichpairoj
Photographers Anuchai Secharunputong
Nok Pipattungkul
Production Remix Studio, Bangkok
Agency Producer Pattaranuch Noimeecharoen
Advertiser Bondex Wood Protector,
"Shake Off"

OMO
dirt is good

Dirt makes good stories

Agency Lowe, Istanbul
Creative Director Can Faga
Copywriter Guven Gurkan
Art Director Cuneyt Ozalp
Illustrator Oscar Ramos
Advertiser Unilever, OMO detergent, "Alice in Wonderland"

Agency Herezie, Paris
Executive CD Andrea Stillacci
Creative Directors Jean-Laurent Py, Sébastien Boutebel
Art Director Christelle Bochet
Head of TV Blaise Izard
Director Pain Surprises, Paris
DOP Pierre Edelmann
Producer Amandine Le Drappier, Henry De Czar, Paris
Post Production Digital District, Paris
Advertiser Henkel, Coloria, "Refreshing Colours"

"Grandpa, please, do it again!" A couple of kids are bothering grandpa, who just wants to read the paper. "OK, one last time!" he agrees. Giving them a mock fierce look, he grabs his sweater from the sofa and pulls it over his head. Suddenly, he looks forty years younger. The younger kid says in an awestruck tone: "Grandpa, do it again please..." Refresh the faded, with Coloria.

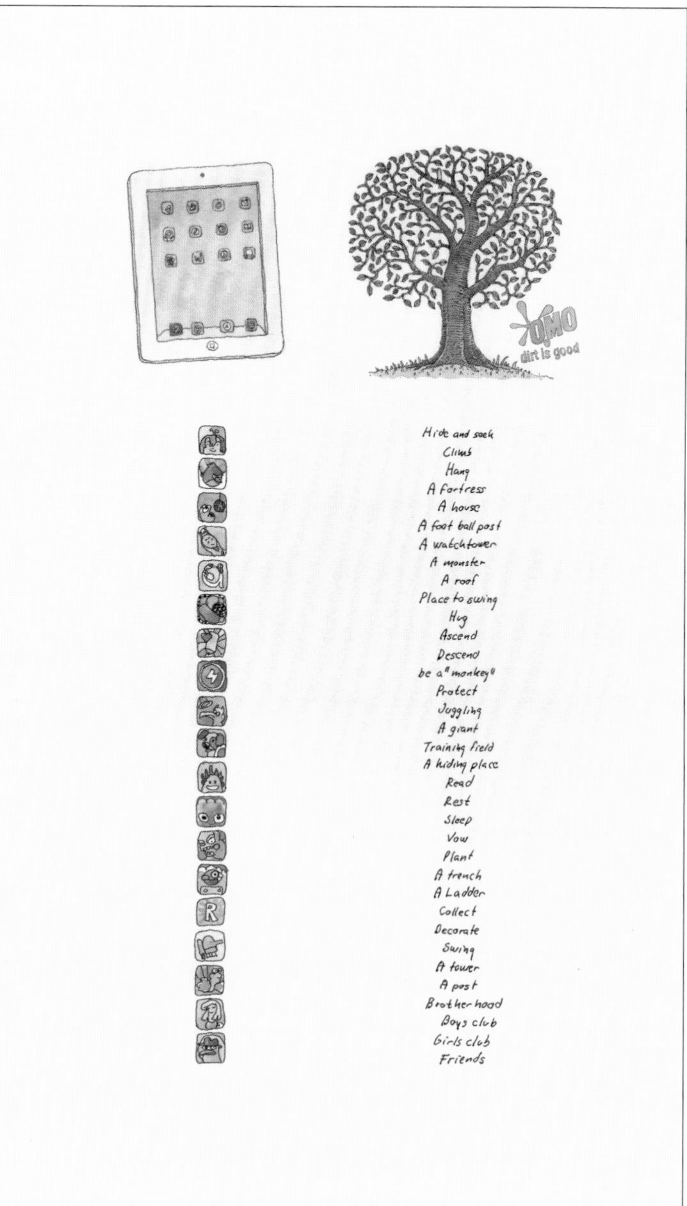

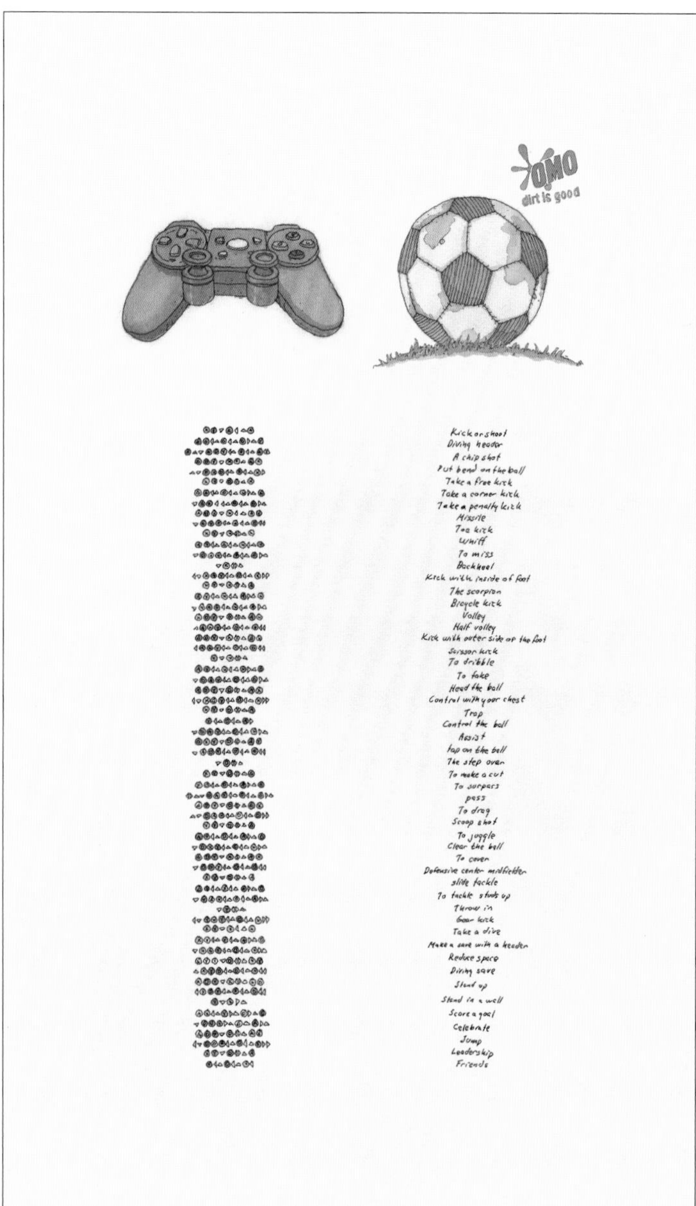

Household Maintenance

Agency Lowe, Ho Chi Minh City
CCO Jose Miguel Sokoloff
Executive CD Carlos Camacho
Copywriter Carlos Camacho
Art Directors Juan Sebastian Otoya
Kumkum Fernando
Illustrator Mattias Adolfsson
Advertiser Unilever, OMO detergent, "Versus"

Agency	Impact BBDO, Dubai
Creative Director	Fadi Yaish
Copywriter	Tomas Almuna
Art Directors	Gonzalo Palavecino Sergio Araya
Production	Garrigosa Studio, Barcelona
Agency Producer	Clarisse Mar Wai May
Advertiser	Vape, Insect Killer, “Widows”

Agency	Lowe, Ho Chi Minh City
Executive CDs	Carlos Camacho Jaime Duque
Copywriter	Carlos Camacho
Art Directors	Jaime Duque
Photographer	Ale Burset
Production	Dragon Films
Producer	Jose Fernando Mafla
Advertiser	Unilever, OMO detergent, “Blackboards”

Agency	FWK, Buenos Aires
Creative Director	Christian Oneto Gaona
Copywriter	Matías Abbondio
Art Director	Matías Fernández
Photographer	Matías Posti
Advertiser	Asurín, Trash Bags, "Chef"

Agency	Herezie, Paris
Executive CD	Andrea Stillacci
Creative Directors	Sébastien Boutebel Jean-Laurent Py
Art Buyer	Johanna Warlus
Production Manager	Capucine Lhermitte
Advertiser	Eparcyl, Toilet Cleaner, "The Dog"

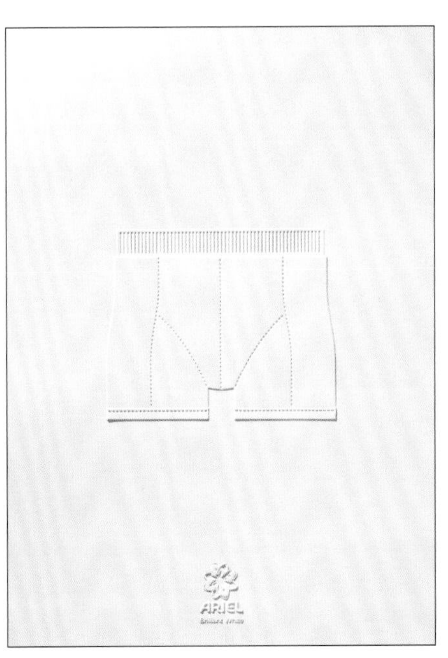

Agency	Saatchi & Saatchi, Dubai
Executive CD	Richard Copping
Copywriter	Sam Hughes
Art Director	Raja Rizkallah
Photographer	Daniel Botezatu
Production	Ali Zayat
Advertiser	Procter & Gamble, Ariel, "White Posters"

Public Interest

Public Interest

Sponsored by euronews

Agency Forsman & Bodenfors, Gothenburg
Copywriter Marcus Hägglöf
Art Directors Agnes Stenberg-Schentz, Johanna Hofman-Bang
Agency Producer Magnus Kennhed
Graphic Design Nina Andersson
Production Acne, Stockholm
Film Directors Torbjörn Martin, Tomas Skoging
Producers Petur Mogensen, Fredrik Skoglund
DOP Christian Haag
Post Production The Chimney Pot, Stockholm
Advertiser UNICEF, "The Good Guys Christmas"

Euronews granted free advertising space to the winner of this category. We're at The House of Goodness. "That's my story," says Jesus, closing the Bible. Listening are Mother Theresa and Ghandi. But who's this other guy? "Now you go," says Jesus. "How did you get here?" He is utterly normal, from his upbringing ("well, I was the middle child, which was pretty rough at times") to his sabbatical year ("partying and surfing") to his non-career. But he did click on a Unicef banner, enabling him to save children's lives. Doing good has never been so easy. Buy your Christmas gifts at Unicef.

Agency	Leo Burnett Tailor Made, Sao Paulo
Creative Directors	Marcelo Reis Guilherme Jahara Vinicius Stanzione Alessandro Bernardo
Copywriter	Christian Fontana
Art Director	Marcelo Rizerio
Photographer	Ale Catan
Advertiser	Fiat, “Don't Make-Up And Drive”

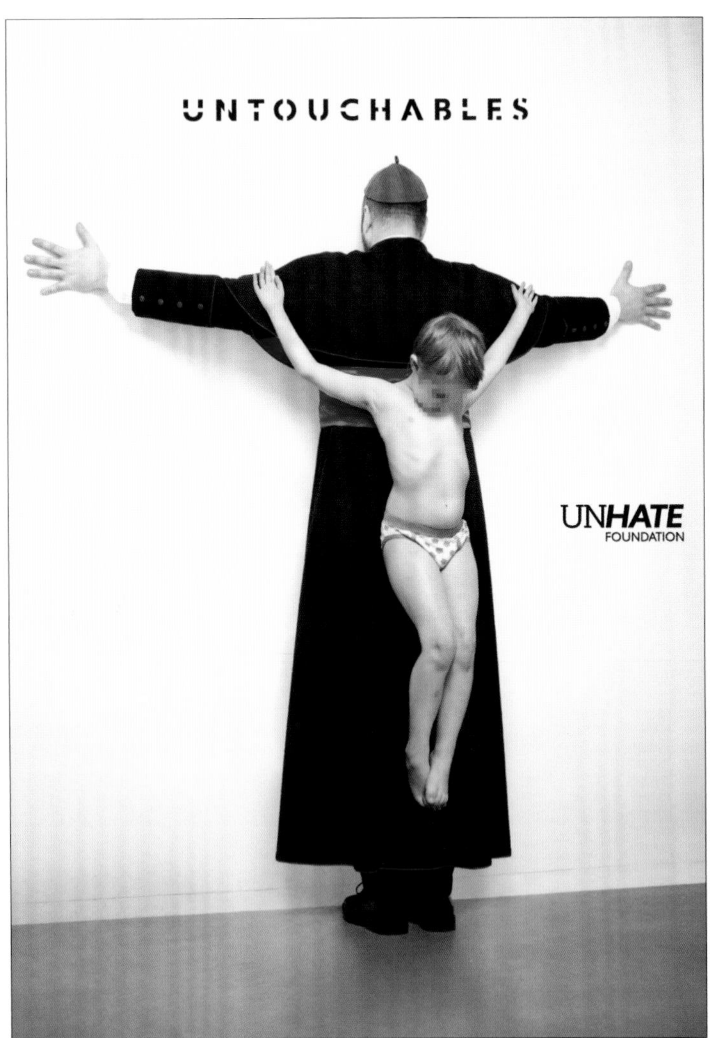

Agency	Fabrica, Treviso
Creative Director	Erik Ravelo
Copywriter	Erik Ravelo
Art Director	Erik Ravelo
Photographers	Erik Ravelo Enrico Bossan
Production	Fabrica, Treviso
Graphic Design	Erik Ravelo
Digital Artwork	Erik Ravelo
Advertiser	UnHate Foundation, "Untouchables"

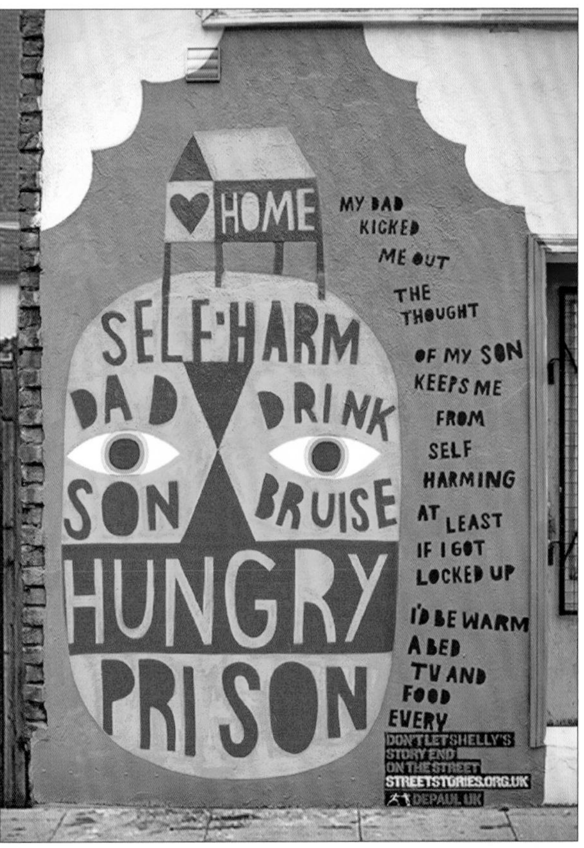

Agency Publicis, London
Executive CD Andy Bird
Copywriter Steve Moss
Art Director Jolyon Finch
Photographer Mark Wesley
Agency Producers Sarah Clifford, Sam Holmes
Producer Colin Hickson
Director/Editor Doug Gillen
Artists Ben Slow, Best Ever, Josh Jeavons, David Shillinglaw
Senior Digital Project Manager Mike Fitzgerald
Head of Technology David Clarke
Digital ECD Pavlos Themistocleous
Head of Design Richie Wykes
Advertiser DePaul UK, "Street Stories"

Homeless charity DePaul UK teamed up with street artists to create illustrations telling the real stories of people who live on the street – and how they got there. Screen prints of the paintings were available for purchase on the charity's site, with proceeds going towards safe accommodation for the homeless.

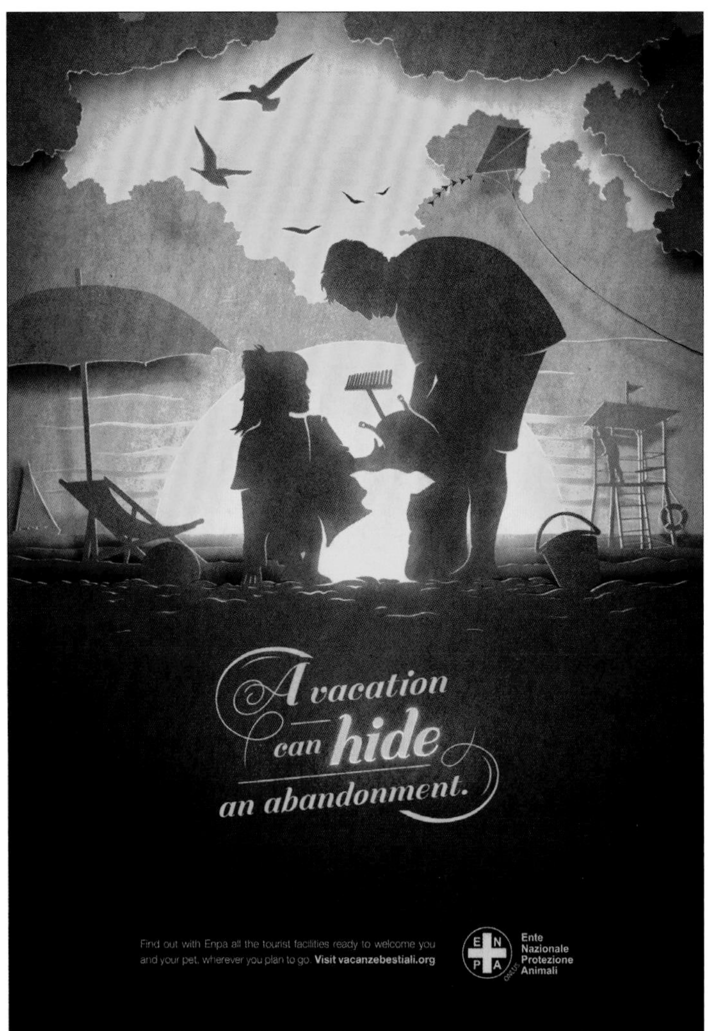

Agency	Cheil Italy, Milan
Creative Director	Alessandro Sironi
Copywriter	Livia Aurora Cappelletti
Art Director	Federico Mariani
Illustrator	Federico Mariani
Digital Artwork	Hyperactive Studio, Milan
Advertiser	Enpa Onlus, Animal protection Association, "Vacation"

Other people make mistakes
Slow down

Agency Clemenger BBDO, Wellington
Creative Directors Philip Andrew, Brigid Alkema
Copywriter Emily Beautrais
Art Directors Emily Beautrais, Philip Andrew
Production Finch, Auckland
Film Director Derin Seale
Producer Karen Bryson
Advertiser New Zealand Transport Agency, "Mistakes"

A car emerges from a side road. Another speeds towards it. The crash will be horrific. But suddenly time stops. The drivers leave their cars to confront one another. "You just pulled out!" says the speeder, "I don't have time to stop! Maybe if I was going a bit slower…" The other driver begs: "Please – I've got my boy in the back." The first man looks helpless. "I'm going too fast. I'm sorry." They return to their cars, brace themselves. Impact. Other people make mistakes. Slow down.

Agency DDB Paris
Executive CD Alexandre Hervé
Creative Director Alexander Kalchev
Copywriter Alexander Kalchev
Art Director Alexander Kalchev
Production Woodblock, Berlin
Film Director Polynoid, Berlin
DOP Tanja Häring
Music World Gang
Advertiser Greenpeace, "New Bees"

This beautifully filmed spot looks like an ad from the future. The soft-toned narration introduces us to "new bees". Thanks to these little marvels of robotics, collapsing honeybee colonies are a thing of the past. They are solar powered, able to defend themselves against predators, and programmed to be harmless to humans. "New bees – the future is already here." In fact, the film is a warning from Greenpeace about the impact of pesticides. Should we create a new world? Or save our own?

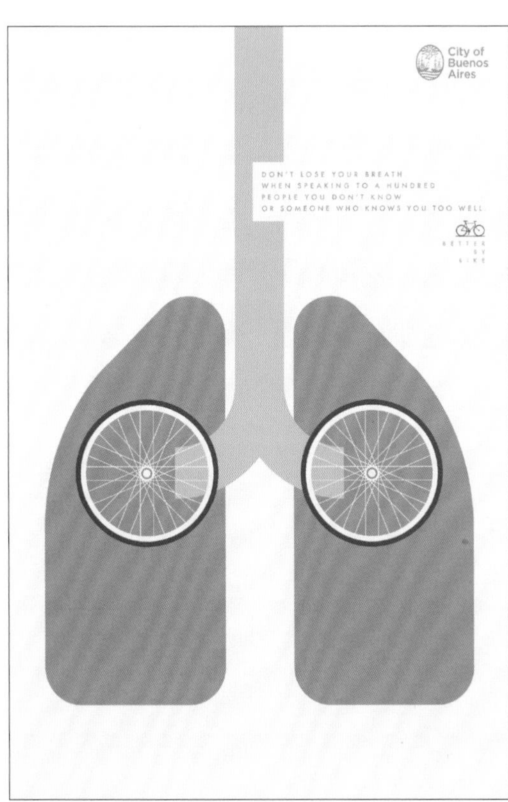

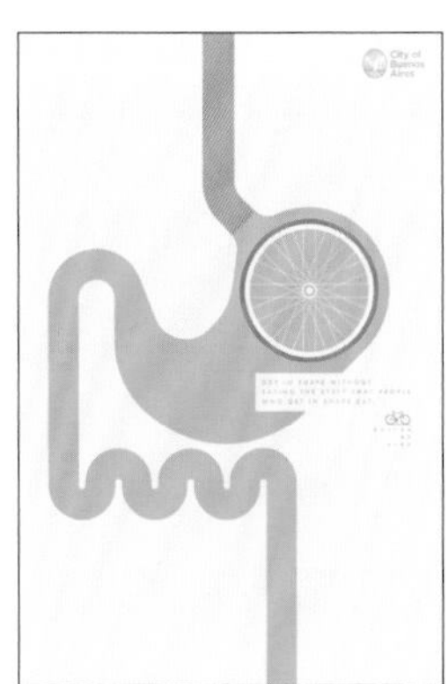

Agency	Synergy Media, Columbus
Creative Directors	Marcus Kon Luke Montgomery
Production	Synergy Media, Dallas
Film Director	Luke Montgomery
Producer	Marcus Kon
Advertiser	FCKH8.com, "Potty-Mouthed Princesses"

Little girls dressed up as princesses: what could be cuter? Except suddenly the girls begin swearing like troopers. "I'm not some ****ing helpless princess in distress, I'm pretty ****ing powerful and ready for success!" The film draws attention to gender stereotypes and sexism. Pay inequality and the fact that one in every five women will be sexually assaulted should be more shocking than a little girl saying the F-word, it points out. Support women by shopping for feminist slogan T-shirts and other merchandise on FCKH8.com.

Agency	La Comunidad, Buenos Aires
Creative Directors	José Mollá Joaquín Mollá Ramiro Raposo Fernando Sosa
Copywriters	Nicolás Larroquet Adrian Rey Aaron Zimroth
Art Director	Dante Zamboni
Illustrator	Guillermo Muñoz
Advertiser	City of Buenos Aires, "Better by Bike"

Agency	Lowe China, Shanghai
Creative Directors	Norman Tan Zeng Qiang
Copywriters	Cherry Wang Willow Yang
Art Directors	Kidd Zhang Hans Han
Photographer	Yang Tan
Production	JT Ideas, Shanghai
Film Director	Eun Taek Cha
Advertiser	Buick, “Human Traffic Signs Campaign”

Agency	Lowe China, Shanghai
Creative Directors	Norman Tan Zeng Qiang
Copywriters	Cherry Wang Willow Yang
Art Directors	Kidd Zhang Hans Han
Cinematographer	Jung Ho Leem
Production	Locus/A New life, Seoul
Film Director	Eun Taek Cha
Advertiser	Buick, “Human Traffic Signs Campaign”

The victims of accidents hold up the traffic signs that could have saved them – if they or the drivers had been paying attention. Traffic signs are there for a reason. Obey the rules. The film was supported by a poster campaign.

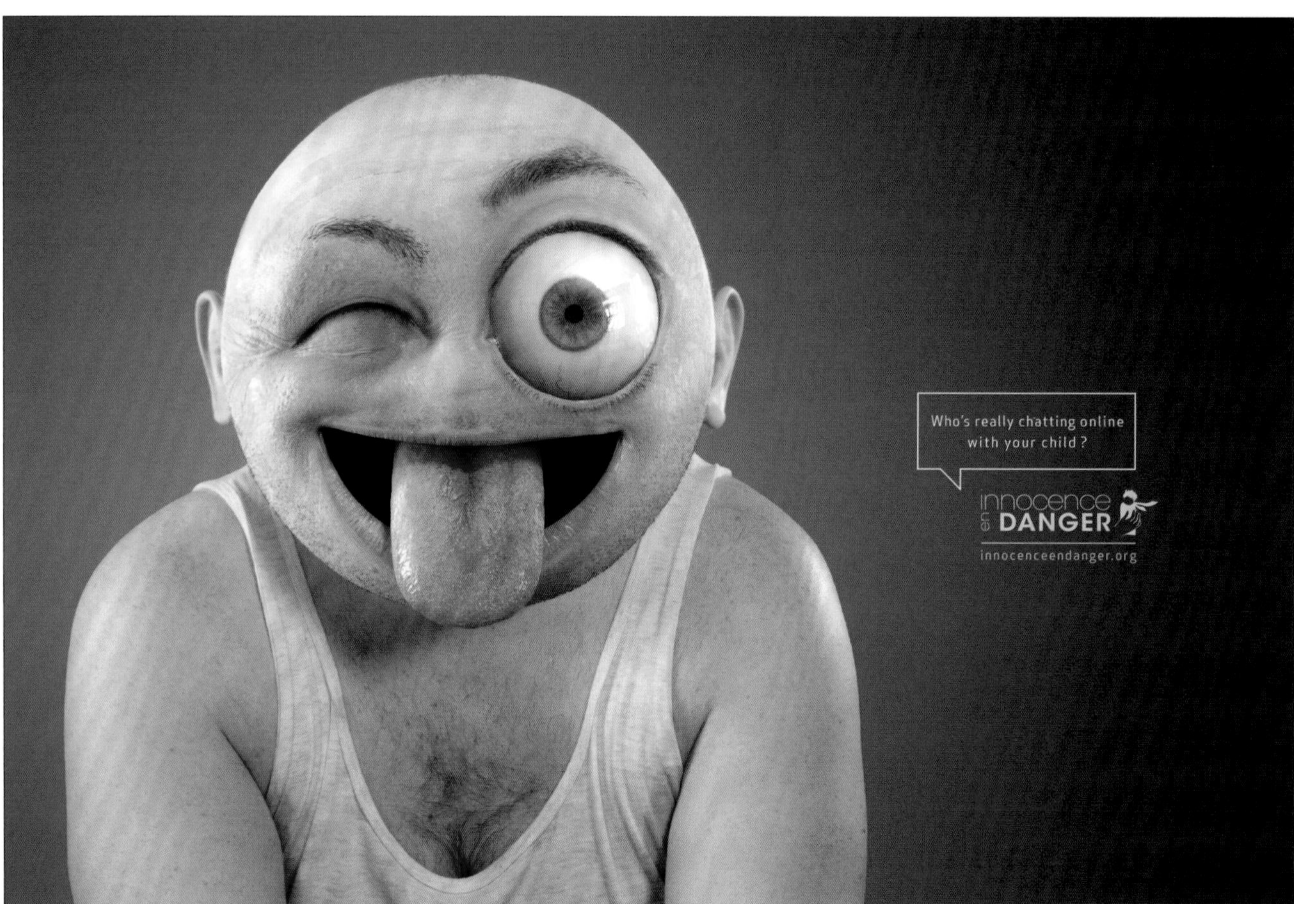

Agency	Rosapark, Paris
Creative Directors	Mark Forgan Jamie Standen
Copywriter	Jamie Standen
Art Director	Mark Forgan
Photographer	Baptiste Massé
Production	Mécanique Générale, Paris
Producer	Emilie Rouault
Agency Producer	Chloé Bartoletti
Illustrator	Baptiste Massé
Typographer	Paul Henri Masson
Digital Artwork	Baptiste Massé
Advertiser	Innocence in Danger, "Emoticons"

Agency	BDDP Unlimited, Paris
Creative Director	Olivier Moine
Copywriter	Caroline Laumont
Art Director	Aurore De Sousa
Photographer	Hervé Plumet
Art Buyer	Marie Ferrara Elise Kubler
Advertiser	Abbé Pierre Foundation, "Find A Future"

Agency	DLVBBDO, Milan
Executive CDs	Stefania Siani Federico Pepe
Copywriter	Matteo Maggiore
Art Director	Valerio Mangiafico
Illustrator	Riccardo Corda
Advertiser	ASA, "Condom Saves Life"

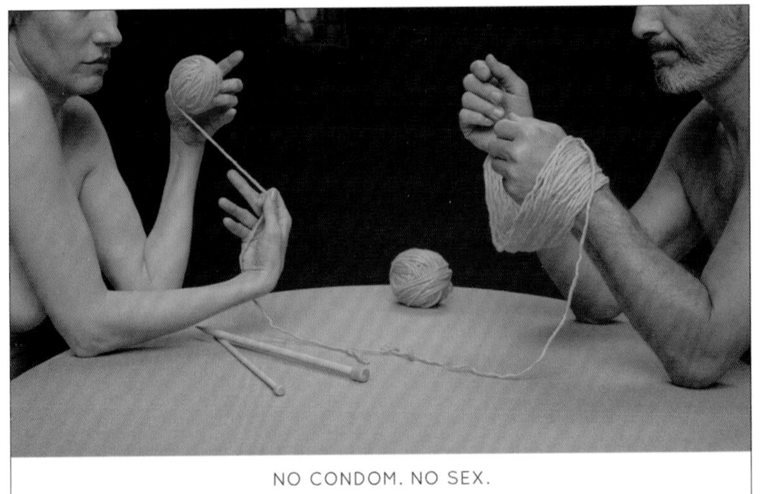

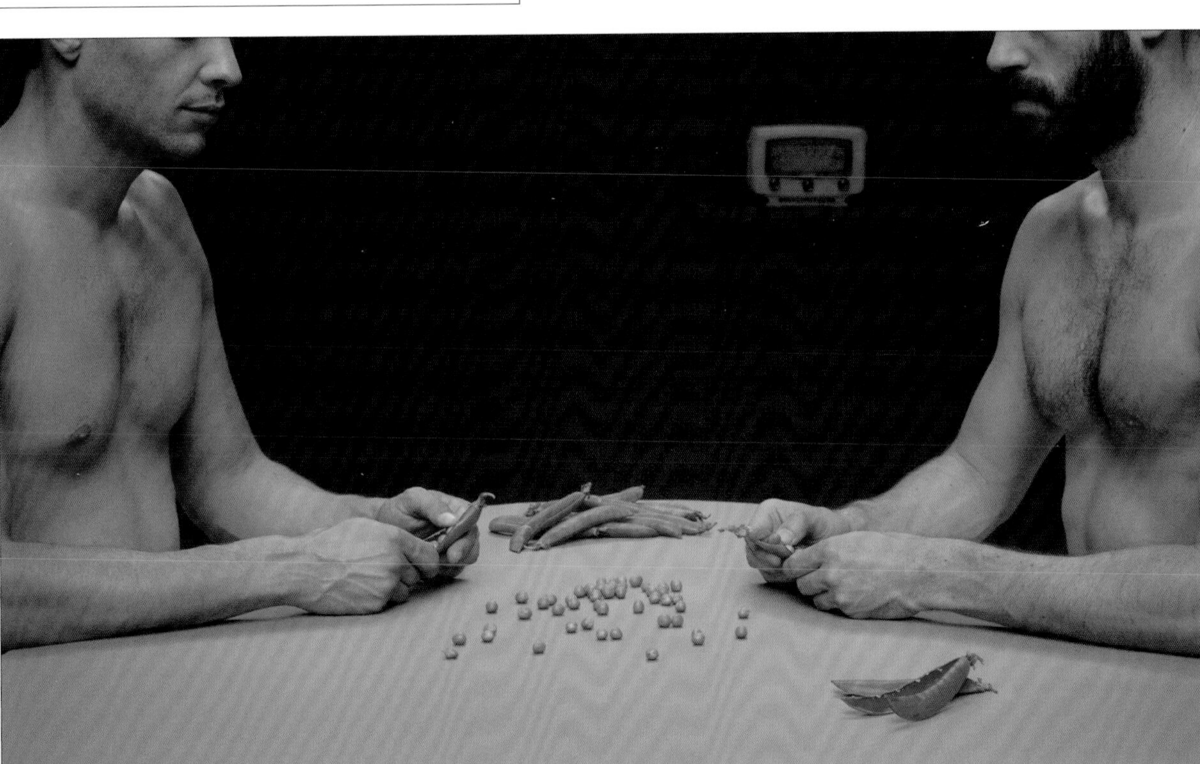

Agency	TBWA\Paris
Creative Director	Jean-François Goize
Copywriter	Antoine Colin
Art Director	Marianne Fonferrier
Photographer	Aurélien Chauvaud
Art Buyer	Julie Champin
Advertiser	AIDES, "No condom, no sex"

29.05.2006
Ablikim Abdiriyim

Political meeting
Arrested with family
Police station
Beaten by police
Secret trial
9 yr sentence
Prison cell
Tortured
Comatose twice

26.03.2008
Dhondup Wangchen

Taken
Arrested
Detention Centre
No trial or charges
Soundproof room
Tied to chair
Beaten in head
Starved
Sleep deprived
Still awaiting trial

04.08.2011
Ales Bialiatski

Political Protest
Bank account blocked
Property seized
Unfair trial
4 1/2 year sentence
Belarus Penal Colony
Solitary confinement
Intimidated
No visitations

11.07.2006
Ebrima B. Manneh

Leaving work
Arrested
Disappeared

18.09.2001
Aster Fissehatsion

Sleeping in bed
Taken by police
Unknown location
No charge or trial
Disappeared

29.06.2007
Johan Teterissa

Peaceful protest
Police van
Police station
Whipped with cables
Snooker ball in mouth
Beaten with guns
Unfair trial
Batu Prison
Overcrowded cell
Concrete bed floor
Denied medical care

03.02.2014
Yevgeny Vitishko

Arrested for
swearing at a bus stop
Unfair trial
3yr sentence
Penal colony

Agency BDDP Unlimited, Paris
Creative Director Olivier Moine
Copywriters Louise Mussot
Simon Delmas
Art Directors Fabien Nunez
Thomas Jouffrit
Advertiser Solidarités International, "The River"

Agency Leo Burnett, London
Creative Directors Adam Tucker
Hugh Todd
Charlie Martin
Copywriter Blake Waters
Art Director Will Thacker
Photographers Andy Rudak
Dirk Rees
Graphic Design Marc Donaldson
Advertiser Amnesty International, "Departure Board"

Monday, 5.30pm. Passengers at London's busy Waterloo Station were surprised when the departure boards began showing the real stories of people who were unable to get home – because they had been imprisoned by repressive regimes for expressing their views. Amnesty International asked commuters to join a petition and share the horrific stories. Within hours, nearly 42,000 people had pledged their support. #helpgethemhome

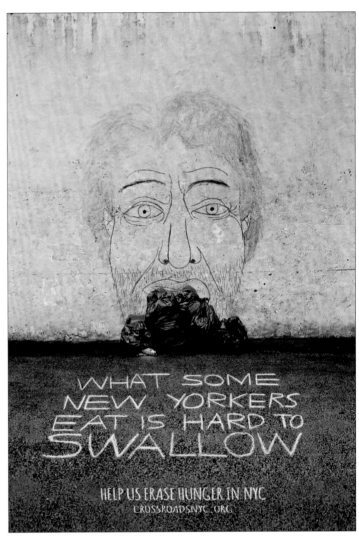

Agency	Saatchi & Saatchi Wellness, New York
CCO	Kathy Delaney
Copywriter	Scott Carlton
Art Director	Carolyn Gargano
Illustrator	Mike Perry
Photographer	Nicolas Maloof
Advertiser	Crossroads Community, "Streetfare Campaign"

Agency	Leo Burnett, Sydney
Copywriter	Guy Futcher
Art Director	Brendan Donnelly
Production	Illusion, Bangkok
Producers	Somsak Pairew Kitidej Rattanasuvansri
Agency Producer	Jeremy Devilliers
Illustrators	Surachai Puthikulangkura Supachai U-Rairat
Typographer	Jason Young
CCO	Andy DiLallo
Advertiser	WWF, "Poachers"

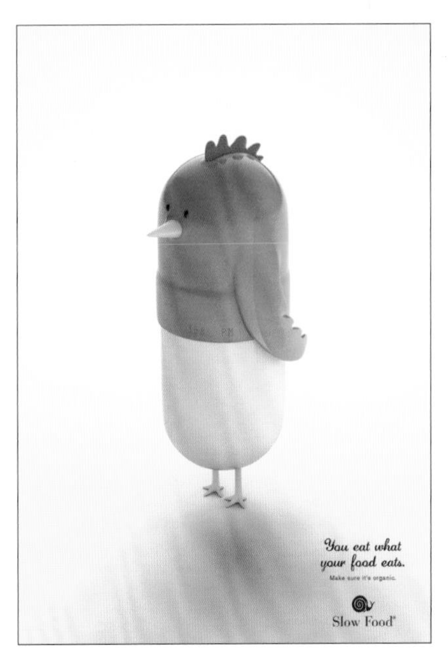

Agency	Leo Burnett, Zurich
Creative Directors	Peter Brönnimann Christian Bircher
Copywriter	Christian Stüdi
Art Director	Pedro Moosmann
Agency Producer	Erasmo Palomba
Illustrator	Linus Schneider Pixelprinz, Zurich
Advertiser	Slow Food, "Animal Pills"

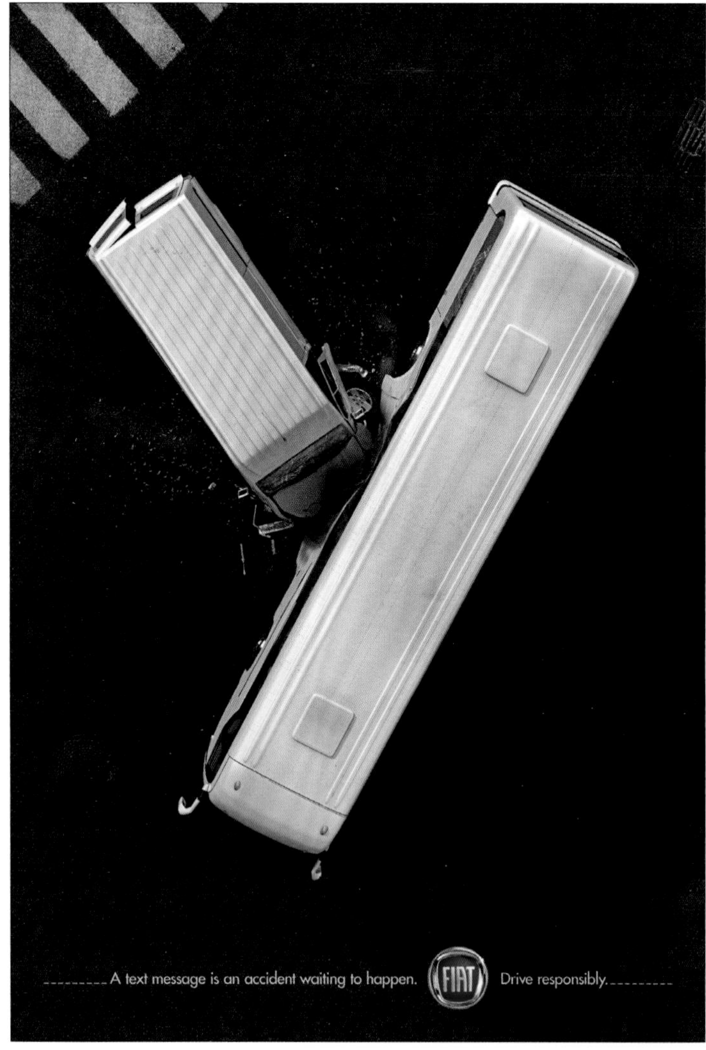

Agency	Leo Burnett Tailor Made, São Paulo
Creative Directors	Marcelo Reis Guilherme Jahara Marcio Juniot Pedro Utzeri
Copywriter	Rafael Genu
Art Directors	Pedro Utzer Luis Paulo Gatti
Illustrator	Big Studios
Advertiser	Fiat, "Letter Crashes"

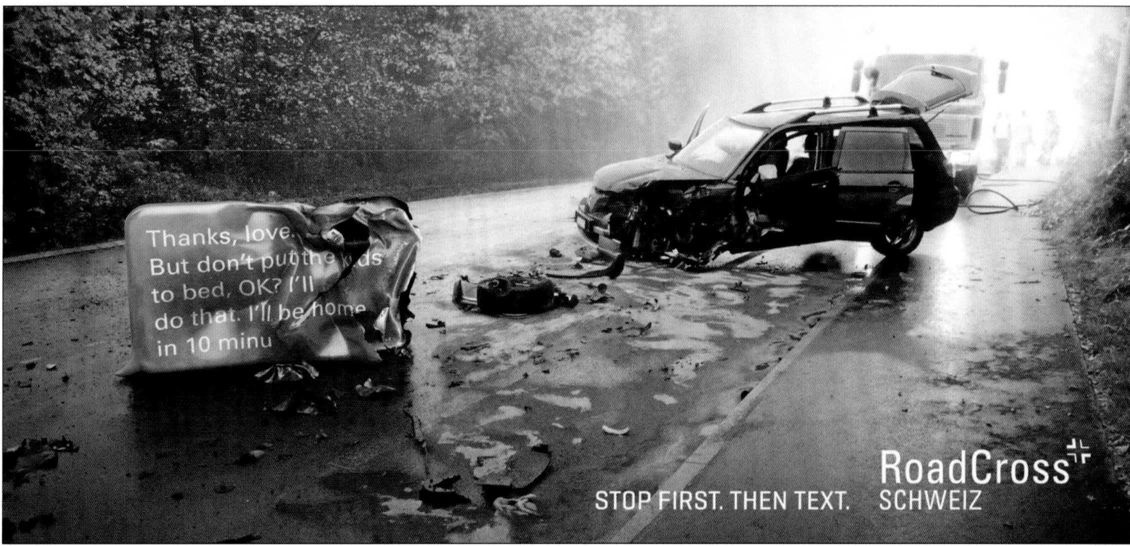

Agency	Wirz/BBDO, Zurich
Executive CD	Philipp Skrabal
Creative Director	Andi Portmann
Copywriter	Wolfgang Bark
Art Director	Isabelle Bühler
Photographer	Markus Heinzer
Art Buyer	Fabienne Huwyler
CGI/3D	Tobias Stierli
Advertiser	RoadCross, "Stop First Then Text"

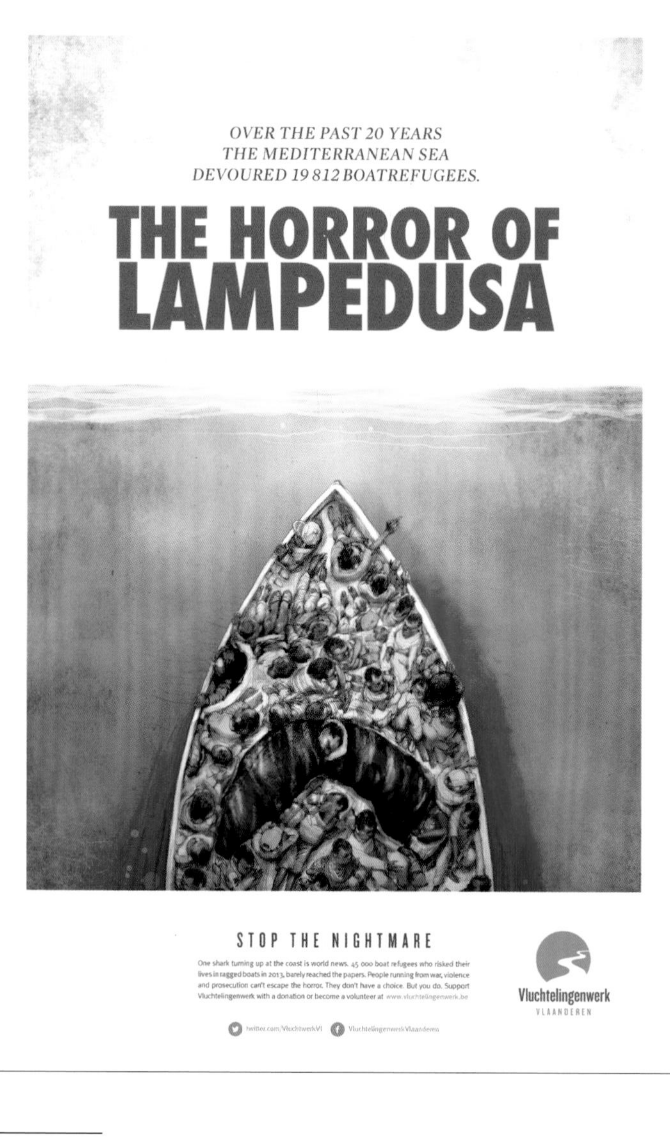

Agency	Cogent Elliott, London
Creative Director	Richard Payne
Copywriter	Craig Wood
Art Director	Simon Fones
Advertiser	Staffordshire Retired Police Dogs Fund, "Teeth"

Agency	Absoluut, Leuven
Creative Director	Ronny Schildermans
Copywriter	Kathleen Bogaerts
Art Director	Frederik De Vlaminck
Illustrator	Paul Van Der Steen
Graphic Design	Frederik De Vlaminck
Advertiser	Vluchtelingenwerk Vlaanderen, "Jaws"

BECAUSE YOU'RE ABOUT

BECAUSE IT'S SOMEBODY'S

Why do you drink?
Test your drinking habits on alcoholprofile.se

IQ

Agency	Forsman & Bodenfors, Gothenburg
Copywriter	Jacob Nelson
Art Director	Ted Mellström
Designers	Ellinor Bjarnolf Axel Söderlund
Production	F&B Factory
Advertiser	IQ, "Because Life is Good"

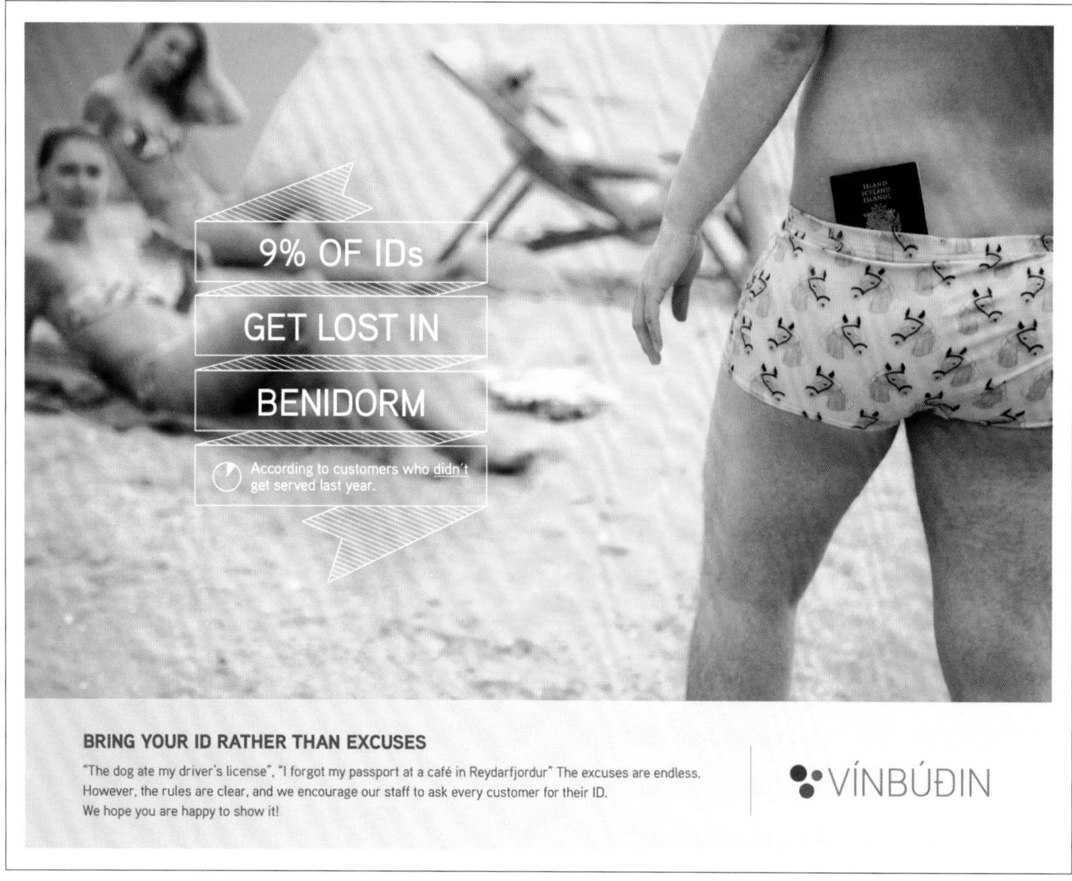

Agency	ENNEMM, Reykjavík
Creative Director	Jón Árnason
Copywriter	Örn Úlfar Sævarsson
Art Director	Hjörvar Harðarson
Photographer	Börkur Sigþórsson
Production	ENNEMM
Advertiser	Vínbúðin Liquor Store, "Bring Your I.D. Rather Than Excuses"

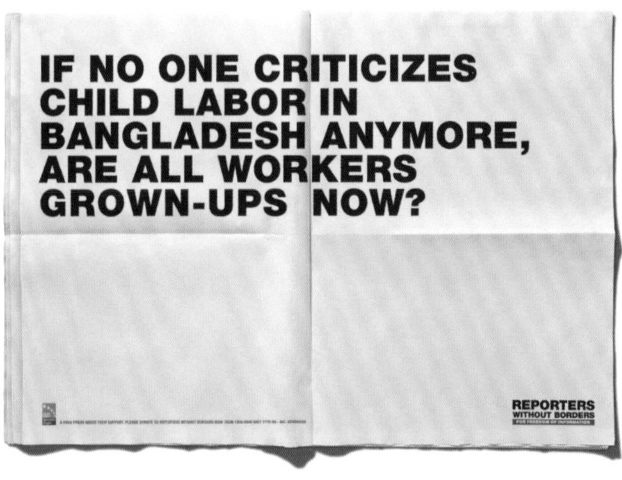
IF NO ONE CRITICIZES
CHILD LABOR IN
BANGLADESH ANYMORE,
ARE ALL WORKERS
GROWN-UPS NOW?
REPORTERS
WITHOUT BORDERS

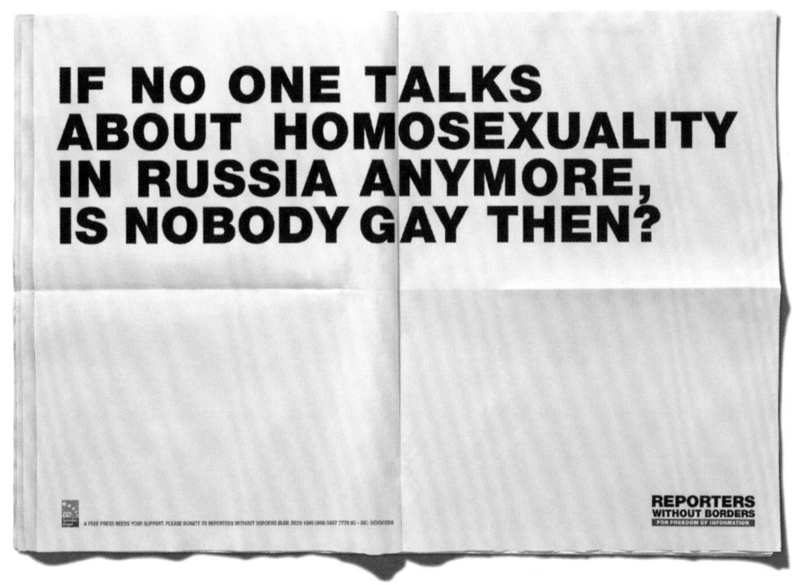
IF NO ONE TALKS
ABOUT HOMOSEXUALITY
IN RUSSIA ANYMORE,
IS NOBODY GAY THEN?
REPORTERS
WITHOUT BORDERS
FOR FREEDOM OF INFORMATION

IF NO ONE REPORTS ON
THE WAR IN SYRIA ANYMORE,
DOES THAT MEAN THERE'S
PEACE NOW?

A FREE PRESS NEEDS YOUR SUPPORT. PLEASE DONATE TO REPORTERS WITHOUT BORDERS IBAN: DE26 1009 0000 5667 7770 80 – BIC: BEVODEBB

REPORTERS
WITHOUT BORDERS
FOR FREEDOM OF INFORMATION

Agency	Leo Burnett, Frankfurt
CCO	Andreas Pauli
Creative Director	Hans-Juergen Kaemmerer
Copywriters	Annina Boettcher Alina Hetzmann Jens Paasen Fridjof Vieth
Art Director	Hans-Juergen Kaemmerer
Photographer	Michael Meisen
Agency Producer	Netti Weber
Advertiser	Reporters Without Borders, "Questions"

NOTHING IS
MORE HORRIFYING
THAN HALLOWEEN
WITHOUT CANDY

Crest + Oral-B

 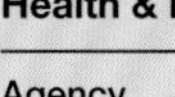

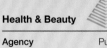

Agency	Publicis Kaplan Thaler, New York	**Executive Producers**	Brian Latt Danielle Peretz Oliver Fuselier Dustin Callif
CCO	Rob Feakins	**Producer**	Luke Mccullough
ECD	David Corr	**Agency Producer**	Noelle Nimrichter
Creative Directors	Rob Feakins David Corr Tony Gomes	**Editor**	John Piccolo
Copywriter	George Logothetis	**Advertiser**	Procter & Gamble - Crest & Oral-B, “Halloween Treats Gone Wrong”
Art Director	Xavier Rodon		
Production	Tool Of North America, Santa Monica		
Film Director	JJ Adler		

Kids traditionally demand treats at Halloween – otherwise they have the right to play a trick. But this year the trick is on them, as these sweet-faced American youngsters take part in a focus group in which they're asked to test “healthy treats” like “veggie fruit chews” and “artichoke buttercups”. They cringe and gag – one of them even throws up – and eventually turn on their tormentor. “I want candy!” Nothing is more horrifying than Halloween without candy. Thank goodness for dental care from Crest and Oral-B.

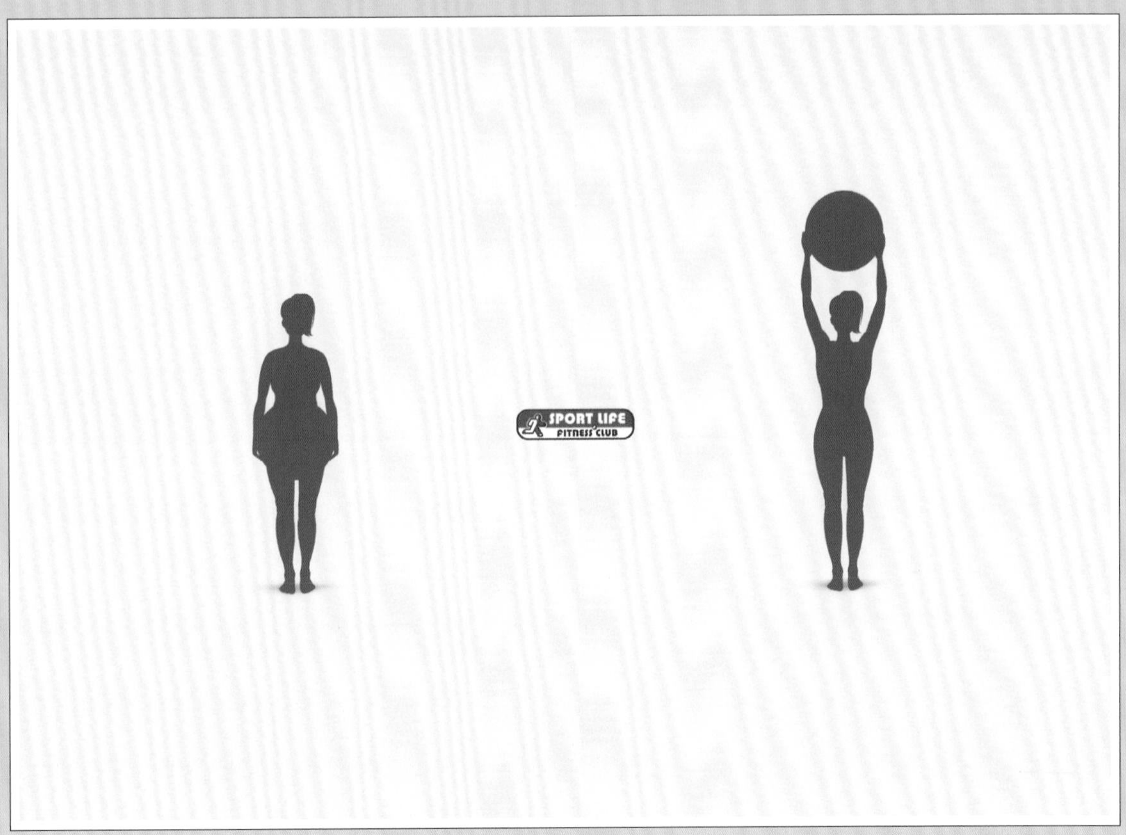

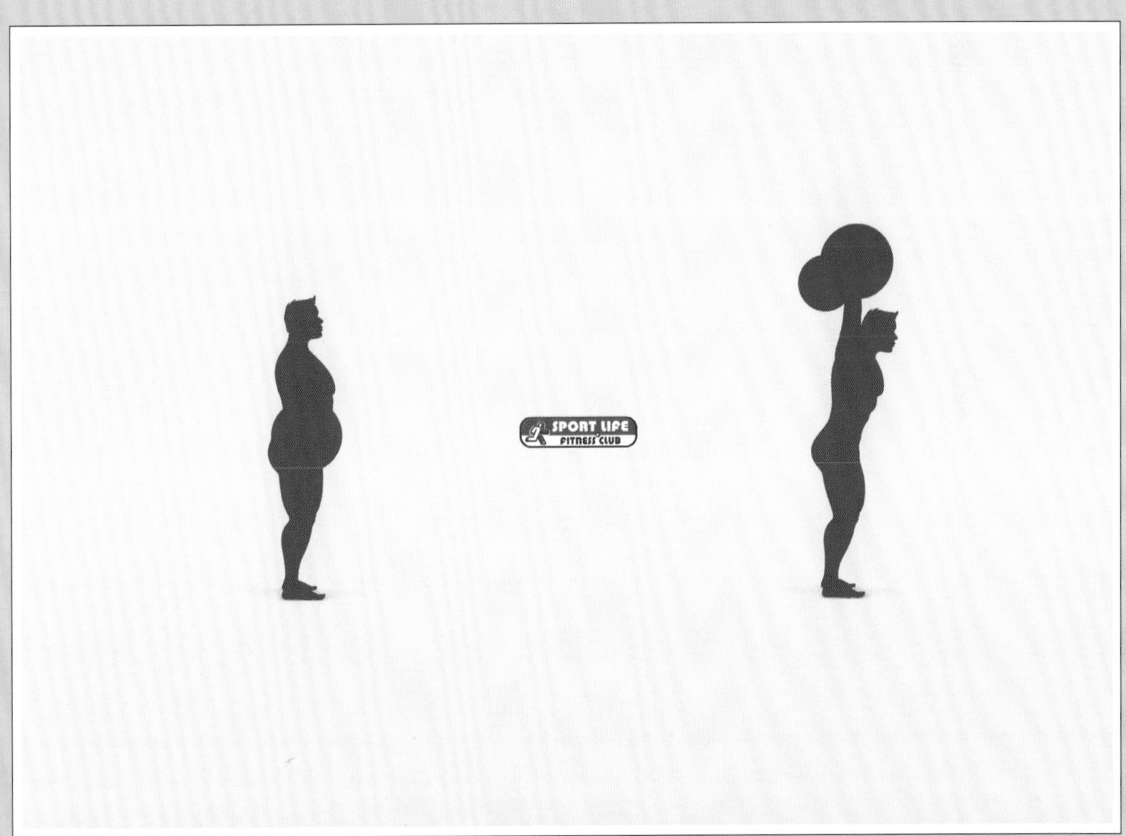

Agency Geometry Global, Kiev
Executive CD Andrew Ushakov
Associate CD Nadia Trikoz
Art Director Sergey Yaroslavtsev
Designer Valentyn Bielienkov
Advertiser Sport Life Fitness Club, "One-Two-Three"

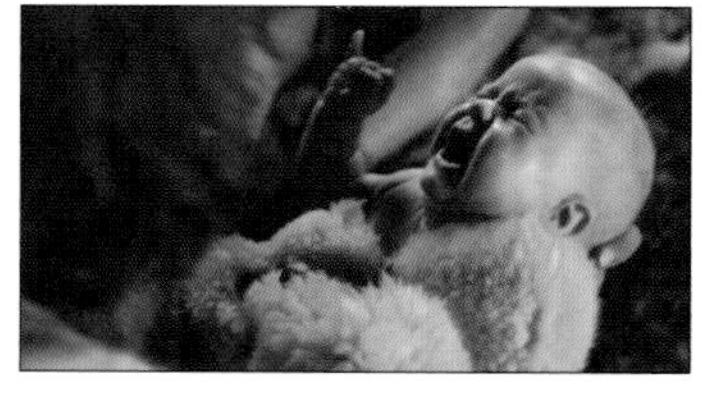

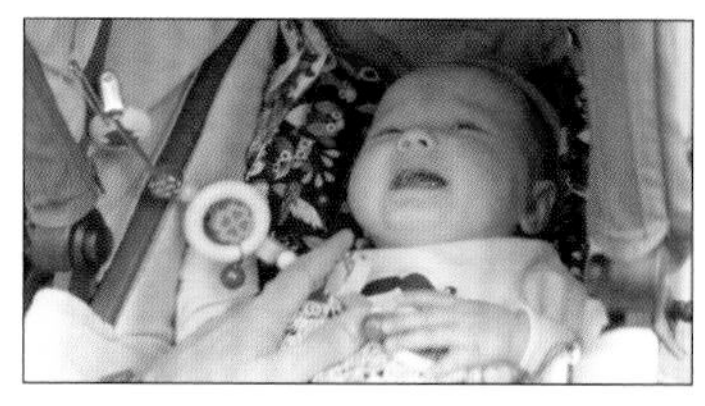

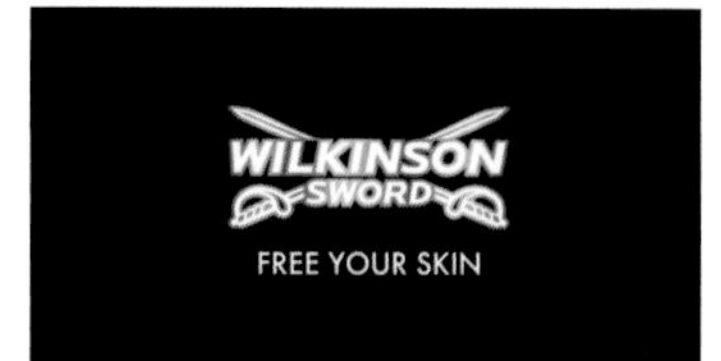

Agency	Labamba Agency, Hamburg
Creative Director	Felix Schulz
Production	Cobblestone Filmproduktion, Hamburg
Film Director	Robert Nylund
Producer	Pieter Lony
DOP	Peter Matjasko
Editor	Alex Kutka
Advertiser	Wilkinson Sword, "First Impression"

Starting in the Stone Age, we witness centuries of bearded men trying to comfort screaming babies. Right up until today's hipster era, the infants are terrified by the bristly faces of dads, grandfathers and other authority figures. Finally, we see a calm and happy baby – touching the smooth jaw of a clean-shaven dad. Free your skin, with Wilkinson Sword razors and blades.

Agency	TBWA\España, Madrid
Creative Directors	Juan Sánchez Guillermo Ginés
Copywriter	Carmen Panero
Art Director	Javier Somoano
Photographer	Gonzalo Puertas
Advertiser	L'Oréal, Vichy "Bald"

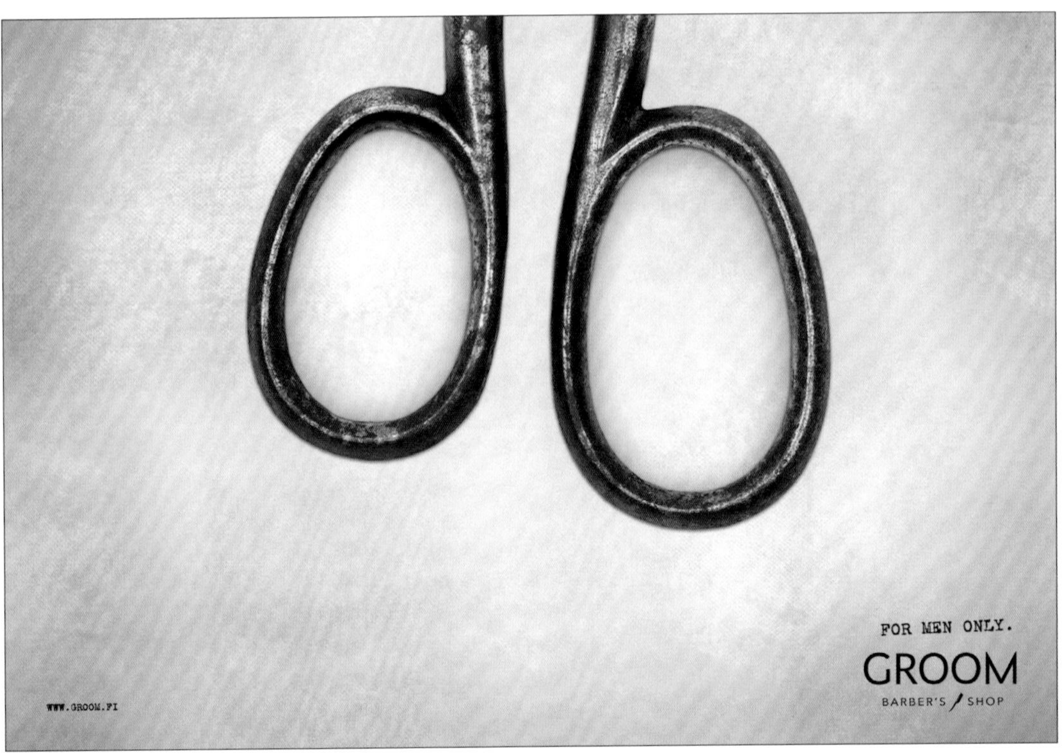

18 Farsta strand
Please move along
On the platform, digital screens were equipped with ultra sonic sensors

Agency	Zeeland, Helsinki
Copywriter	Jusa Valtonen
Art Director	Ari Kivi
Graphic Designer	Ari Kivi
Advertiser	Groom Barber Shop, "For Men Only"

Agency	Åkestam Holst, Stockholm
Creative Director	Andreas Ullenius
Copywriter	Mariette Glodeck
Art Director	Lars Baecklund
Digital Producer	Sofia Swedenborg
Graphic Designers	Lotta Person Jens Sjöbergh
Studio Assistant	Anne-Lie Karl
Production	STOPP/Family, Stockholm
Photographer	Elisabeth Frang
Advertiser	Apotek Hjärtat's, "Blowing in The Wind"

This Swedish subway installation looks like a standard image of a woman with beautiful hair. Then a train rushes into the station, and her locks are blown about by the breeze, just like those of the passengers on the platform. When her hair settles it looks windswept, but she remains lovely, thanks to Apotek Hjärtat's Apolosophy beauty products. The digital poster worked using a sound detector finely tuned to react to arriving trains.

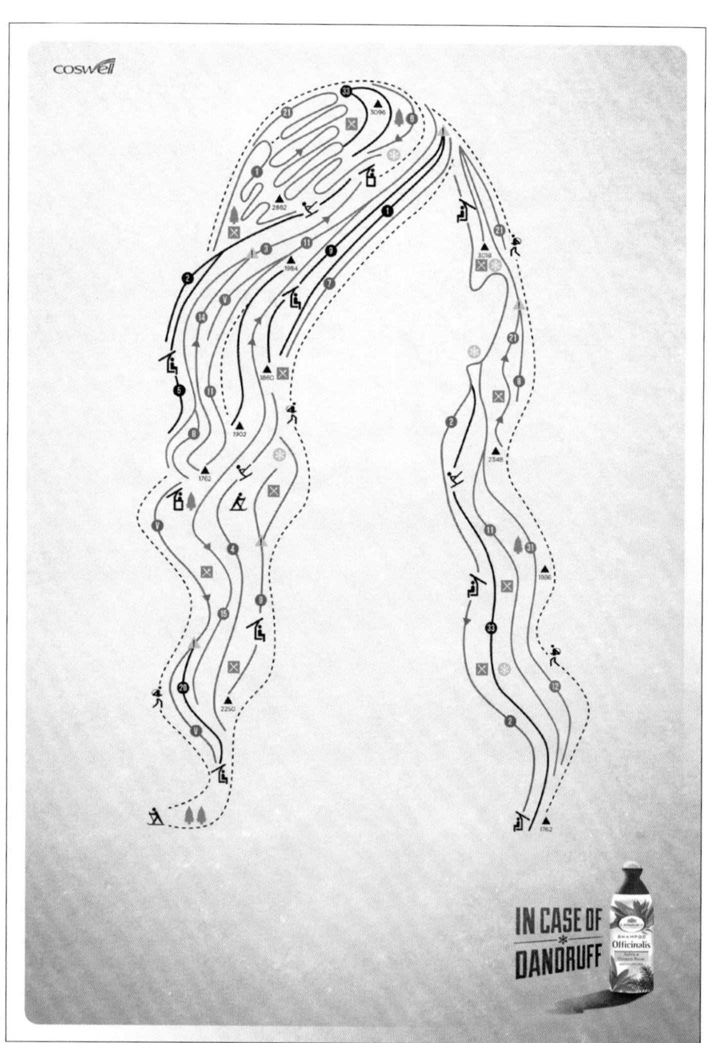

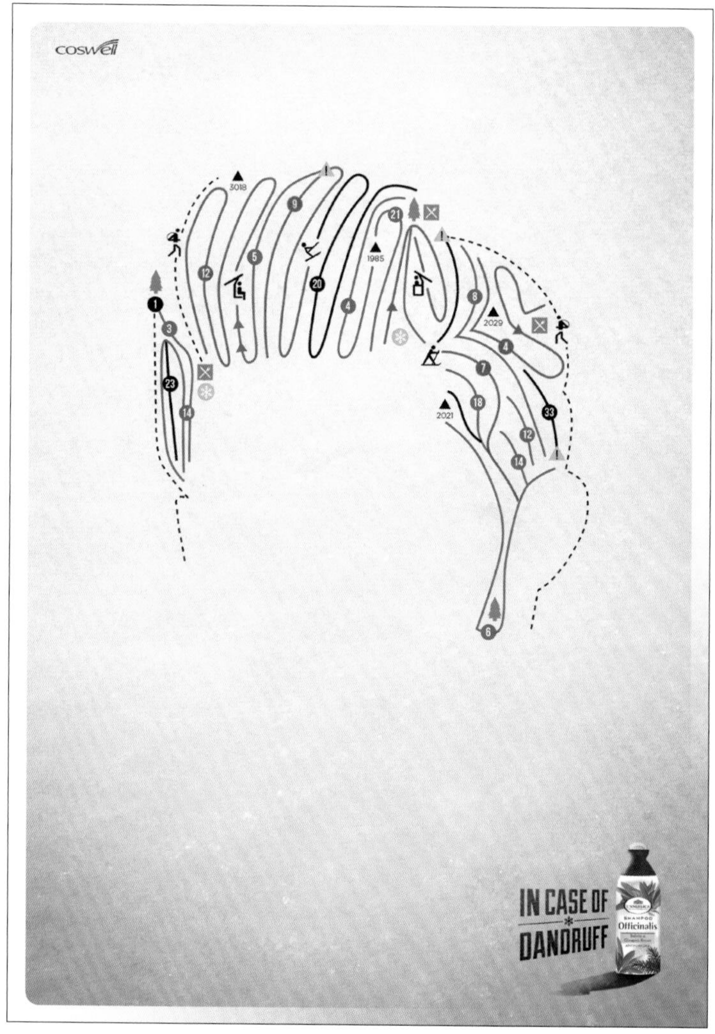

Agency	Leo Burnett, Milan
Executive CDs	Francesco Bozza Alessandro Antonini
Copywriter	Giovanni Salvaggio
Art Director	Luca Ghilino
Senior Art Director	Luca Ghilino
Illustrator	Azzurra Bacchetta
Advertiser	Coswell, "Ski Trail Map"

Agency	DDB Paris
Executive CD	Alexandre Hervé
Copywriter	Alexis Benoit
Art Director	Paul Kreitmann
Production	Carnibird, Paris
Film Director	Daniel Warwick
Producers	Juliette Demarescaux Thomas LePeutrec Adam Lyne
Agency Producer	Sophie Mégrous
DOP	Ross McLennan
Advertiser	Coty, "Playboy VIP"

This ad imagines all the things that might happen when a young guy's parents leave for the weekend and he throws a party. In the first version, a lot of people show up. In the second, a lot of people show up – including his parents, who missed their flight. Then everyone shows up – 88 years late. Next, due to a man-killing virus, only girls show up. Even better, only naked girls show up. Finally, nobody shows up apart from the one girl he wanted to see. Anything can happen when you wear Playboy VIP fragrance. Press to play.

Agency	DLVBBDO, Milan
Executive CDs	Stefania Siani Federico Pepe
Copywriter	Pasquale Frezza
Art Director	Nicola Cellemme
Production	BRW, Milan
Film Director	Alessio Fava
Agency Producer	Marijana Vukomanovic
Advertiser	Marionnaud, "Clap"

A women is chasing a fly around her apartment. She pounces and slaps her hands together. The buzzing stops – she's killed the little menace! But when she uncups her hands, the buzzing begins again. After several unsuccessful attempts, we realise that her hands are so soft they can't even squash a fly. Ultra soft hands, thanks to Marionnaud skincare products.

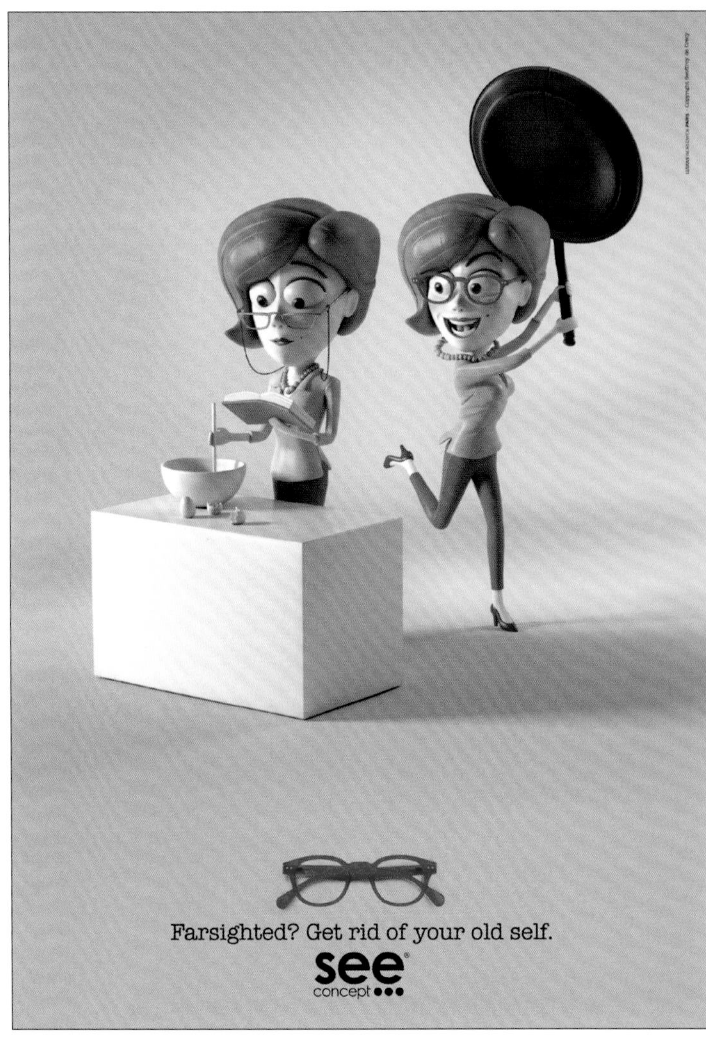

Agency	Havas Paris
Creative Director	Christophe Coffre
Copywriter	Pierre-Louis Messager
Art Director	Guillaume Fillion
Agency Producer	Christine Meneux
3D Illustrator	Geoffroy de Crécy
Advertiser	See Concept, "Farsighted? Get Rid Of Your Old Self"

NOT EVERYONE'S THAT DISTINCTIVE
PRESCRIPTION GLASSES
EYEZONE

NOT EVERYONE'S THAT DISTINCTIVE
PRESCRIPTION GLASSES
EYEZONE

NOT EVERYONE'S THAT DISTINCTIVE
EYEZONE

Agency	BPG/Bates, Dubai
Chief Creative Officer	Leslie James
Creative Group Head	Pushkar Patange
Associate CD	Mriganka Kalita
Advertiser	Rivoli Eyezone, "Guess Who"

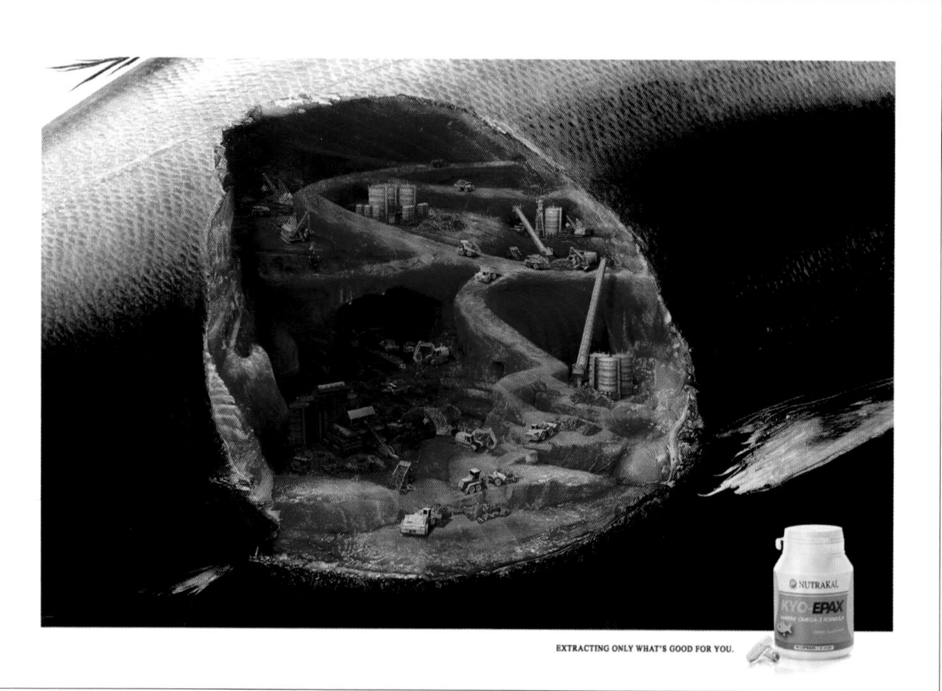

Agency	BrawandRieken, Hamburg
Copywriters	Kornelius Kroll Jan Lamprecht
Art Director	Julian Karliczek
Production	Appel Grafik, Hamburg
Advertiser	A.W. Niemeyer, "Bear"

Agency	Dentsu Plus, Bangkok
CCO	Subun Khow
Creative Director	Supparat Thepparat
Copywriters	Pattarapong Lapjarupong Subun Khow
Art Directors	Naphol Chantapakorn Supparat Thepparat
Photographer	Ekarat Wisuttiwan
Production	Montage Studio, Bangkok
Agency Producer	Virayut Khunvithayapaisal
Illustrator	Somkiat Nathiworasit
Advertiser	Nutramedica, "Salmon Mining"

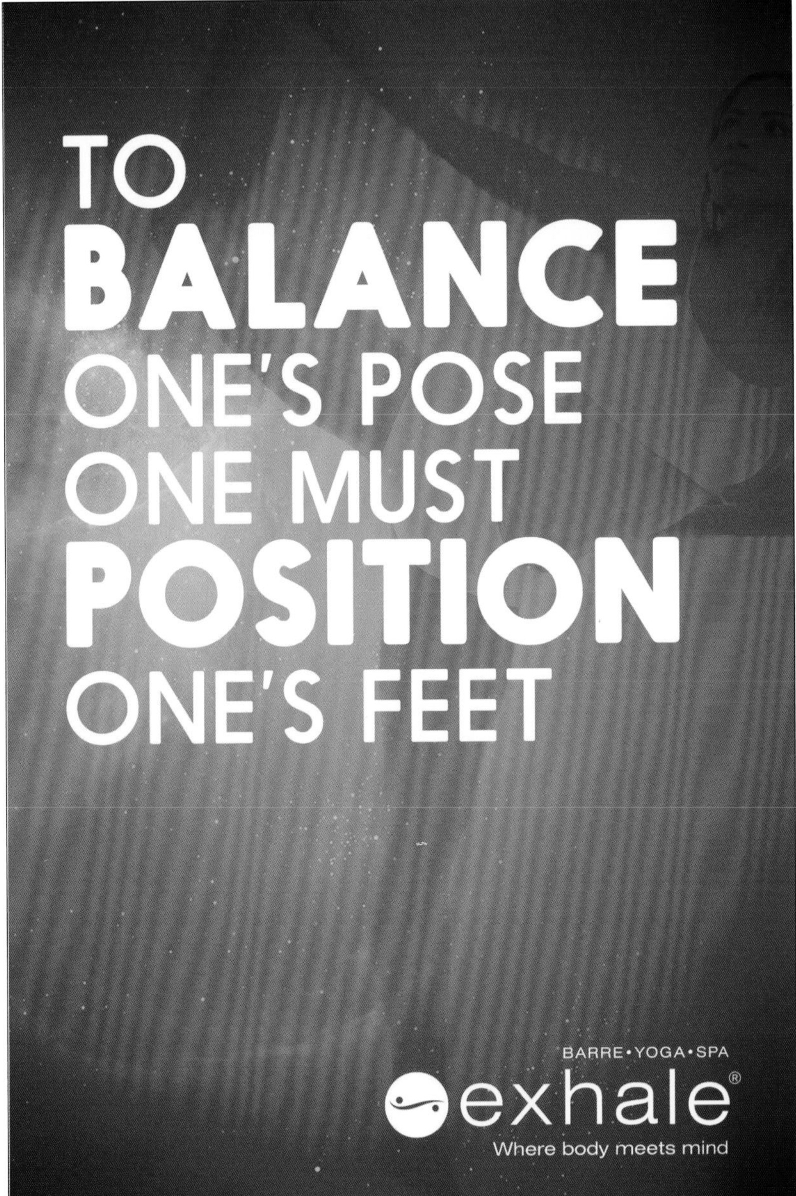

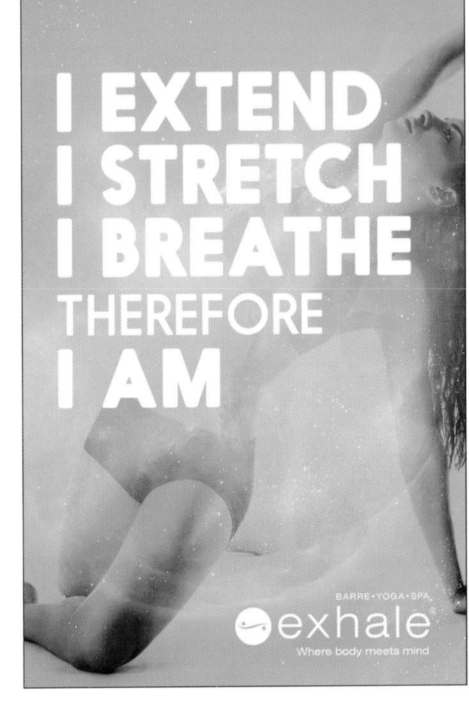

Agency	Saatchi & Saatchi Wellness, New York
CCO	Kathy Delaney
Creative Director	Carol Fiorino
Associate CD	Scott Carlton
Copywriter	Scott Carlton
Advertiser	Exhale Barre Yoga Spa, "Teachings"

Fashion, Footwear & Personal Accessories

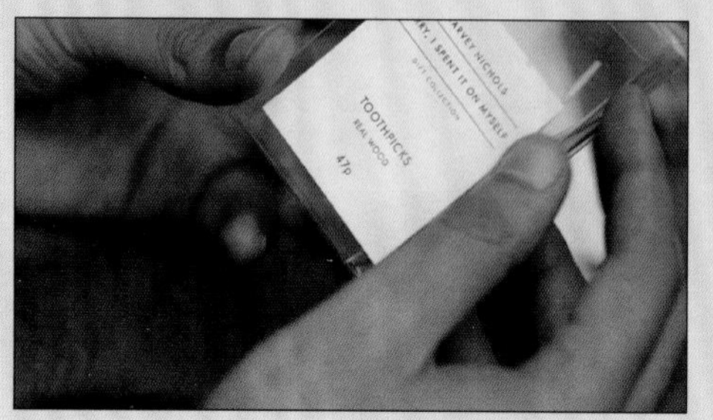

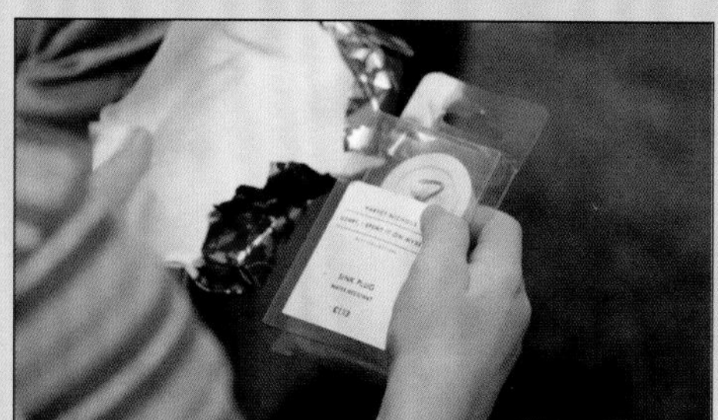

142 **Fashion, Footwear & Personal Accessories**

Agency adam&eveDDB, London
Executive CDs Ben Priest, Ben Tollett, Emer Stamp
Creatives Richard Brim, Daniel Fisher
Agency Producer Victoria Keenan
Production Outsider, London
Film Director James Rouse
Producer Benji Howell
Cameraman Alex Melman
Editor Bill Smedley, Work Post, London
Post Producer Josh King, MPC, London
Sound Factory Studio, London
Advertiser Harvey Nichols, "Sorry, I Spent It On Myself"

We're obliged to buy friends and family presents at Christmas. But what if there was a way to save the bulk of the festive gift budget for ourselves? Introducing the Harvey Nichols "Sorry, I Spent It On Myself" Gift Collection. Cheapskate gifts like paper clips and toothpicks are nicely packaged by the UK luxury store. So everyone wins. Well, not quite, to judge by the reactions of the recipients.

STYX
MENS COMFORTABLE UNDERWEAR

WWW.STYX-UNDERWEAR.CZ

Agency	Havas Worldwide, Prague
Creative Directors	Eda Kauba Pavel Fris
Copywriter	Pavel Fris
Art Directors	Pavel Slovacek Ales Pokorny
Agency Producer	Veronika Brichtova
Illustrator	Progressive FX, Prague
Advertiser	Styx, “A Truly Masculine Living Room”

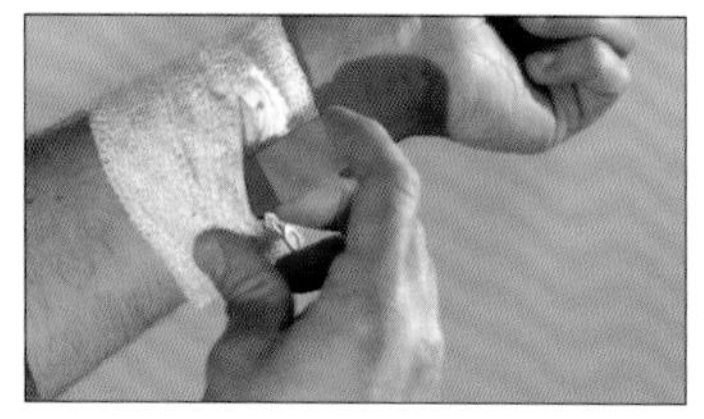
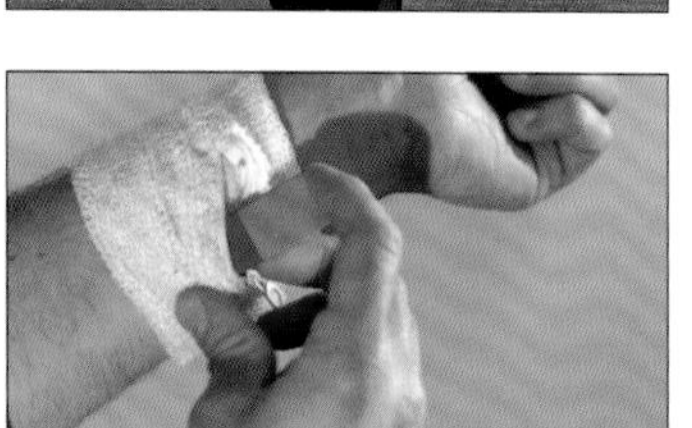

Agency BETC, Paris
Creative Directors Rémi Babinet, Antoine Choque
Copywriters Gabrielle Attia, Damien Bellon
Art Directors Damien Bellon, Gabrielle Attia
Production Wanda, Paris
Film Director Seb Edwards
Agency Producer David Green
Advertiser Lacoste, "The Big Leap"

A nervous guy leans across a café table, clearly intending to kiss the woman in front of him for the first time. He pictures himself jumping from the top of a building. Will she reject him? Will she respond? He's taking a leap of faith. As the two sequences intercut, we see the couple falling together in his imagination, and falling in love in real life. With its roots in sportswear, Lacoste makes fashion that can be worn on every occasion. Because "life is a beautiful sport".

Agencies Cheil Germany, Frankfurt; Cheil UK, London
CCO Roland Rudolf
Executive CD Logan Wilmont
Creative Directors Joern Welle, Thomas Schroeder
Advertiser Bernd Hummel, "Just ROO it - The ROOband"

In this satirical spot, the narrator tells us about his love of running. But just lately, he says, running has become less joyful, mostly due to connected devices. "Why did it become necessary to download software to aid running?" he asks. Now he introduces us to his invention, the RooBand, "the world's first analogue, wearable fitness tracker". It looks suspiciously like a sweat band. Indeed, by squeezing it out, you can measure your performance. But it also has a pocket for your front door key. Just Roo it, with Kangaroo footwear and accessories.

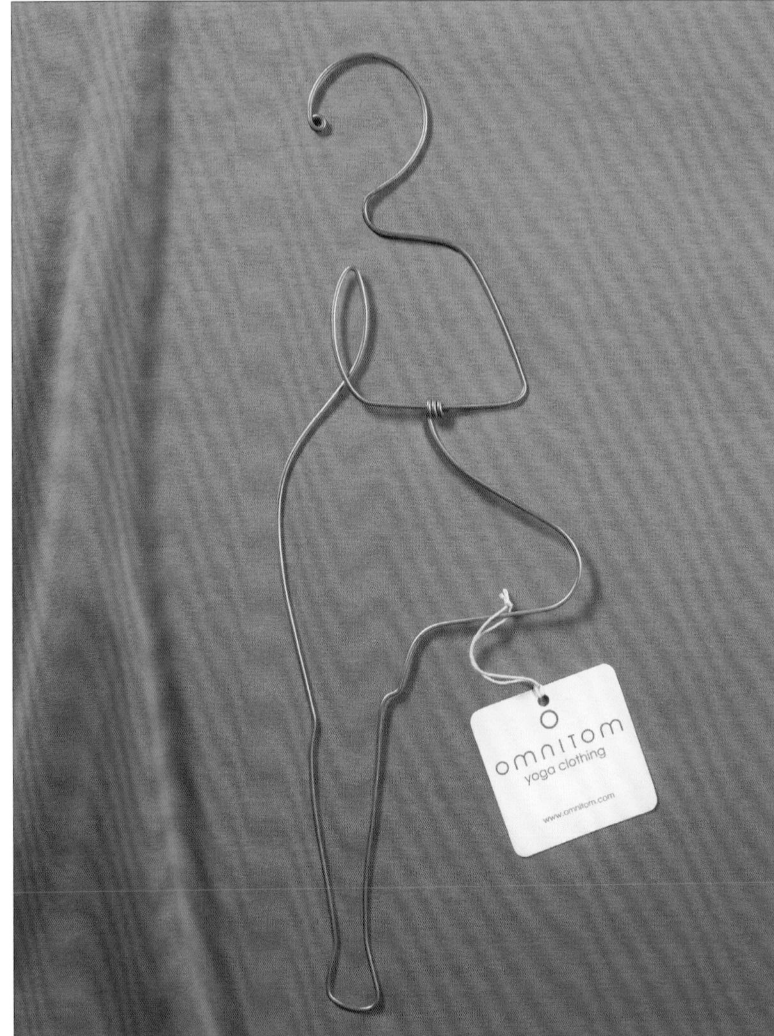

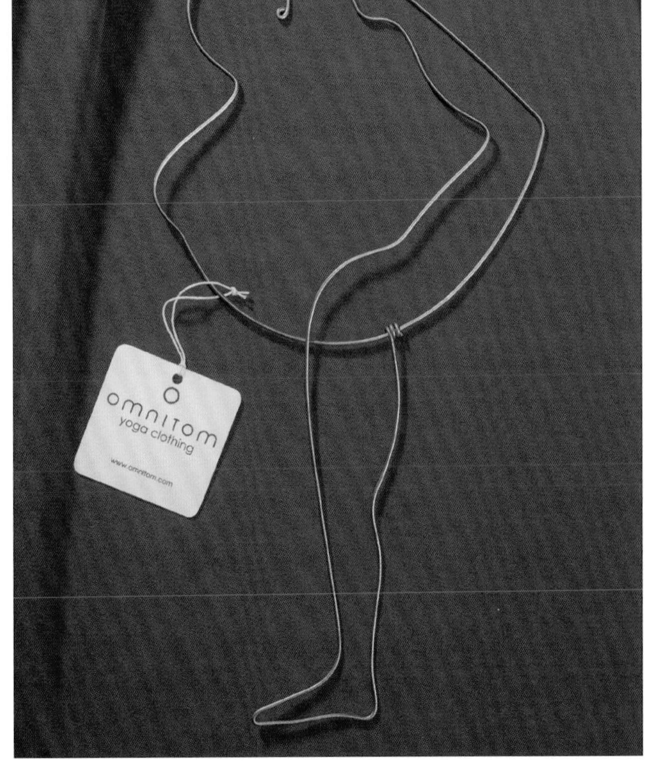

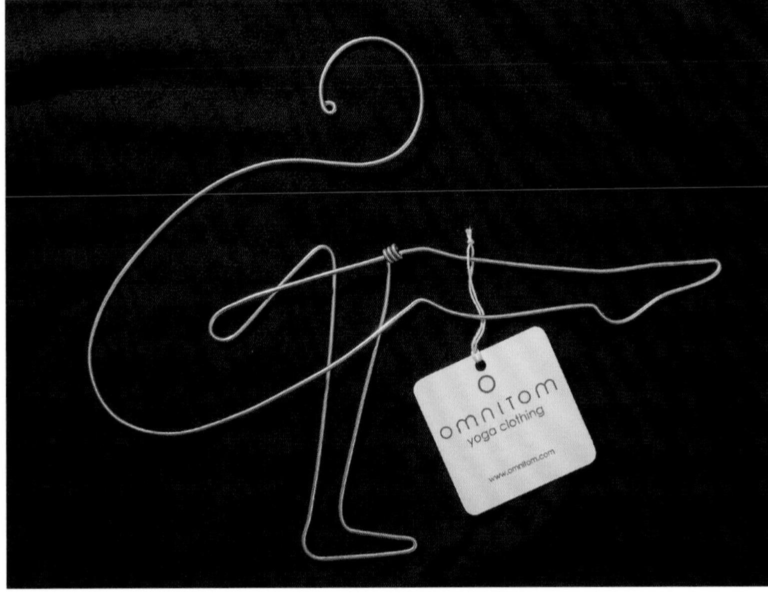

Agency	Noble Graphics, Sofia
Creative Director	Marsel Levi
Copywriter	Penko Kotov
Art Director	Eva Markova
Photographer	Atanas Kanchev
Advertiser	Omnitom, "Hangers"

 Fashion, Footwear & Personal Accessories

Agency	Marcel, Paris
CCO - Publicis Worldwide	Erik Vervroegen
CD - Publicis Worldwide	Erik Vervroegen
Creative Team	Bastien Grisolet Marjorie Vardo Nicolas Feer
Global Print Manager	Jean-Luc Chirio, Publicis
Art Buyer	Lauriane Dula, L'Adresse
Line Producer	Thomas Geffrier
Photographer	Mark Seliger
Production	Prodigious, Paris
Producer	Ruth Levy
Advertiser	Ray-Ban, "Brand Campaign 2014"

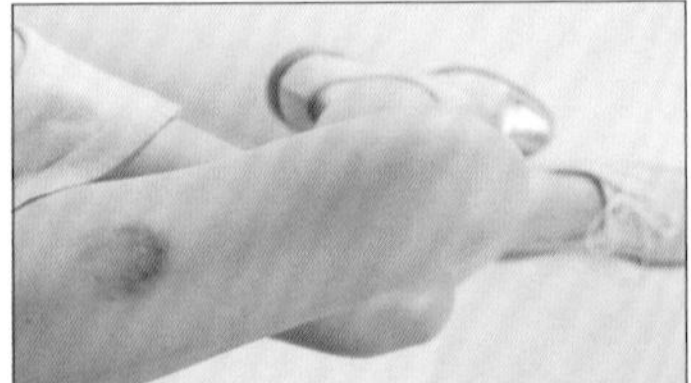

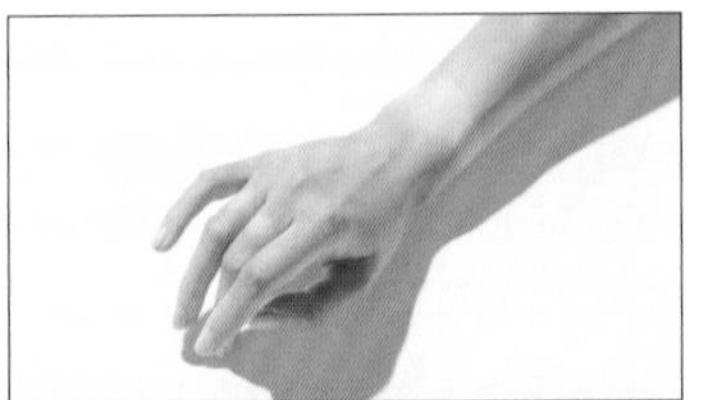

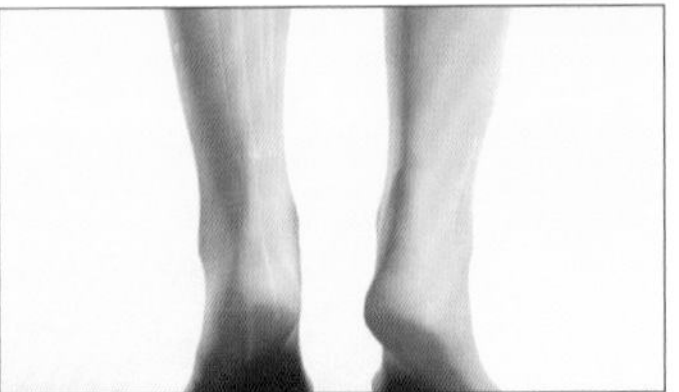

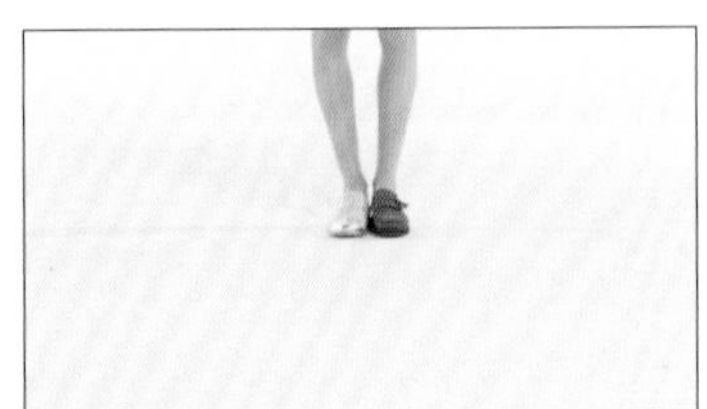

THE BEAUTY OF IMPERFECTION D.EFECT

Welcome
to our world.
arena
SWIMWEAR

Agency New Agency, Vilnius
Creative Director Tomas Ramanauskas
Production PVZ, Vilnius
Film Director Ruta Kiskyte
Producer Justina Briedyte
Art department Laimonas Juzumas, Pasa Leontjevas
Music Vytautas Rasimavicius, Katedra
Advertiser D.Efect, "The Beauty Of Imperfection

Can supposedly imperfect things be beautiful? A smashed teapot, a distorted glass, freckles, bruises, scars, a gap-toothed grin or a multi-coloured car? Of course they can. Fashion brand D.Efect (a play on "defect") provides individualistic women with clothes in unusual shapes and fabrics. It's all about beauty with a difference.

Agency Y&R, Milan
Executive CD Vicky Gitto
Creative Director Vicky Gitto
Copywriter Stefano Guidi
Art Director Andrea Fumagalli
Photographer Justin Lewis
Advertiser Arena Swimwear, "Waterworld"

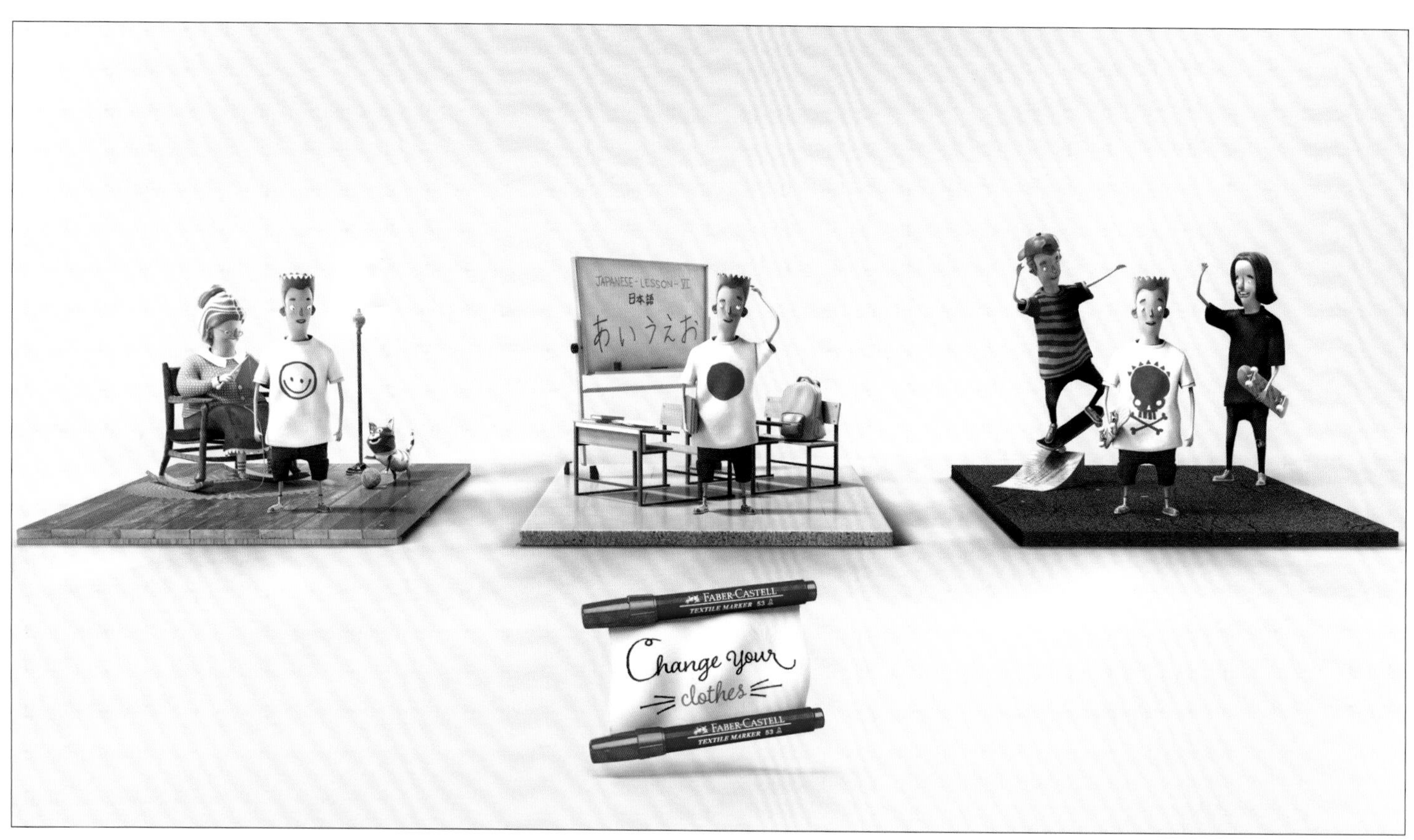

Agency	FCB, Istanbul
Creative Directors	Elif Önay Yavuzhan Gel Çağlar Cengiz
Copywriter	Pınar Cingöz
Art Director	Cem Haşimi
Illustrator	Studio Mutato Art, São Paulo
Advertiser	Faber-Castell, "Change Your Clothes"

Agency	Armando Testa, Turin
Creative Directors	Dario Anania Vincenzo Celli
Copywriters	Federica Saraniti Lana Vincenzo Celli
Art Director	Laura Sironi
Illustrator	Michelangelo Rossino
Advertiser	Cam, "Let's play!"

Agency	FCB, Istanbul
Creative Directors	Elif Önay Yavuzhan Gel Çağlar Cengiz
Copywriter	Yavuzhan Gel
Art Director	Çağlar Cengiz
Photographer	Murat Süyür
Production	Rpresenter, Istanbul
Producer	Bahadır Karataş
Advertiser	Faber-Castell, "Psychological Issues"

1Bag
1Match
French handmade bags
made from recycled sport shirts

1bag1match.com

Agency	Havas Paris
Creative Director	Christophe Coffre
Copywriter	Guillaume Blanc
Art Director	Florian Roussel
Agency Producer	Corinne Dutoit-Costa
Art Buyer	Phitsana Dieu
Advertiser	1Bag1Match, "1Bag1Match Campaign"

 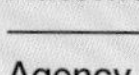

Agency adam&eveDDB, London
Global Executive CD Jeremy Craigen
Copywriters & ADs Nikki Lindman, Toby Brewer
Agency Producer Pamie Wikstrom
Designer/Typographer Oliver Watts, Stanley's King Henry, London
Production The Mob Film Company, Manchester
Film Director Paul WS Anderson
Producer John Brocklehurst
Editor Bled Bujupi
Producer Natalie Dickens, Felt Music, London
Music Composers Ru Pope, Toby Bricheno, Felt Music, London
Sound Designer Chris Southwell, Unit, London
Colourist Simon Astbury, Unit, London
Advertiser Volkswagen, "Made for Real Life"

On a US highway, a bus smashes through a roadblock. We see that it's been hijacked by escaped convicts in a typical action-movie scenario. The good guys are in pursuit in their VW. One of them climbs out of the car's sunroof and onto its bonnet in a heroic attempt to board the bus. But the VW can't get close enough – due to its safe distance technology, which automatically slows it down. Made for real life, not the movies. Perfect for a cinema ad, though.

Agency Fred & Farid, Shangai
Creative Directors Fred & Farid, Feng Huang, Laurent Leccia
Copywriter Laurent Leccia
Art Director Laurent Leccia
Agency Producers Joanne Zhou, Terry Jin
Illustrators Marc Burckhardt, Asaphz
Agency Supervisors Grégoire Chalopin, Vivian Wang, Kylie Wang
Retouching Happy Finish
Advertiser Porsche, "911 Rear Horsepower"

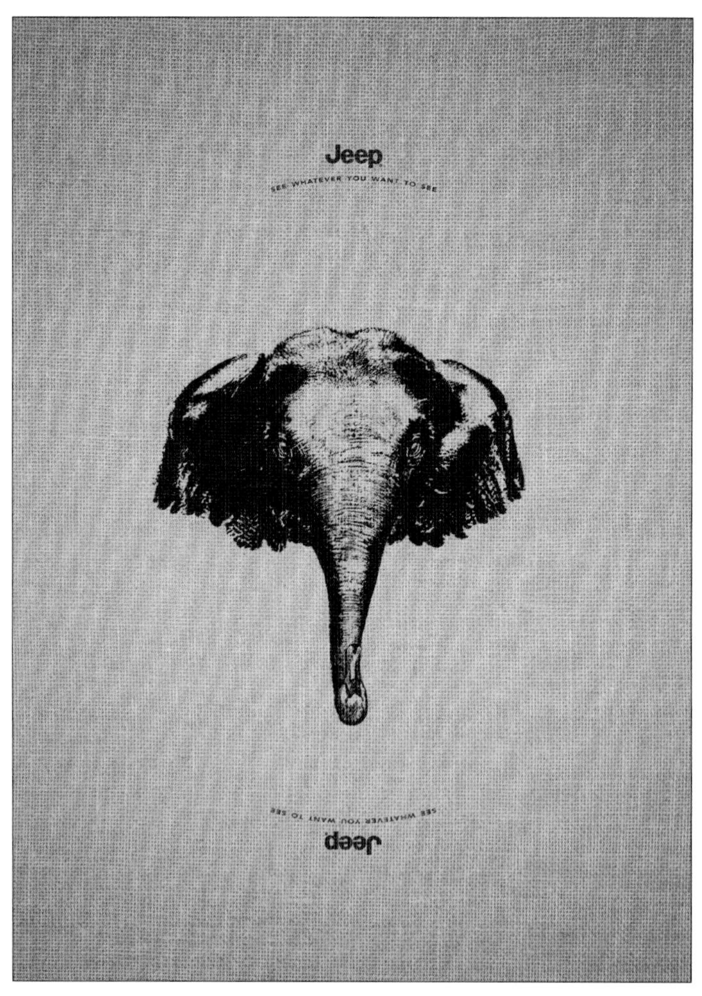

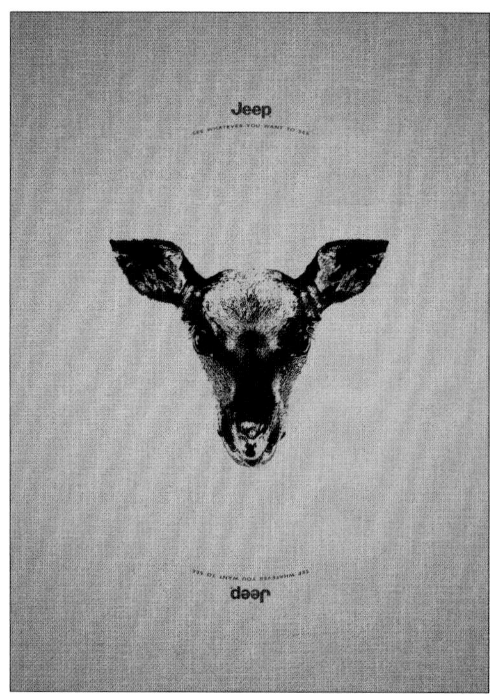

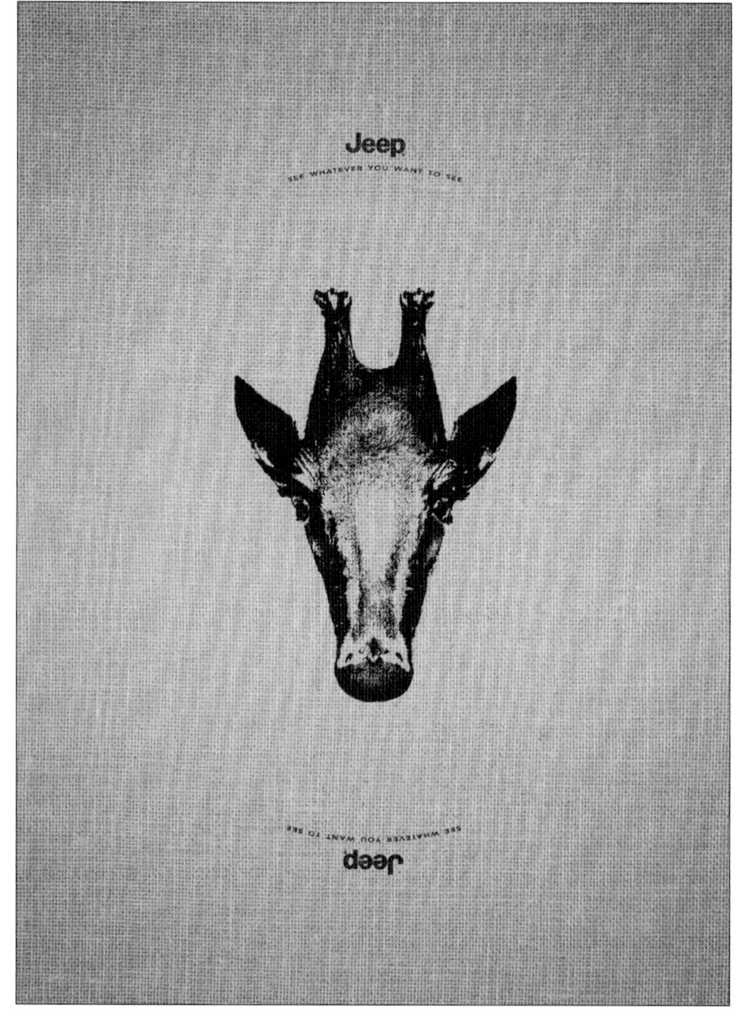

Automobiles

Agency	Leo Burnett, Paris
Executive CD	Xavier Beauregard
Copywriter	Hadi Hassan-Helou
Art Directors	Jérôme Gonfond Rémi Lascault
Illustrator	Jérôme Gonfond
Advertiser	Jeep, “Upside Down”

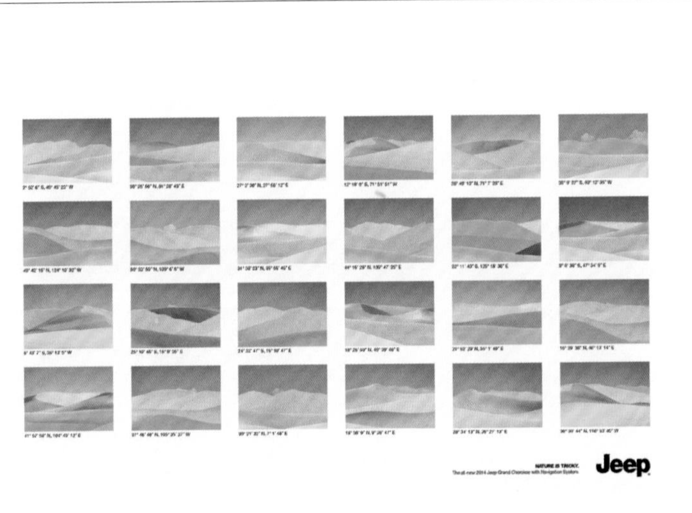

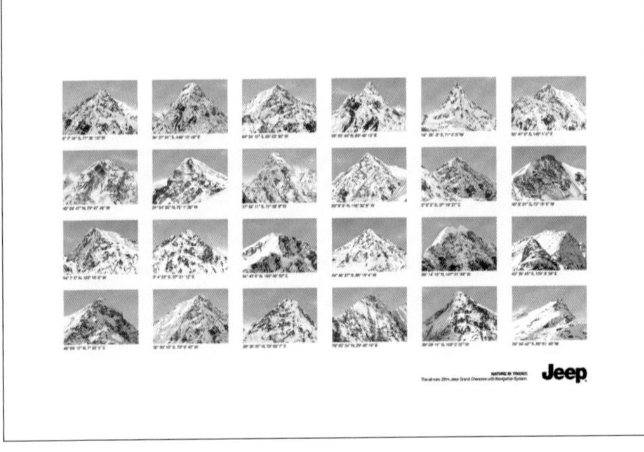

Agency	Leo Burnett Tailor Made, São Paulo
Creative Directors	Marcelo Reis Vinicius Stanzione Alessandro Bernardo
Copywriter	Renato Ramalho
Art Director	Henri Honda
Advertiser	Jeep, "Coordinates"

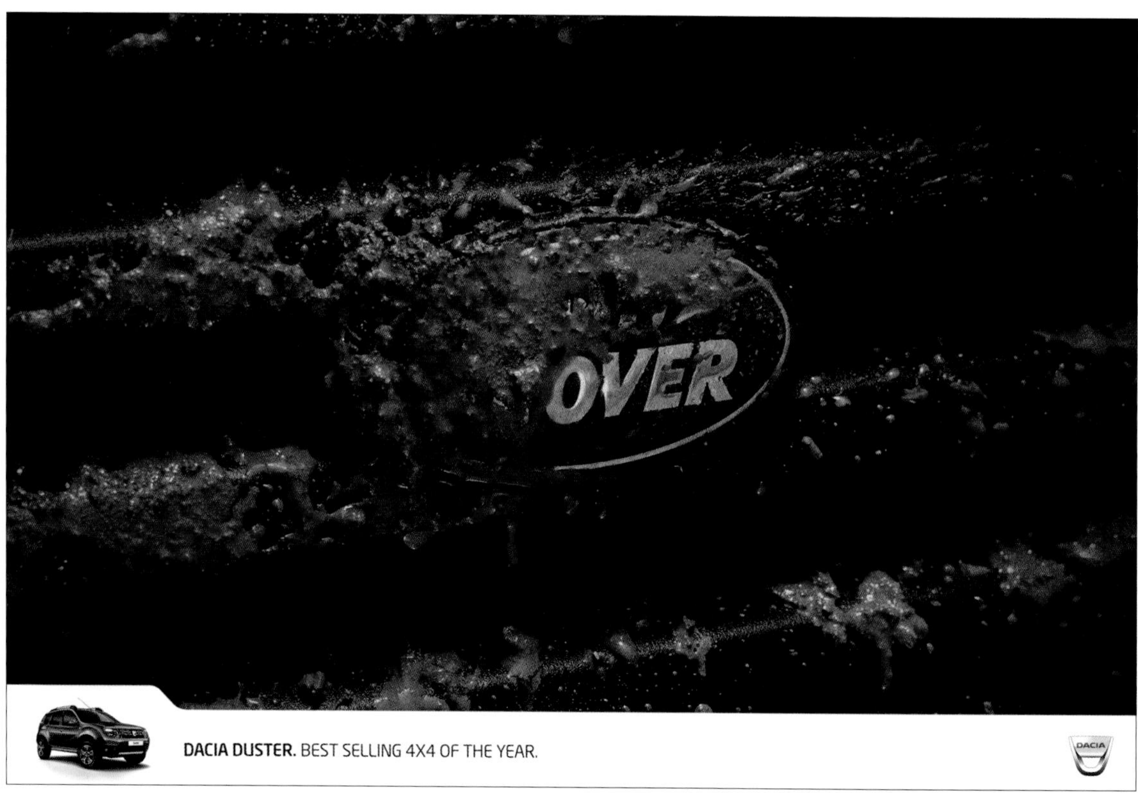

OVER
DACIA DUSTER. BEST SELLING 4X4 OF THE YEAR.
DACIA

Agency Les Gaulois, Paris
Creative Directors Gilbert Scher, Marco Venturelli, Luca Cinquepalmi
Copywriter Ouriel Ferencz
Art Director Marie Donnedieu
Production Wanda, Paris
Director Steve Rogers
Producer Jérôme Denis
Music Supervisor Lionel Dray
Advertiser Citroën, "Daddy"

This father finds it hard to find time for himself. His three kids insist on clinging to him, whether he's bird-watching, playing a sport, learning to dance, water-skiing or horse-riding. Even yoga is a family affair. But then we see him at the wheel of his spacious Citroën C4, finally relaxed with his kids in the back. At least he can still enjoy driving.

Agency Publicis Conseil, Paris
Creative Director Olivier Altmann
Copywriters Olivier Dermaux, Alexandre Hildebrand
Art Directors Martin Darfeuille, Lena Monceau
Photographer Yann Le Pape
Advertiser Land Rover, "Over"

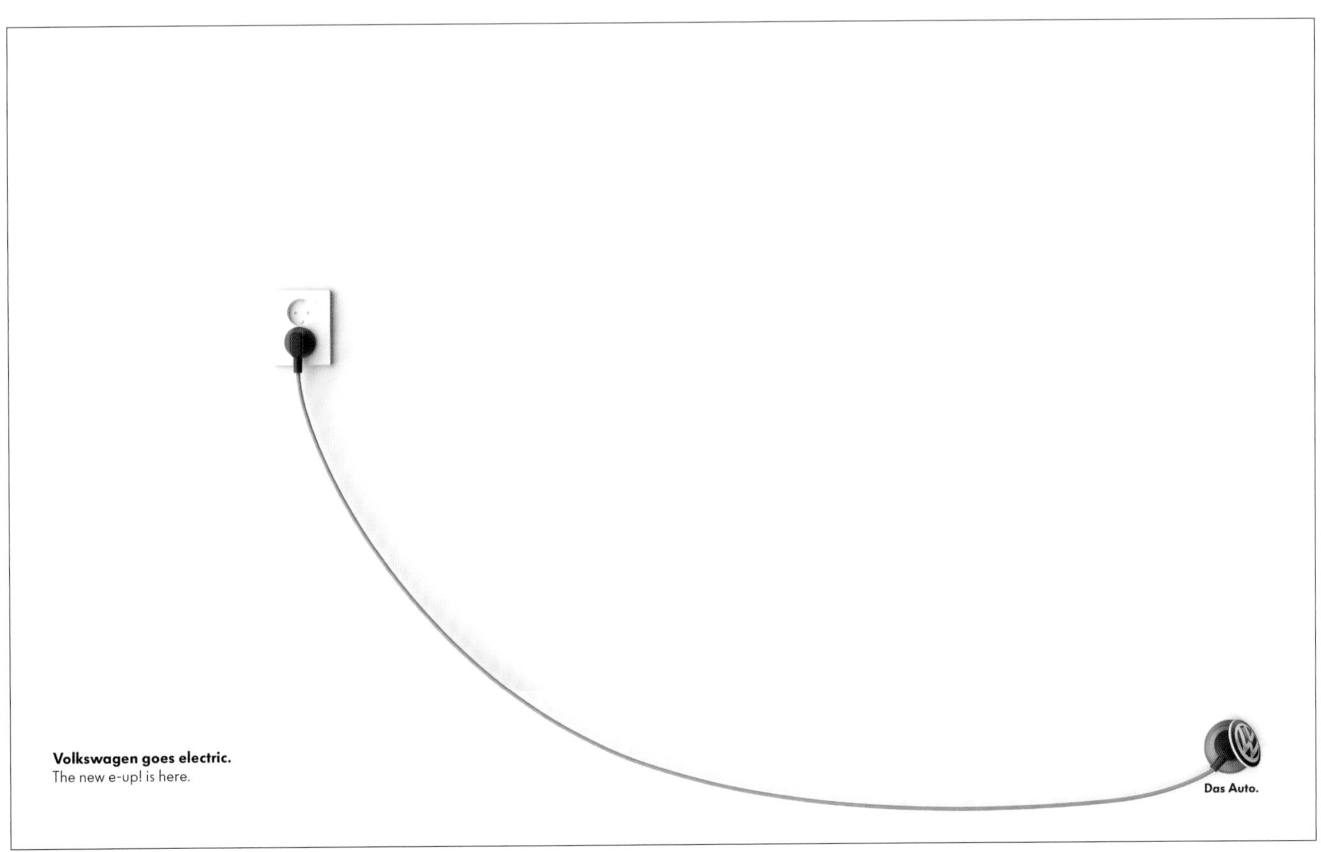

Volkswagen goes electric.
The new e-up! is here.
Das Auto.

Voltswagen.

Volkswagen goes electric.
The new e-up! is here.

Das Auto.

Agency	TRY/Apt/POL, Oslo
Copywriter	Petter Bryde
Art Directors	Thorbjørn Ruud Aleksander Erichsen Thea Emanuelsen
Agency Producer	Cathrine Wennersten
Mac Designer	Thomas Bråten
Advertiser	Volkswagen, "Stick" & "Voltswagen"

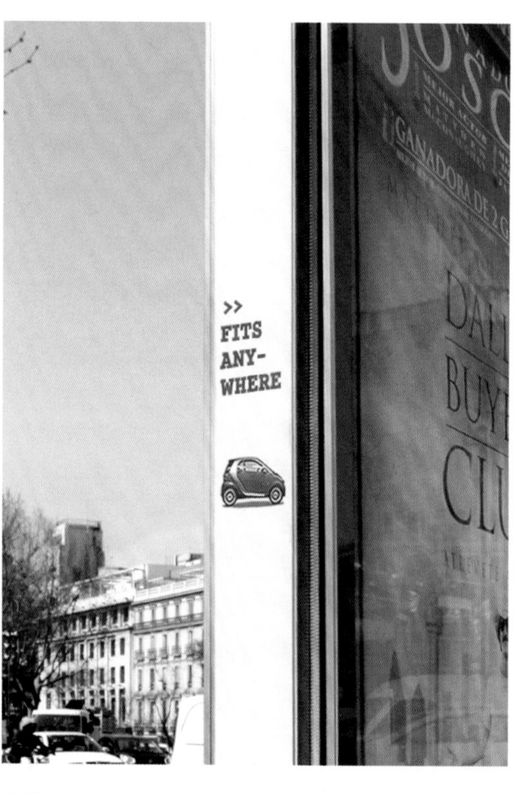

Agency	Contrapunto BBDO, Madrid
Creative Directors	Felix del Valle Carlos Jorge Gorka Fernandez Iriso Gonzalo Urriza
Copywriters	Marta Lopez Samuel Gomez Joao Valente
Art Directors	Africa Lopez Roberto Gabian Gorka Fernandez Iriso
Advertiser	Mercedes-Benz, "Park at the Front Door"

"Park at the front door", instruct these amusingly situated images of the small but cool Smart.

Agency	Contrapunto BBDO, Madrid
Creative Directors	Felix del Valle Carlos Jorge
Copywriters	Raul Lopez Aurora Hidalgo
Art Directors	Raul Lopez Aurora Hidalgo
Graphic Design	Javier Lujan
Advertiser	Mercedes-Benz, "Side"

The Smart is so compact that you can park it almost anywhere. And find ingenious media placements for it too.

>> Park at the front door.

>> Park at the front door.

>> Park at the front door.

Agency	Contrapunto BBDO, Madrid
Creative Directors	Felix del Valle Carlos Jorge
Copywriters	Raul Lopez Aurora Hidalgo
Art Directors	Raul Lopez Aurora Hidalgo
Photographer	Gonzaga Manso
Graphic Designers	Javier Lujan Antonia Belenguer
Advertiser	Mercedes-Benz, "Doors"

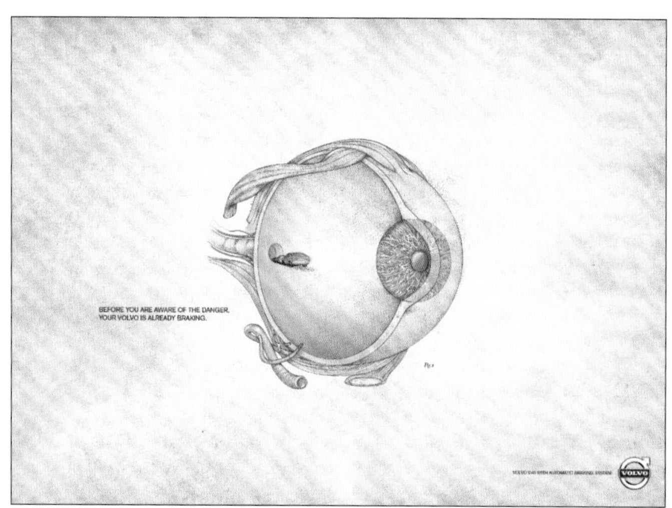

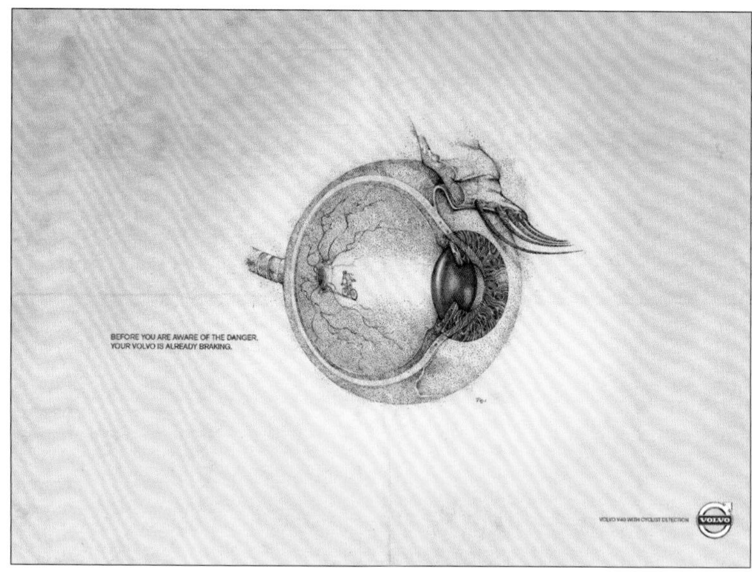

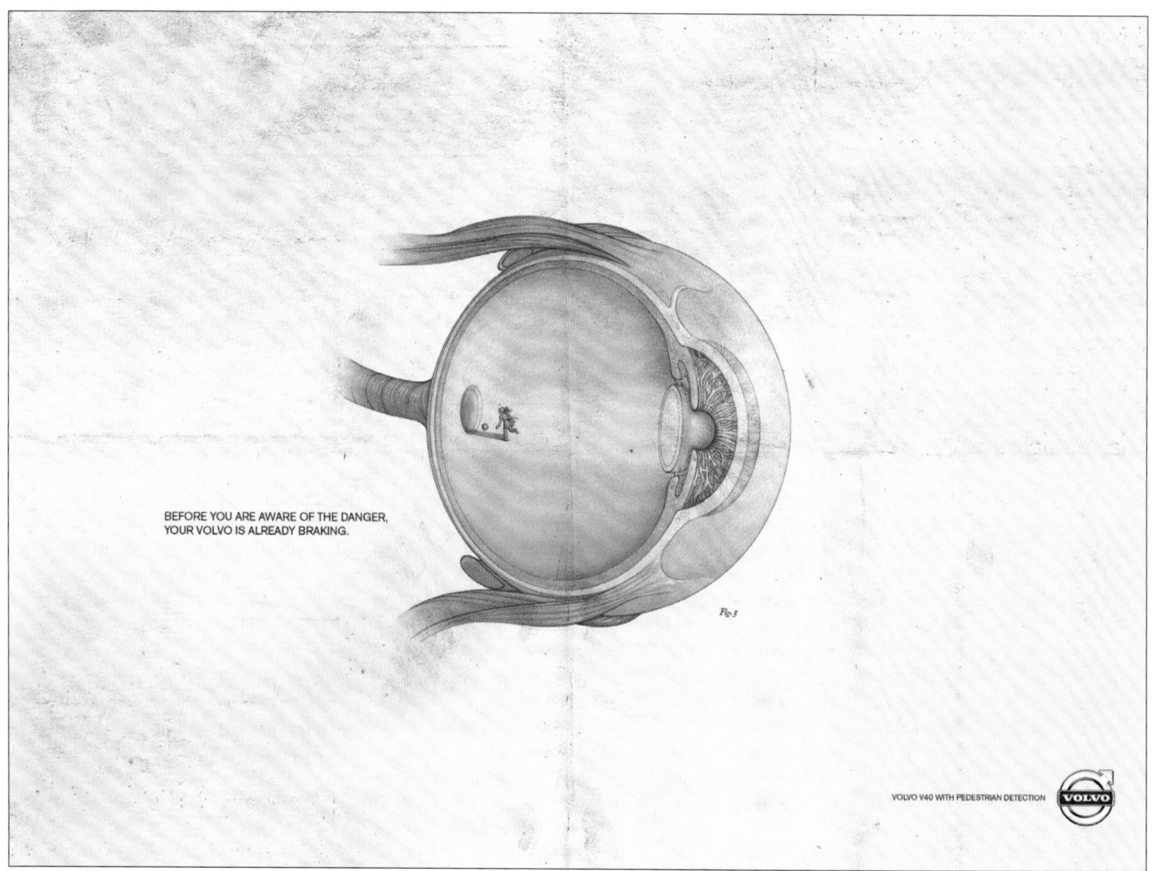

 Automobiles

Agency	BBDO, Brussels
Creative Directors	Arnaud Pitz Sebastien De Valck
Copywriter	Vincent De Roose
Art Director	Cristina Gesulfo
Agency Producer	Leen Van den Brande
Illustrator	Bruno Vergauwen
Graphic Designers	Jorrit Michiels Eric Leurquin
Advertiser	Volvo, “Eyes”

Agency	Impact BBDO, Dubai
Creative Director	Fadi Yaish
Copywriter	Aunindo Sen
Art Director	Gautam Wadher
Photographer	Ralph Baiker
Agency Producer	Clarisse Mar Wai May
Illustrator	Club Production, Zoot
Advertiser	Mercedes-Benz, "Be Warned"

Agency	Lowe GGK, Bratislava
Creative Directors	Jozef Červeň Ondrej Kořínek
Copywriters	Ondrej Kořínek Ivana Polohová
Art Director	Jozef Červeň
Advertiser	Audi, "Lights"

Automobiles

Agency	FCB, Istanbul
Creative Directors	Elif Önay Yavuzhan Gel Çağlar Cengiz
Copywriter	Yavuzhan Gel
Art Director	Çağlar Cengiz
Illustrator	Onay Akmut
Advertiser	Suzuki, "Teeterboard"

Agency DDB Russia, Moscow
Creative Director Holger Paasch
Copywriter Alexander Bozhko
Art Director Alexey Sanzharovskiy
Photographer Sergey Klyosov
Production Belle Ville Creative Production, St. Petersburg
Producer Egor Mikhaylov
Digital Nikita Stepanov, Sergey Klyosov, Sergey Brezhnev
Advertiser Volkswagen, "Discover Your Wild Side"

Agency DDB Russia, Moscow
Creative Director Holger Paasch
Copywriters Alexander Bozhko, Andrey Lee
Art Directors Alexey Sanzharovskiy, Anton Volovsky, Alexey Soroka
Producer Egor Mikhaylov
Digital Nikita Stepanov, Sergey Klyosov
Designer Julia Artamonova
Advertiser Volkswagen, "Escape The City"

Introducing Volvo FH with
I-Shift Dual Clutch

Automotive & Accessories

Agency	Forsman & Bodenfors, Gothenburg
Copywriters	Martin Ringqvist Björn Engström
Art Directors	Anders Eklind Sophia Lindholm
Production	Smuggler, London
Film Director	Henry Alex Rubin
Producer	Drew Santasario
Agency Producer	Alexander Blidner
Designer	Jerry Wass
Web Producer	Peter Gaudiano
Post Production	Absolute Post, London
DOP	Matthew Woolf
Editor	Spencer Ferszt, Marshall Street Editors
Music	"Tighten Up" Al Escobar and His Orchestra, Courtesy of Fania Records
Execut. Producers	Chris Barett Fergus Brown
Advertiser	Volvo, "Casino"

We're assured that this spot was "filmed with hidden cameras on the Italian Riviera". We see a young guy start his first night on the job as a parking valet at a casino. As the red carpet guests arrive for a glamorous event, he accepts their keys and parks their shiny automobiles. But he's totally nonplussed when a giant truck pulls up. He takes the keys, looking unsure what to do next. The new Volvo FH. Under the hood, it's a sports car.

Agency	Grupo Vale Havas, Mexico City
Creative Directors	Alvaro Zunini Daniel Castro
Copywriter	Geraldine Basaldua
Art Directors	Alberto Zárate Luis Matías
Photographer	Roberto Toris
Production	Diagonal, Mexico City
Agency Producer	Marco Esperón
Graphic Designers	Alberto Zárate Luis Matías
Advertiser	Continental Tires, “Grip”

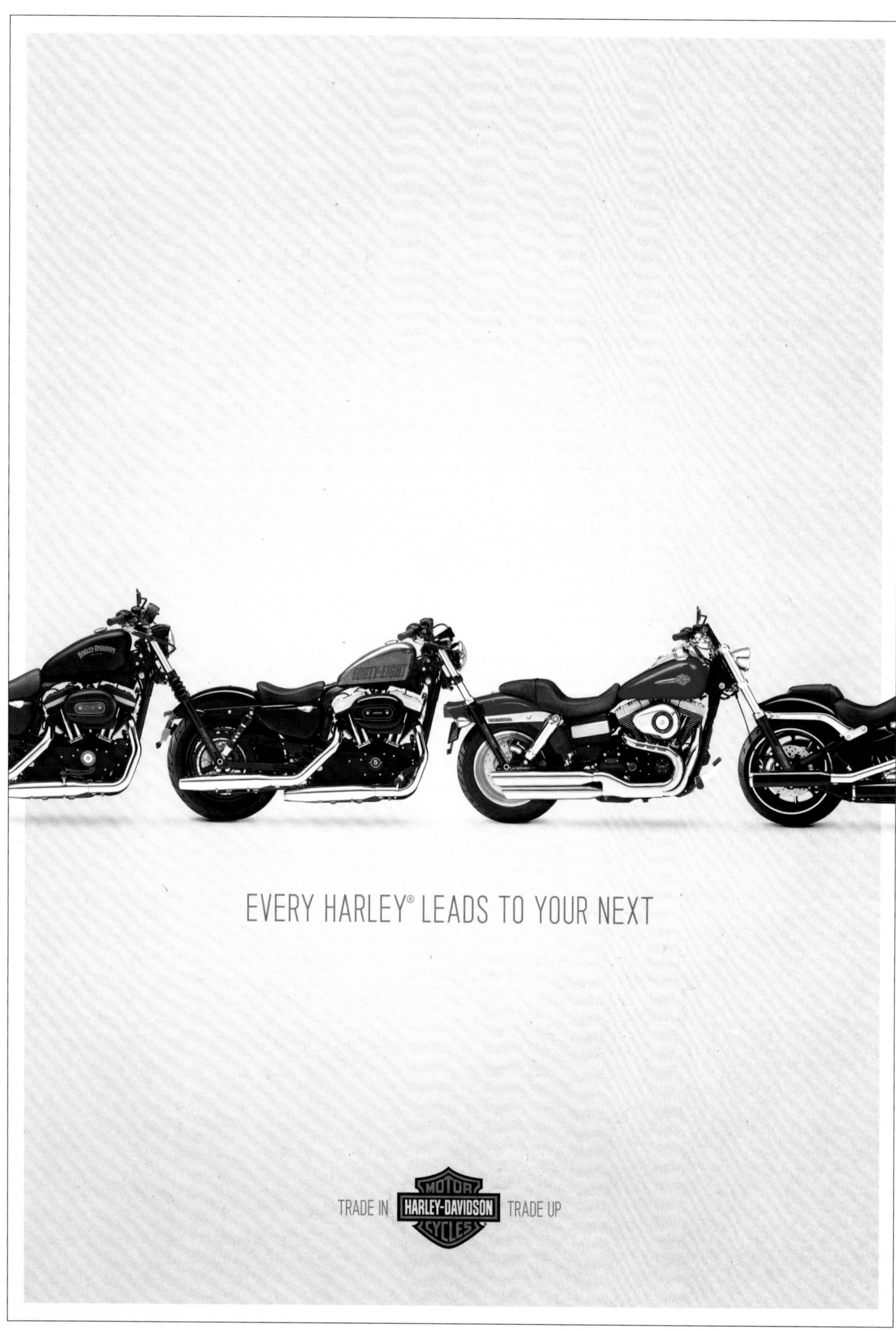

EVERY HARLEY® LEADS TO YOUR NEXT
TRADE IN
MOTOR
HARLEY-DAVIDSON
CYCLES
TRADE UP

Agency Big Communications, London
Creative Director Dylan Bogg
Copywriter James Cross
Art Director Tim Jones
Photographer Benedict Campbell
Advertiser Harley-Davidson, "Trade Up"

Agency DDB Paris
Executive CDs Alexandre Hervé
Copywriters Stéphane Audouin, Emilie Ramain
Art Directors Stéphane Audouin, Emilie Ramain
Illustrators Stéphane Audouin, Emilie Ramain
Advertiser Honda, "Only Gods Think Once"

Agency Lukas Lindemann Rosinski, Hamburg
CCOs Arno Lindemann, Bernhard Lukas
Creative Directors Henry Bose, Philip Simon
Art Directors Damian Kuczmierczyk, Moritz Frehse
Agency Producer Henning Rieseweber
Production Cobblestone Filmproduktion, Hamburg
Advertiser Mercedes-Benz, "Dirty Driving"

A Mercedes S63 AMG Coupé and an Actros truck conduct a romance on wheels to the tune of "Dirty Dancing". After they get physical, the result is the Vito van, which combines the best of the two vehicles, and has unbeatable Mercedes genes.

CANAL+

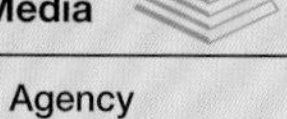

Agency BETC, Paris
Creative Directors Stéphane Xiberras, Olivier Apers
Copywriter Paul Delmas
Art Director Thomas Renaudin
Production Henry de Czar, Paris
Film Director Bart Timmer
Agency Producer David Green
Advertiser Canal+, "Cameramen"

These cameramen really get to the heart of the action. We see them on the football pitch, sprinting, leaping and even diving with the players. They pull out all the stops to ensure that Canal+ viewers don't miss a single second. They even form a wall for the penalty shoot-out. The channel's pledge is to make big matches even bigger.

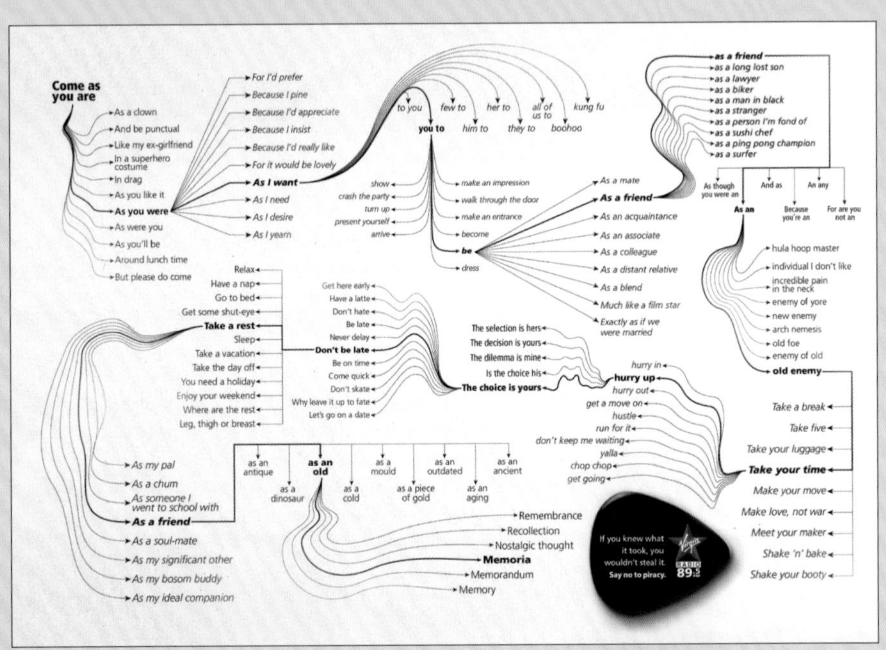

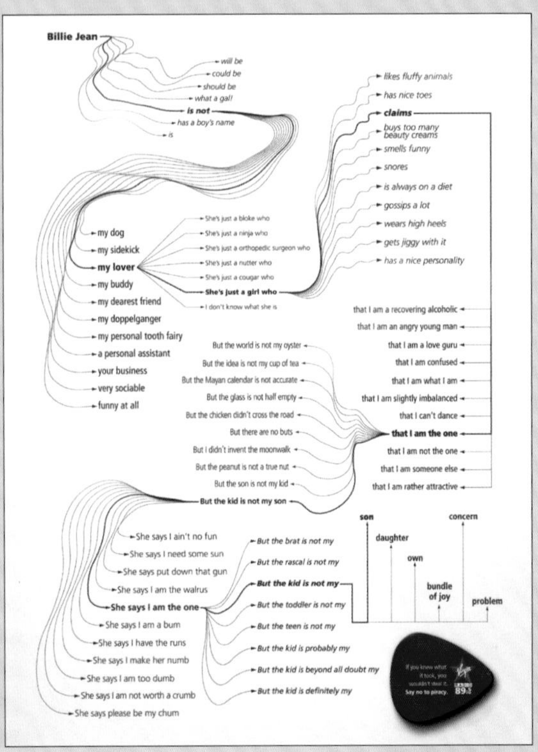

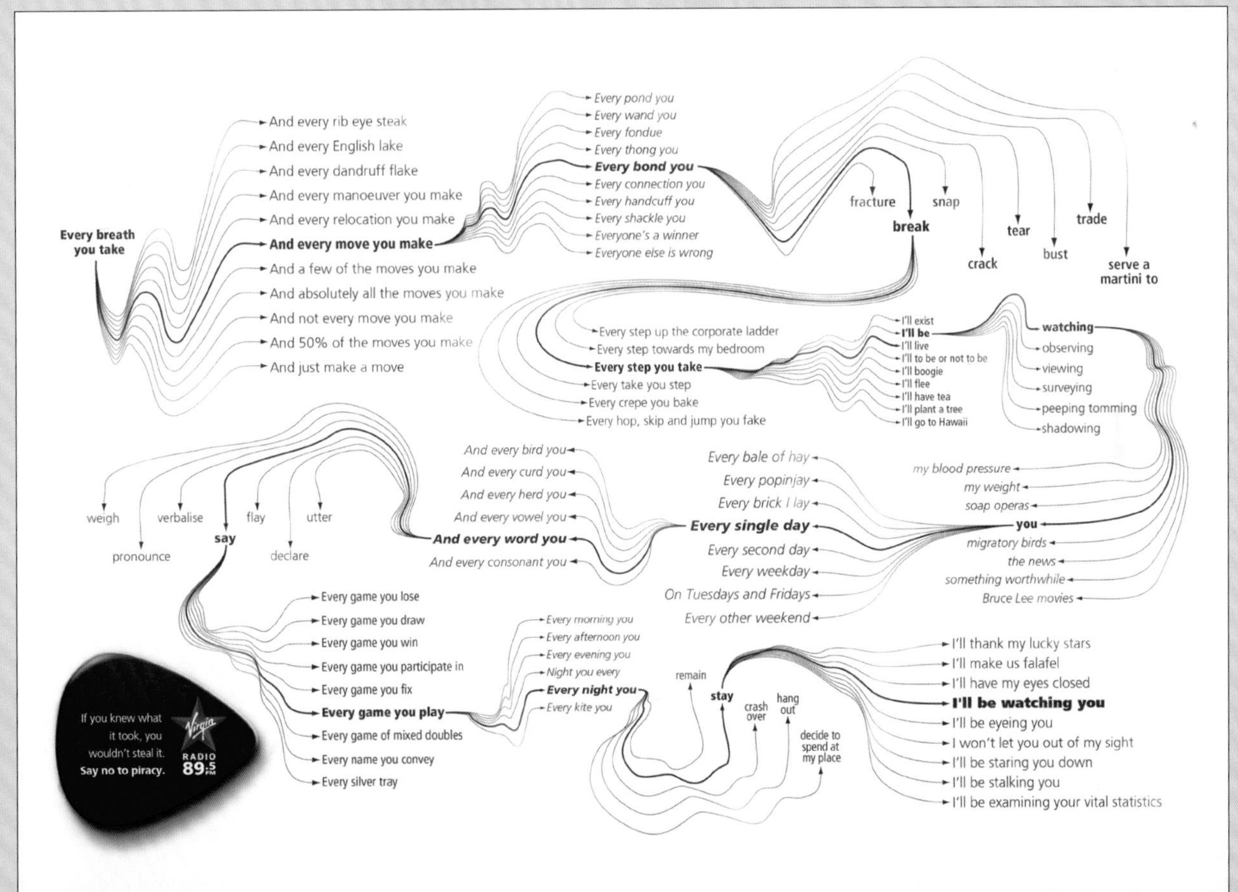

Media

Agency	Leo Burnett, Beirut	
Creative Directors	Bechara Mouzannar Malek Ghorayeb Abraham Varughese	
Copywriters	Zaid Alwan Abraham Varughese Edward Poh	
Art Director	Edward Poh	
Illustrator	Edward Poh	
Advertiser	Virgin Radio, "Making Music"	

How are great songs born? These ingenious ads for Virgin Radio use info-graphics to depict the potential lyrics available to the writers of legendary pop songs by Michael Jackson, The Police and Nirvana. Once you've followed the trail, the pay-off reminds you that creating brilliant music demands extraordinary effort. If you knew what it took, you wouldn't steal it. Say no to piracy.

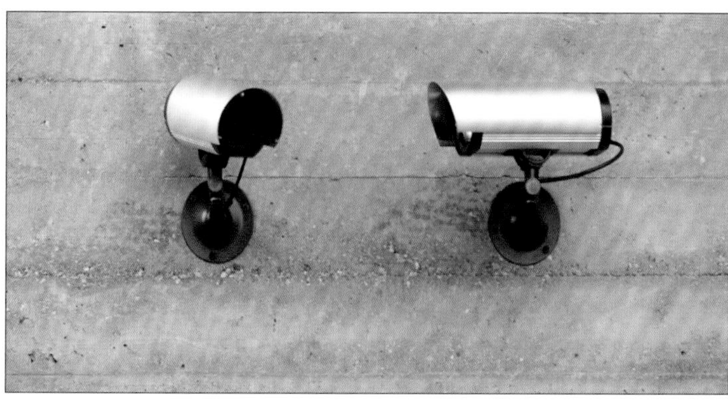

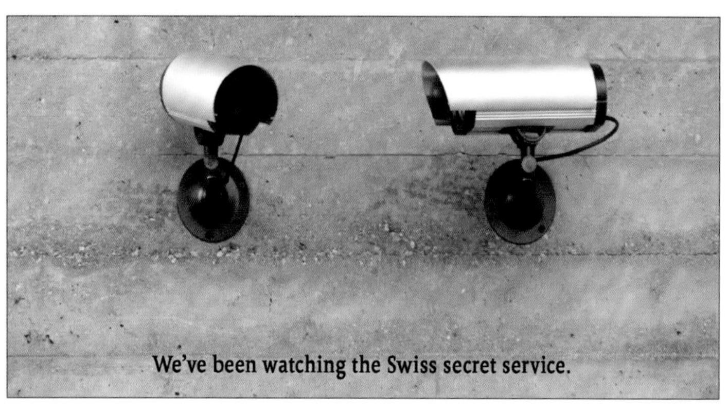

We've been watching the Swiss secret service.

Read the story in our special issue.
WOZ

Media

Agency 358, Helsinki
Copywriters Verneri Leimu
Juuso Janhunen
Art Director Ale Lauraéus
Production Teko Film, Helsinki
Producers Frej Karlson
Jussi Suvanto
Advertiser Melonen Media/ Radio Aalto, "Let the Music Do the Talking"

A car cruises through neon-lit streets. It pulls up beside a woman. "Hello," says the driver. "Is it me you're looking for?" The woman replies: "We are living in a material world, and I am a material girl." "Let's dance," says the driver. Soon they pick up another character. "Up all night to get lucky?" inquires the woman. "I kissed a girl," he admits. "And I liked it." Even the villain talks in song lyrics. "Every breath you take, every move you make, I will be watching you." Radio Aalto – let the music do the talking.

Agency Leo Burnett, Zurich
Creative Directors Johannes Raggio
Pablo Schencke
Copywriter Fabian Windhager
Art Director Barbara Hartmann
Production Plan B Film, Zurich
Advertiser WOZ Newspaper, "Surveillance"

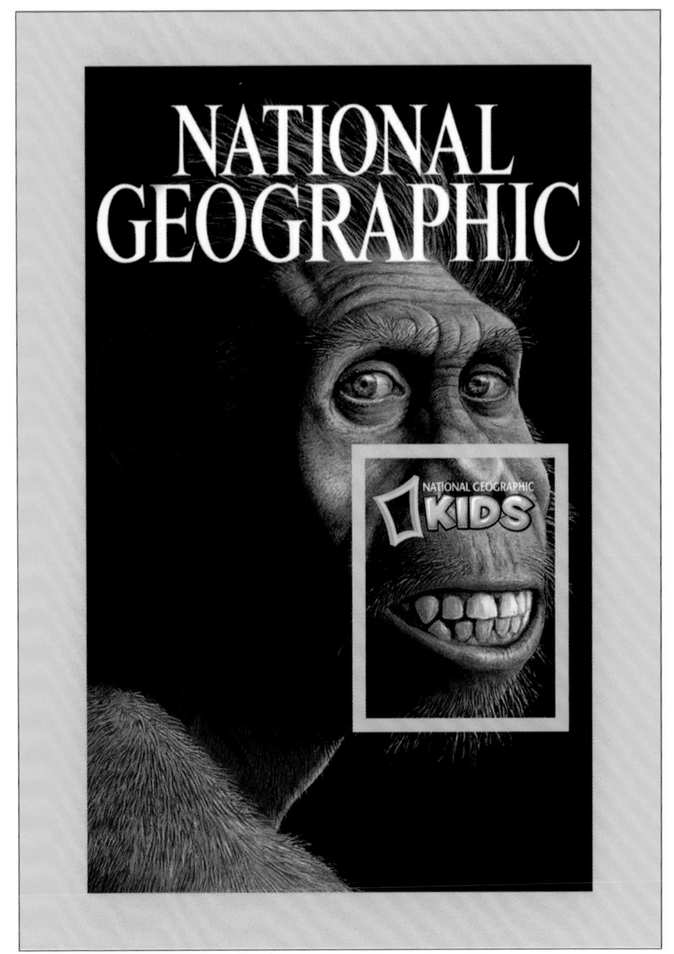

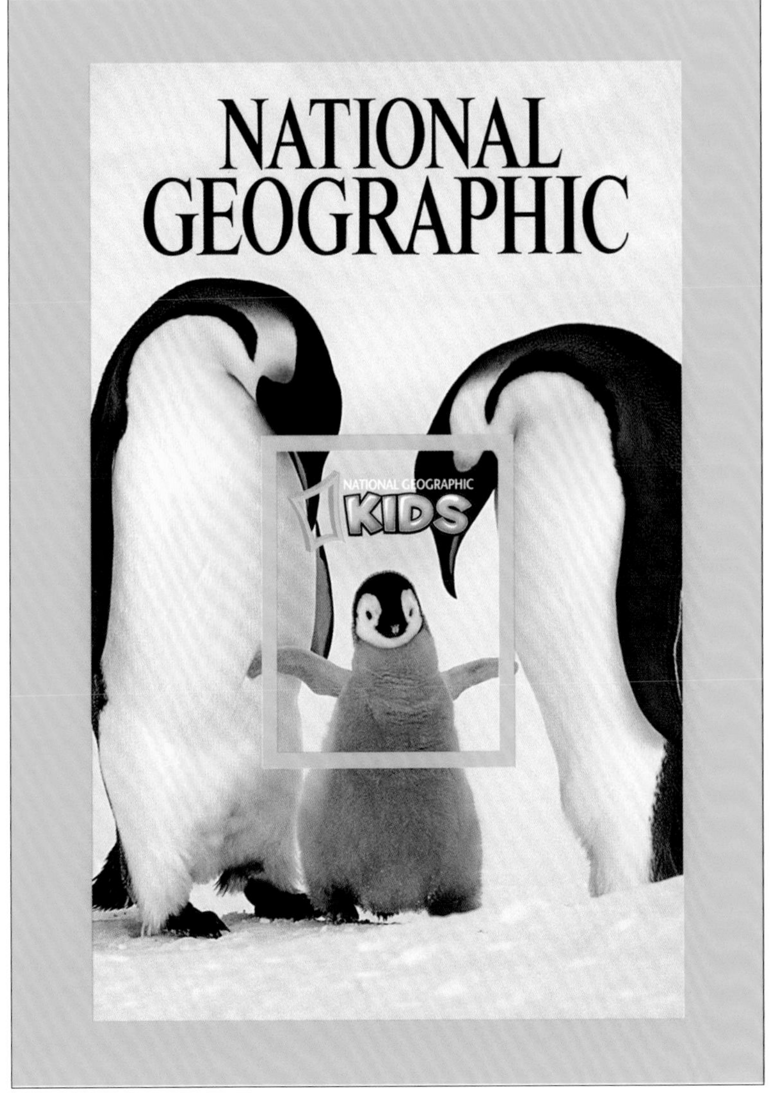

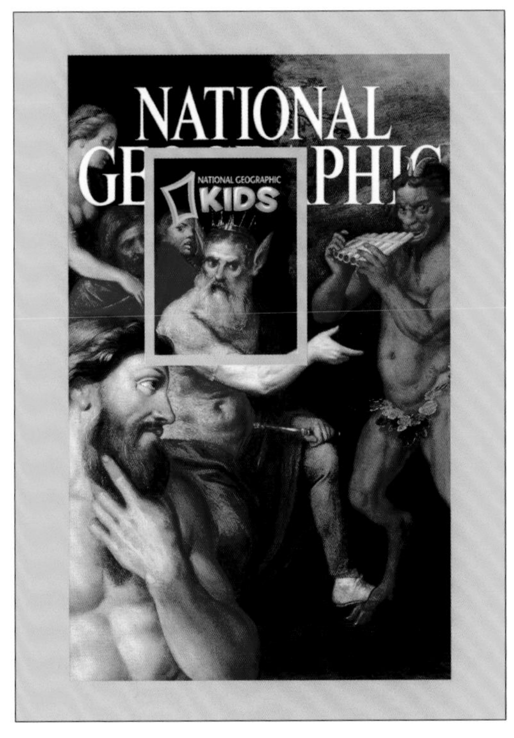

Agency	Rafineri, Istanbul
Creative Director	Ayşe Bali
Copywriter	Gökhan Özdemir
Art Director	Faruk Terzi
Advertiser	National Geographic, "Magazine Covers"

male
diction

The results of 4000 years of male domination
are revealed only in the proper context.

to
get
her

The secret rules of online dating
are revealed only in the proper context.

new
steam

The search for new business models within
the media is revealed only in the proper context.

in
car
nation

The reinvention of the US car industry is
revealed only in the proper context.

Agency	Havas Worldwide, Zurich
Creative Directors	Frank Bodin Michael Kathe
Copywriters	Jan Hertel Beat Gloor
Art Director	Andrea Huber
Graphic Design	Anne-Marie Pappas
Advertiser	Schweizer Monat Magazine, "Word Split"

Print
Send
Comments (632)
AA+
Share 72K
Tweet 90K
Like 94K
Tag: ukraine, europe, reverse
delo ua
News briefly

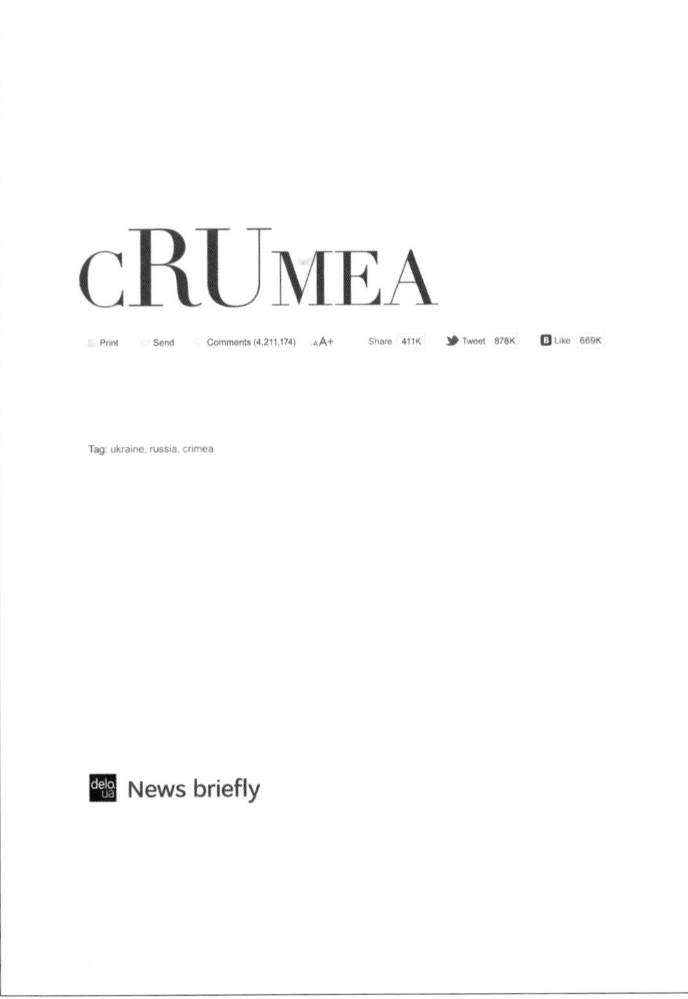

cRUMEA
Print
Send
Comments (4,211,174)
AA+
Share 411K
Tweet 878K
Like 669K
Tag: ukraine, russia, crimea
delo ua
News briefly

Agency Leo Burnett, Kiev
Creative Director Tatiana Fedorenko
Copywriter Vladimir Navrotskyi
Art Director Denys Savchenko
Agency Producer Kateryna Denysenko
Advertiser delo.ua, "Oneword News"

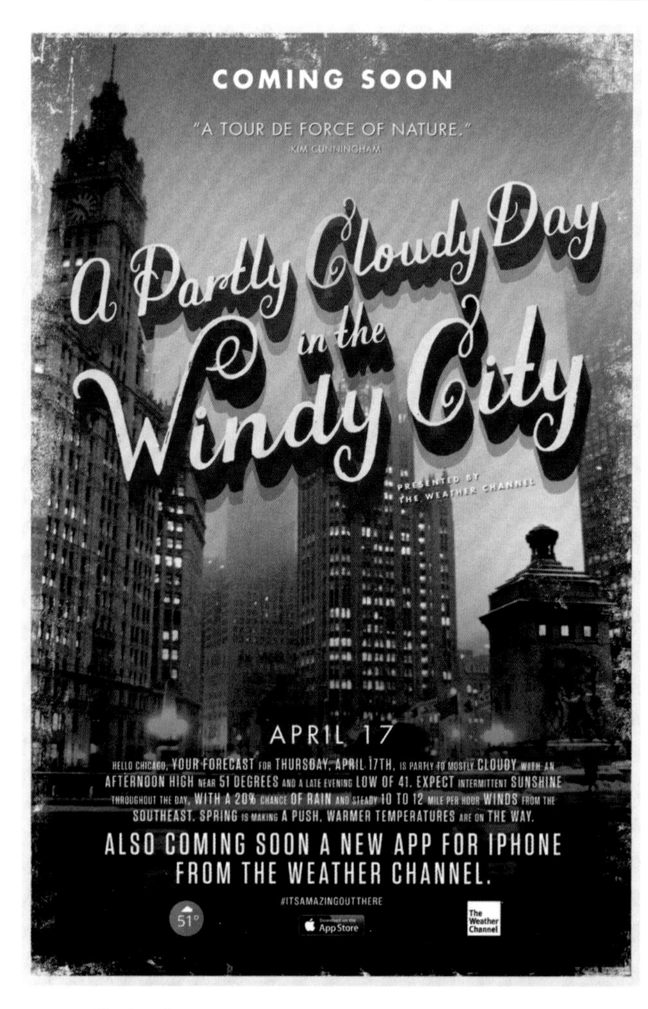

Agency	BBDO New York	**Art Directors**	Camilo De Gafore
CCOs	David Lubars		Lauren Hom
	Greg Hahn	**Sr. Integrated Producer**	Katie Krueger
Executive CD	Tom Markham	**Sr. Print Producer**	Mike Musano
Creative Directors	Peter Albores	**Art Buyer**	Megan Maquera
	Hunter Fine	**Advertiser**	The Weather Channel,
	Andre Massis		"Know the Weather
Copywriter	Lucas Owens		Coming Soon"

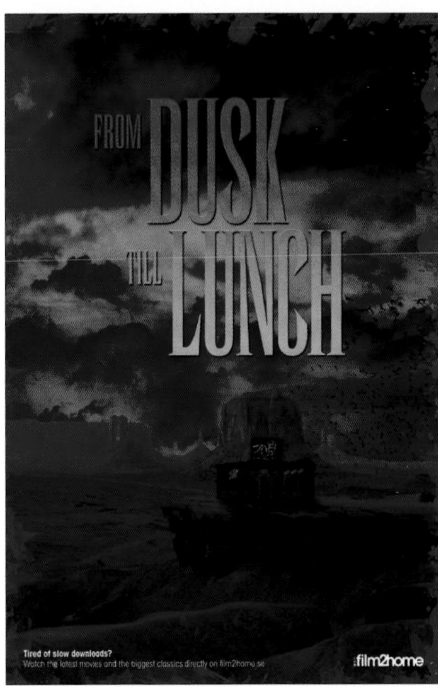

Agency	TBWA\Stockholm
Creative Director	Kalle Widgren
Copywriter	Johannes Ivarsson
Art Directors	Andre Persson Martin Baude Alexander Fredlund
Graphic Designers	Christian Styffe Fanny von Pongracz
Advertiser	Film2home, "Tired of Slow Downloads?"

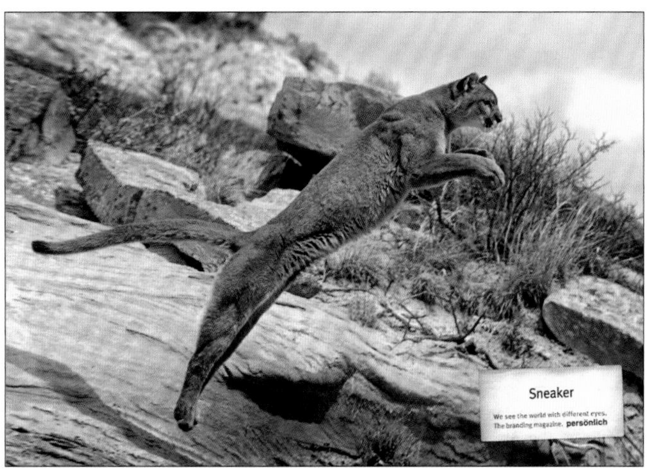

Sneaker
We see the world with different eyes.
The branding magazine. persönlich

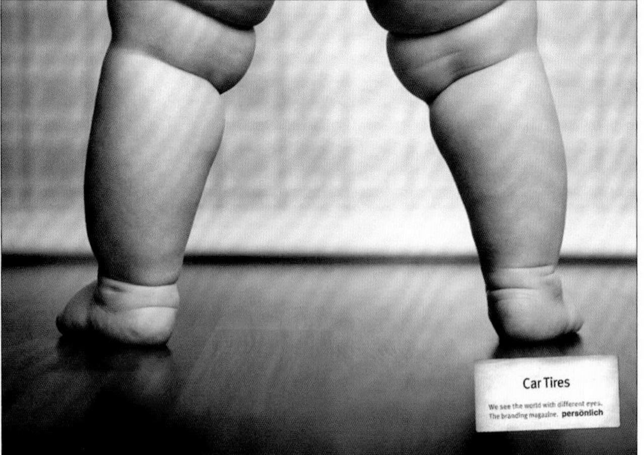

Car Tires
We see the world with different eyes.
The branding magazine. persönlich

Men's Magazine
We see the world with different eyes.
The branding magazine. persönlich

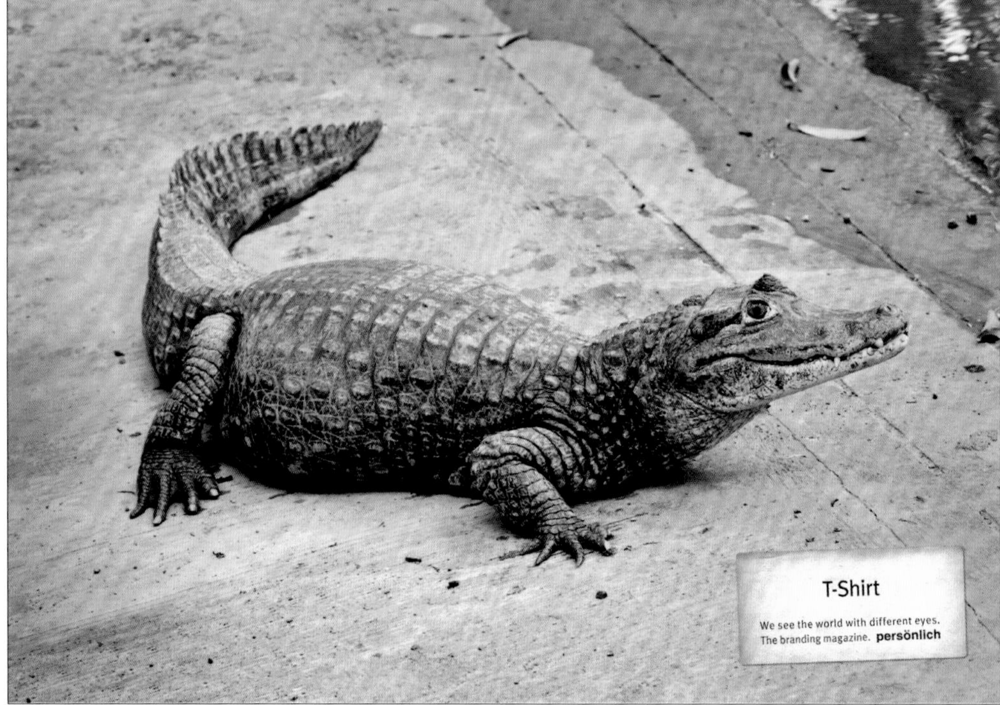

T-Shirt
We see the world with different eyes.
The branding magazine. persönlich

 Media

Agency	Ruf Lanz, Zurich
Creative Directors	Markus Ruf Danielle Lanz
Copywriter	Andreas Hornung
Art Director	Isabelle Hauser
Post Production	Isabelle Hauser
Advertiser	Persoenlich Advertising Magazine, "Image Campaign"

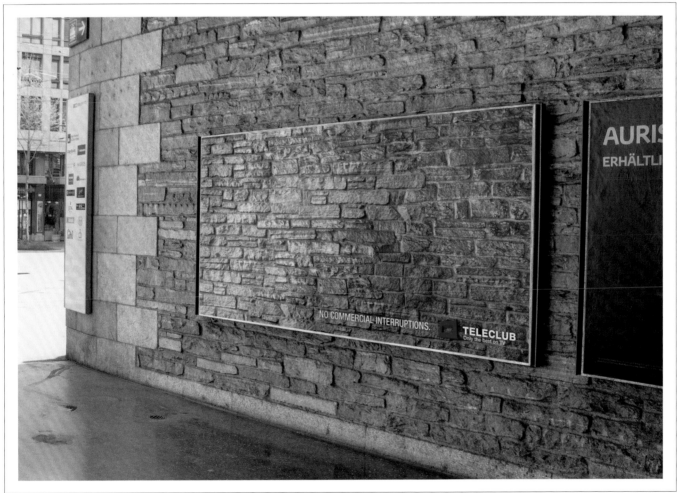

Agency	Y&R, Zurich
CCO	Markus Gut
Executive CD	Dominik Oberwiler
Copywriter	Fabian Küchler
Art Directors	Lukas Wietlisbach Fabian Küchler
Advertiser	Teleclub Pay-TV, "No Interruptions"

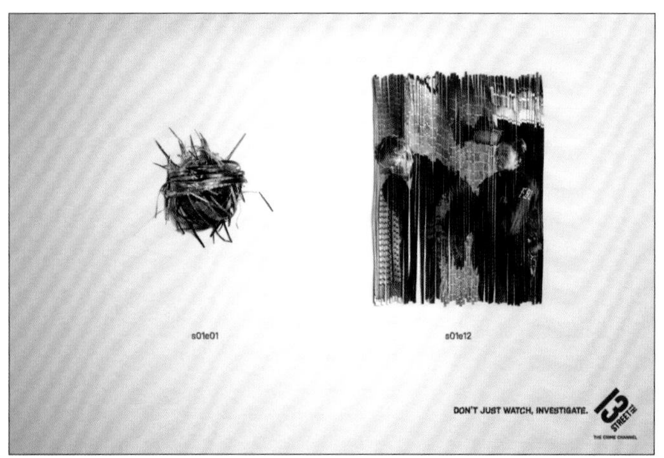

00:00:00

01:42:18

DON'T JUST WATCH, INVESTIGATE.

13 STREET

THE CRIME CHANNEL

Media

Agency	BETC, Paris
Creative Directors	Stéphane Xiberras Olivier Apers
Copywriter	Adrian Skenderovic
Art Director	Alphons Conzen
Advertiser	13e Rue TV Channel, "Reassembled Evidence"

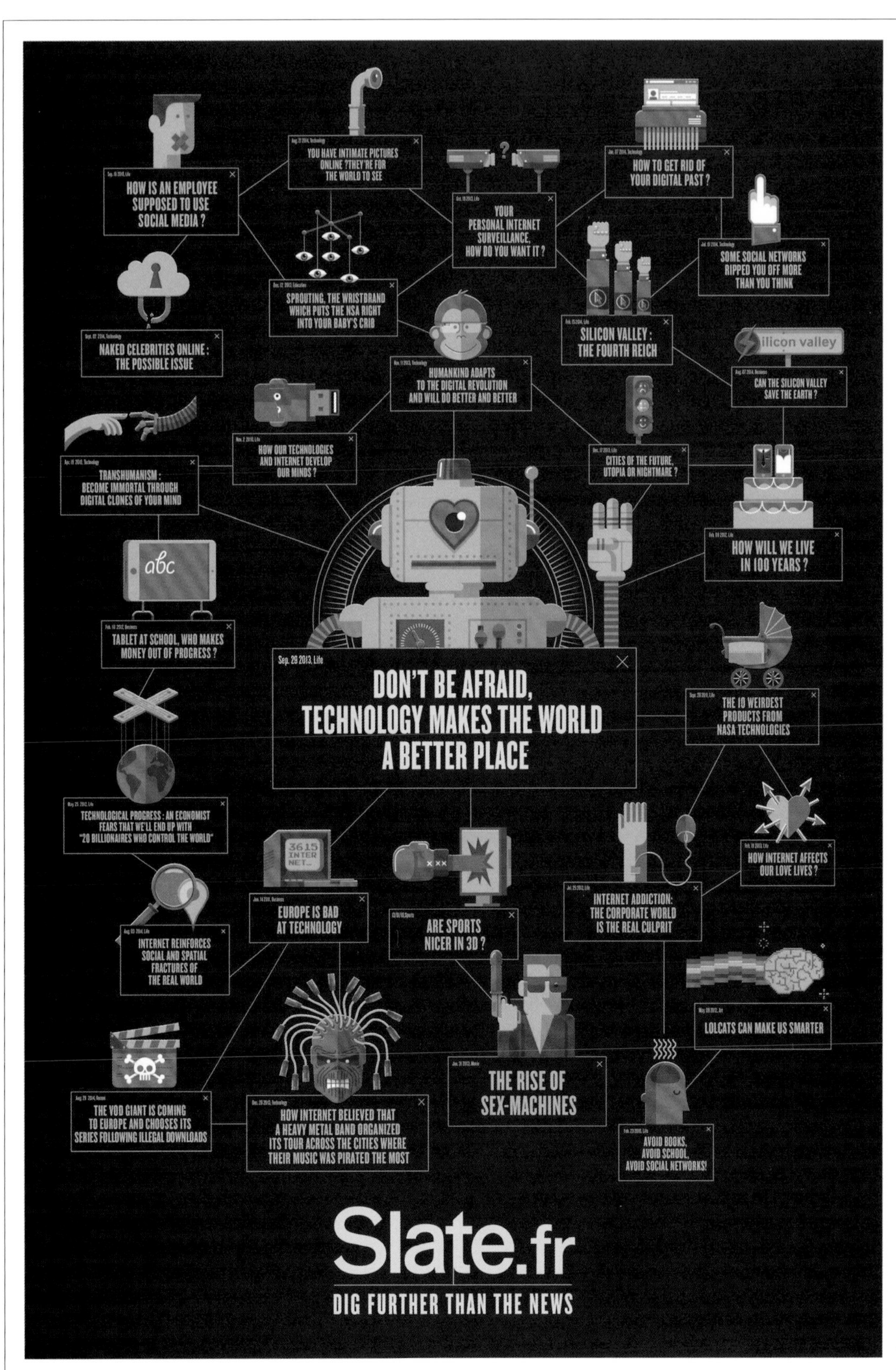

Agency	Havas 360, Paris	Illustrator/Graphic Design	WeAreTed
Executive CD	Thomas Derouault	Agency Producer	Cécile Ousset
Creative Director	Alban Pénicaut	Advertiser	Slate.fr, Online Magazine, "Dig Further Than the News"
Art Directors	Franck Lebraly Alfred Pelamatti		
Copywriters	Alban Pénicaut Antoine Palle Cédric Guillossou		

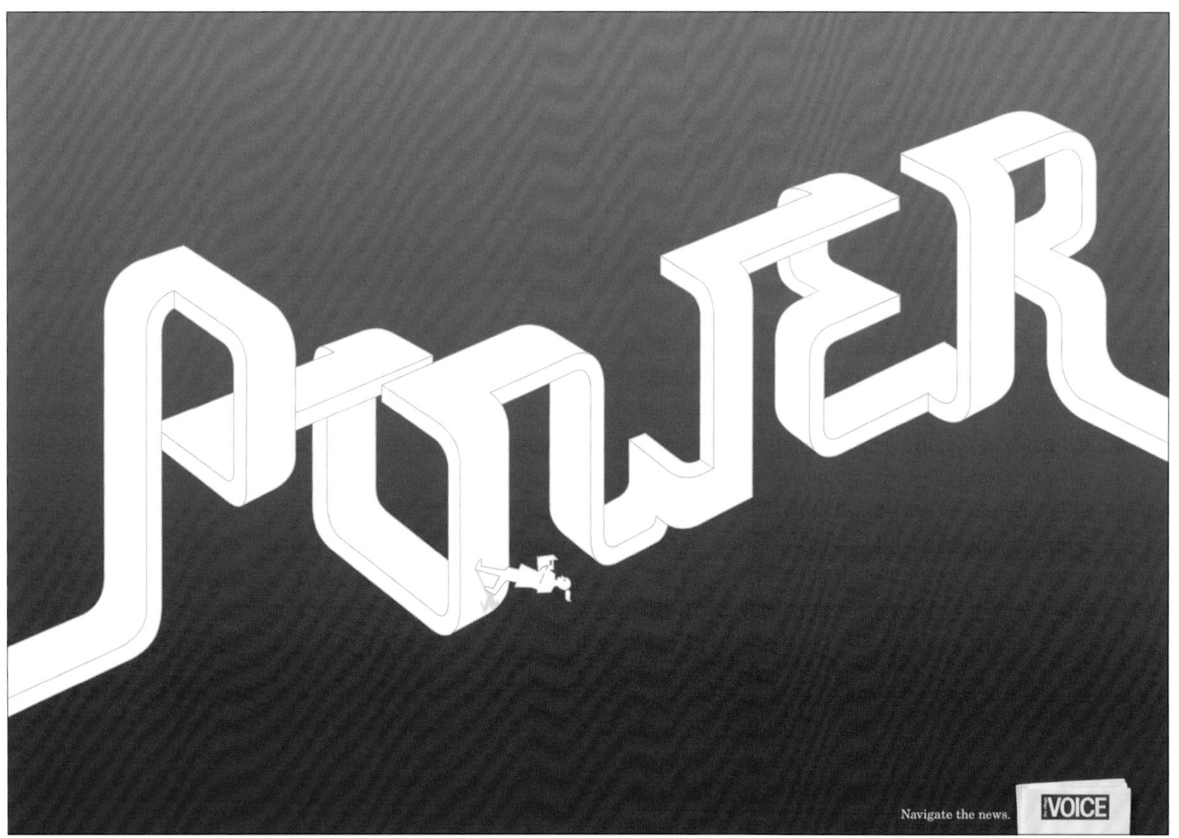

Media

Agency	BBDO New York
Chief Creative Officers	David Lubars Greg Hahn
Senior Creative Directors	Danilo Boer Grant Smith
Copywriter	Grant Smith
Art Director	Danilo Boer
Agency Producer	Casey Flax
Illustrators	Bob Partington Danilo Boer
Advertiser	The Village Voice Newspaper, "Navigate the News"

Agency	TBWA\Stockholm
Creative Director	Kalle Widgren
Copywriters	Nayeli Kremb Andre Persson
Art Directors	Nayeli Kremb Andre Persson
Production	Agent Molly, Stockholm
Illustrator	Thomas Feiner
Graphic Design	Christian Styffe
Advertiser	film2home, "Look Up"

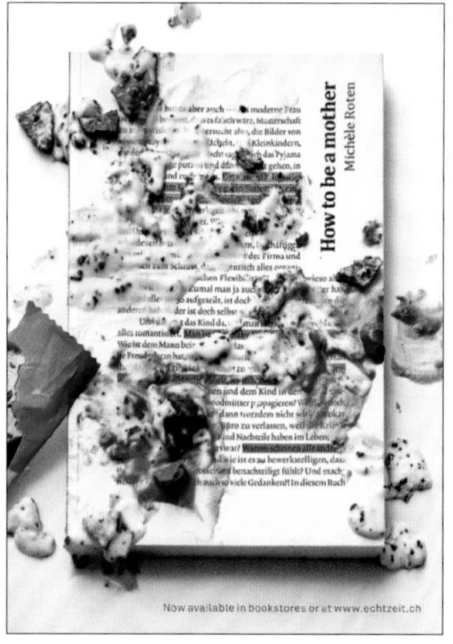

 Media

Agency	Ruf Lanz, Zurich
Creative Directors	Markus Ruf Danielle Lanz
Copywriter	Markus Ruf
Art Director	Isabelle Hauser
Photographer	Marie-Christine Gerber
Illustrators	Luca, Anna, Sara (3 years old), Laura (2 years old), Noah (4 years old)
Advertiser	Echtzeit Publishing, "How To Be a Mother"

Agency	The Newtons Laboratory, Athens
Creative Director	Andreas Dimitroulas
Copywriter	Kostas Binis
Art Directors	Liveris Yiannis Dimitris Vikelis
Advertiser	Parapolitika Newspaper, "Obama", "Merkel", "Putin"

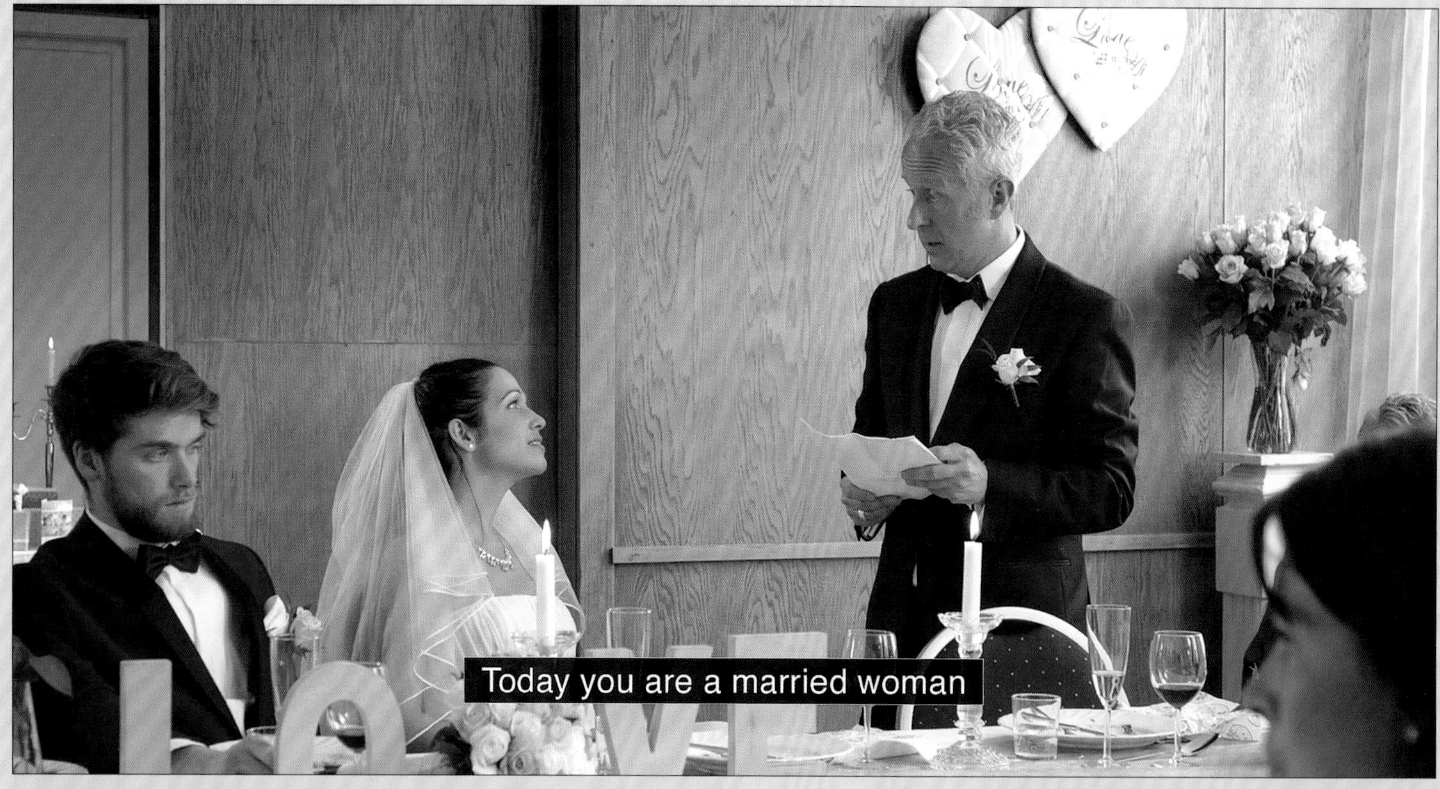
Today you are a married woman

You will allways be my little girl

Her dad will cry like a baby.

If her father cries, I´ll do a striptease after dinner.

Deal!

Life´s more fun when
something´s at stake

Find your next bet at Oddsen

oddsen

Agency	TRY/Apt/POL, Oslo
Copywriter	Jonas Grønnern
Art Director	Lars Kristian Harveg
Production	Bacon, Oslo
Film Director	Andreas Riiser
Producers	Magne Lyngner Mari Grundnes Paus
Advertiser	Oddsen, "The Wedding Speech"

At a wedding reception, the father of the bride is giving a boring speech. "Now you are a married woman…" he drones, as most of the guests look ready to nod off. Except for two guys, who are hanging on his every word. When the father sheds a tear, one of the men looks aghast. "Yes!" says the other under his breath. In a flash-back, we see the guys making a bet: "If her father cries, I'll striptease after dinner." "Deal!" Life is more fun when something's at stake. Place your next bet through Oddsen.

WILDLIFE IS BACK IN TOWN

WILDLIFE IS BACK IN TOWN

WILDLIFE IS BACK IN TOWN

PARIS ZOO
WILDLIFE IS BACK IN TOWN
RE-OPENING IN APRIL

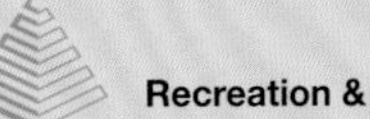

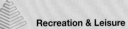

Agency Publicis Conseil, Paris
Creative Directors Olivier Altmann, Frédéric Royer
Copywriter Bangaly Fofana
Art Director Benoît Blumberger
Photographer Ronan Merot
Process Manager Valérie Marquant
Art buyer Jean Luc Chirio, Flore Silberfeld
Retouching Adrien Bénard
Advertiser Paris Zoo, "Paris Zoo-Wildlife is Back in Town"

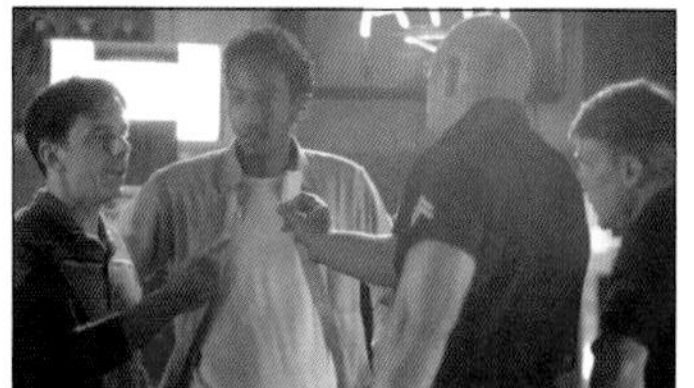

Agency BETC, Paris
Creative Director Stéphane Xiberras
Copywriter Arnaud Assouline
Art Director Benjamin Le Breton
Production Rita Films, Paris
Film Director Cécilia Verheyden
Producer Michel Teicher
Advertiser Watchdogs, "The Amazing Street Hack"

The manager of a telephone repair shop offers "a special gift" to real customers who ask him to fix their phones. One by one, he takes them out onto the street and convinces them that with his new app they are now able to control the street lights. They can also unlock cars and hack ATMs. They can even change the traffic lights, which rapidly causes an accident. When the police arrive, he denies everything, leaving the duped customers to explain. But it's all a prank, filmed with hidden cameras, to promote the videogame Watchdogs.

Agency Leo Burnett, Paris
Executive CD Xavier Beauregard
Copywriter Hadi Hassan-Helou
Art Director Jérôme Gonfond
Production Blue Film Production, Paris
Film Director Jean-Marc Gosse
Producers Patrick André, Marie Archambeaud
Advertiser Bastille Theater, "The Fake Trailer"

This cinema ad looks at first like a rather clichéd film trailer. It's Christmas time, and ageing writer Mr Bates falls for his somewhat younger new housekeeper. Just as they're about to embrace, the wardrobe door opens. Out comes a naked man with a long beard. He parts it to reveal an opera-singing mask in the place of his genitals. The Theatre de la Bastille: really unexpected shows.

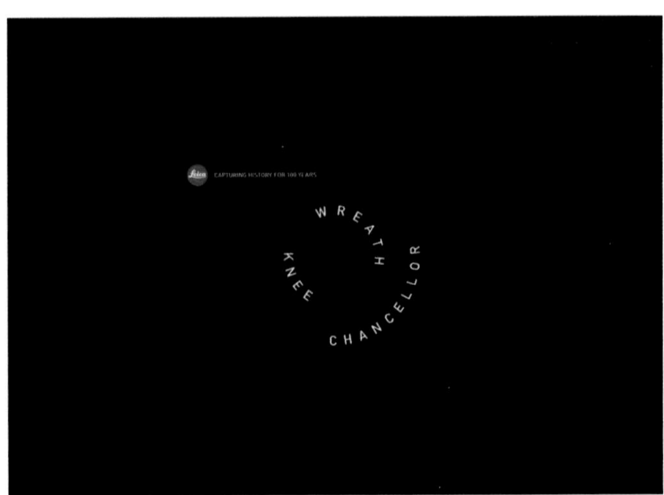

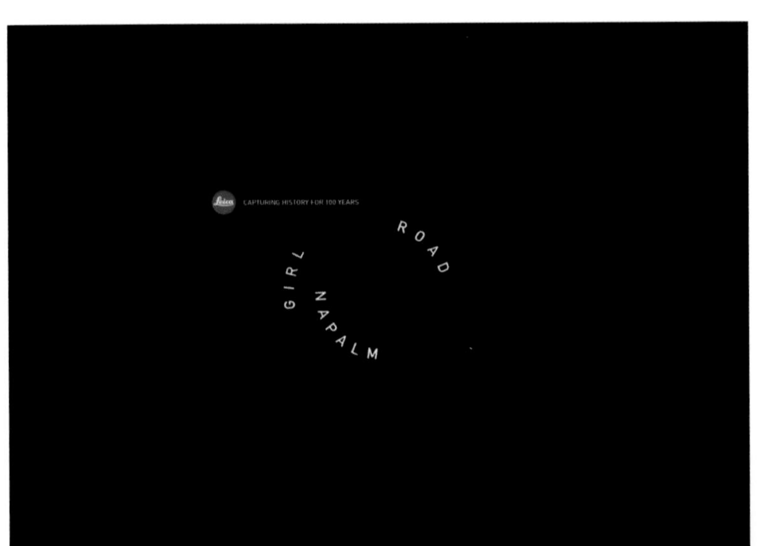

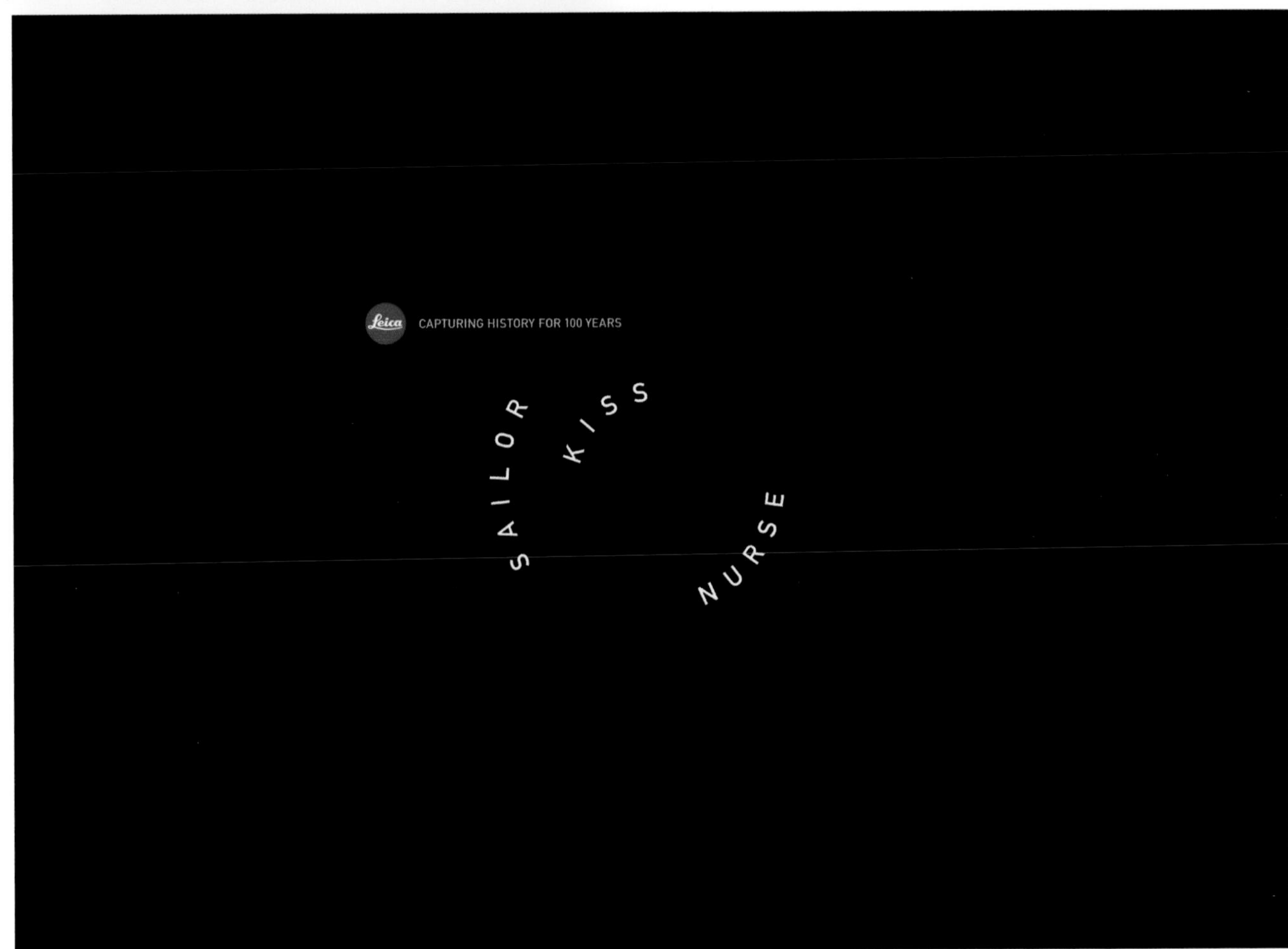

Agency	Geometry Global, Berlin	**Art Directors**	Mona Pust Nina Gruen Sabine Bartels
CCO	Christian Mommertz		
CD Branding & Design	Felix Duerichen	**Advertiser**	Leica Camera, "Iconic Leica Pictures"
Creative Director	Anita Stoll		
Associate CD	Jutta Haeussler		
Senior Copywriter	Phillip von Buttlar		
Senior Art Directors	Sabine Brinkmann Oliver Rapp		

Agency	DDB Paris
Executive CD	Alexandre Hervé
Copywriter	Jean-François Bouchet
Art Director	Emmanuel Courteau
Advertiser	Hasbro, "Trivial Pursuit"

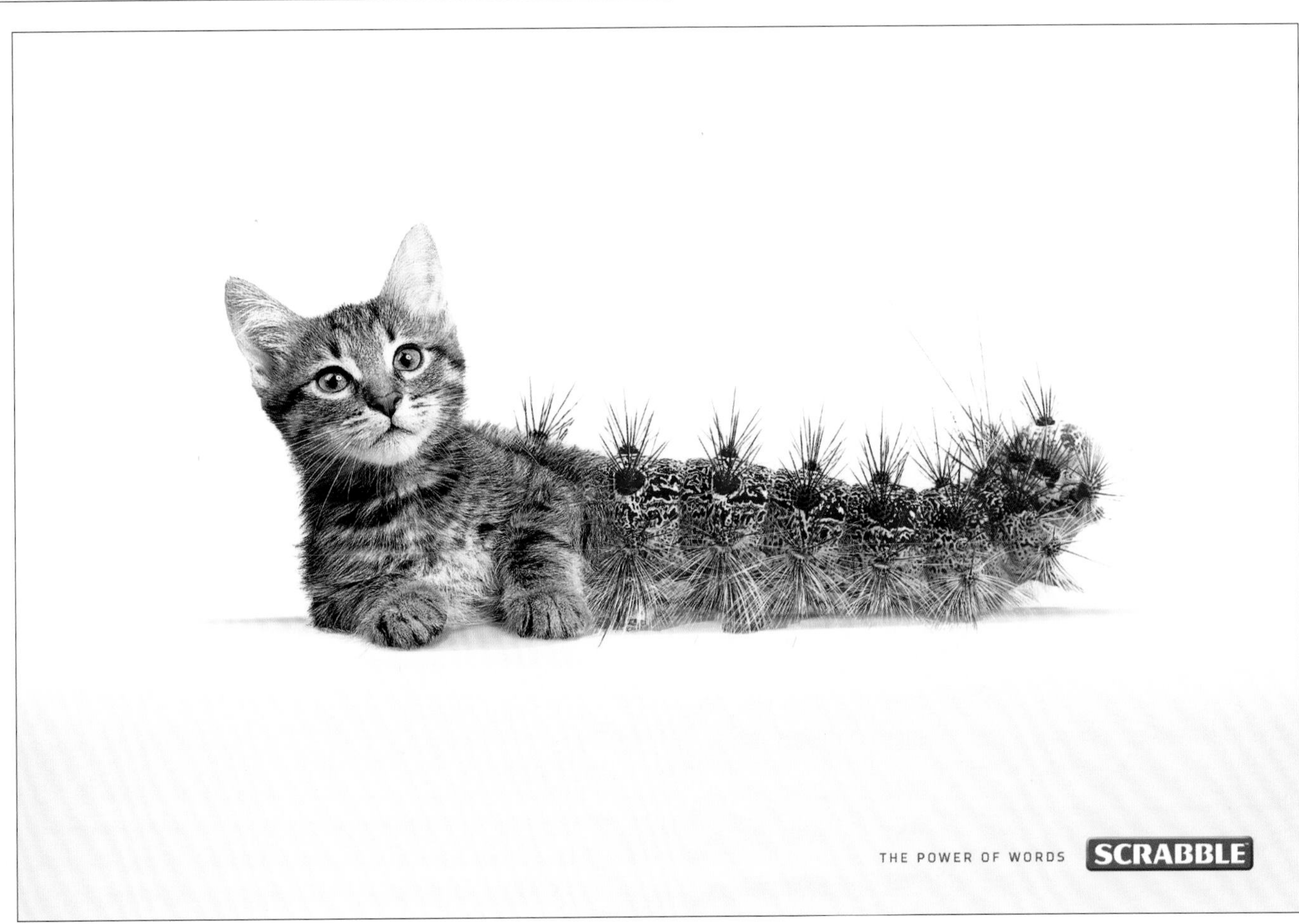

Agency	Twiga, Kiev
Creative Director	Slava Fokin
Copywriters	Slava Fokin Dima Tsapko
Art Director	Dima Tsapko
Production	Tough Slate Design, Kiev
Advertiser	Scrabble, "The Power of Words"

Celebrate the World Cup on Ladbrokes.com

Agency McCann Copenhagen
Creative Directors Cliff Kagawa Holm, Silas Jansson
Art Directors Cliff Kagawa Holm, Silas Jansson
Photographer Johan Palm
Production B-Reel, Stockholm
Film Director Emil Möller
Producers Rikard Äström, Cathrin Holmqvist
Advertiser Ladbrokes.com, "Iconic Celebration"

Something is going on in the night-time streets of Rio, as sewing machines chatter and a swathe of material is loaded into the back of a van. In the morning, a young boy dribbles a soccer ball, imitating the traditional goal celebration by slipping his shirt over his head and extending his arms like wings. Suddenly there's a hubbub on the street, and he follows the crowds to see… Christ the Redeemer, with a football shirt over his head. Celebrate the World Cup on betting site Ladbrokes.com.

Agency TBWA\España, Madrid
Creative Directors Juan Sańchez, Guillermo Ginés, Fran López, Vicente Rodriguez
Copywriter Vicente Rodriguez
Art Director Fran López
Photographer Jesus Alonso
Production Jesus Alonso Studio, Madrid
Agency Producer Nuria Mazarío
Advertiser Sony Playstation, "Fireman"

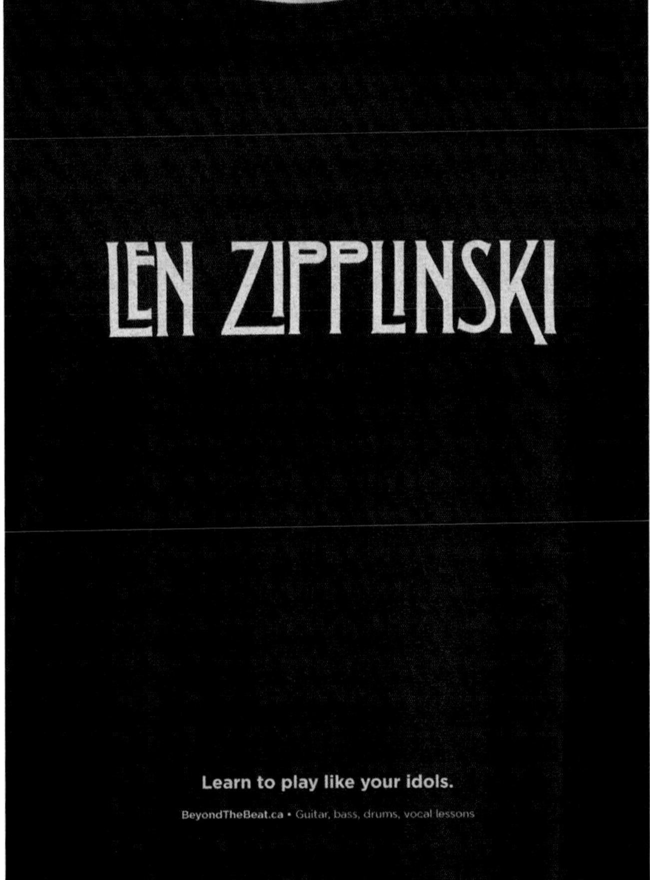

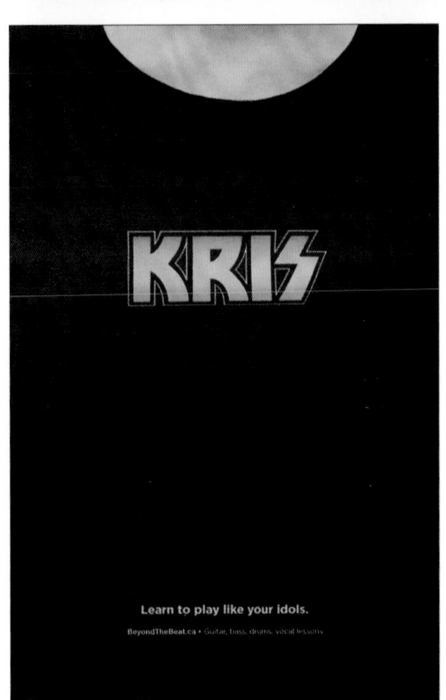

Agency	Zulu Alpha Kilo, Toronto
Creative Director	Zak Mroueh
Copywriter	Jerry Brens
Art Director	Jenny Luong
Photographer	Daniel Ehrenworth
Agency Producer	Kari Macknight Dearborn
Illustrator	Jenny Luong
Studio Artist	Brandon Dyson
Advertiser	Beyond the Beat Music Studio, "Icons"

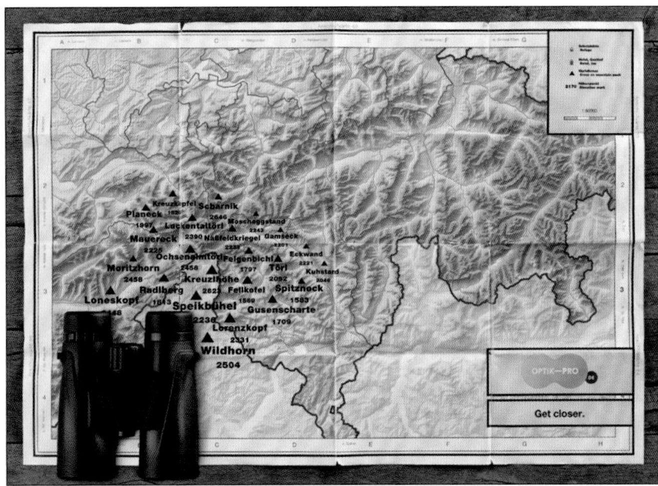

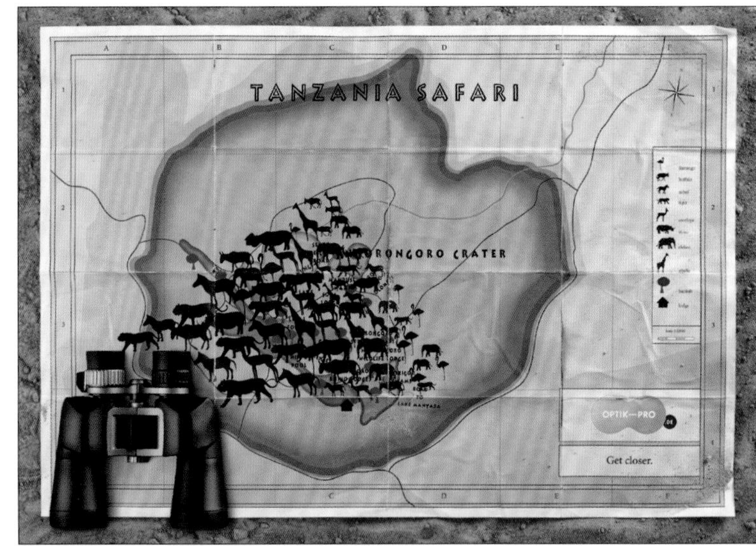

 Recreation & Leisure

Agency	Leo Burnett, Frankfurt
Creative Directors	Andreas Pauli Daniela Ewald Jörg Hoffmann Alexander Haase Irina Schestakov
Copywriter	Julian Windischmann
Art Director	Julian Windischmann
Photographer	Mark Wuchner
Production	Prodigious, Frankfurt
Advertiser	Optik-Pro Binoculars, "Maps"

THE 54° GENOA
INTERNATIONAL
BOAT SHOW
The world of boating meets Italian style.
Genoa, October 1-6, 2014 - genoaboatshow.com

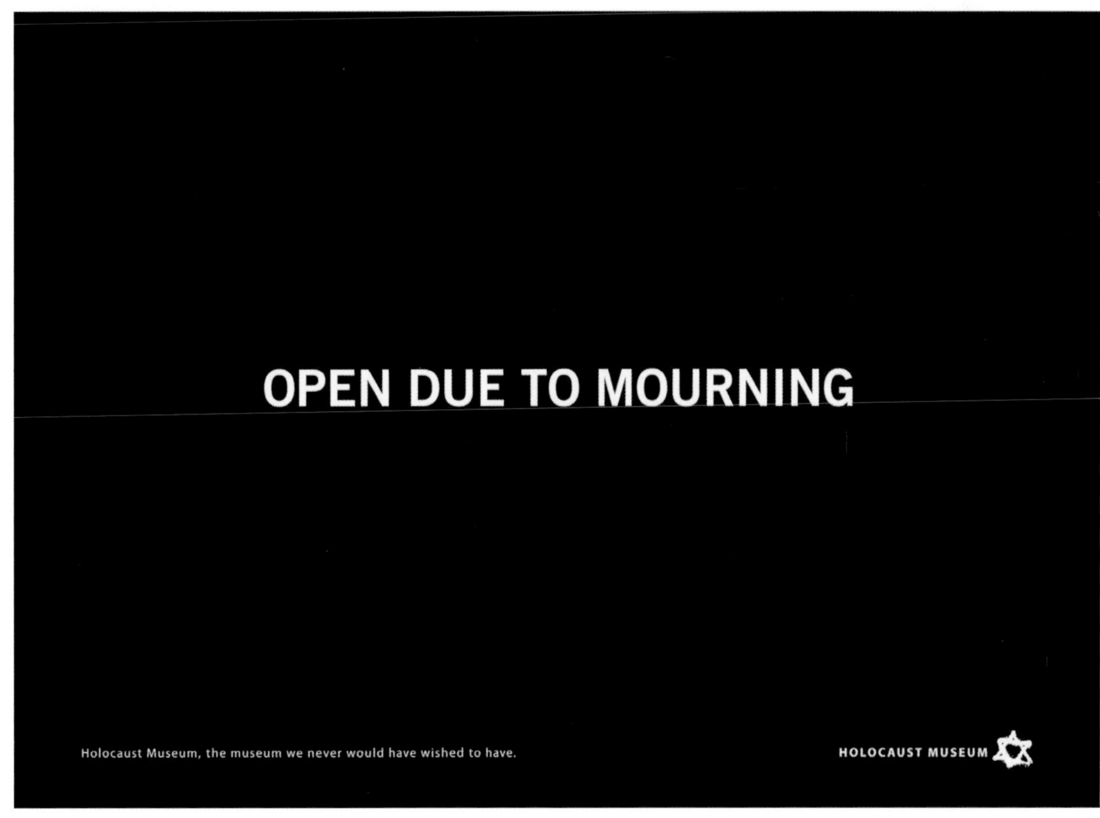

Holocaust Museum, the museum we never would have wished to have.

Agency	Meloria, Genoa
Creative Directors	Livio Gerosa Andrea Rosagni
Copywriters	Marco De Rosa Sara Tetro Manolo Trebaiocchi
Art Directors	Enzo Girardi Tatiana Foroni Fulvio Rumazza
Photographer	Scatto, Milan
Advertiser	54th Genoa International Boat Show, "Swaying"

Agency	FWK Argentina, Buenos Aires
Creative Director	Christian Oneto Gaona
Copywriters	Christian Oneto Gaona Juan Repetto
Art Director	Martin Tortonese
Advertiser	Holocaust Museum, "Open Due to Mourning"

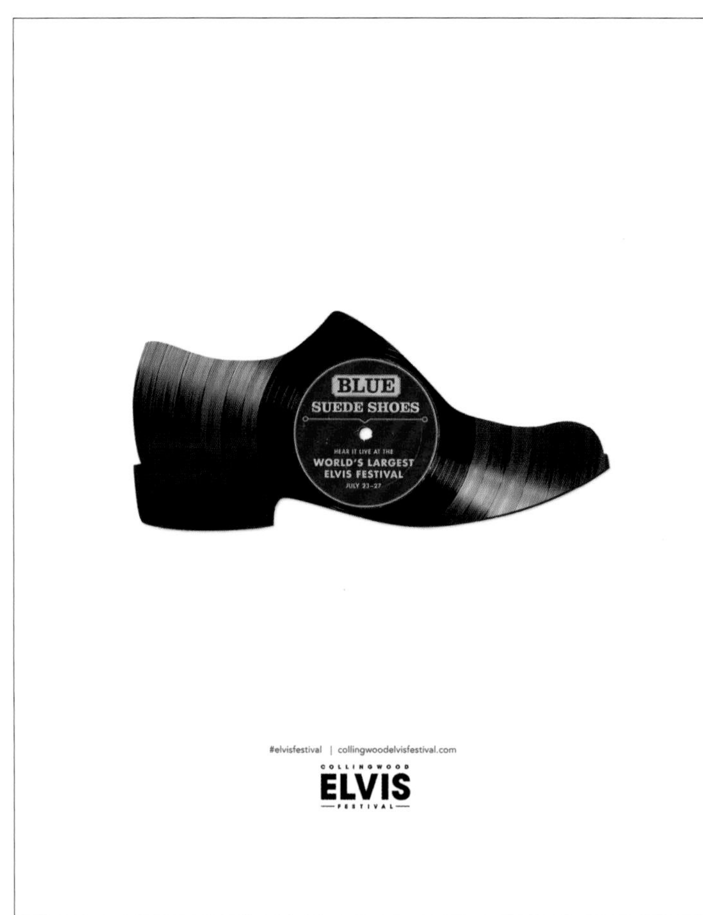

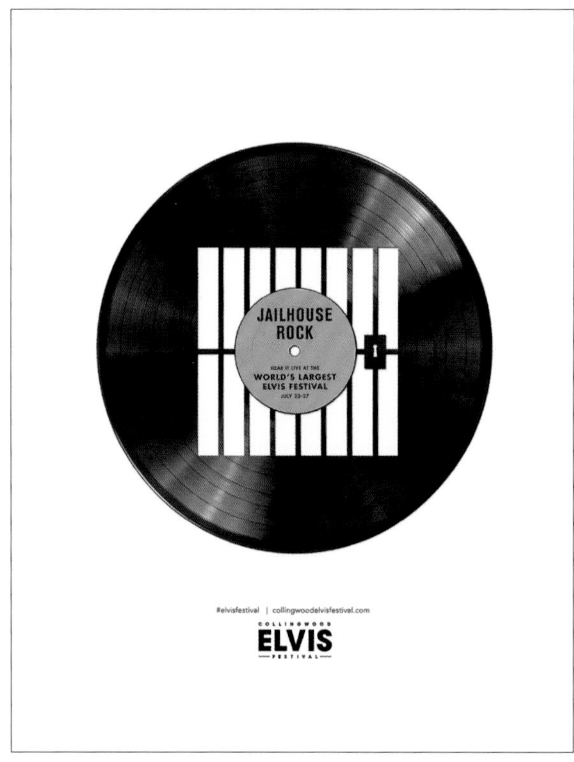

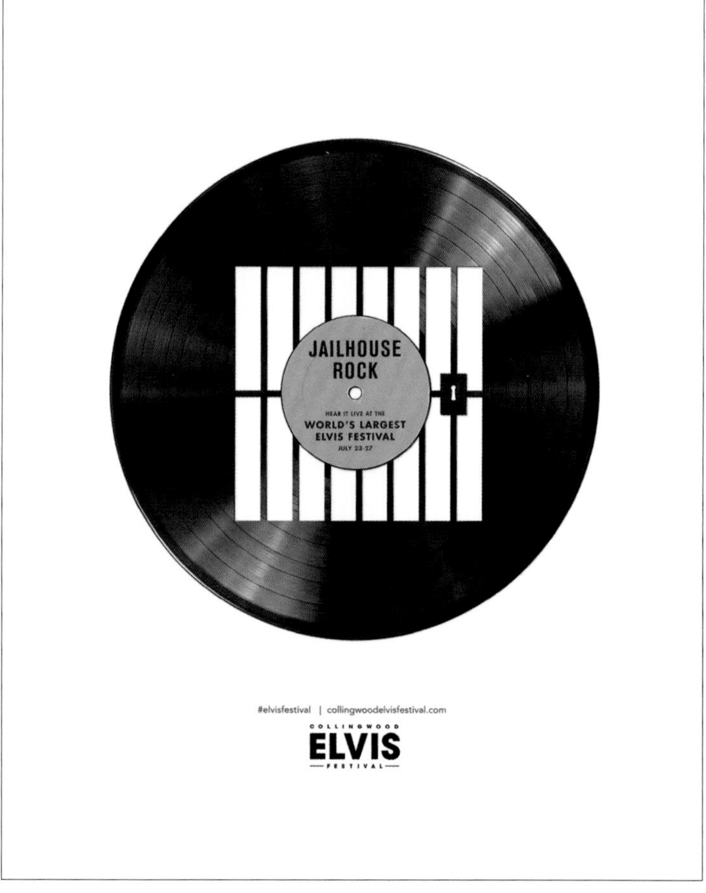

Recreation & Leisure

Agency	Zulu Alpha Kilo, Toronto
Creative Director	Zak Mroueh
Copywriter	Nick Asik
Art Director	Allan Mah
Photographer	Jamie Morren
Digital Imaging	Brandon Dyson
Mac Artist	Greg Heptinstall
Agency Producers	Kari Macknight Dearborn Kate Spencer
Advertiser	Elvis Festival, "Collingwood Elvis Festival"

ARE YOU
KIDDING?
HARDLY
BREATHING.
WHERE IS THIS
LEADING? LOOK,
I DON'T NEED A
HAND. THIS FEELS
GRAND.
HEADSTAND

YOU HAVE IT IN YOU

NOT POSSIBLE.
LOOKS HURTABLE.
KIND OF STABLE.
JUST INCREDIBLE.
EASY AS A PIE I
HAD FOR LUNCH.
STIFFNESS,
CONGE!
LOW LUNGE

YOU HAVE IT IN YOU

NO WAY.
WITH MY
WEIGHT?
I JUST ATE!
HEY, WAIT!
BEFORE YOU
NOTICE.
LOTUS

YOU HAVE IT IN YOU

Agency	New Moment New Ideas Company Y&R, Belgrade
Creative Director	Svetlana Copic
Copywriter	Svetlana Copic
Art Director	Vladimir Radivojevic
Advertiser	Namaste Yoga Studio, "You Have It In You"

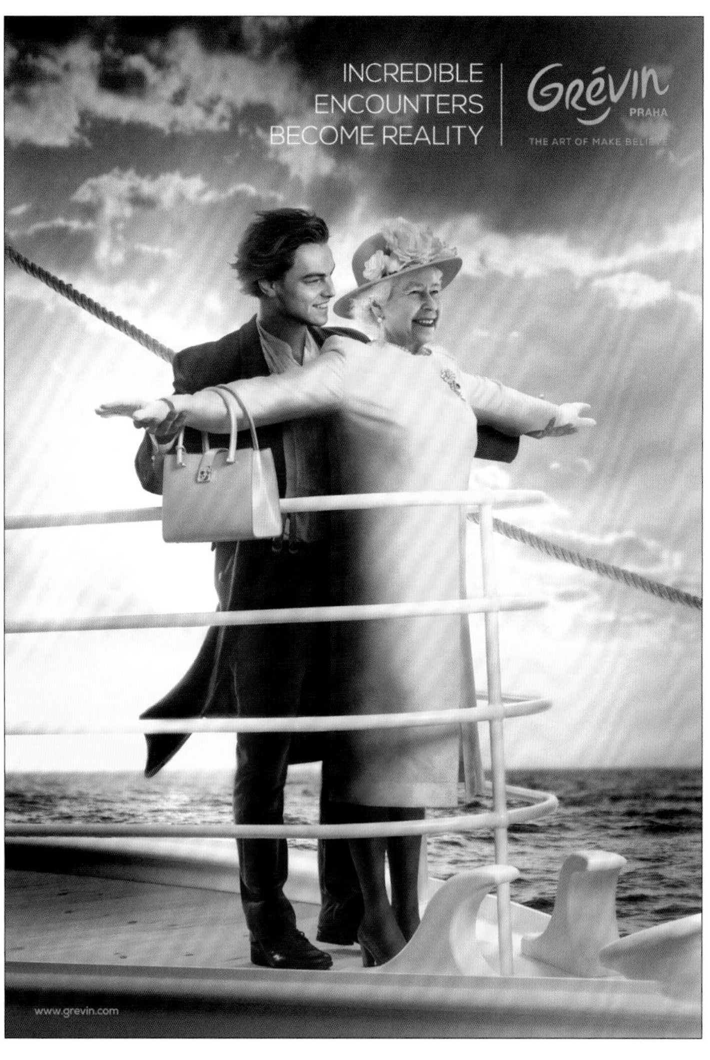

Agency Havas Worldwide, Prague
Creative Directors Eda Kauba, Pavel Fris
Copywriter Zdenek Maly
Art Directors Pavel Slovacek, Jan Lesak
Photographer Roman Dietrich
Agency Producer Barbora Safarikova
Post-Production Playground, Prague
Advertiser Grévin Museum, "Incredible Encounters"

Agency Volt, Stockholm
Copywriter Petter Nylind
Art Director Jörgen Berglund
Photographer Petter Brandt
Production Bsmart, Stockholm
Final Art Åsa Stjärnquist
Advertiser Friskis&Svettis Stockholm Gyms, "The Workout Burger"

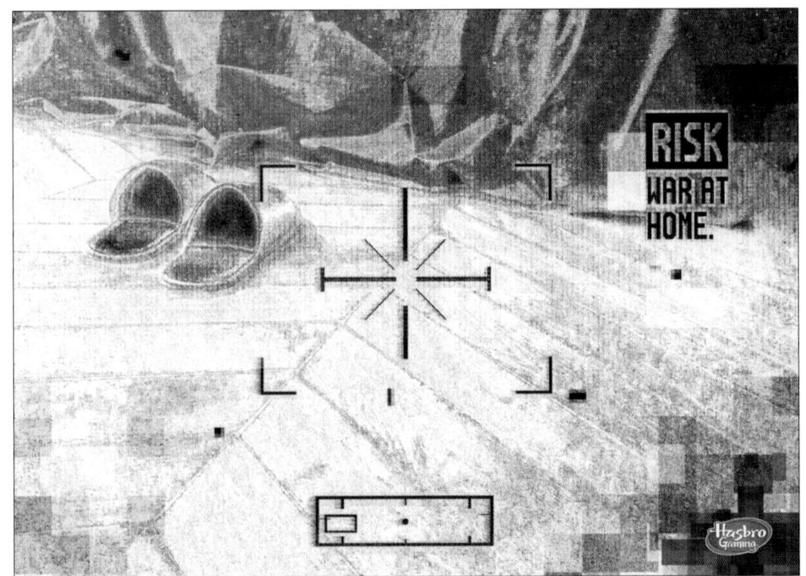

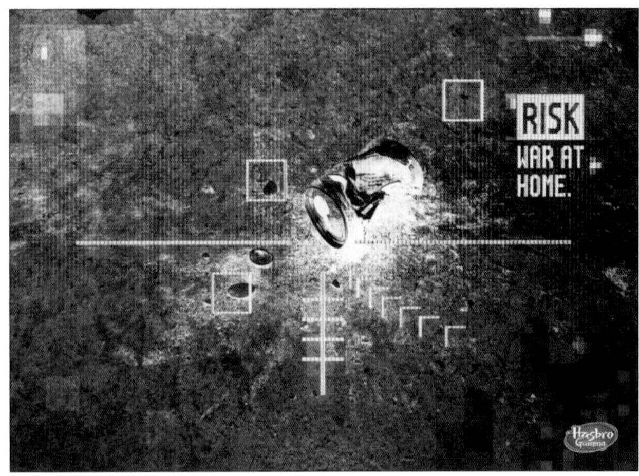

Agency	DDB Paris
Executive CD	Alexandre Hervé
Copywriter	Fabien Teichner
Art Directors	Alexandre Lagoet Francis Pluntz
Advertiser	Hasbro, “Domestic War”

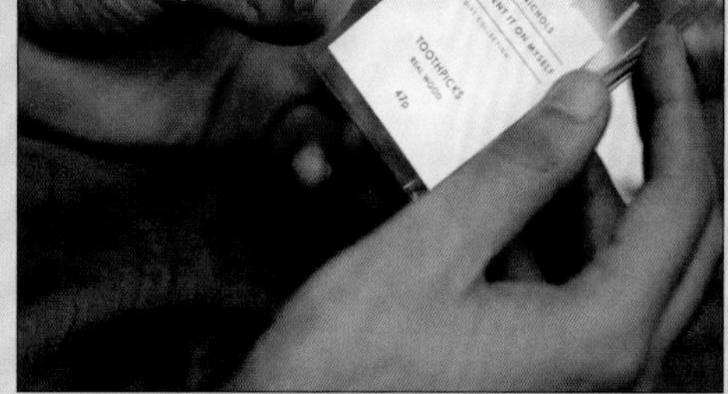

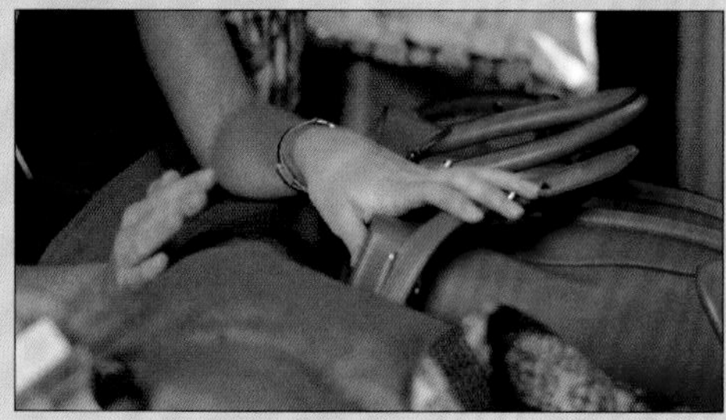

Luxury & Premium Brands

Agency adam&eveDDB, London
Executive CDs Ben Priest, Ben Tollett, Emer Stamp
Creatives Richard Brim, Daniel Fisher
Agency Producer Victoria Keenan
Production Outsider, London
Film Director James Rouse
Producer Benji Howell
Cameraman Alex Melman
Editor Bill Smedley, Work Post, London
Post Producer Josh King, MPC, London
Sound Factory Studio, London
Advertiser Harvey Nichols, "Sorry, I Spent It On Myself"

Presenting a series of selfish shoppers who snapped up nicely packaged but cheap gifts – ranging from elastic bands to a sink plug – from UK luxury store Harvey Nichols. As the faces of the recipients drop, the camera shows us where the money really went: on a posh dress, shoes or bag. The "Sorry, I Spent It On Myself Gift Collection", from Harvey Nichols.

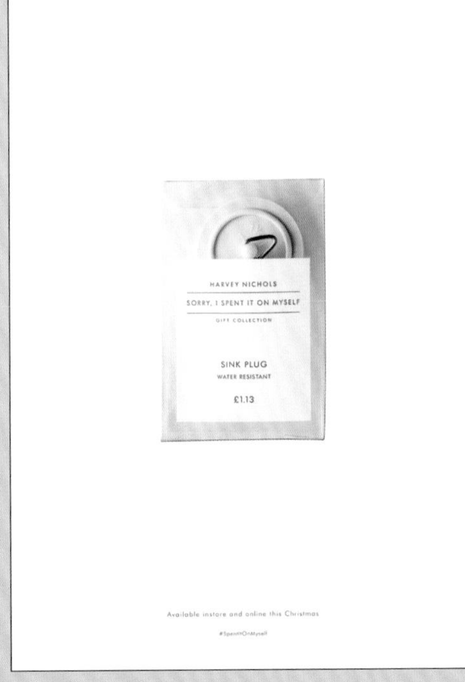

Agency	adam&eveDDB, London
Executive CDs	Ben Priest Ben Tollett Emer Stamp
Creatives	Richard Brim Daniel Fisher
Creative Producer	Kirsty Harris
Head of Print	Daniel Moorey
Designer/Typographer	Alex Fairman, Stanley's King Henry
Retouching	Stanley's King Henry
Photographer	James Day
Advertiser	Harvey Nichols, "Sorry, I Spent It On Myself"

It may be difficult to find a beautiful tooth brush – but would you really want a packet of gravel for Christmas? "Sorry, I Spent It On Myself" was not just a smartly cynical ad, it was also a genuine range of goods, available from "Harvey Nicks" in-store and online, and depicted in these print ads.

Agency Armando Testa, Turin
Executive CD Michele Mariani
Copywriter Federico Bonenti
Art Director Alessandro Padalino
Photographer Serge Guerand
Production BRW Filmland, Milan
Film Director Serge Guerand
Executive Producer Maurizio Coppolecchia
Client Director Tiziana Travo
Advertiser Giorgio Armani Eyewear, "Frames of Life, The Encounter"

This picturesque ad for Armani eyewear, shot in luminous black and white, depicts a woman who leaves her glasses on a subway in Shanghai. She does so quite deliberately, as a lure for a young man who's caught her eye. A cat-and-mouse pursuit through the city follows, featuring numerous changes of eyewear, until the pair are finally united at a chic rooftop bar. He returns her glasses tenderly, and a romance is born.

Agency CHI & Partners, London
Executive CD Jonathan Burley
Creative Director Monty Verdi
Copywriters & ADs Angus Vine, Colin Smith
Production Stink, London
Film Director Adam Berg
Producer Ben Croker
Agency Producer Nicola Ridley
Advertiser Lexus, "Strobe"

A kinetic spot features a series of LED-illuminated mannequins who appear to traverse the urban landscape at night. The amazing light sculptures dive and somersault through trees, across rooftops and among the desks of a deserted office, before landing superhero-style on the roof of the new Lexus. Amazing in motion.

Agency	Ruf Lanz, Zurich
Creative Directors	Danielle Lanz Markus Ruf
Copywriter	Markus Ruf
Art Director	Isabelle Hauser
Photographer	Rico Rosenberger
Post Production	Aschmann Klauser, Zurich
Advertiser	Swiss Deluxe Hotels, "Hidden Guests"

Agency	REM - Ruini e Mariotti, Roma
Creative Director	Riccardo Ruini
Art Director	Li Bjurholm von Euler
Photographer	Terry Richardson
Advertiser	Valentino, "Valentino Accessories Fall Winter 2013"

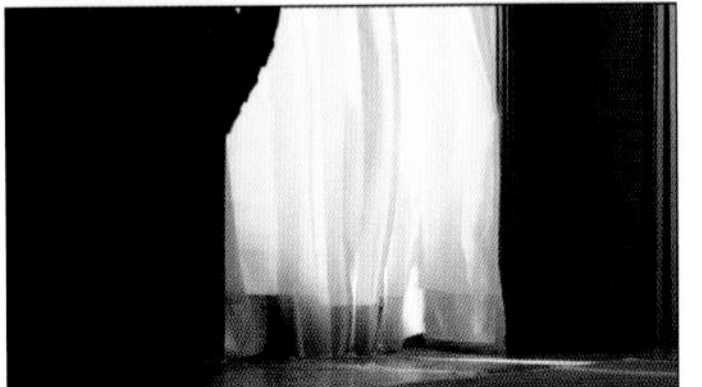

Agency	Mazarine Mlle Noï, Paris
Executive CDs	François Jacquey Valérie Larrondo
Film Director	Johan Renck
Advertiser	Valentino, "Valentino Uomo"

Shades of La Dolce Vita as French actor Louis Garrel gets up to adventures in a beautifully-shot nocturnal Rome. Whether at the wheel of his vintage convertible, hanging out in a subterranean nightclub, or evading the paparazzi with his female companion, Louis always looks impeccable. The pair break into the grounds of an ancient palazzo and indulge in a hedonistic tryst. But in the morning, the palace turns out to be home after all. The universe of Valentino Uomo, a fragrance for men.

Agency	Impact & Echo BBDO, Kuwait
CDs	Cesar Jachan Lokesh Achaiah
Copywriter	Lokesh Achaiah
Art Director	Akram Rehayel
Advertiser	Alghanim Motors Honda Marine Engine, "Quiet Far Away"

Make up is make up

A mufffroom is a mufffroom

Maybe I should use Double A

TOUS LES PAPIERS
NE SE VALENT PAS.
Double A

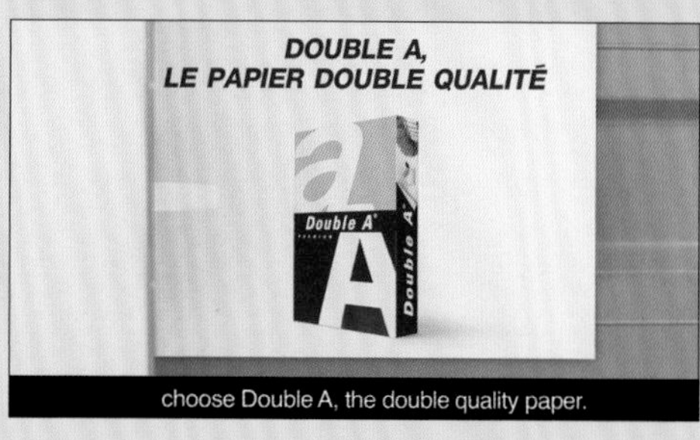

DOUBLE A,
LE PAPIER DOUBLE QUALITÉ
Double A
choose Double A, the double quality paper.

Agency Buzzman, Paris
CEO & CD Georges Mohammed Chérif
Copywriter Régis Boulanger
Art Director Romain Repellin
Art Director Assistant Clément Séchet
TV Producer & Art Buyer Vanessa Barbel
TV Producer Assistant Ayman Jaroudi
Digital Producers Laurent Marcus, Lara-Jane Lelièvre
Film Director Bart Timmer
Production Henry de Czar, Paris
Advertiser Double A, "The Double Quality Paper"

"Don't you use Double A?" a co-worker asks a man who's about to refill the printer. "Paper is paper," the man shrugs. Then he reflects. Transported to the Wild West, he finds himself on a miniature pony. "A horse is a horse," he protests. He takes a Chihuahua on a SWAT raid: "A dog is a dog." As for space exploration: "A helmet is a helmet." He has issues with camouflage make-up too. And when he takes a bite, he realises that, no, a mushroom is not a mushroom. Back in the office, he decides to use Double A paper.

English in 5 weeks

Agency	Vozduh, St. Petersburg
Creative Directors	Valeriy Melnik Viacheslav Nabokov
Art Director	Roman Luzanov
Advertiser	Five O'Clock School of English, "Flags"

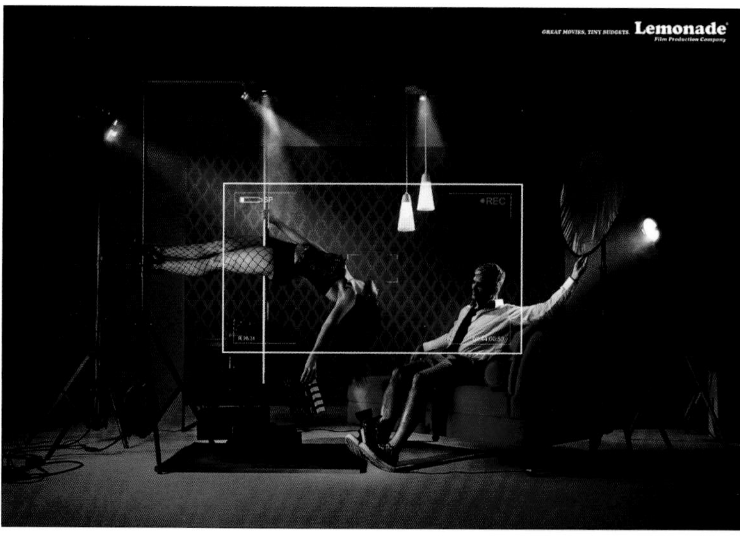

Professional Products & Services

Agency	Leo Burnett Tailor Made, São Paulo
Creative Directors	Marcelo Reis Vinicius Stanzione Alessandro Bernardo
Copywriter	Flavia Coradini
Art Director	Ricardo Alonso
Photographer	Nano Cunha
Advertiser	Lemonade Films, "Low Budget"

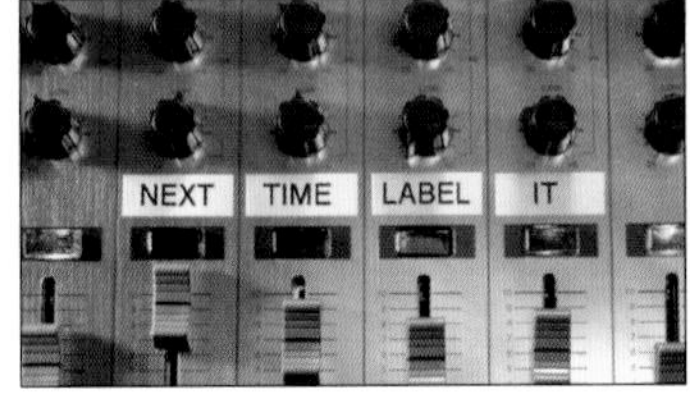

Agency Rosapark, Paris
Co-founders Jean-Patrick Chiquiar, Jean-François Sacco, Gilles Fichteberg
Creative Directors Mark Forgan, Jamie Standen
Copywriter Nicolas Gadesaude
Art Director Julien Saurin
Production Henry de Czar, Paris
Film Director Bart Timmer
Advertiser Brother International, "Next Time Label It"

We're at the circus, and a young chap is about to make his debut in the lighting and effects booth. His colleague shows him the ropes, pats him on the shoulder and leaves him to it. But at show time, he can't remember which button is which. He plunges the trapeze artists into darkness – we hear a scream – and hastily activates the clown music, just as he opens the big cat cages. Clowns, lions and tigers run amok, the crowd panics – and then he lets off the fireworks. Labels are important.

Agency ComZone, Phnom Penh
Creative Director Lundy So
Copywriters Lundy So, Vichit Hong
Art Director Seyhak Seang Sok
Photographer Roger Spooner
Production DigiPost, Vietnam
Film Director Peter Aquilina
Producer Andy Ho
Advertiser Camel Cement, "The Wrecking Ball"

A "deconstruction" worker looks on as a festival of wrecking balls lays waste to a group of skyscrapers. But he looks irritated when one particular ball smashes into a building – and nothing happens. After a couple of seconds, the huge ball drops off its chain, beaten by the tough edifice. Camel Cement: strength you can trust.

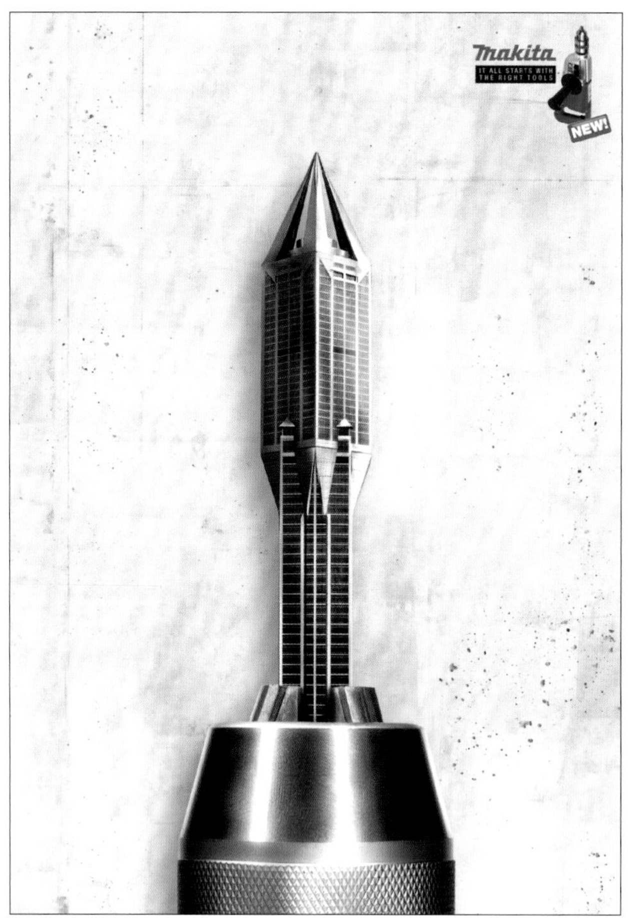

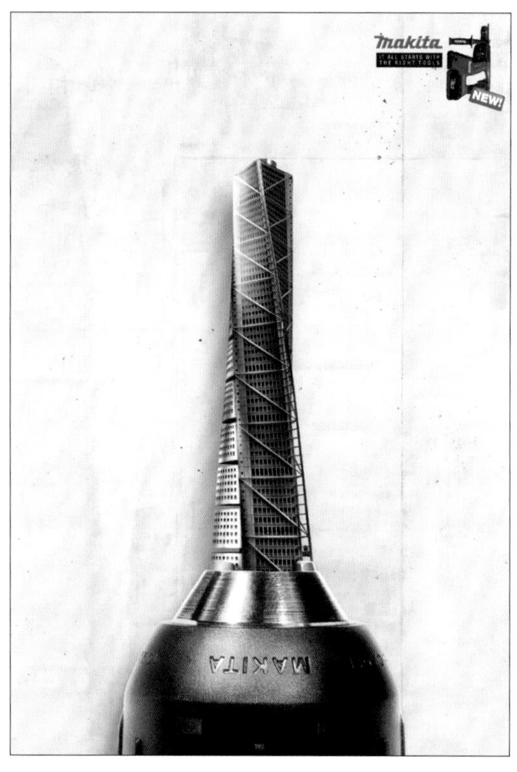

Agency	Leo Burnett, Frankfurt
CCO	Andreas Pauli
Creative Director	Hans-Juergen Kaemmerer
Copywriter	Benjamin Merkel
Art Directors	Hugo Moura Hans-Juergen Kaemmerer
Illustrator	Jack Moik
Photographer	Getty Images
Advertiser	Makita, Power Tools, “Makita – It All Starts With The Right Tools.”

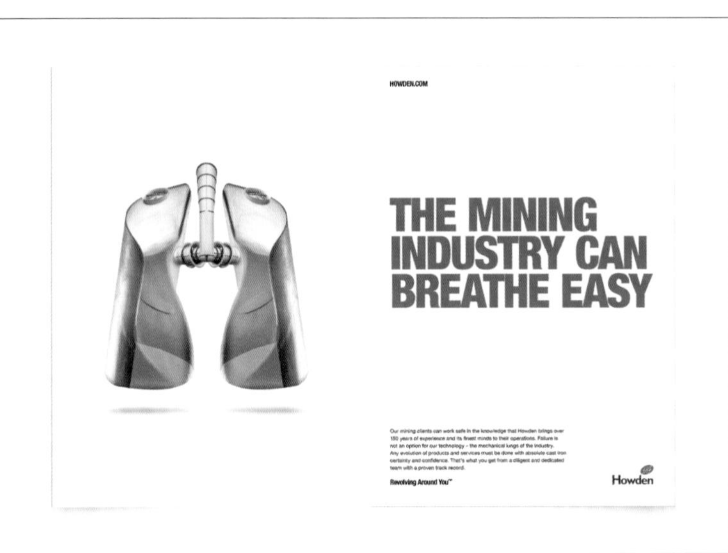

Agency	Stein IAS, Manchester
Creative Director	Reuben Webb
Copywriter	Alex Webb
Art Director	Chris Place
Advertiser	Howden, "Revolving Around You"

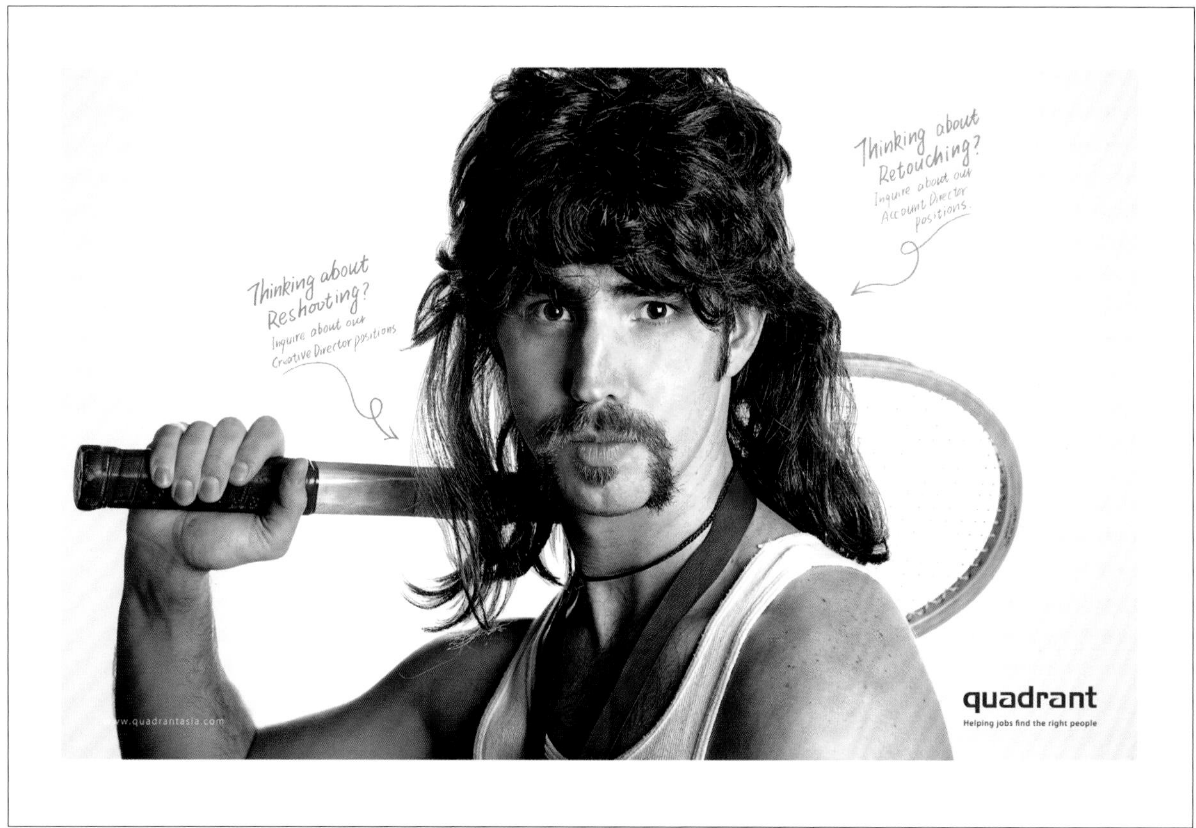

 Professional Products & Services

Agency	BBDO China, Shanghai
Executive CDs	WaiFoong Leong Kevin Lynch
Associate CD	Ben Guo
Copywriter	Kevin Lynch
Advertiser	Quadrant Recruitment Service, “Corporate Ad”

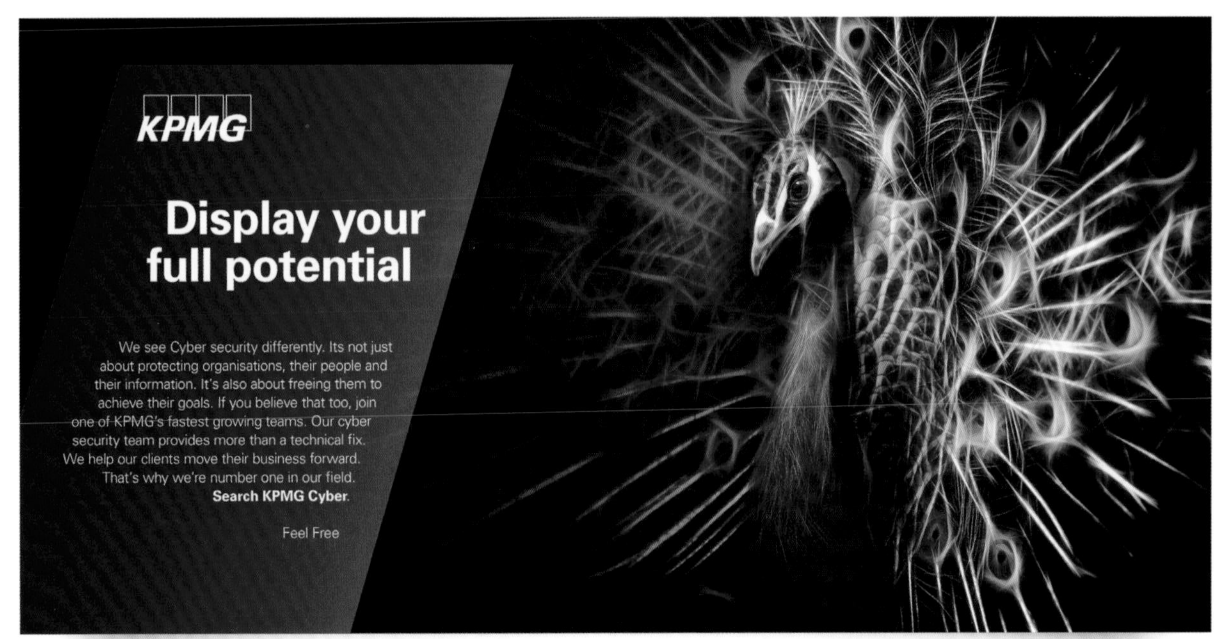

Agency	Stein IAS, Manchester
Creative Director	Reuben Webb
Copywriter	Alex Webb
Art Director	Chris Place
Advertiser	KPMG, Cyber Security Consultancy, "KPMG Cyber – Feel Free"

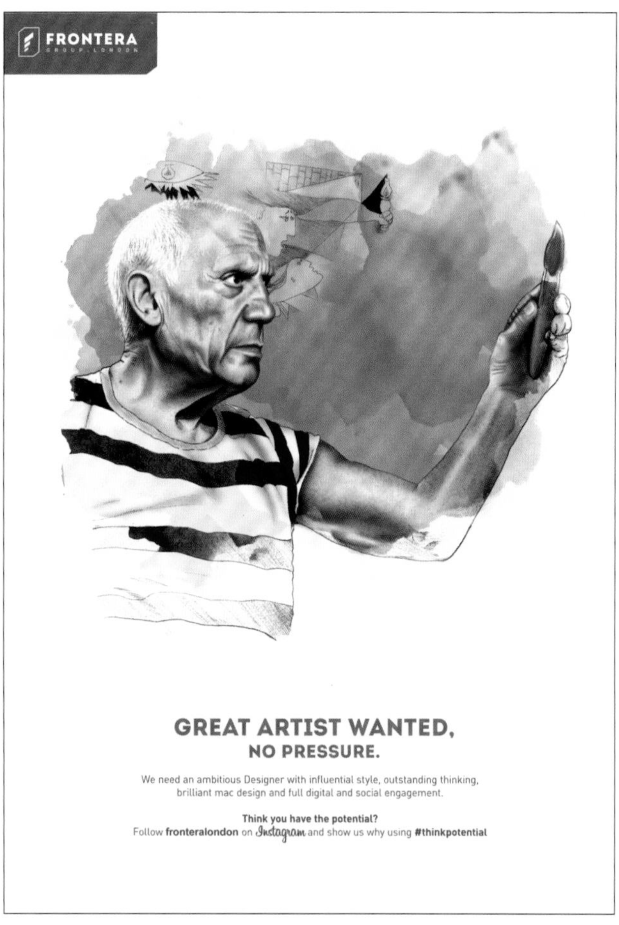

FRONTERA
GROUP.LONDON
GREAT ARTIST WANTED,
NO PRESSURE.
We need an ambitious Designer with influential style, outstanding thinking,
brilliant mac design and full digital and social engagement.
Think you have the potential?
Follow fronteralondon on Instagram and show us why using #thinkpotential

FRONTERA
GROUP.LONDON
GREAT WRITER WANTED,
NO PRESSURE.
We need an ambitious Medical Copywriter with a passion for words and ideas,
who has the ability to think different and believes impossible is nothing.
Think you have the potential?
Follow @frontera_london on twitter and tell us why using #thinkpotential

FRONTERA
GREAT MANAGER WANTED,
NO PRESSURE.
We need an ambitious Account Manager with stamina, who can pick up a big project
and go the extra few yards to recognise exciting new opportunities.
Think you have the potential?
Follow Frontera on LinkedIn and convince us why using #thinkpotential

 Professional Products & Services

Agency	Frontera, London
Executive CD	Frank Walters
Creative Directors	Andy James Francesc Coves
Copywriter	Andy James
Art Directors	Francesc Coves Paul Cleary
Production	Veni, Madrid
Illustrator	Martin Echeverria
Advertiser	Frontera, “Think Potential”

Agency Voskhod, Yekaterinburg
Creative Director Andrey Gubaydullin
Copywriter Egor Gavrilin
Art Director Alexander Solodkiy
Illustrator Catzwolf, Moscow
Advertiser Rabota.ru, Employment Website, "Dismissal"

Agency Dentsu Plus, Bangkok
CCO Subun Khow
Creative Director Supparat Thepparat
Copywriters Pattarapong Lapjarupong, Viraj Swaroop L K, Subun Khow
Art Directors Nattagorn Thairattanasuwan, Supparat Thepparat
Production Remix Studio, Bangkok
Photographers Anuchai Secharunputong, Nok Pipattungkul
Advertiser SECOM, Security Systems, "Jewelry Shop"

NEWS
POLITICS
BUSINESS
ENTERTAINMENT
TECH
MEDIA
WORLD
HEALTH
COMEDY
Menu
NEWS
The Boy Who Beeps
He speaks the language of industry
He's fluent in machine
Companies are thinking if you can talk to machines, you can do great things

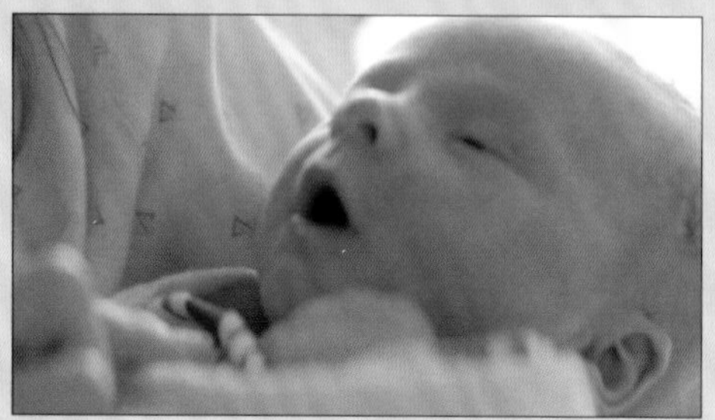

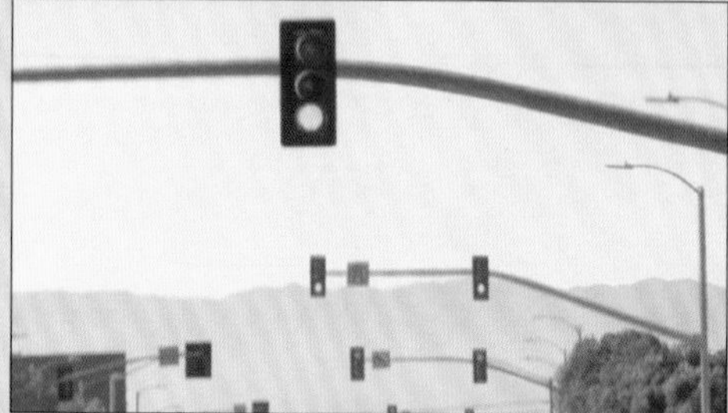

ON TIME
ON TIME
DELAYED
DELAYED

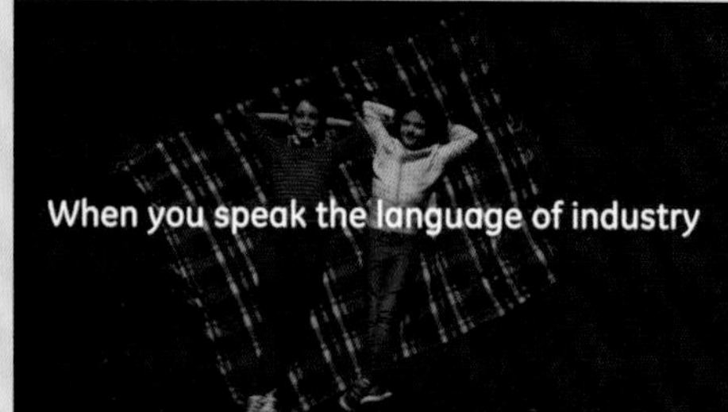
When you speak the language of industry

the conversation can change the world.

Agency	BBDO New York	**Production**	Park Pictures, New York
CCO	David Lubars	**Film Director**	Lance Acord
	Greg Hahn	**Producers**	Jackie Kelman Bisbee
Executive CD	Michael Aimette		MaryAnn Marino
Creative Director	Tim Roan		Caroline Kousidonis
Copywriter	Tim Roan	**Editorial Company**	Exile, Santa Monica
Art Director	Lance Vining	**Editor**	Kirk Baxter
Dir. of Integrated Prod.	David Rolfe	**Composer**	Beck
Executive Producer	Diane Hill	**Sound Designer**	Barking Owl, West Los Angeles
Agency Producer	George Sholley		
Head of Music Prod.	Rani Vaz	**Advertiser**	GE, "The Boy Who Beeps"
Executive Music Prod.	John Melillo		

From birth, a little boy beeps instead of making human sounds. His parents are concerned, but he also has a talent: he can talk to machines. His beeps turn on the TV, control traffic lights, and restore power to the town. Soon he's sought after by industry. But he also uses his talent to win over a little girl. As they watch the stars one night, he turns out the lights. "Thank you," she says. "You're welcome," he replies – his first words. The film is a metaphor for GE technology that allows machines to talk.

Agency	Leo Burnett, Istanbul
Creative Group Head	Ekin Arşiray
Creative Directors	Oktar Akın Emrah Akay
Copywriters	Ömer Siber Ari Koen
Art Director	Mert Özkaner
Graphic Design	Funda Kentuş
Advertiser	Tofaş-Jeep, "Beep, Keep, Deep"

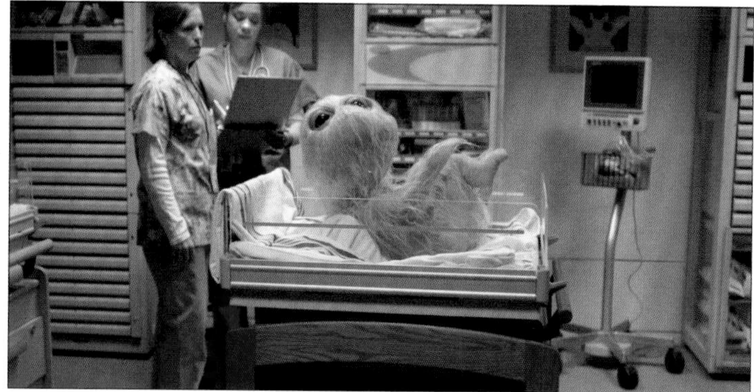

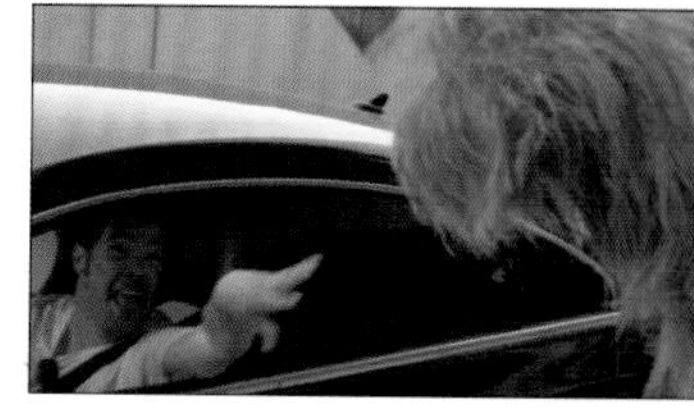

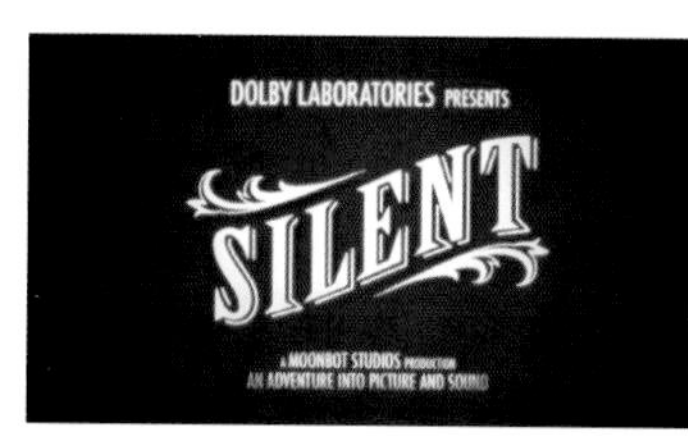

Agency BBDO New York
CCOs David Lubars, Greg Hahn
Executive CD Michael Aimette
Copywriter Greg Hahn
Art Directors Ralph Watson, Matt Vescovo
Executive Producer Diane Hill
Production Biscuit Filmworks, Los Angeles
Film Director Noam Murro
DOP Eric Schmidt
Advertiser GE, "Ideas"

Ideas don't always start out looking great. They need people to nurture them. The concept is shown here in the form of an alien-looking creature who, like many ideas, comes into this world "ugly and messy". For a long time, he is rejected. "Ideas are frightening, because they threaten what is known," observes the narrator. But in his darkest hour, the creature is adopted by GE and becomes "something beautiful". GE embraces new ideas.

Agency CAA Marketing, Los Angeles
Production Moonbot Studios, Shreveport
Execut. Producer William Joyce
Producers Trish Farnsworth-Smith, Lampton Enochs
Directors Brandon Oldenburg, Limbert Fabian
Editor Calvin O'Neal Jr.
Lead Animator Kevin Koch
Sound Designer Steve Boeddeker
Advertiser Dolby, "Silent"

This endearing cartoon begins with the hapless inventor of a primitive silent movie projector and his little girl taking shelter in a magical cinema. The inventor finds himself on the big screen, and with his daughter providing the soundtrack on the organ, he passes through decades of movie history, before bursting out of the screen in a riot of glorious colour and surround sound. Dolby is the name behind the sounds of cinema.

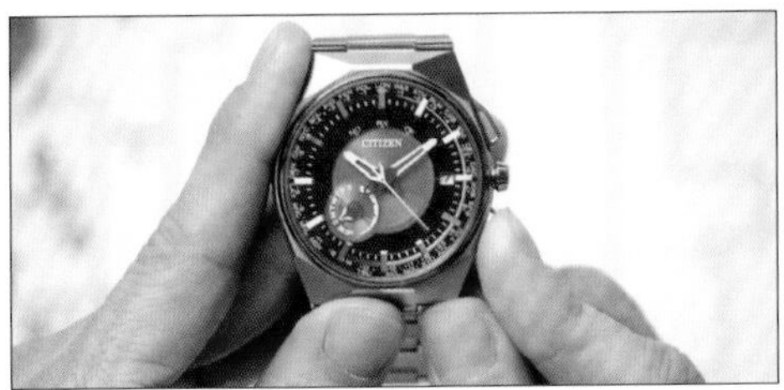

Agencies	Wieden+Kennedy, Amsterdam Wieden+Kennedy, Tokyo
Creative Directors	Mikey Farr Tota Hasegawa
Copywriter	Evgeny Primachenko
Art Director	Vasco Vicente
Agency Producers	Tony Stearns Lars Fabery de Jonge
Production	100% Halal, Amsterdam
Film Director	Johan Kramer
Producers	Gijs Determeijer Christine Anderton
Editor	Kevin Whelan
Titles Designer	Dan Cassaro
Post-Production	MPC, Amsterdam
Composer	Andre Ettema, AME Music
Sound Design	Wave Studios, Amsterdam
Advertiser	Citizen, "Better Starts Now"

A bird's eye shot of a watchmaker's desk is the focus of this journey through time. As we travel through history the desk evolves – and so do the watchmaker's designs, through shockproof, waterproof, solar-powered and satellite-linked. The story of each new invention is concluded with the words "The End". But then the film continues. What if every ending is a chance to start something better? Citizen. Better starts now.

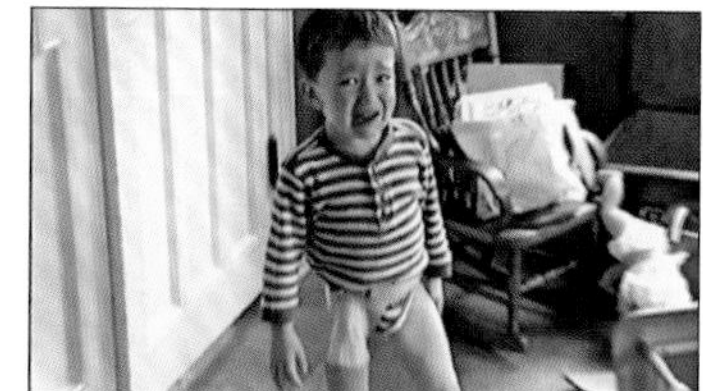

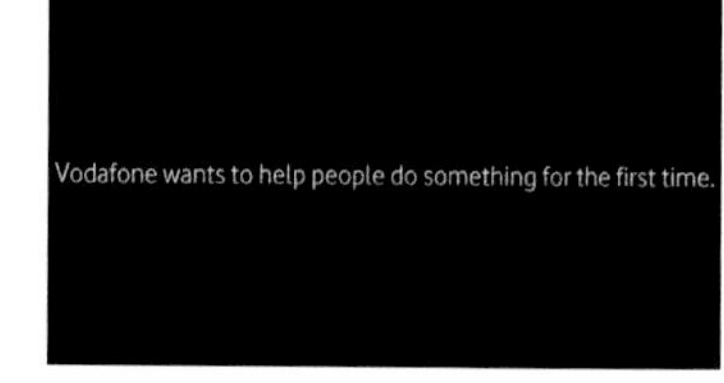

Agency	Wieden+Kennedy, Amsterdam
Executive CDs	Mark Bernath Eric Quennoy
Creative Directors	Alvaro Sotomayor Rosie Bardales
Copywriter	Bernard Hunter
Art Director	Mike Bond
Advertiser	Powerade, "There's Power In Every Game"

Genuine film footage tracks the story of Nico Calabria, who was born with only one leg. Encouraged by his parents and friends, he nonetheless pursues his love of sports. Despite tears and frustration, we see courage, tenacity and good humour blazing out of the kid. He evolves into a spectacular soccer player, exemplifying the Powerade ethos of determination and commitment. There's power in every game.

Agencies	ACHTUNG!, WeFilm, Blyde, Amsterdam
Creative Director	Mervyn ten Dam
Creative	Niels Straatsma Vincent Rang
Art Director	Jort Schutter
Designer	Marten Beerda
Director	Jona Honer
Producer	Sara Nix
Advertiser	Vodafone, "#FirstConcert"

Deaf from birth, Vera received a cochlear implant at 16, which allows her to hear, although some sounds remain difficult. Vodafone wanted to help her attend her first rock concert. Ideas for songs were crowd-sourced, but finally Dutch musician Kyteman worked closely with Vera to devise the perfect concert for her implant-aided hearing. The payoff shows Vera's joyful reaction to the music. Her story was widely shared across social networks and traditional media.

Agency W&Cie, Paris
Creative Director Thomas Stern
Copywriter Asma Kanzari
Art Director Guillaume Dupré
Film Director Jean-Noël Lepoint
Advertiser Paris Orly Airport, "#iamtheguest"

Airports are viewed as impersonal places, and 28 million people pass through Paris Orly every year. How to make the airport a bit more human? Using the omnipresent selfie, of course. For ten days, every passenger was invited to take a selfie. The results were transformed into the biggest "selfie wall" in the world: 7,000 selfies over 3,000 square metres on the airport's exterior. And of course everyone shared their airport selfie experience.

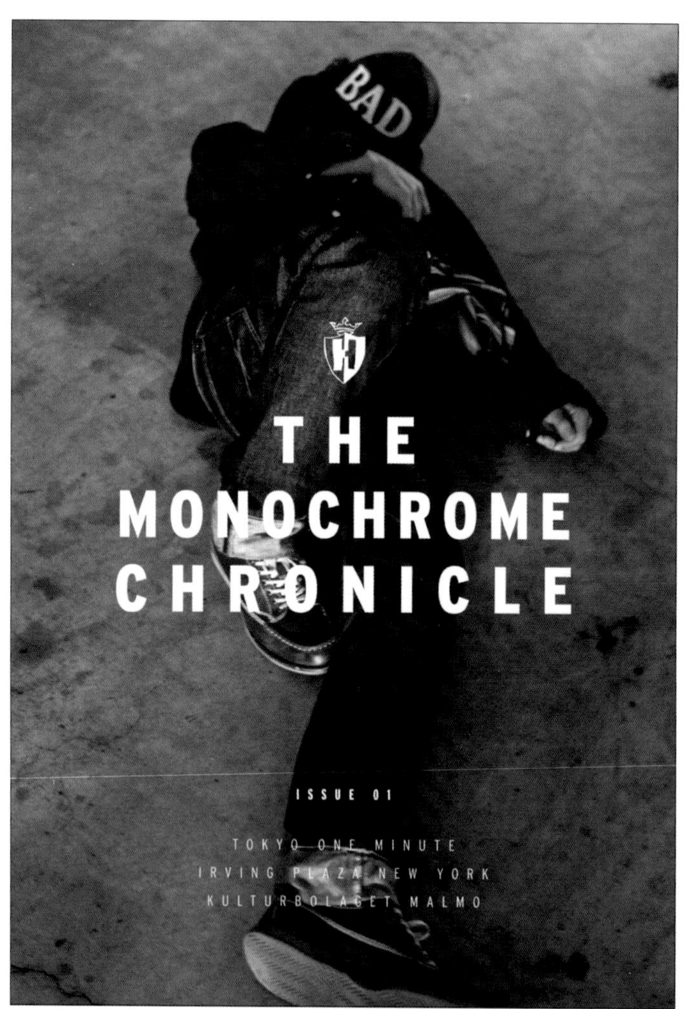

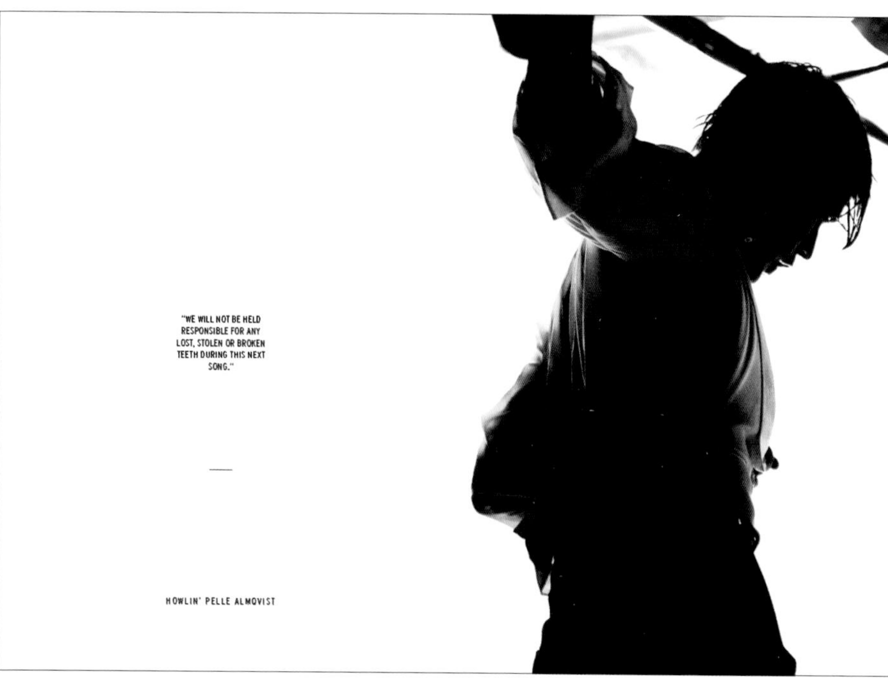

Agency	Göran Broberg, Stockholm
Creative Director	Göran Broberg
Copywriter	The Hives
Art Director	Andreas Fernhede Dagman
Photographer	Göran Broberg
Graphic Design	Andreas Fernhede Dagman
Typographer	Andreas Fernhede Dagman
Advertiser	The Hives, Live Punk Rock, "The Monochrome Chronicle"

Rock band The Hives - famous for their black and white sartorial style - star in their first publication. Get a glimpse of the band's live act and lifestyle in glorious monochrome.

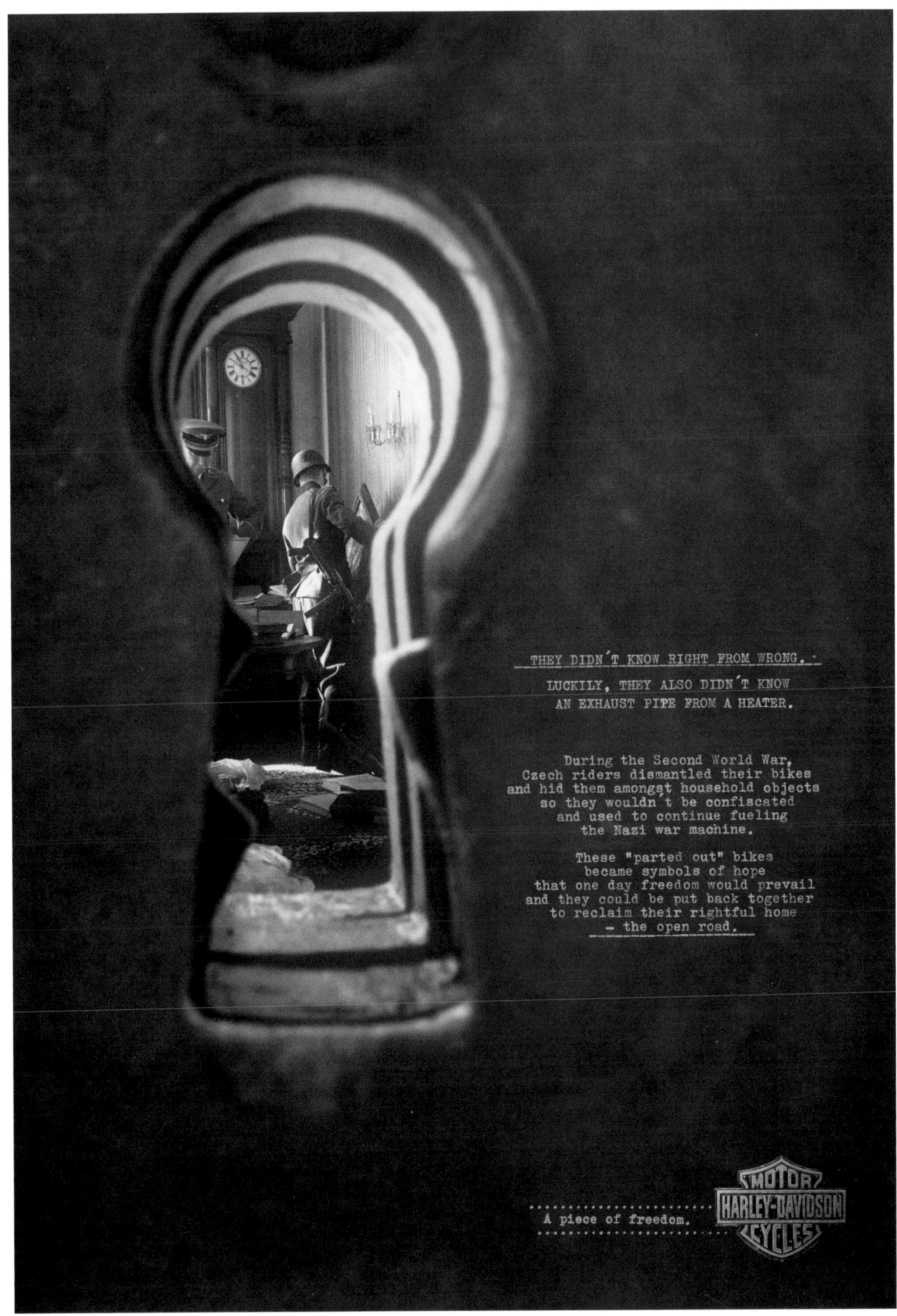
THEY DIDN'T KNOW RIGHT FROM WRONG.
LUCKILY, THEY ALSO DIDN'T KNOW
AN EXHAUST PIPE FROM A HEATER.
During the Second World War,
Czech riders dismantled their bikes
and hid them amongst household objects
so they wouldn't be confiscated
and used to continue fueling
the Nazi war machine.
These "parted out" bikes
became symbols of hope
that one day freedom would prevail
and they could be put back together
to reclaim their rightful home
– the open road.
A piece of freedom.
MOTOR
HARLEY-DAVIDSON
CYCLES

Agency	Y&R, Prague	**Production**	G.P.S. Production, Prague
Chief Creative Officer	Jaime Mandelbaum	**Producer**	Tomas Tomasek
Creative Directors	Jaime Mandelbaum Jaroslav Schovanec	**Designer**	Neil Johnston
Copywriters	Nathan Dills Jaroslav Schovanec Conor Barry Dora Pruzincova	**Typographer**	Neil Johnston
Art Director	Atila Martins	**3D Artist**	Marek Motalik
Photographer	Miro Minarovych	**Advertiser**	Harley-Davidson, "Harley Second World War"

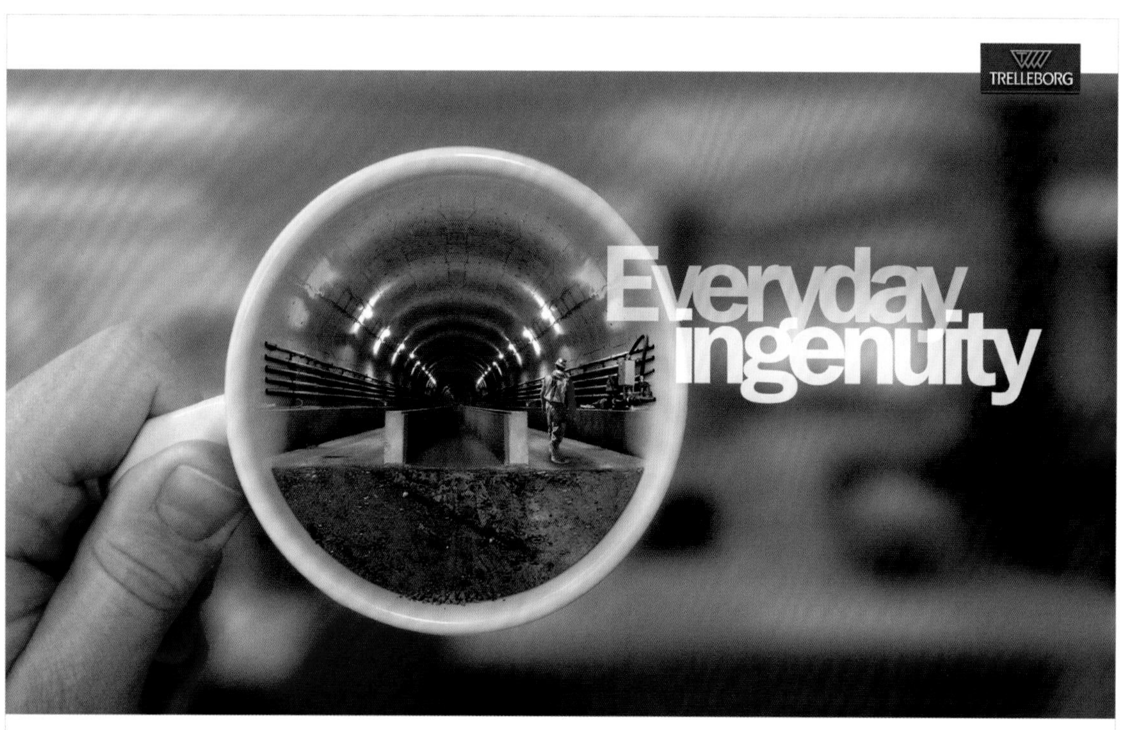

Corporate Image

Agency	Stein IAS, Manchester
Creative Director	Reuben Webb
Copywriters	Matthew Webb Alex Webb
Art Director	Russell Suthers
Photographers	Russell Suthers David Croucher
Advertiser	Trelleborg Engineered Products, "Everyday Ingenuity"

Agency	Paleta de Ideias, Braga	Branding, set design and typography for the 10th edition of Dialética, a biannual summit held by business software solutions provider Primavera. The seminar and working sessions took place in the beautiful Theatro Circo in Braga, Portugal. The branding was subtle, as a contrast to the opulent surroundings, and the lettering struck a nostalgic note to evoke the first event 20 years ago. It was reproduced as a neon installation that gradually faded, marking the boundary between the past and the future of Primavera.
Creative Directors	Abel Rocha Dionísio Monteiro Pedro Matos	
Copywriters	Dionísio Monteiro Pedro Matos	
Graphic Design	Pedro Matos	
Typographer	Pedro Matos	
Advertiser	Primavera, Sofware Solutions Summit, “Dialética 2013”	

Radio Advertising

ZQ Lady:
At ZzzQuil we're committed to help you get your Z's, so we created 1-855-ZZZ-QUIL to gently bore you to sleep.

ZQ Lady
Press '1' for the Fundamental Theorum of Calculus.

TUTOR
Ok. If you have a continuous function on the closed interval A to B, then you define a new function, G of X as the integral from A to X of the function F of T D T, where X is between A and B. Function G is continuous.

ZQ Lady
Press '2' to hear commentary of a checkers game.

Checkers Commentator
Black jumps a red checker. Red jumps the black checker. If that didn't make your eyelids heavy, you could use some ZzzQuil after all.

Checkers Commentator
Black's King moves to the right diagonally.

ZzzQuil Sleep-Aid:
Nighty night.

ZQ Lady:
At ZzzQuil we're committed to help you get your Z's, so we created 1-855-ZZZ-QUIL to gently bore you to sleep.

ZQ Lady
Press '1' to hear about the baby. Again.

Woman:
This is Brayden 12 minutes after delivery.
This is Brayden after his first bath.
This is me and Brayden, our first mother and son picture. Aww..

ZQ Lady
Press '2' to hear someone describe an abstract painting.

Woman
It's... restrained. It tells us almost nothing and yet it communicates so much. It's asking questions of its very existence. Does it? Is it? Will it? The colors, while muted, speak. Also note the sub-notes of Cyan. And look there's cranberry.

If this pointless pontification hasn't put you to sleep, then perhaps you need some ZzzQuil after all.

ZzzQuil Sleep-Aid:
Nighty night.

ZQ Lady:
At ZzzQuil we're committed to help you get your Z's, so we created 1-855-ZZZ-QUIL to gently bore you to sleep.

ZQ Lady
Press '1' for a lesson in the proper usage of a semicolon.

PROFESSOR
The semicolon. Perhaps the most misunderstood piece of punctuation. The semicolon can be used one of three ways. The first is to connect two related sentences.

ZQ Lady
Press '2' to hear the inner musings of a mime.

MIME
I'm in the imaginary box. Ok, hands up, stiff fingers, and walk the hands. Time for panic face. Big eyes, bigger, bigger, and mouth in an O as if I was saying Ooooohh!

If you're still awake after this mind numbing miming, perhaps you should try some ZzzQuil after all.

ZzzQuil Sleep-Aid:
Nighty night.

Agence	Publicis Kaplan Thaler, New York	**Agency Producer**	Lauren Schneidmuller
		Audio House	Phantom Audio, New York
CCO	Rob Feakins		
ECD	Joseph Johnson	**Producer**	Mary Ruth Tomasiewicz
Creative Director	Carlos Figueiredo	**Advertiser**	Procter & Gamble, ZzzQuil, "Sleepline 2.0"
Copywriters	Liz Rosenthal Patrick Merrit Larissa Kirschner James Rothwell		

Treatment Note
One voice coming from the left speaker and another from the right. The voices will seem as if they are moving towards each other throughout the spot and will finally come together at the end.

Left	It's your 30th birthday.
SFX	Birthday celebrations
Right	A baby white shark is born in the Pacific Ocean.
SFX	Underwater ambience
Left	You go to work as usual.
SFX	Elevator,
SFX	Office ambience
Right	The baby shark's parents name him Timmy.
SFX	Underwater ambience
Left:	Your wife plans a surprise for you.
SFX	Home ambience
Right	Timmy is playing hide and seek with his family.
SFX	Underwater ambience
Left	You come home to find tickets for two to Australia.
SFX	Door opening,
SFX	House ambience
Right	Timmy gets lost.
SFX	Underwater ambience
Left	You plan your holiday.
SFX	Home ambience
Right	Timmy is sad.
SFX	Underwater ambience
Left	You reach the airport.
SFX	Airport ambience
Right	Timmy is wandering aimlessly.
SFX	Music,
SFX	Underwater ambience
Left	You land in Australia.
SFX	Airline flying
Right	Timmy is now angry at the world.
SFX	Music,
SFX	Underwater ambience
Left	You head to the beach.
SFX	Waves
Right	Timmy enters the Indian Ocean.
SFX	Music,
SFX	Underwater ambience
Left	You enter the waters.
SFX	Waves
Right	Timmy is hungry.
SFX	Music,
SFX	Underwater ambience
Left:	You feel something brush against your legs.
Right	Timmy sees legs.
Center	
SFX:	Water,
SFX	Gasp.

Center
For when your destinies meet, stay travelled insured, with Commercial Insurance.
Call 1280, 24 hours.

Dog
If Blåkläder were a dog, it wouldn't have been a little bitch called Chanell that was carried around in the purse of a platinum blonde girl.
Nah... It would have been a cross between pit bull and grizzly, that only obeyed the name Psycho, and if Psycho had lifted his leg to mark, flames would have bursted out, and made Pompeii look like a girl's fart in a cub scout's tent.

RomCom
If Blåkläder were a romantic comedy, it wouldn't have been a chick flick starring Hugh Grant.
Nah... The leading role would be played by a beef cake, with no lines, what so ever. It would have been the most violent and bloody romantic comedy ever made.
The movie would have an age limit of 35, and make every single paratrooper in the kingdom of Norway shit their pants.

Agency	Impact BBDO, Dubai
Creative Director	Fadi Yaish
Copywriter	Alok Mohan
Production	Eardrum, Sydney
Agency Producer	Emilie Haddad
Producer	Lesley Chambers
Director	Ralph Van Dijk
Sound Engineer	Simon Kane
Advertiser	Commercial Insurance, "Your Destiny"

Agency	Både Og AS, Oslo
Copywriters	Erik Lysø Joachim Sandvik
Production	Både Og AS, Oslo
Producers	Ola-Per Ekblom Elisabeth Andonov
Sound Designer	Joachim Sandvik
Advertiser	Blåkläder, "The Toughest Workwear on the Market"

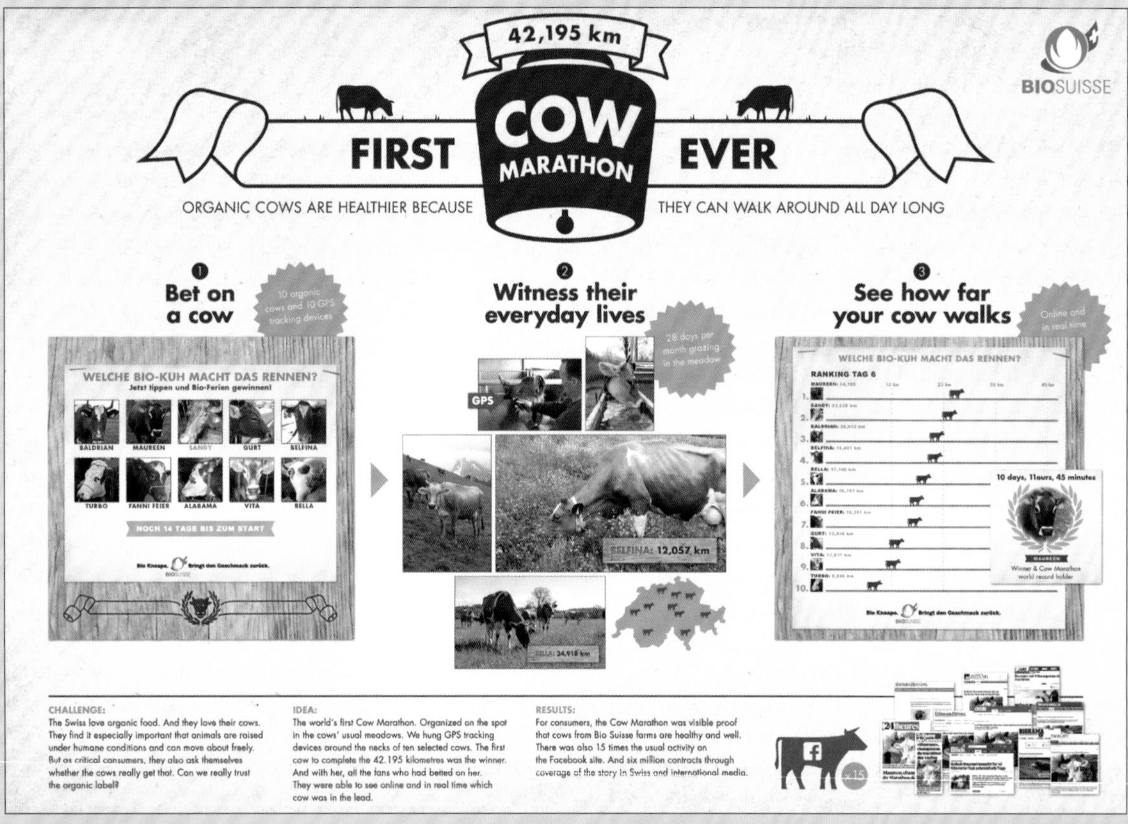

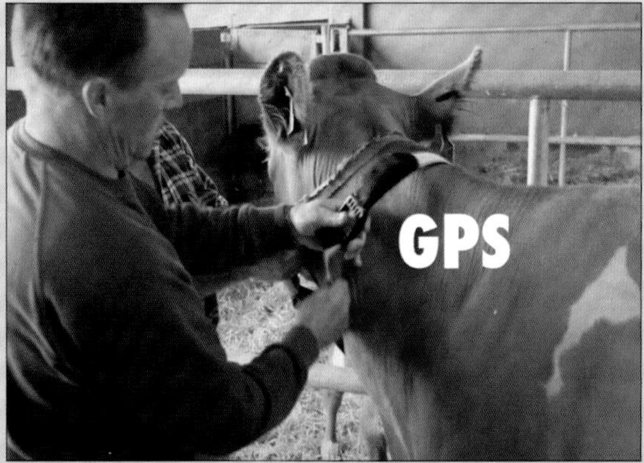

Agency	Leo Burnett, Zurich
CDs	Peter Brönnimann Christian Bircher
Copywriter	Christian Stüdi
Art Director	Pedro Moosmann
Production	Xeit, Zurich
Advertiser	Bio Suisse (Swiss Organic Producers Association), "Cow Marathon"

Organic cows are healthier because they can walk around all day. But how to reassure Swiss consumers that their cows are truly free-range? The Cow Marathon! The first cow to walk 42.195 kilometres (or just over 26.2 miles) wins. It worked by hanging GPS tracking devices around the necks of 10 organic cows. Then people were asked to bet on one of the cows via a website. They could read info about the candidates and check their environment through satellite photos. After just over 10 days of heavily-tweeted action, Maureen was declared the winner.

Are you Klaus-Heidi? Lufthansa

One way ticket to Berlin.
70 m² apartment.
Language course.
Free domestic flights.
Bike.

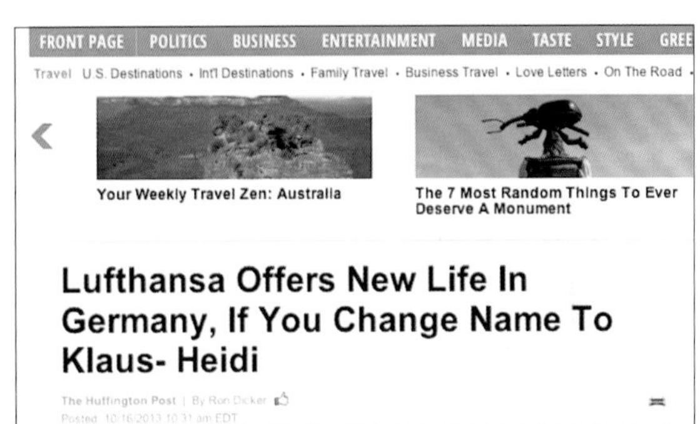

FRONT PAGE | POLITICS | BUSINESS | ENTERTAINMENT | MEDIA | TASTE | STYLE | GREE

Travel U.S. Destinations • Int'l Destinations • Family Travel • Business Travel • Love Letters • On The Road •

Your Weekly Travel Zen: Australia

The 7 Most Random Things To Ever Deserve A Monument

Lufthansa Offers New Life In Germany, If You Change Name To Klaus- Heidi

Agency DDB Stockholm
CDs Jerker Fagerström, Magnus Jakobsson, Fredrik Simonsson
Copywriters Jens Thelfer, Daniel Vaccino
Art Directors Patrik Pagréus, Joakim Khoury, Daniel Mencak
AD Assistant Oskar Pernefeldt
Digital Producer Katarina Mohlin
Digital Designer Martin Runfors
Digital Developers Alexander Ekman, August Björnberg
Technical Dir. Andreas Fabbe
Retouch Christian Björnerhag
Graphic Design Tor Westerlund
Advertiser Lufthansa, "Are You Klaus-Heidi?"

Would you change your name to Klaus-Heidi for a free flight to Berlin? How about a free flight to Berlin and a new life in the city, including an apartment, a language course, free domestic flights and a bike? This was the dare that Lufthansa threw at Swedes to promote Berlin. Launched through PR and word of mouth, the campaign encouraged 42 Swedes to legally change their names. In the end, the newly-minted "Klaus-Heidi Andersson" was picked as the winner.

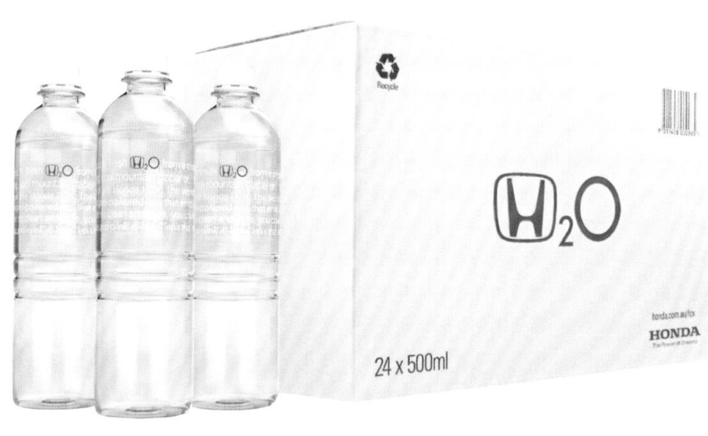

Agency	Leo Burnett, Melbourne
Executive CD	Jason Williams
Head Copy	Sarah Mcgregor
Senior Designer	Matt Portch
Production Manager	John Trifonopoulos
Advertiser	Honda, "Honda H_2O"

The Honda FCX Clarity runs on hydrogen, which means that its only emission is pure water. To reinforce this, Honda and its agency created and packaged a new water brand: H_2O. Launched at cinemas across Australia, where it was given away to demonstrate the car's benefits, it now has pride of place in the fridges of Honda dealerships, where it can be used to spur conversations about hydrogen fuel.

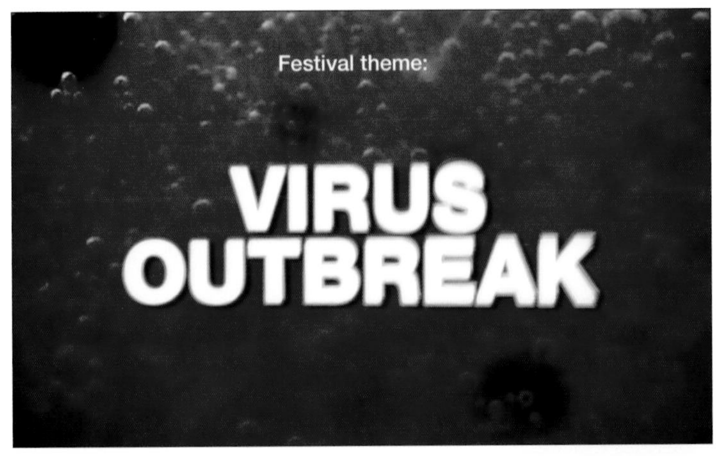

NATIONAL INSTITUTE FOR DISEASE CONTROL

May 20, 2014

YOU MAY BE INFECTED.

Dear Mr. Thermaenius:

We are contacting you because we suspect you may have been infected with a virus we refer to as the TRIlle virus. In this letter you will find informat about the virus and contact information to reach our Institute.

Possible time of infection

It has come to our attention that you spent time in Reims, France in April last year. During that period of time a deployment of the TRIlle virus was reported in the groundwater. The leak was reported from Restaurant L'apostrophe and may have contaminated some of the city's water supply. We are currently treating and containing one American citizen infected by the virus, who visited the same area at that time.

About the virus

The TRIlle virus is likely to be sprung from the Rhabdoviridae family of viruses but may have adapted some of the characteristics of the Herpesviridae family of viruses. We know that it's highly contagious and life threatening without treatment. It has developed more rapidly in some cases and we believe this has to do with an unusual strain of the TRIlle virus, probably due to a mutation.

Early symptoms

Some of the early symptoms we've seen are: hallucinations, odd behavior, not recognizing people's faces, mood swings and personality changes.

Late symptoms

Amongst later symptoms we've seen: extensively paranoid behavior, not only self-destructive behavior but also destructive behavior directed towards other people. Patients in this stage become aggressive, violent and lose their ability to communicate. This state is comparable to the symptoms of a maniac or psychopath.

Report immediately

It is the highest priority to track down every origin of the virus and initiate potential treatment, therefore it's VERY IMPORTANT that you call us immediately at +1 917 725-4046

Yours sincerely,

Dr. H. West
Agent in charge of
Contagious Diseases
and Prevention.

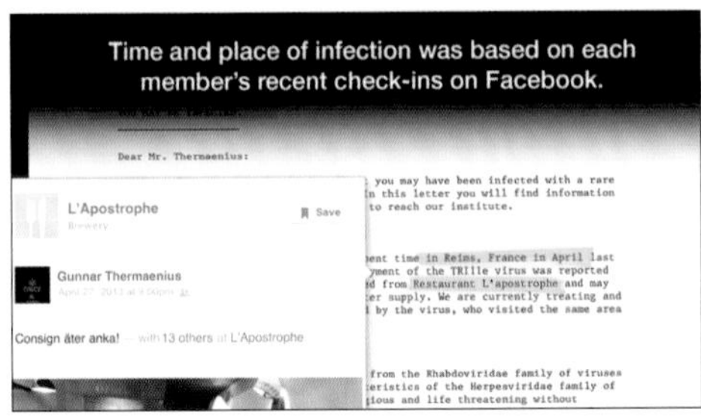

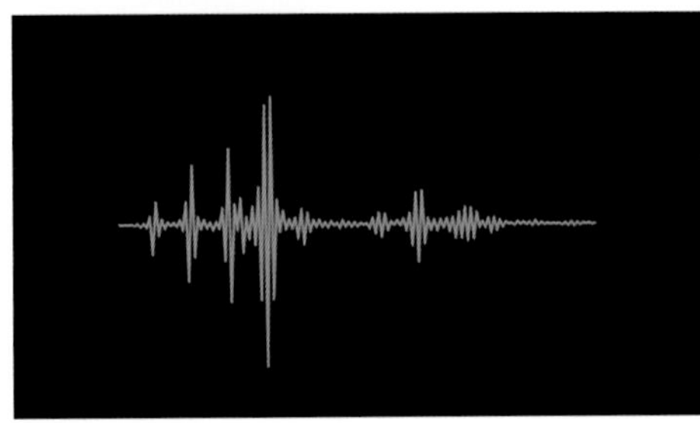

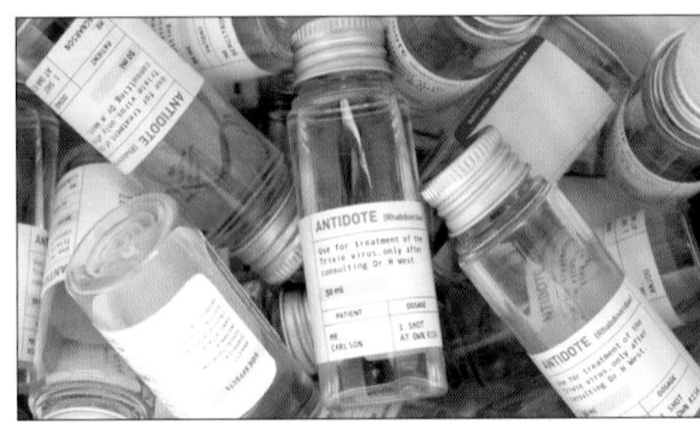

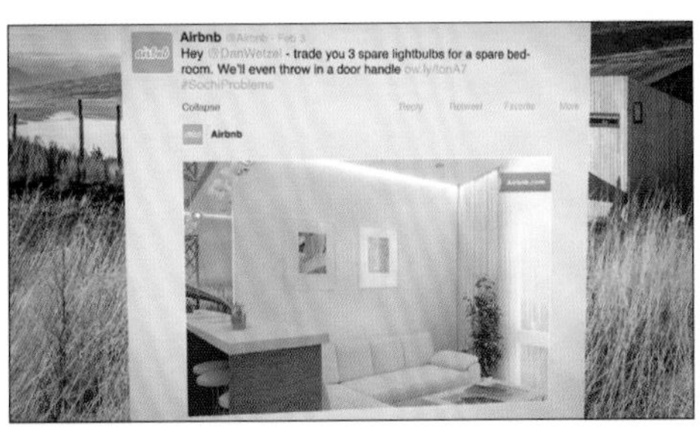

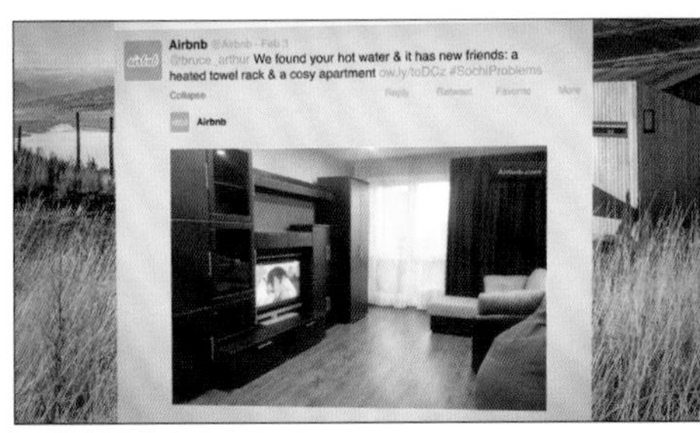

Agency	Saatchi & Saatchi, Stockholm
Creative Director	Gustav Egerstedt
Copywriters	Daniel Jakobsson Petter Dixelius
Art Directors	Felix Nilsson Erik Hiort af Ornäs
Graphic Design	Jacob Hamilton
Advertiser	Elmsta 3000 Horror Festival, "Virus Outbreak"

The Elmsta 3000 Horror Festival is famous for the diabolical ways in which it targets potential attendees. This year, people on its database received a personalised letter from the National Institute for Disease Control, telling them they had contracted a deadly virus. A phone number led to a recorded message by a doctor who told them it was too late – he had already "turned". Their only hope was to attend the festival, where they could pick up the antidote.

Agency	Pereira & O'Dell, San Francisco
CDs	Rafael Rizuto Eduardo Marques
Copywriter	Chris Ryan
Advertiser	Airbnb, "Airbnb#SochiProblems"

The Winter Olympics at Sochi became infamous for its substandard facilities, especially when journalists tweeted pictures of their hotel rooms: unplumbed bathrooms, drooping curtain rails, missing light bulbs and all. Airbnb jumped on the trend by tweeting that it had more than 500 great rooms available. It also responded directly to journalists, offering to replace, say, a missing door handle with an entire apartment: "Take a break from your hotel." As a result, Airbnb was one of the biggest winners at the Olympics.

OUTSIDE
INSIDE
FOLD
&
SEAL
BUY
SOMETHING
NEW
TURN ME INSIDE OUT AND DONATE
SOMETHING OLD.
DONATE
SOMETHING
OLD

Consumer Direct

Agency DDB Stockholm
Executive CD Jerker Fagerström
Copywriters Nick Christiansen, Magnus Jakobsson
Art Directors Joel Ekstrand, Fredrik Simonsson
Design Director Linnea Lofjord
Designer Linus Östberg
Graphic Design Peter Danielsson
Retouch Artist Christian Björnerhag
Advertiser Uniforms for the Dedicated, "The Rag Bag"

Swedish brand Uniforms For The Dedicated makes menswear with an ethical slant, often using recycled fibres. Here it created a shopping bag that encourages recycling. Buy something new, then turn the shopping bag inside out and insert your old clothing. Send the bag to one of the charities listed on it. Postage is already paid. Buy something new, donate something old. And give your unwanted clothes a second life.

Agency McCann Worldgroup, Milan
CDs Alessandro Sabini, Gaetano del Pizzo
Copywriters Alessandro Sabini, Mario Esposito
Art Directors Marco Zilioli, Gaetano Del Pizzo
Photographer Fulvio Bonavia
Production Craft, Milan
Film Director Alessio Fava
Advertiser Smacchiotutto, "The Stain Remover Pizza Box"

Smacchiotutto is an Italian stain remover. To demonstrate its power, it hit Italians where they live – by using pizza. In fact, 20,000 pizza boxes were handed out in some of the most famous pizzerias in Milan. And thanks to a neat little picture of a white shirt on a sheet in the lid of the box, consumers saw just how quickly the product could remove a stain.

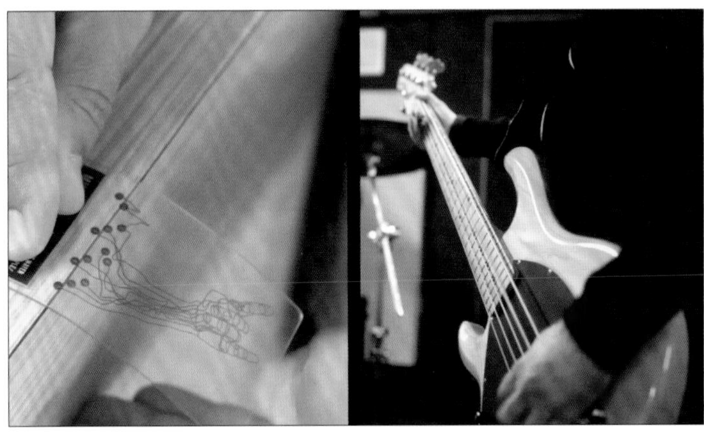

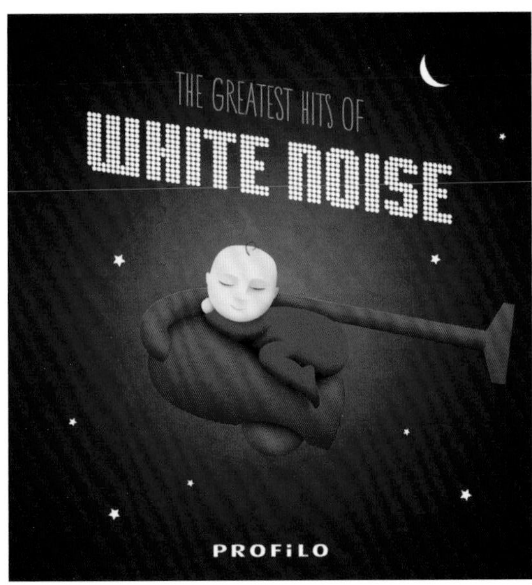

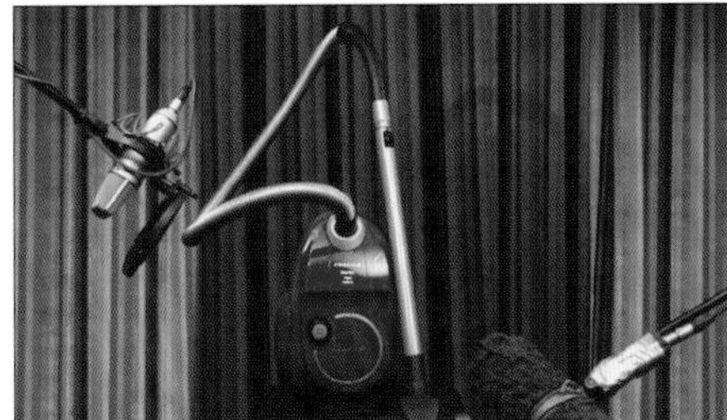

Agency TDI Group Russia, Moscow
Creative Director Alexander Zazheko
Sr. Copywriter Sergey Laputs
Art Director Ekaterina Trapeznikova
Advertiser MuzZone, "Musical Visiting Card"

These highly appropriate business cards were created for musical instruments shop Muzzone. Apart from the usual information, the plastic cards showed a melody in the form of symbols. By changing the positions of the cards, users could twang them to perform tunes by Queen, Nirvana and Deep Purple.

Agency Rafineri, Istanbul
Creative Director Ayşe Bali
Copywriter Melih Ediş
Art Director Cihan Eryılmaz
Agency Producers Kerem Ilbeyli, Selin Ceylan
Advertiser Profilo Home Appliances, "White Noise"

Many parents have found that "white noise" created by normal domestic appliances, such as vacuum cleaners and hair dryers, relaxes babies and sends them off to sleep. But it's not very practical to stand beside your kid with a vacuum cleaner for hours. So Profilo Home Appliances produced a CD containing The Greatest Hits of White Noise and gave them away in-store.

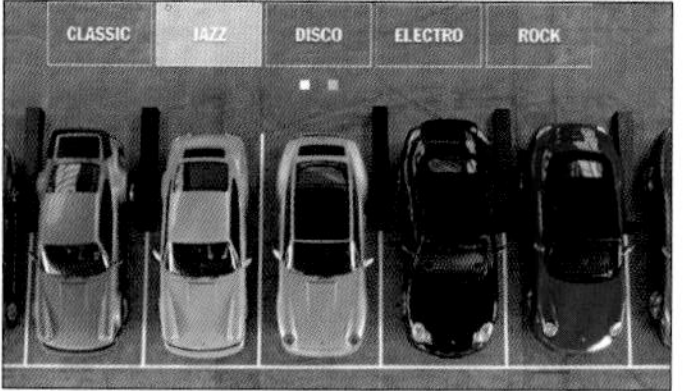

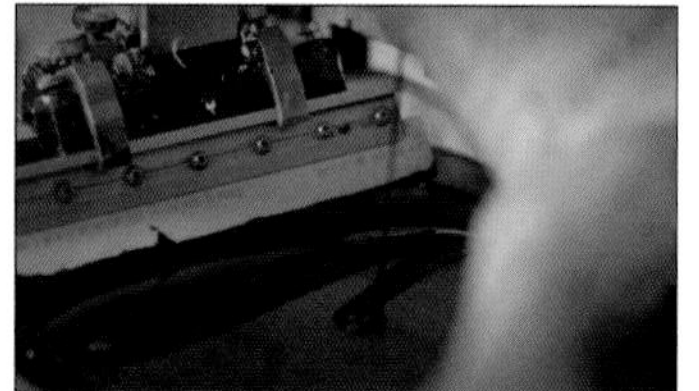

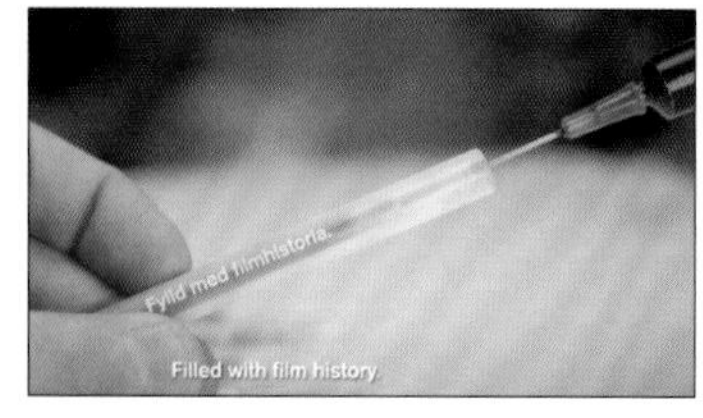

Agency Fred & Farid, Shanghai
CDs Fred & Farid, Feng Huang, Grégoire Chalopin, Laurent Leccia
Copywriters Laurent Leccia, Adrien Goris, Jean-Baptiste Le Divelec
Art Director Laurent Leccia
Production RSA Films Asia, Hong Kong
Film Director Jan Richter-Friis
Advertiser Porsche, "911 Birthday Song"

Although China does not have a large sports car culture, Porsche and its agency felt that potential buyers would respond to the throaty roar of an engine. So it recorded the engine sounds of seven generations of the 911 and turned them into musical notes. A viral video showed the cars "singing" Happy Birthday. Online users were invited to play the Porsche piano, unlocking videos that revealed key moments in Porsche history. They were also challenged to compose and share their own melodies. The game was played 1.5 million times.

Agency Lowe Brindfors, Stockholm
Creative Director Rickard Villard
Copywriter Desiré Engström
Art Director Jeremy Phang
Designers Noel Pretorius, David Drew
Producer Mikaela Rönnberg
Final Art Lena Barthon, Jesper Kewenter
Advertiser Guldbagge Film Awards, "The Film History Ink"

The Guldbagge Awards are the Swedish Oscars. In 2014 the awards turned 50, so the challenge was to create an invitation worthy of the occasion. The idea was to inspire the award-winning scripts of the future. So props from 50 years of Swedish cinema were collected – and ground to dust in an industrial blender. This was transformed into the ink used to print the invitation. The ink also filled a pen sent to the 2000 recipients, inviting them to write the next chapter of Swedish film history.

Agency Friends, Moscow
Creative Directors Alexander Zavatskiy, Maxim Ponomarev
Copywriter Maxim Ponomarev
Art Director Alexander Zavatskiy
Graphic Design Alexey Pushkarev
Film Director Alexander Starostin
Tattoo Artists Andrey Svetov, Scott Move, Valentin Hirsch, Dmitriy Yusin, Sasha Unisex, Mike Kolesnikov, Ien Levin, Dmitry Zakharov, Nikita Broslavskiy, Sergey Gusak, Andrey Yurevich, Herman Ix, Sergey Berlin, Andrey Kichatiy
Web Production Charmer Studio
Video Production Barbershop, Moscow
Advertiser WWF Russia, "Wild Tattoo"

Tattoos have become increasingly popular – and many of them feature animals. The World Wide Fund for Nature (WWF) in Russia took advantage of this by challenging 14 of the world's greatest skin artists to design tattoos of the rarest animals. Online, visitors to a site could share their favourite tattoos with their social community and sign up to get one. Only 14 people could win the prize draw, but news of the project spread around the world.

Agency Alice BBDO, Istanbul
Creative Director Derya Tambay
Copywriters Hasan Cetin, Cengiz Pulgu
Art Directors Ahmet Ulku, Mustafa Baripoglu
Photographer Hakan Dogru
Advertiser Smart, "Being Two Is Enough"

Only two people can sit in the dinky Smart Fortwo. But sometimes two is enough, as these sunshades featuring legendary couples demonstrate. They were sent to Smart Fortwo owners as promotional items.

Agency Leo Burnett, Toronto
CCO & CDs Judy John, Lisa Greenberg
Copywriter Steve Persico
Art Director Anthony Chelvanathan
Photographer Raina+Wilson
Productions Sons & Daughters, Toronto; Beno & Wolf, Toronto
Advertiser TSN/Bell Media - Broadcasters, "Kings and Queens of the Court"

Canadian broadcaster TSN wanted to generate a big audience for the US Open tennis tournament. So it created "tennis art" with these balls placed in wire fencing around courts. Using 15,000 balls, it brought the spirit of the tournament directly to tennis fans, and generated plenty of earned media coverage.

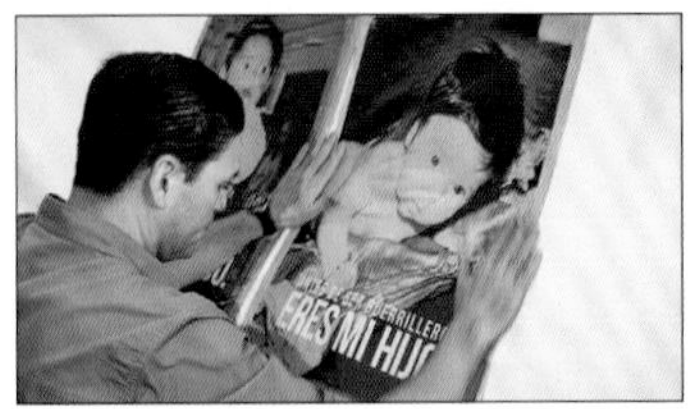

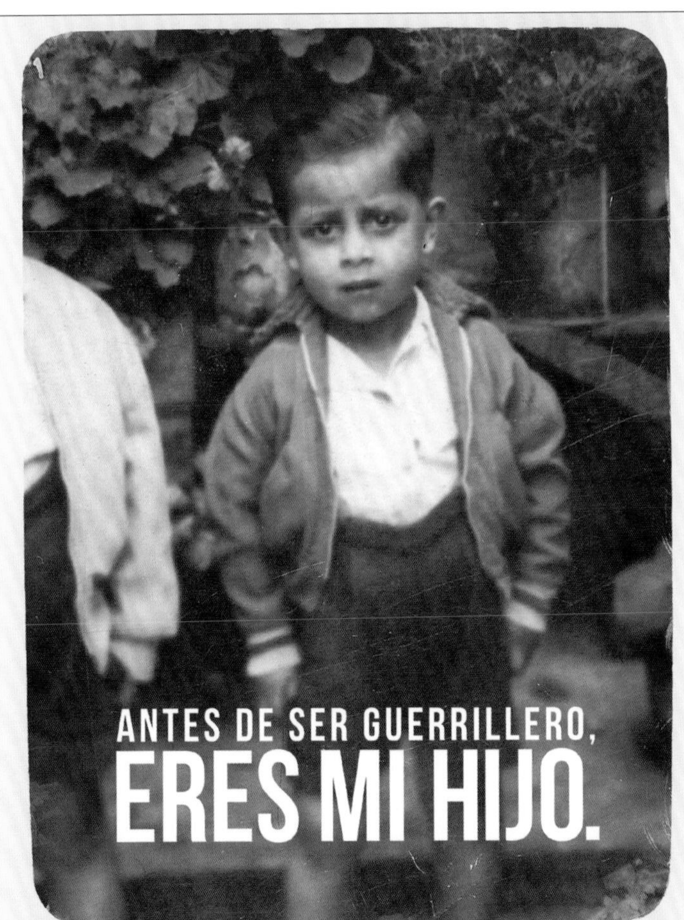

ANTES DE SER GUERRILLERO,
ERES MI HIJO.
MinDefensa
Ministerio de Defensa Nacional
ESTA NAVIDAD TE ESPERO EN CASA.
DESMOVILÍZATE. EN NAVIDAD TODO ES POSIBLE.

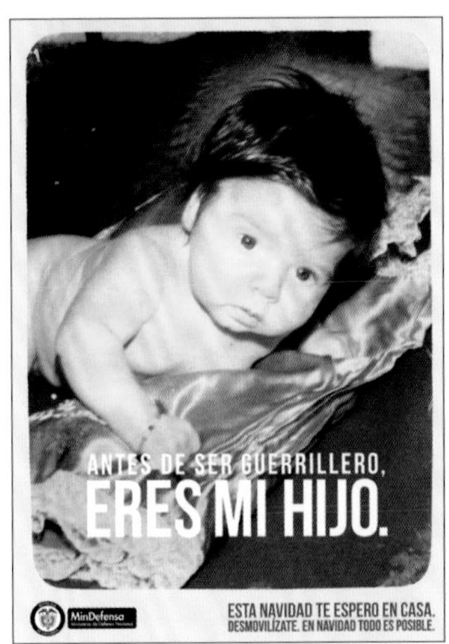

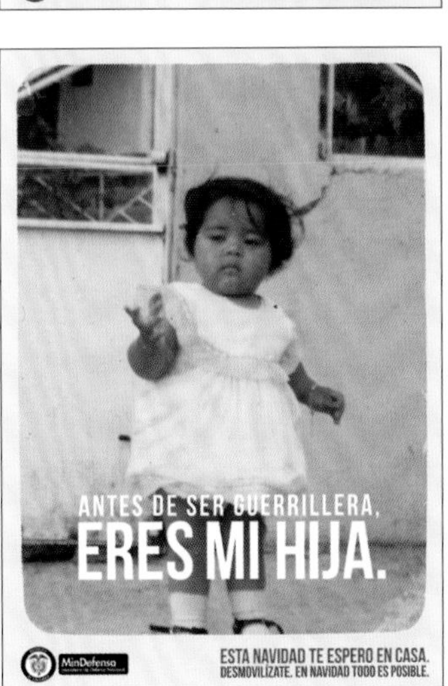

ANTES DE SER GUERRILLERA,
ERES MI HIJA.
MinDefensa
ESTA NAVIDAD TE ESPERO EN CASA.
DESMOVILÍZATE. EN NAVIDAD TODO ES POSIBLE.

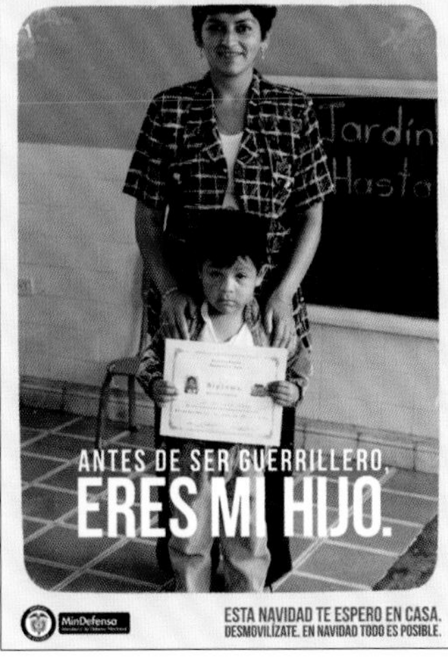

Agency LOWE/SSP3, Bogota
Creative Directors José Miguel Sokoloff, Jaime Duque, Gustavo Marioni, Mario Lagos
Copywriters Mario Lagos, Gustavo Marioni, Alberto Triana
Art Directors Andrés Estepa, Guillermo Siachoque, Andrés Carvajal
Production Guala Films, Bogotá
Film Director Miguel Herrera
Advertiser Colombian Ministry of Defense, "You Are My Son"

Many mothers of FARC guerrillas in Colombia have not seen their children for years. So this Christmas, they urged them to come home. Pictures of their children were turned into posters which were put up in areas were fighting is still going on. Some mothers starred in a TV spot featuring a song made from their words. In all, 218 mothers welcomed their children home.

Business to Business Direct

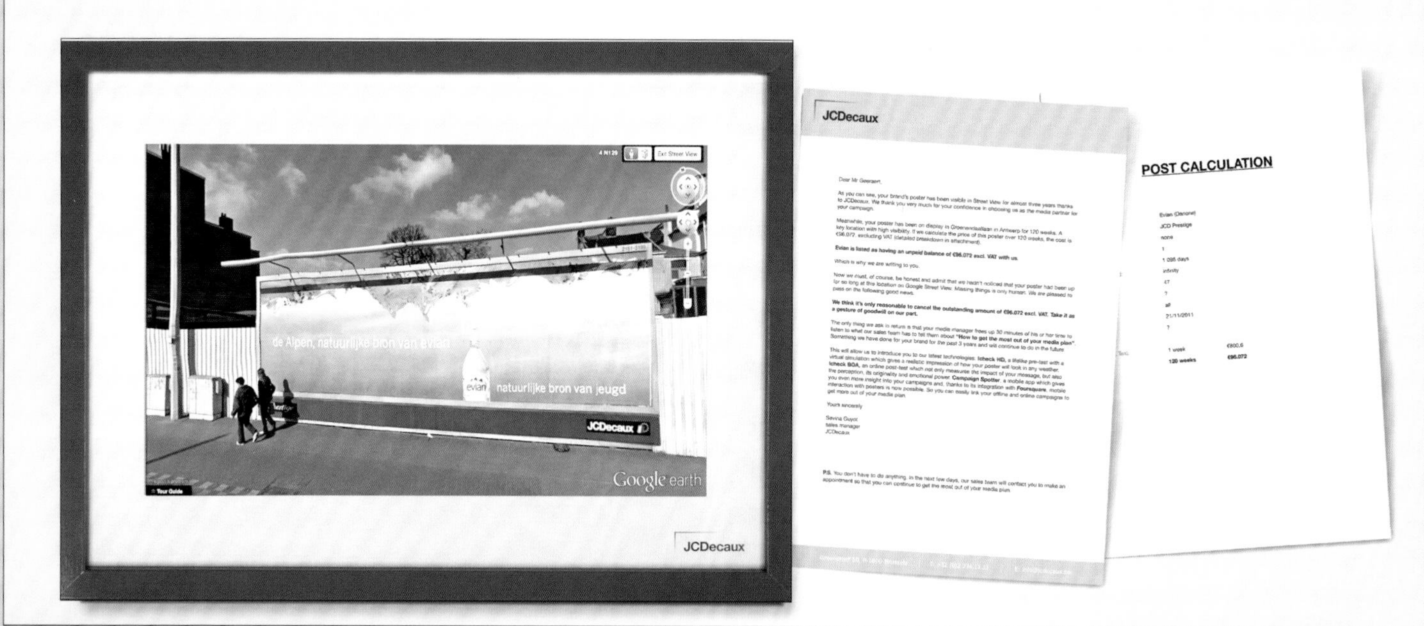

JC DECAUX **STREET VIEW UNPAID BILLS**

Agency	BBDO, Brussels
Creative Directors	Arnaud Pitz Sebastien De Valck
Copywriter	Morgane Choppinet
Art Director	Toon Vanpoucke
Advertiser	JCDecaux, “Street View Unpaid Bills”

Outdoor advertising contractor JC Decaux provides billboards, but it also has a whole range of digital solutions. The company realised that, on Google Street View, many billboards have shown the same ads for years. Which means years of free media space for the advertisers. In order to start a conversation, Decaux sent 53 of Belgium’s biggest advertisers a framed photo of their advertisement on Street View – and an invoice. Of course, the brands weren’t required to pay it. But they were encouraged to take a meeting with a digital expert from Decaux.

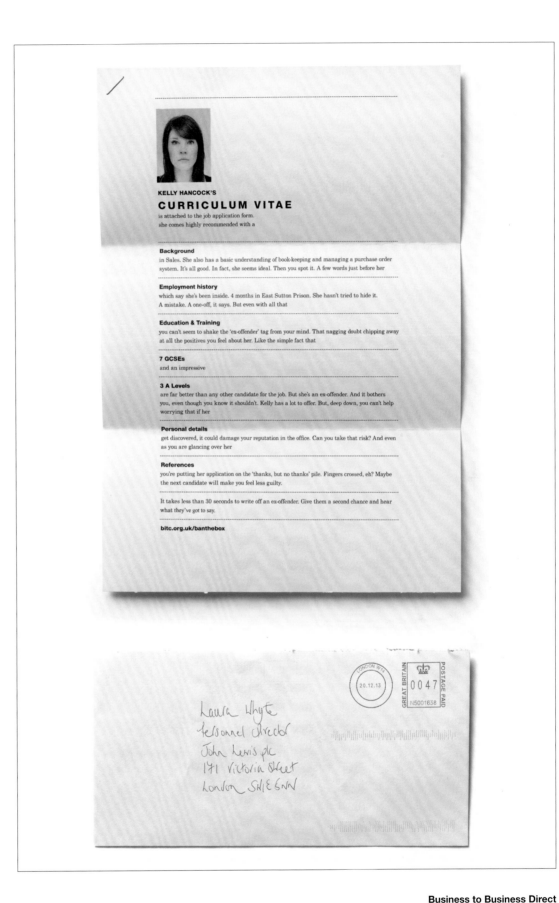

KELLY HANCOCK'S

CURRICULUM VITAE

is attached to the job application form.
she comes highly recommended with a

Background

in Sales. She also has a basic understanding of book-keeping and managing a purchase order system. It's all good. In fact, she seems ideal. Then you spot it. A few words just before her

Employment history

which say she's been inside. 4 months in East Sutton Prison. She hasn't tried to hide it. A mistake. A one-off, it says. But even with all that

Education & Training

you can't seem to shake the 'ex-offender' tag from your mind. That nagging doubt chipping away at all the positives you feel about her. Like the simple fact that

7 GCSEs

and an impressive

3 A Levels

are far better than any other candidate for the job. But she's an ex-offender. And it bothers you, even though you know it shouldn't. Kelly has a lot to offer. But, deep down, you can't help worrying that if her

Personal details

get discovered, it could damage your reputation in the office. Can you take that risk? And even as you are glancing over her

References

you're putting her application on the 'thanks, but no thanks' pile. Fingers crossed, eh? Maybe the next candidate will make you feel less guilty.

It takes less than 30 seconds to write off an ex-offender. Give them a second chance and hear what they've got to say.

bitc.org.uk/banthebox

LONDON W14
20.12.13
GREAT BRITAIN
0047
N5001638
POSTAGE PAID

Laura Whyte
Personnel Director
John Lewis plc
171 Victoria Street
London SW1E 5NN

Agency	Leo Burnett, London	Research shows that people who've spent time in prison are less likely to commit another offence if they find a job. But employers routinely reject former offenders. To highlight this, non-profit organisation Business in the Community sent ordinary-looking CVs to human resources professionals. As they read the document, they discovered a stream-of-consciousness narration from a prospective employer, justifying their rejection of an ex-offender.
Executive CD	Justin Tindall	
Creative Directors	Hugh Todd Adam Tucker	
Copywriter	Adam Tucker	
Art Directors	Lance Crozier Marc Donaldson	
Art Buyer	Leah Mitchell	
Advertiser	Business in the Community, "CVs"	

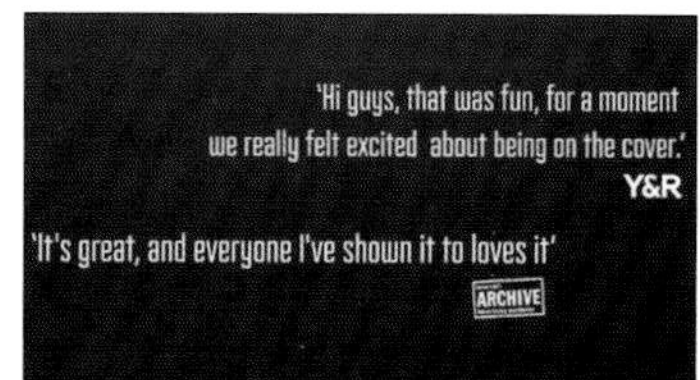

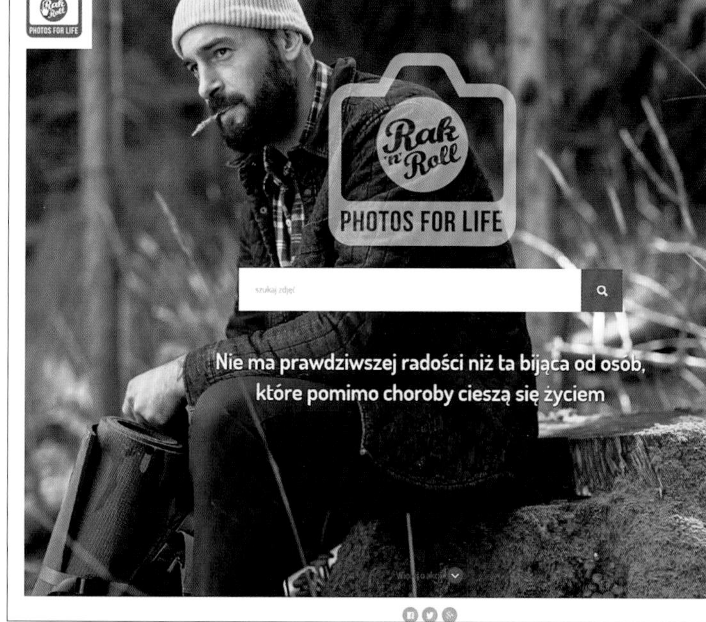

Business to Business Direct

Agency LetsAdvertise.it, Copenhagen
Art Directors Casper Christensen, René Schultz
Advertiser LetsAdvertise.it, "The Disguised Portfolio"

A couple of unemployed creatives wanted to attract the attention of agency creative directors. So they used a medium creative directors appreciate: Lürzer's Archive, a magazine about the world's best advertising. They designed fake editions of the magazine with the targeted creative director's work on the front. But the contents showcased their own portfolio, and even included articles about themselves. The "disguised portfolio" generated buzz around the industry and got its creators a job with one of their favourite agencies.

Agency Isobar, Warsaw
Creative Director Maciej Nowicki
Copywriter Jan Cieślar
Art Director Rafał Ryś
Photographers Paweł Fabjańęski, Łukasz Ziętek, Jacek Poremba, Karol Grygoruk
Production ShootMe, Warsaw
Advertiser Rak'nRoll Cancer Foundation, "Photos for Life - a Charity Photo Bank"

Cancer foundation Rak'n'Roll ("rak" means cancer in Polish) wanted to show that many people recover from cancer and go on to lead full lives. So it created Photos For Life, the world's first charity photo bank, where all the models are cancer patients or survivors. Businesses, magazines, brands and agencies were contacted and invited to use the images, which are far cheaper than those from regular stock services. But the photos come with a signature: "The model in this photo won their fight with cancer. Learn more at www.photosfor.life"

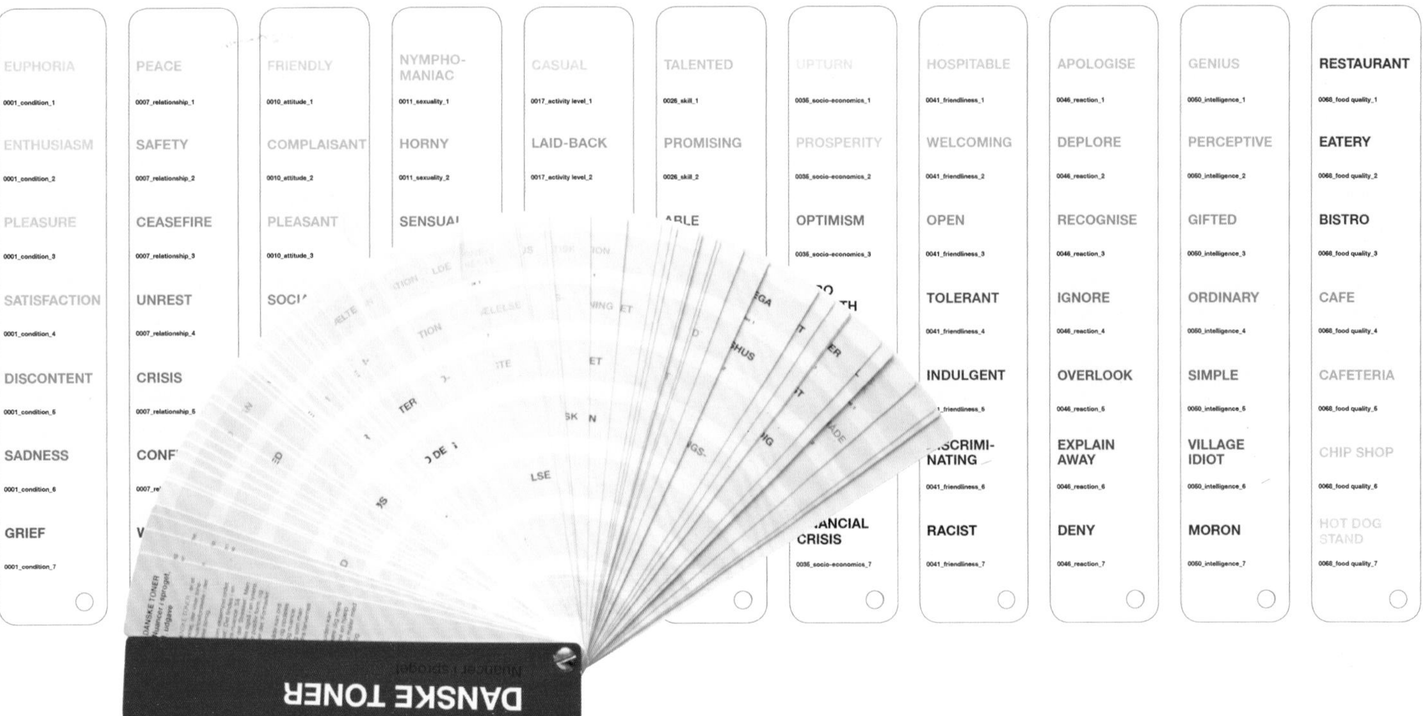

Agency	TN Reklame, Hellerup
Creative Director	Thomas Norgaard
Copywriter	Thomas Norgaard
Art Director	Lisbet Kroll
Photographer	Lisbet Kroll
Graphic Design	Lisbet Kroll
Advertiser	TN Reklame, "World's First Colour Guide Based on Words"

Copywriting agency TN Reklame wanted to promote its skills to potential clients and agency partners. But how to remind them of the power of words? It launched "Danske Toner" (Danish Tones), the first colour guide based on words and their nuances. "Colder" words around subjects like finance are blue, while "warmer" ones like those describing love, romance and happiness are printed in shades of pink or red.

Agency	Cundari, Toronto
Creative Directors	Andrew Simon Dean Martin
Copywriter	Alexandra Manahan
Art Director	Melissa Medwyk
Designer	Melissa Medwyk
Production	Anstey Book Binding, Toronto
Advertiser	Toronto Zoo, "Panda Cups"

The Toronto Zoo's giant panda exhibit was now open to the public. So journalists and opinion leaders were sent this pack, which invited them to raise a cup of tea to "China's most famous natural treasures".

HOW OLD MARKETING BOOKS BECAME
AN INVITATION TO INNOVATION

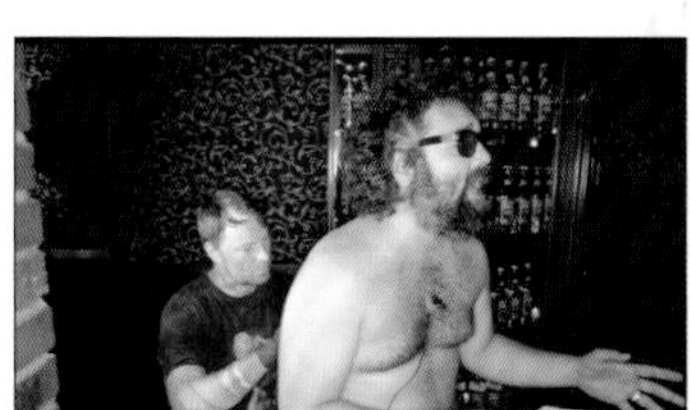

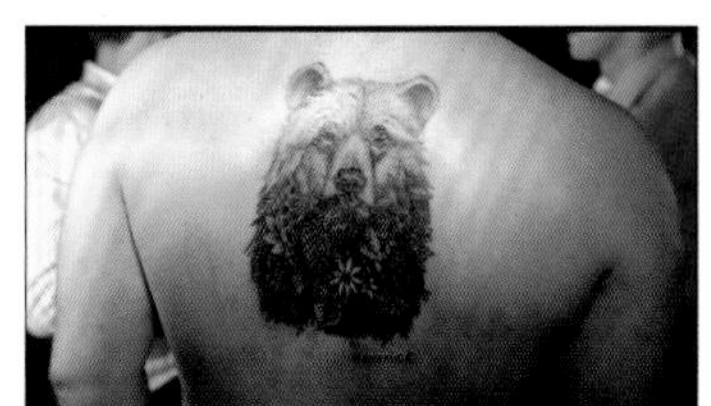

Agency BBDO Brussels
CDs Henny Van Gerwen, Sebastien De Valck, Arnaud Pitz
Copywriters Régine Smetz, Leen Baeten
Art Director Klaartje Galle
Production Jozias Boone, Gent
Advertiser BBDO Connect, “Old Marketing Books. An Invitation to Innovation”

BBDO & Microsoft run BBDO Connect, a marketing seminar about innovative technologies. So the invitation had to be pretty special. In the end, it actually destroyed some examples of traditional media. The pages of old marketing books were torn out and printed upon, becoming invitations to discover new solutions. “Your future sales are not in this book. Join us to stay relevant.”

Agency Mama Agency, New York
Executive CD Yv Corbeil
Production 1ONE Productions, Montreal
Film Directors Matt Jocey, Mael Demarcy
Producer Jean-René Parenteau
Advertiser Heineken, “1 AM Presentation”

Entrepreneur, creative director and speaker Yv Corbeil was challenged by Heineken’s global marketing director Americas to inspire all his marketing directors and get them excited about Desperados beer. So they were “kidnapped” from a bar, flung in the back of a prison van and taken to a nightspot with a distinctly underground vibe. There, Yv got a bear tattooed on his back, live on stage, while giving a talk about the world of Desperados.

Agency Abby Norm, Stockholm
Creative Director Olle Nordell
Copywriter Dan Göransson
Art Directors Oskar Hellqvist, Emil Frid
Typographer Familjen Pangea
Final Art Camilla Thuresson, Emily Pennström
Advertiser Adobe, "This Is Your Type"

The brief was to invite top Nordic creatives to Adobe's event Create Now – Creative Meet Up. Using Adobe software, the agency crafted 239 personalised typefaces inspired by the life and work of the creative invitees themselves. But the invitations made clear that they would have to show up to the event to receive their bespoke typeface on a USB key.

Agency Impact & Echo BBDO, Kuwait City
CDs Cesar Jachan, Lokesh Achaiah
Copywriter Lokesh Achaiah
Art Director Akram Rehayel
Photographer Hani Ali Abdel Satar
Production Chroma, Kuwait City; Hanilens, Kuwait City
Producer Hisham Murtuda
Agency Producer Ahmed Shamsin
Advertiser Wataniya, "The Apron That's Got You Covered"

Hair salons are one of the few places where people are cut off from their mobile devices. On behalf of Wataniya telecom, a special apron was created with a transparent window that allowed users to continue their digital lives while having their hair styled. Happy customers, and a nice little promotional tool for Wataniya.

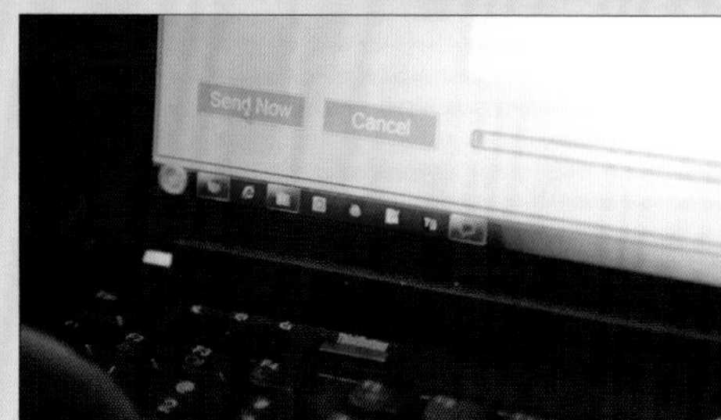
Send Now
Cancel

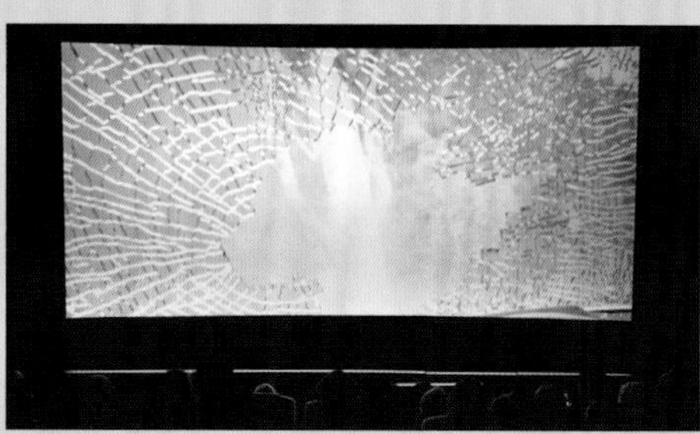

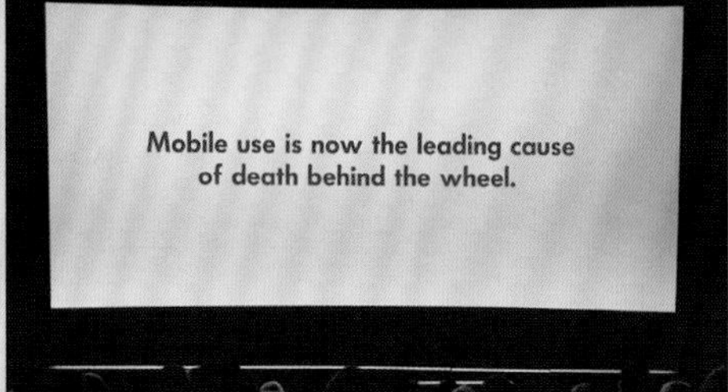
Mobile use is now the leading cause of death behind the wheel.

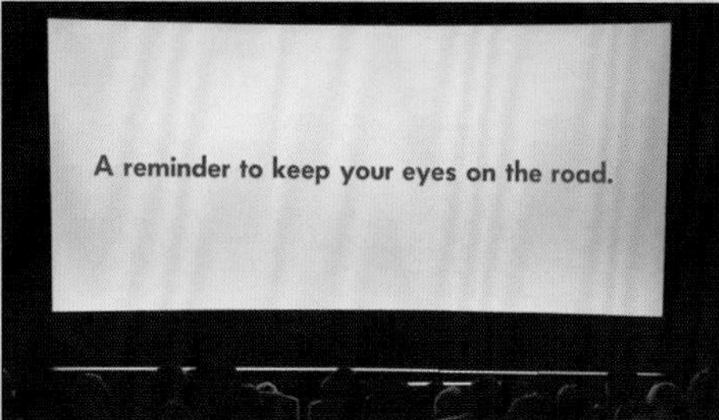
A reminder to keep your eyes on the road.

Das Auto.

244 **Media Innovation-Traditional Media**

Agency	OgilvyOne, Beijing	**Agency Producers**	Morris Ku
CDs	Graham Fink		Rita Yang
	Doug Schiff	**3D Design**	Yu Guo
	Kama Yu		Sun Zhang
	Daqing Wang		Xing Wan
Copywriters	Doug Schiff		Wanqiu Lin
	Lei Song	**DOP**	Alfred Pong
Art Directors	Minsheng Zhang		Jovi Lee
	Xufeng Zhou		Alan Yip
Production	Answermark, Hong Kong	**Sound Effects**	KK Chau
Film Director	Eggtart Chow	**Advertiser**	Volkswagen, "Eyes On The Road"
Producer	Avis Or		

Auto makers are aware that mobile use while driving has become the leading cause of death behind the wheel. Volkswagen wanted to remind young drivers of this in a way they wouldn't soon forget. As the cinema's lights went down, a short film showed a car journey from the driver's point of view. Nothing happened for 15 seconds. Suddenly, the viewers received a message on their phones. As they looked down, they were jolted by the sound of the car on screen having a terrible accident. "A reminder to keep your eyes on the road."

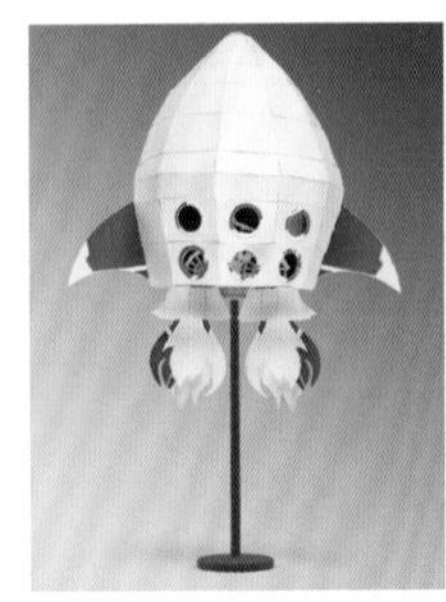

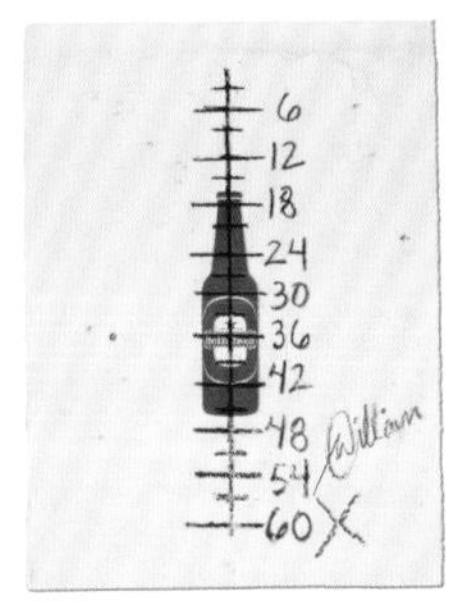

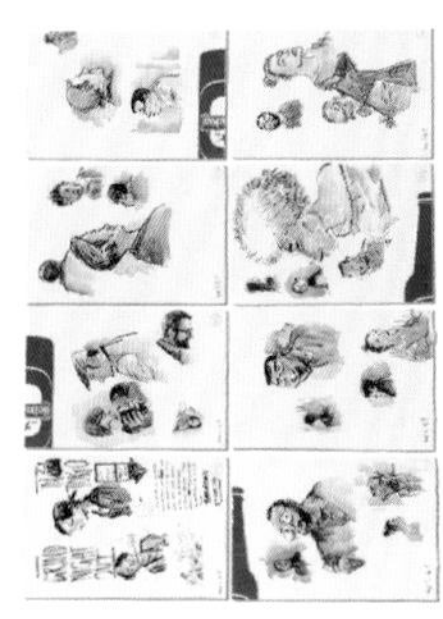

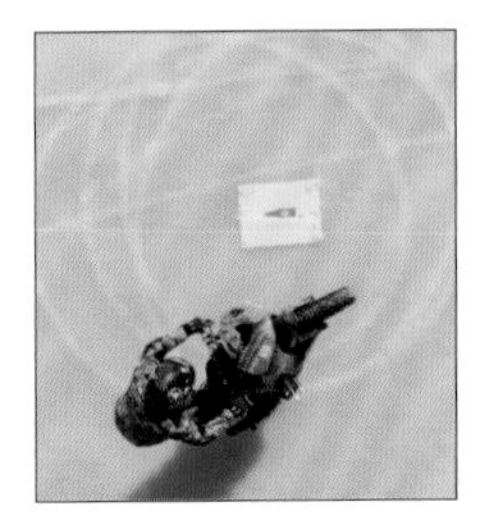

Agency Wieden+Kennedy, Amsterdam
Executive CDs Mark Bernath, Eric Quennoy
Creative Directors Thierry Albert, Faustin Claverie
Head of Creative Innov. Edu Pou
Copywriter Evgeny Primachenko
Art Director Vasco Vicente
Interactive AD Tiago Varandas
Broadcast Prod. Erik Verheijen, Judd Caraway, Stijn Wikkerink
Interactive Prod. Andrew Allen, Matthew Ravenhall
Design/Photography Joe Burrin, Philip Cronerud, Jackie Barbour, Dario Fusnecher
Film Directors Quentin van den Bossche, James "Red" McLeod
Advertiser Heineken, "The Legendary Posters"

Heineken has become famous for its spots introducing us to legendary people. Now, meet the legendary posters. The set of 40 posters travelled the world, had adventures and met extraordinary people. They climbed mountains, plunged deep into the oceans – one of them even went into space. They were exhibited at galleries, on streets and eventually at the Stedelijk Museum in Amsterdam, before being auctioned on a custom-built Tumblr page via eBay, with proceeds going to Reporters Without Borders.

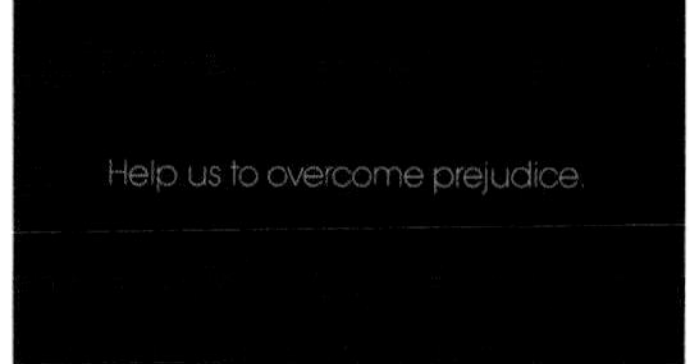

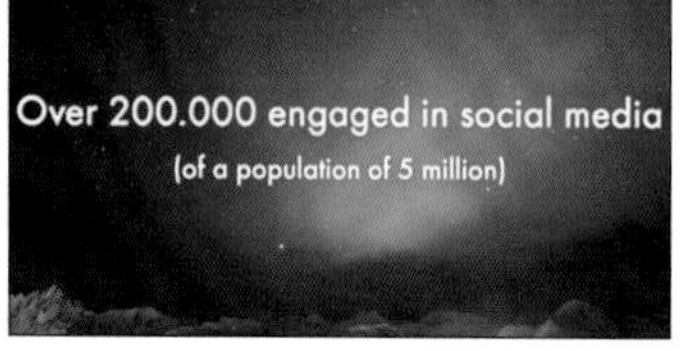

Agency Y&R, Milan
Executive CD Vicky Gitto
Copywriters GB Oneto, Carmela Balestrieri
Art Directors Davide Breghelli, Cinzia Caccia, Giulia Papetti
Production Combocut Film, Milan
Film Director Alessandro Palminiello
Advertiser Pubblicità Progresso Foundation, "The Balloon Trap"

Apparently, 6 out of 10 Italians think gender discrimination doesn't exist. This project involved luring men to make sexist remarks thanks to judiciously placed speech balloons. The posters featured incomplete phrases such as "At work I'd like to…" or "After my degree I'd like to…" The temptation proved too great for some men, driving a digital debate about sexism. The client is a non-profit organisation tackling the problems of society through freely distributed advertising.

Agency TRY/Apt/POL, Oslo
Creative Director Lars Joachim Grimstad
Copywriters Lars Joachim Grimstad, Jonas Grønnern, Camilla Bjornhaug
Art Directors Egil Pay, Lars-Kristian Harveg, Preben Moan
Production Tangrystan, Oslo
Film Director Andrea Eckerbom
Advertiser DNB Bank, "The 24 Hour Ad Break"

Many people toss and turn at night worrying about their finances. But Norwegian bank DNB wanted to let them know that its advice line is open 24 hours a day. So it bought all the ad slots on Norway's leading channel over a 24 hour period, and filled them with normal people offering their advice on all aspects of life. And of course each slot ended with the bank's advice line number.

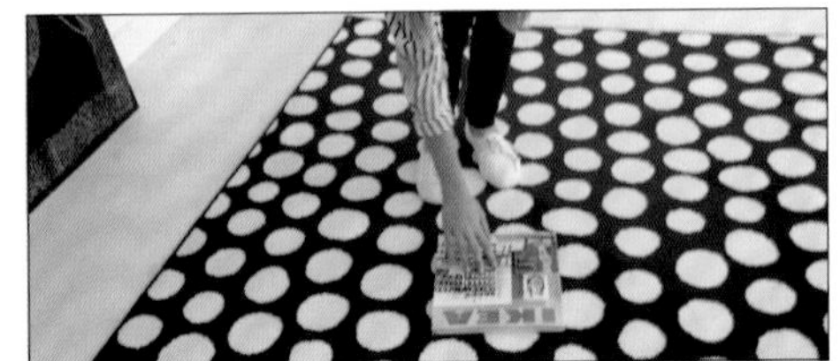

Agency	Leo Burnett, London
CDs	Matt Lee
	Pete Heyes
	Adam Tucker
Copywriters	Phillip Meyler
	Darren Keff
Art Directors	Phillip Meyler
	Darren Keff
Production	Leo Burnett, London
	Grand Visual, London
Graphic Designer	Andy Allen
Advertiser	McDonald's, "See One. Want One."

Once you've decided you fancy a Big Mac, it's pretty difficult to get the idea out your mind. Hence this digital billboard, which automatically detected passers-by and made a thought bubble containing a burger pop up above their heads. And then it followed them until they were out of the poster's range. Then people found it hard to stop talking about the Big Mac, too.

Agency	McCann Copenhagen
CCOs	Linus Karlsson
	Andreas Dahlqvist
Strategic CD	Mark Fallows
Creatives	Eva Wallmark
	Rickard Beskow
	Michal Sitkiewicz
	Rasmus Keger
	Morten Halvorsen
Art Director	Jan Finnesand
Advertiser	IKEA, "Showroom At Home"

Looking at an IKEA catalogue is one thing, but how do you know what the furniture will look like in your own home? This app enabled customers to place a 3D projection of items exactly where they'd sit in real life, thanks to their mobile device. Simply scan the relevant page of the catalogue, select the item you like, and activate the app.

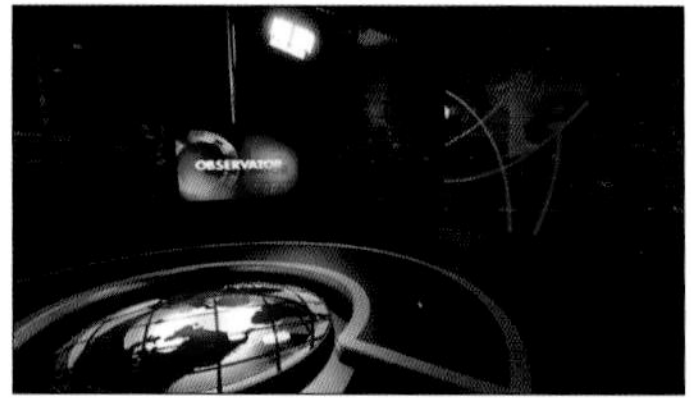

Agency Leo Burnett, London
Creative Director Adam Tucker
Copywriters Hugh Todd, Darren Keff, Phillip Meyler
Art Directors Hugh Todd, Darren Keff, Phillip Meyler
Production Blink, London
Advertiser Business in the Community, "Second Chance"

Ex-offenders are often overlooked by recruiters, but they deserve a second chance. This interactive pre-roll utilises the "Skip Ad" facility on YouTube. A man who has spent time in prison tries to convince an interviewer that he is the right man for the job. If the viewer tries to "skip" him, he returns, less confident every time. But when he's not skipped, his confidence grows.

Agency Geometry Global, Bucharest
Creative Director Mihai Fetcu
Copywriter Sorana Somesan
Art Director Florina Alexandru
Head of Art Stefan Vasilachi
Advertiser Antena1, "The RGB News"

Less than 2% of Romanians donate blood, so the country has a serious shortage. TV station Antena 1 decided to recruit donors through its prime time news program, Observator. When switching on to watch the news, viewers saw that something odd had happened to the colours on their screen. The presenter reassured them: "There's nothing wrong with your set – this is life without red." The initiative reached 14 million Romanians and led to an 80% rise in blood donations.

Agency	Publicis, Skopje	
CD	Vasilije Corluka	
Copywriter	Dejan Spirkoski	
Art Directors	Miki Stefanoski Milan Stojanov	
Photographer	Aleksandar Pulios	
Agency Producer	Aleksandar Jakovlev	
Graphic Design	Gjorgji Janevski	
Advertiser	National Neurological Institute, "Alzheimer's News Editors"	

People with Alzheimer's have difficulty remembering recent events, but can often recall things from the past. For a campaign by the National Neurological Institute, the agency asked Alzheimer's sufferers to share the most recent news stories they could remember. Using the results, on World Alzheimer's Day Macedonia's three leading newspapers ran front pages containing stories from the past. The TV news also featured old stories. Finally, the presenter explained the campaign, raising awareness of the early signs of Alzheimer's.

Agency	BBDO New York	
CCO	David Lubars Greg Hahn	
Associate CDs	Peter Alsante Matthew Zaifert	
Copywriter	Adam Noel	
Art Director	Jon Kubik	
Production	Anonymous + BA Content, LA	
Film Director	Christian Loubek	
Advertiser	Autism Speaks, "Lifetime of Difference Project"	

Spotting autism early and seeking the right advice can make a lifetime of difference. To illustrate this, Autism Speaks teamed up with three different brands (Band Aid, Campbell's and AT&T) to create related ads featuring an autistic boy. Although each of the short spots are apparently self-contained, the full 60 second story shows the boy's journey from childhood to graduation. He leads a happy and fulfilled life. "Learn the early signs of autism today, because an early diagnosis can make a lifetime of difference."

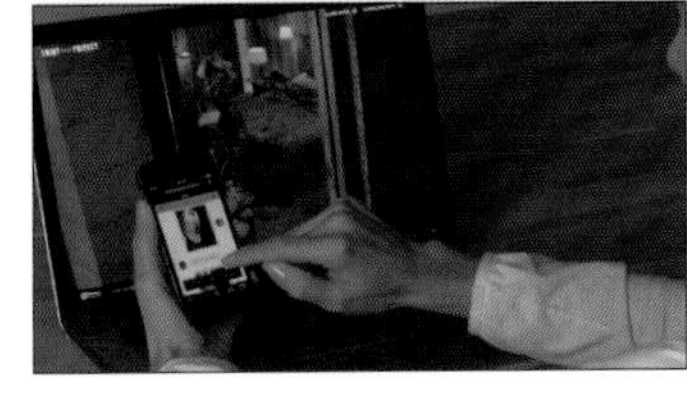

Agency	Leo Burnett, Chicago	
CCO	Susan Credle	
Executive CDs	Jon Wyville Dave Loew	
Creative Directors	Rainer Schmidt Tohru Oyasu	
Executive Producer	Rob Tripas	
Producer	Topher Cochrane	
Director	Mark Molloy	
DOP	Crighton Bone	
Advertiser	Norton, "Enjoy Your Privacy"	

Norton Mobile Security wanted to encourage people to protect their privacy while using mobile devices. The result was a game experience that paired the user's mobile with their PC or tablet. On the screen, peer into the windows of seven different characters. On your phone, select one of their names, and suddenly you have access to all their texts, mails, pictures and financial details. Find out about the unfaithful wife, the shady businessman, and the vegan blogger – who secretly binges on steak.

FOR A WEEK WE HEATED UP THE CITY'S INTEREST
WITH A GIANT PICTURE OF RAW MEAT

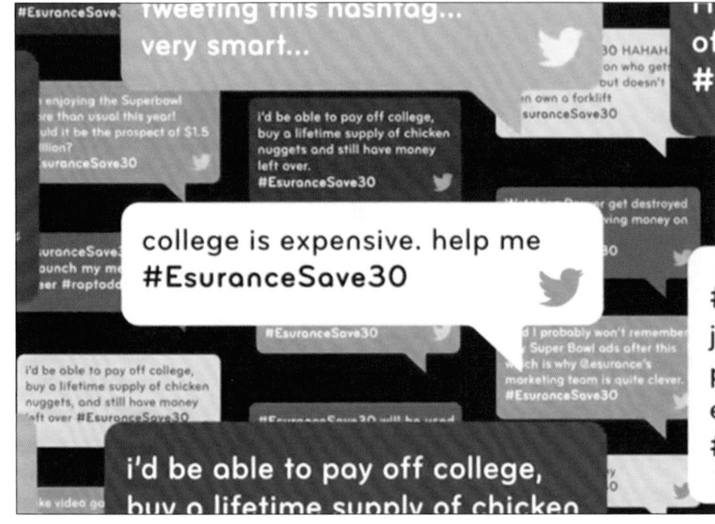

i'd be able to pay off college,

the top twitter trend in the world

Agency	Voskhod, Yekaterinburg
CD	Andrey Gubaydullin
Copywriters	Evgeny Primachenko Andrey Chernyi
Art Directors	Vladislav Derevyannikh Dmitry Maslakov
Designer	Evgeniya Surovtseva
Advertiser	Double Grill & Bar, "Grillboard"

There are a lot of steak houses in Yekaterinburg, Russia, so you have to work hard to stand out. But all this agency needed to promote the Double Grill & Bar was a single billboard. First it gave citizens an appetite by putting up a picture of a juicy raw steak. Then a few days later, it set fire to the billboard and gave the meat a good grilling. Local media were ablaze with the news – and suddenly it became hard to get a table at the restaurant.

Agency	Leo Burnett, Chicago
CCO	Susan Credle
Executive CD	Brian Shembeda
Creative Director	Jeff Candido
Associate CDs	Jesse Dillow Travis Lampe
Executive Prod.	Matt Blitz
Producer	Chance Woodward
Director	Chris Smith
Advertiser	Esurance, "#EsuranceSave30"

Esurance is all about doing things more efficiently, and then passing on the savings to its customers. Which is why it didn't buy a slot in the Super Bowl, one of the most popular (and therefore expensive) live TV broadcasts in the world. Instead, the insurer bought the first slot just after the big game. Then it promised to give the 1.5 million dollars it had saved to a person who tweeted #esurancesave30. The twittersphere went crazy (5.3 million tweets), the media loved the story, and after the prize draw one family couldn't believe their luck.

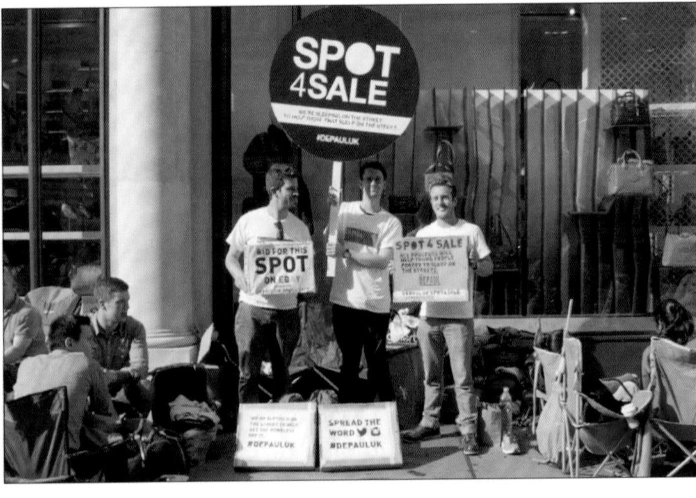

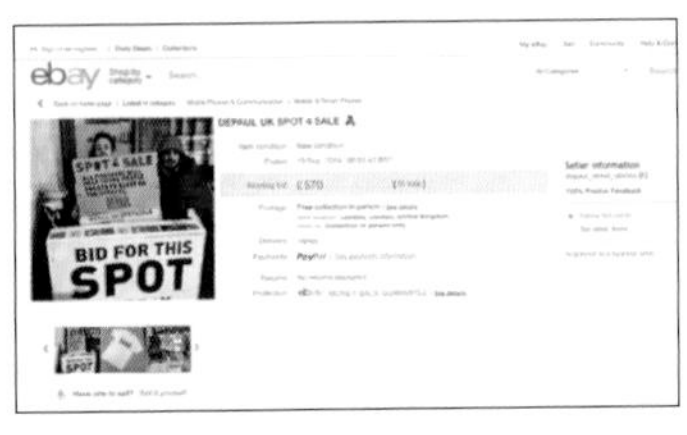

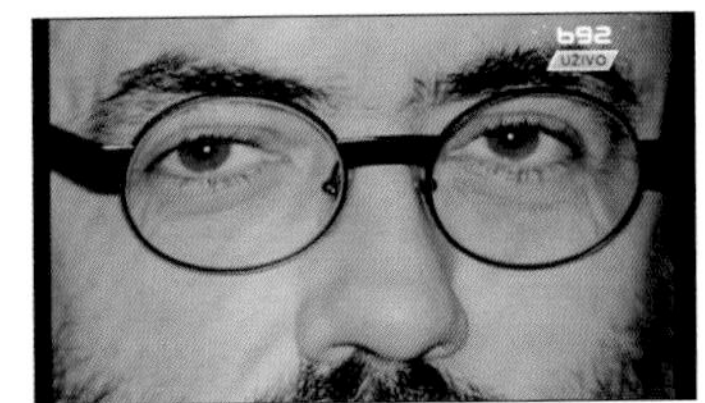

Agency	Publicis, London
Executive CD	Andy Bird
Creatives	Jason Moussalli Adam Balogh
Executive Prod.	Colin Hickon
Operations Director	Debbie Burke
Advertiser	Depaul UK, "Spot 4 Sale"

Some people are forced to live on the streets. Others do so just for one night – for instance, when they camp outside the Apple Store so they can get their hands on its latest device on the day of launch. Playing on this irony, homeless charity Depaul grabbed one of the first spots in the queue at the London Apple Store for the launch of the iPhone 6. Then it auctioned the spot on eBay, raising enough money to keep a homeless person off the streets for 47 nights. Media coverage raised awareness of the charity and amplified the message.

Agency	Saatchi & Saatchi, Belgrade
Executive CD	Veljko Golubović
Regional CD	John Pallant
CDs	Žarko Veljković Ivana Zeković Dragana Petković
Copywriter	Nikola Zmajevć
Producer	Ivan Zornić
Advertiser	OSCE, "Chronicles of Threats"

In Serbia, journalists investigating issues linked to the state are routinely threatened. Three have been murdered. To bring this situation to the fore, a group campaigning for press freedom slipped an authentic "threatening letter" into newspapers. When they opened their daily paper, people initially thought the threats were aimed at them. Many called the police. The next day, the truth was revealed, stoking debate. Unsolved cases were reopened, and the new government formally admitted that "the state" assassinated one of the journalists.

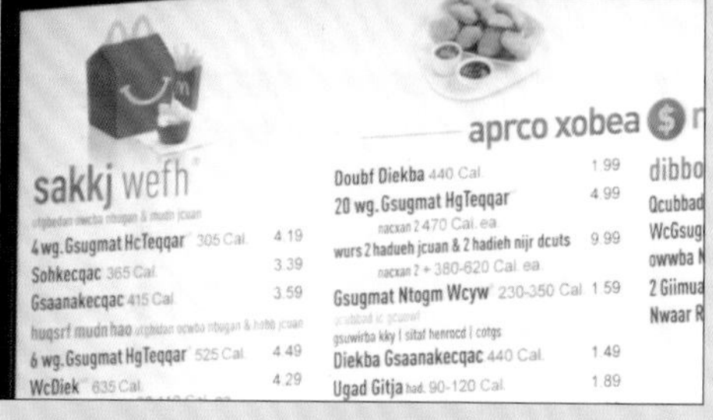

Agency Leo Burnett, Chicago
CCO Susan Credle
Executive CDs Jon Wyville, Dave Loew
CDs John Hansa, Tony Katalinic
Copywriter Kamil Kowalczyk
Art Director Pablo Jimenez
Executive Prod. Denis Giroux
Producers Ross Greenblat, Benjamin Milam
Digital Production Matt Kuttan
Advertiser McDonald's, "Literacy Store"

One in every four children in America grows up without learning to read. McDonald's decided spread the joy of reading by giving away children's books in its Happy Meals. To promote the importance of literacy, a McDonald's store in Chicago became illegible. Regular signage and menu items were replaced with nonsensical, mixed-up words. Even employee nametags and ketchup packets were changed. Customers were baffled, until an announcement explained the operation. "To a child who can't read, the world can be a confusing place."

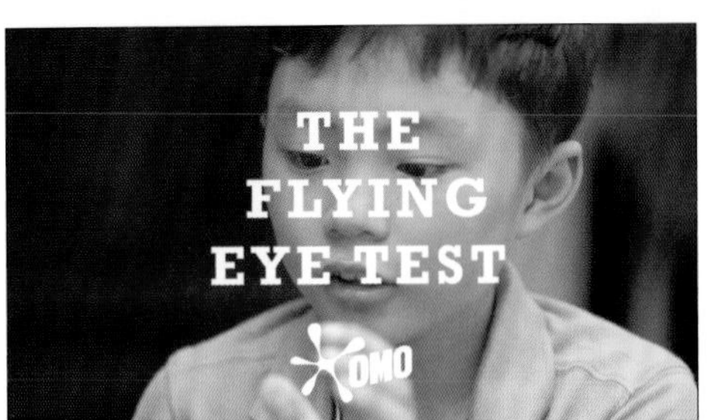

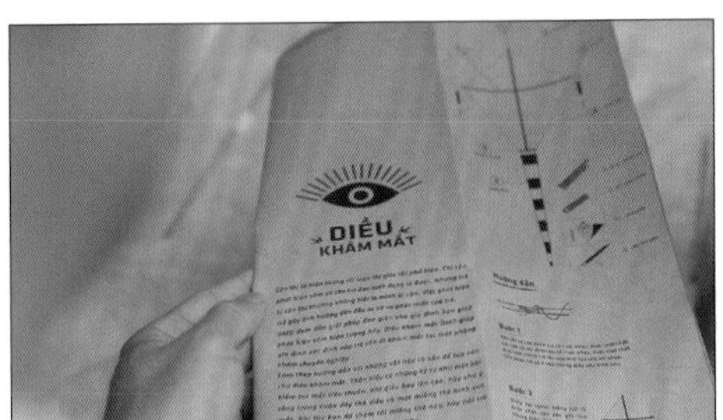

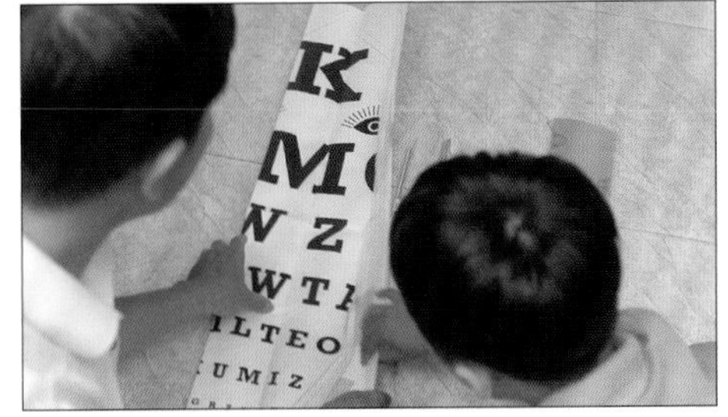

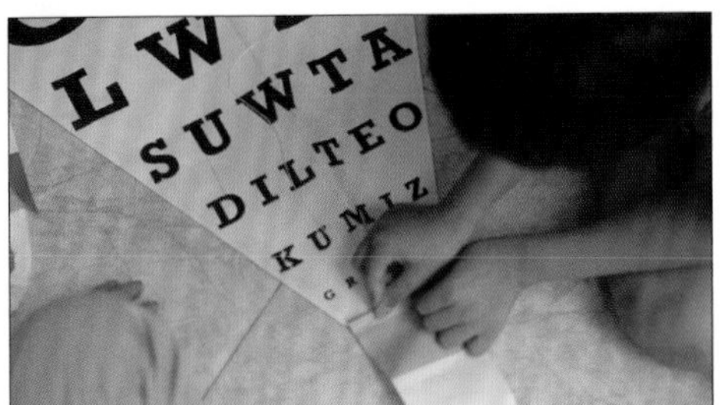

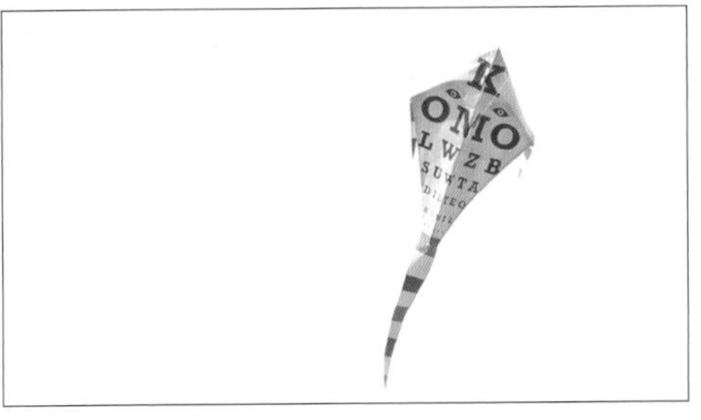

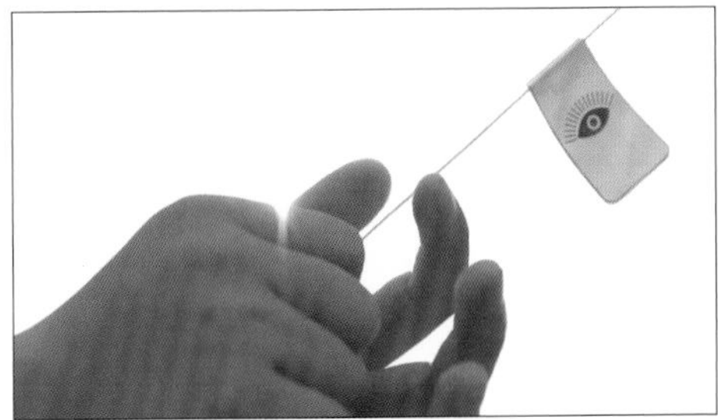

Agency	Lowe Vietnam , Ho Chi Minh City
Executive CD	Carlos Camacho
Art Director	Kumkum Fernando
Photographer	Duy Ho
Production	Frame World, Ho Chi Minh City
Producer	Club House Films
Film Director	Quoc Huy
Agency Producer	Hai Ta
Graphic Design	Kumkum Fernando
Advertiser	Unilever, OMO, "The Flying Eye Test"

In Vietnam, the early detection of myopia among children is a challenge for families, especially in rural areas. OMO, the detergent brand that believes "dirt is good" because kids should play outdoors, teamed up with its agency to create the OMO kite. Costing just one dollar to make, the kite is a flying eye test. A tag on the string indicates the exact distance from where the child should be able to see the letters. In parks and playgrounds, 2000 kites were distributed.

Agency	Rosapark, Paris
CDs	Mark Forgan Jamie Standen Mathilde Carpentier
Copywriters	Jamie Standen Nicolas Gadesaude
Art Directors	Mark Forgan Julien Saurin
Production	So Films, Paris
Film Director	Julian Nodolwsky
Producer	Olivier Bassuet
Advertiser	Monoprix, "Change The Beep"

Cash registers in supermarkets are annoyingly monotonous. As each item is scanned, you hear the same old beep. For this stunt and viral film, when a Monoprix own brand product was scanned, the beep was replaced by a more appropriate sound. Eggs clucked; milk mooed; soda fizzed; English breakfast tea played the UK national anthem. With Monoprix products, the everyday is less "everyday".

Agency	Leo Burnett, Milan
Executive CDs	Francesco Bozza Alessandro Antonini
Associate CD	Andrea Marzagalli
Digital CD	Paolo Boccardi
Creative Team	Andrea Stanich Sergio Spaccavento Serena Micieli Silvia Savoia
Copywriter	Alice Jasmine Crippa
Production	Movie Magic, Milan
Advertiser	WWF, "Pets4pets Project"

Kids are the future, so the WWF (World Wide Fund for Nature) gave its latest advertising brief to a school in Italy. The children pitched their ideas and a winning script was chosen. Then the ad was shot, with a camera crew and professional advice. Finally it was screened on TV. It shows a polar bear wreaking havoc in a normal household. How would you like it if the bears destroyed your home? The kids also produced seven print ads, four radio spots and a web video.

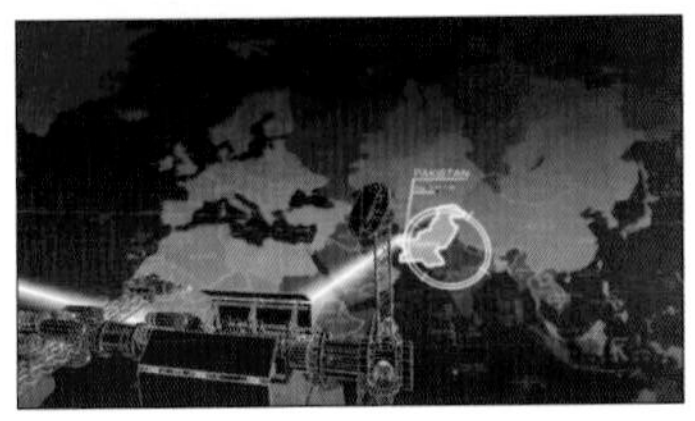

BRIEF:

Sun Hung Kai Properties' East Point City, an environmentally friendly mall in Hong Kong, wanted to help tackle the problem of excessive wrapping paper use during Chinese New Year. They wished to increase mall traffic and sales, whilst raising awareness of recycling and saving trees.

IDEA:

Introducing the world's first Instant Newspaper Recycler. With low-tech silk-screen printing techniques specially powered by all-natural human energy, we transformed old newspapers into unique, beautifully designed eco-friendly wrapping paper in just 30 seconds.

RESULTS:

- In the first 2 days, over 3,000 consumers & 3,600 new wrapping paper
- Queues of over an hour during peak periods
- 30% increase in mall traffic and sales
- Covered by 70 news sites
- HKD1.5 million in free media

AS SEEN ON:

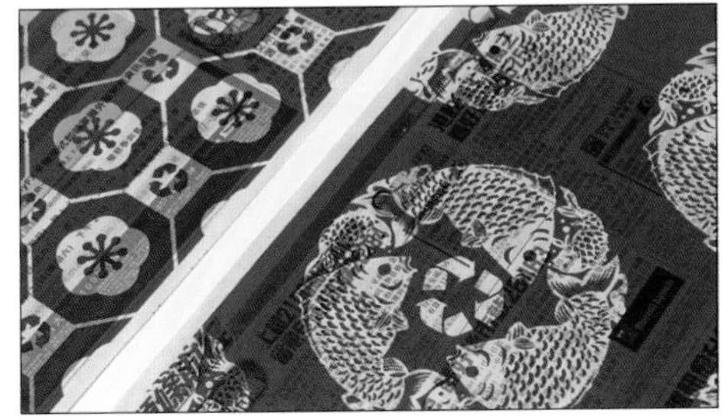

Agency	BBDO Pakistan, Lahore
Creative Director	Ali Rez
Artist	Saks Afridi
Photographers	Insiya Syed Jamil Akhtar Imran Arif Khan Noor Behram
Photographer/Artist	JR
Production	Brave New Films, Culver City
Advertiser	Reprieve, "Not A Bug Splat"

According to the Foundation for Fundamental Rights, drone strikes have killed more than 3,500 people in Pakistan since 2004, including an estimated 200 children. Yet drone operators are so far removed from the field that they sometimes refer to their victims as "bug splats". This giant image of a child was placed in a strategic area of Pakistan. It made a potential victim visible to the drone operators, as well as to the media. Word was spread with the hashtag #NotABugSplat, stirring debate about the morality of drone attacks.

Agency	Saatchi & Saatchi, Hong Kong
CCO	Carol Lam
Head of Creative	Pelie Kwok
Integrated Director	Arion Yau
Copywriters	Adeline Siow Jin Pan
Art Director	Kenneth Foo
Director	Joshua Wong, Laundromatte, HK
Advertiser	SHK Properties, "The Instant Newspaper Recycler"

Three million free newspapers are handed out every day in Hong Kong – and then thrown away. A new "environmentally innovative" shopping mall found an additional use for the unwanted papers. Over Chinese New Year, when everyone gives gifts, it set up an "instant newspaper recycler" in the mall. Pop your paper in and get it reconfigured as free gift wrapping! In fact the recycling "machine" was a mini-atelier in which artists screen-printed the news sheets. The free wrapping bore the store's brand name.

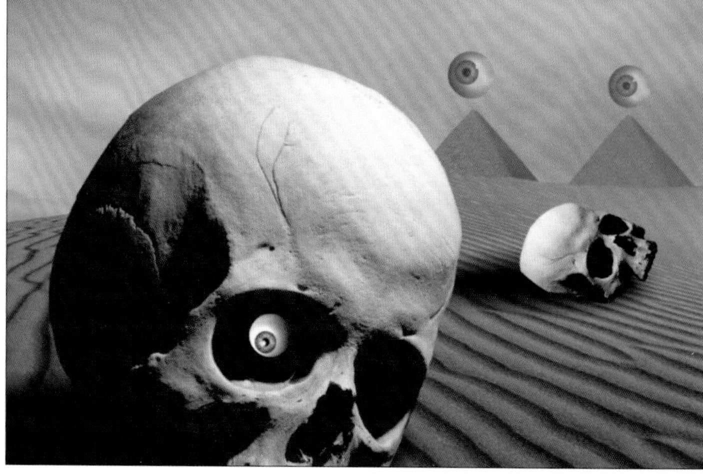

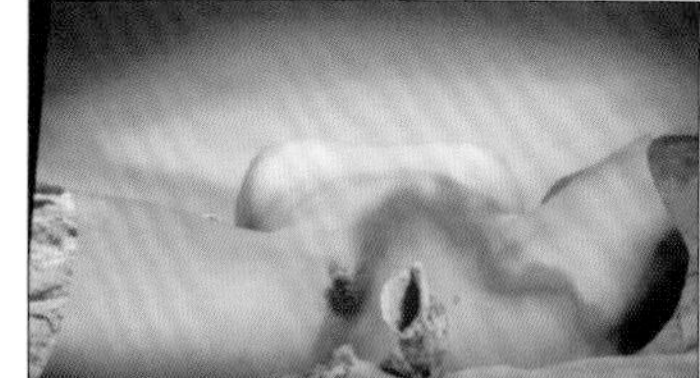

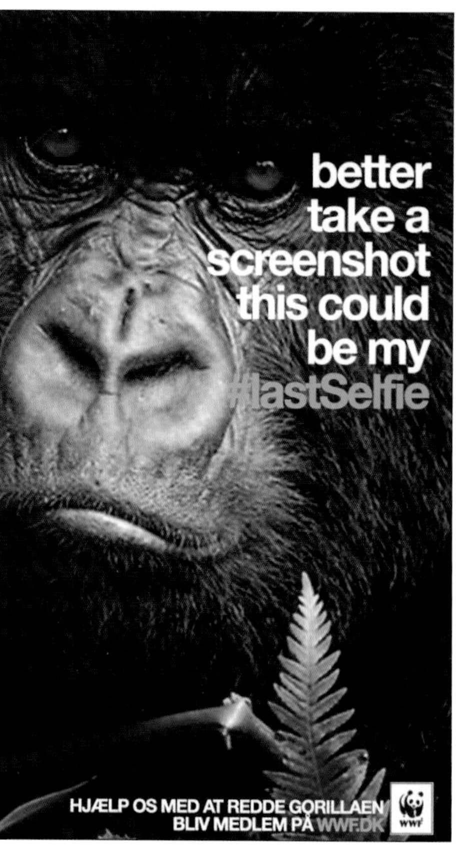

Agency	Rhinofly, Utrecht
CDs	Hugo van de Hoef Bas Gezelle
Copywriter	Bas Gezelle
Photographer	Khalid el Khouani
Film Director	Khalid el Khouani
Agency Producers	Nienke van Heusden Gerben van Heijningen
Animation	Roland Lamers
Digital Artwork	Roland Lamers Nicky Correljé
Advertiser	Centraal Museum, "Braintrip"

For an exhibition of surrealist art at the Centraal Museum in Utrecht, visitors were asked to let go of reality. The "Braintrip" installation used brainwave readers to measure viewer's reactions to surreal scenes on the screen. The device could tell whether they were focused or relaxed. If they managed to relax, they travelled further into the world of surrealism. But if they became agitated, the scenes stayed closer to reality. Afterwards, they could share a record of their brainwave activity during the experience on social media.

Agency	41? 29!, Istanbul
Creative Group Head	Ilyas Eralp
Creative Group Creative Directors	Alperen Altınoz Seren Koroglu Ahmet Terzioglu
Comm. Management	Jesper Hansen
Art Group Head	Elif Kavalci
Art Directors	Muharrem Huner Emir Anarat Ercan Nailoglu
Advertiser	WWF, "#LastSelfie"

On social network Snapchat, "selfie" photos can be seen for only ten seconds. The WWF (World Wide Fund for Nature) took advantage of this by posting pictures of endangered species – which disappeared before viewers' eyes. Each image asked for help: "In ten seconds I'll be gone forever. But you can still save my kind. #LastSelfie." Users could share, adopt an animal, or donate via SMS. The operation attracted 40,000 tweets in one week. Coverage in traditional media around the world also raised awareness.

They're more than Moving Day boxes. They're inspira
Take one. Use it to move. See how it looks in your new home.
MALM
STUVA
MICKE
MALM
STUVA
IKEA

It's not just a Moving Day Box, it's inspiration.
→ Use this box to help you move. Then use it to help you see what a stylish MALM chest with 2 drawers can bring to your new home. Once you find the perfect spot for it, come to IKEA for the real thing, and find all the other home furnishings you'll need to make the most of your new space.

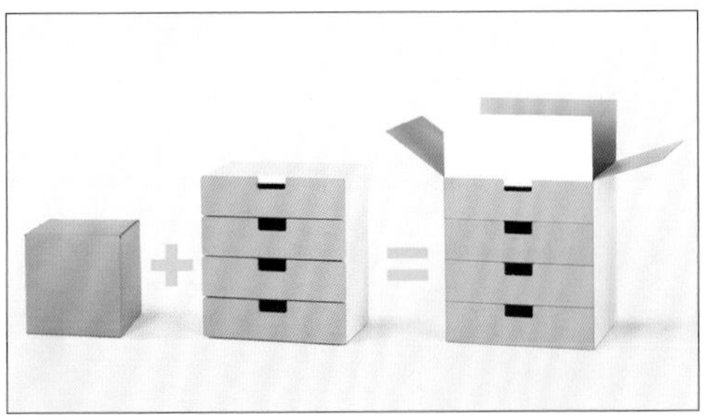

Agency	Leo Burnett, Toronto
CCO	Judy John
Group CDs	Morgan Kurchak Anthony Chelvanathan Steve Persico
CDs	Judy John Lisa Greenberg
Copywriter	Steve Persico
Art Director	Anthony Chelvanathan
Producer	Anne Peck
Advertiser	IKEA, "Inspiration Boxes"

Due to an obscure bylaw in Quebec, residents are only allowed to move house on July 1. As a result, Moving Day sees about 225,000 people shifting their belongings at the same time. IKEA has helped them out over the past couple of years by providing free moving boxes. This year, its boxes resembled IKEA storage units. So if the movers felt like buying one of the units, they could first see what it looked like in their new home.

Agency	Leo Burnett, Hong Kong
CDs	Connie Lo Brian Ma Alfred Wong May Chan Fanny Lau
Copywriter	Fanny Lau
Art Directors	May Chan Daniel Lo
Photographer	Ricky Wong
Advertiser	Crown Relocations, "Gift Box"

When you move house, you tend to throw a lot of your old stuff away. Much better to donate or recycle it – but what if you don't have time? Hong Kong moving service Crown Relocations made it easy. The lids of its moving boxes were printed with two different designs: "Keep" or "Gift", depending on how you seal the flaps. For the things you want to take to your new home, use the "Keep" lid. If you choose the "Gift" option, Crown will deliver the box to the Salvation Army for you.

PLAY THE ROAD
DRIVING MUSIC REINVENTED

Das Auto.

Agency Tribal Worldwide, London
CDs Simon Poett, Simon Richings
Copywriters Paul Robbins, Sam Turk
Art Directors Paul Robbins, Sam Turk
Production B/Reel, London; Framestore, London
Film Director Anders Hallberg
Producers Trine Pillay, B/Reel; Heather Kinal, Framestore
Agency Producer Lucy Westmore
Creative Technologists Matthew Oxley, Andy Best
Original Music Artist Underworld
Music Producer Rick Smith
Audio Specialist & Creative Producer Nick Ryan
Advertiser Volkswagen, "Play The Road - Reinventing Driving Music"

Driving the Volkswagen Golf GTI is a thrilling experience, and listening to music at the same time makes it even better. So what if the music could be tailored to your journey? Play The Road is an app that converts your driving data into music. Every turn of the wheel or burst of acceleration has an impact on the tune; a link with the GPS ensures that the mood of the music suits your surroundings. Technical wizardry, the musical talents of British electro band Underworld and your own driving style merge to provide a unique journey.

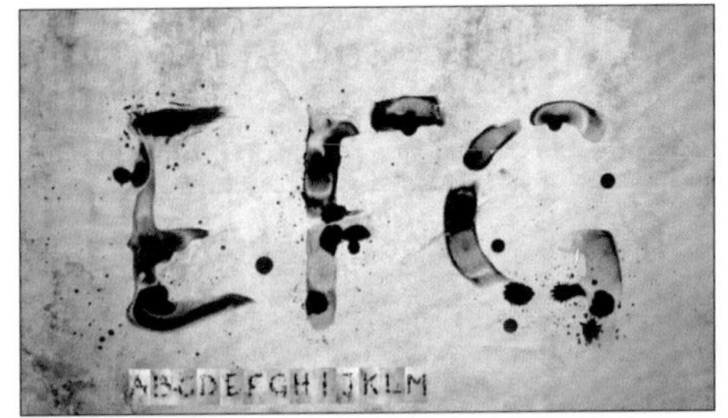

Agency	FCB, Zürich
Creative Director	Dennis Lück
Copywriter	Sören Schröder
Art Director	Marcin Baba
Production	WirzFraeffelPaal, Zürich
Typographer	Stefan Grandjean, Start
Programmer	Sebastian Palka, 3Elemente
Advertiser	MTV Mobile, "The Emography Project"

Everyone knows MTV – but MTV Mobile was less famous. To change that, MTV and FCB created a campaign for the mobile generation. A free messaging service was developed that enabled users to send texts using "emotive" typography. Each typeface reflects a basic emotion: a confetti font to capture surprise; tear-stained letters to depict sadness; romantic letters written with lipstick kisses – and even an angry typeface created with an extended middle finger! "Emography" brought the spirit of emojis to typography. And captured the irreverent energy of MTV Mobile.

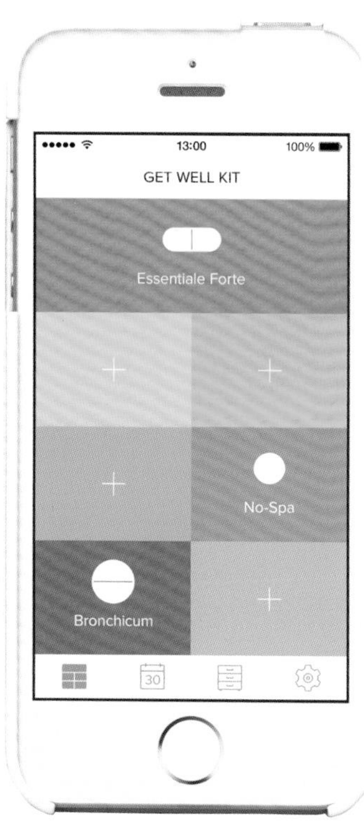

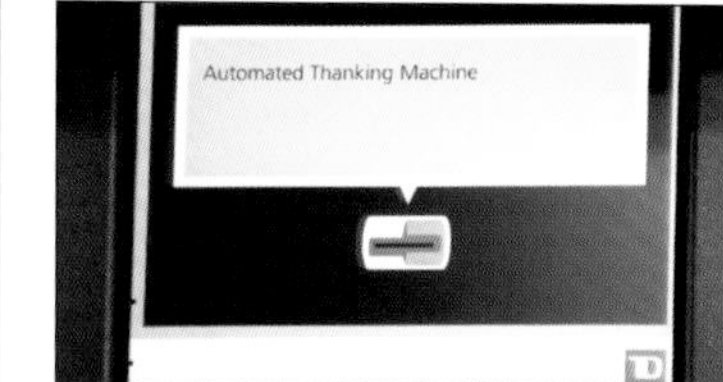

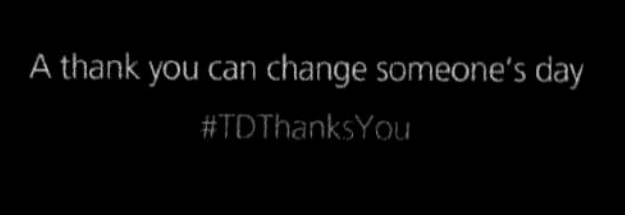

Agency Geometry Global, Moscow
Executive CD Andrew Ushakov
Copywriter Darya Ushakova
Art Director Elena Medvedeva
Digital AD Vitaliy Rynskiy
Product Designers Elena Medvedeva, Ilya Petrov
Advertiser Sanofi-Aventis, "Get Well Kit"

People who need to take a lot of medication often use pill organisers to keep everything in order. But that doesn't help them to remember to take the right pill at the right time. Sanofi teamed with Apple to create an iPhone "Get Well Kit". The colour-coded pill organiser is integrated into a case surrounding the phone. On the phone itself, a dedicated app can be programmed to remind users exactly when they need to take their meds. It even keeps track of their dosage and prescription in case they need to stock up.

Agency Diamond Integrated Marketing, Toronto
Creative Directors David Diamond, Josh Diamond, Mark Vandervoet, Judy John, David Federico
Copywriters Sara Vinton, Mike Johnson
Art Directors Darryl Graham, Jordan Gladman
Advertiser TD Bank, "#TDThanksYou"

Canadian bank TD wanted to thank its customers in a personal way. Having worked with staff to identify loyal customers with compelling backstories, the bank turned two ATMs into Automated Thanking Machines. Gifts were handpicked and delivered to the customers through the machines: for instance, tickets to Disneyland for one hard-working mom. These touching moments were filmed and turned into a heart-warming online film, created for YouTube and widely shared.

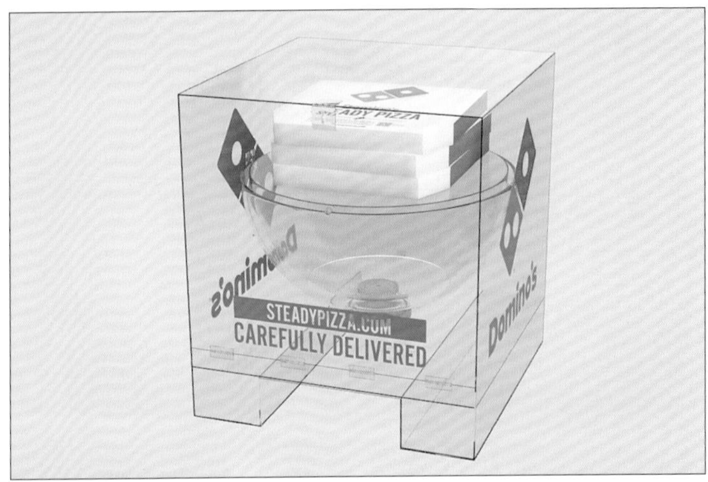

Agency Artplan, Rio de Janeiro
CCO Roberto Vilhena
Creative Directors Gustavo Tirre, Alessandra Sadock
Copywriters Henrique Louzada, Pedro Rosas
Art Director Augusto Correia
Advertiser Domino's, "Domino's Steady Pizza"

Domino's does its best to create great pizzas, but there's nothing more disappointing for customers than a delivery fail, when transport has made their pie look more like a sandwich. Advertising can't solve the problem, but technology can. The brand worked with experts to create this stable delivery system, which keeps pizzas flat even when mopeds are inclined. More than 10,000 stores worldwide will benefit from Steady Pizza – and so will the brand's image. Find out how it works on steadypizza.com.

Agency Rethink, Toronto/Vancouver
Creative Directors Aaron Starkman, Chris Staples, Ian Grais, Dre Labre
Copywriters Aaron Starkman, Mike Dubrick
Art Directors Joel Holtby, Vince Tassone
Advertiser Molson Canadian, "Passport Beer Fridge"

Molson Canadian wears its nationality on its label. To make Canadians even more proud of their brew, the Canadian Passport Beer Fridge was created. A big red fridge full of free beer – which you could only access with a Canadian passport. Simply slot the passport into the scanner, and take a trip to paradise. The beer fridge travelled the world and the experiences of its users were turned into a video that garnered millions of views online.

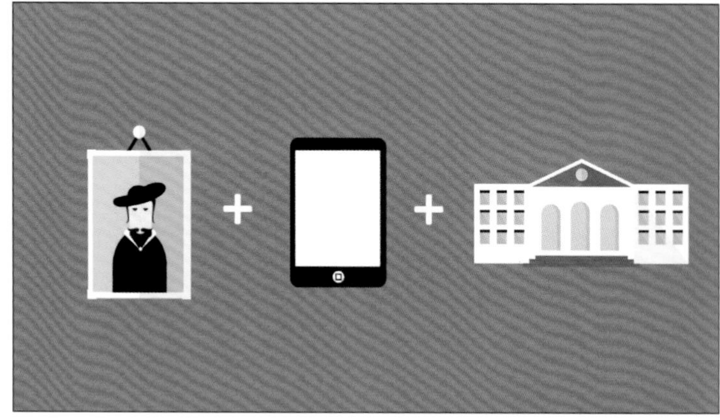

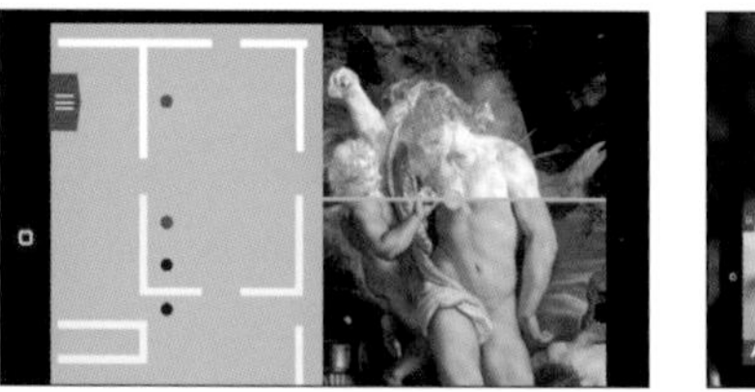

Agency Prophets, Antwerp
Concept Lucas Caessens, Micha Symoens, Samuel Joos
Digital Artwork Micha Symoens
Programmers Samuel Joos, Toon Severijns, Valentijn Steenhoudt
Advertiser The Rubens House, "The Rubens House App"

Visiting the house of the artist Rubens in Antwerp is like taking a trip back in time. But the house is also a centre of expertise, containing extensive archives. These were inaccessible to the general public – until now, thanks to a combination of iBeacon technology and a smartphone app. Approach an exhibit and the iBeacon wirelessly beams new layers of history and augmented reality to your phone. As a result, visitors enjoyed the museum more, stayed longer, and got a fuller grasp of the artist's story.

Agency KBS, New York
CDs Ed Brojerdi, Izzy DeBellis, Kevin Keehn, Cesar Rubin
Copywriter Chris Lane
Art Director Anna Yeager
Production The Armoury, New York
Film Director Kevin Osgood
DOP Matthew Pizzano
Advertiser Parlux Fragrances, "The Jay Z Gold Window"

Gold is the new fragrance from Jay Z, renowned rapper and business tycoon. How does it feel when, like Jay Z, everything you touch turns to gold? This interactive installation in Manhattan turned visitors' reflections into liquid gold, which followed their movements in real time.

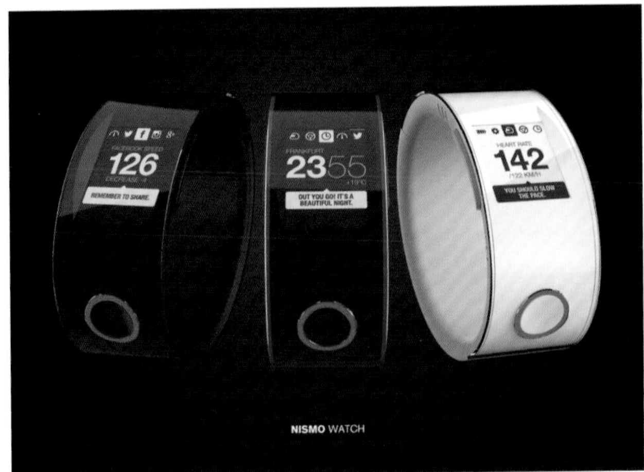

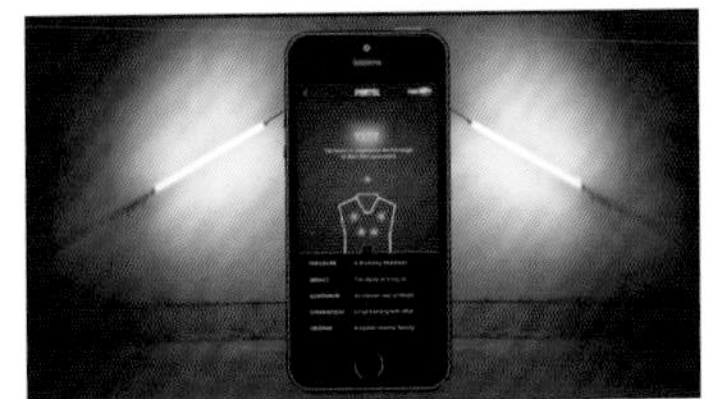

Agencies	TBWA\Helsinki, TBWA\G1, Paris
Creative Directors	Sami Thessman Rudi Anggono
Creative Technologist	Juhana Hokkanen
Designer	Daniel Julier
Strategy Director	Sami Viitamäki
Video Editor	Altti Sjögren
Project Director	Nana Paija
Advertiser	Nissan, "Nissan Nismo Watch"

Nissan wanted to raise awareness and engagement for its Nismo performance car, aimed at connoisseurs of automotive excellence and technology. The prototype Nismo Watch combines both. The wearable tech monitors both the performance of the car and your physical reactions. Track average speed and fuel efficiency, receive weather and road data, stay informed of social messages – and watch your pulse rate when you really put your foot down! The concept was unveiled at the Frankfurt Motor Show and the buzz soon went global.

Agency	CHE Proximity, Melbourne
Creative Director	Leon Wilson
Copywriter	Sam Harris
Art Director	Tom Wenborn
Production	Wearable Experiments, Sydney
Head of Digital Craft	Sam Maguinness
Digital Designer	Tom Lear
Technical Director	Diego Trigo
Head of TV	Di Nash
Advertiser	Foxtel, "Alert Shirt"

Foxtel needed to convince fans of Australian Rules Football – already widely broadcast on free channels – that its pay TV service brought them closer to the game. Hence the Alert Shirt, available to new subscribers. It uses haptic technology to replicate the feelings the players were experiencing on the pitch. Data on key moments in the game are live-streamed to a mobile phone app, which then activate sensors in the shirts. So when a player gets tackled on the screen, you feel the force.

THE
MEN
INSIDE
THE
SUITS.

with the Sape I don't get old

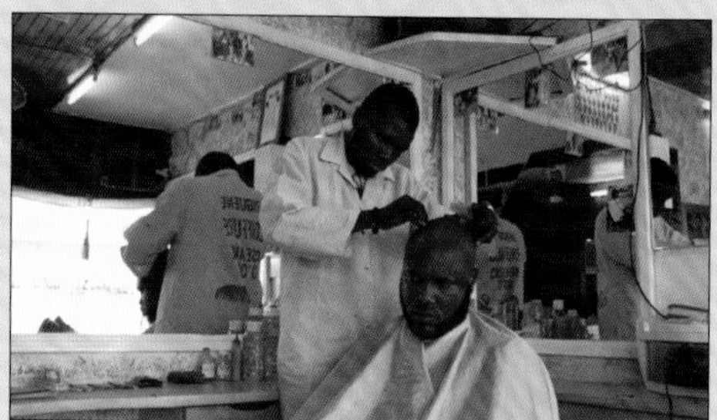

Enjoy GUINNESS Sensibly. Visit
drinkaware.co.uk

Agency AMV BBDO, London
ECD Paul Brazier
Creative Director Dave Buchanan
Creatives Nadja Lossgott, Nicholas Hulley
Agency Producer Yvonne Clayton
Production Stillking, London
Film Director Hector Mediavilla
Producer Rudi Rossouw
Post Production The Mill, London
Editor Russ Clapham
Sound Design Parv Thind, Dugal MacDiarmid, Wave, London
Advertiser Diageo, Guinness, "Sapeurs Documentary"

Guinness and AMVBBDO made an award-winning spot featuring the Sapeurs – the Society of Elegantly Dressed Persons of the Congo. This documentary takes us behind the scenes to meet the Sapeurs and hear their incredible stories. One explains that his father was a Sapeur before him; another shows us the spot where he was forced to bury his fine clothes during the civil war. The Sapeurs are against violence and advocate politeness. Above all, they never forget: "It's not the cost of the suit that counts, it's the worth of the man inside it."

Agency McCann Sydney
Executive CD Dejan Rasic
Copywriter Dejan Rasic
Art Director Dejan Rasic
Film Director Timothy Reckart
Production AMVI & Starburns Industries, Los Angeles
Executive Producer Blaize Saunders
Producer Trever Stewart
Production Manager Nathanael Horton
Paper Engineer Javan Ivey
Concept Designer Lily Pham
Fabricator Maeve Callahan
Visual Effects Supervisor Clint Fanny
DOP Aaron Wong
Assistant Camera Steve Crocker
Additional VFX Kalina Torino
Editor JD Dawson
Advertiser MTV Exit Foundation, "Broken Dreamers"

This beautiful yet chilling animation tells tragic stories that unfold from the pages of a book. We meet a young woman who is promised a job overseas and then forced into prostitution; a man who is tricked into semi-slavery on a construction site; and another woman whose au pair job turns into a form of imprisonment. This is human trafficking, when people are recruited and deceived. You can help put a stop to it by supporting MTV Exit, which campaigns against exploitation and trafficking.

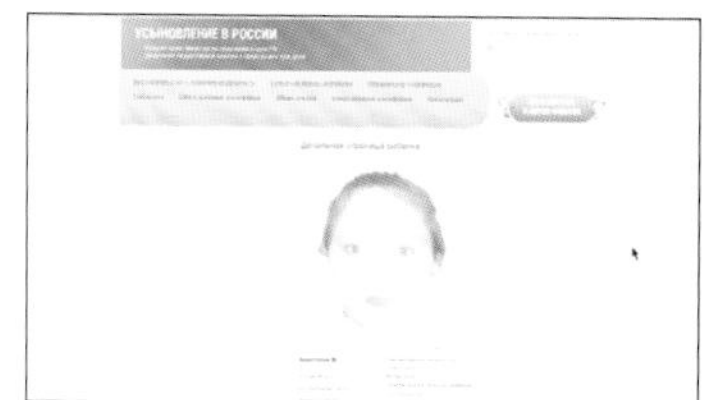

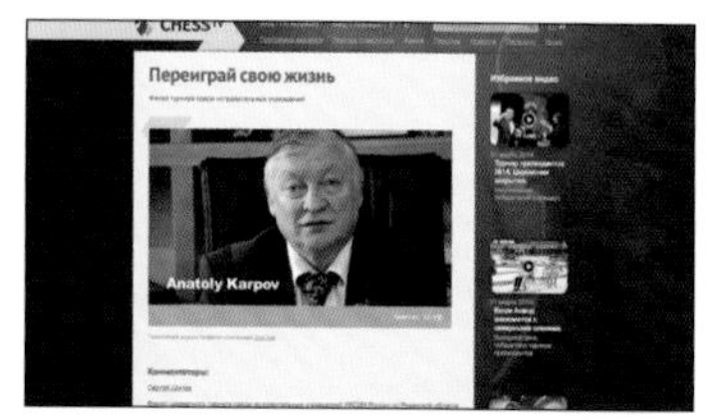

Agency Young & Rubicam FMS, Moscow
Creative Director Marco Cremona
Copywriter Ilya Lebedev
Art Director Federico Fanti
Agency Producer Inna Alperovich Chikhladze
Graphic Design Dmitriy Izotov, Tatiana Vasilieva
Advertiser Change One Life Foundation, "Movies That Change Lives"

There are 105,000 orphans in Russia, but potential parents can only see them on the state's online archive, where the children are represented with a bad picture and a one-line description. Young & Rubicam and the Change One Life Foundation asked ten top Russian movie directors to spend time in the orphanages and create short films featuring the kids. For the first time the children were portrayed as lively personalities. The films got everyone talking, the kids received requests for adoption, and the government promised to update the archive.

Agency TBWA\Moscow
Creative Director Maxim Kolyshev
Copywriter Julia Komolikova
Art Director Natalia Bystrova
Agency Producers Olga Kirillova, Gavriil Spirin
Advertiser Russian Chess Federation, "Jail Chess Cup"

The Russian Chess Federation wanted to raise interest in the game. The agency concluded that chess can teach people to think strategically in their own lives. Hence the Jail Chess Cup: those who had made a mistake in their lives were offered a chance to change their future – the winner would be eligible for early parole. The competition was backed by world chess champ Anatoly Karpov and dramatized by TV spots. Of 200 prisoners who took part, 16 made it to the finals. And at the time of writing, winner Leonid Karol was due to be released.

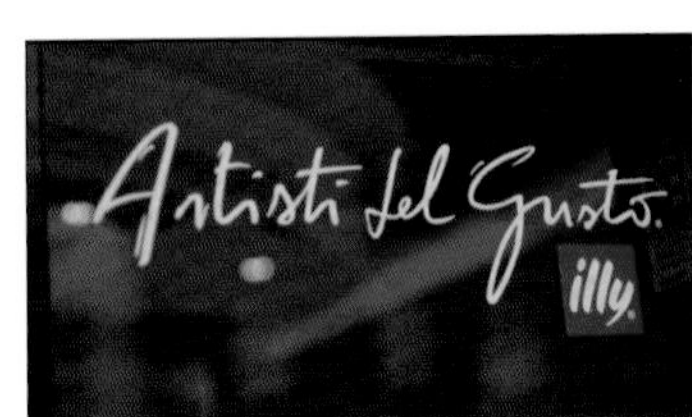

Agency	FOX Factory, Rome
Creative Director	Daniele Borgia
Production	Fluid Produzioni, Rome
Film Directors	Davide Barletti Lorenzo Conte Gabriele Gianni
Agency Producer	Vittoria Festa
Advertiser	Illy, "Artisti del Gusto"

Illy Coffee teamed up with the National Geographic Channel to make a ten-episode documentary reality show, 'Artisti Del Gusto' ('Artists of Taste'). Each ten-minute episode featured the real life of a barista, capturing the art of coffee-making and enhancing the brand's quality positioning. Artisti Del Gusto spoke "not to a target, but to an audience".

Agency	Thinkmodo, New York
Creative Directors	James Percelay, Michael Krivicka
Photographer	Matthew Cady
Production	Thinkmodo, New York
Film Directors	Michael Krivicka James Percelay
Agency Producer	Sam Pezzullo
Advertiser	Sony Pictures, "Telekinetic Coffee Shop Surprise"

Everyone loved this viral promoting the remake of the movie Carrie, which features a girl with telekinetic powers. The stunt involved creating "telekinetic" experiences inside a popular coffee shop and filming the reactions of bystanders. When a female customer is upset, her supernatural powers turn the café upside down and pin a customer halfway up the wall.

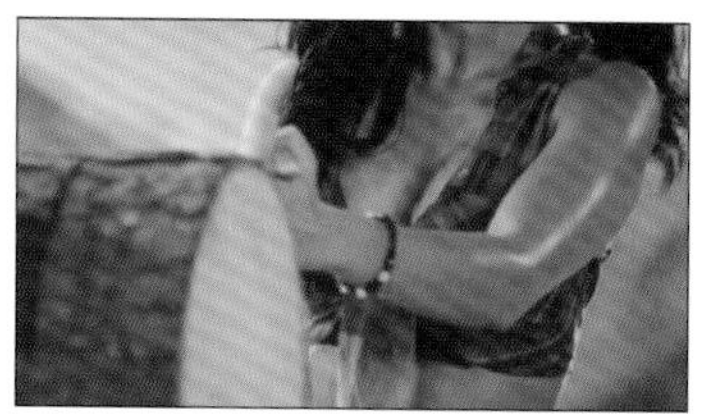

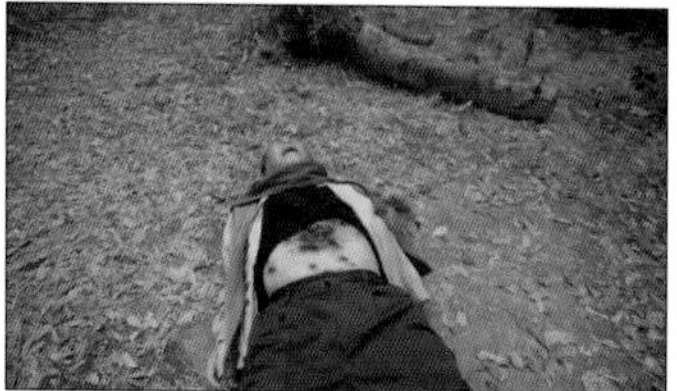

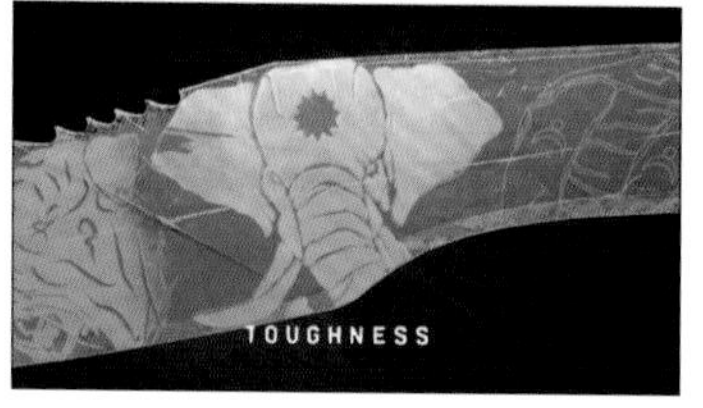

Agency	TBWA\Helsinki
Creative Director	Theodor Arhio
Production	Also Starring, Helsinki
Film Directors	Markus Virpiö Nalle Sjöblad Teemu Niukkanen
Producer	Johannes Lassila
Sitcom Prod. Co.	Fremantle, Finland
Broadcaster	MTV Media
Advertiser	Multiple, "Brändärit (Buy This!)"

Finland's Brändärit is a TV show about an advertising agency – but it's not Mad Men. In fact, TBWA\Helsinki teamed up with a host of its clients to tell the story of a fictional advertising agency that works for real brands. Not only that, but the ads created in the show are aired immediately after each episode. And because they were part of the story, the brands had the opportunity to create crazy campaigns that they would never have signed off in normal circumstances.

Agency	Grey, Paris
Creative Director	Thierry Astier
Copywriters	Dimitri Hekimian Mehdi Benkaci Vicken Adjennian
Art Directors	Quentin Deronzier Mehdi Benkaci Vicken Adjennian Vivien Urtiaga
Production	Stink, Paris Stinkdigital, Paris
Advertiser	Ubisoft, "What Are You Made Of ?"

To promote the fourth edition of first person shooter game Far Cry, a series of four interactive films allowed players to take part in "rites of passage". They include face-to-face combat and a blindfolded chase. The stories evolve depending on the player's decisions, with a total of 42 million variations. At the end of each "rite" an algorithm analyses the player's personality based on five criteria: toughness, violence, bravery, endurance and wisdom.

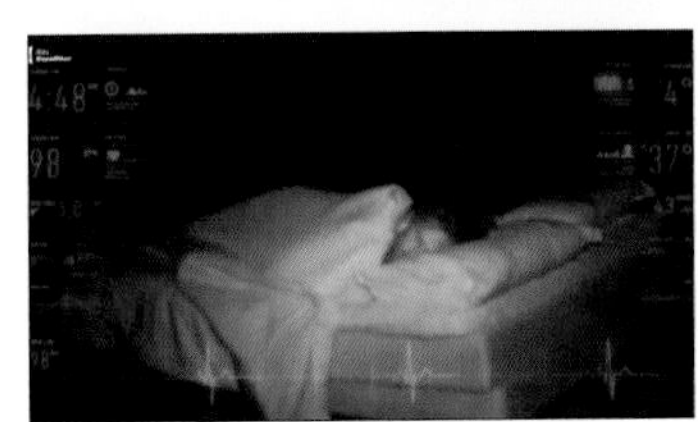

Agency	Wirz/BBDO, Zurich
Executive CD	Philipp Skrabal
Creative Directors	Rob Hartmann Andi Portmann
Copywriter	Marietta Mügge
Art Director	Paul Labun
Graphic Design	Benjamin Staudenmann
Image Editor	Rino Frei
Advertiser	Mobilar Insurance, "Believe It Or Not"

Young people aren't interested in insurance. However, they are interested in many of the things insurance is for: accidents, crashes and explosions. So insurer Mobilar and its agency created "Believe It Or Not", an online TV quiz show inspired by outrageous insurance claims. Participants and online viewers had to watch recreations of unexpected disasters or dangerous household experiments and vote on whether they were real or fake.

Agency	BETC/BETC Digital, Paris
Creative Directors	Stéphane Xiberras Antoine Choque Annick Teboul
Copywriters	Julien Deschamps Guillaume Rebbot
Art Directors	Jordan Lemarchand Sylvain Paradis
Production	Anonymous, Paris
Advertiser	Accor Hotels, Ibis, "The Ultimate Sleep"

When you're a hotel chain, there are many ways of convincing customers that your beds are super comfortable. Such as making an online documentary featuring a real-life adventurer who drags one of your beds up a mountain and sleeps in it while perched on the edge of a cliff. Interactive elements included 360° mountain views, helicopter shots and the ability to monitor the experiment live during the night. He slept like a baby, by the way.

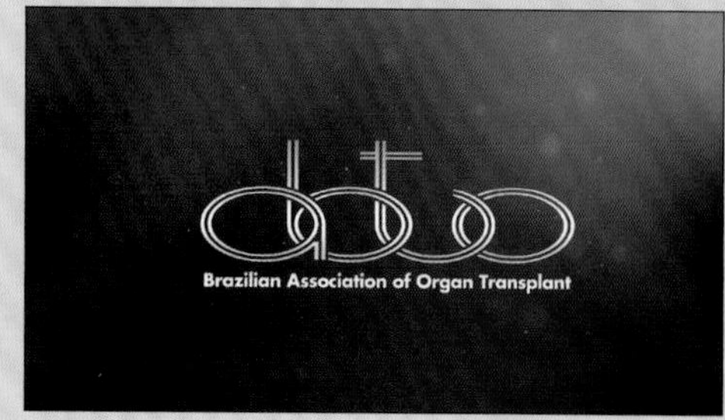

 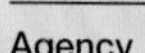

Agency	Leo Burnett Tailor Made, Sao Paulo
Creative Directors	Marcelo Reis Guilherme Jahara Rodrigo Jatene
Copywriter	Christian Fontana
Art Director	Marcelo Rizerio
Editors	Paulo Staliano Gregorio Szalontai Jack La Noyée Christian Balzano
Agency Producers	Celso Groba Rafael Messias Stella Violla
Advertiser	ABTO, "Bentley Burial"

In Brazil, people could hardly believe their ears when eccentric billionaire Count Chiquinho Scarpa announced he was planning to ritually bury his Bentley so it could be with him "in the afterlife". The media frenzy built as he invited the press to attend the event. But on the day, the Count halted the burial with an unexpected statement: people bury something far more valuable every day – their organs. The stunt for the Brazilian Association of Organ Transplantation generated millions of dollars' worth of earned media coverage. Organ donations rose 31.5% in a month.

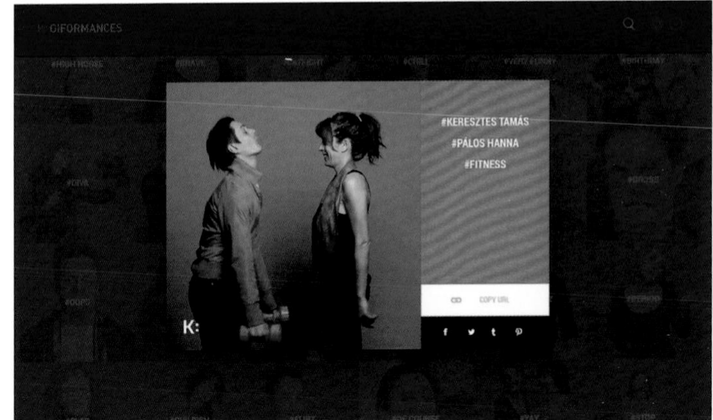

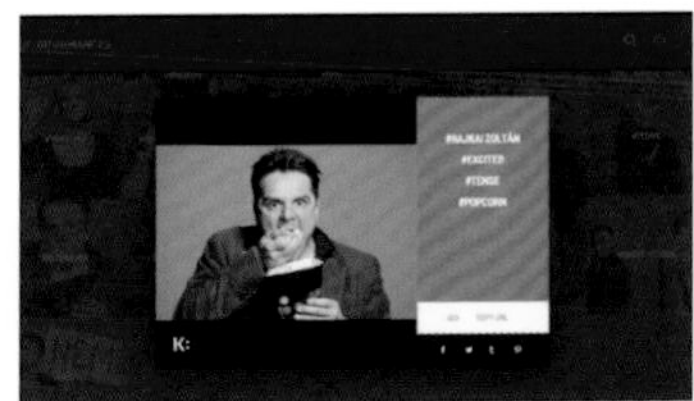

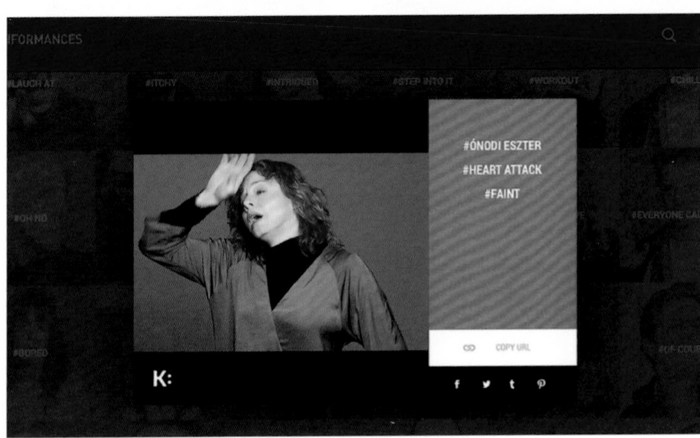

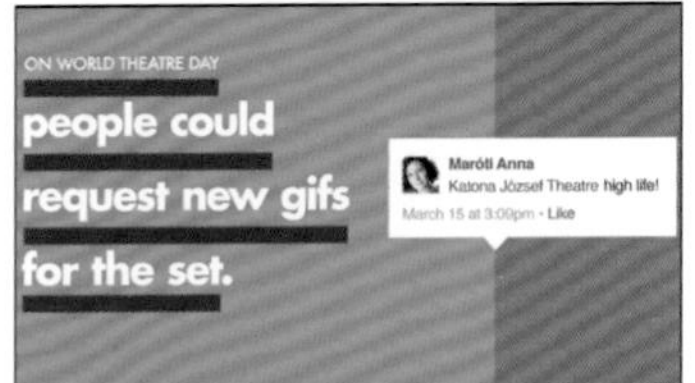

Agency: Leo Burnett, Milan
Creative Directors: Christopher Jones, Anna Meneguzzo, Cristiano Tonnarelli
Digital CD: Paolo Boccardi
Copywriter: Alice Jasmine Crippa
Art Directors: Gianluca Ignazzi, Alessia Casini
Production: Magnolia, Milan
Advertiser: Samsung, "The Maestros Academy"

Samsung wants to empower people through technology, but many younger consumers are losing interest in traditional crafts thanks to their immersion in the digital world. To reconnect these two cultures, Samsung and Leo Burnett created The Maestros Academy: a digital platform enabling young talents to learn the secrets of their chosen trade from legendary Italian craftsmen. Five artisans gave video tutorials and live interactive lessons. The masters and their apprentices were also featured in a 12-episode TV show on Discovery.

Agency: Y&R, Budapest
Creative Directors: László Falvay, Karolina Galácz
Copywriter: Karolina Galácz
Art Directors: László Polgár, Áron Hujber
Agency Producer: Péter László
Digital Producer: Dániel Somogyi
DOPs: Dávid Lukács, Tamás Kovács
Advertiser: Katona József Theatre, "Giformances"

The theatre and technology seem to be a long way apart. To reach a younger audience, Katona József Theatre created Giformances, an online catalogue of emotional gifs featuring the theatre's actors. Users could express their emotions by sending their friends dramatic scenes acted by the stage stars. And on International Theatre Day, people could suggest emotional gifs, which were immediately recorded by the actors and posted back via Facebook.

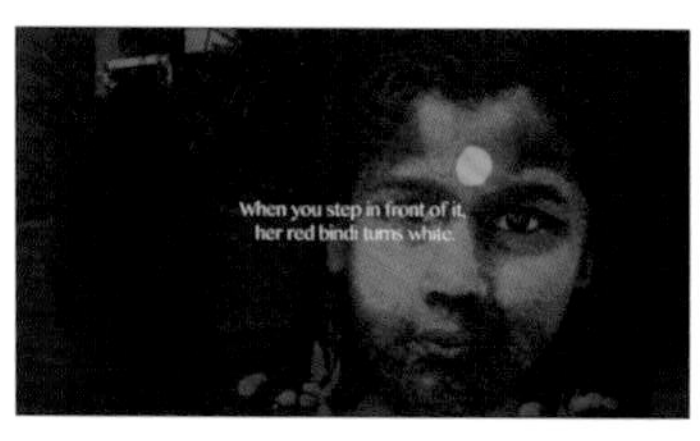

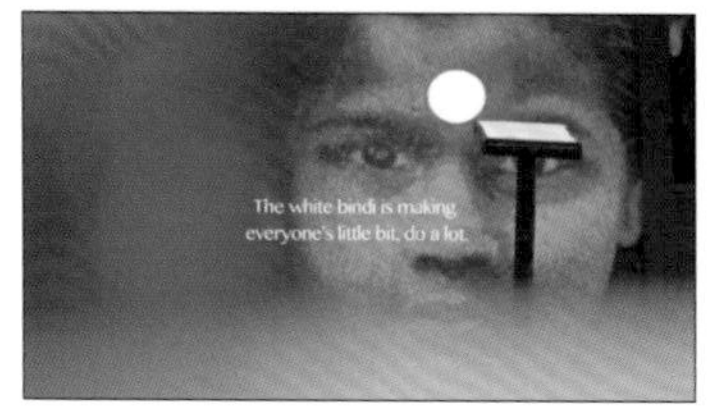

STILL SHARING
"WENT TOO FAST, GONE TOO SOON"

Agency Havas Worldwide, Gurgaon
CDs Satbir Singh, Ravi Raghavendra
Copywriter Nikhil Guha
Art Directors Prakhar Kant Jain, Sumit Sond
Illustrators Prakhar Kant Jain, Sumit Sond
Production UnCommonSense Films, Delhi
Advertiser Child Survival India, "No Child Brides"

In India, it's said that 39,000 girls become child brides every day. Married Indian women typically wear a red bindi (a dot on their forehead). This campaign turned the white bindi into a powerful protest against child marriage. To kick it off, a giant picture of a young girl made up of 39,000 white dots was taken on the road. The single red dot on the picture's forehead turns white when you approach. Bollywood actresses and models at Indian Fashion Week also supported the cause by wearing white bindis.

Agency 20Something, Brussels
Creative Director Benoît Vancauwenberghe
Art Director Jean-Pol Lejeune
Copywriters Quentin Watelet, Birgit Fonteyn
Production Zoom Production, Brussels
Advertiser Belgian Institute for Road Safety, "Went Too Fast. Gone Too Soon"

Driving over the speed limit can of course have fatal consequences. To underline this, speeders were invited to a unique event – their own funerals. The moving services were filmed and turned into a viral that attracted international media coverage. "Went Too Fast. Gone Too Soon" became Belgium's "most talked-about safe driving campaign ever".

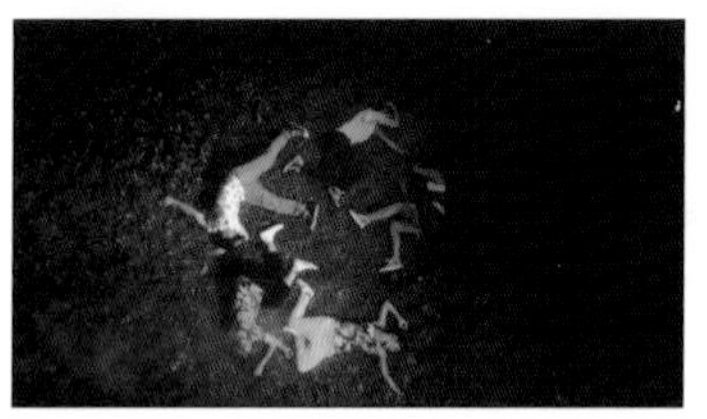

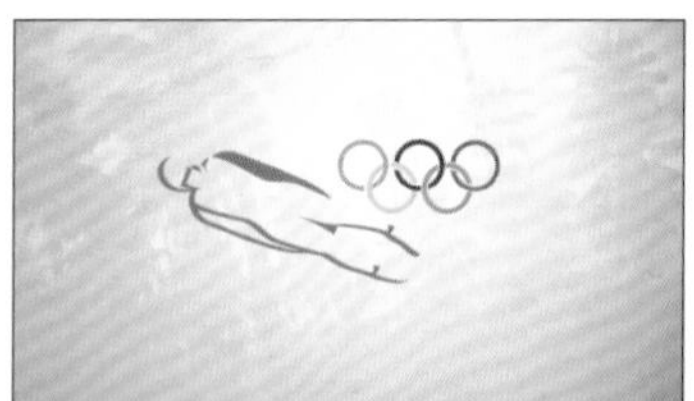

Agency Isobar, Warsaw
Creative Director Maciej Nowicki
Copywriter Konrad Słonecki
Art Director Patryk Kościelniak
Photographer Borysław Georgijew
Agency Producers Marta Kartasińska, Magdalena Długowolska, Katarzyna Kołtuniewicz, Krzysztof Szymczak
Advertiser Kujawski Cooking Oil, "Dance For Life"

Bees are dying as a result of pollution. Cooking oil brand Kujawski wanted to highlight their plight as it depends on the bees to pollinate its vast fields of oilseed. Since bees actually communicate by dancing, the solution became "Dance For Life", a contemporary dance based on the movement of bees. YouTube tutorials showed people how to do the dance, which caught on. When the buzz was at its height, an additional video showed the climax of the dance – the death of the bees.

Agency makai Europe, Leipzig
Creative Director Mathias Ihle
Agency Producers Mathias Ihle, Christian Belter
Photographers Josephine Heyde, Andreas Schmidt
Film Directors Jörg Junge, Susann Wentzlaff
Graphic Design Twosyde Media
Advertiser Bruno Banani, "Bruno Banani Goes Olympic"

How can you crash the Winter Olympics when you're not an official sponsor? And how can you attract the world's attention when you're the far-flung tropical archipelago of Tonga? This campaign achieved both aims. An athlete from Tonga with an unlikely talent for the luge agreed to change his name to Bruno Banani, a German underwear brand, in return for sponsorship. So luge racer Bruno Banani became Tonga's first and only participant at the Winter Olympics in Sochi. Now the world knows their names.

Promotions & Incentives

In fact, Danes have 46% more sex on city holidays

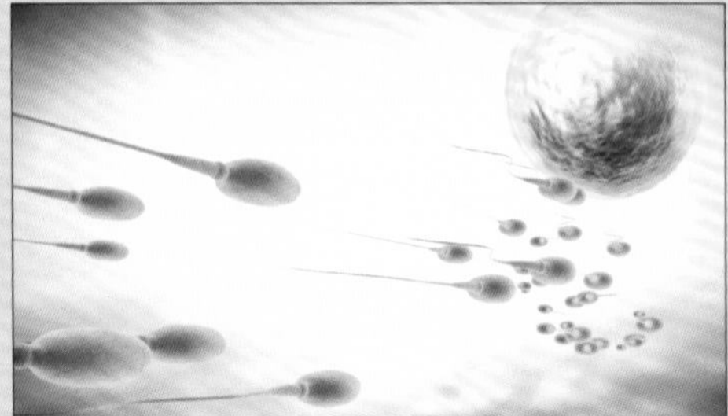

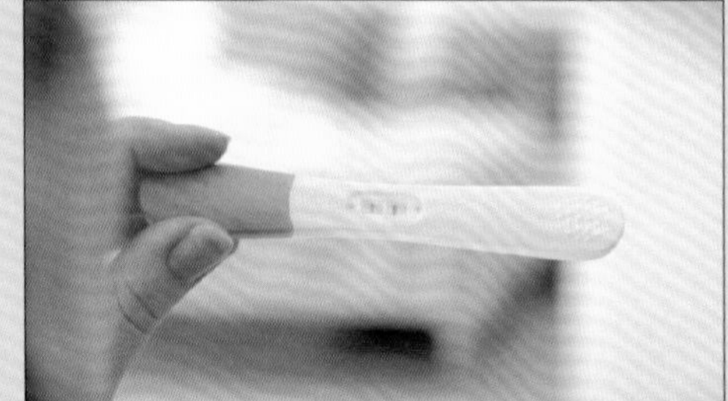

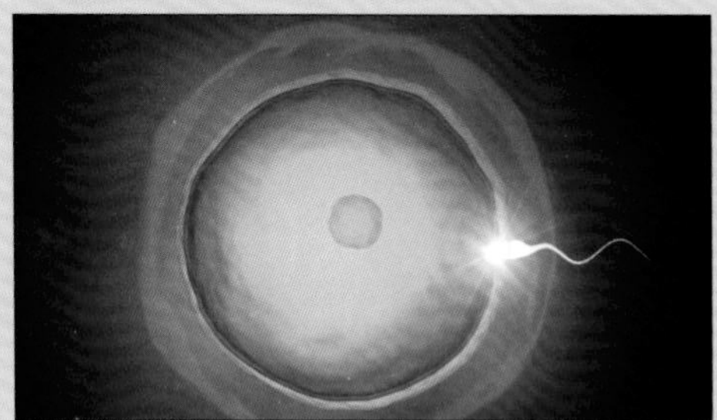

CAN SEX SAVE DENMARK'S FUTURE

Agency Robert Boisen & Like-minded, Copenhagen
Executive CD Michael Robert
Creative Director Heinrich Vejlgaard
Copywriter James Godfrey
Dir. Of Creative Technology Michael Bugaj
Designer Morten Grundsøe
Production Gobsmack Productions, Copenhagen
Film Director Niels Nørløv
DOP Niels Thastum
Editor Theis Schmidt
Line Producer Cille Silverwood-Cope
Executive Producer Christina Erritzøe
VFX Magnus Sveinn Jonsonn
Sound Jason Luke, P47 Sound
Music Upright Music
Seeding Be On, Copenhagen
Website Nao Studios, Stockholm
Advertiser Spies Travels, "Do It For Denmark"

Denmark's birth rate is falling, but research shows that Danes are more likely to make love while on vacation. 46% more, to be exact. Armed with this information, holiday Spies company offered couples "an ovulation discount". And if they could prove they conceived a child while on vacation, they won three years' worth of baby supplies and a child-friendly holiday. Needless to say, the media loved the story, which went global.

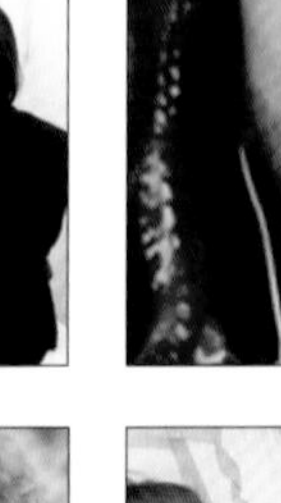

Agency Agency 222, Doha
Creative Directors Tim Styles, Fergus O'Hare
Copywriter Muhammad El Ayat
Arabic Copywriter Hossam El Gharably
Art Director Baher Raouf
Photographer Sadie Packer
Production Agency 222, Doha
Illustrators Allan Santiago, Nomer Tamayo, Narayanan Nair Manoj
Advertiser Novo Nordisk, "Fingers To Diabetes"

Qatar has a high rate of diabetes, but many people won't take the blood test because they have a fear of needles. This became the inspiration for "Give a finger to diabetes", launched to create awareness of a major screening event. Using Facebook, key influencers were invited to spread the word by changing their profile pictures to "finger portrait" caricatures. At the event, participants had their own funny finger portraits created by the professionals. The portraits continued to spread via social media.

Agency GPY&R, Brisbane
Chief Creative Officer Ben Coulson
Creative Group Head Jim McKeown
Creative Director Brendan Greaney
Art Director Joshua Bartlett
Production Michelle Short
Advertiser SP Brewery, "Mozzie Box"

In Papua New Guinea, blokes like nothing more than swigging SP Lager around the barbecue. Unfortunately, mosquitos tend to join the party – and they often carry malaria. The lager brand solved the problem by coating its cardboard boxes with eucalyptus, which mosquitos hate. So as the drinkers emptied the box, they could also burn it, sending out eucalyptus-infused smoke that kept the mozzies at bay.

IKEA
SHOWROOM AT
HOME
AN INTERACTIVE IKEA CATALOGUE EXPERIENCE

In Sweden every child knows what "Saturday candy" is.
Most families stick to the rule candy only on Saturdays or holidays.
But that is a rule for kids – being a grown-up has it's benefits!

Agency McCann Copenhagen
CCOs Linus Karlsson, Andreas Dahlqvist
Strategic CD Mark Fallows
Creatives Eva Wallmark, Rickard Beskow, Michal Sitkiewicz, Rasmus Keger, Morten Halvorsen
Art Director Jan Finnesand
Advertiser IKEA, "Showroom At Home"

This technological marvel allowed IKEA customers to isolate an item of furniture from its online catalogue and – using their mobile or tablet – project a 3D rendering of it into their own homes, so they could see if it would suit their space. The app impressed technology writers everywhere, and attracted one million downloads in its first week.

Agency King, Stockholm
Creative Director Frank Hollingworth
Copywriter Hedvig Hagwall Bruckner
Art Director Lotta Ågerup
Production Segerfeldt Film AB, Malmo
Producer Jenny Sernerholt, Colony, Stockholm
Web Director Thomas Larsson
Advertiser Malaco, "18 Years Age Limit On Candy"

In Sweden, there's a rule that kids are only allowed to eat sweets on Saturday or holidays. Candy brand Malaco decided to take this to its logical conclusion by imposing the ban on everyone aged under 18. TVCs showed adults sneaking a candy treat. And for a viral filmed in a store, a cashier refused to sell candy to children, because it was a Tuesday. Of course this had the desired effect of making everyone crave candy.

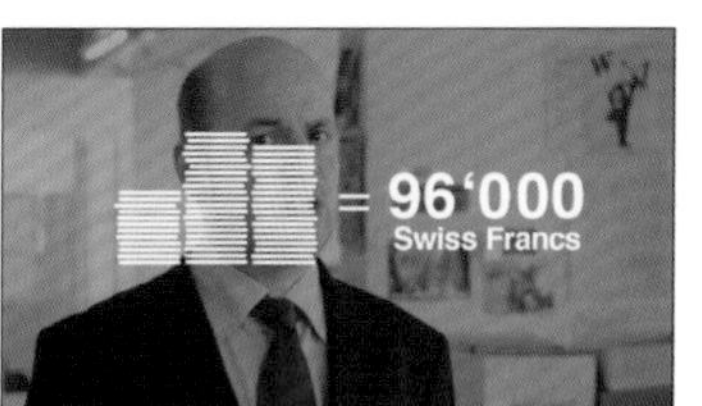

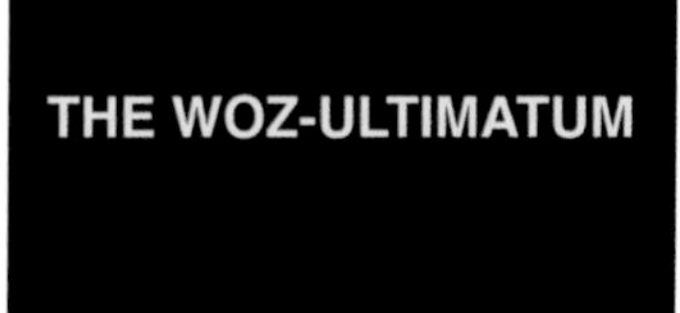

Agency	Welcom, Gothenburg
Creative Director	Jonas Sjövall
Copywriter	Niclas Hallgren
Art Director	Andreas Larsson
Advertiser	Bokon, "Kill Billy"

Bokon is Sweden's largest e-book store, and so it naturally competes with traditional bookstores. This bag and flyer were distributed during the Gothenburg Book Fair. It refers to Billy, the bestselling IKEA bookshelf. Which you won't need, of course, if you switch to e-books.

Agency	Leo Burnett, Zurich
Creative Directors	Peter Brönnimann Johannes Raggio Pablo Schencke
Copywriters	Johannes Raggio Fabian Windhager
Art Director	Barbara Hartmann
Advertiser	Woz, "The Ultimatum"

Left-leaning Swiss weekly WOZ decided to take a stand against the surveillance state. Its reporters gathered information about the life of Markus Seiler, chief of the Swiss secret service. Via a viral video, it announced that it would publish its findings in a special edition. But the video also told Seiler that he could "buy the entire edition of 16,000 copies before publication, if you wish to prevent the general public from finding out all about you". Seiler did not buy the entire print run. But it sold anyway, to the intrigued public.

Agency Dallas, Antwerp
CDs Stijn Gansemans, Paul Popelier
Creatives Stijn Gansemans, Paul Popelier, Joeri Van Den Broeck, Wesley Kuystermans, Yannick Schoch
Film Director Michael Bombeeck
Film Producers Annemie Decorte, Tuyen Pham Xuan
Advertiser JOE FM, "99 Luftballons"

To celebrate its fifth birthday, Belgian radio station JOE FM asked listeners to nominate the "greatest hit" they'd like to experience for real. Out of hundreds of suggestions, one song was randomly selected: "99 Luftballons", by Nena. A TVC and print ad gave listeners a chance to fly in one of the balloons. But could JOE really do it? Yes they could – on the station's birthday, 99 balloons soared into the sky. And the station's slogan, "Your Greatest Hits", was brought to life.

Agency Heimat, Berlin
CCO Guido Heffels
CDs Guido Heffels, Ramin Schmiedekampf, Frank Hose
Copywriter Mirjam Kundt
Art Director Susanna Fill
Production Czar, Berlin
Film Director Lionel Goldstein
Producers Jan Fincke, Boerge Heesemann
Advertiser Hornbach, "Act Against Ugliness"

Spring is a popular period for home improvements, but it has a fallout – ugly DIY-related garbage waiting for collection on the streets, from planks to paint cans. German home improvements brand Hornbach decided to act. It distributed a total of 1.5 million "Act Against Ugliness" garbage bags via newspaper inserts, direct mail and its own stores. The bags became a solution, a message and a weapon in the war against littering.

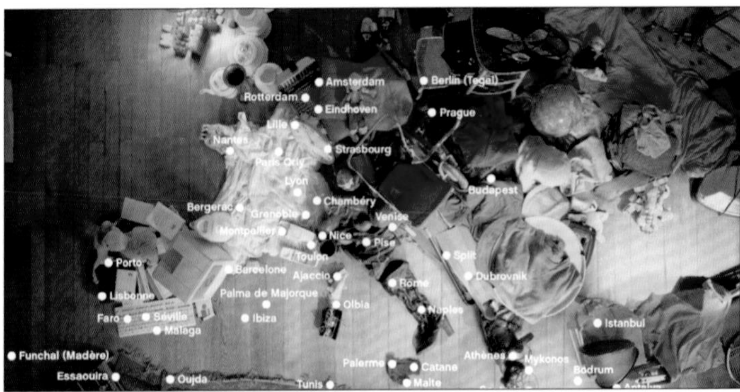

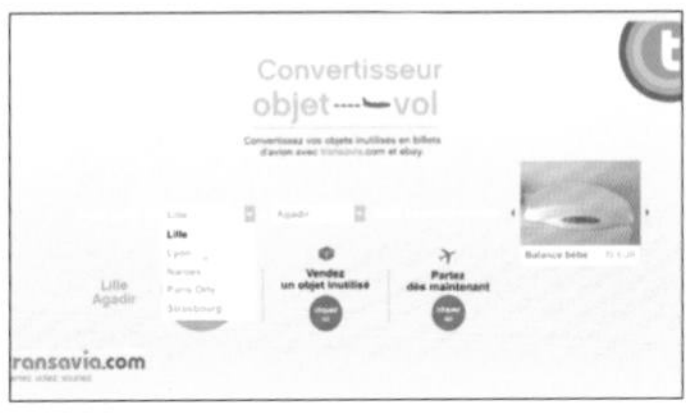

This is a beach in Marrakech.

transavia.com
Travel with the first object-flight converter.

SURPRISING CONTENT SHALL
MOTIVATE THE SWISS TO TELL
THEIR PERSONAL STORY

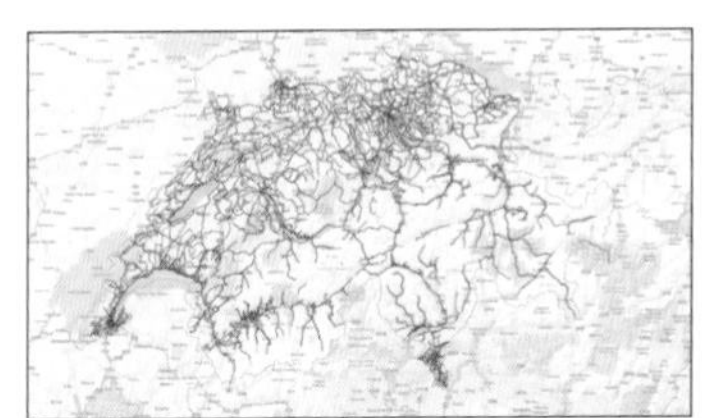

Agency	Les Gaulois, Paris
CDs	Gilbert Scher Marco Venturelli Luca Cinquepalmi
Copywriter	Ouriel Ferencz
Art Director	Marie Donnedieu
Copywriter Web	Julia Ben Rabah
Art Director Web	Sabrina Bourzat
Head of Digital	Olivier Tewfik
Art Buyer	Milène Araujo
Advertiser	Transavia, "Transavia Ebay"

When you have something you no longer need, you can always sell it on eBay. But airline Transavia teamed up with the site to create something different: BYE-BYE, the first object-to-flight converter. Place an object on the site, and when it's sold, the amount on your PayPal account can be converted directly into a flight ticket, without the need for a credit card. So even during an economic crisis, people still found the means to take a break.

Agency	JWT/FABRIKANT, Zurich
Creative Director	Michele Salati
Copywriters	Heinz Helle Urs Zwyssig
Art Directors	Noèlie Martin Cagdas Cakmaktas
Digital Director	Sabrina Schoenfelder
DTP	David Guntern
Digital Manager	Pascal Kuptz
Graphic Design	Vanessa Benvenuto
Advertiser	Mazda, "Voilà ma Suisse"

Mazda in Switzerland wanted to show off its cars while also creating an alternative portrait of the country. So it equipped ten cars with street view cameras and invited people to sign up to drive them. As they drove, the volunteers contributing to a new interactive map of Switzerland told their stories to a second camera inside the car. These became branded content on YouTube. Media coverage on TV, in print and by bloggers supported the project, which became a Swiss phenomenon.

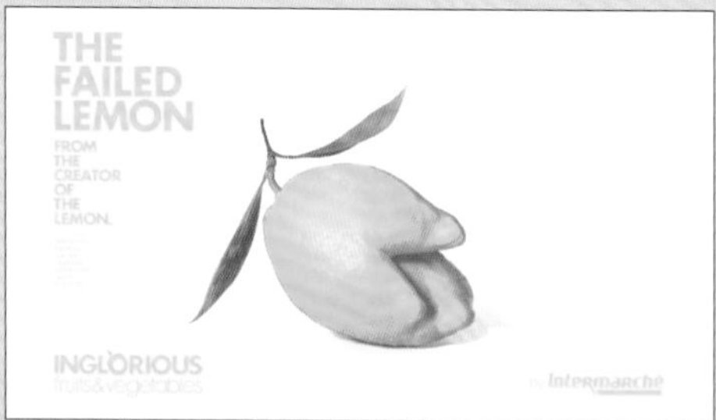

Intermarché

Agency Marcel, Paris
CCO Publicis Worldwide Erik Vervroegen
CCO Anne de Maupeou
Executive CD Dimitri Guerassimov
Creative Director Julien Benmoussa
Copywriters Julien Benmoussa, Gaëtan du Peloux, Youri Guerassimov
Art Directors Youri Guerassimov, Gaëtan du Peloux, Anaïs Boileau, Leoda Esteve
Production Prodigious, Paris; Indaprod, Paris
Producer Justine Beaussart
Photographer Patrice de Villiers
Directors Cédric Dubourg, Fabien Dubois
Advertiser Intermarché, "Inglorious Fruits and Vegetables"

Ridiculous though it may seem, supermarkets often throw away fruit and vegetables simply because they are "non-calibrated and imperfect". French supermarket Intermarché decided to combat food waste by turning the oddities into heroes: "The Inglorious Fruits & Vegetables". The weird-looking but perfectly edible items were sold 30% cheaper and promoted via an advertising campaign. In the end customers couldn't get enough of the malformed foodstuffs: 1.2 tons were sold per store in two days.

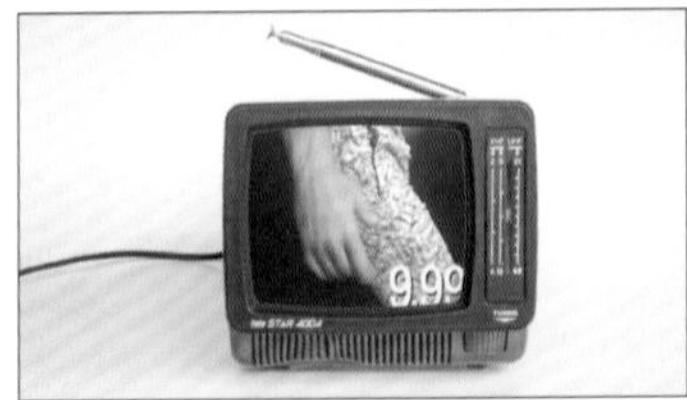

B&L

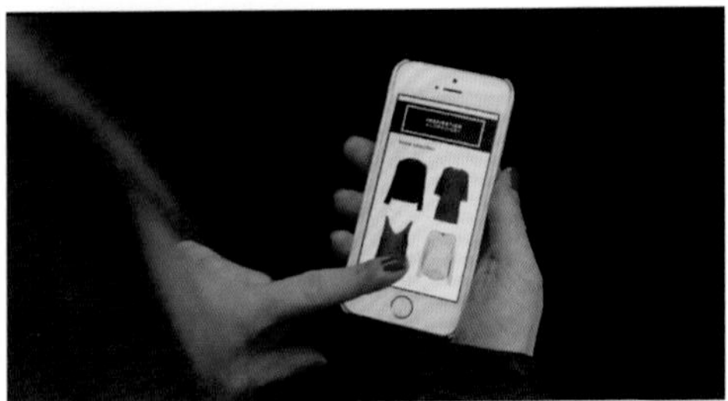

Agency	Edelman, Sydney
Creative Director	Jamal Hamidi
Creative Partner	Banjo Advertising, Sidney
Creative Director	Georgia Arnott,
Copywriter	Lewis Farrar,
Art Director	Casey Schweikert,
Director	Matt Weston, Syndicate Films
Advertiser	Best&Less, "The LAB Experiment"

Most Australian fashionistas wouldn't be seen dead at the Best&Less low cost store, because they think high fashion means high prices. To show them the error of their ways, Best&Less clothes were placed in a pop-up luxury store called LAB, in the heart of Sydney's fashion district. The items were disguised with expensive labels. But when shoppers got to the checkout, the prices were slashed and the truth was revealed. Their reactions were filmed for an online video. The event made national news.

Agency	DigitasLBi, Paris
Creative Director	Patrick Dacquin
Creative Technologist	Julien Terraz
Director	Diego Verastegui
Motion Designer	Jeremy Vissio
Designer	Nolwenn de la Pintière
Advertiser	Klepierre, "Inspiration Corridor"

Klepierre malls updated the personal shopper with a physical digital experience called "The Inspiration Corridor". On entering the corridor, a full body scan registers the shopper's dimensions and gender, as well as the colour of their clothes. Using this profile, it suggests suitable clothing and accessories from across the mall. Shoppers can also scan recently purchased items for suggestions on how to complete their outfit. Touch an item to add it to a shopping list on your phone, which then guides you to the right place in the mall.

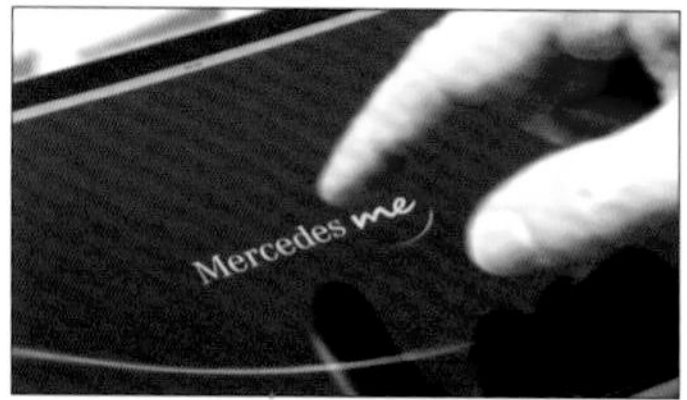

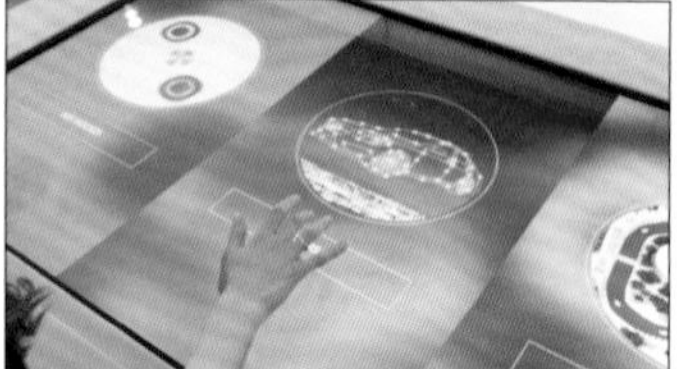

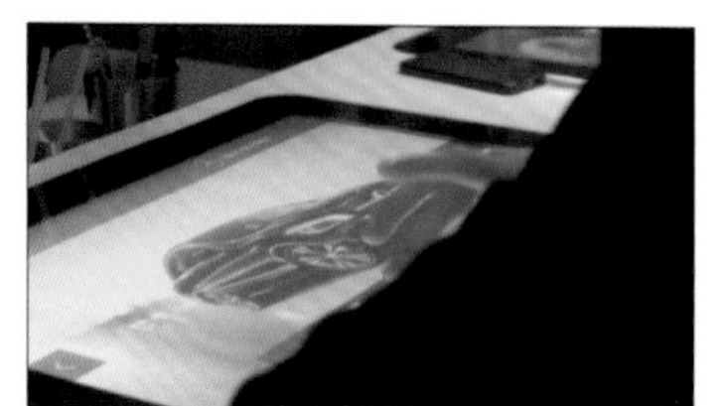

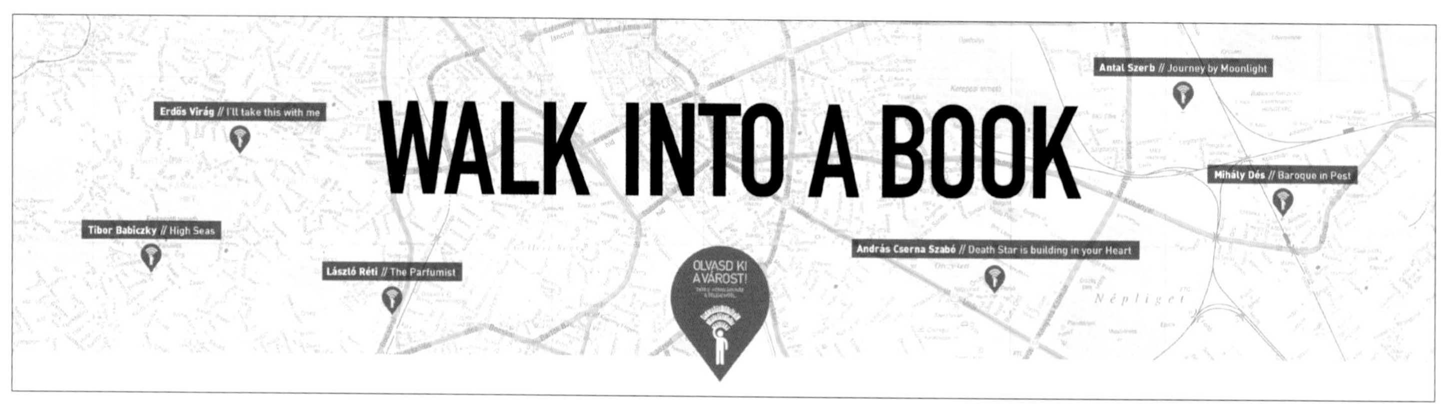

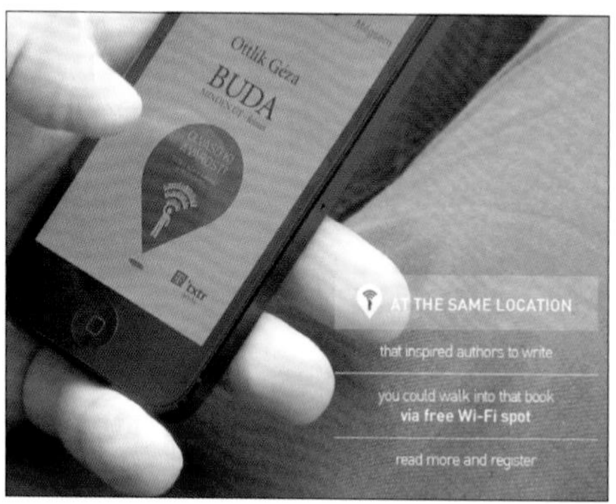

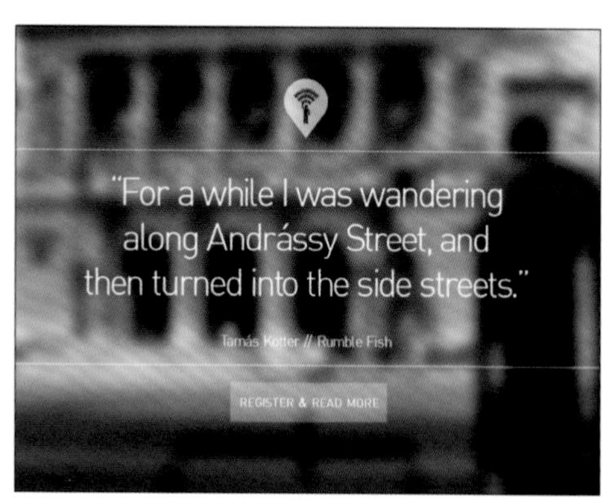

Agencies Ark Connect, Moscow; Leto Agency, Moscow
Creative Group Head Ilya Provkin
Digital Production Vitaly Shirokov
Art Director Dmitiry Konakhovsky
Advertiser Mercedes, "Mercedes me Cafe Moscow"

The Mercedes me café in the heart of Moscow connects the auto brand to individuals. Interactive terminals allow guests to make orders, play games, catch up with Mercedes news and access their social networks. A live feed on the café's giant interactive screen shows user-generated content. Best of all, the E-Motion device can analyse the profile of guests based on their facial expressions and suggest the ideal Mercedes for them – at which point they can book a test drive.

Agency Isobar, Budapest
Creative Director Marton Jedlicska
Copywriters Orsolya Nagymáté, Balázs Vizi
Art Director Dóra Suhai
Programmers Gergő Kiss, Tamás Uhrin, István Lovas, Krisztián Nagy
Editors Róbert Tóth, Gyula Tóth
Advertiser HungarianTelekom, "Walk into a book"

Telekom asked Isobar Budapest to help it collect more members for its e-book service. The agency thought places that had inspired great authors might also inspire readers; so spots around Budapest became virtual books. A real quote from a book caught the attention of strollers and encouraged them to download the full chapter on their phone via Wi-Fi. Then they could read the literary event in the very spot where it took place.

Agency	SapientNitro / Second Story, New York	
Worldwide CCO	Gaston Legorburu	
Creative Director	Perry Chan	
Copywriter	Susan Phuvasitkul	
Art Director	Radu Becas	
Strategy	Daniela Lobo Billie Edington	
Technical Director	Thomas Wester, 2S	
Experience Designer	Mustafa Bagdatli	
Senior Interactive Developer	Matthew Fargo, 2S	
Producer	Alyssa Glass	
Developers	Matthew Fargo Donald Richardson	
Advertiser	Hermes, "A Man's World"	

French luxury brand Hermès asked the agency to customise two events with interactive experiences that would live in guests' memories long afterwards. In Miami, for the launch of the menswear collection, there were RFID-enabled interactive mirrors, including fog mirrors that could be doodled on. At a store opening in Beverly Hills, attendees received RFID tokens that unlocked content throughout the evening. Highlights included Hollywood-style musical numbers seen through peepholes and the chance to drive a vintage Mercedes against a movie-style backdrop.

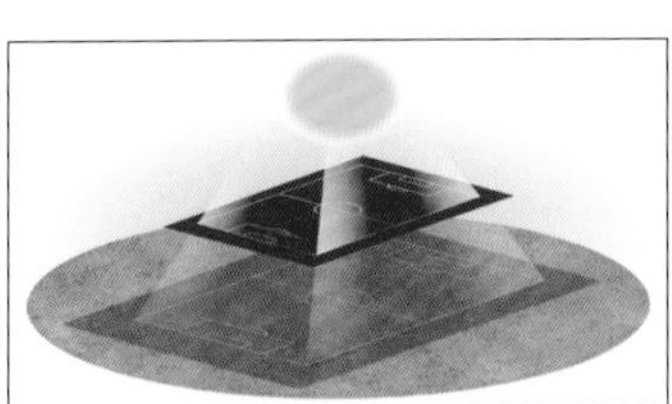

Agency	Volontaire, Stockholm
Production	Meshugene Brothers, Stockholm
Event agency	Ryska Posten Event, Stockholm
Construction	Kosmonaut Event, Falkenberg
Advertiser	Swedish Cancer Association, "Play In The Shade"

When summer comes to Sweden, people understandably want to play in the sunshine. But this can lead to melanoma, as the Swedish Cancer Association wanted to point out. The solution was an installation that used sun and shade to create the markings on a soccer pitch. Participants could stay outdoors while playing safely in the shade. The installation sparked comment across social and traditional media.

Agency	INGO, Stockholm
Creative Director	Björn Ståhl
Copywriter	Josefine Richards
Art Director	Rikard Holst
Production	Acne, Stockholm
Film Director	Markus Svanberg
Agency Producer	Markus Ahlm
Designer	Kerstin Engberg
Graphic Design	Andreas Mandahus
Digital Producer	Daniel Rytz
Digital Artwork	Fredrik Lundberg
Advertiser	Lidl, "Dill - The restaurant"

Lidl is a discount food store, but people have a hard time believing that low prices and high quality can go together. So a pop-up restaurant called Dill opened its doors for three weeks in Stockholm, with top chef Michael Wignall in the kitchen. Unbeknown to customers, all his ingredients came from Lidl. The restaurant was booked solid and the truth was only revealed five days before closing. Media coverage exploded and Dill provoked a debate about food quality and low prices.

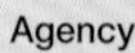

Agency Forsman & Bodenfors, Gothenburg
Copywriter Marcus Hägglöf
Art Directors Agnes Stenberg-Schentz, Johanna Hofman-Bang
Agency Producer Magnus Kennhed
Graphic Design Nina Andersson
Production Acne, Stockholm
Film Directors Torbjörn Martin, Tomas Skoging
Producers Petur Mogensen, Fredrik Skoglund
DOP Christian Haag
Post Production The Chimney Pot
Advertiser UNICEF Sweden, "The Good Guys Christmas"

We find ourselves at The House of Goodness, where Jesus, Mother Theresa and Ghandi are exchanging the stories of their lives. But how did an ordinary bloke from the suburbs of Stockholm end up in such illustrious company? He explains that after a life of dissolution everything changed when he saw a UNICEF banner ad. He just had to click on it to save children's lives. "It's almost too simple," he admits. But the other good guys approve.

In a sequel to the spot, the new guy shows Jesus how to click on the UNICEF banner. Unfortunately the saviour of mankind is not very internet-savvy and clicks the wrong one. "Not all banners save lives," explains our hero. And now Ghandi wants a go.

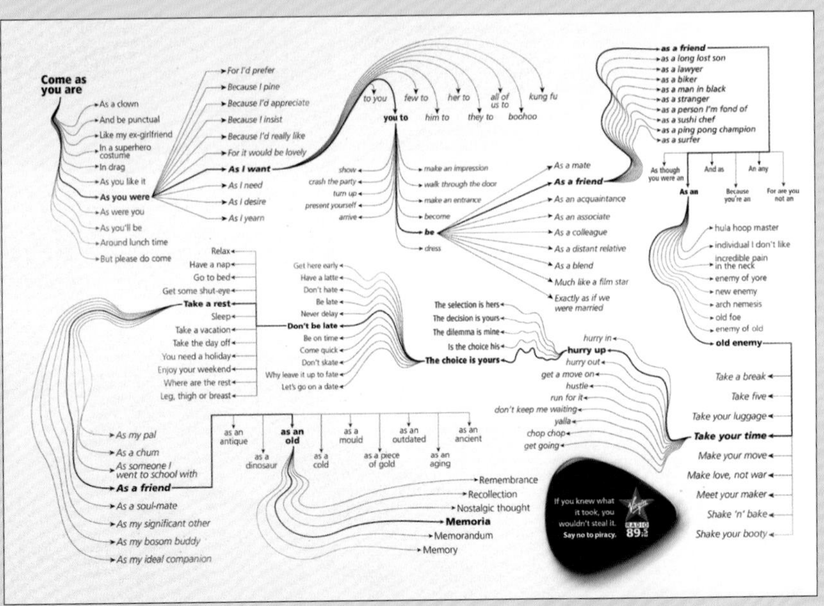

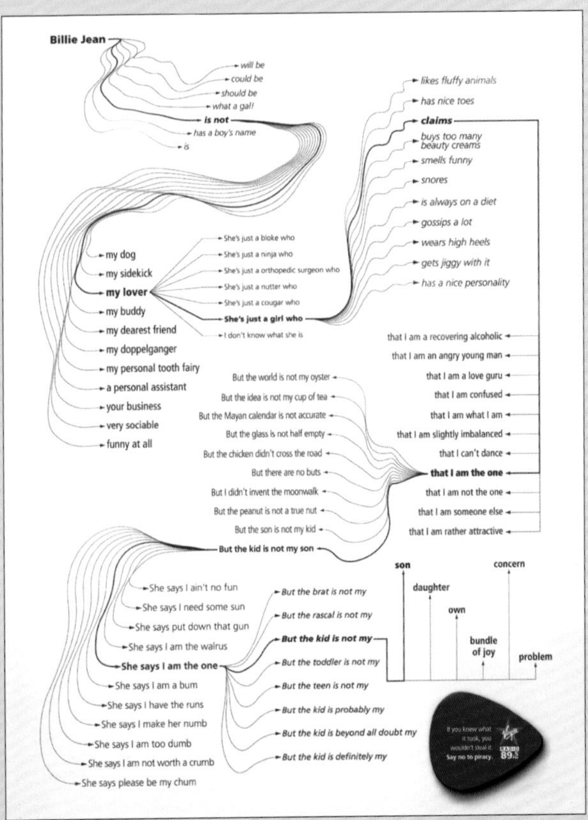

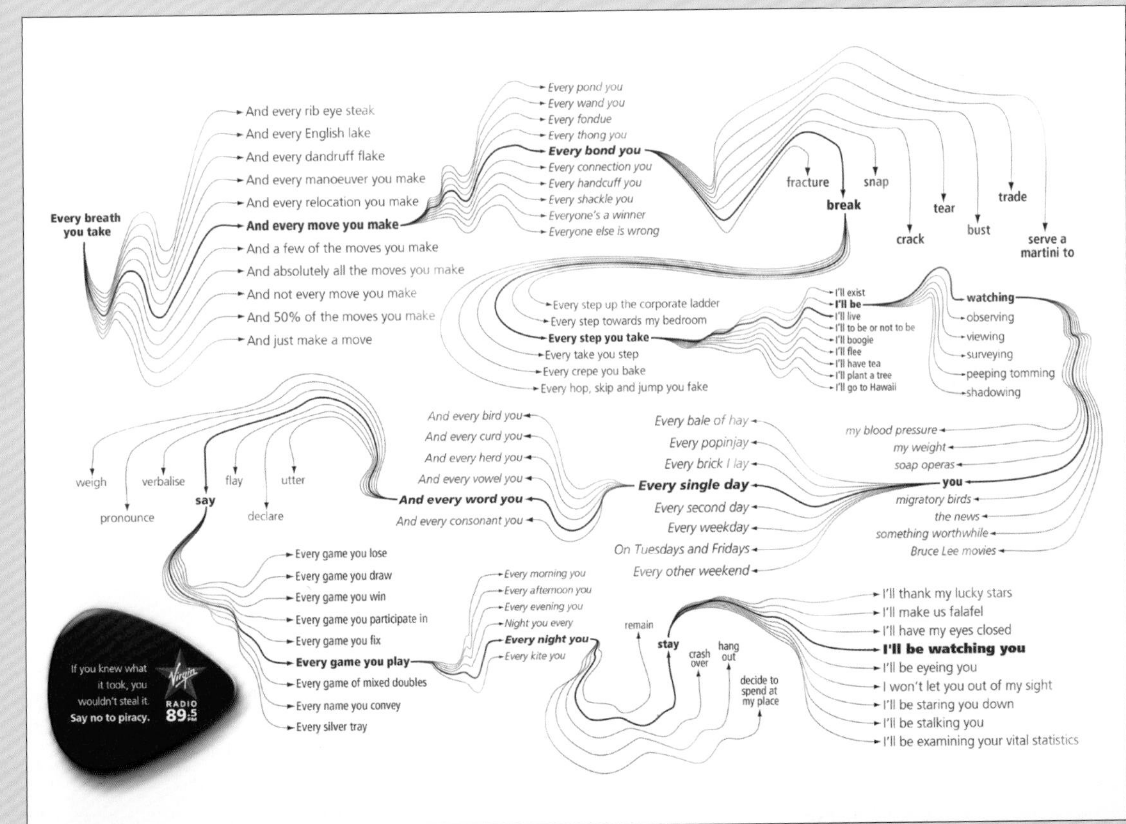

sponsored by MONT BLANC

Agency	Leo Burnett, Beirut
Creative Directors	Bechara Mouzannar Malek Ghorayeb Abraham Varughese
Copywriters	Zaid Alwan Abraham Varughese Edward Poh
Art Director	Edward Poh
Illustrator	Edward Poh
Advertiser	Virgin Radio, "Making Music"

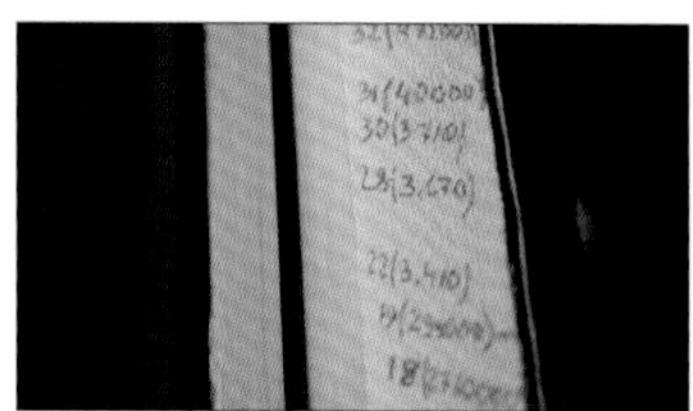

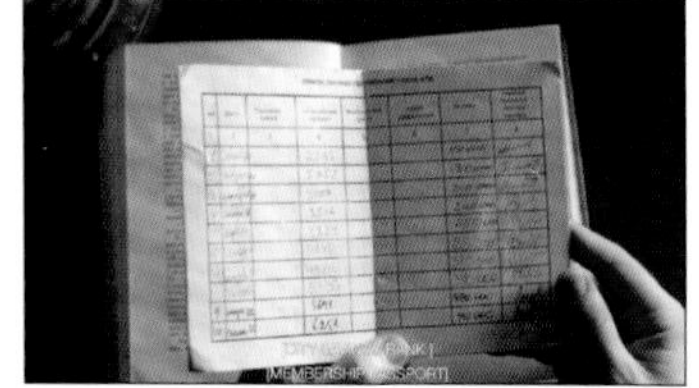

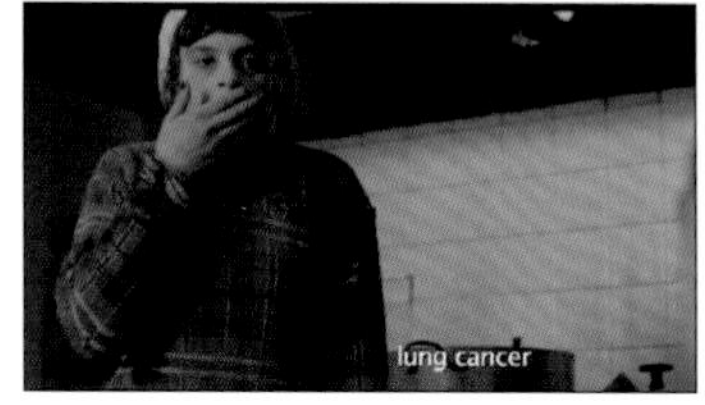

Agency	Irma Film, Moscow
Copywriter	Eugene Korchagin
Art Director	Eugene Korchagin
Photographer	Alexander Nosovsky
Production	Look Film, Moscow
Film Director	Eugene Korchagin
Producer	Anna Ryzhikova
Illustrator	Mikhail Loskutov
Advertiser	City Savings Bank, "The Notches"

A young guy explores his grandfather's apartment, soon after the older man has passed away. He recalls his grandfather's wisdom, imagination and love of books. His eye strays to the figures pencilled on the wall, where he was regularly measured as he grew up. Picking his grandfather's favourite book off the shelf, he discovers a savings book tucked into its pages. The figures correspond to the numbers on the wall. All those years, his grandfather was saving for his future.

Agency	Leo Burnett, Dubai
CCO	Bechara Mouzannar
Creative Directors	Abraham Varughese Hesham Ezzat
Copywriters	Maged Nassar Hesham Ezzat
Art Director	Hesham Ezzat
Production	Manasvi Gosalia Wadih Safieddine
Advertiser	Du Telecommunications, "Du Tuesday - The Two For One Tickets Campaign"

A depressing scene in a dreary kitchen, where a mother is dishing out slops for her crippled son. It turns out she's mute, so she signs: "This is the last soup we'll have this month." Then she accidentally drops it. She's horrified, but there's worse to come. The equally mute son signs: "But mom, I have lung cancer." Cut to an appalled viewer in a cinema. Some movies are too depressing to watch alone. But on Du Tuesdays, thanks to a special offer from UAE telecoms brand Du, you can bring a friend for free.

The future's bright.
At least that's what we imagine when we bag our first job
in this unpredictable industry. We join the professionals. We want to be the best
and so we work our socks off. Impossible is nothing we think to ourselves as we wade
enthusiastically into pitches, new business and anything else that promises reward and
recognition. That thrill, that sense of excitement and achievement, it's the real thing.
And when our bosses demand that it absolutely, positively has to be there overnight we
just do it because, as we know, every little helps us get on. So we're there at our desks early,
late, weekends, on call anytime, anyplace, anywhere, inching our way up the greasy pole.
And we try harder and harder, pushing ourselves to get that promotion, grab that award or
win that account in our relentless pursuit of perfection. Sure, we love it, hate it sometimes,
but we are driven people so we do more and climb higher. Besides, it goes a long, long way to
furthering our career and it's all good, isn't it? And though we may have a break occasionally,
though we may promise ourselves we'll cut down on our hours, though we think we might
one day take that sabbatical, deep, deep down we're convinced this job is like no other.
Hey, we're Madmen and we think different. Worry? Not us. Admit to stress? No way. And anyway,
What's the worst that could happen? The fact is, we don't really notice the damage
that can happen to our pot noodles and that sometimes the effect is shattering.
Which is precisely why we need to try something new today, something called
a NABS Resilience Programme. It's not a miracle treatment. It doesn't offer
an easy cure for anxiety. Instead, it does exactly what it says on the tin and
equips us with the tools to deal with this occasionally crazy business.
Because, after all the years we've spent foisting promises, slogans and
smart phrases onto others maybe, just maybe it's time we took
on board some wise words for our own well-being.
And haven't we always said
it's good to talk?

NABS
RESILIENCE
PROGRAMME
0845 602 4497
Charity reg No 1070556

BrandRepublic

Agency	SapientNitro, London
Worldwide CCO	Gaston Legorburu
Creative Director	Paul Hodgkinson
Copywriter	Paul Hodgkinson
Typographer	Adam Brewster
Advertiser	NABS, "Resilience Program"

This print ad for the National Advertising Benevolent Society uses famous slogans from advertising history to draw attention to a new programme designed to help those who work in the industry cope with anxiety and stress.

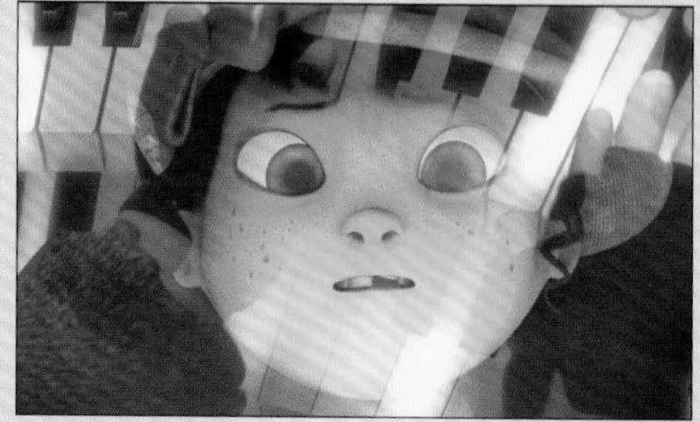

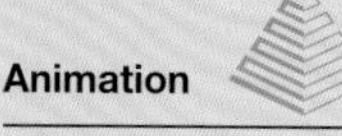

Agency CAA Marketing, Los Angeles
Production Moonbot Studios, Shreveport
Executive Producer William Joyce
Producers Trish Farnsworth-Smith, Lampton Enochs
Directors Brandon Oldenburg, Limbert Fabian
Editor Calvin O'Neal Jr.
Lead Animator Kevin Koch
Sound Designer Steve Boeddeker
Music Company Breed Music, Dallas
Composer John Hunter
Colorist John Daro
Advertiser Dolby, "Silent"

This beautifully animated tale takes us into a magical movie house. The owner of a primitive silent film projector plunges into the silver screen and becomes the star of famous scenes from the history of cinema, as his little girl provides the soundtrack. Finally he re-emerges to wild applause from the crowd. The film reminds us that Dolby has enhanced some of our greatest movie experiences.

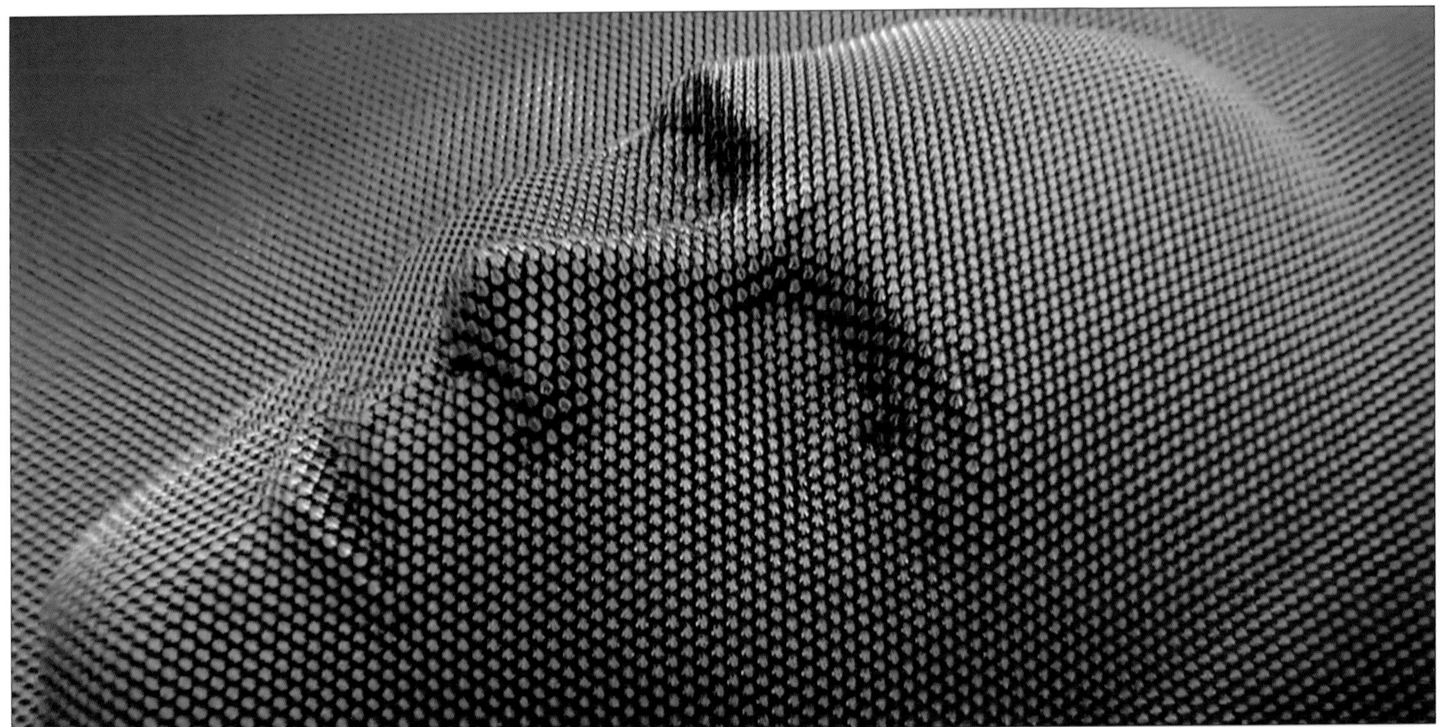

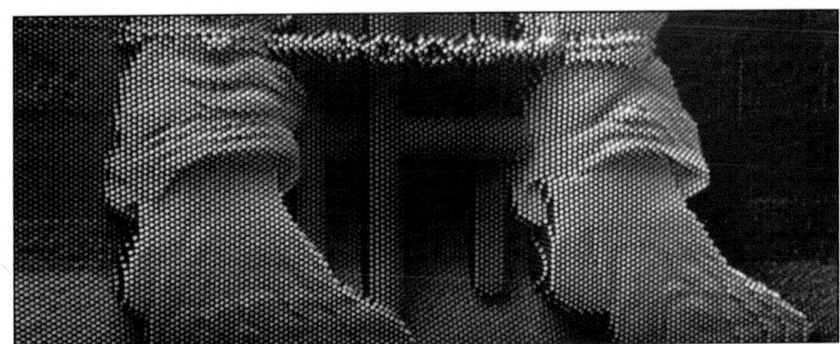

Agency TBWA\Paris
Creative Directors Philippe Taroux, Benoît Leroux
Copywriter Ingrid Varetz
Art Director Ingrid Varetz
Production Troublemakers TV, Paris
Film Director Onur Senturk
Producer James Hagger
2nd Prod. Co. \Else, Paris
Head of TV Maxime Boiron
TV Producer Amer Zoghbi
Music & Sound Olivier Lefebvre
Sound Producer Benoît Dunaigre
Music Art Direction Philippe Mineur, Ferdinand Huet
3rd Prod. Co. One More Co. Production, Paris
Post Producer Benjamin Darras
VFX Supervisor Johnny Alves
Editors Nicolas Larrouquere, Romain Bouileau
Advertiser Amnesty International, "Amnesty Pens"

Pens become pixels in this harrowing drama, which begins with a demonstration against oppression. One of the demonstrators is imprisoned and brutally tortured. The pens rise up in protest and signatures swirl on the screen. Now we see the demonstrator again, this time free and victorious. For 50 years, thousands of signatures on Amnesty petitions have led to thousands of releases. Pens can have power.

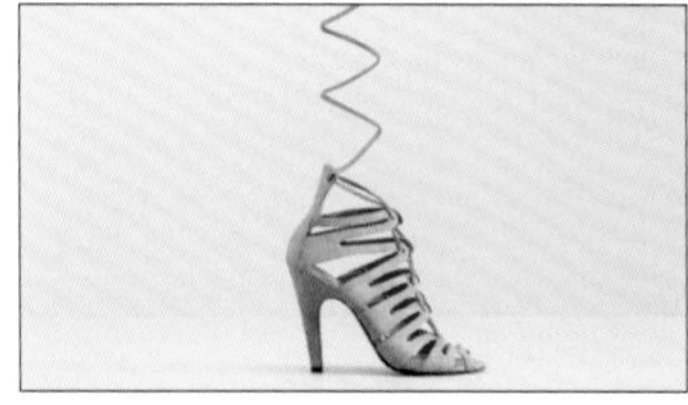

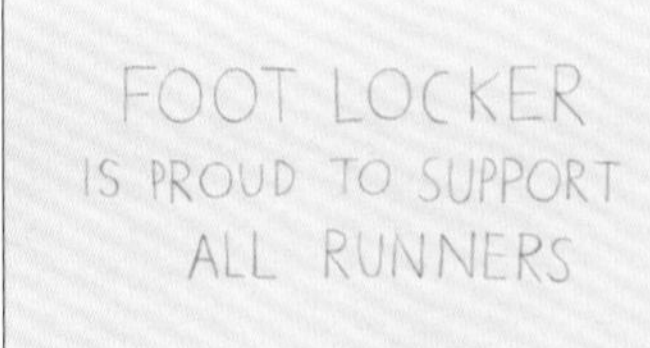

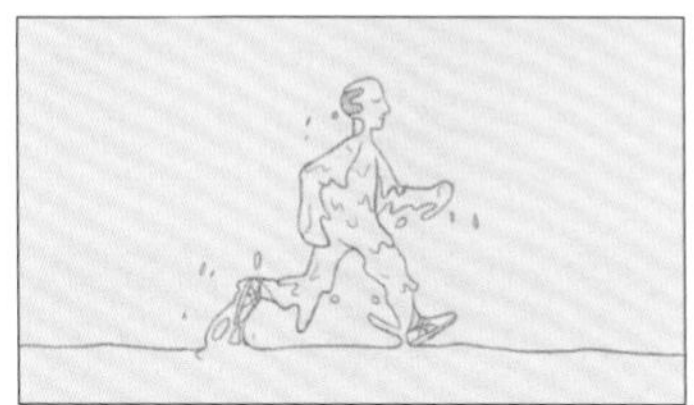

Agency DigitasLBi, Paris
CCO Bridget Jung
Creative Director Nicolas Thiboutot
Art Directors Frederic Roux, Chisato Tsuchiya
Agency Publicis&Nous, Paris
Creative Director Fabien Mouillard
TV Producer Alexandra Marik
Advertiser Hermès, "2014 Spring Summer Collection"

Every year, luxury fashion house Hermès crafts its collection around one theme. This film was designed to capture the theme of metamorphosis. We see Hermès gifts like rings, shoes, handkerchiefs and ties evolving into strange creatures or starring in surrealistic tableaus. The film was created using hand-made techniques inspired by Hermès craftsmanship.

Agency BBDO New York
CCO David Lubars, Greg Hahn
Executive CD Chris Beresford-Hill, Dan Lucey
Creative Directors Grant Smith, Danilo Boer
Copywriter Grant Smith
Art Director Danilo Boer
Executive ±Producer Tricia Lentini
Advertiser Foot Locker, "Runners"

Foot Locker is proud to support all runners. This cartoon shows us some of them, including silly runners, runners who follow others too closely, proudly muddy runners, high-fiving runners, sweaty runners, bearded runners, runners who run so they can eat a lot, and costumed runners who feel awkward around runners with conflicting costumes. Not to mention runners who can't stop looking at their new shoes. All these and more can expect a warm welcome at Foot Locker.

Agencies BETC, Paris
Havas, Dusseldorf
CCO Rémi Babinet
CD Vincent Behaeghel
Creatives Marcus Herrmann
Oliver Hilbring
Stefan Muhl
Art Director Juliette Courty
Production Wizzdesign, Paris
Producer Matthieu Poirier
Advertiser Peugeot,
"The Legend Returns"

Thirty years ago, the Peugeot 205 GTi starred in a much-loved Bond-style spot. We open with the original ad – but then the older car is overtaken by the new generation: the 208 GTi. Driving on thin ice, the Bond-esque hero in his sporty runabout survives attacks by jet, bomber and helicopter gunship, before inevitably getting the girl. "You made me wait," she says. "I know," he replies, archly. "About 30 years." The action is made credible by animation that recalls the coolest video games.

Agency Bray Leino, Devon
Creative Director Jon Elsom
Copywriter Henry Challender
Art Director Scott Franklin
Production th1ng, London
Film Director Peter Szewczyk
Producer Ru Warner
Advertiser Freederm,
"Geese"

A flock of geese are flying in their usual formation. One of them looks bored – and then suddenly plunges away from the crew to do his own thing. After some aerial acrobatics and wave-skimming, he visits the city, flies with kites, loops the loop on a roller-coaster and even soars into space. Finally, after breaking the world geese record, he rides off into the sunset on a chopper. Geese-y rider? There's nothing like feeling free. Freederm – for spot-free skin.

Direction & Cinematography

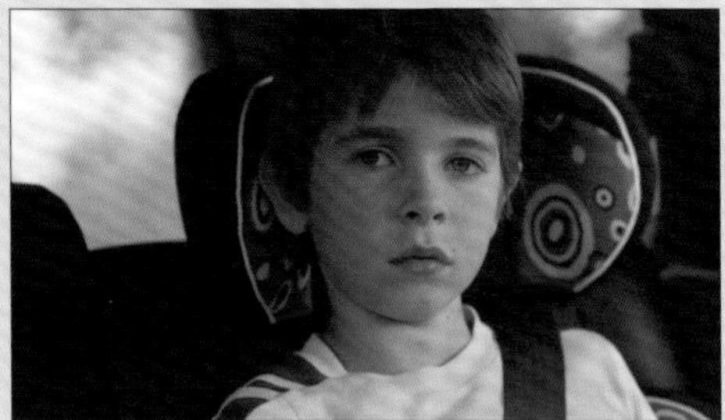

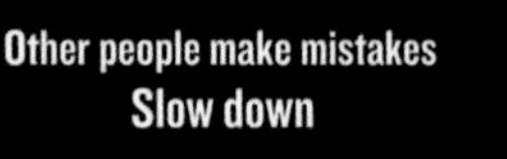

Agency Finch, Paddington
Executive CD Philip Andrew
Creative Director Brigid Alkema
Copywriter Emily Beautrais
Art Directors Emily Beautrais, Philip Andrew
Agency Producer Marty Gray
Dir. of Digital Innovation Thomas Scovell
Director Derin Seale
Producer Karen Bryson
Executive Producer Robert Galluzzo
DOP Stefan Duscio
Editor Drew Thompson
Spec. Effects Supervisor Stuart White
Colourist Ben Eagleton
Sound Design Simon Lister
Advertiser New Zealand Transport Agency, "Mistakes"

This chilling spot freezes the action as two cars are about to collide. The drivers leave their stilled vehicles and talk in a bid to prevent the inevitable. One pleads that he has his son in the back of his car. The other admits that he's going too fast to prevent the crash: "I'm sorry." Reluctantly, they turn their backs and trudge back to their cars. Time unsticks, and the tragedy runs its course.

Agency	BBDO New York	From birth, a boy emits beeps instead of human sounds. As he grows up, we discover that he can talk to machines. This has advantages when you're faced with a broken TV, but his parents are worried and his gift elicits sniggers at school. When he restores electricity to his town, he becomes a hero. But only his first sweetheart can give him the power of speech. A corporate image movie that packs in all the emotion of a big screen classic.
CCOs	David Lubars Greg Hahn	
Executive CD	Michael Aimette	
Creative Director	Tim Roan	
Copywriter	Tim Roan	
Art Director	Lance Vining	
Dir. of Integrated Prod.	David Rolfe	
Executive Producer	Diane Hill	
Production	Park Pictures, New York	
Film Director	Lance Acord	
Advertiser	GE, "The Boy Who Beeps"	

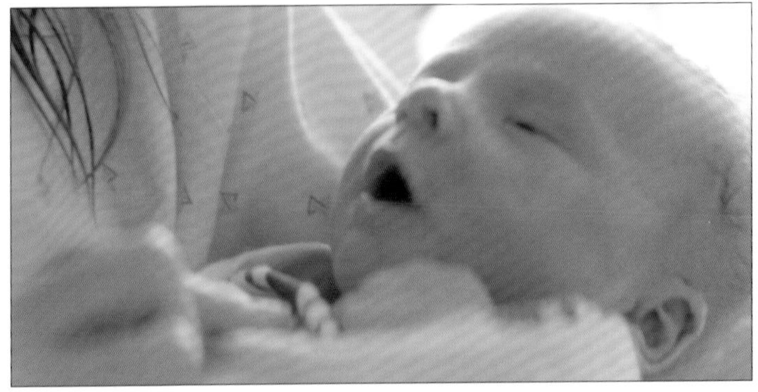

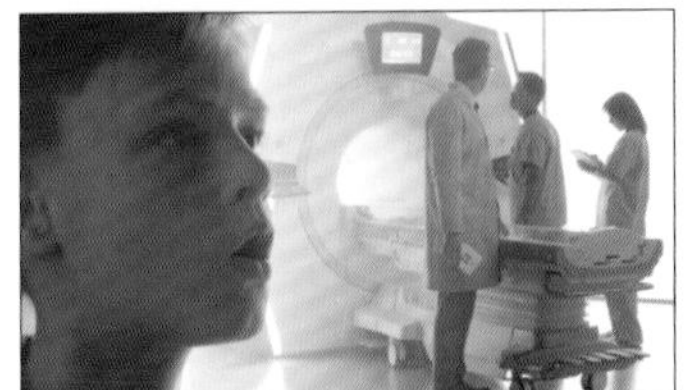

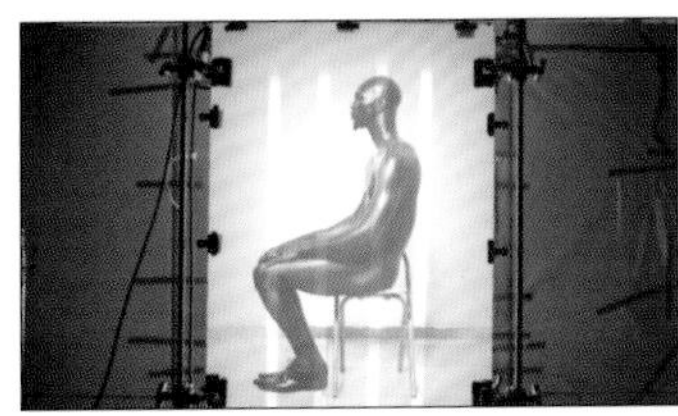

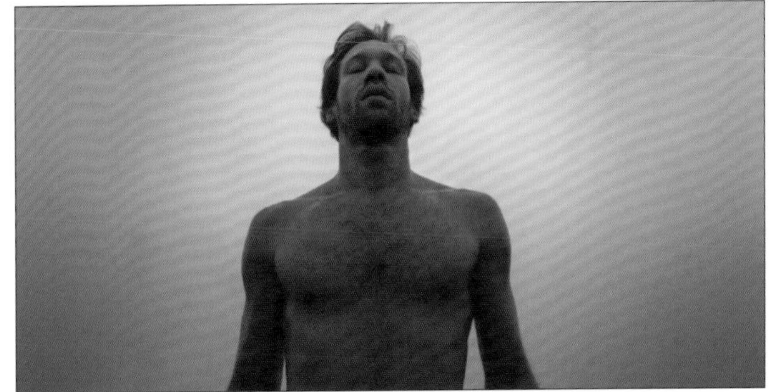

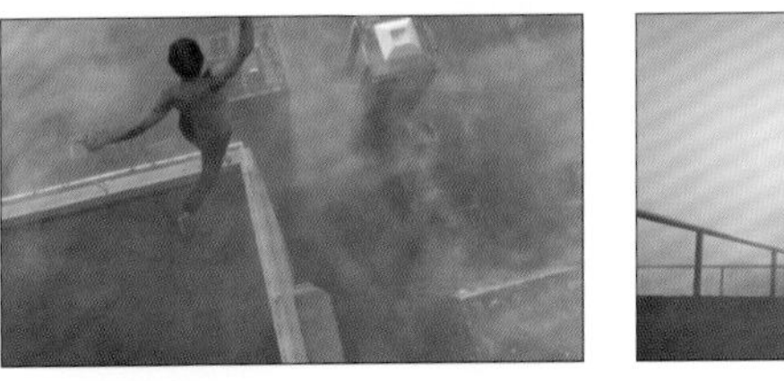

Agencies	BBDO Africa, AMVBBDO, London	A dynamic film with a rock video verve portrays black not as a colour, but an attitude. Black "dances to a different beat" and "writes its own rules". Machine-gun fast editing, eye-popping vignettes and a soundtrack of Kanye West's "Black Skinhead" guarantee an exciting experience. And it's all for Guinness, which is made of black. It was part of a pan-African campaign for Guinness Africa.
Creative Director	Mike Schalit	
Creatives	Ant Nelson Mike Sutherland	
Production	Rogue Films	
Producers	Nick Godden James Howland	
Film Director	Sam Brown	
Post Production	The Mill, London	
Editing House	Final Cut, London	
Advertiser	Diageo, Guinness, "Made Of Black"	

Agency	BETC, Paris	We're taken inside a young man's emotions as he leans across a café table for the kiss that may start a new relationship. For him, the gesture is akin to jumping from a tall building – a leap of faith. But the girl responds and soon we see them falling together, and for each other. The soundtrack is both lush and intense: the Flume remix of "You & Me" by Disclosure.
Creative Directors	Rémi Babinet Antoine Choque	
Copywriters	Gabrielle Attia Damien Bellon	
Art Directors	Gabrielle Attia Damien Bellon	
Production	Wanda, Paris	
Film Director	Seb Edwards	
Advertiser	Lacoste, "The Big Leap"	

Editing & Special Effects

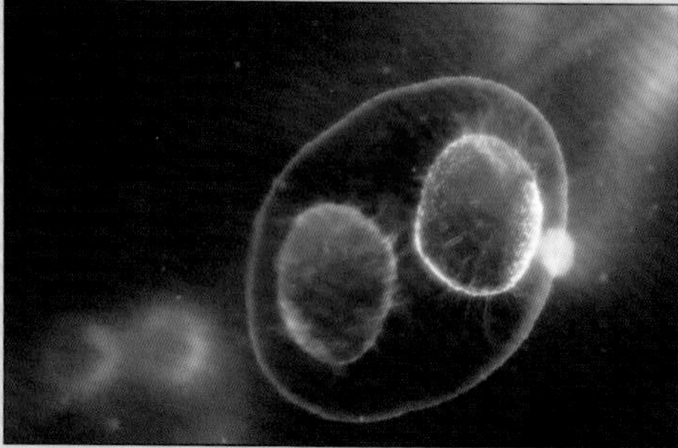

Agency Y&R, Paris
Creative Director Pierrette Diaz
Production Gang Films, Paris
Producers Jean Villiers, Nathalie Lecaer
Agency Producers Valerie Montiel, Estelle Diot
DOP Joost Van Gelder
Production Design Pirra
Editors Walter Mauriot, Fred Baudet
Post Production Digital District, Paris; Lardux
Sound Design Dir. Sam Ashwell,750Mph
Music Supervision Vincent Nayrolles, Matthieu Devos
Advertiser Danone, Volvic, "Volvic The Giant"

This epic film takes us through the history of Earth itself as we watch quakes, eruptions, evolutions and conquests. The subject, however, is eternal: Volvic mineral water, "born from time" and supremely indifferent to the foibles of Man. Handy for quenching his thirst, though.

Agency	Bazelevs, Moscow
Film Director	Timur Bekmambetov
Producer	Aleksey Borisov
Executive Producer	Ekaterina Tkachenko
DOP	Sergey Trofimov
Production Designer	Dmitry Onishenko
Wardrobe Designer	Natalya Dzubenko
Post Production	Ludmyla Vereykina
Composer	Oleg Litvishko
Sound Design Supervisor	Roland Kazaryan
Sound Designer	Oleg Karpachev
General Producer VFX	Aleksandr Gorokhov
VFX Supervisor	Timofey Penkov
Advertiser	Donstroy, "The Heart Of The Capital - Dream Away"

This may be the ultimate ad for a real estate company. Through the windows of a glass tower, we see a child sleeping. The building dissolves, showing us all the sleepers inside. We follow one young woman through a dreamlike landscape: spider-webs that turn to glass, buses that resemble toys, and even a passing dragon. Time and perspective slip, taking us to a ballet, a blossom-filled glade, and finally home. Donstroy: all facets of life at the heart of the capital.

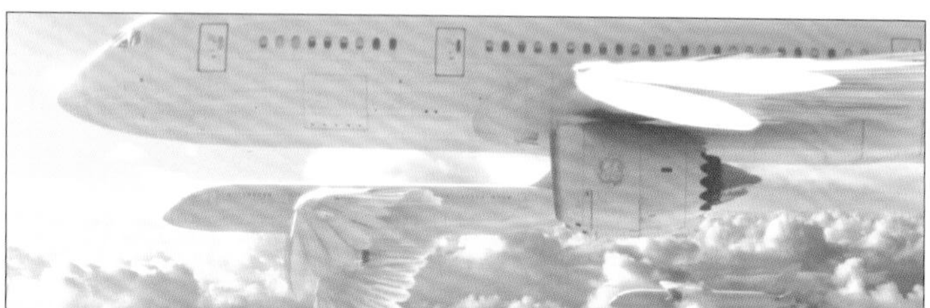

Agency	BBDO New York
CCOs	David Lubars Greg Hahn
Executive CD	Michael Aimette
Senior CD	Eric Cosper
CDs	Nick Sonderup Eric Goldstein
Copywriter	Nick Sonderup
Art Director	Eric Goldstein
Executive Producer	Anthony Nelson
Music Production	Rani Vaz Peter McCallum Sam White

Production	MJZ, New York
Film Director	Dante Ariola
DOP	Benoit Delhomme
Editorial Company	Whitehouse
Editor	Rick Lawley
Music Company	Barking Owl
Sound Mixer	Philip Loeb, Heard City
VFX Company	Method Studios
Advertiser	GE, "Childlike Imagination"

Special effects create a world of childlike wonder. A little girl narrates. "My mom? She makes underwater fans that are powered by the moon." Each real invention from GE is given a new twist by the child's imagination. "She makes airplane engines that can talk... hospitals you can hold in your hand." She can also print jet engines from her computer and makes trains that are "friends with trees". The payoff? "My mom works at GE." Imagination at work.

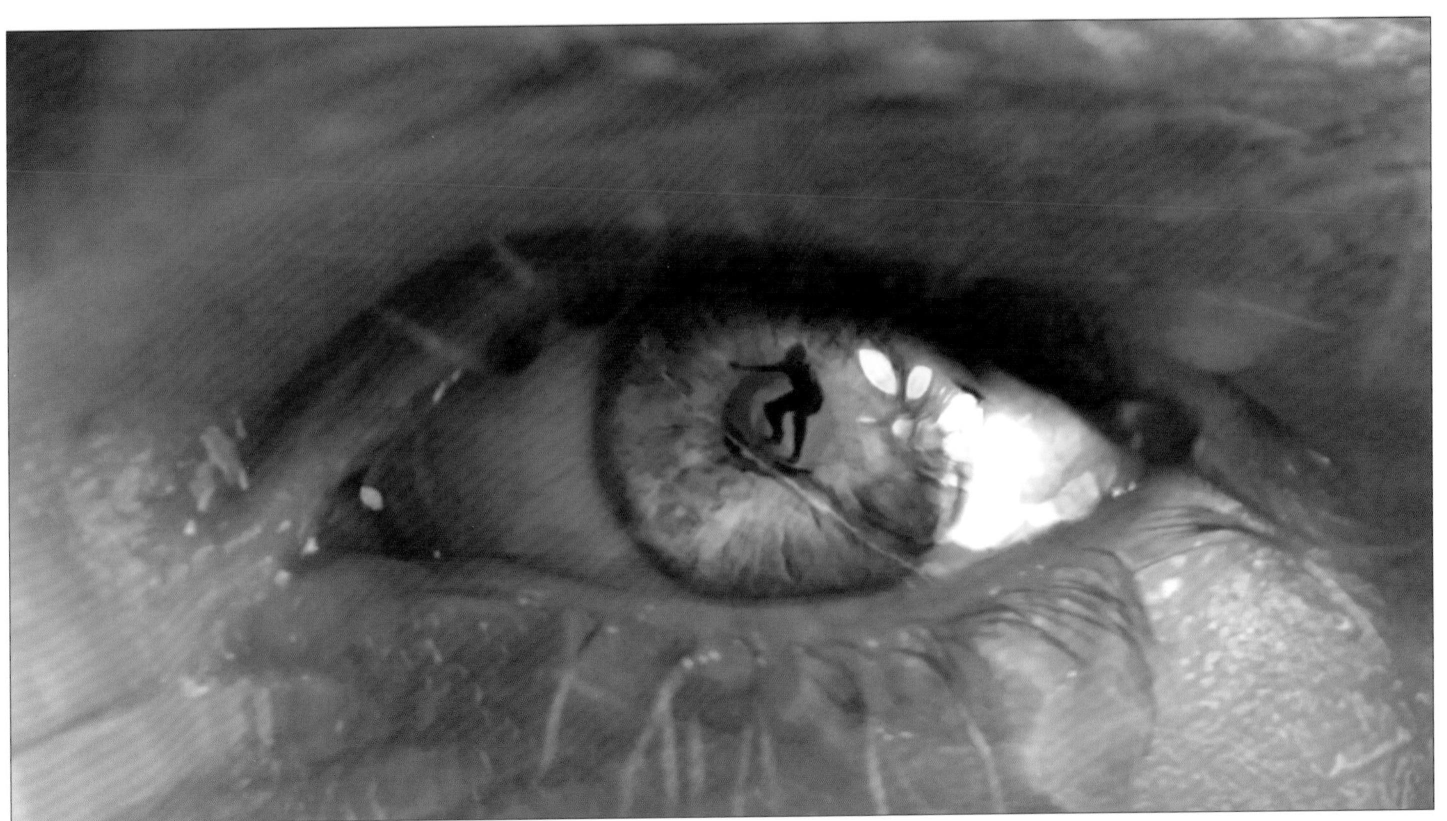

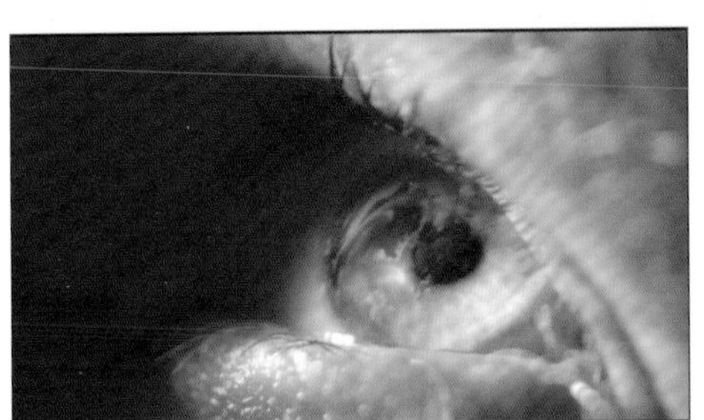

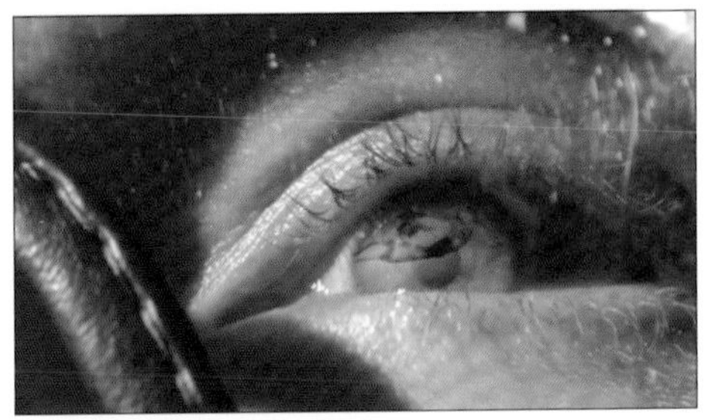

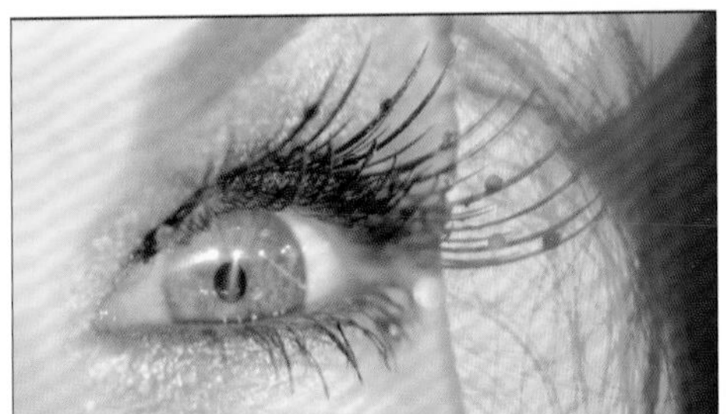

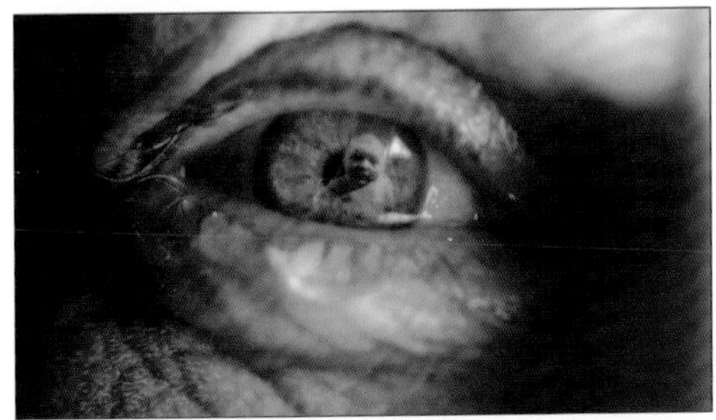

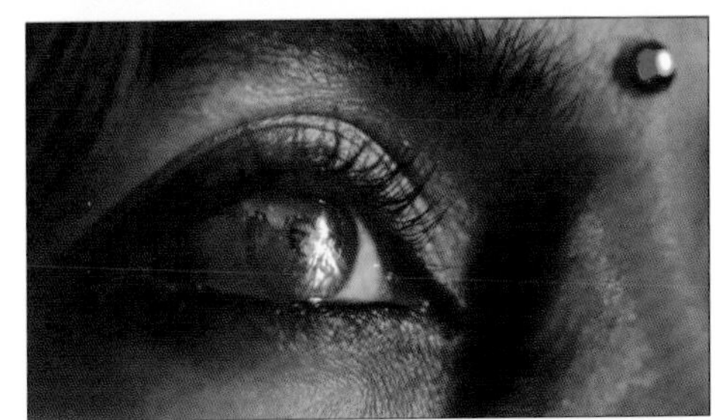

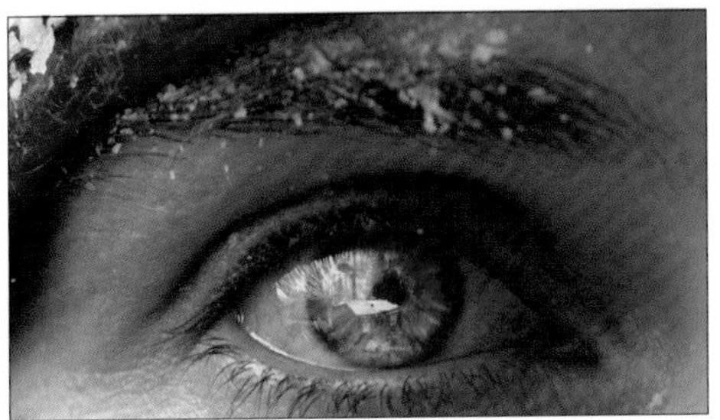

no one sees it
like you

Canon
facebook.com/canonaustralia

Agency Leo Burnett, Sydney
Chief CD Andy Dilallo
Creative Director Tim Green
Copywriter Gary Williams
Art Director Jim Walsh
TV Producer Renata Barbosa
Rita Gagliardi
Production Playbig, Sydney
Film Director Rey Carlson
VFX Supervisor Colin Renshaw
VFX Executive Prod. Takeshi Takada
Composer Ramesh Sathiah
Sound Design Abigail Sie
Advertiser Canon,
"Seeing"

Close-up on an eye. A young girl says: "There are over seven billion people on our planet… all looking at the world in our own way." More eyes appear, each one unique. "What do you see? Is it adventure?" Reflections in the eyes mirror her words. "Danger? Is it passion? Or tradition?" Look carefully and you'll see the answers. "Beauty? A new beginning? Or ending?" From celebrations to freedom, fame to potential, "no-one sees it like you". Canon cameras enable you to take what you see.

Best Use of Music

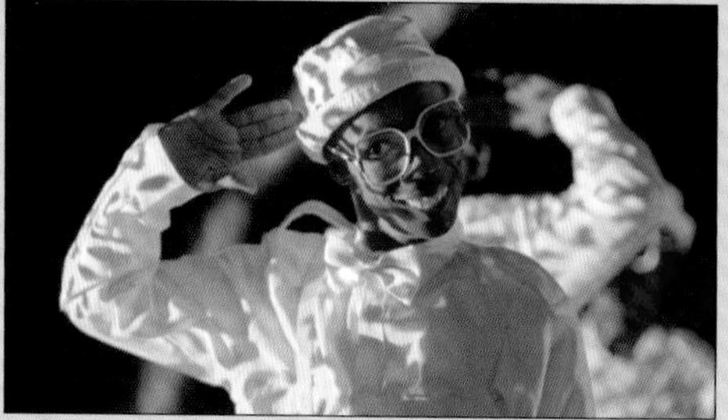

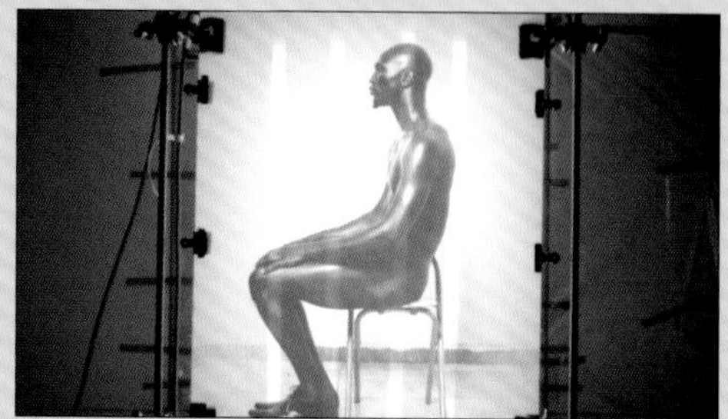

 Best Use of Music 

Agencies	BBDO Africa, AMV BBDO, London	**Producers**	James Howland
Production	Rogue Films	**Post Prod.**	The Mill, London
CD	Mike Schalit	**Editing House**	Final Cut, London
Creatives	Ant Nelson, Mike Sutherland	**Editor**	Amanda James
Producer	Nick Godden	**Sound Design**	Aaron Reynolds, Wave Studios,London
Film Director	Sam Brown	**Advertiser**	Diageo, Guinness, "Made Of Black"

Kanye West's "Black Skinhead" is the track that powers this kinetic celebration of all things black. But black here is not a colour, it's an attitude: creative, rebellious and cutting edge. This is an African campaign for Guinness, "Made Of Black". It's also the perfect meld of sound and image.

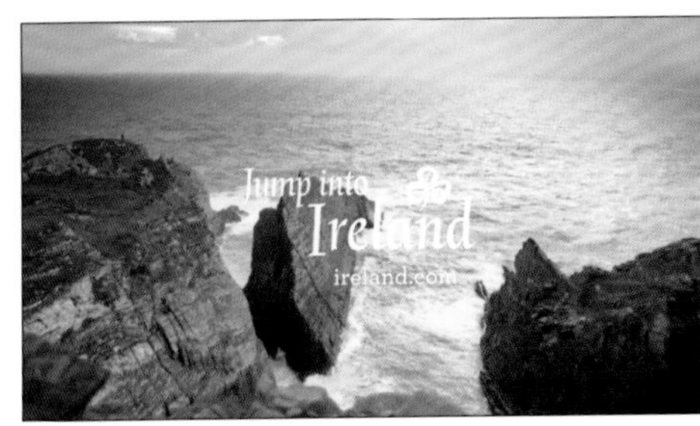

Agency	Publicis, London
ECD	Andy Bird
Creative Director	Dave Sullivan
Creatives	Adam Balogh Jason Moussalli
Digital ECD	Pavlos Themistocleous
Production	Friend, London
Film Director	Georgi Banks-Davies
Producer	Mikey Levelle
Agency Producer	Joshua Sanders
Agency Executive Prod.	Colin Hickson
Production Assistant	Charlotte McConnell
DOP	Todd Banzhal
In-House Editor	Myles Painter
Post-Production	George K Cynthia Lee, The Moving Picture Company
Sound Designer	Phil Bolland
Sound House	750MPH
Offline Editor	Sam Ostrove
Advertiser	Tourism Ireland, "Wild Atlantic Way"

The Wild Atlantic Way is a beautiful route down the west coast of Ireland. To create a unique piece of branded content for Tourism Ireland, the band Solomon Grey were sent on a road trip with a mobile studio and the mission of capturing the Wild Atlantic Way in audio form. They recorded sounds and worked with local musicians, often placing them in unusual locations. The result was an album available on social platforms and Ireland.com, as well as an evocative online film.

When breaking news, it's better with music

Best Use of Music

Agency	Dimensión, San Sebastián
Creative Director	Guillermo Viglione
Copywriter	Guillermo Viglione
Art Director	Guillermo Viglione
Production	Debolex, San Sebastián
Agency Producer	Laura Aristeguieta
Advertiser	Radio Euskadi, "Better With Music - Obama"

The wittier side of Barack Obama is shown as he recounts an incident from the campaign trail, when a woman in the crowd shouts, "Fire it up!" and the crowd responds, "Ready to go!" But his anecdote becomes more compelling with the addition of music, turning it into a kind of rap. Radio Euskadi believes news is better with music.

Agency	BBDO, Brussels
CDs	Sebastien De Valck Arnaud Pitz
Copywriter	Nicolas Gaspart
Art Director	Frederic Zouag
Production	Caviar, Brussels
Film Director	Arnaud Uyttenhove
Producer	Caviar, Brussels
Agency Producer	Leen Van den Brande
DOP	Dimitri Karakatsanis
Advertiser	Belgian Olympic Commitee, "Belgian Mountains"

Legendary Belgian singer Jacques Brel provides the soundtrack to this gritty film, which shows snowboarders practicing in a rural landscape where snow is noticeably absent. Hills, fields, cows and mud are more the order of the day. "The flat land which is mine," as Brel puts it. But Belgians don't need mountains to win a medal. Sochi Belgian Olympic Team 2014.

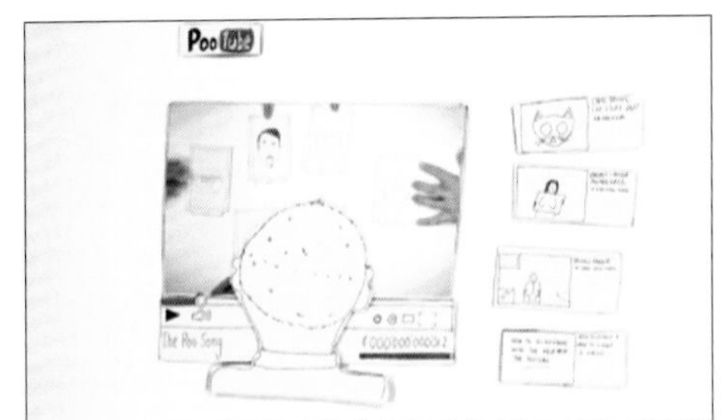

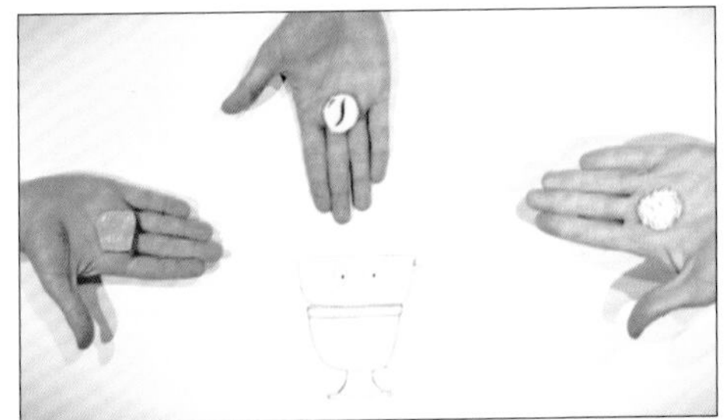

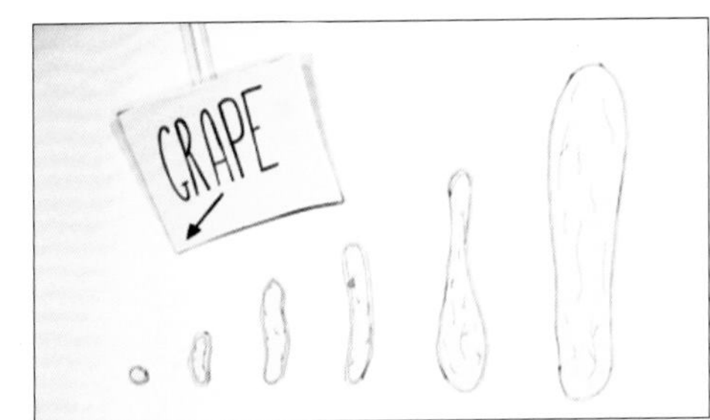

Agency The Leith Agency, Edinburgh
Creative Director Gerry Farrell
Production The Leith Agency
Freakworks,
Edinburgh
Creative Team Jordan Laird
Ian Greenhill
Film Directors Jordan Laird
Ian Greenhill
Erik Ravaglia
Advertiser The Scottish Bowel
Screening Service,
"The Poo Song"

How do you convince people to test themselves for bowel cancer, when it's a somewhat intimate process? You address the problem head on, with a scatological ode called "The Poo Song" and a funny cartoon. "Tell your mum, tell your dad, tell your second uncle Vlad: there's no need to be sad, it may not be so bad. When you're next on the loo, tell them what to do, spin yourself around – and test your latest poo." By making us laugh, the song takes the taboo out of poo.

Title & Credits

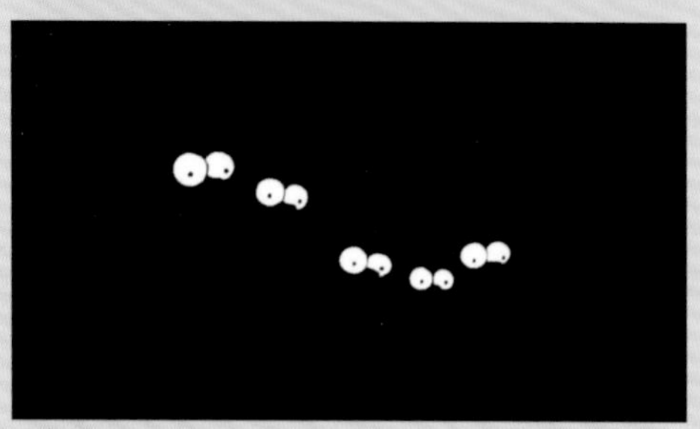

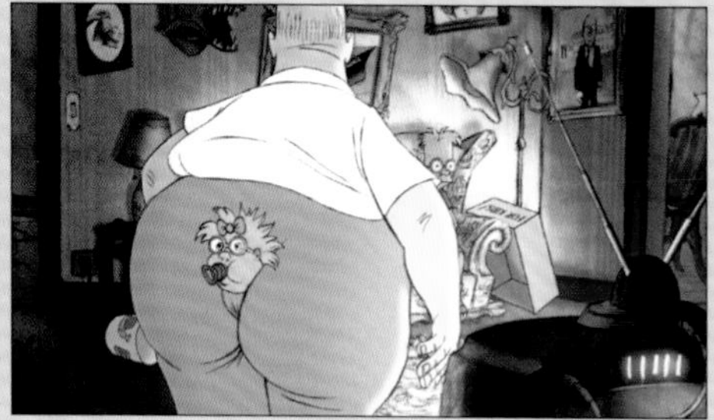

Agency	Fox Entertainment, LA
Production	th1ng, London
Film Director	Sylvain Chomet
Producers	Dominic Buttimore Ru Warner
Agency Producers	James L. Brooks Matt Groening Al Jean
Advertiser	The Simpsons, "Chomet Couch Gag"

The Simpsons opening sequences are renowned for their playful adaptions of the same format, including contributions from guest directors. Here, French director Sylvain Chomet – of the animated tale The Triplets of Belleville – takes his turn, giving the Simpsons' household a distinctly Gallic touch. Snails play the role of popcorn and an unfortunate goose becomes a plaything.

PARIS ZOO
WILDLIFE IS BACK IN TOWN
RE-OPENING IN APRIL

WILDLIFE IS BACK IN TOWN

WILDLIFE IS BACK IN TOWN

WILDLIFE IS BACK IN TOWN

Agency	Publicis Conseil, Paris	**Artbuyer**	Jean Luc Chirio Flore Silberfeld
Creative Directors	Olivier Altmann Frederic Royer	**Retouching**	Adrien Benard
Copywriter	Bangaly Fofana	**Advertiser**	Paris Zoo, "Paris Zoo" Campaign
Art Director	Benoit Blumberger		
Photographer	Ronan Merot		
Process Manager	Valerie Marquant		
Advertiser Supervisors	Thomas Grenon Frederic Vernhes Fanny Decobert Cecile Brissaud, National Museum of Natural History		

With our prices you can do more.

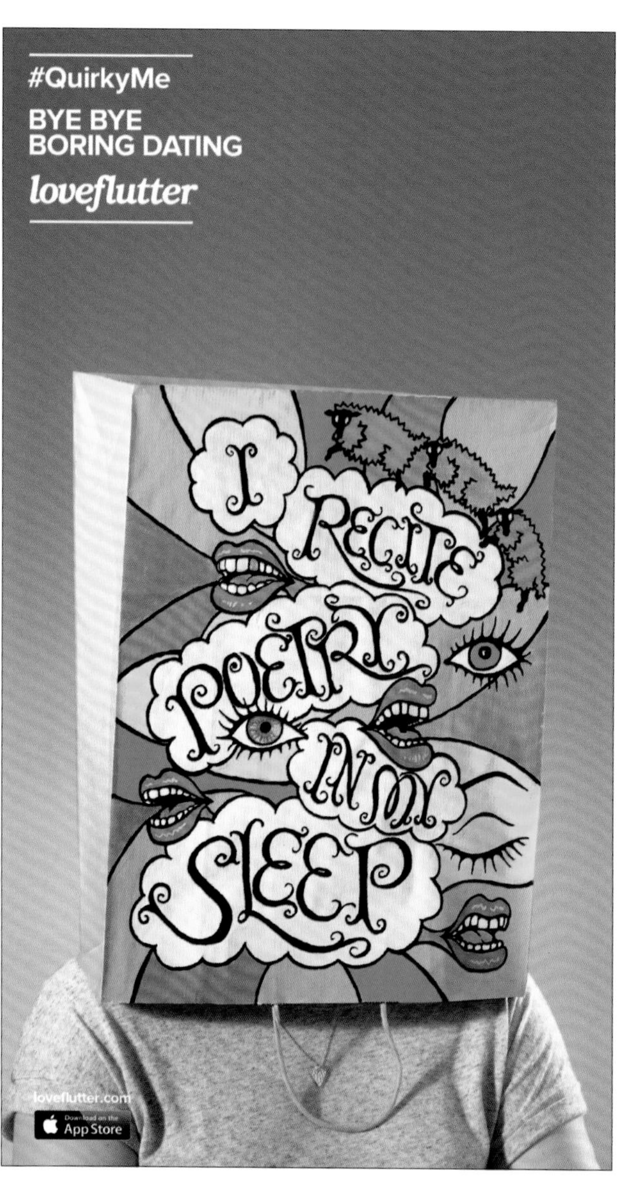
#QuirkyMe
BYE BYE
BORING DATING
loveflutter
I RECITE POETRY IN MY SLEEP
loveflutter.com
App Store

#QuirkyMe
BYE BYE
BORING DATING
loveflutter

#QuirkyMe
BYE BYE
BORING DATING
loveflutter
NO ONE can PRONOUNCE my NAME!

Agency	Leo Burnett, Moscow
Executive CD	Mikhail Kudashkin
Senior Art Director	Max Kitaev
Junior Art Director	Leyla Mukhametzianova
CD of Design Studio	Dmitry Jakovlev
Producer	Anna Flankina
Production	Catzwolf Production & Lacewing Studio, Moscow
Advertiser	Leroy Merlin, "Ark"

Agency	Havas Worldwide London
Executive CD	Mark Fairbanks
Copywriter	Andy Mcananey
Art Director	Christian Sewell
Photographer	Alan Powdrill
Art Buyers	Kate Blumer Raine Allen Miller
Illustrator	Christian Sewell
Typographer	Christian Sewell
Advertiser	Loveflutter, "Bags" Campaign

Loveflutter is a dating app with a difference: instead of flicking through photos of people, you scroll through interesting facts about them. The agency used paper bags and enlisted talented designers and illustrators to bring peoples' crazy facts to life.

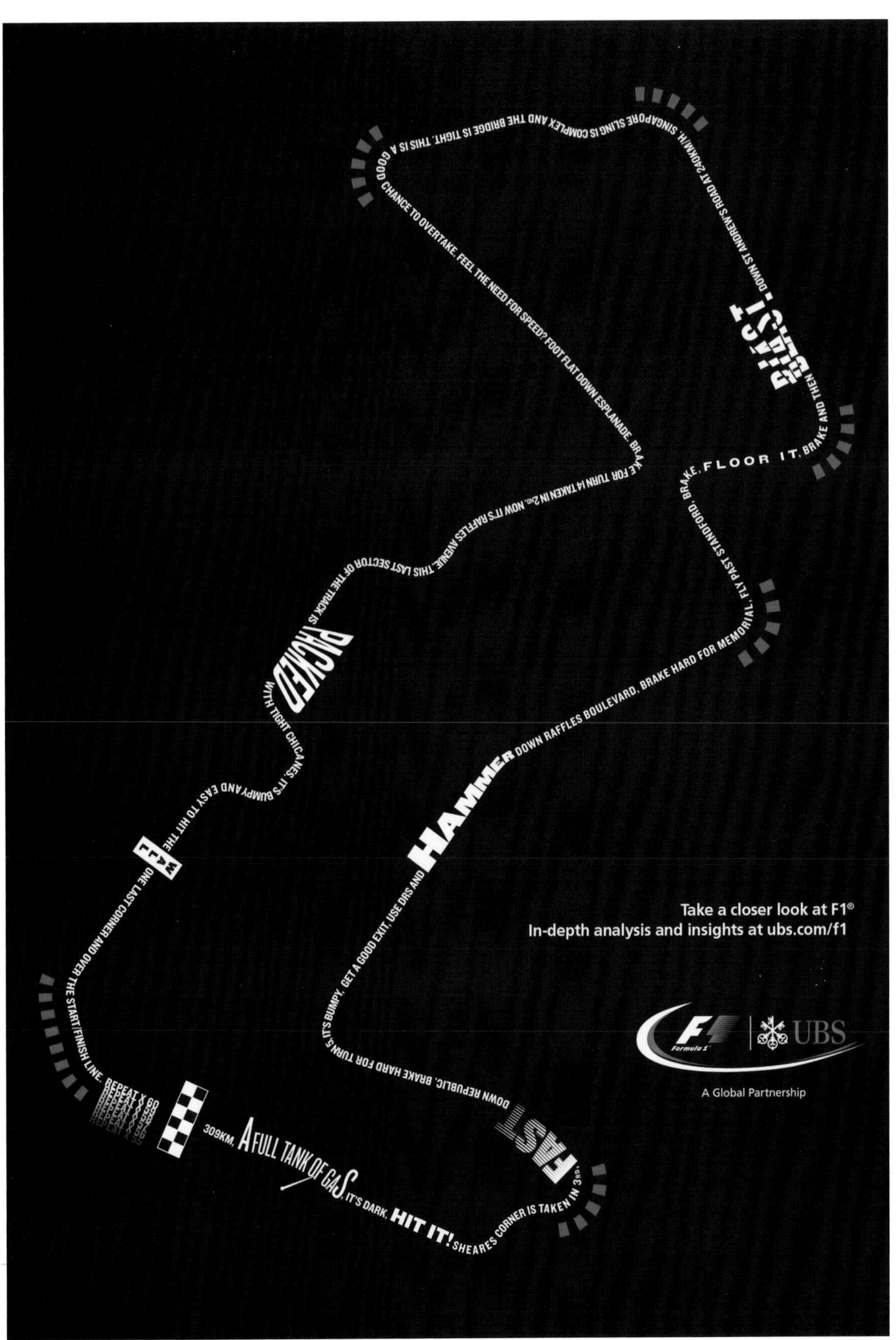
Take a closer look at F1®
In-depth analysis and insights at ubs.com/f1
UBS
A Global Partnership

Agency	Publicis, London
ECD	Andy Bird
Creative Directors	Richard Baynham Ian Gabaldoni
Copywriter	Adam Balogh
Art Director	Jason Moussalli
Head of Art/Design	Andy Breese
Agency Producer	Debbie Graves
Graphic Design	Mara Vojnovic
Advertiser	UBS, "F1 Insights"

Rear horsepower

911

Agency	Fred & Farid, Shanghai	Agency Supervisors	Gregoire Chalopin
Creative Directors	Fred & Farid		Vivian Wang
	Feng Huang		Kylie Wang
	Laurent Leccia	Retouching	Happy Finish
Copywriter	Laurent Leccia	Brand Supervisors	Deesch Papke
Art Director	Laurent Leccia		Carsten Balmes
Agency Producers	Joanne Zhou		Estella Yang
	Terry Jin	Advertiser	Porsche,
Illustrators	Marc Burckhardt		"911 Rear
	Asaphz		Horsepower"

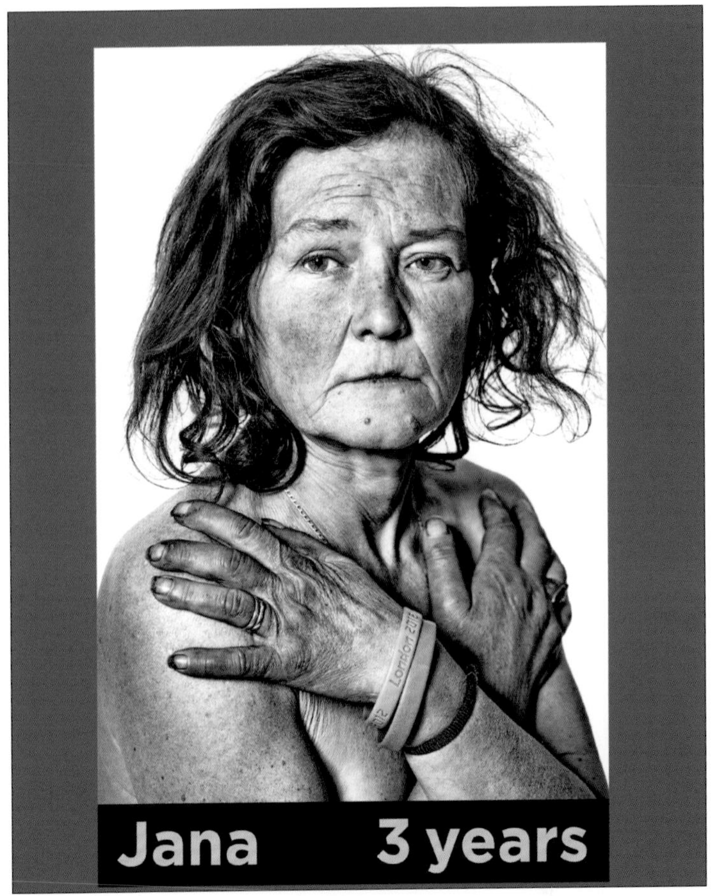

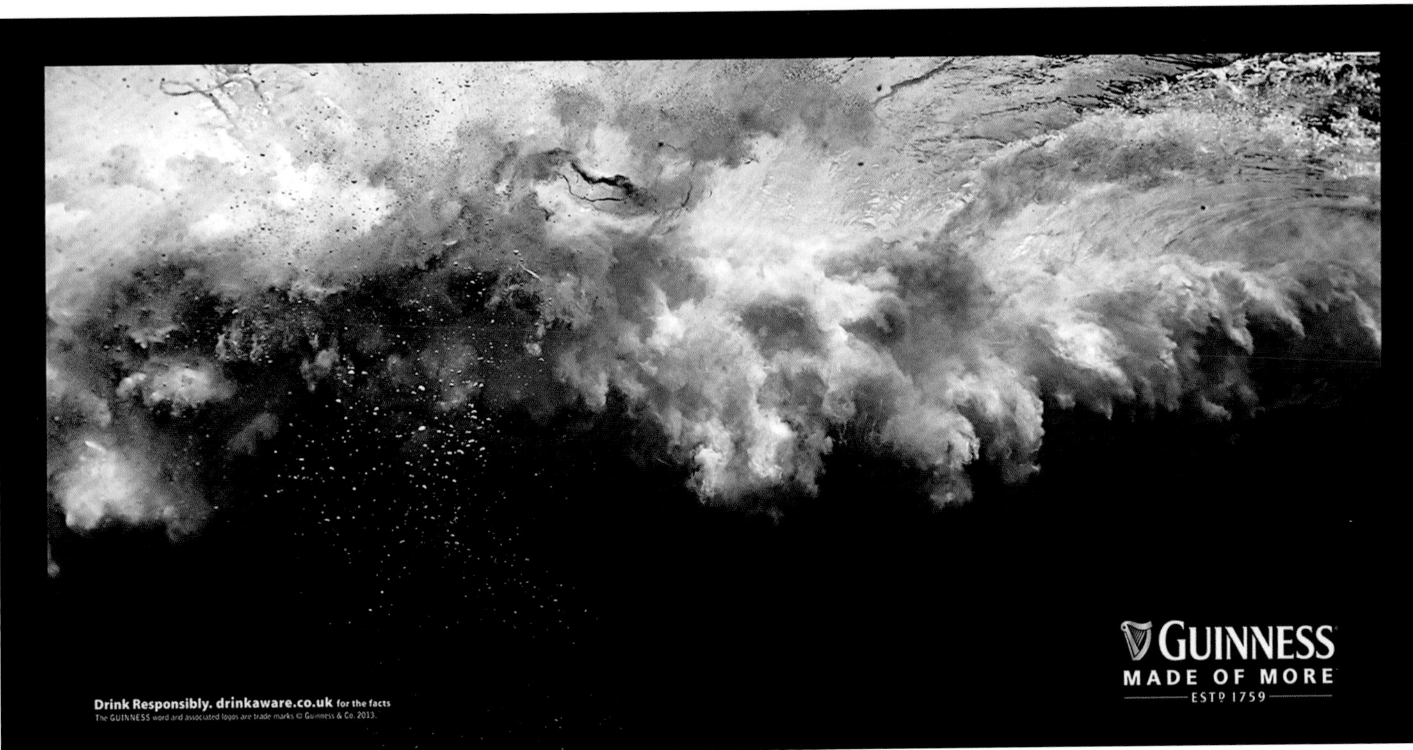

GUINNESS
MADE OF MORE
ESTD 1759
Drink Responsibly. drinkaware.co.uk for the facts
The GUINNESS word and associated logos are trade marks © Guinness & Co. 2013.

Agency	Letensti Holobradci, Prague
Creative Directors	Tomas Trestik Eda Kauba
Art Directors	Tomas Trestik Vilem Kabzan
Photographer	Tomas Trestik
Production	Pink Productions, Prague
Postproduction	Holubowicz Studio
Advertiser	Czech Helsinki Committee, "Not Living, Just Surviving"

Agency	AMV BBDO, London
Creative Director	Dave Buchanan
Copywriter	Nicholas Hulley
Art Director	Nadja Lossgott
Directors	Scott Mortensen Daren Crawford
Agency Producer	James Robley
Photographer	Brian Bielmann
Designer	Richard Holgate
Advertising Managers	Stephen O'Kelly Nick Britton
Advertiser	Guinness, "Surge"

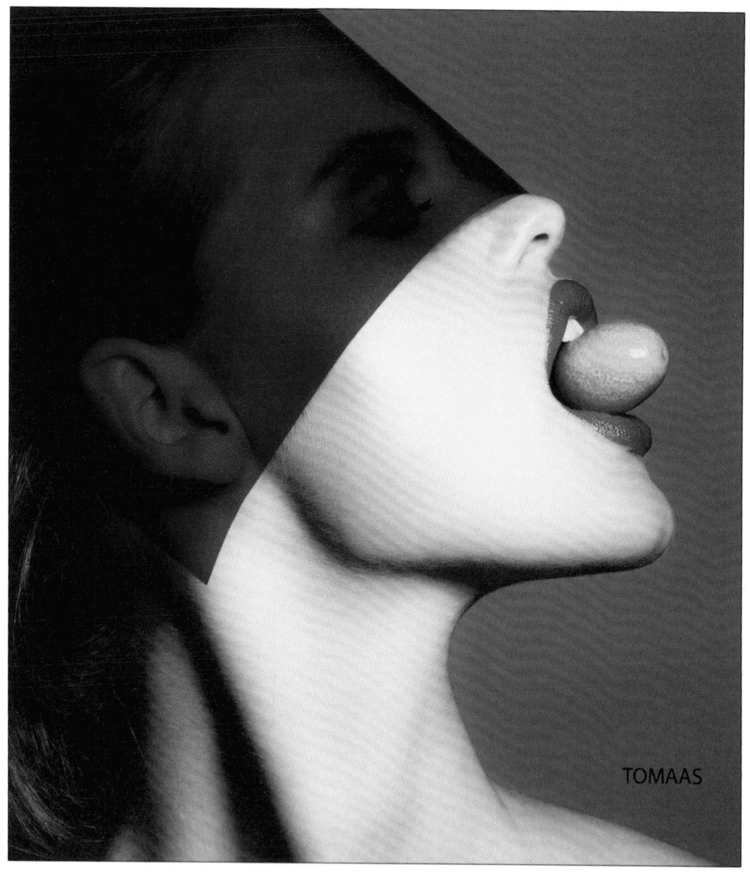

Creative Director	TOMAAS	**Retoucher**	Elena Levenets TOMAAS
Art Director	TOMAAS	**Advertiser**	TOMAAS, "TOMAAS"
Photographer	TOMAAS		
Hairstylist	Seiji Uehara Represented By Ennis, Inc. NYC		
Make up	Nevio Raggazini, Next Artists, NYC		
Models	Lisette, Ford Models Staz Lindes, Request Models Kim, IMG Models		

Agency	Publicis, Paris
Art Director	Pierre Penicaud
Photographer	Nadav Kander
Art Buyer	Marion Venot
Advertiser	Orange, "Fibre"

Photographs by loyal Epica contributor Nadav Kander illustrated a campaign for French telecom brand Orange.

 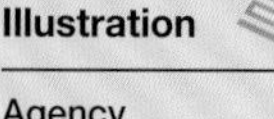

Agency	TBWA\Italia, Milan	**Artist**	Gionata "Ozmo" Gesi
Executive CDs	Nicola Lampugnani Francesco Guerrera	**Artist Assistant**	Mattia Turco
		Production	First Floor Under, Milan
Copywriter	Mirco Pagano	**Experience Design**	Dadomani Studio, Milan
Art Director	Moreno De Turco	**Video Maker**	Flash Factory
Web Developer	Chiara Villotta	**Music Artist**	Sheldon Coper
Digital Art Director	Federico Gatto	**Advertiser**	Humanitas Hospital and Cancer Center, "Smok-ink"
Digital CD	Michele La Fiandra		
Agency Producer	Federico Fornasari		
Calligrapher	Virginia Ottina		

A special machine "smoked" 4000 cigarettes and the residue was transformed into a noxious black liquid. This was used to create a giant mural at an exhibit for Humanitas, the Italian hospital and cancer centre. Referring to iconic pictures from art history, the detailed infographic warned teens about the dangers of smoking. The paint actually smelled of smoke.

Franz Liszt
TUESDAY, 20. MAY 2014, CHUR
ST. MARTIN`S CHURCH, 8 P.M.
Swiss Youth Symphony Orchestra.
CLASSICAL, YOUNGER THAN EVER.

TSCHAIKOWSKY
SWAN LAKE
SATURDAY, 17. MAY 2014, SOLOTHURN
• KONZERTSAAL, 8 P.M. •
Swiss Youth Symphony Orchestra.
CLASSICAL, YOUNGER THAN EVER.

VERDI
LA TRAVIATA
MONDAY, 19. MAY 2014, ZÜRICH
TONHALLE, 7.30 P.M.
Swiss Youth Symphony Orchestra.
CLASSICAL, YOUNGER THAN EVER.

Richard Wagner
TRISTAN & ISOLDE
SUNDAY, 11. MAY 2014, ST. GALLEN
TONHALLE, 5 P.M.
Swiss Youth Symphony Orchestra.
CLASSICAL, YOUNGER THAN EVER.

Agency FCB, Zurich
Creative Director Dennis Lück
Copywriters Fabienne Arnold, Clara Garnier, Maximilian Kortmann
Art Directors Christoff Strukamp, Marcin Baba, Dyane Gremaud, Cinthia Stettler, Elgee David Wee
Illustrators Amadeus Waltenspühl, Richard Phipps, Andreas Preis,
Gordei Illustrations Vince Ray
Advertiser Swiss Youth Symphony Orchestra, "Classical Band Merchandise"

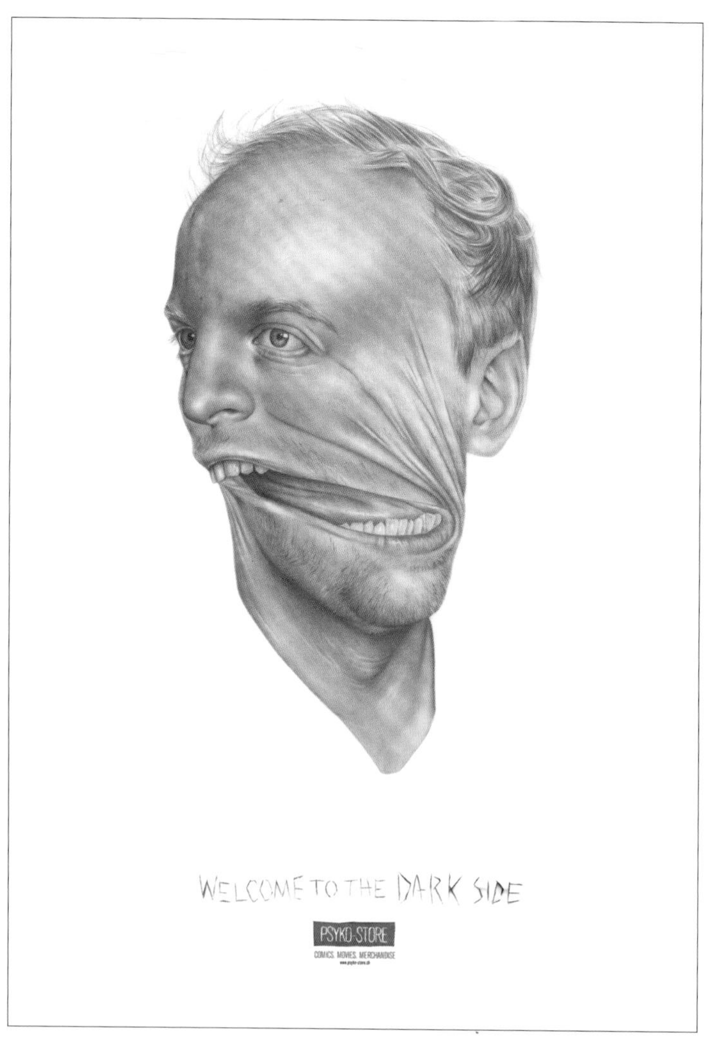

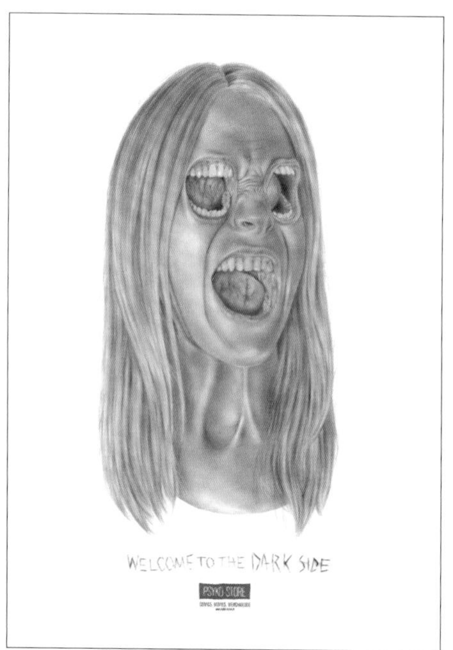

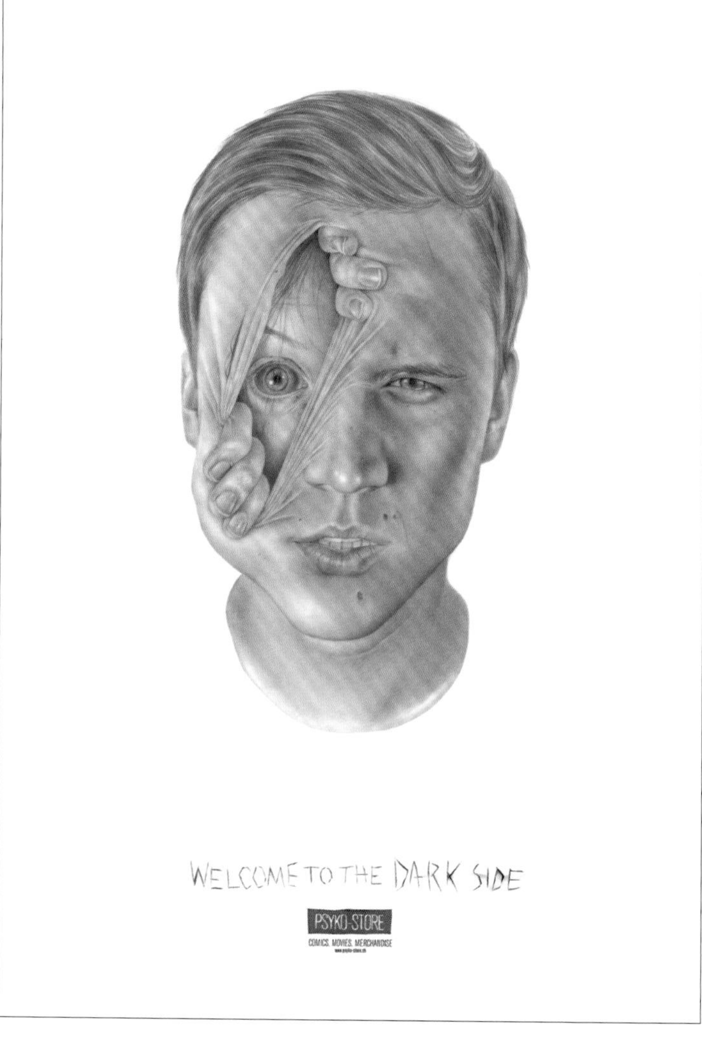

Agency	Y&R, Zurich
CCO	Markus Gut
Executive CD	Dominik Oberwiler
Director	Martin Stulz
Art Directors	Jeremy Küng Lukas Wietlisbach
Copywriter	Martin Stulz
Consulting	Pascal Trütsch
Illustrator	Jeremy Küng
Advertiser	Psyko-Store, "Dark side"

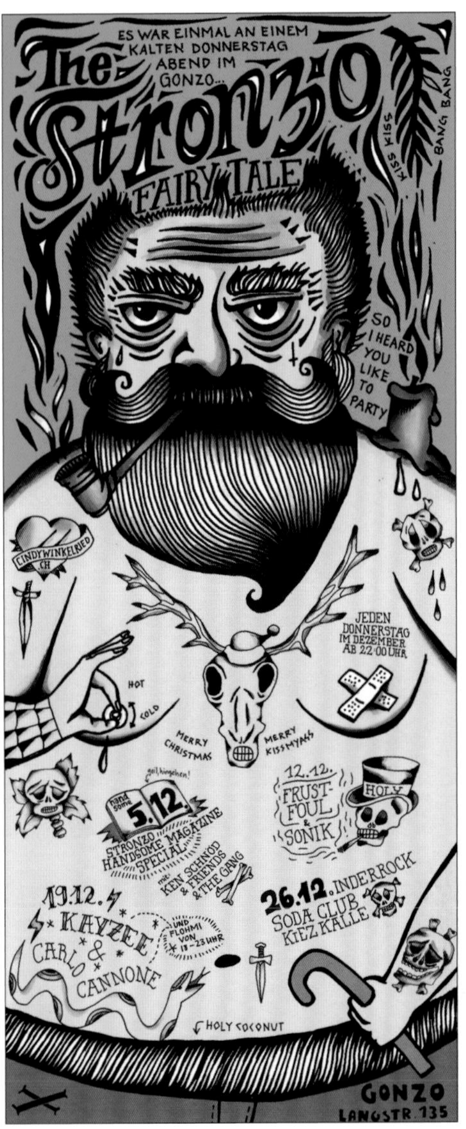

Agency	Wirz BBDO, Zurich	These anarchic posters for the Gonzo Club in Zurich provide a good indication of the decadent and fun atmosphere at the venue.
Art Director	Katrin von Niederhäusern	
Illustrator	Katrin von Niederhäusern	
Advertiser	Gonzo Club Zurich, "Fairy Tale"	

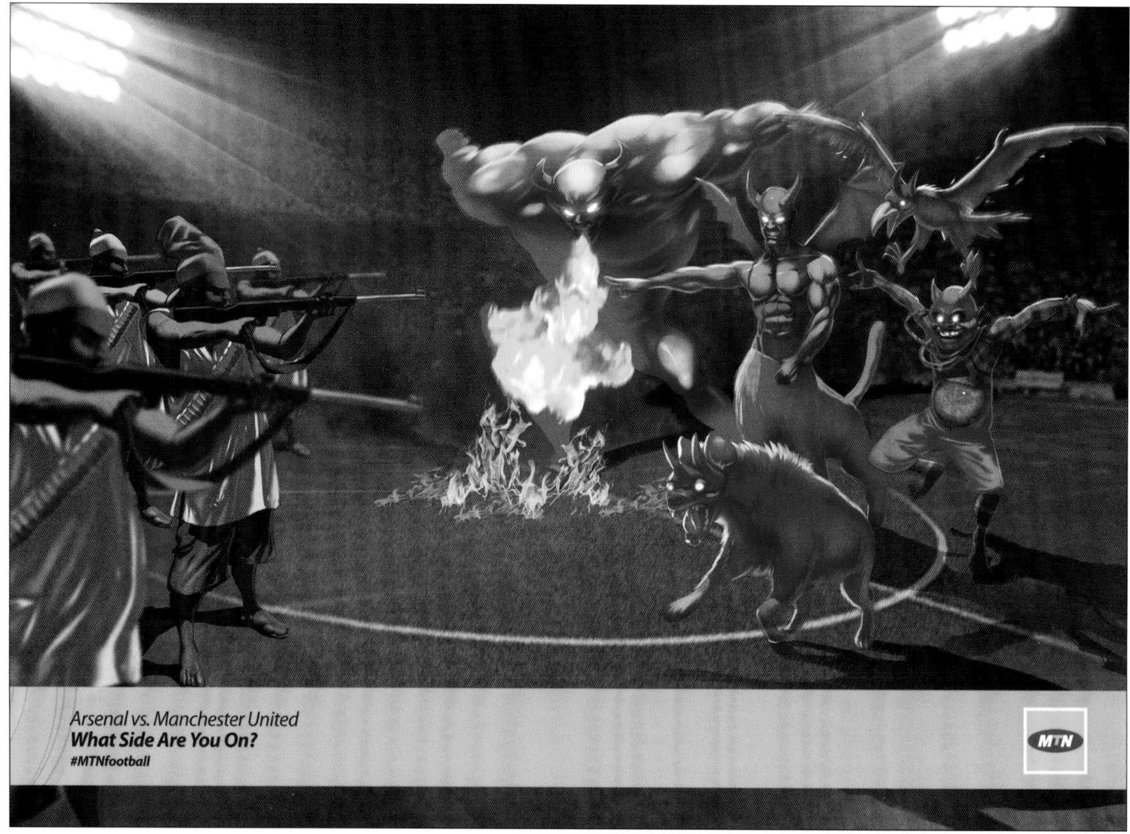
Arsenal vs. Manchester United
What Side Are You On?
#MTNfootball
MTN

Arsenal vs. Chelsea
What Side Are You On?
#MTNfootball
MTN

Agency	DDB Lagos
Creative Director	Babatunde Sule
Copywriter	Chuka Obi
Art Director	Emmanuel Ogabi
Illustrator	Jide-Obi Okonkwo
Advertiser	MTN, "MTN Football Battles"

Two soccer clashes: Arsenal are known as The Gunners after the cannon symbol on their club crest. Meanwhile, Manchester United's symbol is a red devil, and the district of Chelsea is famous for its distinctive bridge across the Thames.

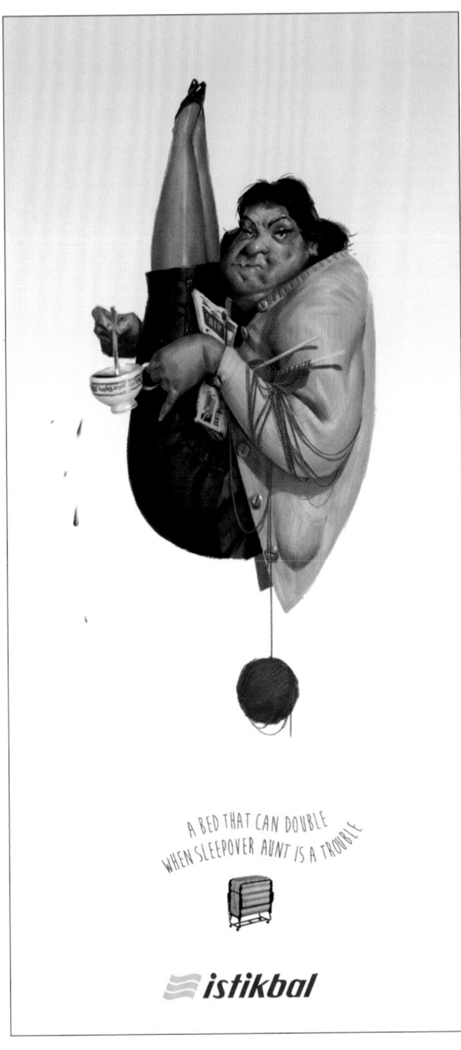

Agency	Havas Worldwide Istanbul
Creative Director	Ergin Binyildiz
Copywriters	Merve Selamet Ozlem Ozel
Art Director	Çetin Yildiz
Agency Producers	Özge Göksel Sıla Salgın
Illustrator	Michal Lisowski
Graphic Design	Hasan Yildirim
Advertiser	Istikbal, "The Unexpected Guest"

The words that can kill a child.

One single word of love can change your whole day. In the same way, words like "whore", "fatso" or "nigger" can tear up large wounds when thrown at someone with full power. Especially if they are aimed against a child.

To become a target of harsh words in school, at the recreation center and in social media is more than anyone should have to endure. Often, the wounds become permanent. Occasionally, the harsh words lead to something even worse.

Suicide is the leading cause of death among young people in Sweden. Many times as a result of bullying. One of those who could not take it anymore was Måns. He had a great smile, liked old French cars and enjoyed listening to music. Måns was only 13 when he took his life.

This text is written in Måns' handwriting. We made the letters from his notes live on, to remind us that sometimes we need to look at the world from a child's perspective. When children no longer want to share our world, then we as adults have failed. For Måns' sake, and the sake of all the others - it's time to learn from our failures. You can spread a clear message.

Support the work against bullying, buy a Winged Word at friends.se

FRIENDS IS A NON-PROFIT ORGANIZATION WORKING TO PREVENT BULLYING.

DO YOU NEED SOMEONE TO TALK TO? CONTACT THE SUICIDE PREVENTION (MIND.SE) OR BRIS (BRIS.SE). SUICIDE CAN BE PREVENTED. MORE INFO AT SUICIDEZERO.SE

friends

Agency Lowe Brindfors, Stockholm
Copywriter Martin Bartholf
Art Directors Petter Lublin, Rikard Linder, Jeremy Phang
Graphic Designer Noel Pretorius
Final Art Patrik Oscarsson
Executive Digital Prod. Sofia Jönsson
Technical Producer Tobias Löfgren
Advertiser Friends - Anti Bullying Organization, "Anti-Bullying Typeface"

This poster for an anti-bullying campaign is written in a typeface created by sampling the handwriting of a boy who, tragically, committed suicide rather than endure further bullying.

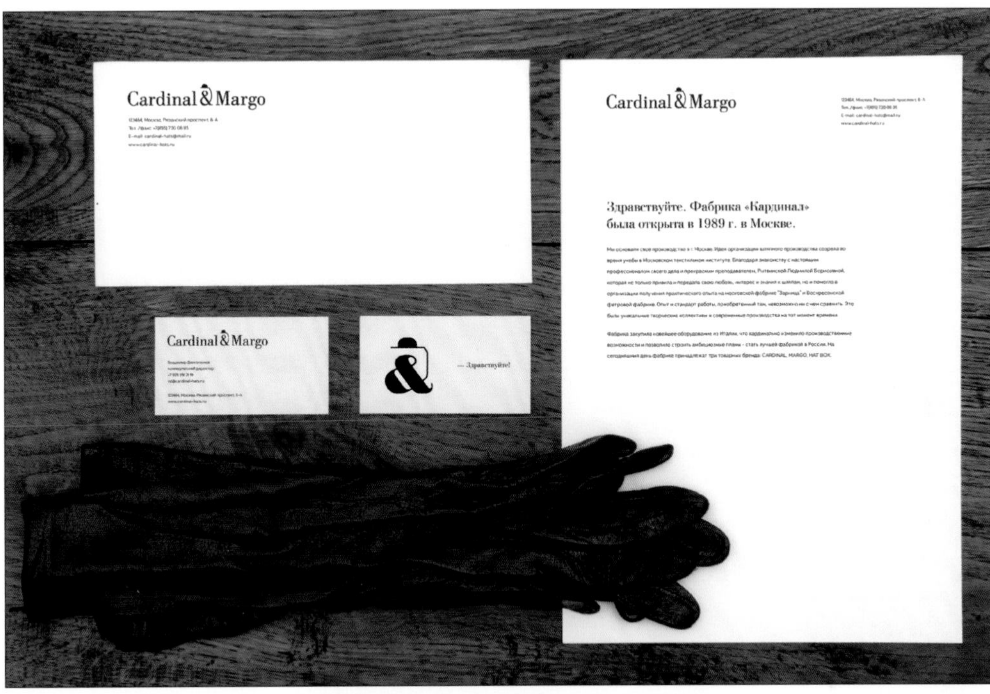

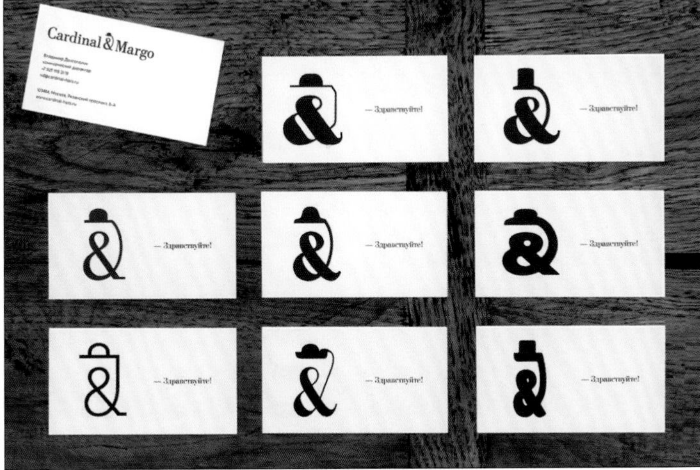

Agency	Suprematika, Moscow
Creative Director	Vova Lifanov
Advertiser	Cardinal&Margo, "Cardinal&Margo"

Cardinal & Margo is a Moscow hat shop founded in 1989. Its hats for men and women are made with felt, suede, angora, straw – and with love. For the brand's new identity, the ampersand in the name became a gentleman tipping his hat.

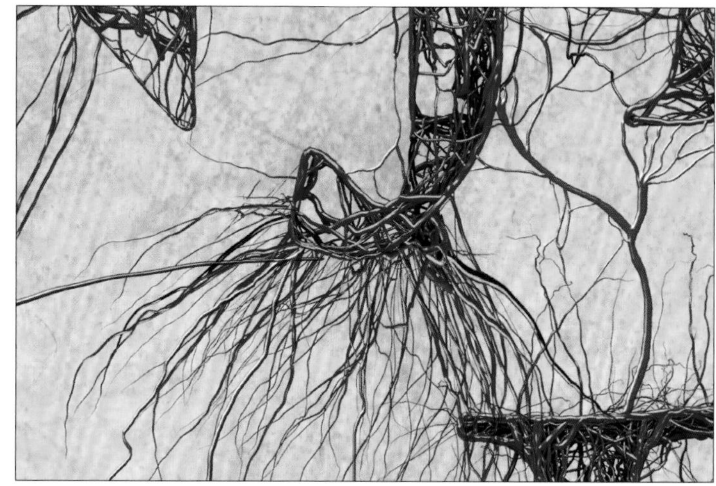

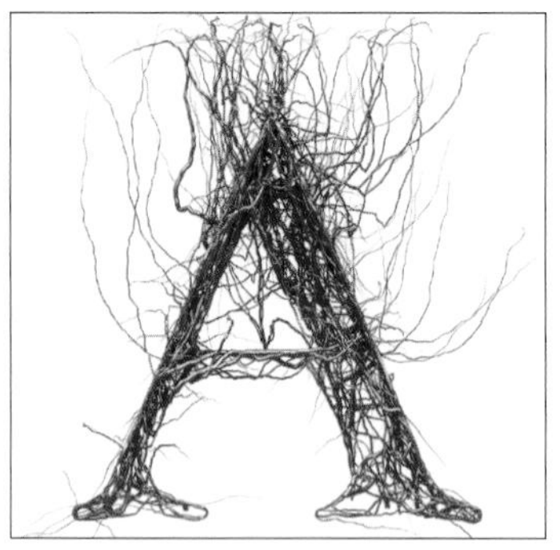

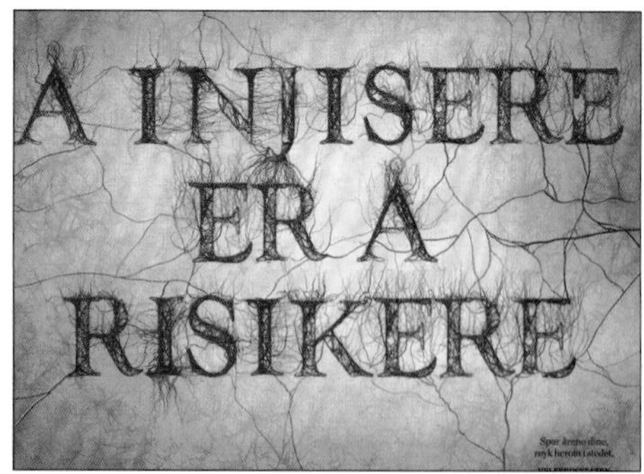

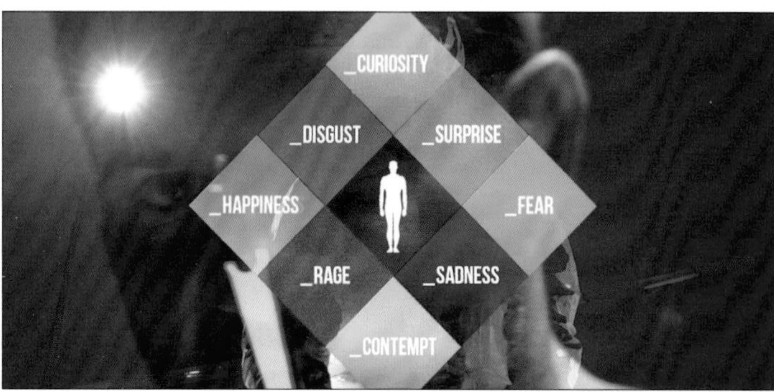

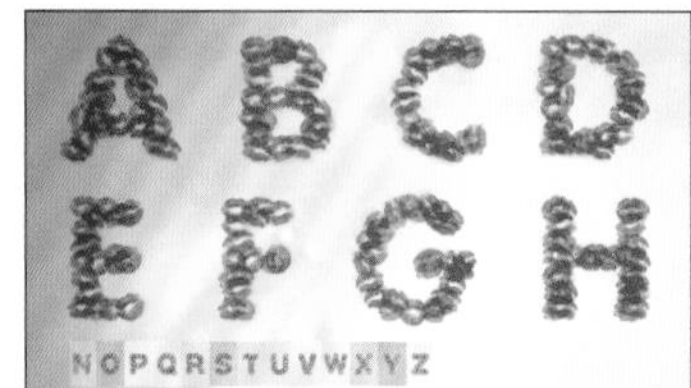

Agency Kitchen Leo Burnett, Oslo
CDs Per Erik Jarl, Christian Hygen
Copywriters Christian Hygen, Carina Lindberg
Art Director Per Erik Jarl
Production Kill Your Image
Illustrator Even
Graphic Design Pia Lystad
Typographer Vrender
Advertiser The Norwegian Agency of Welfare, "Written in The Veins"

Drawing attention to the dangers of injecting heroin by creating "vein letters". The posters were put up in places where heroin users often go to shoot up.

Agency FCB, Zurich
Creative Director Dennis Lück
Copywriter Sören Schröder
Art Director Marcin Baba
Production WirzFraeffelPaal, Zurich
Typographer Stefan Grandjean, START
Programmer Sebastian Palka
Advertiser MTV Mobile, "The Emography Project"

Text messages are pretty boring unless you add an emoji or two. But this design put the emotions in the letters themselves. The new "emography" featured tear-stained letters, kiss letters, and even letters written with an angry raised middle finger. The client was MTV Mobile.

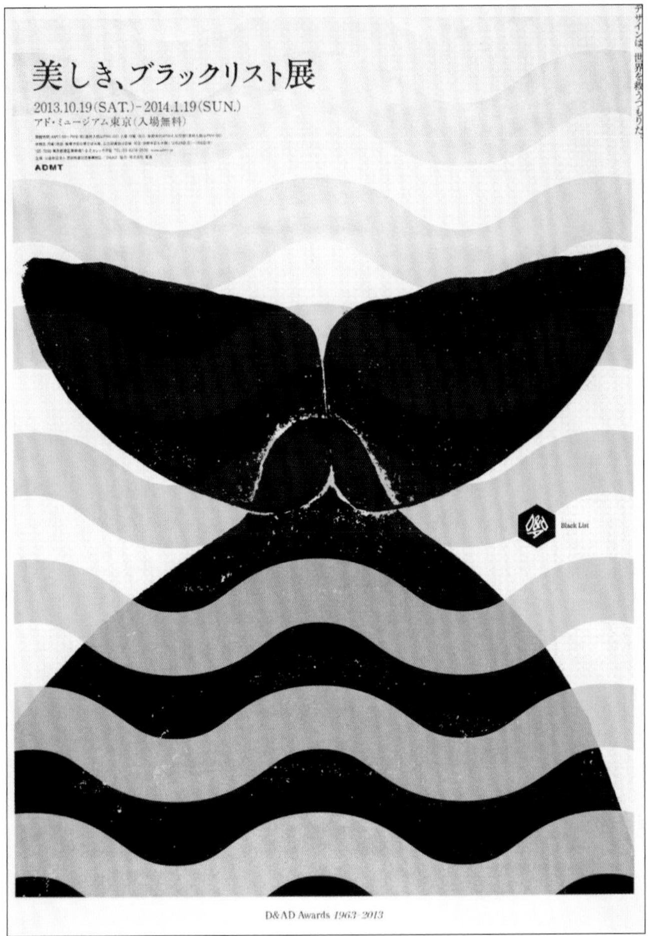

Agency	Dentsu, Tokyo
Executive CD	Yuya Furukawa
Creative Director	Yoshihiro Yagi
Copywriters	Haruko Tsutsui
	Nao Sakamoto
Art Director	Yoshihiro Yagi
Producer	Yoshiko Tomita
Production	Creative Power Unit, Tokyo
Illustrator	Nao Morimi
Graphic Design	Minami Otsuka
	Daisuke Hatakeyama
Typographer	Yoshihiro Ito
Printing Producer	Shinya Tamura
Advertiser	Yoshida Hideo Memorial Foundation/Advertising Museum Tokyo, D&AD 2013 Exhibition in Japan, "The Beautiful Black List"

The Beautiful Black List was an exhibition in Japan celebrating the 50th anniversary of the D&AD by showing winners of the Black Pencil, its highest award. To promote the show, the whale was chosen as a design motif for its extraordinary power. The agency also designed the exhibition itself.

Agency	CHI & Partners, London
Executive CD	Jonathan Burley
Creative Directors	Jay Phillips Neil Clarke Richard Brim Daniel Fisher
Copywriter	Matt Searle
Art Director	Sarah Levitt
Graphic Design	Matt Hunt
Advertiser	The Prince's Trust, "The Tomorrow Project"

With youth unemployment in the UK at 1.2 million, the Prince's Trust (Prince Charles's charity) wanted to invest in the future of young people. The solution was the Tomorrow project. Established designers partnered with young talents to create "tomorrow's products". These were sold online and in a pop-up "Tomorrow's Store" in London. The space was modular, enabling each of the young designers to customise it, showcase their products and tell their story.

Agency	Bold, Stockholm
Creative Director	Oskar Lübeck
Brand Strategist	Carl-Fredrik af Sandeberg
Designers	Nick Greening Richard Feldéus
Photographers	Bsmart Elisabeth Toll
Advertiser	The Shirt Factory, "The Shirt Factory - Visual Identity"

A new visual identity designed to take the wrinkles out of The Shirt Factory, a brand launched in 1988. The focal point is a detailed crest made of tailoring equipment, paired with a strong yellow colour. The crest signals attention to detail, while the colour suggests youth and confidence.

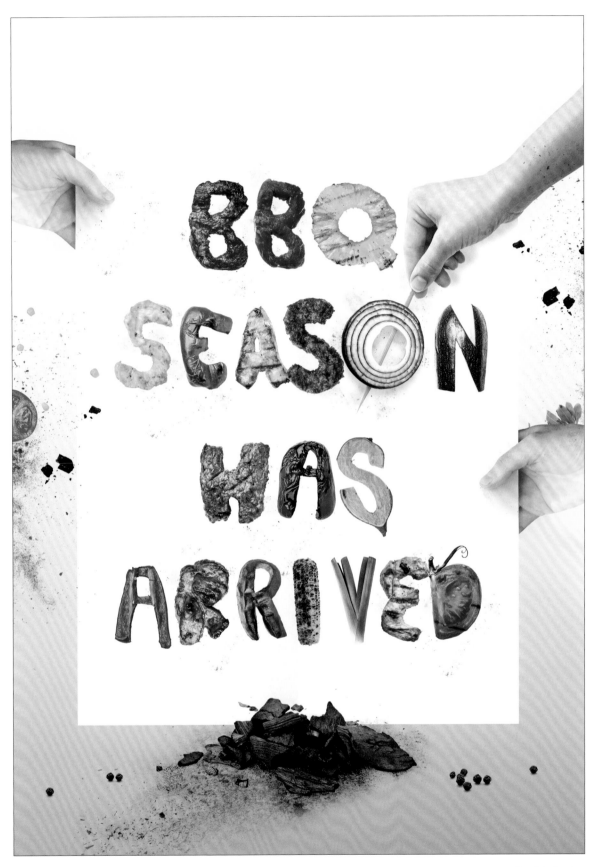

Agency Anti Inc., Oslo
Creative Directors Erik Heisholt, Kjetil Wold
Copywriter Erik Heisholt
Art Directors Kjetil Wold, Jason Kinsella
Photographer Colin Eick
Production Handverk AS, Sande
Film Director Anders Bergh Halvorsen
Agency Producer Kjersti Brinch Lund
Illustrator Handverk AS
Graphic Design Mats Ottdal, Fredrik Melby, Magnus Henriksen
Typographer Handverk AS
Advertiser Rimi, "Grillography"

For a poster campaign for Norwegian grocery chain Rimi, the designers of Anti Inc focused on barbecue season, a national tradition. They bought products from the store, meticulously hand-carved them into an alphabet, and grilled them. The letters were then photographed for the campaign. "Grillography" – a new typographic language for Rimi.

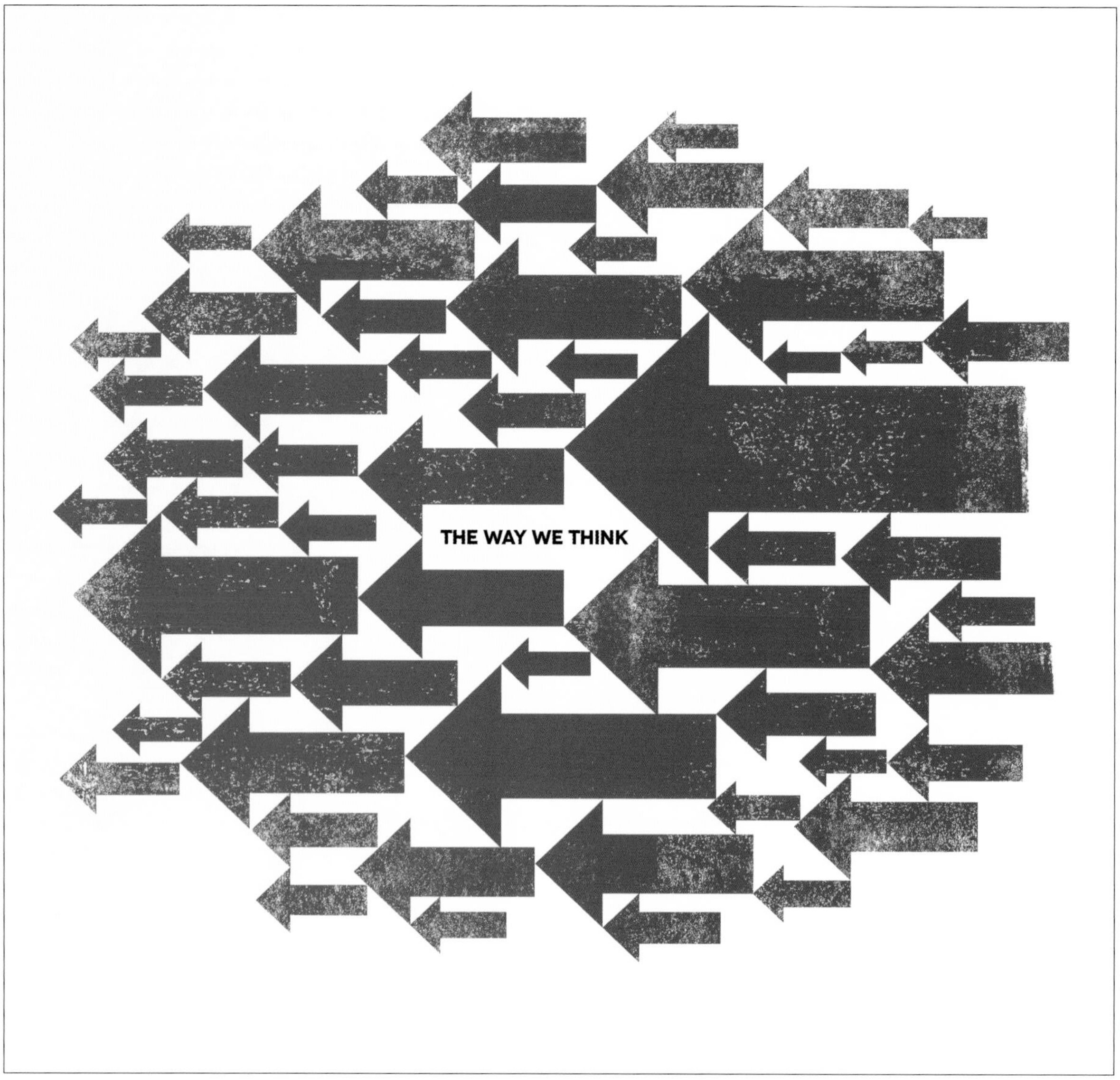

THE WAY WE THINK

Agency Turner Duckworth, London & San Francisco
Executive CDs David Turner, Bruce Duckworth
Designer David Blakemore
Artworker James Norris
Advertiser Turner Duckworth, London & San Francisco
Poster,
"The Way We Think"

Bruce Duckworth, co-founder of brand design studio Turner Duckworth, gave a lecture at the Mudam modern art museum in Luxembourg.

Agency Turner Duckworth, London & San Francisco
Executive CDs David Turner, Bruce Duckworth
Creative Director Paula Talford
Designers Mathilde Solanet, David Blakemore
Artworker James Norris
Advertiser Kim and John Buckland, Sandpiper,
"Sandpiper Logo"

Agency	New Agency, Vilnius
Creative Director	Tomas Ramanauskas
Copywriter	Tomas Ramanauskas
Designer	Lina Marcinonyte
Photographer	Darius Petrulaitis
Illustrator	David Schiesser
Advertiser	Drama Burger, Restaurant Design, "Drama Burger"

There are fast food burgers – and then there are gourmet burgers, like the ones served up by Drama Burger in Vilnius. The store identity features plenty of drama, from the crossed-out letter in the name to the illustrations, accompanied by phrases describing the drama of choosing your favourite dish.

Agency	Kira Alleinova Advertising Agency, St. Petersburg
Creative Director	Ruben Monakhov
Art Director	Milena Gogolitsyna
Advertiser	Sigma Video, "The Gymnastics in Office"

Promotional material for a group of personal trainers who will come to your office and exercise with your staff.

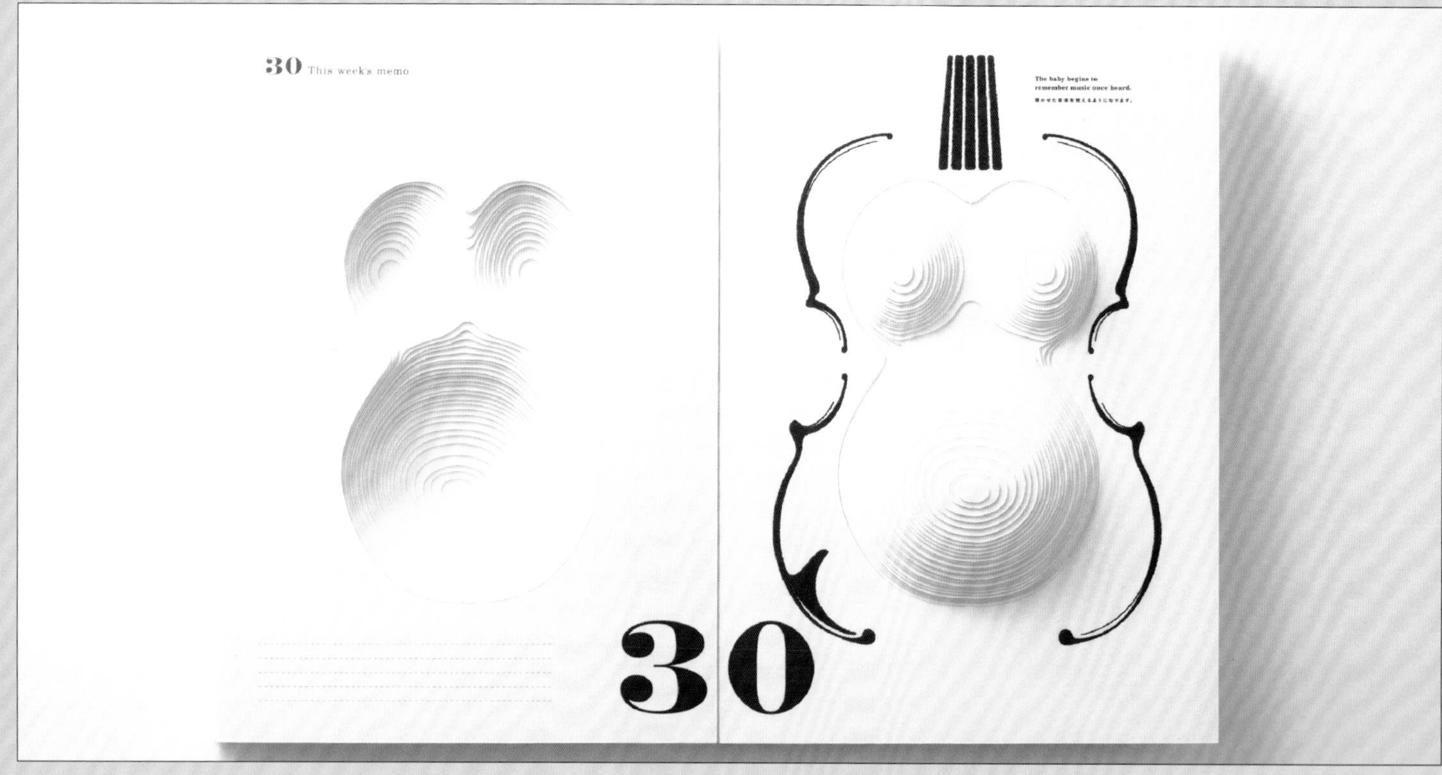

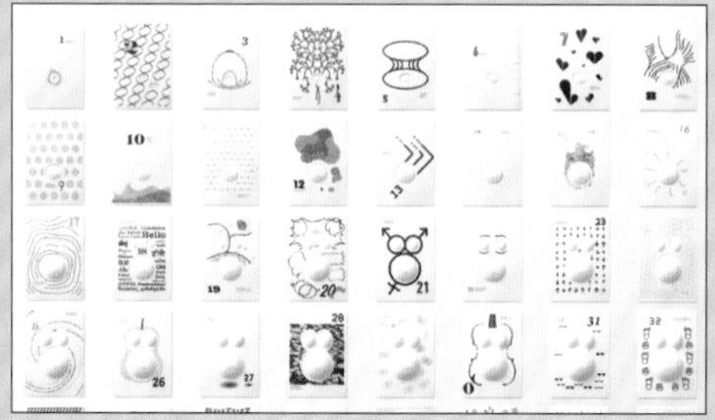

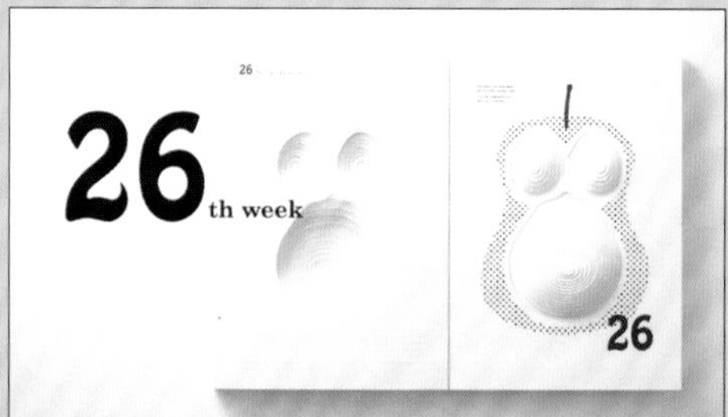

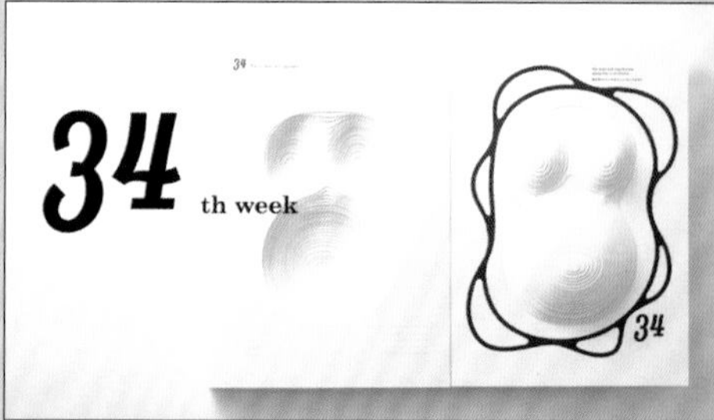

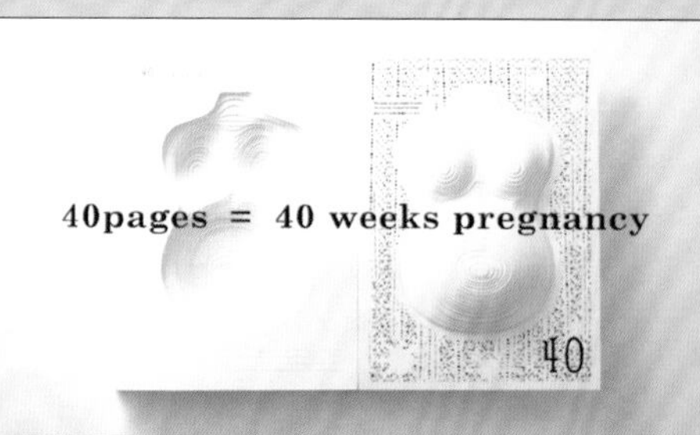

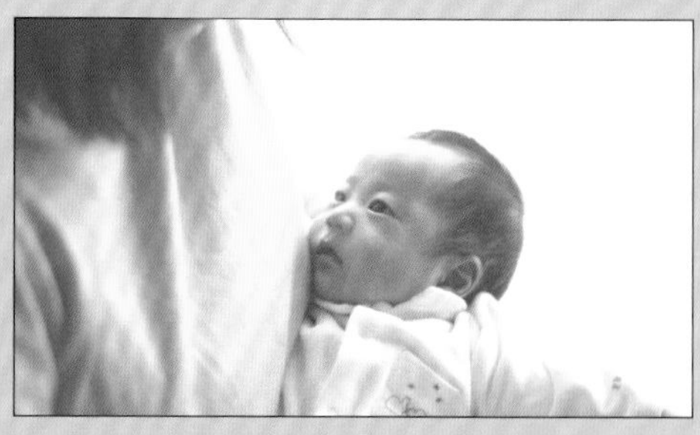

 Publication Design 

Agency Dentsu, Nagoya
CCOs Kazunari Nagatomo, Tomio Nakaue
Executive CD Mamoru Yamashita
Creative Directors Kishiomi Wakahara, Michihito Dobashi
Copywriters Jyunichi Tawara, Kanako Wada, Kotoha Tanaka
Art Director Michihito Dobashi
Agency Producers Shigeki Wada, Ryuhei Torii
Designers Masao Shirasawa, Tomoko Takeda
Photographer Yoshihiro Ozaki
Retouchers Tomohiro Koyama, Hiroaki Ishikawa, Runa Inagaki
Director Yoshitaka Kondo
Cinematographer Yoshihiro Ozaki
Film Producer Tsutomu Kondo
Advertiser Kishokai Medical Corporation, Bell-Net Obstetrics, "Mother Book"

Bell-Net Obstetrics wanted to capture the magic of pregnancy and childbirth. Hence The Mother Book: 40 pages to match the weeks of the gestation period. Each page informs mothers about the current stage of their pregnancy, with room for a diary entry. And as you can see, the book grows with the baby.

Agency Marimo, Rome
Creative Directors Paola Manfroni, Assunta Squitieri
Copywriter Alessandro Canale
Art Director Paola Manfroni
Production Fabrizio Guadagnoli, Rome
Illustrator Tommaso Guerra
Graphic Design Giampiero Quaini
Advertiser Studio Universal, Satellite TV Channel, "Goodbye Film"

Celluloid film has been replaced with digital formats. The Studio Universal film calendar is a tribute to film and to the magical work of the film editor. Created using 12 pieces of genuine celluloid, each representing a cinematic genre, and all bearing the marks of the film editor's pencil.

Agency Leo Burnett, Colombo
CCO Trevor Kennedy
CDs Eraj Wirasinha, Athula Kathriarachchi
Art Directors Sithum Walter, Shayani Obeyesekera
Copywriters Malaka Samith, Farzad Mohideen, Dileep Kulathunga
Advertiser Mawbima, "The World's First Mosquito Repellent Newspaper"

To promote National Dengue Week in Sri Lanka, the newspaper Mawiba was printed with a mix of citronella – a natural mosquito repellent – and ink, thus protecting readers while informing them. Posters at bus shelters and patches for kids were also printed with the special ink. The idea spread beyond Sri Lanka and inspired other newspaper owners to do the same. Print is not dead – and it can even save lives.

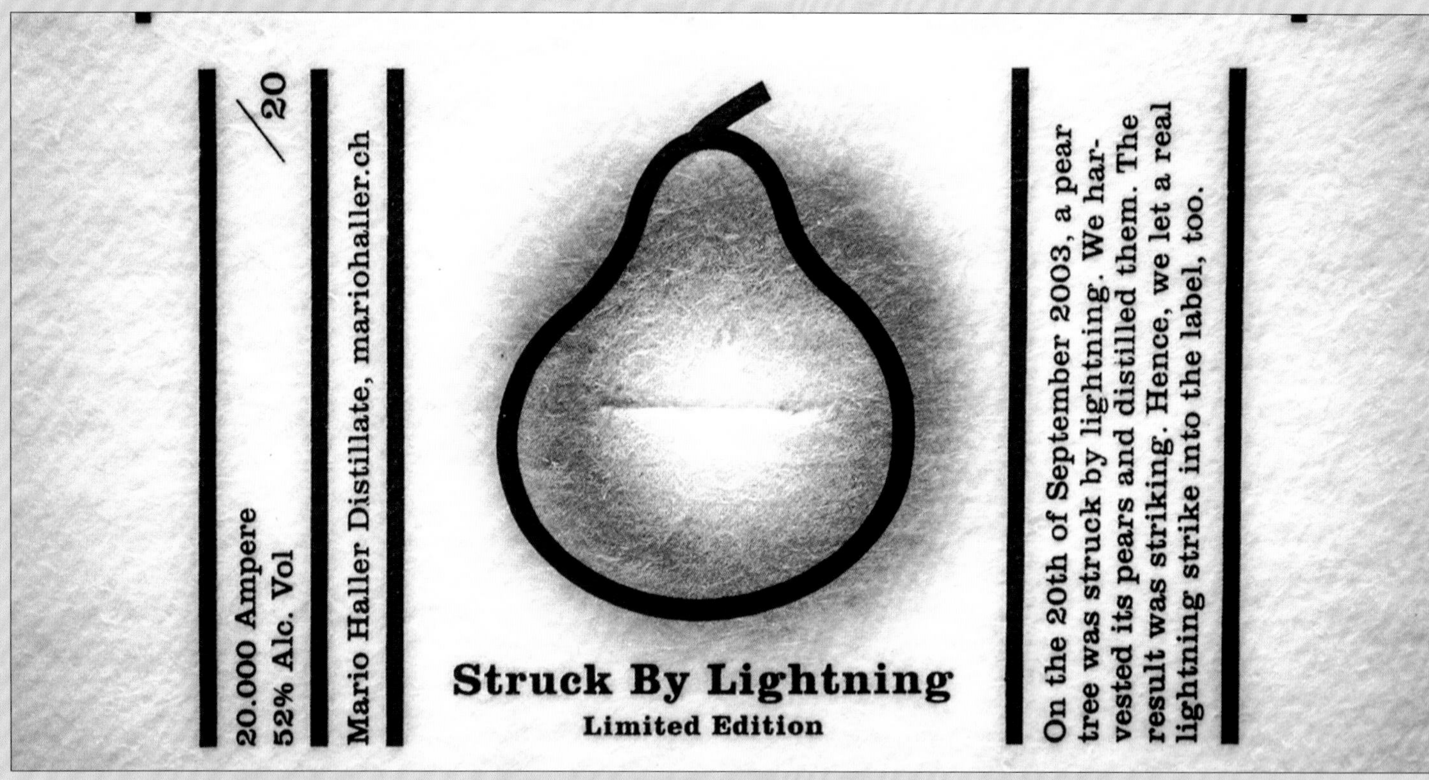

20.000 Ampere
52% Alc. Vol
/20
Mario Haller Distillate, mariohaller.ch
Struck By Lightning
Limited Edition
On the 20th of September 2003, a pear tree was struck by lightning. We harvested its pears and distilled them. The result was striking. Hence, we let a real lightning strike into the label, too.

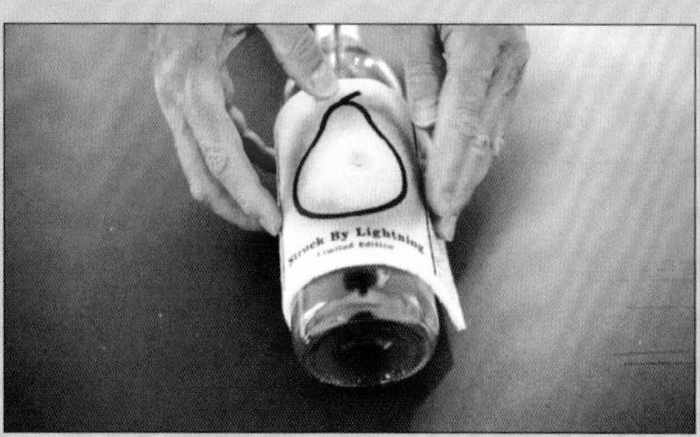

326 Packaging Design

Agency Leo Burnett, Zurich
Creative Directors Axel Eckstein, Christian Bircher
Copywriter Bastian Otter
Art Director Christian Bircher
Illustrator Christian Bircher
Advertiser Mario Haller, "Lightning"

When a pear tree in Mario Haller's orchard was hit by lightning, he decided to distil a limited edition batch of brandy from its fruit. The agency responded by creating a unique label. A sheath of heat-resistant paper was attached to a lightning rod. When a bolt of lightning finally struck the rod it left a burn mark on every sheet of paper. These were then used for the labels.

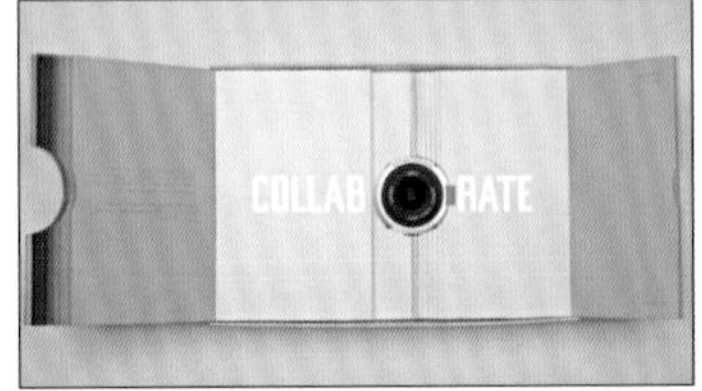

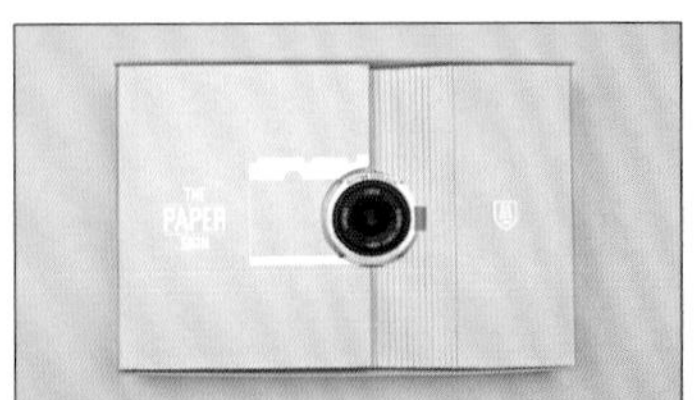

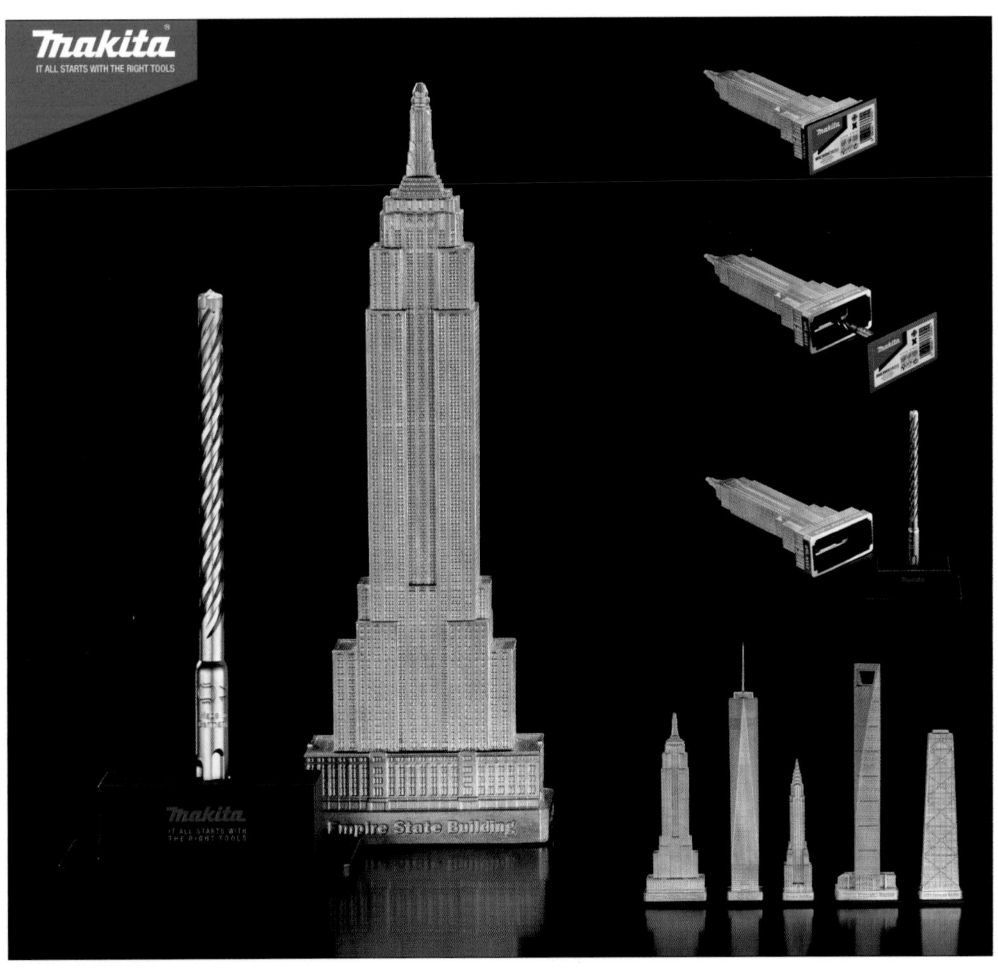

Agency	Geometry Global, Berlin
CCO	Christian Mommertz
CD Branding & Design	Felix Dürichen
Sr. Copywriter	Sabine Weber
Sr. Art Director	Sabine Brinkmann
Art Director	Martin Wojciechowski
Media Designer	Johanna Woetzel
Type Design	Stefan Hecht
Advertiser	Fedrigoni Fine Paper, "The Paper Skin"

To demonstrate the amazingly resistant qualities of Fedrigoni's "constellation jade" packaging paper, the material was used in place of the leather facing on the Leica X2 – the camera of adventurers. The camera was then placed inside a limited edition sample book, which also told the story of the Fedrigoni brand. The books were used as a PR tool and sold for 3,900 euros each.

Agency	Leo Burnett, Frankfurt
Creative Directors	Hans-Juergen Kaemmerer
CCO	Andreas Pauli
Copywriter	Benjamin Merkel
Art Directors	Hugo Moura Hans-Juergen Kaemmerer
Photographer	Thomas Balzer
Agency Producer	Netti Weber
Artbuyer	Cornelia Richter
Advertiser	Makita, "Makita Drill Packagings"

The greatest skyscrapers began with the right tools. Makita has been making tools, including drills, since 1915. This special edition pack was placed on the shelves of Makita dealers and sent as a direct mailing to architects, contractors, journalists and bloggers.

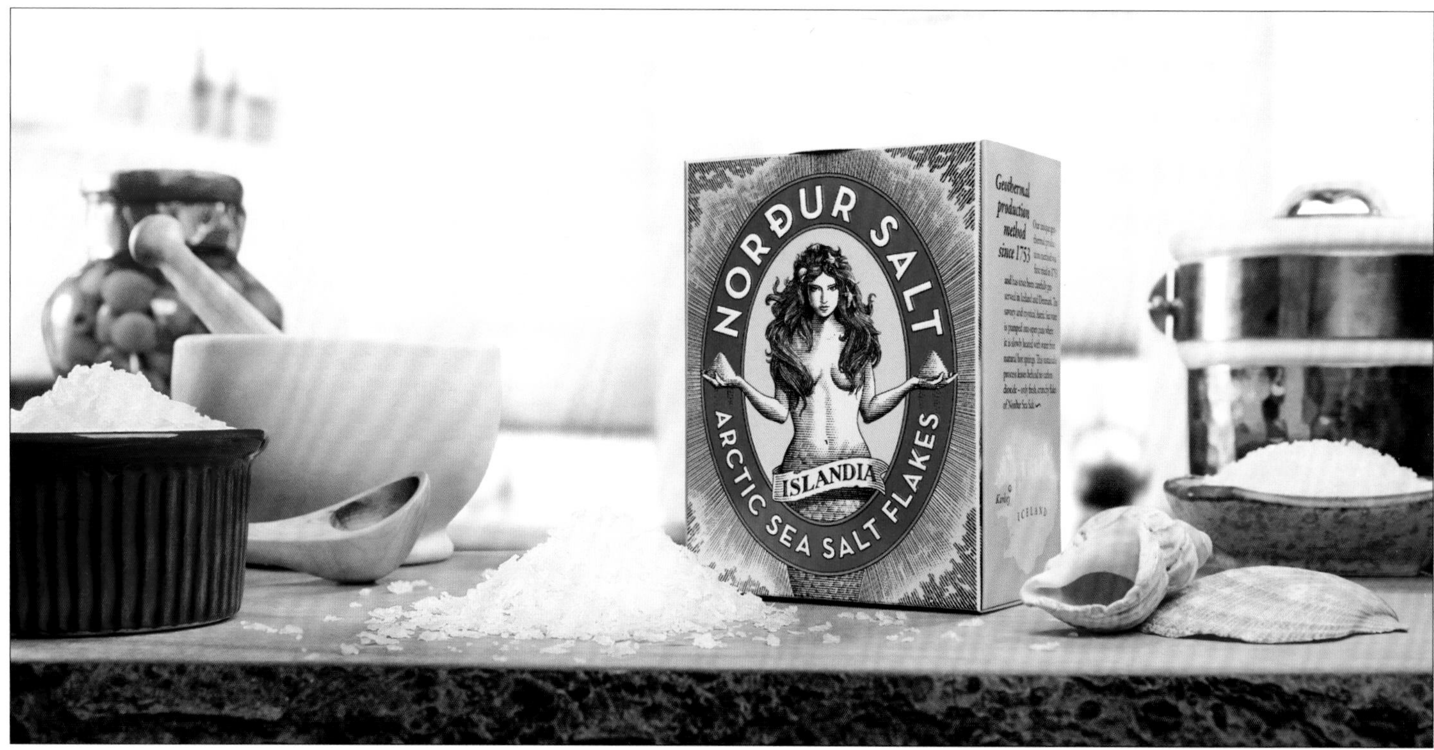

Agency Ohmybrand, Moscow
Creative Director Nadie Parshina
Copywriter Svetlana Chugunova
Photographer Polina Tverdaya
Illustrator Dmitry Hendrikson
Advertiser TrueGlove, "TrueGlove"

TrueGlove domestic gloves are printed with tattoos for a fun and fashionable vintage touch. The packaging is designed to look like the cover of a fashion magazine. It includes a QR code that leads to the manufacturer's website, where consumers can shop for more tattooed gloves for their collection.

Agency Jónsson & Le'macks, Reykjavík
Creative Director Albert Muñoz
Copywriter Huldar Breiðfjörð
Art Director Siggi Odds
Illustrator Mark Summers
Graphic Design Thorleifur Gunnar Gíslason
Product designer Jón Helgi Hólmgeirsson
Advertiser Norðursalt, "Norðursalt packaging"

Agency Artemov Artel, Kiev
Art Directors Sergii Artemov
Gera Artemova
Designer Sergii Artemov
Illustrator Sergii Artemov
Advertiser Paradise. Gourmet-Club™, "Exotic Coffee Collection"

Exotic coffee packaging featuring mystical figures from each country, such as Tiki (Hawaii) and Mahakala (Nepal).

Agency Brand Union, Stockholm
Executive CD Mattias Lindstedt
Production No Picnic
Design Director Jesper Klarin
Designer Dag Forsberg
Client Director Ted Carlström
Advertiser The Absolut Company, "Absolut Contemporary Flavors"

Images of fruit on a fruit-flavoured vodka? Not for an innovative brand like Absolut. Instead a "hand-made" approach was taken to capture the essence of each flavour using paper, pen and brush.

Agency	Vozduh, St. Petersburg
Creative Director	Valeriy Melnik
Art Director	Roman Luzanov
Advertiser	TM VIZIT condoms, "VIZIT"

Agency	Amelung Design, Hamburg
Executive CD	Jonathan Sven Amelung
Editor	Alicia Maritza Amelung
Idea & Concept	Jonathan Sven Amelung
Illustrator	Angela Wittchen
Design	Jonathan Sven Amelung
3D Artist	Daniel Yaqub
Advertiser	Lingua Simplex, "Language Play. Language Learning."

Packaging for a "pairs" card game which involves matching verbs with pictures of the corresponding action. The act of opening the boxes made the characters come to life.

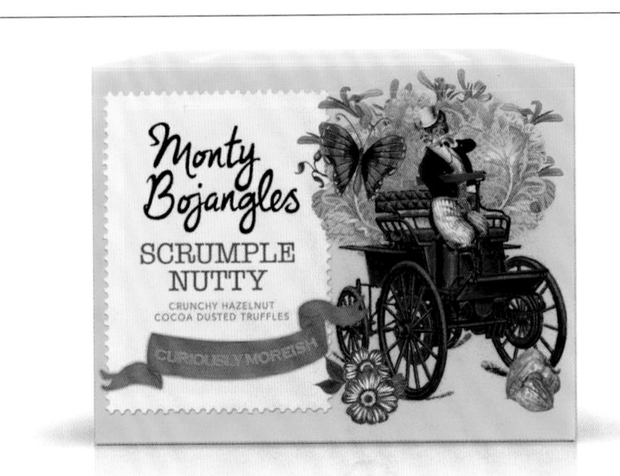

Agency	Springetts Brand Design Consultants, London
Creative Directors	Andy Black Sue Bicknell
Illustrator	Amy Matthews
Graphic Design	Amy Matthews
Advertiser	Monty Bojangles, "Monty Bojangles"

Each box shows a new "adventure in taste" with a mixture of Victorian etchings, original botanical drawings and hand-painted illustrations.

Agency	Geometry Global, Moscow
Executive CD	Andrew Ushakov
Copywriter	Darya Ushakova
Art Director	Alexandra Istratova
Illustrators	Alexandra Istratova Alexander Koshkin
Advertiser	Moscow Farmer, "Layer Hen"

Agency	Depot WPF, Moscow
Creative Director	Alexey Fadeev
Art Director	Vera Zvereva
Designer	Maria Ponomareva
Advertiser	Milk & Honey Land, Organic products delivery, "Delivery Of Meat And Emotions"

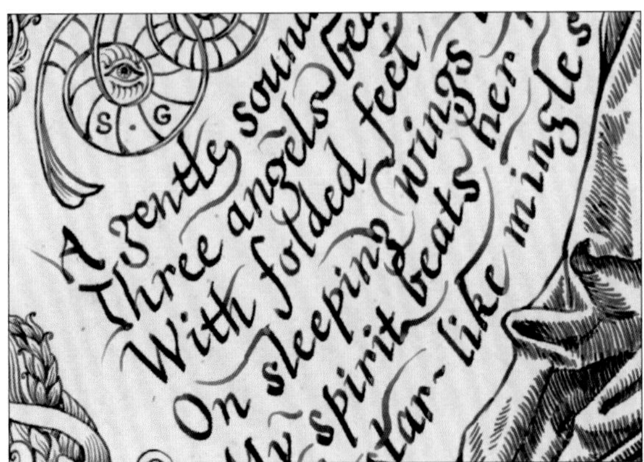

Agency Depot WPF, Moscow
Creative Director Alexey Fadeev
Copywriter Ekaterina Lavrova
Art Director Alexandr Zagorsky
Illustrator Vadim Briksin
Typographer Julia Zhdanova
Advertiser Crianzas y Viñedos R. Reverte, "Label Gap"

Agency SeriesNemo, Barcelona
Creative Director Jokin Arregui
Art Director Jokin Arregui
Branding SeriesNemo
Naming SeriesNemo
Graphic Design SeriesNemo
Advertiser Mediterranean Premium Spirits GINRAW, "GINRAW, Gastronomic Gin"

Agency TBWA\España, Madrid
Creative Directors Juan Sañchez, Guillermo Ginés, Vicente Rodriguez
Copywriter Desirée Heranz
Art Director Miguel De María, Raquel Benito
Production TBWA\España, Madrid
Agency Producer Nuria Mazarío
Illustrator Oscar Gutiérrez
Advertiser DYC, "Málaga Fair Special Edition Bottle"

A special edition of DYC 8 whisky celebrating Malaga, birthplace of Picasso, for the city's annual feria. Illustrator Óscar Gutiérrez provided drawings inspired by the artist.

Agency	STUDIOIN, Moscow
Creative Director	Arthur Schreiber
Graphic Design	Pavla Chuykina
Digital Artwork	Maksim Kadashov
General Director	Roman Inkeles
Advertiser	Comon Sava Wine, "Comon Sava"

Russian wine brand Comon Sava takes its name from the French expression "Comment ça va?" or "How's it going?" But "sava" also sounds like the Russian word for "owl".

Agency	:OTVETDESIGN, Saint-Petersburg
Creative Director	Vladimir Fedoseev
Art Director	Arina Yushkevich
Illustrators	Vladimir Fedoseev Elena Kobeleva Suzanna Belkina
Graphic Design	Vladimir Fedoseev
Typographer	Vladimir Fedoseev
Advertiser	Sunfeel Horticultural Canned Food, "Sunfeel"

Sunfeel fruit and vegetables have no additives or chemicals and are grown the natural way, under real sunshine.

Agency	Voskhod, Yekaterinburg
Creative Director	Andrey Gubaydullin
Art Director	Vladislav Derevyannikh
Advertiser	Sansara Indie-Band, "The Best Of"

Agency	Pearlfisher, New York
Creative Director	Hamish Campbell
Advertiser	Blue Bottle Coffee, Blue Bottle New Orleans Iced Coffee, "Pearlfisher designs Blue Bottle RTD"

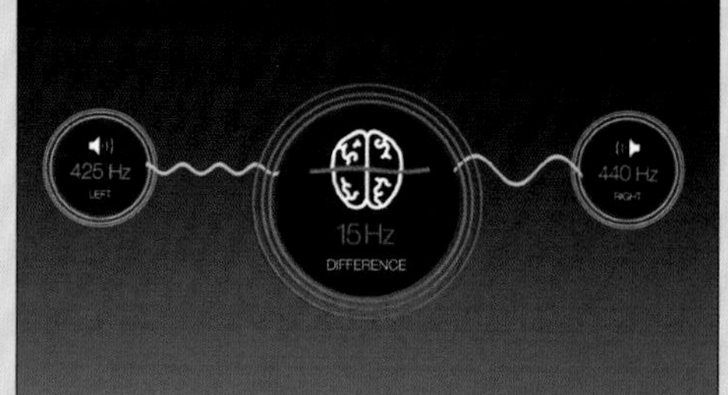

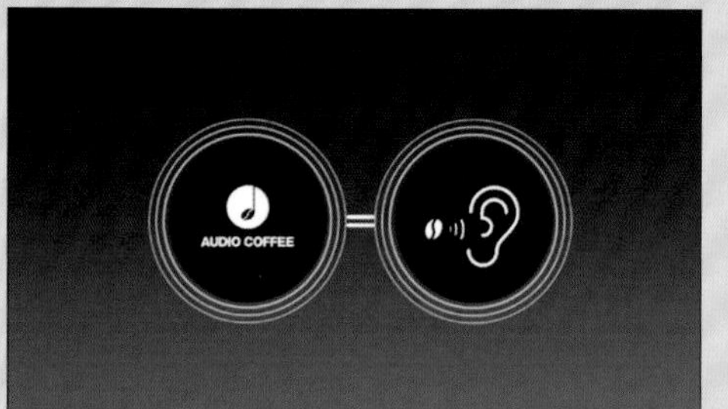

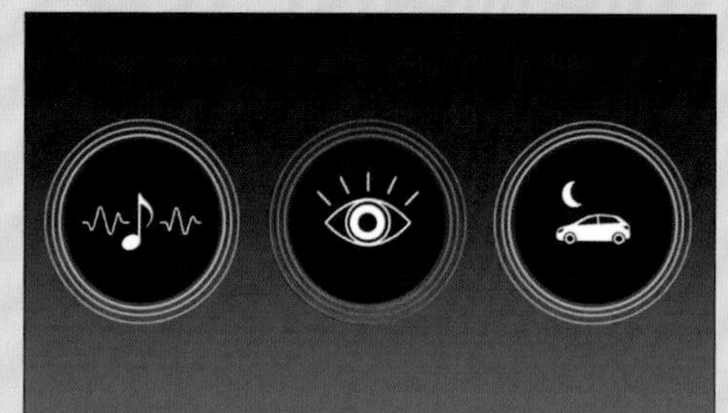

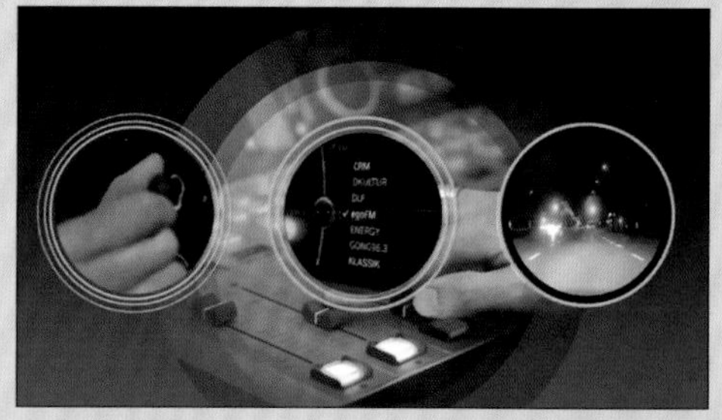

Agency plan.net / Serviceplan, Munich
CCO Alexander Schill
Executive CDs Christoph Everke, Matthias Harbeck, Till Diestel
CDs Nicolas Becker, Andreas Balog
Copywriters Michael Schoepf, Christoph Bohlender, Carola Luettringhaus
Art Director Walter Ziegler
Programmers Markus Mrugalla, Felix Ohr, Ret Lauterbach
Agency Producer Katy Pergelt
Executive Creative Prod. Florian Panier
Sound Design Infrasonics, Cologne; zimmerli sounds, Dusseldorf; m-sound, Munich
Advertiser Deli Star Bagel & Coffee, "Audio Coffee"

Audio Coffee, designed for night drivers, is "coffee" you can listen to. The music, created by famous deejays in partnership with Serviceplan Gruppe, played on the radio at night and included "binaural beats" to stimulate the brain – proven to keep people awake longer.

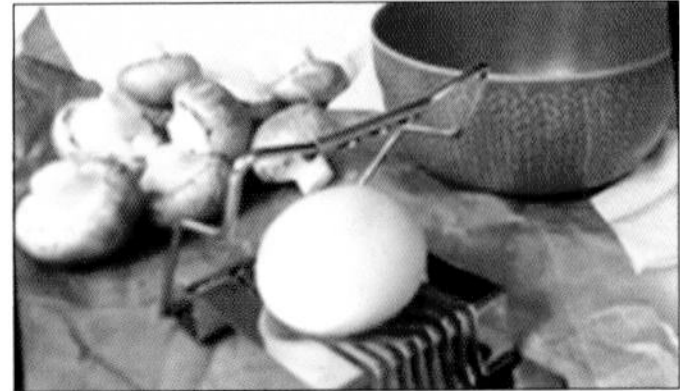

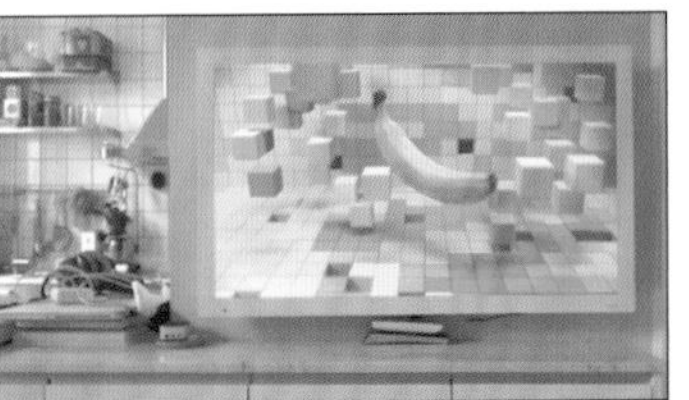

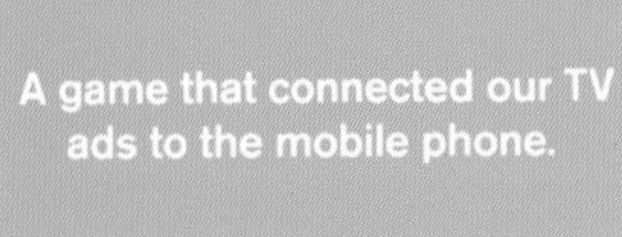

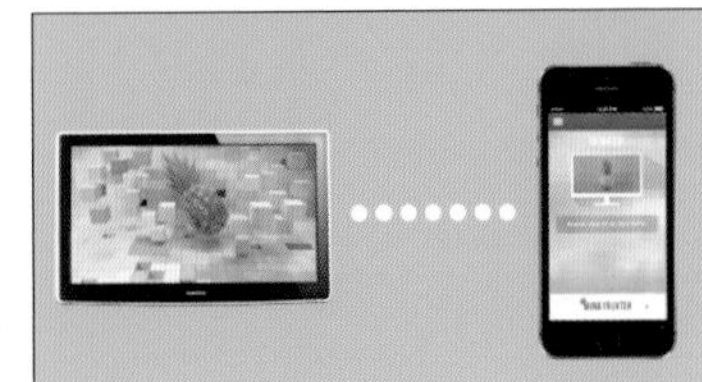

Agency Razorfish, Frankfurt
Creative Director Andreas Schmidl
Copywriters Guido Schröpel, Boris Jäger, Britta Seidel
Art Directors Leonore von Kalkreuth, Daniel Lichtmess
Photographer Anna Wegelin
Programmer Thorsten Diegel
Advertiser Nestlé, Maggi, "Maggi #Cookinghacks"

How do you transform instant food preparation into something inspirational? By providing "food hacks" online! Alongside Razorfish Germany, Maggi used Vine to teach pro cooking secrets in seconds, boosting social engagement by 250%.

Agency DDB Stockholm
Copywriter Stefan Gustafsson
Art Director Simon Higby
Digital Director Jon Dranger
Graphic Design Daniel Liljas
Designer Dennis Phang
Digital Producer Elisabet Halming
Retouch Christian Björnerhag
Director Kalle Haglund
3D Bastian Zakolski
Advertiser McDonald's, "Fruit Match"

This ingenious way of selling McDonald's fruit smoothies featured a TV ad that synced with a fruit-tastic gaming app, where users could win free smoothies. People could "up" their chances of winning by catching the ad on other channels.

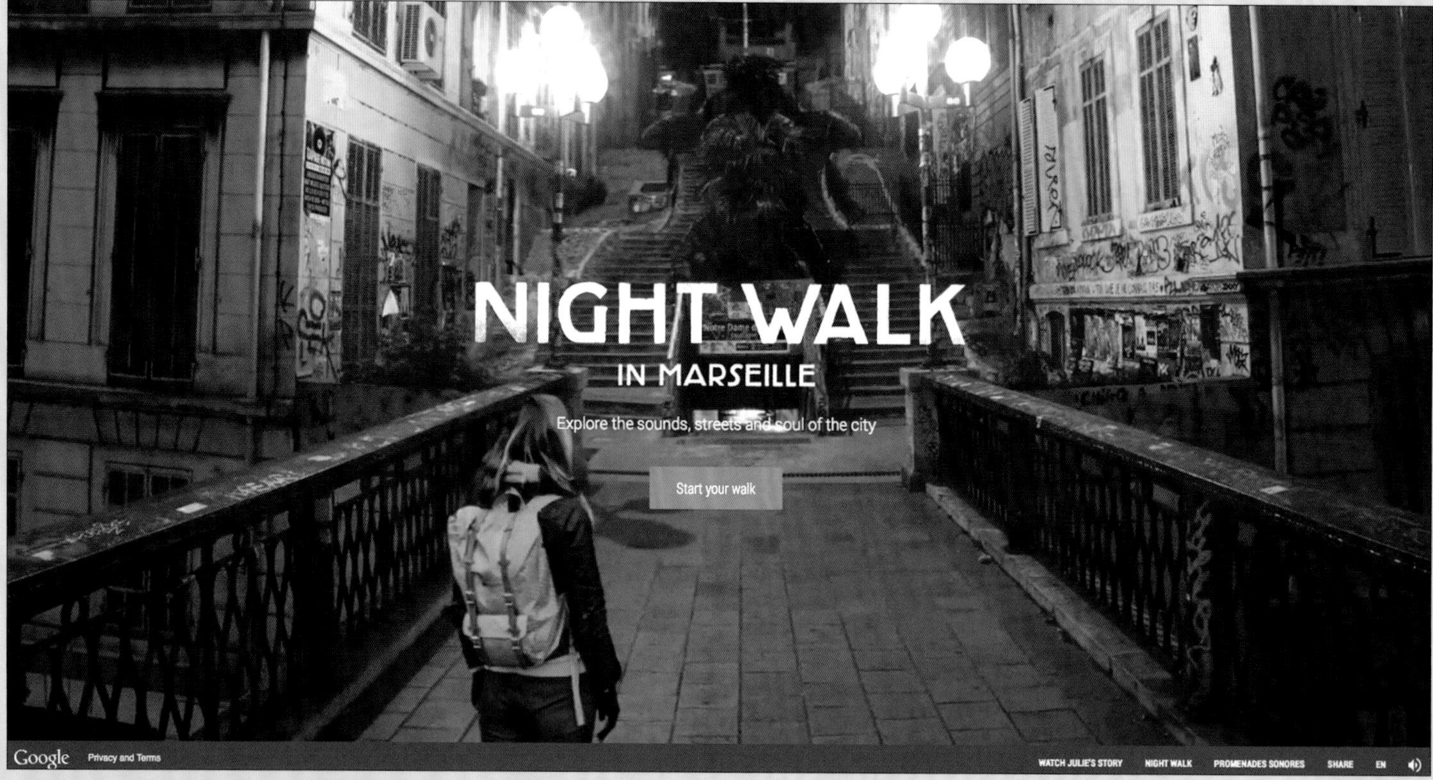

Agency	72andSunny, Amsterdam
Executive CD	Carlo Cavallone
Creative Directors	Gregg Clampffer Micky Coyne
Art Director	Patric Franz
Lead Writer	Yann Corlay
Broadcast Producer	Phil Mccluney
Digital Executive Prod.	Sanne Drogtrop
Creative Technologist	Gabor Szalatnyai
Film Production	Epoch Films, London
Directors	Lucid / Producer David Knox
Digital Production	Mediamonks, Amsterdam
Digital Producer	Xander Amo
Interactive Director	Jeroen Van De Meer
Production	Brenninkmeijer Issaacs, Amsterdam
Film Director	Joe Roberts
Photographer	Martijn Baudoin
2nd Contributing Co.	Google Creative Lab, London
Executive CD	Steve Vranakis
Senior Creative	David Bruno
Advertiser	Google, "Night Walk In Marseille"

Marseille: it's a misunderstood city, but it has its charms. Local resident and Google user Julie de Muer created an Audio Walks map to share what makes the city special. Impressed by her work, Google upped the ante, adding a visual layer to her maps that transformed her neighbourhood into a magical 360° experience. It generated over 88 million PR impressions… and hopefully a new perspective on Julie's hometown.

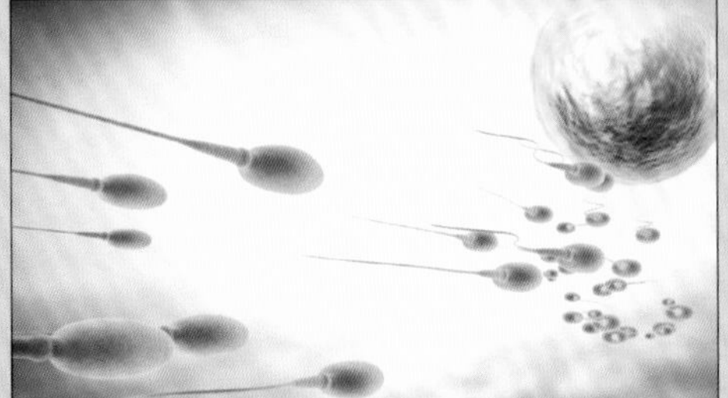

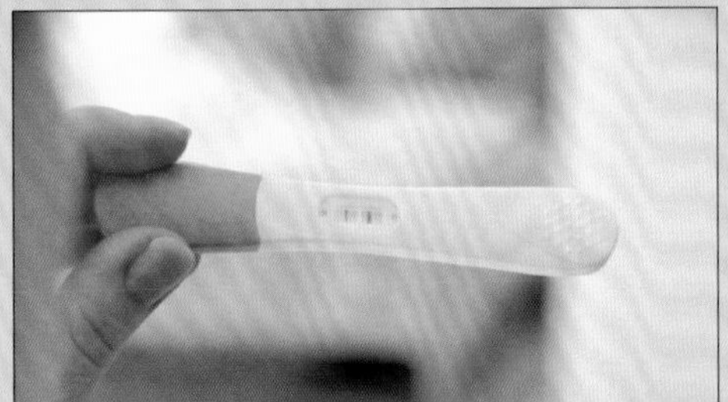

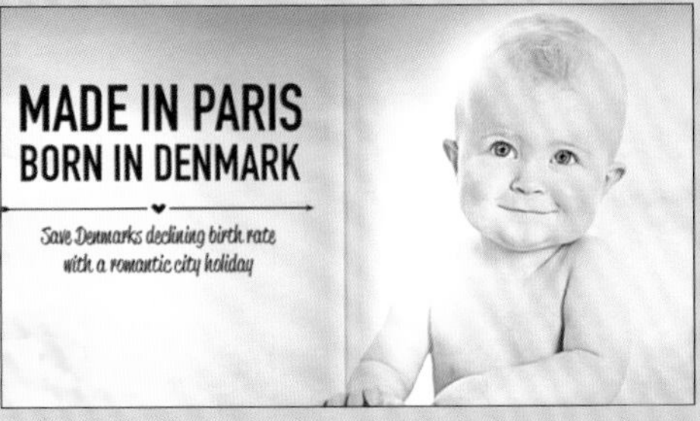

MADE IN PARIS
BORN IN DENMARK
Save Denmarks declining birth rate
with a romantic city holiday

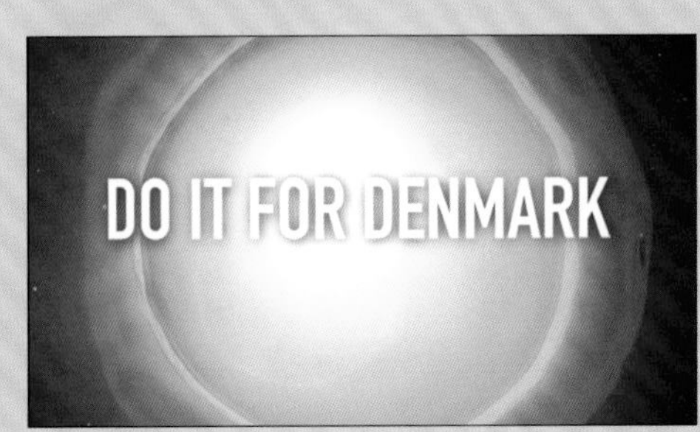

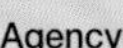

Agency	Robert Boisen & Like-minded, Copenhagen
Executive CD	Michael Robert
Creative Director	Heinrich Vejlgaard
Copywriter	James Godfrey
Designer	Morten Grundsøe
Dir. of Creative Tech.	Michael Bugaj
Production	Gobsmack Productions, Copenhagen
Film Director	Niels Nørløv
Executive Producer	Christina Erritzøe
DOP	Niels Thastum
Editor	Theis Schmidt
Line Producer	Cille Silverwood-Cope
VFX	Magnus Sveinn Jonsonn
Sound	Jason Luke, P47 Sound
Music	Upright Music
Seeding	Be On, Copenhagen
Advertiser	Spies Travels, "Do It For Denmark"

Spies Travel had an ambitious mission: improving Denmark's low birthrate. Using the insight that 10% of Danish children are conceived on holidays (thanks to a 46% higher likelihood of lovemaking), it launched a campaign encouraging people not just to book holidays, but to prove they'd conceived while away—with hopes of winning three years' worth of free baby supplies. Intrepid ladies who happened to be ovulating during vacation time got a special discount. The jury's still out on whether the work resulted in a baby-boost, but the Danes are working on it: holiday bookings rose by 107%.

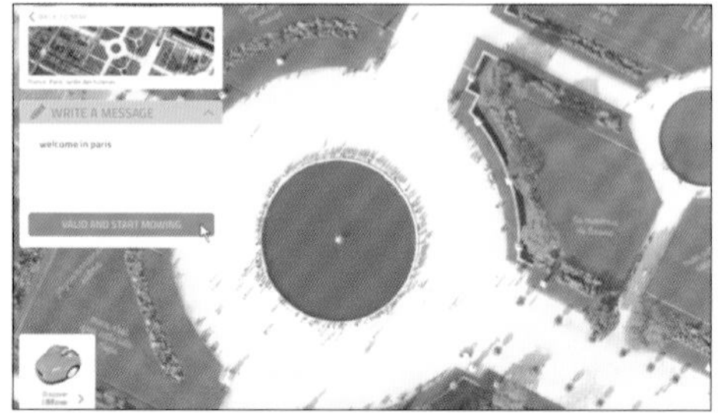

Agency	Publicis Conseil, Paris
Creative Director	Olivier Altmann
Copywriter	Didier Aerts
Art Director	Alexandra Offe
Assisting AD	Camille Vernier
Creative Technologist	Julien Chaillou
Digital Producers	Aurelie Mazodier, Minda Bouanda, Bastien Chanot
Production	Le Lab Marcel, Paris
Technical Chief	Christophe Serret, Le Lab Marcel
Lead Programmers	Vivien Ripoche, Cédric Fressin, Le Lab Marcel
Advertiser	Viking, "IMowssages"

To raise awareness of Viking's iMow, Publicis Conseil produced iMowssages. In partnership with Google Maps, people could choose any lawn on earth to mow a message across. (The word's still out on who mowed that message "from" Putin onto the White House lawn, but we're sure it didn't do foreign policy any harm.) The work generated a "larger than expected" audience of 160,000 site visits – and plenty of interest in the iMow.

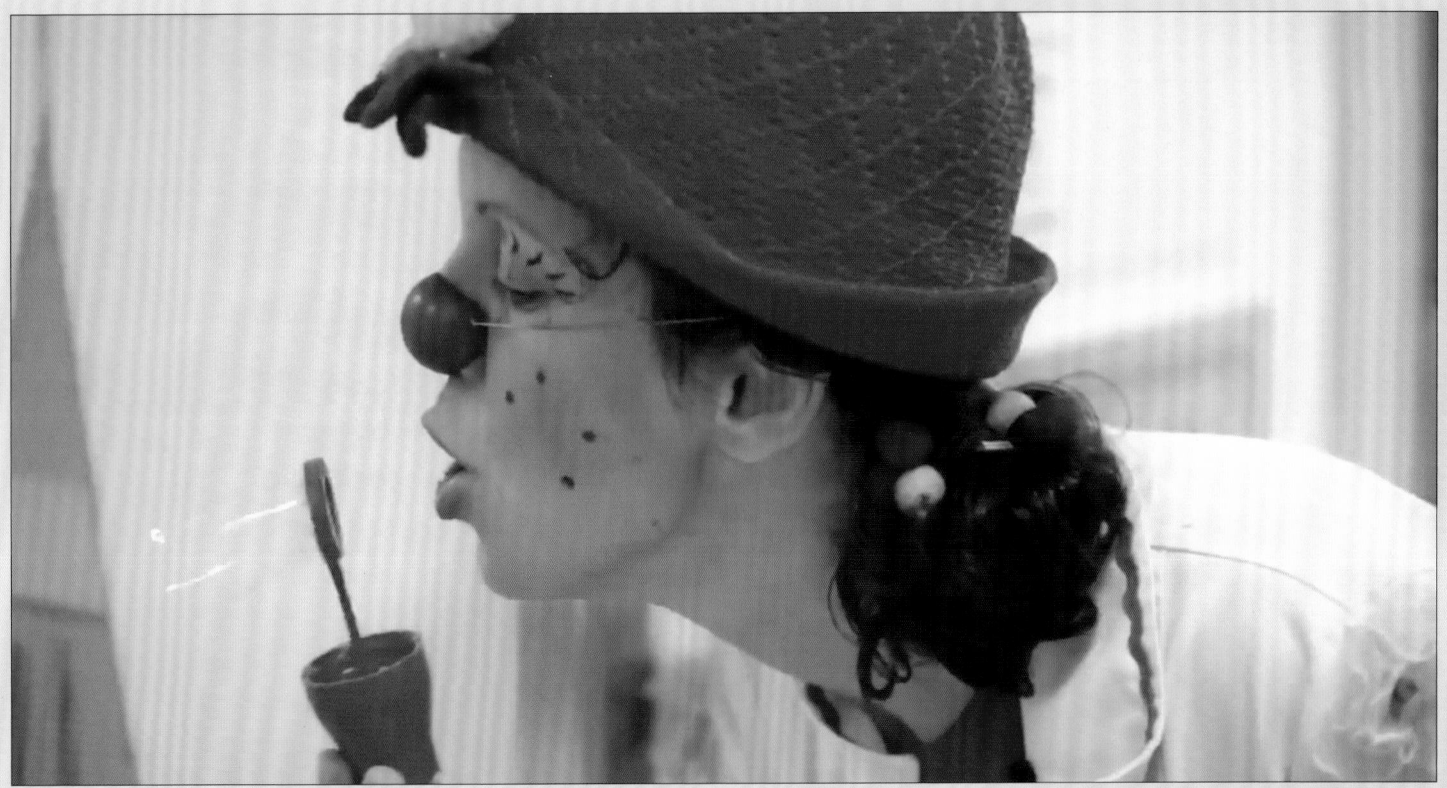

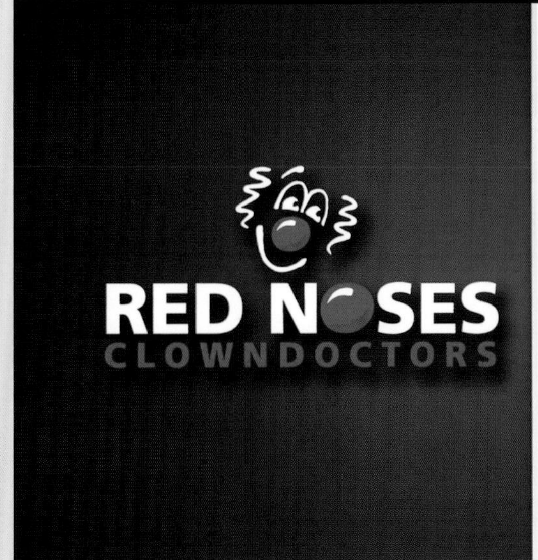

Agency Demner, Merlicek & Bergmann, Vienna
CDs Robert Dassel, Arno Reisenbuechler, Roman Steiner, Francesco Bestagno, Alexander Hofmann, Franz Merlicek
Copywriters Arno Reisenbuechler, Hieronymus Kloss
Art Director Robert Dassel
Photographer Robert Staudinger
Agency Producers Juergen Madl, Katharina Luerzer
Graphic Design Robert Dassel
Digital Creative Robert Dassel, Rene Wegscheider
Filmproduction Ping Pong Communications, Vienna
Sound Studio Tic Music, Vienna
Advertiser Red Noses Clown Doctors, "Red Noses. Red Button."

Red Noses Clown Doctors is an organisation that visits children in hospital to draw smiles out of sad situations. It relies entirely on donations, which are difficult to obtain via TV because of all the steps viewers are required to take. So agency Denmer Merlicek & Bergmann came up with the "Red Button". With help from telco partner A1, people could donate simply by touching the red button on their remote controls. The amount was charged to the user's cable bill, making account details unnecessary. Afterwards, a clown personally thanked the contributor on-screen.

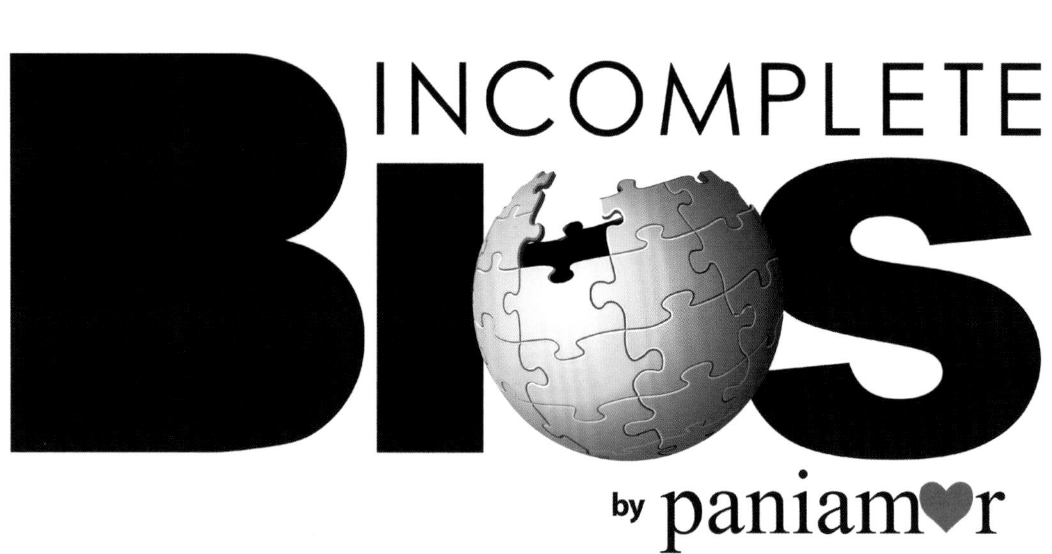

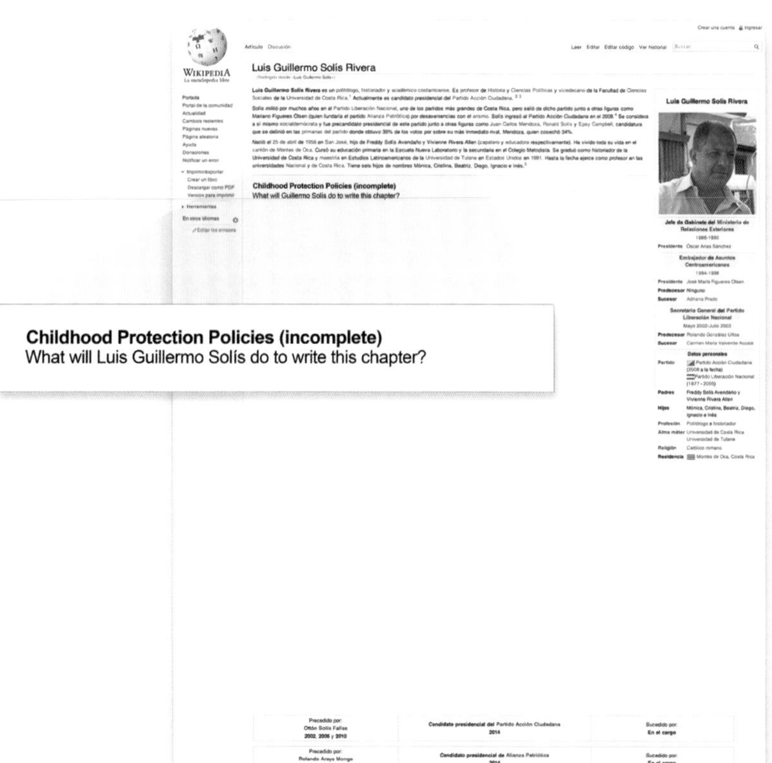

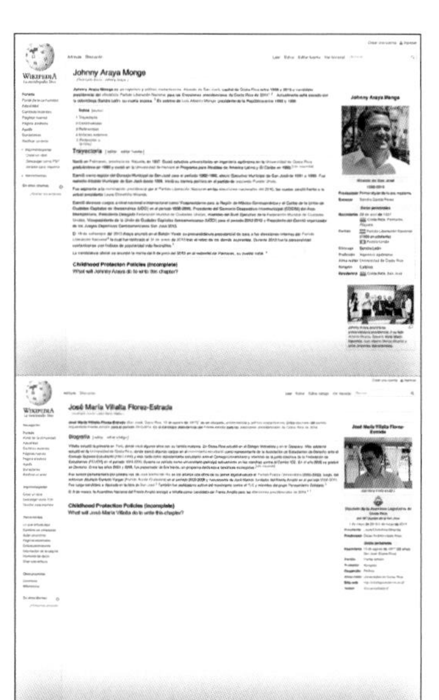

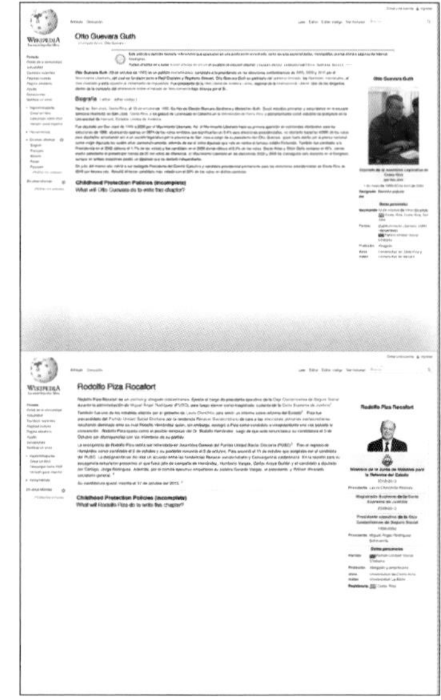

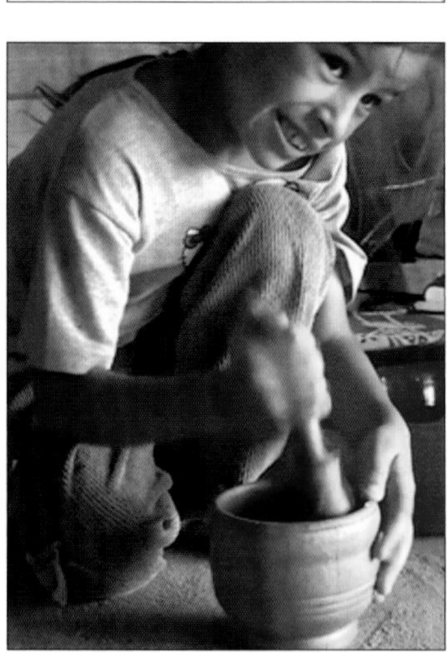

Agency Leo Burnett, San José
CCO Alexis Ospina
CD Jorge Carrera
Copywriters Alexis Ospina, Jorge Carrera, Jose Pablo Huertas
Art Director Daniel Flores
Graphic Design Manuel Berrocal
Advertiser Paniamor Foundation for Child Protection, "Incomplete Bios"

It's no secret that aspiring presidents base campaign speeches on what generates the most votes. Foundation Paniamor manipulated this tendency for a crucial sector that cannot vote: children. Leo Burnett Costa Rica added a new Wikipedia category to the biographies of the country's 2014 Presidential candidates: "Childhood Protection Policies". This was deliberately left blank. Using the hashtag #incompletebios, they drew attention to the policy gap and created a public stir.

Within a month all candidates filled out their bios with clear actions for protecting children, and included them in their campaigns. They included Costa Rica's new President, Luis Guillermo.

IT TAKES LESS THAN 30 SECONDS TO WRITE OFF AN EX-OFFENDER

BUSINESS
IN THE
COMMUNITY
bitc.org.uk/banthebox

Agency	Leo Burnett, London
Creative Director	Adam Tucker
Copywriters	Hugh Todd Darren Keff Phillip Meyler
Art Directors	Hugh Todd Darren Keff Phillip Meyler
Production	Blink, London
Film Director	Dougal Wilson
Producers	Patrick Craig James Studholm
Agency Producers	Natalie Kozlowska Camille Simms
Technical Director	Peter Eichhorn
DOP	Benjamin Todd
Editor	Ed Cheeseman, Final Cut, London
Sound Engineers	Miles Kempton Milos Stojanovic Grand Central, London
Advertiser	Business in the Community, "Second Chance"

Ex-convicts don't have an easy time rebuilding their lives, and part of this is because it's so difficult to find work after spending time in prison. Business in the Community came up with "Second Chance", a digital campaign that exposes you to the voices, and CVs, of former convicts. The work is moving and impossible to ignore.

Online Campaigns - Health, Beauty & Fashion

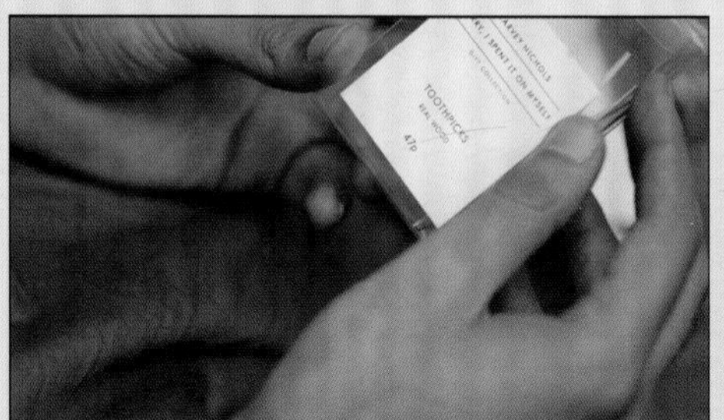

 Online Campaigns - Health, Beauty & Fashion

Agency adam&eveDDB, London
Executive CDs Ben Priest, Ben Tollett, Emer Stamp
Creatives Richard Brim, Daniel Fisher
Production Outsider, London
Producer Daniel Moorey
Agency Producer Victoria Keenan
Film Director James Rouse
Cameraman Alex Melman
Editor Bill Smedley, Work Post, London
Post Producer Josh King, MPC, London
Sound Factory Studio, London
Photographer James Day
Advertiser Harvey Nichols, "Sorry, I Spent It On Myself"

For client Harvey Nichols, adam&eveDDB took the concept of holiday giving and turned it on its head: In "Sorry, I Spent It On Myself", people are depicted giving obviously thoughtless gifts (toothpicks, paperclips) to loved ones under the same brand name as the campaign. A few choice shots show where the money really went (to themselves, of course).

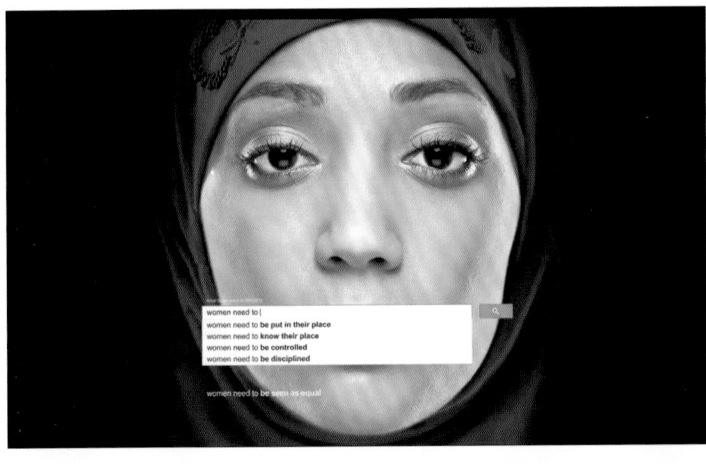

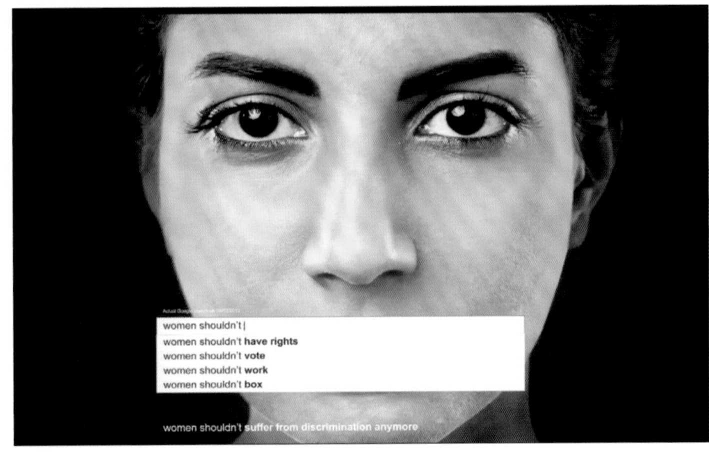

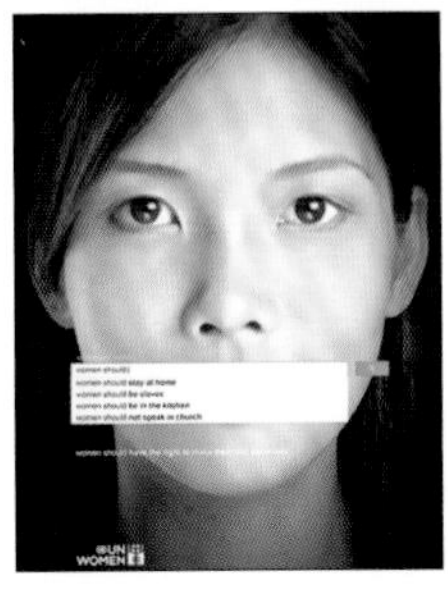

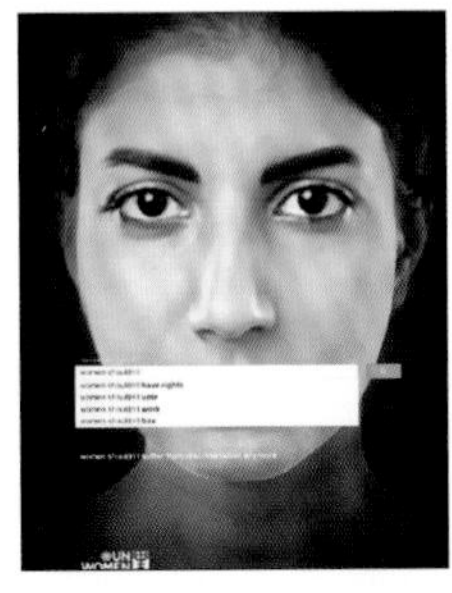

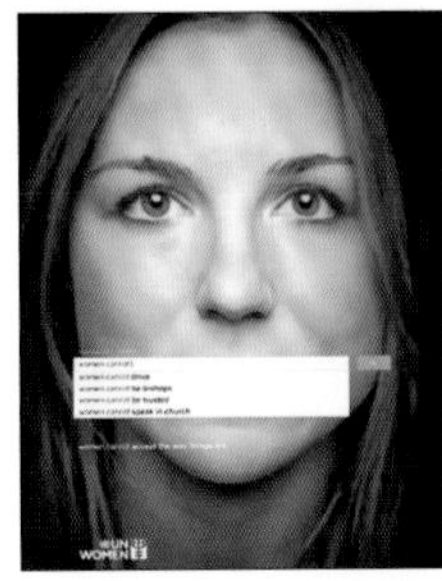

Agency Memac Ogilvy & Mather, Dubai
Executive CD Ramzi Moutran
Creative Director Sascha Kuntze
Copywriter Kareem Shuhaibar
Art Directors Sabia Fatayri, Christopher Hunt, Leonardo Borges
Studio Tarek Bawab
Agency Producer Carmel Missilmany
Editor Souheil Zahreddine
Advertiser UN Women, "The Autocomplete Truth"

Not convinced that there's still a gender equality problem? This UN Women campaign by Memac Ogilvy & Mather puts the situation in perspective by showcasing the Google Autocomplete phrases for terms like "women should". Autocomplete provides the most common search terms that complete the phrase you've entered. And since women should apparently "stay at home", "be slaves" or "be in the kitchen", it looks like we've still got a lot of work to do.

Agency BBDO New York
Chief Creative Officers David Lubars, Greg Hahn
Creative Directors Jason Stefanik, Alex Taylor
Copywriter Ryan Lawrence
Art Director James Kuczynski
Executive Prod. Julian Katz
Interactive Prod. Eric Berg
Advertiser Champs Sports, "Hard Hinting"

If you're a sports fan, and have trouble getting your parents to give you what you really want for Christmas, Champs Sports is here to help. Say hello to "Hard Hinting", which uses banner ads and other marketing collateral to send a message straight to your parents (with your face on it!), along with the items they really need to put on the list. (All conveniently available at Champs.)

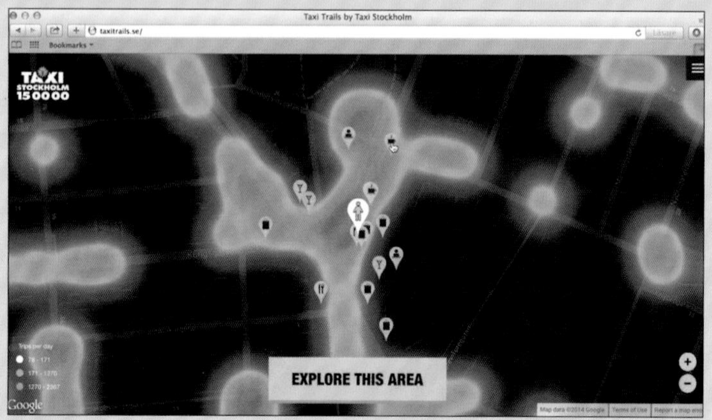

Agency	King, Stockholm
Creative Director	Frank Hollingworth
Copywriter	Christoffer Dymling
Art Director	Josephine Wallin
Production	Yours, Stockholm
Digital Creative	Johan Tesch
Advertiser	Taxi Stockholm, "Taxi Trails"

Taxi drivers are a wealth of local information, but it's difficult to take advantage of their knowledge. That's why, with help from agency King, Taxi Stockholm launched "Taxi Trails": A tourist guide that uses GPS data from eight million taxi trips to show you where real Stockholmers like to go. It's never been easier to navigate like a local.

It's not how far or fast you go,
it's who follows you.

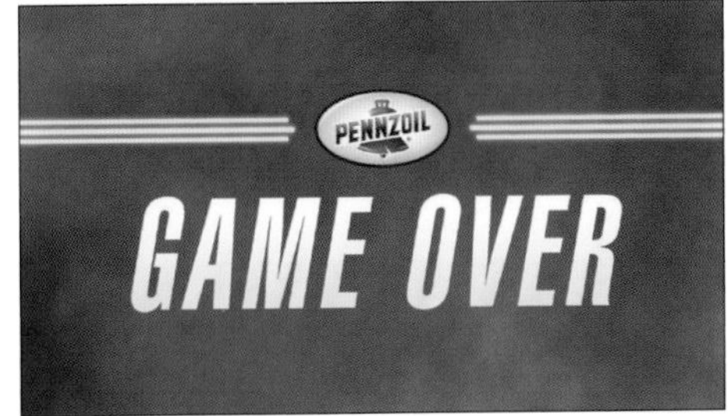

Agency Razorfish, New York
Executive CD Frederic Bonn
Creative Director Alex Bodman
Associate CD Penn Li
Copywriter Nick Elliott
Art Directors Lauren Race, Nicole Berke, Thomas Dudon
Advertiser Mercedes-Benz, "Take The Wheel"

Hoping to reach a new generation of driver, Mercedes-Benz launched "Take The Wheel" for its affordable new CLA model. It asked five of Instagram's best photographers to spend five days piloting a CLA, sharing six photos a day on both their own accounts and that of Mercedes-Benz. The content generated 87 million organic Instagram impressions and two million likes. The CLA broke sales records when it launched.

Agency MediaCom, New York
Creative Agency J. Walter Thompson, Atlanta
Advertiser Shell, "Mario Karting Reimagined"

To promote Pennzoil's new motor oil, made from natural gas, Shell took advantage of the hype around the SXSW (South by Southwest) creative and technology festival in Austin, Texas. "Mario Karting Reimagined" let festival attendees play Mario Kart 8 in real life by crashing around in bumper cars. In the meantime, via RFID technology, they learned about the benefits of Pennzoil's new technology through power-ups that made them better racers.

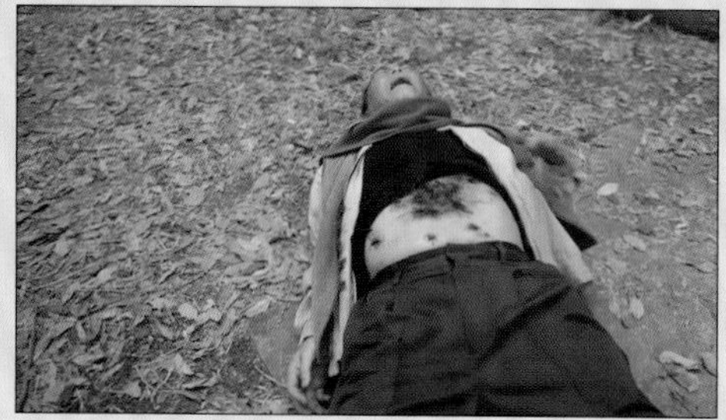

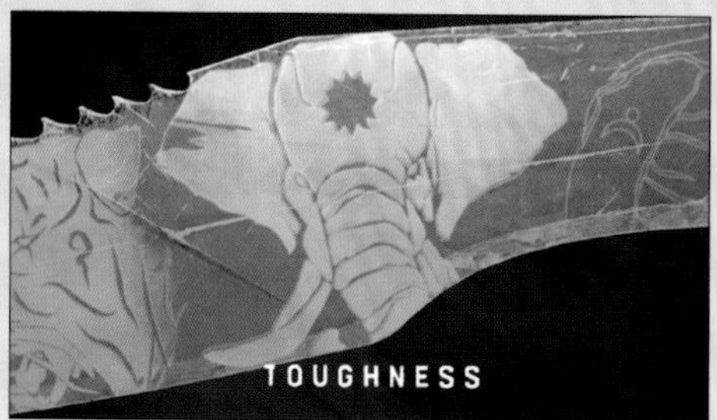

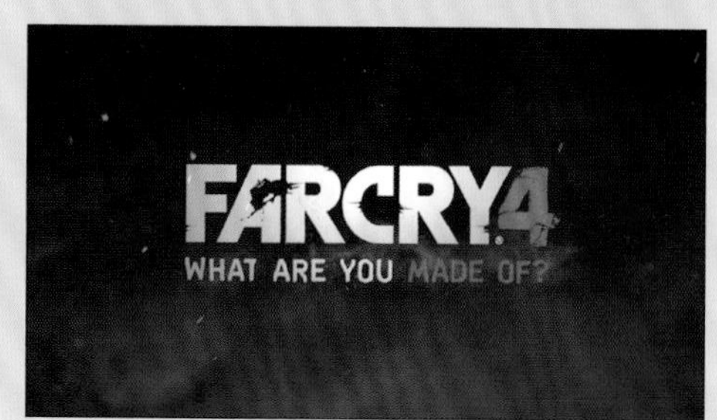

Agency Grey, Paris
Creative Director Thierry Astier
Copywriters Dimitri Hekimian, Mehdi Benkaci, Vicken Adjennian
Art Directors Quentin Deronzier, Mehdi Benkaci, Vicken Adjennian, Vivien Urtiaga
Production Stink, Paris, Stinkdigital, Paris
Film Director Luis Nieto
Producers Sophie Gaaloul, Greg Panteix
Agency Producer Laurent Dailloux
Graphic Design Charlie Montagut
Advertiser Ubisoft, "What Are You Made Of ?"

For the launch of the latest Far Cry game, Ubisoft and Grey Paris hijacked its artificial-intelligence theme and created "What Are You Made Of?". The digital platform includes four rites of passage, with 168 interactive video sequences (totaling 42 million possible outcomes). Users have only a few seconds to decide what to do in any given situation. Based on each decision, an algorithm provides analysis on their personality. Far Cry 4 was heralded a top five game based on sales as soon as it launched.

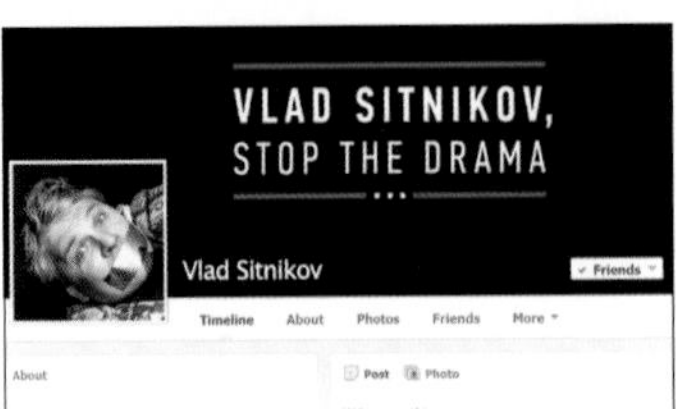

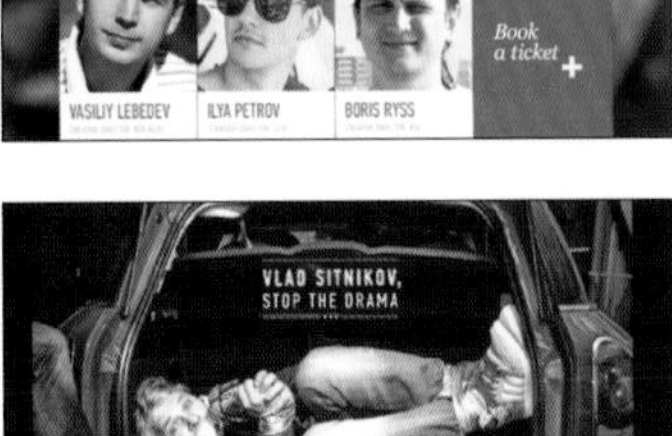

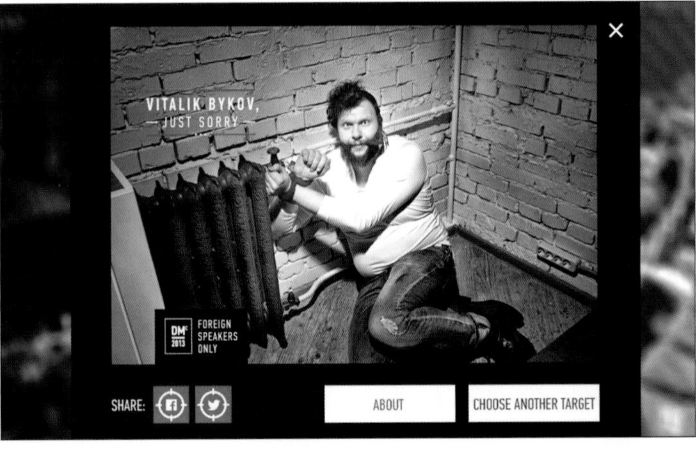

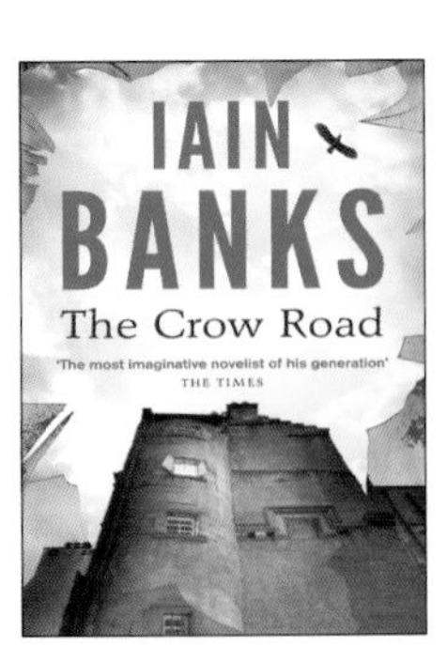

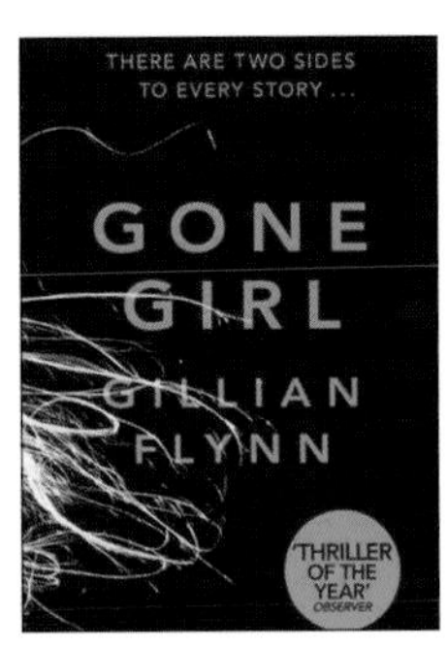

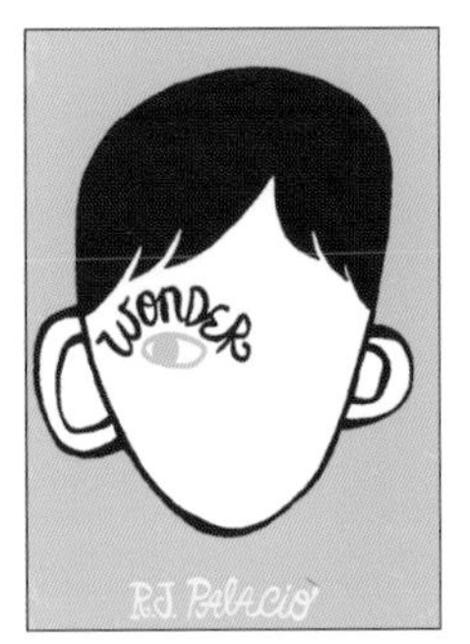

Agency Grape, Moscow
Creative Director Vladimir Garev
Copywriter Artem Tsaregorogsev
Art Director Vsevolod Navashin
Photographer Victor Molodtsov
Production GrandReport, Moscow
Agency Producer Anton Kopylov
Graphic Design Alexander Stogov
Advertiser Digital Marketing Conference, "Captured!"

The Russian Federation had a problem with its Digital Marketing Conference: it's the biggest event for Russian digital marketers, but nobody wanted to attend because they were fed up with local speakers. So the "Captured!" campaign amusingly highlighted the fact that only foreign speakers would be invited to the latest conference. Ironic photos showed local professionals gagged, kidnapped or otherwise detained. Ticket sales rose by 90%.

Agency 34, Cape Town
Executive CD Richard Phillips
Creative Directors Geraint Gronow, Wilton Ackeer
Copywriter Wilton Ackeer
Art Director Geraint Gronow
Digital Artwork Derick Botha, Warren Deyzel
Programmers Derick Botha, Warren Deyzel
Advertiser Exclusive Books, "Opening Lines"

Long-form books are losing out to short, quickly-consumed media like Twitter. To resolve this, Exclusive Books tweeted the opening lines of great novels to reconnect people with books they might love. The campaign also featured YouTube pre-rolls using opening lines – because as any book lover knows, it only takes a couple of seconds to read one, and that's plenty of time to get hooked.

Online Campaigns - Luxury

Agency adam&eveDDB, London
Executive CDs Ben Priest, Ben Tollett, Emer Stamp
Creatives Richard Brim, Daniel Fisher
Producer Daniel Moorey
Agency Producer Victoria Keenan
Production Outsider, London
Film Director James Rouse
Producer Benji Howell
Cameraman Alex Melman
Editor Bill Smedley, Work Post, London
Post Producer Josh King, MPC, London
Sound Factory Studio, London
Photographer James Day
Advertiser Harvey Nichols, "Sorry, I Spent It On Myself"

Why spend your hard-earned cash on others? For Harvey Nichols, adam&eveDDB encouraged people to allocate their Christmas money a little differently. "Sorry, I Spent It On Myself" is both a campaign and a bespoke brand. Buy small (but lovingly-packed) baggies of paperclips or toothpicks for those you love. The larger portion of your budget can then go to the person who really deserves it: you.

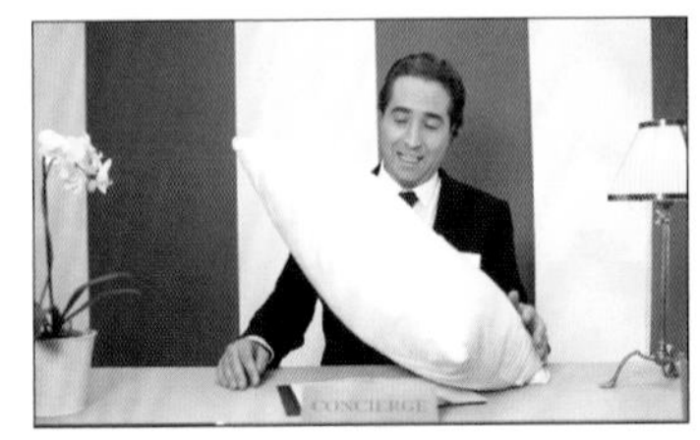

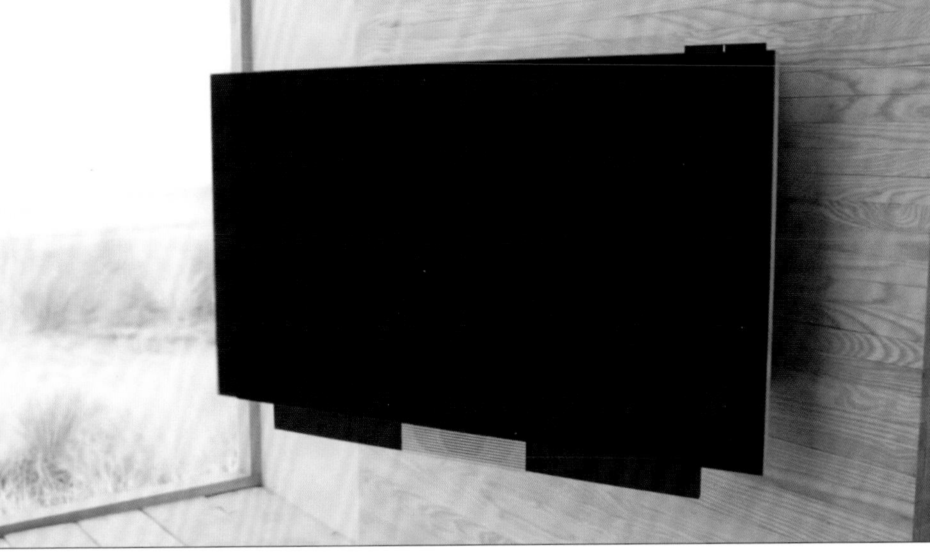

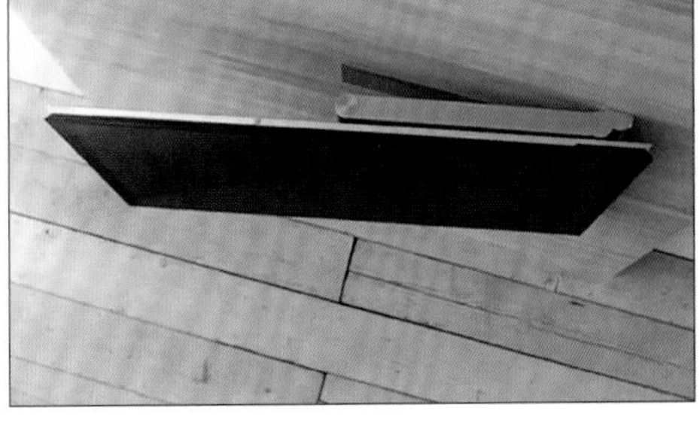

BANG & OLUFSEN
wunderman

Agency	We Are Social, Paris
Art Director	Max Vedel
Advertiser	Hyatt Hotels, "#HYATTaDream"

To raise awareness of Hyatt in France (and of the hotel's delightful service), We Are Social created a social media concierge. Tweet your deepest desires to #HYATTaDream and he might answer you with a personalised video. Some dreams even came true...in a Hyatt hotel, of course.

Agency	Wunderman, Copenhagen
Creative Director	Kenneth Pøhler
Copywriter	Signe Bloch Lysgaard
Art Director	Rune Guldbrand Pedersen
Photographer	Niels Buchholzer
Production	The Lab, Copenhagen
Film Director	Rune Guldbrand Pedersen
Advertiser	Bang & Olufsen, "A Moving Digital Experience of BeoVision Avant"

To demonstrate the magic of Bang & Olufsen's new BeoVision Avant TV, whose screen can be easily adjusted to suit your viewing needs, Wunderman Copenhagen compiled a film documenting its movements over time, then put the footage on a sub-site and banner ads to illustrate just how sensitive the set is to viewers' movements and desires.

Online Campaigns - Business to Business & Corporate

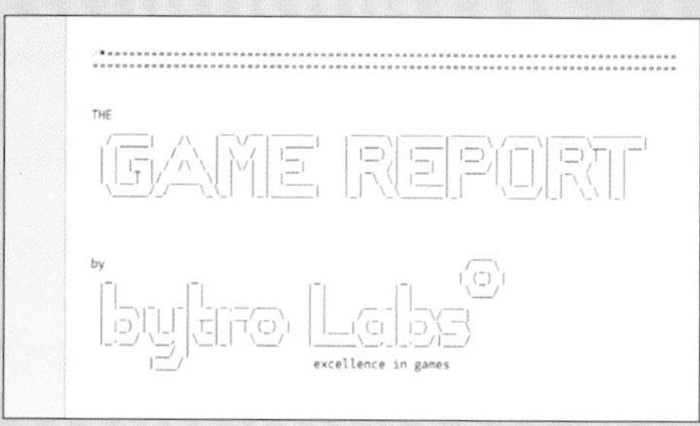

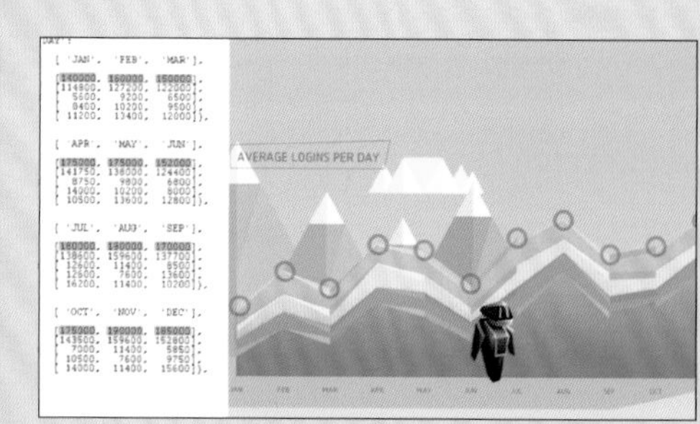

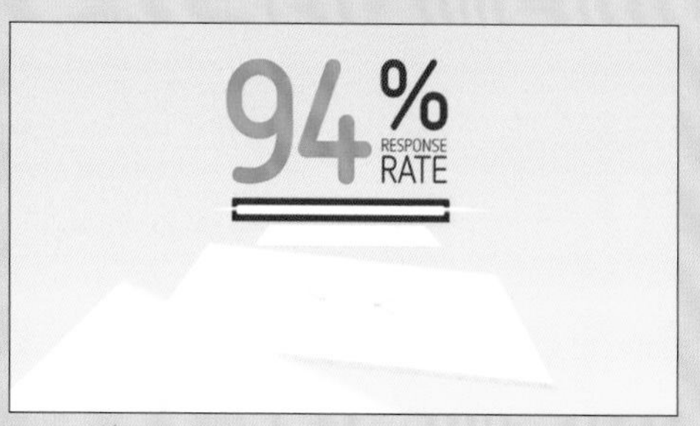

Agency plan.net / Serviceplan, Munich
CCO Alexander Schill
Executive CDs Matthias Harbeck, Till Diestel
Creative Director Marcell Francke
Copywriters Lorenz Langgartner, Gabriel Doell
Art Directors Franz Roeppischer, Andreas Heuschneider
Illustration Frank Graefe, Eat, Sleep + Design, Berlin
Programmer Philipp Schmidt
Production LIGA 01, Munich
Creative Producer Sarah Neuner
Sound Design German Wahnsinn, Hamburg
Special Effects Constantin von Zitzewitz, Sven Wellbrock, Johannes Peter, Florian Dehmel
Advertiser Bytro Labs, "The Game Report"

Who likes reading business reports? Hardly anyone. So agency Serviceplan transformed the business report of developer startup Bytro Labs into a game. The report went out to journalists as a simple text file. But when they changed the file extension from .txt to .html, it became a game that let them experience the Bytro Labs adventure for themselves.

CHARYTATYWNI.ALLEGRO LAUNCH
SHARE THE BEST YOU HAVE

The launch of the CSR platform charytatywni.allegro.pl.
How to reach 500 top brands and be distinctive?

1 Our solution: an extraordinary delivery consisting of two envelopes: I HELP and I DO NOT HELP.

I help

2 An electronic timer counting down 72 hours. PR managers with no choice but to start a charity auction.

Natalia Hatalska

Maciej Budzich

3 On the website there was a guide on how to start the charity auction and the information on the benefits of using the platform. Companies' actions were gauged by top marketing bloggers.

4 Hundreds of auctions appeared on the platform and press articles have been published about the launch.

127 PR publications

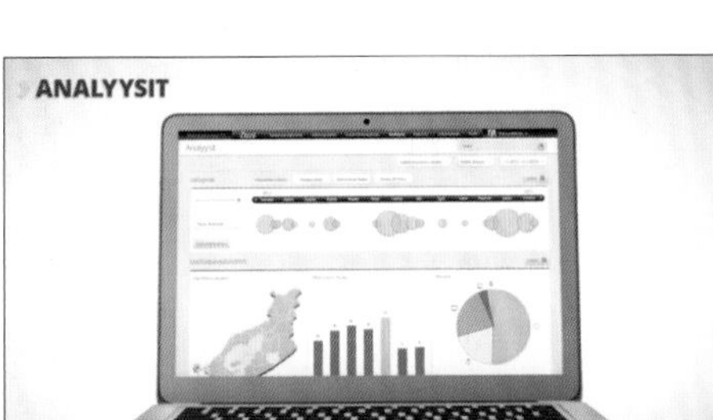

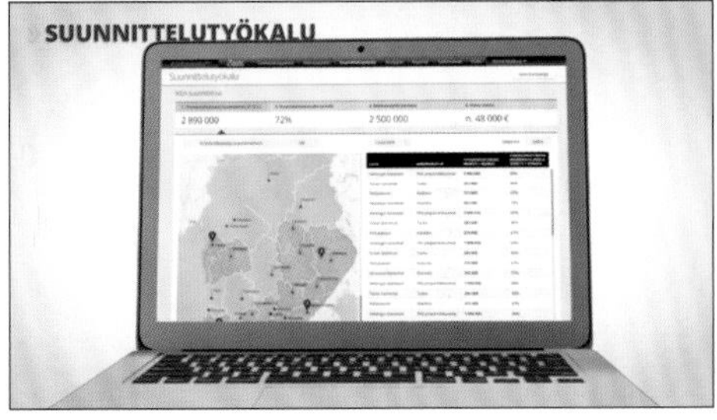

Agency Biuro Podróży Reklamy, Warsaw
Creative Director Łukasz Ludkowski
Sr Graphic Designer Anna Żołnierowicz
Photographer Agnieszka Sosnowska
Advertiser Allegro Group, "Share The Best You Have"

For the launch of Allegro Group's new CSR platform, Biuro Podróży Reklamy sent two envelopes to the PR representatives of 500 major brands. The envelopes gave them the option "I Help" or "I Do Not Help". When they chose "I Help", they were sent to a website with detailed instructions about how to launch a charity auction. Each of their efforts was gauged by top marketing bloggers.

Agency Citat, Helsinki
Creative Director Jyri Niemi
Copywriter Vesa Pakkanen
Art Director Niko Airaksinen
Concept Designer Hong Ding
Production Futurice, Helsinki
Producers Mari Piirainen, Mikko Viikari
Agency Producer Aleksis Moisio
Programmers Lauri Kainulainen, Touko Vainio-Kaila
Advertiser Kärkimedia, "Baari"

For client Kärkimedia, agency Citat Oy created Baari, a digital platform that offers relevant information and tools to media designers and account managers in a single dashboard. The work was attractive and functional – a rarity in B2B, where people often forget that businesses are customers, too.

Agency Grey, Paris
Creative Director Thierry Astier
Copywriters Dimitri Hekimian, Mehdi Benkaci, Vicken Adjennian
Art Directors Quentin Deronzier, Mehdi Benkaci, Vicken Adjennian, Vivien Urtiaga
Production Stink, Paris, Stinkdigital, Paris
Film Director Luis Nieto
Producers Sophie Gaaloul, Greg Panteix
Agency Producer Laurent Dailloux
Graphic Design Charlie Montagut
Advertiser Ubisoft, "What Are You Made Of ?"

For the launch of Ubisoft's Far Cry 4, Grey Paris produced "What Are You Made Of?", a site that uses the game's artificial intelligence theme by pushing users to make decisions in four dramatic situations. At the end of each choice, it provides an analysis of their personality. The site enjoyed over 1 million visitors in just 4 weeks, 30% of whom returned to play again, and Far Cry 4 numbered among the top-five games as soon as it launched.

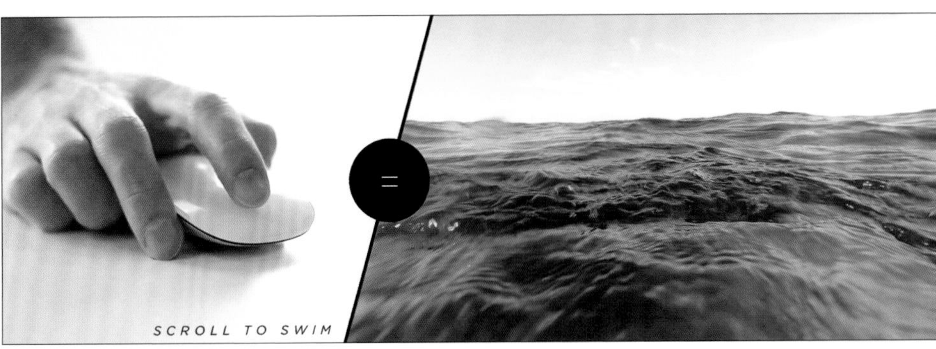

Agency	Publicis, London
ECD	Andy Bird
Digital ECD	Pavlos Themistocleous
Creative Director	Dave Sullivan
Creatives	Adam Balogh Jason Moussalli
Production	Friend, London
Film Director	Georgi Banks-Davies
Producer	Mikey Levelle
Agency Producer	Joshua Sanders
DOP	Todd Banzhal
Advertiser	Tourism Ireland, "Wild Atlantic Way"

Created by Publicis London for Tourism Ireland, the epic "Wild Atlantic Way" website follows a road trip down the west coast of Ireland. It features an exceptional soundtrack inspired by the people and places along the route, with new tracks being made available to followers each step of the way. The site explores both the trip, the inspiration for the music, and – as a stunning complement – previously unseen shots of Ireland and its people.

Agency	CLM BBDO, Paris
Production	Wanda Digital, Paris
Film Director	Ben Strebel
Producers	Perrine Schwartz Helene Segol
Advertiser	Guy Cotten, "Trip Out To Sea"

Here's an approach you don't see everyday. For marine wear vendor Guy Cotten, Wanda Digital created sortieenmer.com (French for "trip out to sea"), a stunning – and effective – website experience that provides a first-hand sense of what it feels like to drown. The message? At sea, you tire faster than you think. Wear a life vest.

COULD YOU AVOID THAT?
2.5 MILLION PEOPLE
COULDN'T EITHER

 Online Ads 

Agency Grey, Moscow
Creative Directors Alexey Artyukhov, Andrey Sivkov
Art Director Ivan Zarutsky
Production Simple Minds, Moscow
Advertiser Opel, "Skiptest"

When did you last watch a YouTube pre-roll ad? For the launch of the Opel Mokka, Grey Moscow took advantage of one big insight: people only watch the "skip" button as it counts down, so they can jump to their content as fast as possible. The "Skiptest" promotion is a set of pre-rolls during which the Opel Mokka interacts with the "skip" button as if it were an actual obstacle – sometimes even crashing into it.

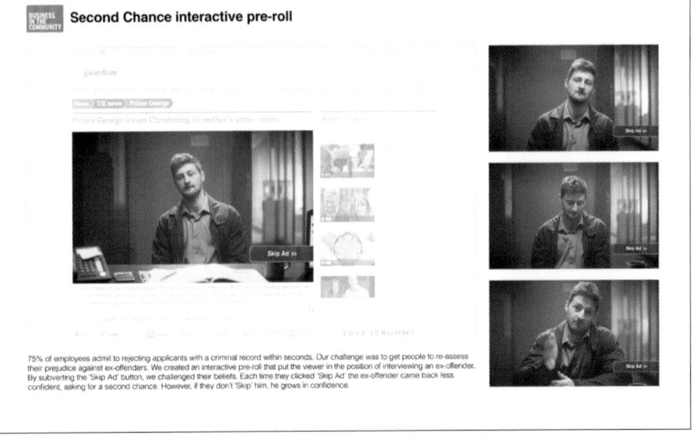

BUSINESS IN THE COMMUNITY
Second Chance interactive pre-roll
guardian
Skip Ad >>
75% of employees admit to rejecting applicants with a criminal record within seconds. Our challenge was to get people to re-assess their prejudice against ex-offenders. We created an interactive pre-roll that put the viewer in the position of interviewing an ex-offender. By subverting the 'Skip Ad' button, we challenged their beliefs. Each time they clicked 'Skip Ad' the ex-offender came back less confident, asking for a second chance. However, if they don't 'Skip' him, he grows in confidence.

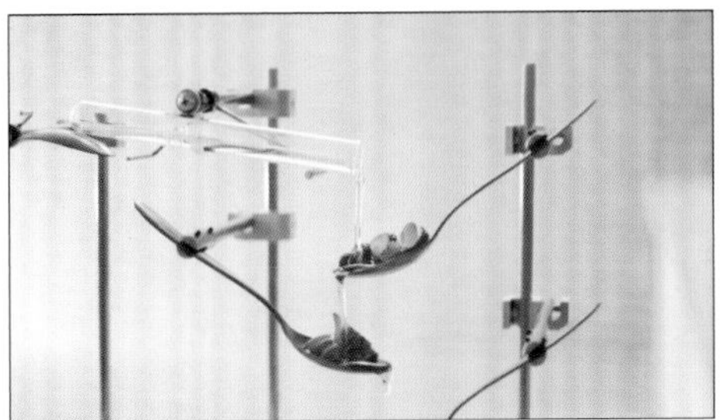

Agency Leo Burnett, London
Creative Director Adam Tucker
Copywriters & ADs Hugh Todd, Darren Keff, Phillip Meyler
Production Blink, London
Film Director Dougal Wilson
Producers Patrick Craig, James Studholm
Advertiser Business in the Community, "Second Chance"

As a compelling reinforcement to Business in the Community's "Second Chance" campaign, which seeks to humanise job applicants with criminal records, Leo Burnett London created interactive pre-rolls that put viewers in the position of interviewing an ex-offender. When you click "skip ad", the ex-offender reappears, less confident, asking for a second chance. If you don't skip him, his confidence grows.

Agency Grey, Tokyo
Regional CD Javier Bonilla
Creative Directors Kanji Miyagawa, Jun Ogasawara
Art Directors Gaku Takai, Keiji Sakamoto
Photographer Hiroki Ando
Production C3 Film, Tokyo, AOI Pro., Tokyo
Producers Shinkichi Yokoyama, Yuki Iizumi
Advertiser Procter & Gamble, "Precise Recipe"

To win visibility for the curiously-named Hair Recipe, a new haircare brand from Procter & Gamble, Grey Tokyo launched "Precise Recipe". The promotion used a Rube Goldberg-style machine, made of basic kitchenware and product ingredients, to illustrate how the product was made – the better to illustrate its "food for hair" manifesto.

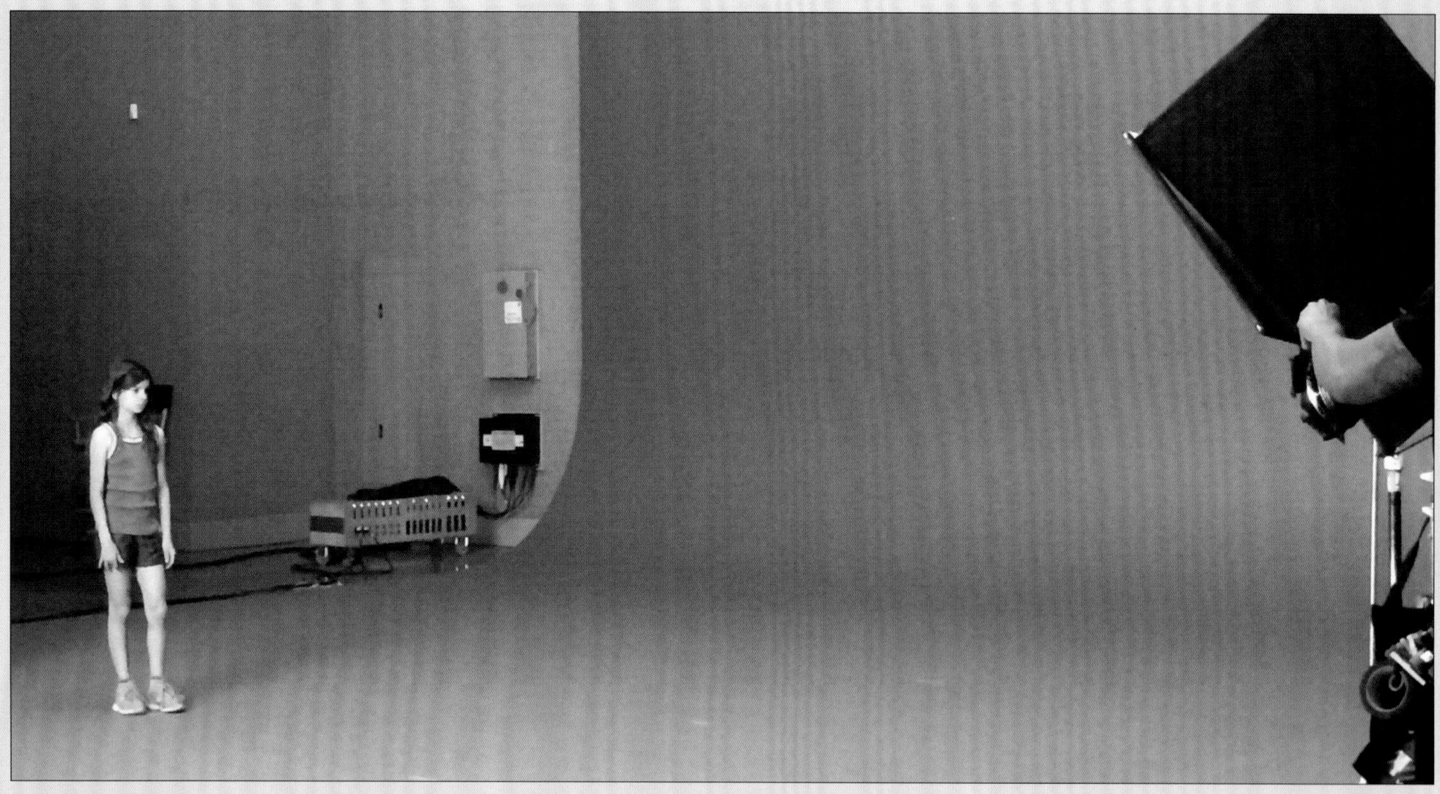

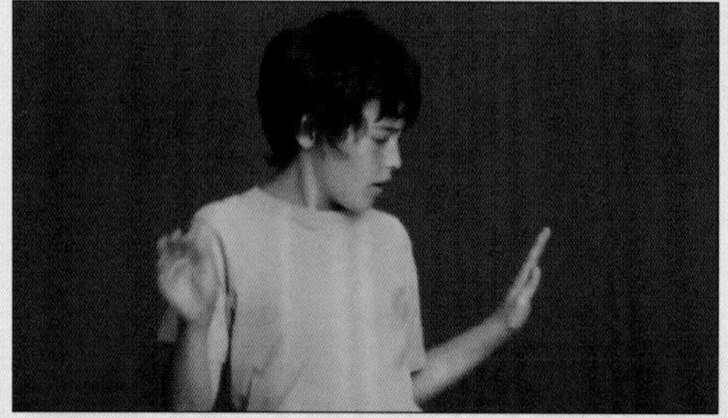

32

LET'S MAKE #LIKEAGIRL MEAN AMAZING THINGS.

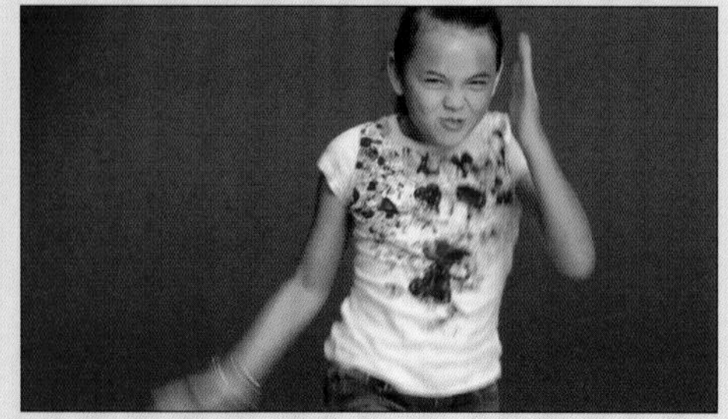

Rewrite the Rules
always

358 **Online & Viral Films**

Agencies	Leo Burnett, Toronto Leo Burnett, Chicago Holler, London	**Agency Producer**	Adine Becker
CCO	Judy John	**Film Director**	Lauren Greenfield
Creative Directors	Judy John Becky Swanson	**Production**	Chelsea Films, Los Angeles
Digital CD	Milos Obradovic	**Editor**	Kathryn Hempel Cutters, Chicago
Copywriters	AJ Hassan Angel Capobianco	**Advertiser**	Procter & Gamble, Always, "#LikeAGirl"
Art Directors	Hmi Hmi Gibbs Nick Bygraves		

Based on the insight that the self-esteem of young girls plummets when they hit puberty, Always and Leo Burnett Toronto created #Likeagirl, a video that illustrates how young girls – versus women and boys – define running, jumping, hitting, and fighting like a girl. The video generated over 10 million views in four days. More importantly, it illustrated how small comments that most people take for granted reinforce constricting societal norms.

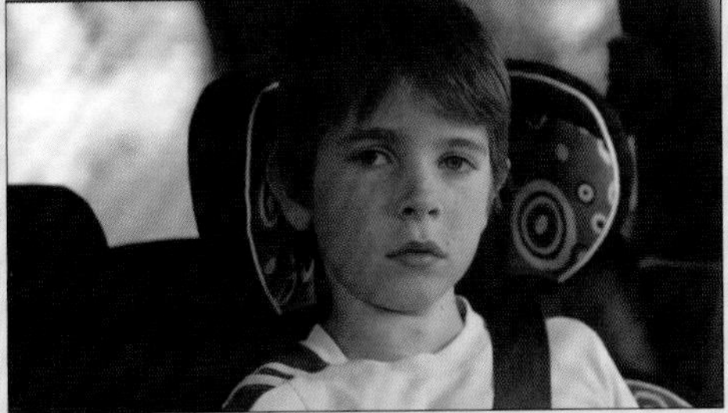

Other people make mistakes
Slow down

Agency	Clemenger BBDO, Wellington	**Executive Producer**	Rob Galluzzo
Creative Directors	Philip Andrew Brigid Alkema	**Producer**	Karen Bryson
Copywriter	Emily Beautrais	**DOP**	Stefan Duscio
Art Directors	Emily Beautrais Philip Andrew	**VFX Supervisor**	Stuart White
Agency Producer	Marty Gray	**Prod. Designer**	Rob Key
Dir. of Digit. Innovation	Thomas Scovell	**Editor**	Drew Thompson
Production	Finch, Auckland	**VFX**	Fin Design
Film Director	Derin Seale	**Sound Design**	Simon Lister
		Advertiser	New Zealand Transport Agency, "Mistakes"

A mistake shouldn't cost you your life. This provocative online video for the New Zealand Transport Agency freeze-frames a car accident in which one driver pulls out of a side turning, and another is going too fast to stop. The frozen moment gives both drivers an opportunity to reflect on the smash that may be about to cost both of them their lives. Most tragically of all, the son of one of the drivers is sitting innocently in the back seat.

Agency	Thinkmodo, New York
Creative Directors	James Percelay Michael Krivicka
Photographer	Matthew Cady
Production	Thinkmodo, New York
Film Directors	Michael Krivicka James Percelay
Agency Producer	Sam Pezzullo
Advertiser	Sony Pictures, “Telekinetic Coffee Shop Surprise”

We'll never get tired of this Thinkmodo video for Sony's latest version of Carrie, which features a girl in a coffee shop losing her cool and wreaking telekinetic havoc, just like the heroine of the movie. The video itself lets you in on the joke, showing how the stunts were prepared in advance, so you can fully enjoy the terror of unwitting coffee shop customers.

Agency	adam&eveDDB, London
Executive CDs	Ben Priest Ben Tollett Emer Stamp
Creatives	Richard Brim Daniel Fisher
Producers	Daniel Moorey Benji Howell
Agency Producer	Victoria Keenan
Production	Outsider, London
Film Director	James Rouse
Cameraman	Alex Melman
Editor	Bill Smedley, Work Post, London
Post Producer	Josh King, MPC, London
Sound	Factory Studio, London
Photographer	James Day
Advertiser	Harvey Nichols, "Sorry, I Spent It On Myself"

In this quirky multi Epica Award winning film for Harvey Nichols, we're introduced to a tongue-in-cheek Christmas product line: "Sorry, I Spent It On Myself". This lets you buy small, artfully-branded bags of toothpicks and other inexpensive oddities for your loved ones from the luxury store while you pick up something rather more pricey for your good self.

BENTLEY
BURIAL

ENTERRO CHIQUINHO SCARPA
THE VAST MAJORITY OF PEOPLE BURY THEIR ORGANS.

SEMANA
NACIONAL
DE DOAÇÃO
DE ÓRGÃOS
DE 23 A 29 DE SETEMBRO
NATIONAL WEEK OF ORGANS DONATION

abto
Brazilian Association of Organ Transplant

Agency Leo Burnett Tailor Made, Sao Paulo
Creative Directors Marcelo Reis, Guilherme Jahara, Rodrigo Jatene
Copywriter Christian Fontana
Art Director Marcelo Rizerio
Editors Paulo Staliano, Gregorio Szalontai, Jack La Noyée, Christian Balzano
Agency Producers Celso Groba, Rafael Messias, Stella Violla
Advertiser ABTO, "Bentley Burial"

Media attention reached fever pitch when eccentric billionaire Count Scarpa announced via Facebook that he would soon bury his beloved Bentley in his backyard "for use in the afterlife". Helicopters circled his house to check on the progress of the burial; but on the big day, he held a press conference pointing out that people bury things far more important than his Bentley each day: their organs. Scarpa became an organ donation champion overnight.

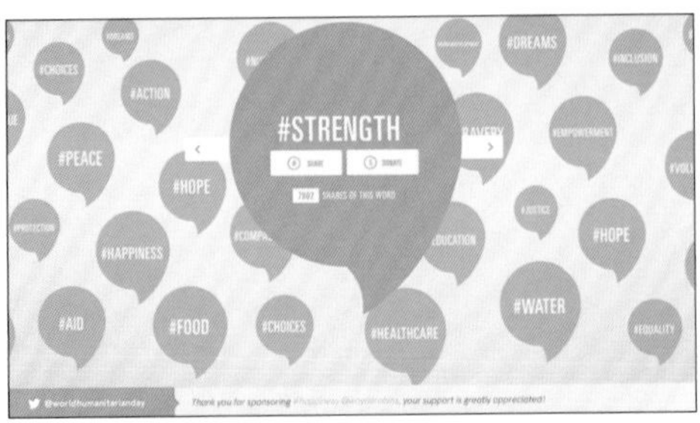

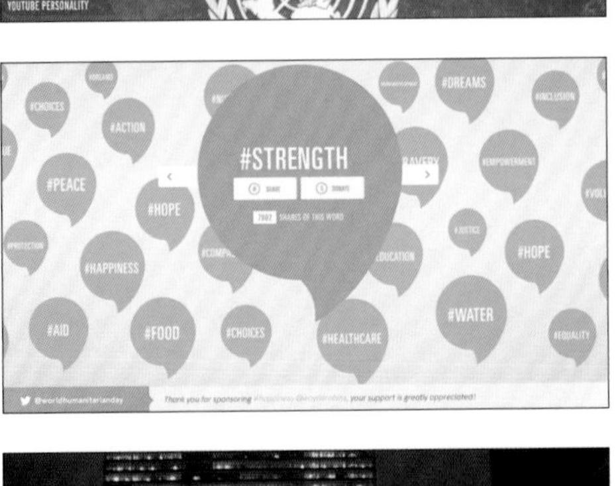

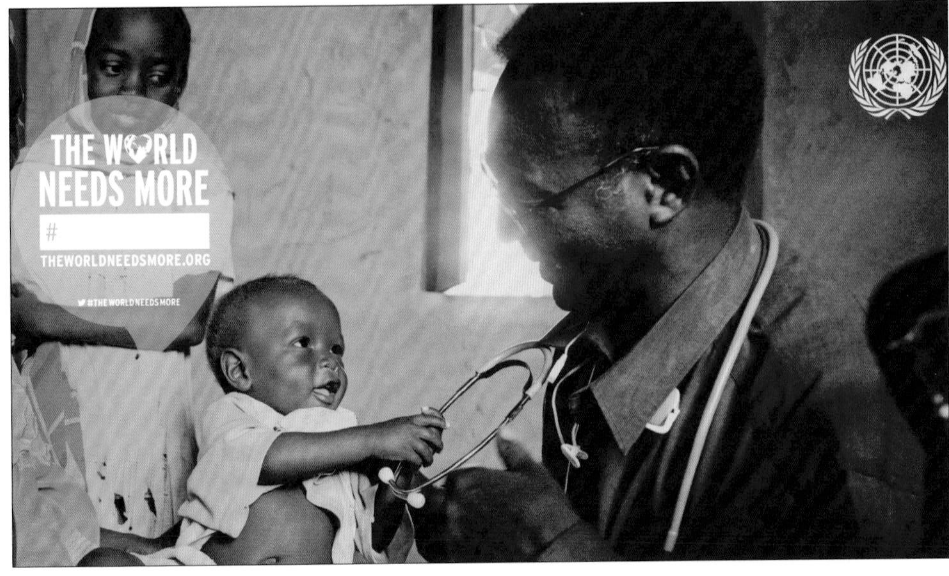

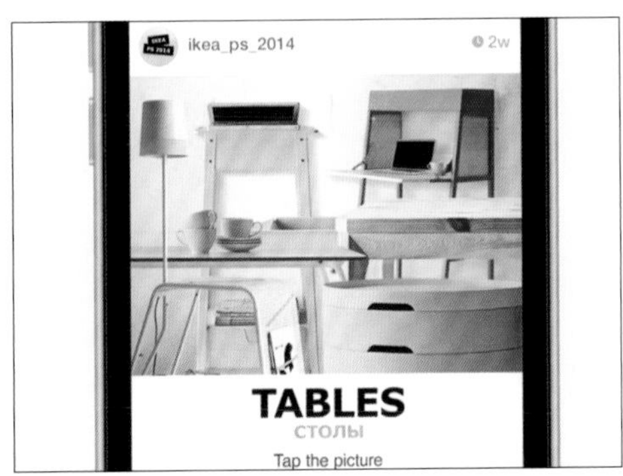

Agency	Leo Burnett, New York
CCO	Jay Benjamin
Executive CDs	Kieran Antill Michael Canning Darren Wright David Skinner
Art Director	Andre Gidoin
Studio Designer	Steven Jordao
Agency Producers	Jeremy Fox
Advertiser	United Nations, "#TheWorldNeeds More"

To generate funding for humanitarian aid, the United Nations worked with Leo Burnett to conceive #theworldneedsmore, a unique marketplace that transformed words of support into action. To take part, people used the hashtag to share a word they felt the world needed more of (such as "love", or "education"). Each word was sponsored by a brand or an individual, and every time it was shared a percentage of the amount donated was unlocked. In the end 2.5 million words were shared, resulting in US$700,000 in donations over three months.

Agency	Instinct, Moscow
Creative Directors	Roman Firainer Yaroslav Orlov
Digital CD	Nikolai Fabrika
Copywriter	Dmitry Moiseev
Art Directors	Timur Abdusheev Max Demkin
Advertiser	IKEA, "IKEA PS 2014"

For the designer collection IKEA PS, agency Instinct produced a dedicated Instagram account. Each of the items in the collection also had its own account, making it easy for others to tag and share items they had purchased. The primary account quickly garnered 30,000 followers—all without a dedicated budget.

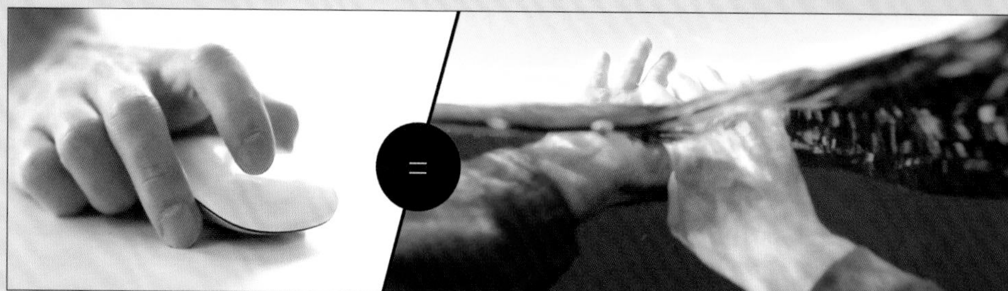

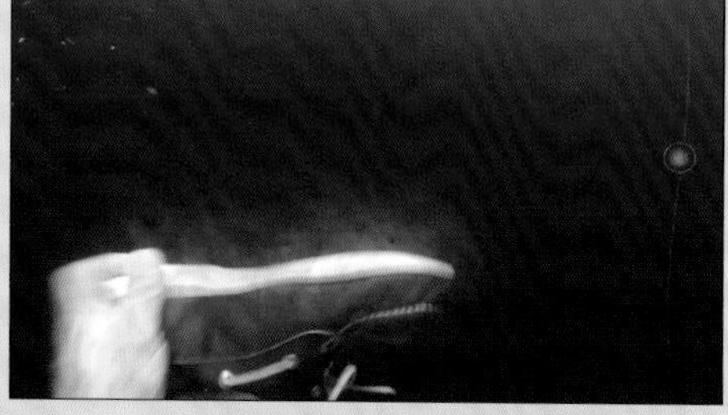

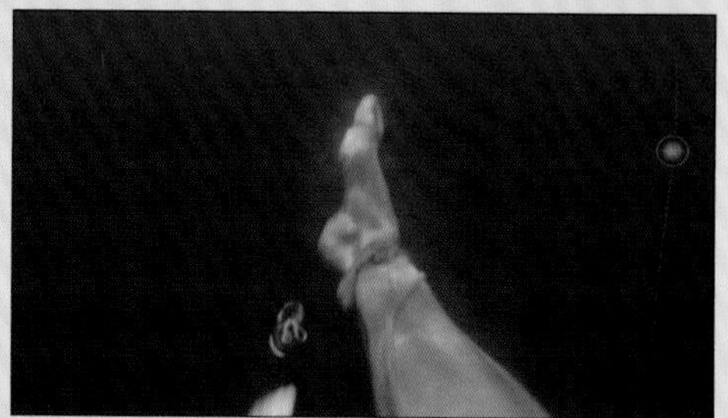

WHENEVER YOU GO OUT TO SEA, WEAR YOUR LIFE JACKET.

Agency CLM BBDO, Paris
Production Wanda Digital, Paris
Film Director Ben Strebel
Producers Perrine Schwartz, Hélène Segol
Advertiser Guy Cotten, "Trip Out To Sea"

To promote the importance of wearing a life vest, French seafaring apparel vendor Guy Cotten worked with Wanda Digital to create sortieenmer.com ("trip out to sea"). Visit the site for a disturbingly real example of what it feels like to drown; use the scrolling feature to try to stay above water. The site effectively plunges the user into a situation that few encounter and fewer still are prepared for.

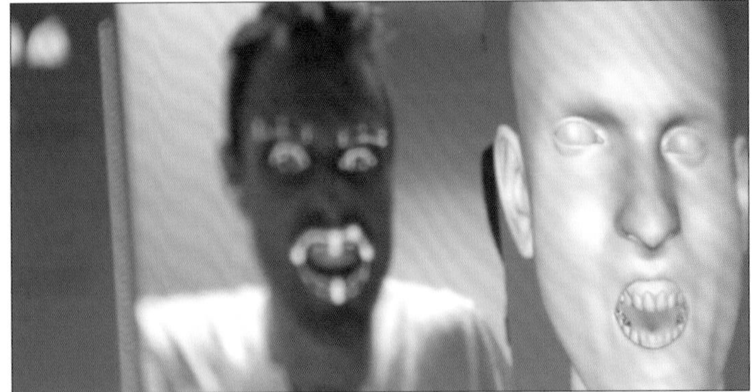
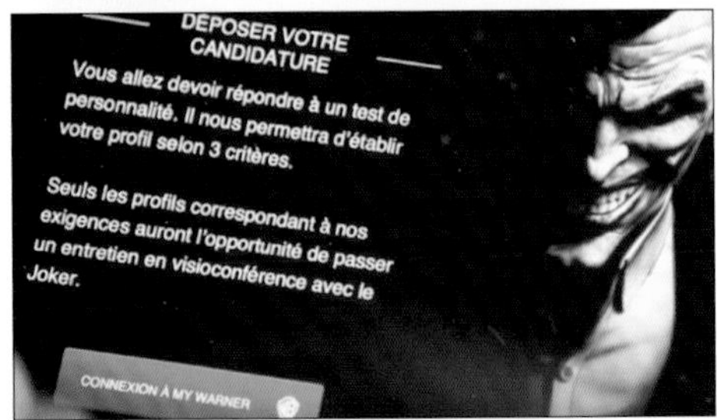

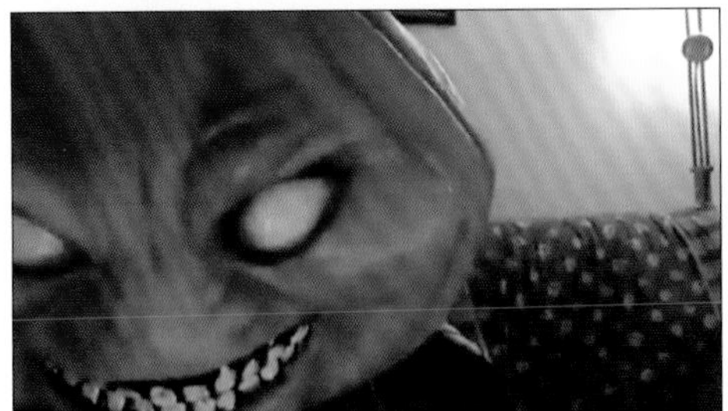

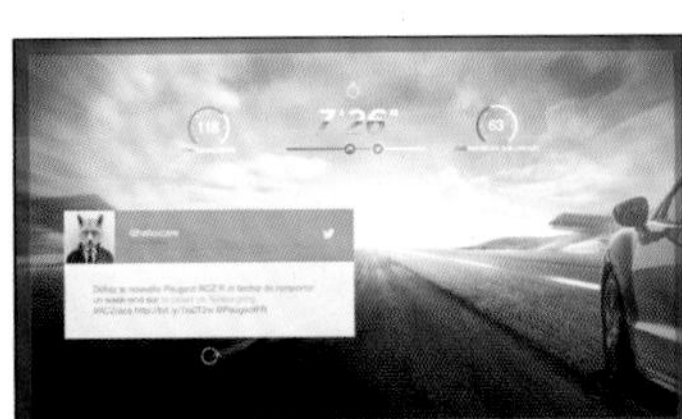

Agency Sid Lee, Paris
Production Wanda Digital, Paris
Film Director Julien Rocher
Producer Hélène Segol
Advertiser Warner Bros, "Batman Arkham"

For the Warner Bros. "Batman Arkham" video game, Wanda Digital created a unique opportunity: apply for the job of hunting Batman down. To take part, users submitted an application to a sub-site and were given job interviews via Google Hangouts. The interviewer was The Joker himself. The winner earned €2000 for hunting Batman down in an actual game.

Agency BETC Digital, Paris
Creative Directors Ivan Beczkowski, Frédéric Sounillac, Vincent Behaeghel
Copywriter Romain Pergeaux
Art Directors Sylvain Paradis, Damien Paris
Production 60 FPS
3D Yan Blary
Motion Design Marc Rodriguez
Advertiser Peugeot, "#RCZRace"

Are you faster than the Peugeot RCZ-R? To promote the car's speed, BETC ran a contest during which Twitter users "raced" the car. Participants had to rewrite one of fifteen 140-character tweets faster than it took the car to get to 140 kph (less than 11 seconds, to be exact). The campaign generated over 12,000 tweets.

Agency	McCann Copenhagen
CCOs	Linus Karlsson Andreas Dahlqvist
Strategic CD	Mark Fallows
Creatives	Eva Wallmark Rickard Beskow Michal Sitkiewicz Rasmus Keger Morten Halvorsen
Art Director	Jan Finnesand
Advertiser	IKEA, "Showroom At Home"

The hardest thing about buying furniture in a showroom is trying to imagine how it'll look once it's in your home. McCann Copenhagen solved this problem with "Showroom At Home". By scanning pages in your IKEA catalogue, you could select the items you wanted and use an augmented reality feature to "place" them in your actual house. No fuss, no risk.

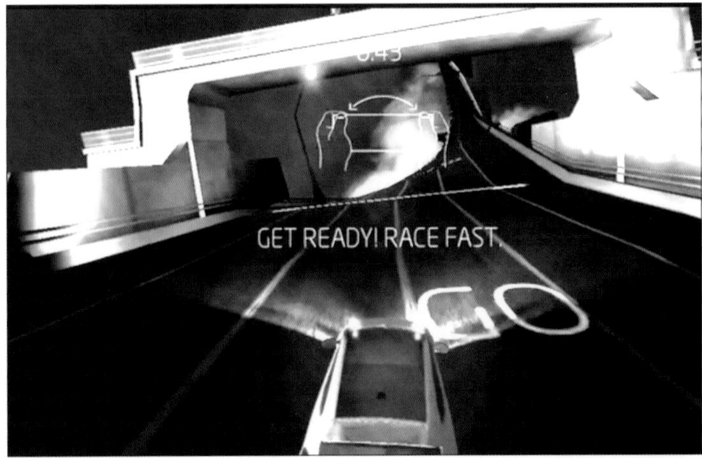

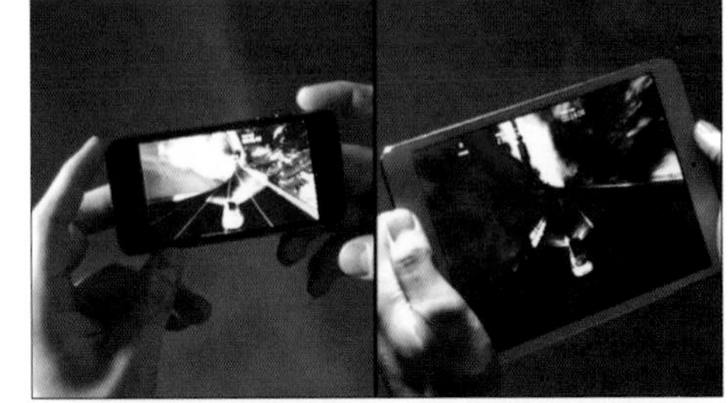

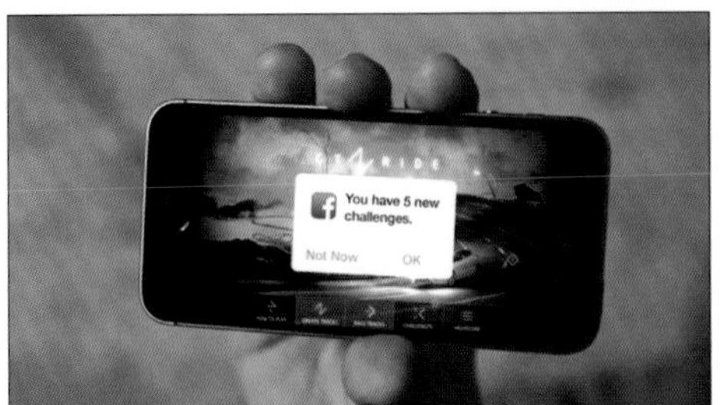

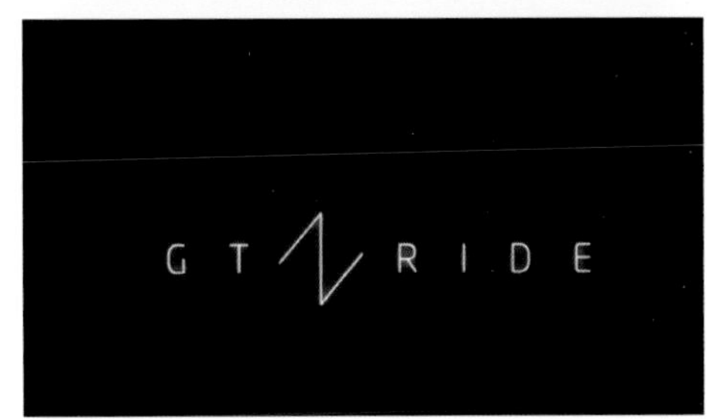

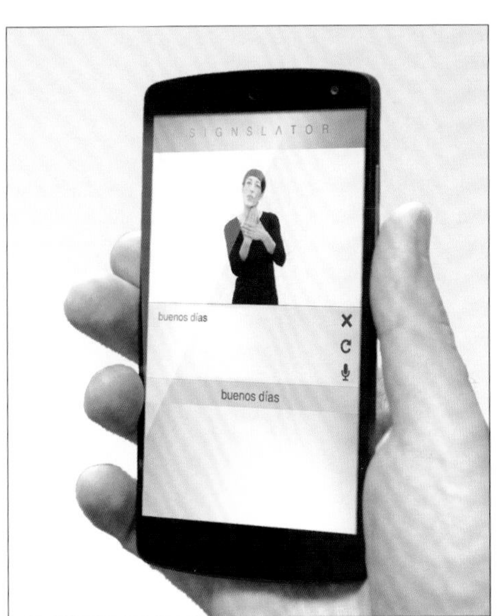

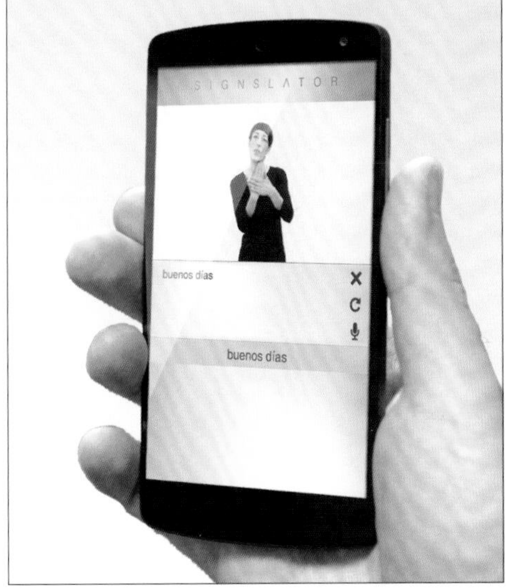

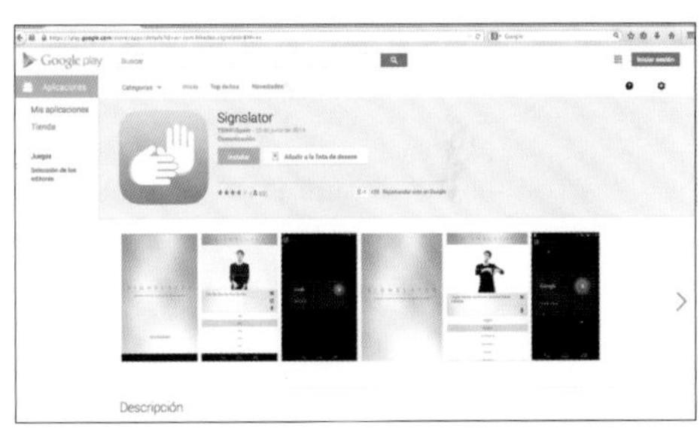

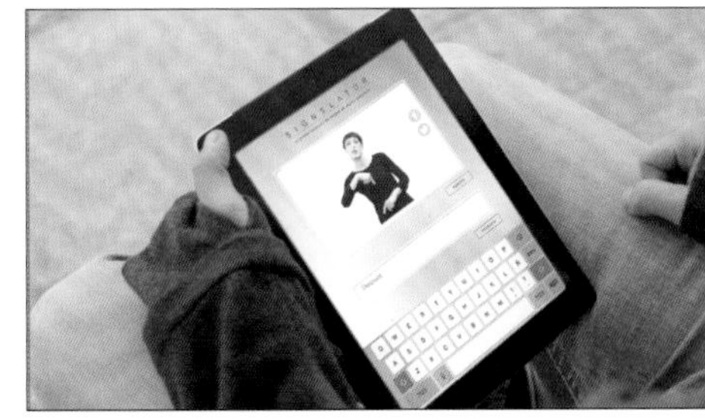

Agency LA RED, Hamburg
Creative Directors Margit Schroeder, Matthias Maurer, Dirk Hoffmann, Patrik De Jong
Copywriter Marco Gabriel
Art Director Christoph Mäder
Production Artificial Rome, Berlin
Advertiser Kia Motors, "GT Ride - Viral Gaming for Kia"

For Kia, LA RED created a mobile racing app to attract hardcore GT fans. "GT Ride" let users build their own virtual racetrack by waving their smartphones through the air. The app recreates a 3D racetrack, then enables you to challenge your Facebook friends to "drive" it in a wheel-screeching mobile game.

Agency TBWA\España, Madrid
Creative Directors Juan Sánchez, Guillermo Ginés, Cristina Davila
Copywriter Inés Méndez
Art Director Urtzi Iñurrita
Production Taco De Perro, Madrid
Film Director Victor Manuel Gulia
Digital CD Noelia Meltzer
Advertiser Anicols, "Signslator"

"Signslator," created for sign language association Anicols by TBWA\España, is the first app to translate the Spanish language into sign language. As well as translating spoken or written Spanish into signs in real time, the app is also a dictionary and a learning aid. Type a word or phrase into the app and the screen shows a woman making the appropriate sign. You can also send sign language messages via Facebook and Twitter. The app allows deaf people in Spain to converse more easily with their friends and family.

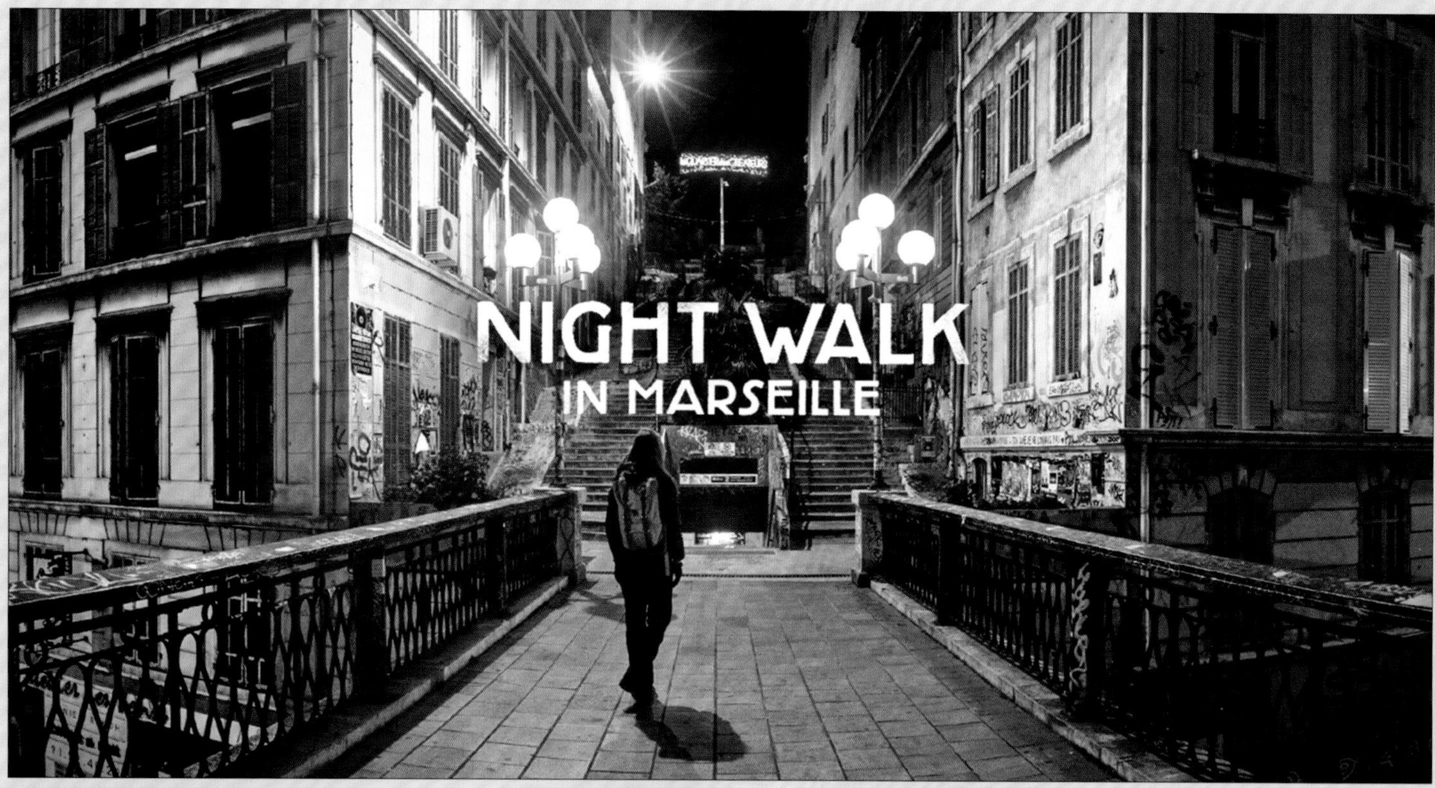

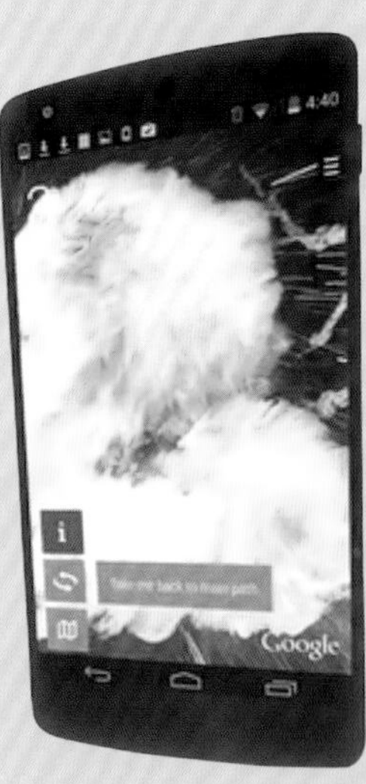

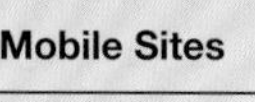

Agency 72andSunny, Amsterdam
Executive CD Carlo Cavallone
Creative Directors Gregg Clampffer, Micky Coyne
Art Director Patric Franz
Lead Writer Yann Corlay
Broadcast Producer Phil Mccluney
Digital Executive Prod. Sanne Drogtrop
Creative Technologist Gabor Szalatnyai
Contributing Company Google Creative Lab, London
Executive CD Steve Vranakis
Senior Creative David Bruno
Film Production Co. Epoch Films, London
Digital Production Co. Mediamonks, Amsterdam
Production Brenninkmeijer, Issaacs, Amsterdam
Advertiser Google, "Night Walk In Marseille"

To share her vision of the city, one Marseille resident created an Audio Walks Google Map offering a tour of unique and surprising local spots. Google picked up on her project and supercharged it with a visual layer. The Night Walk is now an immersive 3D experience, during which users can meet local Marseille street artists or travel back in time to discover the city's history.

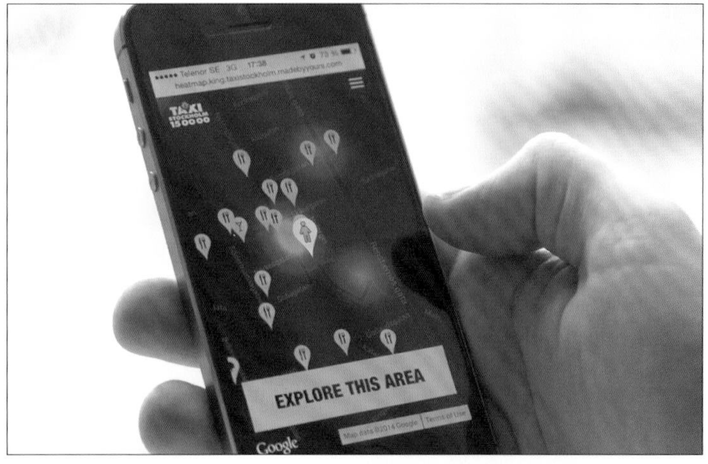

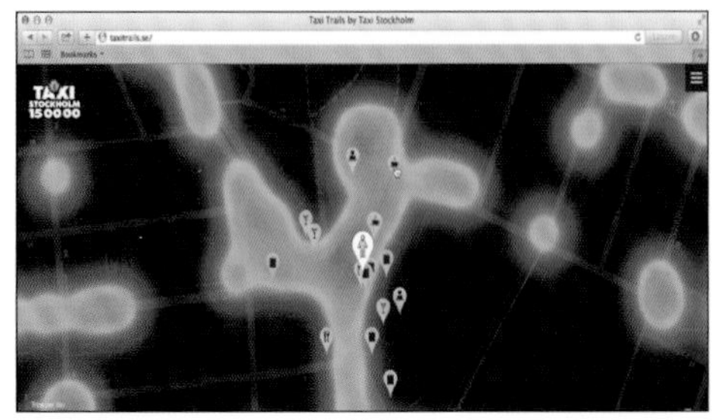

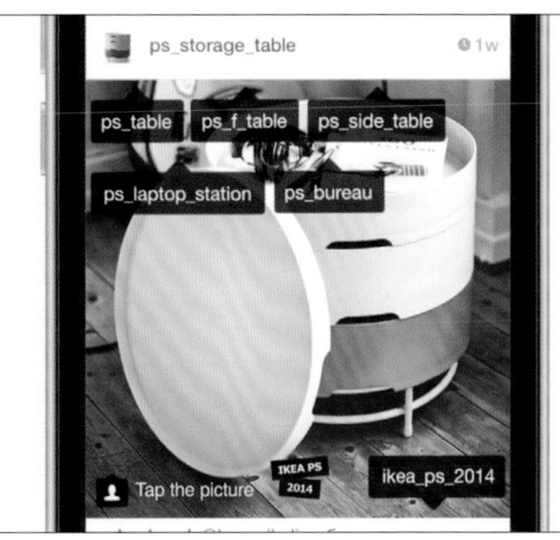

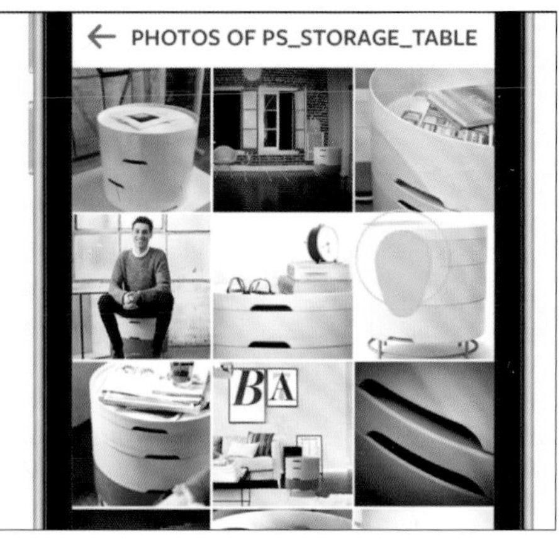

Agency King, Stockholm
Creative Director Frank Hollingworth
Copywriter Christoffer Dymling
Art Director Josephine Wallin
Production Yours, Stockholm
Digital Creative Johan Tesch
Advertiser Taxi Stockholm, "Taxi Trails"

Taxi drivers know more about their cities than anybody, but it's not always easy to access this wealth of knowledge. Alongside agency King, Taxi Stockholm launched "Taxi Trails", a smart tourist-oriented website that uses GPS data from over eight million taxi trips to show you where real Stockholmers like to go. Now all you have to do is follow them.

Agency Instinct, Moscow
Creative Directors Roman Firainer, Yaroslav Orlov
Copywriter Dmitry Moiseev
Art Directors Timur Abdusheev, Max Demkin
Digital CD Nikolai Fabrika
Advertiser IKEA, "IKEA PS 2014"

For the IKEA PS designer collection, IKEA and agency Instinct transformed Instagram into the go-to site for potential buyers. Each of the 34 items in the collection had its own Instagram account, making it easy for others to tag and share items they purchased.

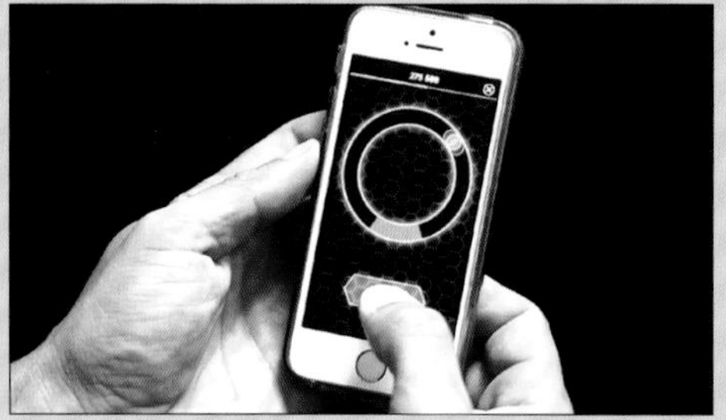

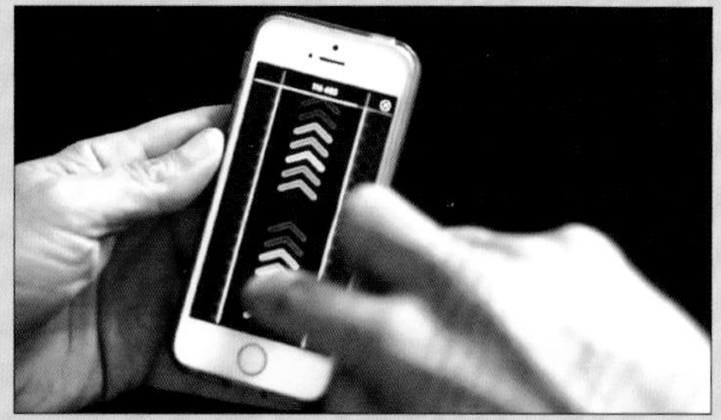

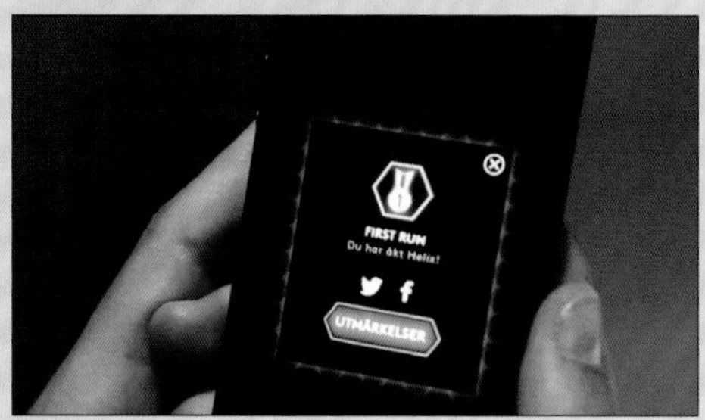

Mobile Games

Agency Shout, Gothenburg
Copywriter Pontus Caresten
Art Directors Calle Österberg, Martin Hummel-Gradén
Final Art Malin Svensson, Johanna Levin
Production Sticky Beat, Karlstad
Developers Nisse Bryngfors, Anders Hammar, Örjan Classon
Art Director Robert Schlyter
Advertiser Liseberg Park, "The Fun Queue"

Theme park attractions are obviously fun – but the queues, not so much. For the debut of Helix, a new rollercoaster, Liseberg park and Shout Advertising turned waiting into a game. Visitors could access a mobile game that could only be played while they stood in line. Each element was based on the attributes of the rollercoaster, with twists, turns and surprises. Every 15 minutes, the highest scoring player won a VIP shortcut to the front of the line.

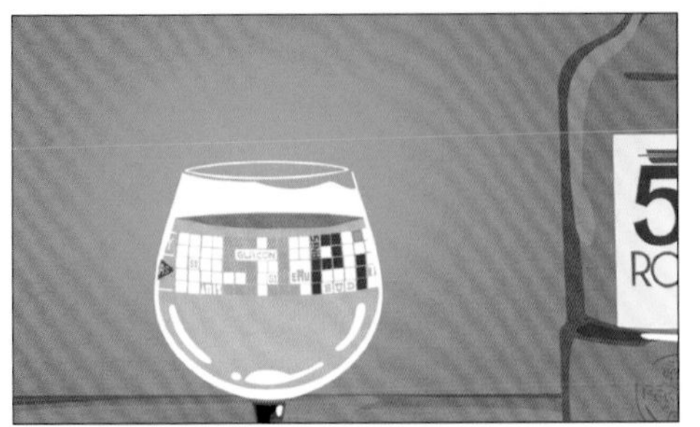

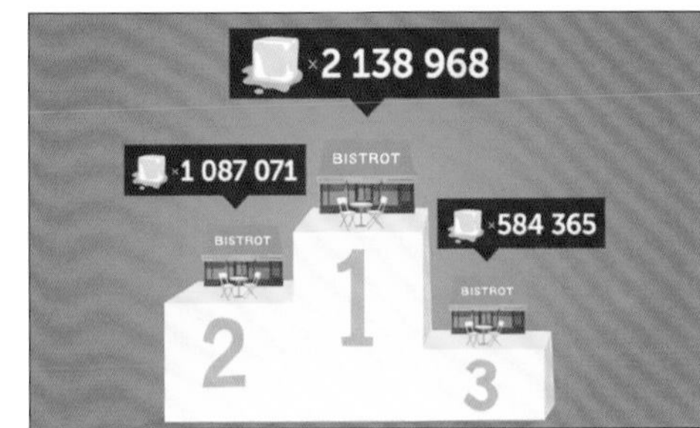

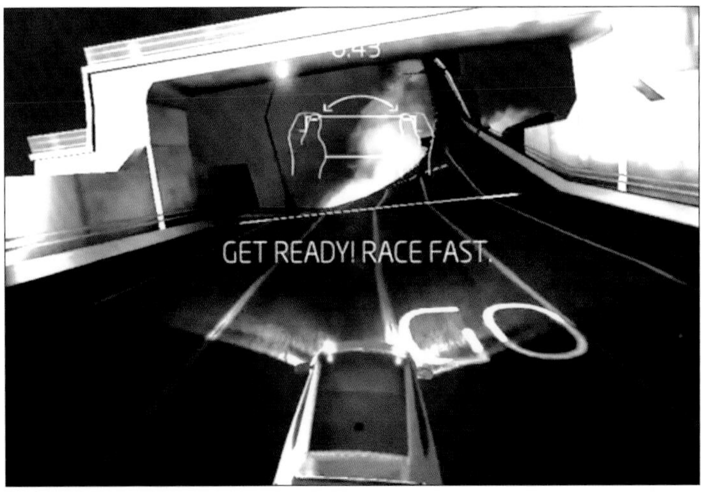

Agency DigitasLBi, Paris
CCO Bridget Jung
Creative Director Nicolas Thiboutot
Creatives Frederick Lung, Philippe Pinel
Art Director Chisato Tsuchiya
Motion Designers Jeremy Vissio, Diego Verastegui
Graphic Design Aline Kesting
Advertiser Pernod Ricard, "The Ice Cube Throwing Championship"

When the sun shines in France everyone wants to sit at a café terrace, which means service can be slow. This problem was transformed into a chance to promote Pernod Ricard's 51 Rosé. "The Ice Cube Throwing Championship" is an augmented reality mobile game in which users must throw ice cubes from their smartphones into a virtual glass that appears on their café tables. They have 51 seconds to fill the glass, while also learning that the best way to enjoy 51 Rosé is over ice.

Agency LA RED, Hamburg
Creative Directors Margit Schroeder, Matthias Maurer, Dirk Hoffmann, Patrik De Jong
Copywriter Marco Gabriel
Art Director Christoph Mäder
Production Artificial Rome, Berlin
Advertiser Kia, "GT Ride - Viral Gaming for Kia"

To draw hardcore GT fans to the Kia brand, LA RED built "GT Ride", a mobile racing app that lets users build a virtual racetrack by moving their smartphones through the air. The app users then challenged their Facebook friends to test the sinuous tracks.

Agency CJ WORX, Bangkok
CCO Saharath Sawadatikom
Creative Director Thanasorn Janekankit
Copywriters Thanasorn Janekankit, Palap Sa Ngaim
Art Directors Saharath Sawadatikom, Chotika Ophaswongse
Agency Producer Nutcha Mauthorn
Web Designer Varamol Chanakitkarnchai
Digital Designer Supalak Threemek
Flash Programmer Wichit Auttaponpijit
Web Programmer Thanawat Soisakhoo
Advertiser Seub Nakhasathien Foundation, "The Virtual Fence Project"

The world's first anti-deforestation social network, "The Virtual Fence Project" created virtual borders for protected forests in Thailand. Via Foursquare, users were asked to check in and share a location if they ever spotted trespassers. They also drew attention to sites that had been illegally built on. The initiative transformed tourists into volunteers actively engaged in forest conservation, thanks to social networking.

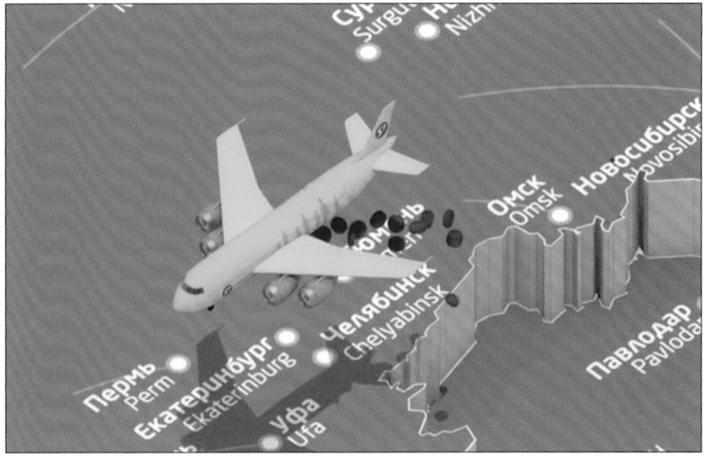

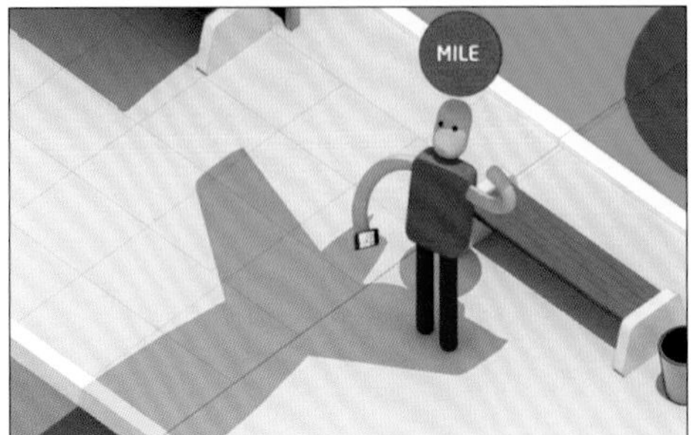

Agency Leo Burnett, Moscow
Creative Director Grisha Sorokin
Art Directors Grisha Sorokin, Michail Derkach
Production Unreal Mojo, St. Petersburg
Advertiser S7 Airlines, "Catch-A-Plane"

After years of bans, the skies above Moscow were recently opened to passenger flights. To celebrate, S7 Airlines and Leo Burnett Moscow created the "Catch-A-Plane" app. Each S7 plane was "loaded" with bonus air miles that players could win. Whenever one flew overhead, app users would get a push notification telling them how many miles they could collect, where the plane was headed, and what the flight cost. All miles collected could be exchanged for real flight tickets.

Agency plan.net / Serviceplan, Munich/Vienna
CCO Alexander Schill
Executive CD Christian Gosch
Creative Directors Christian Gosch, Matthaeus Frost
Copywriters Christian Gosch, Werner Eisenbock
Art Director Jan Paepke
Production Ping Pong, Vienna
Creative Producer Florian Panier
Advertiser Parship.at, "No Fake Profiles"

Dating sites are packed with people embellishing their profile descriptions jn order to seem more attractive. But dating site Parship vets each profile manually. To draw attention to this, Serviceplan created a Shazam promotion inviting users to both listen to potential "mates" and see them at the same time. Often, the dashing six-foot guy proved older and squatter than he claimed!

Agency	Leo Burnett, Melbourne
Executive CD	Jason Williams
Creative Director	Andrew Woodhead
Copywriter	Callum Fitzhardinge
Digital Art Director	Tim Shelley
Community Manager	Chris Steele
Digital Designer	Matt Peters
Digital Executive Prod.	Nicole Ross
Advertiser	SPC Ardmona, "#SPCSunday"

SPC, Australia's oldest fruit and vegetables processing company, was threatened by new, cheaper competitors. A concerned onlooker, Linda Drummond, created the #SPCSunday hashtag, encouraging others to eat SPC products in solidarity. Leo Burnett Melbourne pushed the hashtag further and amplified the campaign. Eventually celebrities joined the fray and the hashtag took on a patriotic bent. The government eventually offered SPC a rescue package.

Agencies	Havas Worldwide, Sydney One Green Bean, Sydney
Executive CDs	Steve Coll Kat Thomas
CD	Christopher Johnson
Copywriters	Simon Fowler Christopher Johnson
Art Directors	Nicole Hetherington Paris Giannakis
Digital CD	Jay Morgan
Digit. Creative	Frida Engstrom
Advertiser	Virgin Mobile, "#Mealforameal"

The #mealforameal campaign turned pictures of food – the third most common images in social media newsfeeds – into real meals for the needy. In partnership with Oz Harvest, every food picture uploaded onto social media with the #mealforameal hashtag became a meal donation by Virgin Mobile Australia to a less-fortunate person.

Agency	Leo Burnett, New York
CCO	Jay Benjamin
Executive CDs	Kieran Antill Michael Canning Darren Wright David Skinner
Art Director	Andre Gidoin
Studio Designer	Steven Jordao
Agency Producer	Jeremy Fox
Advertiser	United Nations, "#TheWorldNeeds More"

For the United Nations initiative #theworldneedsmore, words on social media were turned into aid opportunities. Using the hashtag, people could share a word they felt the world needed more of. Each word ("love", "education" and so on) was sponsored by a brand or an individual, and every time it was shared a percentage of the amount donated was unlocked. In total, 2.5 million words were shared, unlocking US$700.000 in donations over three months.

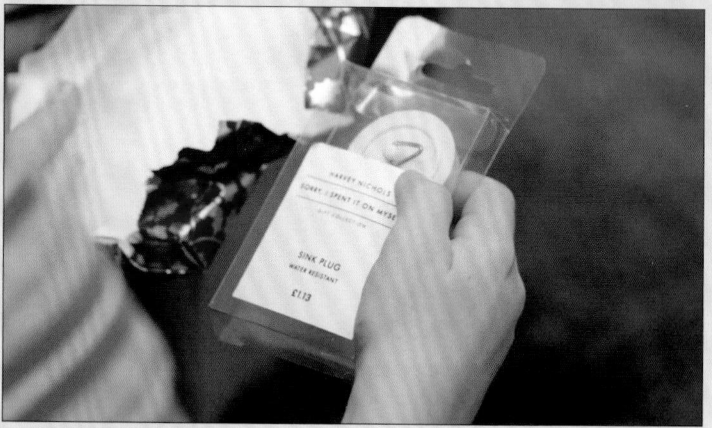

Agency adam&eveDDB, London
Executive CDs Ben Priest, Ben Tollett, Emer Stamp
Creatives Richard Brim, Daniel Fisher
Producer Daniel Moorey
Agency Producer Victoria Keenan
Production Outsider, London
Creative Producer Kirsty Harris
Film Director James Rouse
Cameraman Alex Melman
DOP Steve Smith
Editor Bill Smedley, Work Post, London
Post Producer Josh King, MPC, London
Sound Factory Studio, London
Photographer James Day
Retouching Stanley's King Henry, London
Advertiser Harvey Nichols, "Sorry, I Spent It On Myself"

This playfully cynical campaign for luxury store Harvey Nichols tapped into our occasional ambivalence about Christmas. Both a film and a product line, "Sorry, I Spent It On Myself" gave people the chance to buy fancily packaged but cheap gifts (toothpicks, paperclips, wire wool) for their loved ones, while spending the saved cash on something glam for themselves. In the film, the camera moves from the underwhelmed recipient's face to where the money really went.

Agency Leo Burnett Tailor Made, Sao Paulo
Creative Directors Marcelo Reis, Guilherme Jahara, Rodrigo Jatene
Copywriter Christian Fontana
Art Director Marcelo Rizerio
Editors Paulo Staliano, Gregorio Szalontai, Jack La Noyée, Christian Balzano
Advertiser ABTO, "Bentley Burial"

Brazilian organ transplant charity ABTO worked alongside eccentric local billionaire Count Scarpa to encourage organ donation. Scarpa posted a series of Facebook updates saying he intended to bury his Bentley in his backyard "for the afterlife". The media and an incensed public followed the story obsessively. But on the day of the "burial", Scarpa gave a press statement about how people bury far more important things than his Bentley each day, namely their organs.

Agency Robert/Boisen & Like-minded, Copenhagen
Executive CD Michael Robert
Creative Director Heinrich Vejlgaard
Copywriter James Godfrey
Creative Technology Michael Bugaj
Designer Morten Grundsøe
Production Gobsmack Productions, Copenhagen
Film Director Niels Nørløv
Advertiser Spies Travels, "Do It For Denmark"

Denmark's birthrate is plummeting, but Spies Travel knew that 10% of Danish children are conceived on holidays. So through its agency Robert/Boisen & Like-minded it launched a campaign encouraging people not just to book a vacation, but to prove they'd conceived while they were away – in the hope of winning three years' worth of free baby supplies. Women who could prove they were ovulating during vacation time got a special discount. Holiday bookings rose 107%!

World Cup

Agency	Razorfish, Frankfurt	**Social Strategy**	Kathrin Stieler
Executive CD	Preethi Mariappan	**Social Concept**	Jakob Lips
Group CD	Chris May	**Developers**	Anna Dressler
Associate CD	Viktor Wahl		René Lamberti
Production	Park Design, Washington D.C.	**Advertiser**	Audi, "Audi LED Scoreboard"
Tech. Company	Moey, Brooklyn		
Design & Production	Cyril Keating		
Technology	Joey Stein		
Chief Strategy & Innovation Officer	Alina Hueckelkamp		

Audi wanted to start conversations about its LED headlight technology while joining the soccer love-in that is the World Cup. Simple: at a prime location in Greenpoint, Brooklyn – across the East River from Manhattan – it transformed shipping containers into garages for Audi A8s and stacked them to make the world's largest scoreboard. Their headlights formed four storey high numbers with a live link to the football scores. All the World Cup's 171 goals were beamed across New York City. The scoreboard also lit up social networks.

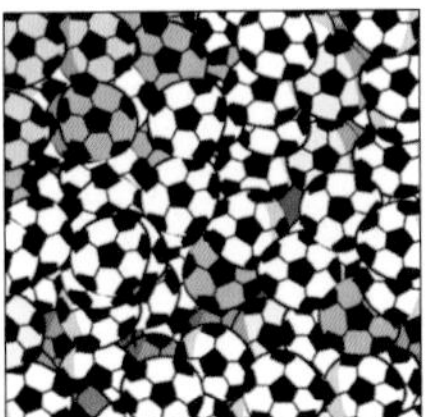

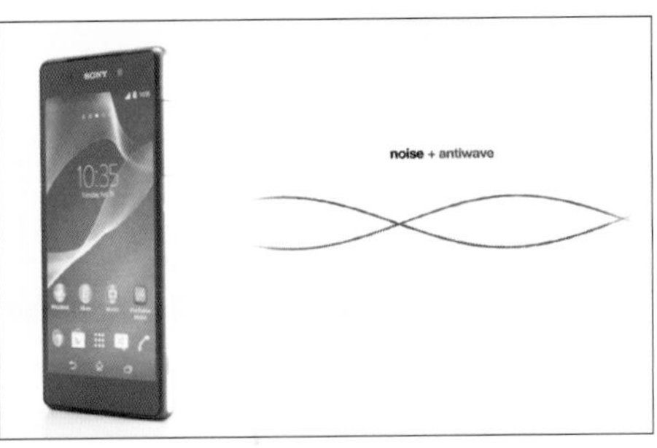

Agency	CP+B, Stockholm
ECD	Björn Höglund
Creative Directors	Tobias Carlson Jonas Wittenmark
Copywriters	Tobias Carlson Jonas Wittenmark Jimmy Hellkvist
Art Directors	Tobias Carlson Jonas Wittenmark Jakob Eriksson
Sr. Integrated Producer	Marcus Åslund
Flash	David Forss
Final Art	Per Westlund
Advertiser	Sony, "Xperia Football Cancellation"

Sony was one of the sponsors of the FIFA World Cup. But it didn't just want to connect with people who loved football. What about those who actively disliked it? The Experia Z2 phone has digital noise cancellation. So in a partnership with Swedish newspaper Aftonbladet, Sony introduced "football cancellation". A simple switch on the newspaper's site or mobile app let users erase all the soccer news, in return for a banner promoting the phone's unique qualities.

Agency	TRY/Apt, Oslo
Creatives	Bård Rostrup Gabrielsen Maja Folgerø
Art Directors	Sindre Fosse Rosness Erik Winn
Programmers	Thomas Lein Simen Lysebo
Motion Graphics	Roy Kristoffersen
Agency Producer	Lisa Canneaux
Advertiser	The Rainforest Foundation, "The Rainforest Cut"

Every three seconds an area the size of a football pitch is lost in the rainforest. But most football fans are more interested in the players' crazy haircuts than in deforestation. So the Rainforest Foundation created its own haircut: The Rainforest Cut. Thick on top, deforested around the sides. First, players from the Swedish national team offered to get their hair cut on national TV in return for donations. Then 130 hair salons offered the charity cut. In the end, 15,000 football pitches worth of rainforest were saved.

Agency	Phantasia Wunderman, Lima
Executive CD	José Aburto
CDs	Bryan Chistopherson Jorge Borrero
Copywriters	Sergio Inamine Diego Fernández-Maldonado
Art Director	Rocio Heredia
Production	Cine 70, Lima
Advertiser	Coca-Cola, "The Maracana Of The Real Tahuantinsuyo"

The kids of Real Tahuantinsuyo, a soccer team from the district of Independencia in Lima, have to play on a stony and dishevelled pitch. Coca-Cola and the Peruvian Sports Institute wanted to help them. It took a square of turf from the iconic Maracanã Stadium in Rio, Brazil and cultivated it as part of a new pitch for the team. Pieces of the turf were also sent out to the media as a direct mailing, generating articles about the story.

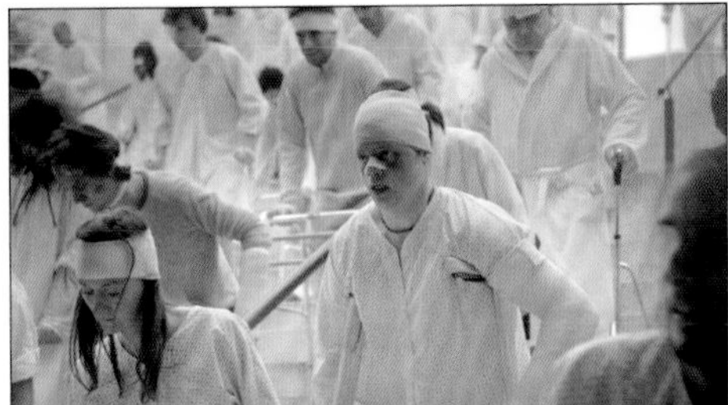

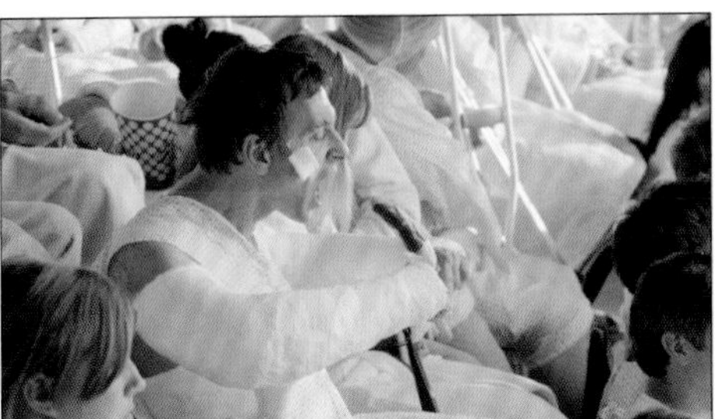

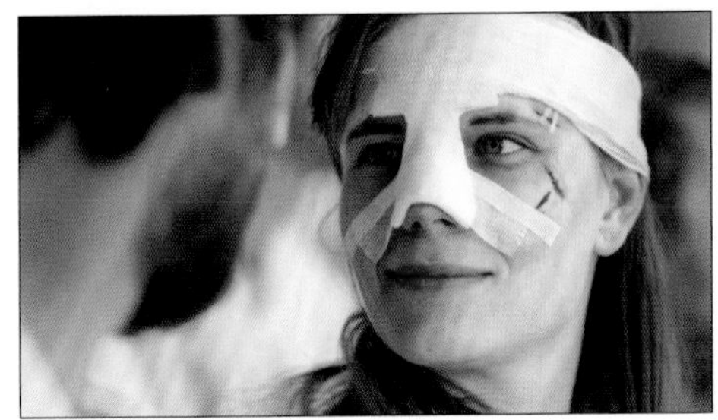

World Cup

Agency	Ruf Lanz, Zurich
Creative Directors	Markus Ruf Danielle Lanz
Copywriters	Markus Ruf Maren Beck
Art Director	Isabelle Hauser
Production	Stories, Zurich
Film Director	Michael Fueter
Producer	Yves Bollag
Production Design	Ursa Loboda
Camera	Michael Mieke
Editing	Marko Strihic
Sound Design	Spacetrain, Zurich
Advertiser	Suva Insurance, "Football Stadium"

Limping, hobbling and rolling in wheelchairs, hundreds of invalids make their way through the streets, all clad in white hospital gowns. Some are even in stretchers. We soon become aware that they are filing into a football stadium. Getting into position is a bit awkward, thanks to all the plaster casts. The narrator explains that 45,000 football players are taken out of the game by injury every year. Don't play dangerous. A message from Suva Insurance.

Agency	Havas Paris
Creative Director	Christophe Coffre
Copywriter	Alain Picard
Art Director	Nicolas Harlamoff
Agency Producer	Thierry Grouleaud
Illustrator	Ludovic Trebalag
Sound Production	La Maison De Production, Paris
Advertiser	Museum of Architecture & Heritage, "The Architecture's World Cup"

The Museum of Architecture & Heritage in Paris pays homage to the World Cup.

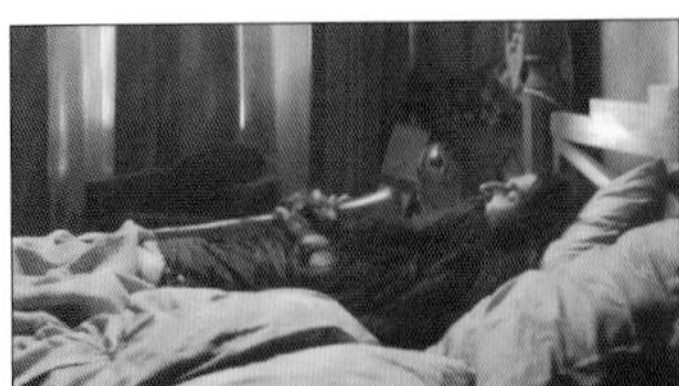

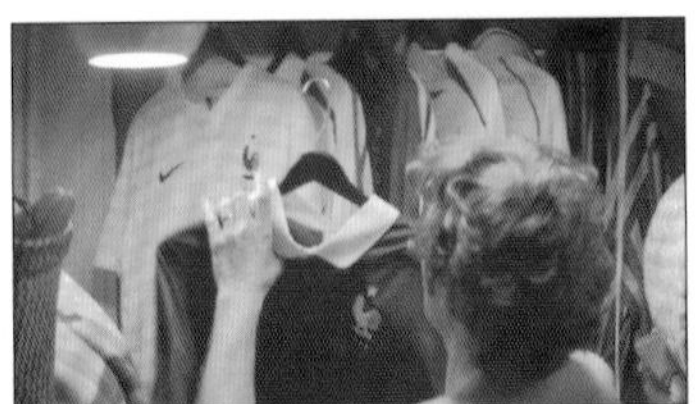

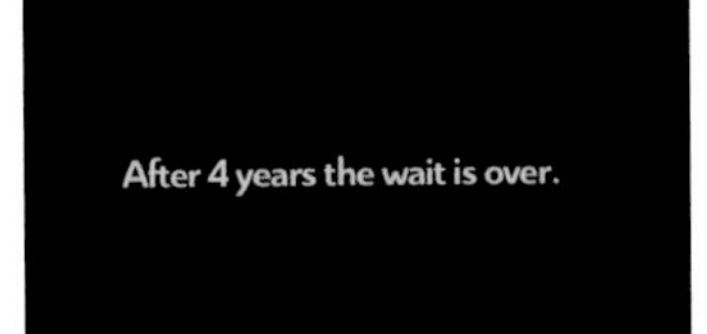

Agency Les Gaulois, Paris
Creative Directors Gilbert Scher, Marco Venturelli, Luca Cinquepalmi
Copywriter Ouriel Ferencz
Art Director Marie Donnedieu
Production Partizan Paris
Film Director Eric Lynne
Sound Design Kouz, Paris
Advertiser Citroën, "Sleeping Supporter"

Somewhere in France, a man is sleeping, a long beard curling to his chest. He is wearing a football shirt and clutching a vuvuzela horn. Stirred by the roar of a crowd, he finally wakes up. He cuts his hair, shaves, selects a new football shirt. From the way his family greets him, it's clear he's been absent for a while. Barely acknowledging them, he turns on the TV – for the World Cup. After four years, the wait is over. An ad from Citroën, sponsor of the French team in Brazil.

Agency McCann Birmingham
Creative Director Vince McSweeney
Copywriters Tim Jarvis, Vince McSweeney, Jon Leigh
Art Director Barrie Robinson
Production The Gate, Manchester
Film Director Cosmo Wallace
Producer Sarah Jarvis
Advertiser Vauxhall, "Stand Together"

"For every doubter, there is a believer," intones the narrator, over idyllic sun-filled shots of England preparing for the World Cup. "For every cynic, a supporter." Fish and chip shop owners, mums and dads, city dwellers and country folk, from north and south – they all stand together. "This is never a team of 11, it's a nation of millions." The England team file out onto the pitch. "For we are England, and we are proud." Auto brand Vauxhall sponsors the England team.

There's peace. Then there's football.

World Cup

Agency	BBDO New York
CCO	David Lubars Greg Hahn
Executive CD	Toygar Bazarkaya
Creative Directors	Jamie McGaw Mike Folino
Copywriter	Mike Folino
Art Director	Jamie McGaw
Group Executive Prod.	Brian Mitchell
Executive Music Prod.	Rani Vaz
Production	Moxie Pictures, New York
Film Director	Errol Morris
DOP	Pavel Edelman
Executive Producer	Robert Fernandez
Producer	Julie Ahlberg
VFX Company	Arcade Edit
Editor	Kim Bica
Editorial Producers	Sila Soyer Fanny Cruz
Music Company	John Kusiak Music
Composer	John Kusiak
SFX Company	Sonic Union, New York
Advertiser	Visa, "United In Rivalry"

"Can a Nobel peace laureate be a rabid fan?" asks the narrator, over scenes of David Trimble (1998) and Lech Walesa (1983) putting on their national scarves. "Of course," says Trimble, "we're still human beings." Leymah Gbowee (2011) says: "We pride ourselves in being united, except when football is involved." Both Lech Walesa and Oscar Arias (1987) admit they want to crush the opposing team. "Look, football isn't life and death," says Bob Geldof (Nobel Prize nominee). "It's much more important than that." There's peace. Then there's football.

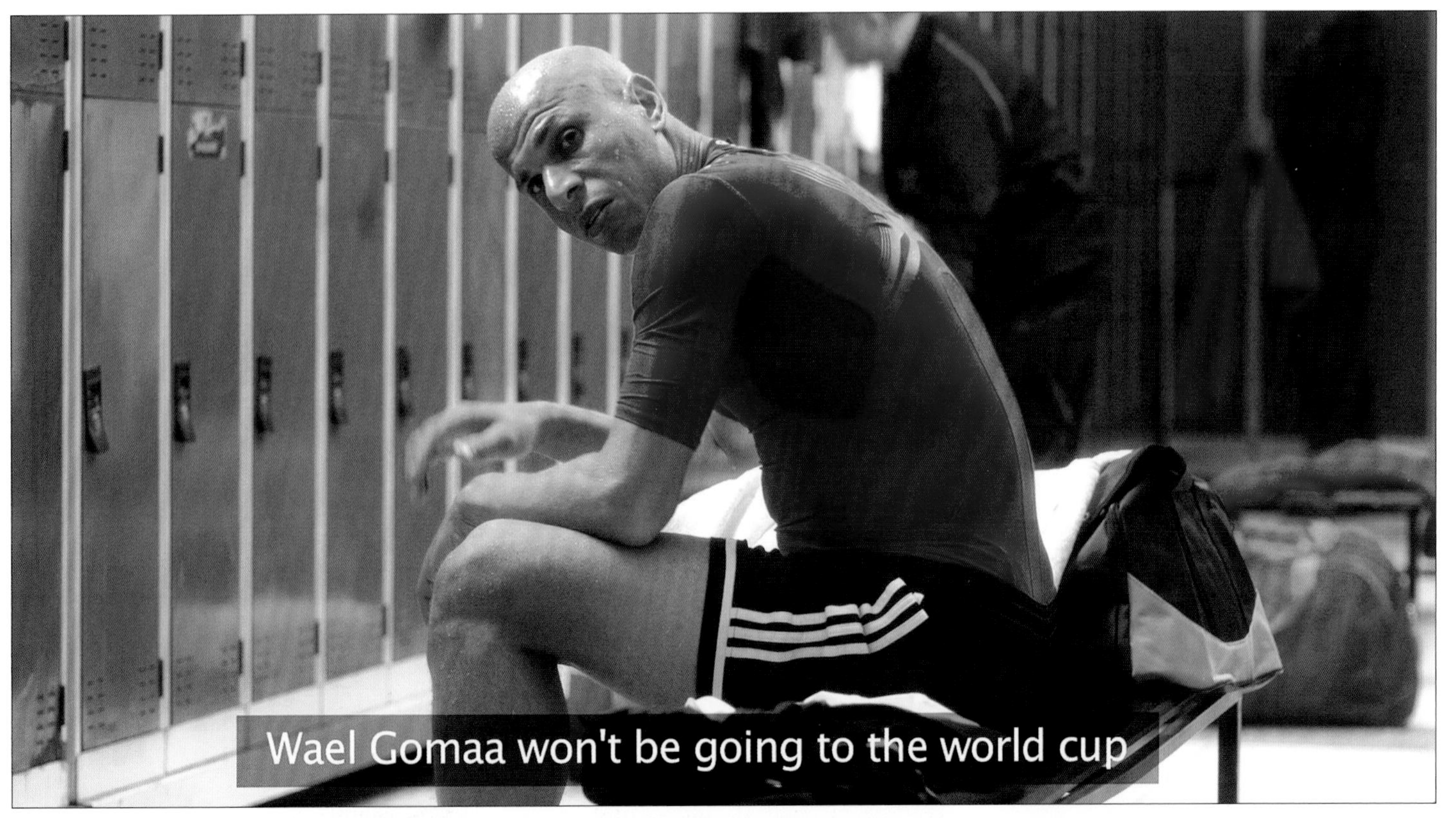

Wael Gomaa won't be going to the world cup

But Shamel Gomaa could go

kamal Gomaa

Ramez Gomaa and his neice Jihan could go

Ibrahim Gomaa

Khamis Gomaa

And Salah Gomaa

Coca-Cola
Your bottle will take you to the world cup

Agency FP7/CAI, Cairo
Creative Directors Maged Nassar, Tameem Youness
Copywriters Maged Nassar, Tameem Youness
Sr. Art Director Sherif Youssef
Production Film Marshals, Cairo
Film Director Omar Hilal
Producers Moataz Thabet, Nihal Sabr
Agency Producers Heba Radwan, Inas Nagy, Mahmoud Enayet, Ashraf Hosafy
Graphic Design Mohamed AbdelHameed, Ezzat Soliman
Advertiser Coca-Cola, "Anyone But Gomaa"

When Egypt failed to qualify for the World Cup, nobody wanted to talk about the tournament any more. But sponsor Coca-Cola needed them to do just that. So it turned to national team captain Wael Gomaa, known for his sombre and serious demeanour. In the spot, Gomaa plays several namesakes who, unlike him, plan to join in the World Cup fun. In fact anyone can go to the World Cup with Coca-Cola: check your bottle cap for a chance to win tickets to Brazil. If Wael Gomaa can't go, maybe you can.

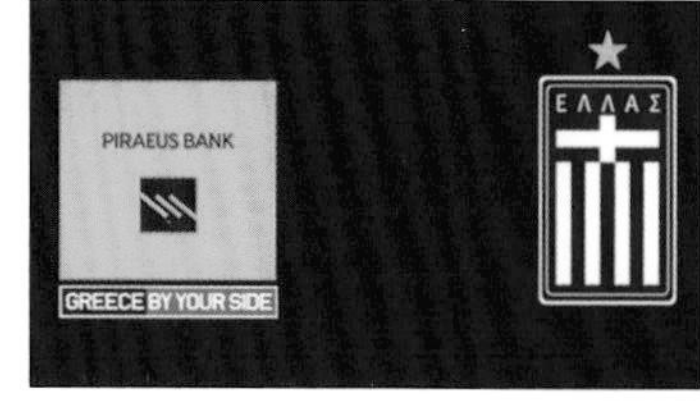

World Cup

Agency	41? 29!, Istanbul
Creative Group Heads	Ilyas Eralp Elif Kavalci
Creative Group	Alperen Altınoz Ahmet Terzioglu
Creative Director	Seren Koroglu
Art Directors	Ufuk Cetincan Emir Anarat Ercan Nailoglu Nilay Oguz Esra Bayramoglu
Advertiser	Akbank T.A.S, "The Legendary Journey"

Turkey did not qualify for the 2014 World Cup. When the Cup was last held in Brazil, 64 years ago, Turkey couldn't go either – even though its team had qualified, they didn't have enough money. This time Akbank decided to step in. In a TV spot it recreated the 1950 match against Syria that secured Turkey's qualification. It found the two surviving players and promised to take them to Brazil at last. Short documentaries about them were supported by a website. The winners of a competition joined the heroes.

Agency	The Newtons Laboratory, Athens
CD	Sorotos Giannis
Copywriters	Liapi Atalanti Vafea Sandra Theodorakopoulos Giorgos
Art Directors	Godenopoulos Paris Karagianni Dimitra
Photographer	Kiriakou Dimitris
Production	Stefi Productions, Athens
Film Director	Giorgos Zafiris
Advertiser	Piraeus Bank, "Manos Sergios"

The Greek team was off to the World Cup with Piraeus Bank as its sponsor and the slogan "By Your Side". But how to make Greeks feel truly involved? Enter Manos Sergios, an "ordinary" Greek who was officially announced as the 24th player of the squad. Everyone was stunned by his rise to fame. A TV spot continued the story. Manos went to Greece with the team; he even launched his own brand and made ads for Nike. Even though he turned out to be fictional, normal Greeks identified with him and felt part of the Cup.

ONE PIC for the WHOLE CUP
THE FIRST COLLECTABLE WORLD CUP AD CAMPAIGN.
by PlayStation.
THIS IS FOR THE CHAMPIONS
A CRAZY WAY
OF SUMMING UP EVERY MATCH
OF THE FIFA WORLD CUP 2014.
ILLUSTRATED LIVE DURING
THE WHOLE COMPETITION.
PUBLISHED EVERY 4 DAYS
ON THE BACK COVER
OF THE SPORT NEWSPAPER : L'ÉQUIPE.
7 COLLECTABLE ADS
IN TOTAL.
NEYMAR'S INJURY.
URUGUAY 1-0 ITALY • SUAREZ BITES CHIELLINI.
BRAZIL 0-0 MEXICO • OCHOA STOPS EVERY BALL.

Agency	TBWA\Paris
Creative Director	Philippe Simonet
Copywriters	Nicolas Roncerel Stéphane Kaczorowski Romain Duler
Art Directors	Jérémy Armand Sébastien Skrzypczak
Advertiser	Sony Playstation, "One Pic For The Whole Cup"

Published every four days on the back page of the French sports newspaper L'Equipe, this was the first collectible ad campaign. Each poster was drawn during the World Cup, with details reflecting the latest events on the pitch. There were seven in total, forming a crazy visual record of the Cup's highlights (and occasionally lowlights).

MONT
BLANC
StarWalker Urban Speed
and Hugh Jackman
Crafted for New Heights
Meticulously crafted with a body made of
black precious resin, PVD-coated metal
fittings and a hand-lacquered red stripe
on the clip – the Montblanc StarWalker
Urban Speed ballpoint pen is bound
to become a true lifetime companion.
Visit and shop at Montblanc.com